The Meaning of Sociology

A READER

Joel M. Charon
Professor Emeritus
Minnesota State University, Moorhead

Prentice
Hall

Upper Saddle River, New Jersey 07458

Library of Congress Cataloging-in-Publication Data
 The meaning of sociology: a reader / Joel M. Charon, editor—7th ed.
  p. cm.
 Includes bibliographical references.
 ISBN 0-13-033676-9
 1. Sociology. I. Charon, Joel M., [date]
HM585 .M43 2002
301—dc21 2001040034

VP / Editorial Director: *Laura Pearson*
AVP / Publisher: *Nancy Roberts*
Senior Acquisitions Editor: *Christopher DeJohn*
Managing Editor: *Sharon Chambliss*
Editorial/Production Supervision: *Joanne Riker*
Prepress and Manufacturing Buyer: *Mary Ann Gloriande*
Marketing Manager: *Chris Barker*
Cover Director: *Jayne Conte*
Cover Designer: *Bruce Kenselaar*
Cover Art: *Doree Loschiavo 2001*

This book was set in 10/11 Electra LH by East End Publishing Services, Inc.,
and was printed and bound by The Hamilton Printing Company. The cover was
printed by Phoenix Color Corp.

 © 2002, 1999, 1996, 1993, 1990, 1987, 1980 by Pearson Education, Inc.
Upper Saddle River, New Jersey 07458

Printed in the United States of America

10 9 8 7 6 5 4 3

ISBN 0-13-033676-9

Pearson Education LTD., *London*
Pearson Education Australia PTY, Limited, *Sydney*
Pearson Education Singapore, Pte. Ltd
Pearson Education North Asia Ltd, *Hong Kong*
Pearson Education Canada, Ltd., *Toronto*
Pearson Educación de Mexico, S.A. de C.V.
Pearson Education — Japan, *Tokyo*
Pearson Education Malaysia, Pte. Ltd
Pearson Education, *Upper Saddle River, New Jersey*

Contents

PART III Social Organization   71

PART IV Social Structure   103

PART V Social Class   145

PART VI Ethnic and Racial Inequality   171

PART VII Gender Inequality   209

PART VIII Culture   237

PART IX Social Control and Social Deviance   257

PART X Social Institutions: Political and Economic   293

Preface

The purpose of this reader is to share the excitement of sociology. Each selection has been chosen carefully according to the following criteria: Is it interesting? Is it a good example of sociology? Does it illustrate an idea or concept that is central to the sociological perspective? Is it written at a level that can be understood by a student who does not have an extensive background in sociology?

Sociology can be applied to every aspect of our lives. It is the study of society and the individual, interaction and organization, social patterns and institutions, social issues and social problems, social order and social change. The selections in this reader attempt to capture this diversity.

Some selections are written by professional sociologists, and some are written by people who think like sociologists. Some are very recent; whereas some happen to be older. Some are theoretical; whereas, some are empirical. Diversity and balance have been my aim.

I also have tried to take selections from a wide variety of sources. The experience of writing seven editions has led me to rely more and more on selections taken from books rather than journals. Always, my concern is to include what I consider to be good representatives of how sociologists think about the human being, and to include articles that students can understand and apply to their lives.

This is the seventh edition of this reader. It is always difficult to know which selections should be kept and which should be replaced. In making decisions for this edition, I relied heavily on a poll of several users of the sixth edition. Although I did not always take their suggestions, they caused me to question my choices, and they gave me good leads. In the end, I decided to use forty-one selections from the sixth edition. Twenty-four selections are new.

I really believe that the selections here are interesting and contribute to an understanding of sociology and society. If some are especially relevant to your life, please let me know. If some are either not interesting or non-relevant I would like to know that too. Please contact me at charonj@mnstate.edu.

I would like to thank Sharon Chambliss, Nancy Roberts, and the staff at Prentice Hall for their confidence in me and for their encouragement and advice. I also thank the Prentice Hall reviewers Russell L. Curtis, Jr., University of Houston; Jonathon Epstein, University of Southern Indiana; Sharon L. Hardesty, Eastern Kentucky University; Mark Jones, Indiana University at South Bend; Ginger E. Macheski, Valdosta State University; and William F. Poley, Jr., Kent State University, for their helpful suggestions for this revision.

I would like to dedicate this book to Denise Krause—friend, colleague, and supporter.

Joel M. Charon

PART I

The Meaning of Sociology

The first two readings in Part I are classic statements about the discipline of sociology. Peter Berger calls sociology a "passion," a "demon" that captures those interested in understanding the human condition. C. Wright Mills calls it a very special "imagination," a creative and important way of understanding the human being and his or her relationship with the larger society. Both statements reveal an excitement that many of us feel about the perspective of sociology, and both also reveal the ultimate purpose of sociology: to understand the human being in a social context, carefully and systematically.

Berger emphasizes that sociology is misunderstood and that it is often confused with social work and social reform. His point is basic: Sociology is an attempt to understand society, it is a science, and it is a unique way of looking at a familiar world.

Mills argues that more than just understanding our social life, sociology must be concerned with human problems. It must sensitize the individual to the fact that society exists and is important for what we do—that our individual lives and our personal problems are part of a much larger history and are embedded in a society. Our problems, in large part, are created in history and in the patterns of society.

The third selection is by Allan G Johnson, who reminds us of the importance of sociology to his life and to many of the rest of us who practice it. It is, in my opinion, an inspiration.

The last three chapters concern science, social science, and sociology as a social science. Erich Goode contrasts science with paranormalism, and in the process reminds us all of the basic assumptions and strengths of science. My own selection supports the importance of carefully generalizing about human beings and claims that social science has as its primary purpose not to stereotype. Robert Alford gives us a brief and excellent introduction to three model sociologists: Karl Marx, Emile Durkheim, and Max Weber.

1. SOCIOLOGY AS A PASSION TO UNDERSTAND

PETER L. BERGER

The sociological perspective is more like a demon that possesses one, that drives one compellingly, again and again, to the questions that are its own.

This first reading is Chapter 1 from the excellent book by Peter L. Berger, *Invitation to Sociology*. There, the chapter is entitled "Sociology as an Individual Pastime," but Berger's point is that it is much more than that—it is an exciting passion, a perspective that truly helps us understand our social world. In this selection, Berger shows us the many misunderstandings about sociology, emphasizing always that it is a scientific attempt to understand. "The sociologist," he says, "is someone concerned with understanding society in a disciplined way." It "will be satisfying, in the long run, only to those who can think of nothing more entrancing than to watch men and to understand things human."

1. What are the misconceptions people have about sociology? Why are they misconceptions?
2. What is sociology? What do sociologists do?
3. Why do sociologists do what they do? What drives them?

(By the way, you might notice that Berger uses the term he, not he or she. Things have changed a great deal in society and in sociology since 1963, when this article was written. Today, few people would attempt to publish a work in sociology that makes it appear that only men contribute to the world. This problem reappears in many other selections in this book too. It is very difficult for me to change other people's work in this book for the purposes of inclusion—sometimes, it is impossible. Please do not let this detract from your enjoyment or learning.)

If one asks undergraduate students why they are taking sociology as a major, one often gets the reply, "because I like to work with people." If one then goes on to ask such students about their occupational future, as they envisage it, one often hears that they intend to go into social work. Of this, more in a moment. Other answers are more vague and general, but all indicate that the student in question would rather deal with people than with things. Occupations mentioned in this con-

nection include personnel work, human relations in industry, public relations, advertising, community planning, or religious work of the unordained variety. The common assumption is that in all these lines of endeavor, one might "do something for people," "help people," "do work that is useful for the community." The image of the sociologist involved here could be described as a secularized version of the liberal Protestant ministry, with the YMCA secretary perhaps furnishing the connecting link between sacred and profane benevolence. Sociology is seen as an up-to-date variation on the classic American theme of "uplift." The sociologist is understood as someone professionally con-

From *An Invitation to Sociology*, by Peter L. Berger. Copyright © 1963 by Peter L. Berger. Used by permission of Doubleday, a division of Random House, Inc.

cerned with edifying activities on behalf of individuals and of the community at large....

It is, of course, true that some Boy Scout types have become sociologists. It is also true that a benevolent interest in people could be the biographical starting point for sociological studies. But it is important to point out that a malevolent and misanthropic outlook could serve just as well. Sociological insights are valuable to anyone concerned with action in society. But this action need not be particularly humanitarian. Some American sociologists today are employed by governmental agencies seeking to plan more livable communities for the nation. Other American sociologists are employed by governmental agencies concerned with wiping communities of hostile nations off the map, if and when the necessity should arise. Whatever the moral implications of these respective activities may be, there is no reason why interesting sociological studies could not be carried on in both. Similarly, criminology, as a special field within sociology, has uncovered valuable information about processes of crime in modern society. This information is as valuable for those seeking to fight crime as it would be for those interested in promoting it. The fact that more criminologists have been employed by the police than by gangsters can be ascribed to the ethical bias of the criminologists themselves, the public relations of the police, and perhaps the lack of scientific sophistication of the gangsters. It has nothing to do with the character of the information itself. In sum, "working with people" can mean getting them out of slums or getting them into jail, selling them propaganda or robbing them of their money (be it legally or illegally), making them produce better automobiles or making them better bomber pilots. As an image of the sociologist, then, the phrase leaves something to be desired, even though it may serve to describe at least the initial impulse as a result of which some people turn to the study of sociology....

Social work, whatever its theoretical rationalization, is a certain *practice* in society. Sociology is not a practice, but an *attempt to understand*. Certainly, this understanding may have use for the practitioner. For that matter, we would contend that a more profound grasp of sociology would be of great use to the social worker, and

that such a grasp would obviate the necessity of his descending into the mythological depths of the "subconscious" to explain matters that are typically quite conscious, much more simple, and indeed social in nature. But there is nothing inherent in the sociological enterprise of trying to understand society that necessarily leads to this practice or to any other. Sociological understanding can be recommended to social workers, but also to salesmen, nurses, evangelists, and politicians—in fact, to anyone whose goals involve the manipulation of men, for whatever purpose and with whatever moral justification.

This conception of the sociological enterprise is implied in the classic statement by Max Weber, one of the most important figures in the development of the field, to the effect that sociology is "value-free." Since it will be necessary to return to this a number of times later, it may be well to explicate it a little further at this point. Certainly the statement does not mean that the sociologist has or should have no values. In any case, it is just about impossible for a human being to exist without any values at all, although, of course, there can be tremendous variation in the values one may hold. The sociologist will normally have many values as a citizen, a private person, a member of a religious group, or as an adherent of some other association of people. But within the limits of his activities as a sociologist, there is one fundamental value only—that of scientific integrity. Even there, of course, the sociologist, being human, will have to reckon with his convictions, emotions, and prejudices. But it is part of his intellectual training that he tries to understand and control these as *biases* that ought to be eliminated, as far as possible, from his work. It goes without saying that this is not always easy to do, but it is not impossible. The sociologist tries to see what is there. He may have hopes or fears concerning what he may find. But he will try to see, regardless of his hopes or fears. It is thus an act of pure perception, as pure as humanly limited means allow, toward which sociology strives....

We would stress strongly that saying this does not imply that the sociologist has no responsibility to ask about the goals of his employers or the use to which they will put his work. But this asking is not sociological asking. It is asking the same questions that any man ought to ask himself about his actions in society. Again, in the same way, biological knowledge can be employed to heal or to kill. This does not mean that the biologist is free of responsibility as to which use he serves. But when he asks himself about this responsibility, he is not asking a biological question.

Another image of the sociologist, related to the two already discussed, is that of social reformer.…

It is gratifying from certain value positions (including some of this writer's) that sociological insights have served in a number of instances to improve the lot of groups of human beings by uncovering morally shocking conditions, or by clearing away collective illusions, or by showing that socially desired results could be obtained in a more humane fashion. One might point, for example, to some applications of sociological knowledge in the penological practice of Western countries. Or one might cite the use made of sociological studies in the Supreme Court decision of 1954 on racial segregation in the public schools. Or one could look at the applications of other sociological studies to the humane planning of urban redevelopment. Certainly, the sociologist who is morally and politically sensitive will derive gratification from such instances. But, once more, it will be well to keep in mind that what is at issue here is not sociological understanding as such but certain applications of this understanding. It is not difficult to see how the same understanding could be applied with opposite intentions. Thus the sociological understanding of the dynamics of racial prejudice can be applied effectively by those promoting intragroup hatred as well as by those wanting to spread tolerance. And the sociological understanding of the nature of human solidarity can be employed in the service of both totalitarian and democratic regimes. It is sobering to realize that the same processes that generate consensus can be manipulated by a social group worker in a summer camp in the Adirondacks and by a communist brainwasher in a prisoner camp in China. One may readily grant that the sociologist can sometimes be called upon to give advice when it comes to changing certain social conditions deemed undesirable. But the image of the sociologist as social reformer suffers from the

same confusion as the image of him as social worker.

If these images of the sociologist all have an element of "cultural lag" about them, we can now turn to some other images that are of more recent date and that refer themselves to more recent developments in the discipline. One such image is that of the sociologist as a gatherer of statistics about human behavior. The sociologist is here seen essentially as an aide-de-camp to an IBM machine. He goes out with a questionnaire, interviews people selected at random, then goes home, enters his tabulations onto innumerable punch cards, which are then fed into a machine. In all of this, of course, he is supported by a large staff and a very large budget. Included in this image is the implication that the results of all this effort are picayune, a pedantic restatement of what everybody knows anyway. As one observer remarked pithily, a sociologist is a fellow who spends $100,000 to find his way to a house of ill repute.

This image of the sociologist has been strengthened in the public mind by the activities of many agencies that might well be called parasociological—mainly agencies concerned with public opinion and market trends. The pollster has become a well-known figure in American life, importuning people about their views from foreign policy to toilet paper. Because the methods used in the pollster business bear close resemblance to sociological research, the growth of this image of the sociologist is understandable. The Kinsey studies of American sexual behavior have probably greatly augmented the impact of this image. The fundamental sociological question, whether concerned with premarital petting or with Republican votes or with the incidence of gang knifings, is always presumed to be "how often?" or "how many?" (Incidentally, the very few jokes current about sociologists usually relate to this statistical image… which jokes had better be left to the imagination of the reader.)

Statistical data by themselves do not make sociology. They become sociology only when they are sociologically interpreted, put within a theoretical frame of reference that is sociological. Simple counting, or even correlating different items that one counts, is not sociology. There is almost no sociology in the Kinsey reports. This does not mean that the data in these studies are not true or that they cannot be relevant to sociological understanding. They are, taken by themselves, raw materials that can be used in sociological interpretation. The interpretation, however, must be broader than the data themselves. So the sociologist cannot arrest himself at the frequency tables of premarital petting or extramarital pederasty. These enumerations are meaningful to him only in terms of their much broader implications for an understanding of institutions and values in our society. To arrive at such understanding, the sociologist will often have to apply statistical techniques, especially when he is dealing with the mass phenomena of modern social life. But sociology consists of statistics as little as philology consists of conjugating irregular verbs or chemistry of making nasty smells in test tubes....

How, then, are we to conceive of the sociologist? In discussing the various images of him that abound in the popular mind, we have already brought out certain elements that would have to go into our conception. We can now put them together. In doing so, we shall construct what sociologists themselves call an "ideal type." This means that what we delineate will not be found in reality in its pure form. Instead, one will find approximations to it and deviations from it, in varying degrees. Nor is it to be understood as an empirical average. We would not even claim that all individuals who now call themselves sociologists will recognize themselves without reservations in our conception, nor would we dispute the right of those who do not so recognize themselves to use the appellation. Our business is not excommunication. We would, however, contend that our "ideal type" corresponds to the self-conception of most sociologists in the mainstream of the discipline, both historically (at least in this century) and today.

The sociologist, then, is someone concerned with understanding society in a disciplined way. The nature of this discipline is scientific. This means that what the sociologist finds and says about the social phenomena he studies occurs with a certain rather strictly defined frame of reference. One of the main characteristics of this scientific frame of reference is that operations are bound by certain rules of evidence. As a scientist,

the sociologist tries to be objective, to control his personal preferences and prejudices, to perceive clearly rather than to judge normatively. This restraint, of course, does not embrace the totality of the sociologist's existence as a human being but is limited to his operations as sociologist. Nor does the sociologist claim that his frame of reference is the only one within which society can be looked at. For that matter, very few scientists in any field would claim today that one should look at the world only scientifically. The botanist looking at a daffodil has no reason to dispute the right of the poet to look at the same object in a very different manner. There are many ways of playing....

The game of the sociologist, then, uses scientific rules. As a result, the sociologist must be clear in his own mind as to the meaning of these rules.

... [T]he interest of the sociologist is primarily theoretical. That is, he is interested in understanding for its own sake. He may be aware of or even concerned with the practical applicability and consequences of his findings—but at that point, he leaves the sociological frame of reference as such and moves into realms of values, beliefs, and ideas that he shares with other men who are not sociologists....

The sociologist ... is a person intensively, endlessly, shamelessly interested in the doings of men. His natural habitat is all the human gathering places of the world, wherever men come together. The sociologist may be interested in many other things. But his consuming interest remains in the world of men, their institutions, their history, their passions. And because he is interested in men, nothing that men do can be altogether tedious for him. He will naturally be interested in the events that engage men's ultimate beliefs, their moments of tragedy and grandeur and ecstasy. But he will also be fascinated by the commonplace, the everyday. He will know reverence, but this reverence will not prevent him from wanting to see and to understand. He may sometimes feel revulsion or contempt, but this also will not deter him from wanting to have his questions answered. The sociologist, in his quest for understanding, moves through the world of men without respect for the usual lines of demarcation. Nobility and degradation, power and obscurity, intelligence and folly—these are equally interesting to him, however unequal they may be in his personal values or tastes. Thus his questions may lead him to all possible levels of society, the best and least known places, the most respected and the most despised. And, if he is a good sociologist, he will find himself in all these places because his own questions have so taken possession of him that he has little choice but to seek for answers.

It would be possible to say the same things in a lower key. We could say that the sociologist, but for the grace of his academic title, is the man who must listen to gossip despite himself, who is tempted to look through keyholes, to read other people's mail, to open closed cabinets. Before some otherwise unoccupied psychologist sets out now to construct an aptitude test for sociologists on the basis of sublimated voyeurism, let us quickly say that we are speaking merely by way of analogy. Perhaps some little boys consumed with curiosity to watch their maiden aunts in the bathroom later become inveterate sociologists. This is quite uninteresting. What interests us is the curiosity that grips any sociologist in front of a closed door behind which there are human voices. If he is a good sociologist, he will want to open that door, to understand these voices. Behind each closed door he will anticipate some new facet of human life not yet perceived and understood.

The sociologist will occupy himself with matters that others regard as too sacred or as too distasteful for dispassionate investigation. He will find rewarding the company of priests or of prostitutes, depending not on his personal preferences but on the questions he happens to be asking at the moment. He will also concern himself with matters that others may find much too boring. He will be interested in the human interaction that goes with warfare or with great intellectual discoveries, but also be interested in the relations between people employed in a restaurant or between a group of little girls playing with their dolls. His main focus of attention is not the ultimate significance of what men do, but the action in itself, as another example of the infinite richness of human conduct. So much for the image of our playmate.

In these journeys through the world of men, the sociologist will inevitably encounter other professional Peeping Toms. Sometimes, these will resent his presence, feeling that he is poaching on their preserves. In some places, the sociologist will meet up with the economist; in others, with the political scientist; in yet others, with the psychologist or the ethnologist. Yet chances are that the questions that have brought him to these same places are different from the ones that propelled his fellow trespassers. The sociologist's questions always remain essentially the same: "What are people doing with each other here?" "What are their relationships to each other?" "How are these relationships organized in institutions?" "What are the collective ideas that move men and institutions?" In trying to answer these questions in specific instances, the sociologist will, of course, have to deal with economic or political matters, but he will do so in a way rather different from that of the economist or the political scientist.…

The fascination of sociology lies in the fact that its perspective makes us see in a new light the very world in which we have lived all our lives. This also constitutes a transformation of consciousness. Moreover, this transformation is more relevant existentially than that of many other intellectual disciplines because it is more difficult to segregate in some special compartment of the mind. The astronomer does not live in the remote galaxies, and the nuclear physicist can, outside his laboratory, eat and laugh and marry and vote without thinking about the insides of the atom. The geologist looks at rocks only at appropriate times, and the linguist speaks English with his wife. The sociologist lives in society, on the job and off it. His own life, inevitably, is part of his subject matter. Men being what they are, sociologists manage to segregate their professional insights from their everyday affairs. But it is a rather difficult feat to perform in good faith.

The sociologist moves in the common world of men, close to what most of them would call *real*. The categories he employs in his analyses are only refinements of the categories by which other men live: power, class, status, race, ethnicity. As a result, there is a deceptive simplicity and obviousness about some sociological investigations. One reads them, nods at the familiar scene, remarks that one has heard all this before and don't people have better things to do than to waste their time on truisms—until one is suddenly brought up against an insight that radically questions everything one had previously assumed about this familiar scene. This is the point at which one begins to sense the excitement of sociology.

Let us take a specific example. Imagine a sociology class in a southern college at which almost all the students are white southerners. Imagine a lecture on the subject of the racial system of the South. The lecturer is talking here of matters that have been familiar to his students from the time of their infancy. Indeed, it may be that they are much more familiar with the minutiae of this system than he is. They are quite bored as a result. It seems to them that he is only using more pretentious words to describe what they already know. Thus he may use the term "caste," one commonly used now by American sociologists to describe the southern racial system. But in explaining the term, he shifts to traditional Hindu society, to make it clearer. He then goes on to analyze the magical beliefs inherent in caste taboos, the social dynamics of commensalism and connubium, the economic interests concealed within the system, the way in which religious beliefs relate to the taboos, the effects of the caste system on the industrial development of the society and vice versa—all in India. Suddenly, India is not very far away at all. The lecture then goes back to its southern theme. The familiar now seems not quite so familiar any more. Questions are raised that are new, perhaps raised angrily, but raised all the same. And at least some of the students have begun to understand that there are functions involved in this business of race that they have not read about in the newspapers (at least not those in their hometowns) and that their parents have not told them—partly, at least, because neither the newspapers nor the parents knew about them.

It can be said that the first wisdom of sociology is this: Things are not what they seem. This, too, is a deceptively simple statement. It ceases to be simple after a while. Social reality turns out to have many layers of meaning. The discovery of each new layer changes the perception of the whole....

People who like to avoid shocking discoveries, who prefer to believe that society is just what they were taught in Sunday School, who like the safety of the rules and the maxims of what Alfred Schuetz has called the "world-taken-for-granted," should stay away from sociology. People who feel no temptation before closed doors, who have no curiosity about human beings, who are content to admire scenery without wondering about the people who live in those houses on the other side of that river, should probably also stay away from sociology. They will find it unpleasant or, at any rate, unrewarding. People who are interested in human beings only if they can change, convert, or reform them should also be warned, for they will find sociology much less useful than they hoped. And people whose interest is mainly in their own conceptual constructions will do just as well to turn to the study of little white mice. Sociology will be satisfying, in the long run, only to those who can think of nothing more entrancing than to watch men and to understand things human.

It may now be clear that we have, albeit deliberately, understated the case in the title of this chapter. To be sure, sociology is an individual pastime in the sense that it interests some men and bores others. Some like to observe human beings, others like to experiment with mice. The world is big enough to hold all kinds, and there is no logical priority for one interest as against another. But the word *pastime* is weak in describing what we mean. Sociology is more like a passion. The sociological perspective is more like a demon that possesses one, that drives one compellingly, again and again, to the questions that are its own. An introduction to sociology is, therefore, an invitation to a very special kind of passion....

2. THE SOCIOLOGICAL IMAGINATION

C. WRIGHT MILLS

The individual can ... know his own chances in life only by becoming aware of those of all individuals in his circumstances.

C. Wright Mills, who died in 1962 at the age of 46, published two classic sociological works: *The Power Elite* and *The Sociological Imagination*. The first of these proved to be extremely important for studying the power structure in the United States. It inspired many sociologists to do research on power and inequality. It is also to Mills's credit that he saw that sociology, in its attempt to be scientific, was losing a spirit that had to be recovered. He called this spirit the "sociological imagination." In his book by that name, he criticized those of us who have lost that imagination, and he called for a renewed effort to help people deal with human problems through sharing the sociological perspective. The section that follows is most of Chapter I from *The Sociological Imagination*, entitled "The Promise." Here Mills, like Berger, shows us the possibilities that sociology holds for those who come to understand it. What people need, Mills contends, "is a quality of mind that will help them use information and to develop reason" to better understand the world and "what may be happening within themselves." This quality is "the sociological imagination."

Here is Mills's organization. It might help you to keep it in mind as you read:

1. "Ordinary men" have problems looking beyond their immediate situation at history and society.
2. The sociological imagination includes three questions that can be applied to a number of human situations.
3. The sociological imagination is the linking of personal problems to public issues.

(Mills, too, used the language of his time; again, you might notice the use of *he*, *him*, and *his*. Mills gives one the impression that only men can have the sociological imagination, but I am positive that he did not intend this.)

Nowadays, men often feel that their private lives are a series of traps. They sense that within their everyday worlds, they cannot overcome their troubles, and in this feeling, they are often quite correct: What ordinary men are directly aware of and what they try to do are bounded by the private orbits in which they live. Their visions and their powers are limited to the close-up scenes of job, family, neighborhood. In other milieux, they move vicariously and remain spectators. And the more aware they become, however vaguely, of ambitions and of threats that transcend their immediate locales, the more trapped they seem to feel.

Underlying this sense of being trapped are seemingly impersonal changes in the very structure of continent-wide societies. The facts of contemporary history are also facts about the success and the failure of individual men and women. When a society is industrialized, a peasant becomes a worker; a feudal lord is liquidated or becomes a businessman. When classes rise or fall, a man is employed or unemployed; when the rate of investment goes up or down, a man takes new heart or goes broke. When wars happen, an insurance salesman becomes a rocket launcher; a store clerk, a radar man; a wife lives alone; a child grows up without a father. Neither the life of an individual nor the history of a society can be understood without understanding both.

Yet men do not usually define the troubles they endure in terms of historical change and institutional contradiction. The well-being they enjoy, they do not usually impute to the big ups and downs of the societies in which they live. Seldom aware of the intricate connection between the patterns of their own lives and the course of world history, ordinary men do not usually know what this connection means for the kinds of men they are becoming and for the kinds of history-making in which they might take part. They do not possess the quality of mind essential to grasp the interplay of man and society, of biography and history, of self and world. They cannot cope with their personal troubles in such ways as to control the structural transformations that usually lie behind them.

Surely it is no wonder. In what period have so many men been so totally exposed at so fast a pace to such earthquakes of change? That Americans have not known such catastrophic changes as have the men and women of other societies is caused by historical facts that are now quickly becoming "merely history." The history that now affects every man is world history. Within this scene and this period, in the course of a single generation, one-sixth of mankind is transformed from all that is feudal and backward into all that is modern, advanced, and fearful. Political colonies are freed, new and less visible forms of imperialism are installed. Revolutions occur; men feel the intimate grip of new kinds of authority. Totalitarian societies rise and are smashed to bits—or succeed fabulously. After two centuries of ascendancy, capitalism is shown up as only one way to make society into an industrial apparatus. After two centuries of hope, even

formal democracy is restricted to a quite small portion of mankind. Everywhere in the underdeveloped world, ancient ways of life are broken up and vague expectations become urgent demands. Everywhere in the overdeveloped world, the means of authority and of violence become total in scope and bureaucratic in form. Humanity itself now lies before us, the supernation at either pole concentrating its most coordinated and massive efforts on the preparation of World War III.

The very shaping of history now outpaces the ability of men to orient themselves in accordance with cherished values. And which values? Even when they do not panic, men often sense that older ways of feeling and thinking have collapsed and that newer beginnings are ambiguous to the point of moral stasis. Is it any wonder that ordinary men feel they cannot cope with the larger worlds with which they are so suddenly confronted? That they cannot understand the meaning of their epoch for their own lives? That—in defense of selfhood—they become morally insensible, trying to remain altogether private men? Is it any wonder that they come to be possessed by a sense of the trap?

It is not only information that they need. In this Age of Fact, information often dominates their attention and overwhelms their capacities to assimilate it. It is not only the skills of reason that they need—although their struggles to acquire these often exhaust their limited moral energy.

What they need, and what they feel they need, is a quality of mind that will help them to use information and to develop reason in order to achieve lucid summations of what is going on in the world and of what may be happening within themselves. It is this quality, I am going to contend, that journalists and scholars, artists and publics, scientists and editors are coming to expect of what may be called the *sociological imagination*.

The sociological imagination enables its possessor to understand the larger historical scene in terms of its meaning for the inner life and the external career of a variety of individuals. It enables him to take into account how individuals, in the welter of their daily experience, often become falsely conscious of their social positions. Within that welter, the framework of modern society is sought; within that framework, the psychologies of a variety of men and women are formulated. By such means the personal uneasiness of individuals is focused on explicit troubles, and the indifference of publics is transformed into involvement with public issues.

The first fruit of this imagination—and the first lesson of the social science that embodies it—is the idea that the individual can understand his own experience and gauge his own fate only by locating himself within his period, that he can know his own chances in life only by becoming aware of those of all individuals in his circumstances. In many ways, it is a terrible lesson; in many ways, a magnificent one. We do not know the limits of man's capacities for supreme effort or willing degradation, for agony or glee, for pleasurable brutality or the sweetness of reason. But in our time, we have come to know that the limits of "human nature" are frighteningly broad. We have come to know that every individual lives, from one generation to the next, in some society; that he lives out a biography, and that he lives it out within some historical sequence. By the fact of his living, he contributes—however minutely—to the shaping of this society and to the course of its history, even as he is made by society and by its historical push and shove.

The sociological imagination enables us to grasp history and biography and the relations between the two within society. That is its task and its promise. To recognize this task and this promise is the mark of the classic social analyst. It is characteristic of Herbert Spencer—turgid, polysyllabic, comprehensive; of E. A. Ross—graceful, muckraking, upright; of Auguste Comte and Emile Durkheim; of the intricate and subtle Karl Mannheim. It is the quality of all that is intellectually excellent in Karl Marx; it is the clue to Thorstein Veblen's brilliant and ironic insight, to Joseph Schumpeter's many-sided constructions of reality; it is the basis of the psychological sweep of W. E. H. Lecky no less than of the profundity and clarity of Max Weber. And it is the signal of what is best in contemporary studies of man and society.

No social study that does not come back to the problems of biography, of history, and of their intersections within a society has completed its intellectual journey. Whatever the specific problems of the classic social analysts, however limited or however broad the features of social reality they have examined, those who have been imaginatively aware of the promise of their work have consistently asked three sorts of questions:

1. What is the structure of this particular society as a whole? What are its essential components, and how are they related to one another? How does it differ from other varieties of social order? Within it, what is the meaning of any particular feature for its continuance and for its change?
2. Where does this society stand in human history? What are the mechanics by which it is changing? What is its place within and its meaning for the development of humanity as a whole? How does any particular feature we are examining affect—and how is it affected by—the historical period in which it moves? And this period—what are its essential features? How does it differ from other periods? What are its characteristic ways of history making?
3. What varieties of men and women now prevail in this society and in this period? And what varieties are coming to prevail? In what ways are they selected and formed, liberated and repressed, made sensitive and blunted? What kinds of "human nature" are revealed in the conduct and character we observe in this society in this period? And what is the meaning for "human nature" of each and every feature of the society we are examining?

Whether the point of interest is a great power state or a minor literary mood, a family, a prison, a creed—these are the kinds of questions the best social analysts have asked. They are the intellectual pivots of classic studies of man in society—and they are the questions inevitably raised by any mind possessing the sociological imagination. For that imagination is the capacity to shift from one perspective to another—from the political to the psychological; from the examination of a single family to the comparative assessment of the national budgets of the world; from the theological school to the military establishment; from considerations of an oil industry to studies of contemporary poetry. It is the capacity to range from the most impersonal and remote transformations to the most intimate features of the human self—and to see the relations between the two. Back of its use there is always the urge to know the social and historical meaning of the individual in the society and in the period in which he has his quality and his being.

That, in brief, is why it is by means of the sociological imagination that men now hope to grasp what is going on in the world, and to understand what is happening in themselves as minute points of the intersections of biography and history within society. In large part, contemporary man's self-conscious view of himself as at least an outsider, if not a permanent stranger, rests on an absorbed realization of social relativity and of the transformative power of history. The sociological imagination is the most fruitful form of this self-consciousness. By its use, men whose mentalities have swept only a series of limited orbits often come to feel as if suddenly awakened in a house with which they had only supposed themselves to be familiar. Correctly or incorrectly, they often come to feel that they can now provide themselves with adequate summations, cohesive assessments, comprehensive orientations. Older decisions that once appeared sound now seem to them products of a mind unaccountably dense. Their capacity for astonishment is made lively again. They acquire a new way of thinking, they experience a transvaluation of values. In a word, by their reflection and by their sensibility, they realize the cultural meaning of the social sciences.

Perhaps the most fruitful distinction with which the sociological imagination works is between "the personal troubles of milieu" and "the public issues of social structure." This distinction is an essential tool of the sociological imagination and a feature of all classic work in social science.

Troubles occur within the character of the individual and within the range of his immediate relations with others; they have to do with his self and with those limited areas of social life of which he is directly and personally aware. Accordingly, the statement and the resolution of troubles properly lie within the individual as a biographical entity and within the scope of his immediate milieu—the social setting that is directly open to his personal experience and, to some extent, his willful activity. A trouble is a private matter: values cherished by an individual are felt by him to be threatened.

Issues have to do with matters that transcend these local environments of the individual and the range of his inner life. They have to do with the organization of many such milieux into the institutions of an historical society as a whole, with the ways in which various milieux overlap and interpenetrate to form the larger structure of social and historical life. An issue is a public matter: some value cherished by publics is felt to be threatened. Often, there is a debate about what that value really is and about what it is that really threatens it. This debate is often without focus if only because it is the very nature of an issue, unlike even widespread trouble, that it cannot be very well defined in terms of the immediate and everyday environments of ordinary men. An issue, in fact, often involves a crisis in institutional arrangements; often, it also involves what Marxists call "contradictions" or "antagonisms."

In these terms, consider unemployment. When, in a city of 100,000, only one man is unemployed, that is his personal trouble. For its relief, we properly look to the character of the man, his skills, and his immediate opportunities. But when in a nation of 50 million employees, 15 million are unemployed, that is an issue, and we may not hope to find its solution within the range of opportunities open to any one individual. The very structure of opportunities has collapsed. Both the correct statement of the problem and the range of possible solutions require us to consider the economic and political institutions of the society, not merely the personal situation and character of a scatter of individuals.

Consider war. The personal problem of war, when it occurs, may be how to survive it or how to die in it with honor; how to make money out of it; how to climb into the higher safety of the military apparatus; or how to contribute to the war's termination. In short, according to one's values, to find a set of milieux and within it to survive the war or make one's death in it meaningful. But the structural issues of war have to do with its causes; with what types of men it throws up into command; with its effects on economic, political, family, and religious institutions; with the unorganized irresponsibility of a world of nation-states.

Consider marriage. Inside a marriage, a man and a woman may experience personal troubles, but when the divorce rate during the first four years of marriage is 250 out of every 1,000 attempts, this is an indication of a structural issue having to do with the institutions of marriage and family and other institutions that bear upon them.

Or consider the metropolis—the horrible, beautiful, ugly, magnificent sprawl of the great city. For many upper-class people, the personal solution to "the problem of the city" is to have an apartment with a private garage under it in the heart of the city, and forty miles out, a house by Henry Hill, garden by Garrett Eckbo, on a hundred acres of private land. In these two controlled environments—with a small staff at each end and a private helicopter connection—most people could solve many of the problems of personal milieux caused by the facts of the city. But all this, however splendid, does not solve the public issues that the structural fact of the city poses. What should be done with this wonderful monstrosity? Break it all up into scattered units, combining residence and work? Refurbish it as it stands? Or, after evacuation, dynamite it and build new cities according to new plans in new places? What should those plans be? And who is to decide and to accomplish whatever choice is made? These are structural issues; to confront them and to solve them requires us to consider political and economic issues that affect innumerable milieux.

Insofar as an economy is so arranged that slumps occur, the problem of unemployment becomes incapable of personal solution. Insofar as war is inherent in the nation-state system and in the uneven industrialization of the world, the ordinary individual in his restricted milieu will be powerless—with or without psychiatric aid—to solve the troubles this system (or lack of system) imposes on him. Insofar as the family as an institution turns women into darling little slaves and men into their chief providers and unweaned dependents, the problem of a satisfactory marriage remains incapable of purely private solution. Insofar as the overdeveloped megalopolis and the overdeveloped automobile are built-in features of the overdeveloped society, the issues of urban living will not be solved by personal ingenuity and private wealth.

What we experience in various and specific milieux, I have noted, is often caused by structural changes. Accordingly, to understand the changes of many personal milieux, we are required to look beyond them. And the number and variety of such structural changes increase as the institutions within which we live become more embracing and more intricately connected with one another. To be aware of the idea of social structure and to use it with sensibility is to be capable of tracing such linkages among a great variety of milieux. To be able to do that is to possess the sociological imagination....

3.   THE PERSPECTIVE OF SOCIOLOGY

ALLAN G. JOHNSON

I believe that the choices we make as individuals matter beyond our lives more than we can imagine, that things don't have to be the way they are, but that they won't get better all by themselves. We need to do something, and what we do needs to be based on more than hunches and personal opinion and prejudice. We need systematic ways to figure things out, and that's what sociological practice offers.

Allan Johnson's book is about the *practice* of sociology in the sense that he uses sociology in every aspect of his life. To Johnson it is important to use sociology to understand the world in order to make it better. It is a practice that helps him understand himself and the world he lives in. Johnson is sensitive to an issue that almost all sociologists will agree with: we all participate "in something larger than ourselves...."

I am a practicing sociologist. This book is about what it is that I practice and what it means and why it matters to practice it. This book is about how the practice finds its way into almost every aspect of life, from headlines in the morning paper to the experience of growing older to the ravages of social oppression in the world. It is about things small and things large, things simple and things complex well past what we can imagine.

I practice sociology in many ways. I practice it when I think about how social life works, when I write, when I work with people trying to see what's going on in the world and our lives in it. I practice as a consultant in corporations to help solve the dilemmas of a diverse and difficult world in which race, gender, sexual orientation, and other issues of difference cast dark shadows over people's lives. I practice when I walk down a street, shop in a market, or sit in a sidewalk restaurant, sip a cup of coffee, and watch the world go by and wonder what life *really* is all about, what this stream of interconnected peo-

ple's lives consists of, what knits it all together and what tears it apart, and what, as my students would say, it's got to do with me.

I practice sociology for many reasons. I practice it because there is so much unnecessary suffering in the world, and to do something about it we need to understand where it comes from. In this sense, practicing sociology has a profoundly moral dimension. I don't mean this in the sense that it's about being good instead of bad. I mean it in a deeper and broader sense of morality that touches on the essence of what we're about as human beings and what our life together consists of. It is impossible to study social life for very long without coming up against the consequences that social life produces, and a lot of these consequences do such damage to people's lives that, unless we find ways to deny or ignore the reality of it, we feel compelled to ask "why?" And once we ask that question, we need tools to help make sense of where it leads and to imagine how we might go from there toward something better. We can't help but be part of the problem; practicing sociology is a way to also be part of the solution. This not only helps the world, but makes it easier to live in, especially given how crazy a place it can seem. It helps to be able to see how one thing

From *The Forest and the Trees: Sociology as Life, Practice and Promise*, by Allan G. Johnson, Temple University Press, 1997. By permission.

13

is connected to another, and, in that, how to find ways to make some small difference. We can't change the world all by ourselves, but we can make informed decisions about how to participate in it, and how that can help turn the world toward something better, even if it's just in our neighborhoods or families or where we work.

I wouldn't do all this if I didn't believe something better was possible, so I have to add faith to my list of reasons for practicing sociology. I believe that the choices we make as individuals matter beyond our lives more than we can imagine, that things don't have to be the way they are, but that they won't get better all by themselves. We need to do something, and what we do needs to be based on more than hunches and personal opinion and prejudice. We need systematic ways to figure things out, and that's what sociological practice offers.

I also practice sociology because it helps to keep me in touch with the essence of my own life in the world, for sociology isn't simply about some larger world "out there." It's also about us in the world and the connection between the two, which means it can take us toward basic truths about who we are and what our lives are about. I practice it because it reminds me that for all that we think we know about things, beneath that is all that we don't know, which is good reason to feel awed from time to time. On some level, for example, I'm amazed that social life works at all, that we're able to live and work together as much as we do, to talk, dream, imagine, fight, and create. There is something miraculous about the simplest conversation, miraculous in the sense that there is a core truth about how it happens that we can never get to. We can contemplate the miracle of things by taking ourselves toward the limit of what we can know. And we can feel the fringe of core truths and how our lives are part of them. So, while my practice is usually "about" understanding the world, it is also about keeping myself in touch with the essentially unknowable essence of human existence that lies beneath.

Practicing sociology is a way to observe the world and to think about and make sense of it. It is a way to be in the world and *of* the world, to play a meaningful role in the life of our species as it shapes and reshapes itself into the mystery of what's going on and what it's got to do with us....

THE ONE THING

If sociology could teach everyone just one thing with the best chance to lead toward everything else we could know about social life, it would, I believe, be this: *We are always participating in something larger than ourselves, and if we want to understand social life and what happens to people in it, we have to understand what it is that we're participating in and how we participate in it.* In other words, the key to understanding social life isn't just the forest and it isn't just the trees. It's the forest and the trees and how they're related to one another. Sociology is the study of how all this happens.

The "larger" things we participate in are called social systems, and they come in all shapes and sizes. In general, the concept of a system refers to any collection of parts or elements that are connected in ways that cohere into some kind of whole. We can think of the engine in a car as a system, for example, a collection of parts arranged in ways that make the car "go." Or we could think of a language as a system, with words and punctuation and rules for how to combine them into sentences that mean something. We can also think of a family as a system—a collection of elements related to one another in a way that leads us to think of it as a unit. These include things such as the positions of mother, father, wife, husband, parent, child, daughter, son, sister, and brother. Elements also include shared ideas that tie those positions together to make relationships, such as how "good mothers" are supposed to act in relation to children or what a "family" is and what makes family members "related" to one another as kin. If we take the positions and the ideas and other elements, then we can think of what results as a whole and call it a social system.

In similar ways, we can think of corporations or societies as social systems. They differ from one another—and from families—in the kinds of elements they include and how those are arranged in relation to one another. Corporations have positions such as CEOs and stockholders, for example; but the position of "mother" isn't part of the corporate system. People who work in corporations can certainly be mothers in families, but that isn't a position that connects them to a corporation. Such differences are a key to seeing how systems work and produce different kinds of consequences. Corporations are sometimes referred to as "families," for example, but if you look at how families and corporations are actually put together as systems, it's easy to see how unrealistic such notions are. Families don't usually "lay off" their members when times are tough or to boost the bottom line, and they usually don't divide the food on the dinner table according to who's the strongest and best able to grab the lion's share for themselves.[1] But corporations dispense with workers all the time as a way to raise dividends and the value of stock, and top managers routinely take a huge share of each year's profits even while putting other members of the corporate "family" out of work.

What social life comes down to, then, is social systems and how people participate in and relate to them. Note that people *participate* in systems without being *parts* of the systems themselves. In this sense, "father" is a position in my family, and I, Allan, am a person who actually occupies that position. It's a crucial distinction that's easy to lose sight of. It's easy to lose sight of because we're so used to thinking solely in terms of individuals. It's crucial because it means that people aren't systems, and systems aren't people, and if we forget that, we're likely to focus on the wrong thing in trying to solve our problems.

Thinking of systems as just people is why members of privileged groups often take it personally when someone points out that society is racist or sexist or classist. "The United States is a racist society that privileges whites over other racial groups" is a statement that describes the United States as a social system. It does *not* thereby describe me or anyone else as an individual, for that has more to do with how each of us participates in society. As an individual, I can't avoid participating and can't help but be affected and shaped by that. But how all that plays out in practice depends on many things, including the choices I make about *how* to participate. Born in 1946, I grew up listening to the radio shows of the day, including *Amos and Andy*, which was full of racist stereotypes about blacks (the actors were white). Like any other child, I looked to my environment to define

what was "funny." Since this show was clearly defined as "funny" from a white perspective in a white society, and since I was born white, I laughed along with everyone else as we drove down the highway listening to the car radio. I even learned to "do" the voices of "black" characters and regaled my family with renditions of classic lines from the show.

More than forty years later, those racist images are firmly lodged in my memory; once they get in, there's no way to get them out. With the benefit of hindsight, I see the racism in them and how they're connected to massive injustice and suffering in the society I participate in. As an individual, I can't undo the past and I can't undo my childhood. I can, however, choose what to do about race and racism *now*. I can't make my society or the place where I live or work suddenly nonracist, but I can decide how to live as a white person in relation to my privileged *position* as a white person. I can decide whether to laugh or object when I hear racist "humor"; I can decide how to treat people who aren't classified as "white"; I can decide what to do about the consequences that racism produces for people, whether to be part of the solution or merely part of the problem. I don't feel guilty because my country is racist, because that wasn't my doing. But as a white person who *participates* in that society, I feel responsible to consider what to do about it. The only way to get past the potential for guilt and see how I can make a difference is to realize that the system isn't me and I'm not the system.

Nonetheless, systems and people are closely connected to each other, and seeing how that works is a basic part of sociological practice. One way to see this is to compare social systems to a game such as Monopoly. We can think of Monopoly as a social system. It has positions (players, banker); it has a material reality (the board, the pieces, the dice, play money, property deeds, houses and hotels); and it has ideas that connect all of this together in a set of relationships. There are values that define the point of the game—to win—and rules that spell out what's allowed in pursuit of winning, including the idea of cheating. Notice that we can describe the game without saying anything about the personalities, intentions, attitudes, or other characteristics of the people who might play it. The game, in other words, has an existence that we can describe all by itself. "It" exists whether or not anyone is playing it at the moment. The same is true of social systems. We don't have to describe actual basketball players in order to describe "a basketball team" as a kind of system that has characteristics that distinguish it from other systems.

I don't play Monopoly anymore, mostly because I don't like the way I behave when I do. When I used to play Monopoly, I'd try to win, even against my own children, and I couldn't resist feeling good when I did (we're *supposed* to feel good) even if I also felt guilty about it. Why did I act and feel this way? It wasn't because I have a greedy, mercenary personality, because I know that I don't behave this way when I'm not playing Monopoly. Clearly I am *capable* of behaving this way as an individual, which is part of the explanation. But the rest of it comes down to the simple fact that I behaved that way because winning is what Monopoly is about. When I participate in that system, greedy behavior is presented to me as a path of least resistance. As defined by the game, it's what you're supposed to do; it's the point. And when I play the game, I feel obliged to go by its rules and pursue the values it promotes. I look upon the game as having some kind of authority over the people who play it, which becomes apparent when I consider how rare it is for people to suggest changing the rules ("I'm sorry, honey," I say as I take my kid's last dollar, "but that's just the way the game is played"). If *we* were the game, then we'd feel free to play by any rules we liked. But we tend not to see games—or systems—in that way. We tend to see them as external to us and therefore not ours to shape however we please....

IT'S ABOUT US AND
IT'S NOT ABOUT US

If we start from the idea that we're always participating in something larger than ourselves and that social life flows from this relationship, then we have to consider that we're all involved—even if only indirectly—in the social consequences that result, both the good and the bad. By defini-

tion, if I participate in a racist society—no matter what my race—then I'm involved in white privilege and racist consequences. As an individual, I may not feel or act in racist ways and in my heart I may even hate racism; but that's beside the core sociological point. I'm *involved* in one way or another by virtue of my participation in society itself.[2] If someone takes what I say more seriously because I'm white, then I've received a benefit of racism whether I'm aware of it or not, and in doing so, I've unwittingly participated in racism. This raises the question of how society works *and* how I participate in it—whether I actively defend white privilege or let people know I'm against racism or just go about my business and pretend there's no problem to begin with.

In diversity training sessions, this simple insight can dramatically alter how people see potentially painful issues and themselves in relation to them. This is especially true for people in privileged groups who otherwise resist looking at the nature and consequences of privilege. Their defensive resistance is probably the biggest single barrier to ending racism, sexism, and other forms of social oppression. Most of the time it happens because, like everyone else, they're stuck in an individualistic model of the world and can't see a way to acknowledge racial privilege as a fact of social life without also feeling personally blamed and guilty for it. And the people who are most likely to feel this way are often the ones who are otherwise most open to doing something to make things better. When they look at a problem like racism sociologically, however, they can see how it's both about them and not about them. It's not about them in the sense that they didn't create the racist society we all live in. As I was growing up white, no one asked me if it was OK with me for white people to use *Amos and Andy* to make fun of black people and keep them in their place beneath white privilege. And if they *had* asked me, I doubt that as a child I'd have known enough to object. In this sense, white people who've grown up in a racist environment have no reason to feel guilty when they hear anger about the existence of white racism and the harm and suffering it causes.

Racism *is* about me personally, however, because whether or not I'm conscious of it, I'm always making choices about how to participate in a society that is organized in racist ways and that makes behavior that perpetuates white privilege a path of least resistance. Regardless of how I behave, as a white person I have privileges that are at the expense of people of other races. Race privilege is built into the system itself, which means I don't have to like it or believe in it or even do anything to receive it. When I go shopping at the mall, sales people and store detectives don't follow me around as if I was going to steal something. They don't swoop down on me and pointedly ask "Can I help you?" as if I was a suspicious character or something other than a serious customer. But black people are mistreated this way all the time, and it usually doesn't matter how well they dress or how much money they have to spend.[3] Most people would agree that everyone should be treated decently, but when some are and some aren't simply because of which group they belong to, then social privilege is at work. And whether I like it or not, as a white person I benefit from that by getting something of value that's denied to them. Once I see this, it's hard to avoid asking about how I participate in the system that produces such racist consequences. What are my responsibilities? What could I do differently that would contribute to different outcomes? How can I be part of the solution to racism rather than merely part of the problem?

In other words, by making me aware that I'm involved in something larger than myself, sociological practice gets me off the hook of personal guilt and blame for a world that I didn't create and that isn't my fault. At the same time, however, it makes me aware of how I choose to participate in that world and how and why that matters. I have no reason to feel guilty simply because I'm white; but I also don't have the luxury of thinking that racism and race privilege have nothing to do with me.[4]...

NOTES

1. There are of course numerous examples of cultures and historical periods where families have behaved in this way, especially in relation to daughters. But in places like the United States where organizations are routinely likened to families, this is not how normal family life is viewed.
2. For more on this way of looking at racism, see David T. Wellman, *Portraits of White Racism*, 2nd ed. (New York: Cambridge University Press, 1993).
3. See, for example, Ellis Cose, *The Rage of a Privileged Class* (New York: HarperCollins, 1993); Joe R. Feagin, "The Continuing Significance of Race: Antiblack Discrimination in Public Places," *American Sociological Review* 56, 1 (1991): 101–116; and Joe R. Feagin and Melvin P. Sikes, *Living with Racism: The Black Middle-Class Experience* (Boston: Beacon Press, 1994).
4. For useful perspectives on how white people can become more aware of how they're connected to a racist society on a personal level, see Paul Kivel, *Uprooting Racism: How White People Can Work for Racial Justice* (Philadelphia: New Society Publishers, 1996).

4. SCIENCE AND PARANORMALISM

ERICH GOODE

Scientists have devised theories or explanatory accounts of how the world works that exclude or prohibit paranormal phenomena or events. Within the framework of traditional or conventional science, many of the events or phenomena that paranormalists say take place are all but impossible. Science has supplied accounts of how one factor or variable influences or causes another. Paranormalism supplies accounts that the universe works in a different way.

Erich Goode is one of the clearest writers of sociology I have read. The difficult topic of science that he writes about in this selection challenges the reader, educates the reader, and clearly introduces the reader to the meaning and importance of science.

Goode emphasizes the fact that science like paranormalism is a very unique approach to understanding. He shows us that science tries to explain why things happen in nature, and since science has become central to Western thinking, that which explains events outside of natural cause is called paranormal. This does not make science right and paranormalism wrong. However, since sociology is a social science, it does not accept paranormal explanation.

The real essence of Goode's selection is his clear explanation of science as empirical and explanatory, taking us a long way to understanding the meaning of science.

"How to Tell if You've Been Raped by a Space Alien!"
"Baby Born with Angel Wings"
"Captured Alien Warns of Invasion from Space"
"Snake Tattoo Chokes Man"
"Orphan Ghost Tortures Couple"
"Half-human Half-fish Are Washing up in Florida!"
"Amazing Dog Levitates in Mid-Air"
"10,000-Year-Old UFO Found in Jungle"
"Brain Doc Cuts Man's Head Open and Removes Demon"
"Chernobyl Chicken Is 6 Ft. Tall"
"Real-Life Flying Nun Floats in the Air & Heals the Sick!"
"Cat Eats Parrot—Now It Talks"

"UFOs Found Hiding in Circus Freak Show"
"Robot Gives Birth to a Human Baby"
"Ants Are Aliens from Space!"
"Sex-Change Woman Makes Self Pregnant"
"Town Beamed Up by UFO"
"Guardian Angel's Halo Blinds Sniper Targeting Cop"
"Eleven People Disappear in Connecticut 'Time Tunnel'"
"Four Space Aliens Held by CIA at Secret Compound in Maryland!"
"Painting of Elvis Weeps Real Tears"
"Woman Goes to Heaven—And Comes Back with Handful of Gold!"

These are a few headlines from articles published recently in tabloid newspapers. Each one makes a claim about events that scientists would say are improbable or all but impossible. While many people read these stories mainly as entertainment (Bird, 1992), a number of such claims are believed to be true by a sizeable proportion of the public. Events, phenomena, or powers that scientists regard as contrary to the laws of nature are referred to as "paranormal."

The prefix "para" is taken from ancient Greek and means "next to" (as in "paraprofessional," "paralegal," or "paramedical"); "similar to" (as in a reference to the police as a "paramilitary" force); or "outside of" or "beyond," which is where "paranormal" comes in. The dictionary defines *paranormal* as that which is "outside of," lies "beyond," or cannot be explained by, routine, ordinary, known, or recognized scientific laws or natural forces. Paranormal claims or stories invoke or make use of forces, factors, dynamics, or causes that scientists regard as inconsistent with a satisfying, naturalistic or materialistic, cause-and-effect explanation. Gray (1991, p.78) defines the paranormal as that which "apparently transcend the explanatory power of mainstream science and stem from unknown or hidden causes." Says Hines, what characterizes the paranormal "is a reliance on explanations for alleged phenomena that are well outside the bounds of established science" (1988, p. 7)....

The word "paranormal" refers, first, to the subject matter itself, as in paranormal *phenomena*—the events or powers that are alluded to. Second, it refers to how paranormal claims are *approached*—that is, whether the validity of these events is accepted, validated, or believed. Thus, when we read a headline that a woman who ate cat food turned into a cat, this narrative or story or claim refers, first, to a paranormal *event* (a woman turning into a cat) and, second, to a paranormal *belief* (the conviction that this event actually took place). Paranormalism is *a non- or extra-scientific approach to a phenomenon*—a scientifically implausible event is believed to be valid and literally and concretely true. Thus, the hallucinations a person under the influence of a psychedelic drug experiences would not be a paranormal phenomenon, since these effects are pharmacological in origin. But believing these visions to be concretely and literally real might very well represent a form of paranormalism.

The definition of paranormalism I offer uses terms that are commonly understood to explain

a concept that addresses events that fall outside the ordinary. Classic science is more frequently identified with linear causality—a mechanical view of the universe where observation reveals what action causes what reaction. This definition is based on what scientists *believe* or *judge* to be beyond the workings of nature. My definition of a scientist is a person with a doctorate in one of the natural sciences who conducts research that is or could be published in the professional journals in these fields. This definition rests squarely in the subjective realm or dimension. That is, it is based on what a sector of the society, scientists, *believe*. Society often assumes that science is objective, based on observable fact—that scientists can point to concrete reasons as to *why* a given assertion is paranormal and another one is not. However, what scientists *believe* is an assertion, not a fact. It is possible that their belief is wrong. One day their label of paranormal (as something outside the boundary of how nature works) may be rejected. Currently that label is a reality and has important sociological consequences....

In the 1700s, farmers and peasants reported that stones fell from the sky. Scientists claimed that such a thing was impossible. The peasants were right. The "stones" did fall; of course; today, we call them meteorites (Westrum, 1978). As a sociologist, I am interested less in whether a given claim is true and more in the struggle to establish a given claim *as* true. Knowing that it is true (and keeping in mind the fact that science was not fully dominant in Western society in the 1700s), I nonetheless have no hesitation to refer to the assertion about stones falling from the sky *at that time* as paranormal, if such an event were to invoke forces or powers that scientists then regarded as a violation of nature's workings. What is thought to be paranormalism in one era can become mainstream science in another. My definition is relative to what scientists think at a given time, and scientists, being human, are fallible. I'll return to this issue a number of times throughout this book. Right now, I'd like to qualify these remarks very slightly.

Belief in the efficacy of powers or phenomena that Western scientists now say are improbable or extremely unlikely have been around since the dawn of humanity, of course. Anthropological textbooks are full of descriptions of religious and magical beliefs that are or were prevalent in nonliterate societies around the world. Does practicing witchcraft cause your enemy to get sick and die? Does the volcano that looms above the village erupt when the volcano god becomes angry? Does animal sacrifice keep the evil spirits away? Were all the stars in the heavens created by the tears of a love-sick wizard? Can examining chicken entrails predict whether an expectant mother will bear a girl or a boy? Most of us today would answer no to these questions; we would argue that science demonstrates them to be empirically or factually without foundation. Most of us believe science has far more valid explanations for these matters than those offered by tribal, ancient, or folk peoples. Does that make these earlier beliefs about how the universe operates examples of paranormalism?

The answer is, no, not quite, at least not as I've defined the term. Most researchers of the paranormal do not investigate the non-scientific beliefs of small, tribal, preliterate, or preindustrial societies — at least not *as* a form of paranormalism. They would insist that the concept of paranormalism is meaningful only when traditional science is established as the norm and it competes with non-scientific beliefs in the same society. Persons who grow up in a society that socializes them to believe that witches, wizards, gods, and spirits have special powers are not able to weigh the validity of such beliefs against a scientific alternative, since science does not exist in that society. Simply by being functioning members of Druid society 2,000 years ago, we would have believed that priestly prayers ensure an abundant crop. As an instance of paranormalism, at a time when science did not exist, the acceptance of non-scientific beliefs is not especially interesting, problematic, or even meaningful.

Paranormalism becomes an intellectual issue only in a society where the scientific method is *hegemonic*, that is, the dominant belief. In Druid society, Western science did not exist; hence, there was no perspective *then* that could have labeled its beliefs *as* paranormal. The same is not true of the modern world. Why do so many people in the world today embrace beliefs that modern science says are false? It is an interesting question, but it was not even a *meaningful* question 2,000 years ago. I'll be raising and attempting to answer similar questions throughout this book. Therefore, when I refer to paranormal beliefs, I do so only within the context of the modern world. I will refer to paranormalism only as a belief system that *contrasts* with what scientists believe is likely *within* a scientifically oriented society.

At what point in the history of the West did science become established as the dominant or hegemonic belief system? When did it obtain the approval and support of the political institution, that is, the government? When did a scientific view of things become the major perspective in the public school system, as well as in higher education? In the mainstream or most authoritative media?

Science became more or less fully institutionalized in the western world roughly a century ago. There is no way of measuring this precisely, but in 1873, authorities at Johns Hopkins University announced that evolution would henceforth be taught as the valid interpretation of the origin of species. Within a few decades, this perspective became the dominant perspective in biology courses. A second date, 1910, is important. In this year the Flexner Report, which was a major step in the professionalization of medical education in the United States, was published. It announced the dominance of Western science in the field of medicine and established medicine as a scientific discipline. For good or ill, and whether their version of reality was valid or not, by some time at the beginning of the twentieth century, mainstream, positivistic Western science and medicine became legitimate, institutionalized, dominant, and hegemonic.

Once again, notice that I am not focusing on the issue of whether Western science or paranormalism is right or wrong. Instead, I am interested in a hegemonic versus a counter-hegemonic view of reality. How does an alternative interpretation of reality become established, legitimated? Given that it runs contrary to the dominant perspective, how does it get its message across? To which segments of the society does it appeal? This approach raises a host of important implications, which I'll explore throughout this book.

THE POPULARITY OF PARANORMAL BELIEFS

This book is a sociological investigation into paranormal beliefs—the view that under certain circumstances what are regarded by traditional scientists as the laws of nature can be bent, broken, suspended, violated, superseded, or subsumed under entirely different principles. A few examples of paranormalism include belief in the truth, reality, or validity of: psychics, occult prophecies, tarot cards, "automatic" writing, parapsychology, ESP (extrasensory perception), remote viewing or clairvoyance (seeing objects outside one's line of vision), time travel, a flat earth, a hollow earth, King Tut's "curse," weeping icons and statues, ancient astronauts, ghosts, seances, hauntings, spiritism (communication with the dead), telepathy (communicating with someone else, living or dead, without the aid of the five senses), precognition and retrocognition (the ability to "see" or intuit the past or to predict the future with one's mind alone, without the assistance of relevant data), channeling (speaking with the voice of a dead person's soul or spirit), spiritual possession, faith healing, dowsing (using a forked stick to determine where water or minerals are located in the ground), witches and witchcraft, angels, the devil as a material-world being, out-of-body experiences, past lives, reincarnation, karma, teleportation, PK (psychokinesis, or moving physical matter with the power of one's mind), lucky numbers, astral projection, unaided voyages to distant places, the physical appearance or earthly manifestation of dead people, miracles, Scientology, dianetics, theosophy, spontaneous combustion, seeing visions of physically nonexistent phenomena, immortality, synchronicity (coincidence, or the special significance or meaning of the appearance of related phenomena above and beyond the laws of chance), the occult origin of crop circles, pyramid power, crystal power, the "Bermuda Triangle," plant perception, astrology, the "lunar" effect (the belief that the position of the moon influences what happens on earth, beyond its gravitational pull), the "Mars" effect (the same for the position of Mars), the "Jupiter" effect (ditto for Jupiter), fairies, the transformation of humans or animals into fantastic creatures such as vampires and werewolves, UFOs as spaceships of extraplanetary origin, alien abductions, numerology (the special significance of certain sequences of numbers), and strict creationism.

Perhaps the most dramatic and memorable examples of paranormal assertions can be found in the pages of supermarket tabloids, of which the *Sun* and the *Weekly World News* are the most clear-cut examples. The headlines quoted at the beginning of this chapter were taken from these two tabloids. (Except for articles on astrology, miraculous healing, and psychic predictions, *The National Enquirer* has abandoned paranormal material and sticks pretty much to gossip about celebrities.) However, a substantial proportion (although far from all) the readers of these papers take these fantastic claims with a grain of salt and read them mainly for entertainment purposes.

Less dramatic but at least as revealing are the surveys taken by polling organizations on whether members of their samples hold paranormal beliefs. The Gallup poll is the most well-known of all polling organizations. In 1996, Gallup surveyed a nationally-representative sample of Americans on a number of paranormal beliefs (Gallup, 1997, pp. 204–207). The results are quite illuminating. Nearly half the sample (48 percent) said that they believe in ESP; a third (35 percent) believed in telepathy; a third (33 percent) believed that houses "can be haunted"; three in ten (30 percent) believed in ghosts; a quarter (27 percent) believed in clairvoyance, "or the power of the mind to know the past and predict the future" and astrology (25 percent); and a fifth said that they believe in reincarnation (22 percent), mental communication with the dead (20 percent), psychokinesis (also called telekinesis, 17 percent), and witches (19 percent). Nearly half believed that UFOs are "something real" (48 percent), and have visited earth (45 percent). Over half (56 percent) believed in the reality of the devil, and four in ten (42 percent) believed that some people have been possessed by the devil. Just under three-quarters (72 percent) said they believe in the reality of angels. It is entirely likely that the size of nearly all of these beliefs have grown since these polls were conducted. (See also Gallup and Newport, 1991; Miller, 1987; Bainbridge and Stark, 1980). Other surveys on college students have turned up similar findings (for instance, Gray, 1995; Harrold and Eve, 1995; Goode, 1999).

Two things are noteworthy about the results of these surveys. First, all these assertions contradict what scientists argue is the way the universe works. And second, the percentage of respondents who believe these claims, both in the Gallup polls and in my survey among undergraduates, is substantial. Clearly, then, in the general population as well as in fairly well-educated segments of the public, paranormal beliefs are popular and extremely widespread.

Obviously, paranormal beliefs cover an immense territory. It is unlikely that a single explanation can account for all of them. However, their common thread is the fact that mainstream, conventional, or traditional science regards their existence or validity so improbable as to be all but impossible. In order to understand how paranormalism operates, therefore, it is necessary to understand the reasoning that undergirds its opposite—conventional or traditional science.

THE SCIENTIFIC APPROACH

Since paranormalism is defined by its contradiction with traditional science, it becomes necessary to say a few words about how scientists approach the world. (I'll expand on this subject in the next two chapters.) For now, two points should be sufficient. One, science is *empirical*. And two, science is *theoretical*. These two points might seem contradictory, but they are two sides of the same coin.

Empirical means that which is informed or guided by information derived from one or more of the five senses; empirical is sensory, what you can see, feel, smell, hear, or taste. To the empiricist, the senses determine what is true. Of course, there are times when you can't see or hear something directly; the senses sometimes need assistance. For instance, you may want to observe tiny pond creatures, but you can only see them with a microscope. If you want to see distant stars or areas of planets and the moon, you will need to use a telescope. Other types of observation may entail using certain chemicals, instruments

(such as an electrocardiogram or an oscilloscope), or even questionnaires or interview schedules to find out what people say they have done or believe. Still others require examining the traces or remains of past events, such as fossils, shards of pottery, or ancient manuscripts. Thus, the "observation" that empiricists do may be indirect as well as direct; it may entail relying on what machines measure, what people say they did, or material that is left behind. (The demand that *all* events be *directly* observable is a fallacy; the pseudoscience on which it is based is referred to as "one-eyed" or "Baconian" science. It will assume importance in our discussion of creationism.) In short, observation (assisted by the necessary aids) is the watchword of the empiricist. "Observe and you shall know" is the empiricist's motto.

Being empirical isn't as easy as it sounds. The relevant information isn't always easy to observe. Sometimes it seems to be hiding in an inaccessible location. Very often, information is spotty, patchy, scattered; it comes in bits and pieces. Many of the things we might want to observe are not so homogeneous that they always appear the same way. We may observe certain things, but our observations may be flawed by the fact that we have seen only a small part of their reality. You've been told that John is a nasty person, but he's extremely nice to you. The Texas Grille has a reputation for efficient service, but the one time you ate at that restaurant you waited an hour to be served. You know it rains a lot in Seattle, but you stayed there for a week and didn't see a drop of rain. Your observations were empirical—you used the data of your senses. But they were very partial, very selective, and not a good cross-section of the things you observed. Scientific theories or explanations are a kind of "schematic diagram" of how reality operates; it is impossible for humans to take in and understand how all the details of a given phenomenon work simultaneously.

Scientists refer to evidence that is slanted or skewed as *biased*. When we use examples to tell us about the way something is, we ought to know that one or two examples are often biased. They may not look like or represent the whole of the thing we are talking about. You can always find one or two examples of almost anything. To scientists, the lesson of a few examples is not persuasive. They refer to evidence based exclusively on examples as "anecdotal." Instead of anecdotes, they say, we need *systematic* evidence—a good cross-section of what we are looking at. So, to determine John's character, we have to observe evidence of his relationships with a wide range of people, not just one. To find out if the service in the Texas Grille is good, we have to eat there a number of times, not just once. And to know about the rainfall in Seattle, we have to look at it year-round, not just during a single week.

Science does not just gather empirical information. Scientists would regard some facts, even if based on systematic observation, as useless. What would be the point of counting every grain of sand on a beach? It would be silly, even if the count were accurate. Scientists seek to tie their observations into an *explanatory* framework—a theory. It makes no difference to any theoretical framework that there are a trillion grains of sand on that beach or a trillion and one.

To many non-scientists, the word "theory" sounds like a guess, little more than wild speculation. Calling something a theory is to admit that it is unproven, as in "That's just a theory." To a scientist, a theory is not a guess, it is an *explanation* or *account* for a general class of phenomena. Why are things the way they are? A theory attempts to answer this question. Why did the dinosaurs die out? What causes AIDS? How did the universe begin? Theories are absolutely necessary in science. An explanatory or theoretical approach is precisely the opposite of mindless fact-gathering.

To a scientist, theories and facts are not opposites. Some theories are explanations that are empirically grounded—they are *facts*. Others are explanations that have not been confirmed; that is, they are theories but not yet regarded as facts. Still others have already been discarded because they were factually wrong. Theories may be wrong or right, they may have been confirmed or disconfirmed, but they, along with evidence, are the lifeblood of science.

Scientists argue that paranormal claims are false because they are not supported by plausible theories or explanations. This is more significant than the lack of evidence to support paranormal claims. Claims of levitation are always and automatically false, scientists would say, not *merely* because empirical observation of such an event is lacking or flawed, but because such an event would violate what is known about how the universe works. Claims that astrology can summarize people's character and predict their fate are false, not merely because the data to support such a claim are lacking but also because the claim cannot be supported by any plausible explanation. Scientists take evidence and theories equally seriously. If a claim violates the currently accepted theoretical framework, scientists become extremely suspicious of it. If the theory is wrong, the supposed data to support it must be flawed. On the other hand, if new evidence fit into a new theoretical scheme that articulates with established frameworks, scientists are likely to accept it. In other words, there is something of a dialectical tension between evidence and theories that often lead to a new synthesis.

Scientists have devised theories or explanatory accounts of how the world works that *exclude* or *prohibit* paranormal phenomena or events. Within the framework of traditional or conventional science, many of the events or phenomena that paranormalists say take place are all but impossible. Science has supplied accounts of how one factor or variable influences or causes another. Paranormalism supplies accounts that the universe works in a very different way. When someone claims that if a person lies underneath a pyramid-shaped structure, his or her intelligence will increase, scientists want to know *how* this process works. What are the precise *forces* or *mechanisms* that emanate from the pyramid to boost the intelligence of the person underneath it? What are the chemicals, the rays, or the molecules, that create the effect? Can they be detected, observed, measured? Where do they come from and how do they work? When such a claim is made, the scientist looks not only for empirical evidence or data relevant to the claim but also for a plausible account or explanation—a *theory*—of how it takes place. Anecdotal evidence that something has taken place more than once or twice is not enough. Without an explanatory theory, scientists inevitably remain unimpressed by paranormal claims. Some scientists go so far as to say, "I don't care *what* evidence you have! What you say is all but impossible!" Many non-scientists or paranormalists see this stance as closed-minded.

ABSOLUTES VERSUS PROBABILITIES

Science cannot definitively disprove the existence of paranormal forces. Scientists rarely use the word "impossible" when they refer to paranormal claims. (They may do so informally, but *as scientists*, they hardly ever do so.) They are more likely to use the phrase "highly unlikely" or perhaps "extremely improbable." Scientists refer to a claim as disconfirmed (but not absolutely disproven) when the evidence looks very strong against it. Scientists look for *degrees of probability*; they do not claim certainty. A critic can always come up with alternate explanations for why a given objection to a paranormal claim doesn't invalidate it.

Scientists do not make a claim to absolute, eternal truth. To a scientist, absolutes exist only in theology, logic, mathematics, political campaigns, and the popular mind. If a given proposition has been verified with extremely strong evidence, scientists say that it is true *beyond all reasonable doubt*. They grant that it is always possible for new and contradictory evidence to be dug up at some point in the future, but it is extremely unlikely. Once a given proposition is accepted as a fact, it has been "confirmed to such a degree that it would be perverse [or contrary] to withhold provisional assent.... I suppose that apples might start to rise tomorrow [instead of fall]," says biologist Stephen Jay Gould, "but the possibility does not merit equal time in the classroom" (1984, p. 255). Scientists then move on to another issue. Even what are referred to as "paradigm shifts" do not toss out old theories so much as subsume them under more general principles. For instance, Newton's theories were not refuted but subsumed by Einstein's theory of relativity. Under specific and clearly stipulated conditions, scientists would say, apples *always* fall. But it's possible that conditions not yet conceived of may enter the picture, and scientists are willing to grant their power to change the picture.

WHAT IS TRUE VERSUS WHAT SCIENTISTS BELIEVE

Here's another point I'd like to reiterate: when I use phrases such as "scientists say," or "science would conclude" or "according to the scientific method," I am not claiming that whatever scientists believe to be true *is* true in some deep, fundamental, or absolute sense. With respect to paranormal beliefs, "rejected by the majority of scientists" does not mean that it is false in the objective, factual sense.

The first statement ("rejected by scientists") is descriptive; it refers to a belief or judgment held by a certain category or community—scientists. The second ("false") is a judgment or *conclusion* about a given assertion. When I say that paranormal beliefs are defined by the fact that scientists *regard* them as false, I mean what I say and no more: that scientists *do* believe that paranormal beliefs are contrary to the laws of nature. Their feeling that this is so is a fact. Whether this feeling is true or valid in some ultimate or absolute sense is a separate issue. Paranormalism is *defined* by its contrast with what the scientific community believes are the workings of nature. If scientists, taken as a whole, believe that a given assertion is true, then it is *not* an example of paranormalism.

Thus, when I refer to the beliefs of scientists, I imply nothing about their absolute truth, only that scientists do hold these beliefs. Their validity is a separate issue (and my feelings about them, likewise, are separate). The fact that some people reject what scientists hold to be true by holding paranormal beliefs is itself a sociologically interesting and important question. So, again, keep in mind that when I say, "scientists believe," I mean that and only that. I do not mean that if scientists believe something to be true, it is always automatically true, or that if someone believes something else, it is by its very nature false. In fact, as we'll see in the next chapter, scientists are often wrong. Science is defined not by the *content* of scientific beliefs but by the *method* by which evidence is gathered and their conclusions are reached. This method is often violated; even when followed, it sometimes produces incorrect results. There is nothing sacred about the views of scientists, but a study of their views, as well as the beliefs that contrast with them, is a sociologically interesting and important topic.

Another way of saying this is that the sociological study of both science and paranormalism are studies of *claims-making*. By that I mean that both science and paranormalism make claims about the nature of reality. Both assert that certain statements, and certain *kinds* of statements, are true. Our perspective does not automatically privilege one type of claim over another. Scientists and psychics are both in the business of convincing audiences that their assertions have validity. They describe the way things are, what the universe looks like, and how it behaves. While both make claims, they don't always make use of the same types of evidence, nor do they reason in the same way. Their audiences also differ in the type of evidence and reasoning processes they find convincing. All these things are sociologically and psychologically patterned, and must be understood as phenomena in their own right. Our interest is in the different approaches to reality. The conventional scientific approach and the paranormal approach make certain claims, use certain kinds of evidence and reasoning processes, and attract certain audiences. It is our job to understand how all this works.

SOCIOLOGISTS, SCIENTISTS, AND PARANORMALISTS

One last point: *the approach most sociologists use to study beliefs* is similar to the way traditional scientists gather evidence and draw conclusions. Sociologists of the paranormal are generally *empirical* in their approach; they ask questions, gather evidence, use science-like reasoning processes, make inferences, test theories, draw conclusions, and appeal to fairly traditional audiences. The sociologist's first response to claims that someone has levitated or communicated with the dead is to try to understand the sort of person who might make such a statement. But his or her *second* response is likely to be much the same as that of most natural scientists: "Show me the evidence."

I am a sociologist and an empiricist. I seek explanations for events in the social world that rely on cause-and-effect mechanisms. The way I do

my intellectual work is not radically different from the way that traditional natural scientists conduct research. However, there are other aspects of my approach that diverge sharply from the conventional scientific perspective. I feel that the study of social behavior is not merely a scrutiny of the mechanical, cause-and-effect motions of a species of being, namely, humans. At least two things make the study of social life different from the study of the natural order.

One is that humans are thinking, reasoning, symbol-using creatures who devise beliefs and ways of life that must be understood in the context in which they were created. The fact that a given belief is accepted among a specific social circle must be understood in these terms. We need go no further than hormones, anatomy, and triggering environmental cues to understand why the bullfrog croaks. But when a survivalist in Idaho believes that United Nations troops are poised to invade and conquer the United States, that belief is an announcement about particular perceptions about the world, how it operates, and what it means. Beliefs both generate and represent meaning-systems; to understand them, we have to get inside them—in a way, *appreciate* them. The survivalist's world is *socially constructed* (Berger and Luckmann, 1966), and the nature of that construction process is the sociologist's stock-in-trade.

A second way in which the study of human behavior and belief is different from the study of natural phenomena is that social scientists are part of the world they study. Our social entanglements in the lives of the people we study are a factor in the way we view those lives. Political, ideological, and ethical considerations play a role in all investigation, scientific or otherwise, but they play a special role for sociologists. Will our research validate or discredit the groups we study? Will they support or harm a certain political cause? What if the publication of our study of a gang of drug dealers or delinquents results in their arrest? How will the social categories to which we belong (for instance, sex, race, age, socioeconomic status) influence what we see and report? Is it right or proper to snoop into anyone's sex life? How much should we cooperate with the police? The government? The media? What if the people we study ask us to do things we feel are unethical or improper? Should we participate in the very behavior we study? These are very difficult questions, almost impossible to answer in a straightforward fashion. While the natural scientist is *sometimes* entangled in political, moral, and ideological issues (consider the subject evolutionists study), the social scientist *almost always* has to struggle with them, and this struggle is often painful.

A FEW CONCLUDING THOUGHTS

Many definitions of the paranormal are possible, and many have been proposed. I've defined paranormalism the non-scientific approach to a scientifically implausible event believed to be literally true. It is the operation of a principle or force that scientists say violates the laws of nature. Two camps or factions may object to this definition: traditional scientists and supporters of paranormalism.

Traditional scientists will argue that my definition relativizes science. To reiterate, notice that I do not say that paranormalism is a view that *violates* one or more laws of nature. Instead, I say that it is a view that violates what scientists *believe* are one or more laws of nature. I also insist that our definition is relative to *today*, not to 1600 or 1800; paranormalism is what scientists *now* regard as all but impossible. Remember, I am interested in how advocates of an alternative perspective (that is, paranormalism) struggle against a dominant perspective's interpretations and their consequences. Therefore, defining paranormalism relative to science in 1600 or 1800 is not entirely relevant. Why? Because science was not the dominant perspective in 1600, or even in 1800.

Many paranormalists, too, will object to my definition. Its point of departure is based on what scientists, not what paranormalists, believe. It is a negative definition, taking its meaning from the lack of correspondence with the mainstream, status-quo thinking. Why not define paranormalism positively by how its advocates rather than its opponents think? After all, if we followed my definition, any heterodox or heretical scientific theory that is later accepted will be defined as paranormal.

It is not my job here to endorse one or another perspective, view, or theory. (Although, as I said,

the very foundation of my thinking is more scientific than paranormal.) The question of the validity of one or another assertion about how nature works is not my primary interest here. I am *mainly* interested in how views of true and false are regarded, debated, and fought over. Science is currently the dominant view and its opposite, paranormalism, represents a deviation from the norm, whose proponents must struggle to achieve for it acceptance and legitimacy. How proponents of these two perspectives fight it out and to what conclusion is our central issue here. All good definitions apply *more or less* to the phenomena they define. None fit perfectly, all are fuzzy around the edges. If readers come up with a better definition of paranormalism than mine that is fairly airtight and addresses the issues with which I am concerned (centrality versus marginality, conventionality versus deviance, and the struggle to maintain dominance versus the struggle for acceptance), I would welcome the input.

REFERENCES

Bainbridge, William Sims, and Rodney Stark. 1980. "Superstitions: New and Old." *Skeptical Inquirer,* 4 (Summer): 18–31.

Berger, Peter L., and Thomas Luckmann. 1966. *The Social Construction of Reality.* Garden City, NY: Doubleday.

Bird, S. Elizabeth. 1992. *For Enquiring Minds: A Cultural Study of Supermarket Tabloids.* Knoxville, TN: University of Tennessee Press.

Gallup, George, Jr. 1997. *Public Opinion 1996.* Wilmington, DE: Scholarly Resources.

Gallup, George, Jr., and Frank Newport. 1991. "Belief in Paranormal Phenomena Among Adult Americans," *Skeptical Inquirer,* 15 (Winter): 137–146.

Goode, Erich. 1999. "Two Paranormalisms or Two and a Half? An Empirical Examination," *Skeptical Inquirer,* 23 (November/December).

Gould, Stephen Jay. 1984. *Hen's Teeth and Horses' Toes: Further Reflections on Natural History.* New York: W. W. Norton.

Gray, Thomas. 1995. "Educational Experiences and Belief in Paranormal Phenomena." In Francis B. Harrold and Raymond A. Eve (eds.), *Cult Archaeology and Creationism: Understanding Pseudoscientific Beliefs About the Past* (exp. ed.). Iowa City: University of Iowa Press, pp. 21–33.

Gray, William D. 1991. *Thinking Critically About New Age Ideas.* Belmont, CA: Wadsworth.

Harrold, Francis B., and Raymond A. Eve. 1995. "Patterns of Creationist Belief Among College

Students." In Francis B. Harrold and Raymond A. Eve (eds.), *Cult Archaeology and Creationism: Understanding Pseudoscientific Beliefs about the Past.* Iowa City: University of Iowa Press.

Hines, Terence. 1988. *Pseudoscience and the Paranormal: A Critical Examination of the Evidence.* Buffalo, NY: Prometheus Books.

Miller, Jon D. 1987. "The Scientifically Illiterate." *American Demographics*, 9 (June): 26–31.

Westrum, Ron. 1978. "Science and Social Intelligence About Anomalies: The Case of Meteorites." *Social Studies of Science*, 8 (4): 461–493.

5. GENERALIZING, STEREOTYPING, AND SOCIAL SCIENCE

JOEL M. CHARON

Social science is a highly disciplined process of investigation whose purpose is to question many of our uncritically accepted stereotypes and generalizations.... The whole thrust and spirit of social science is to control personal bias, to uncover unfounded assumptions about people, and to understand as objectively as possible.

We all generalize. Generalization is basic to all human understanding. We all stereotype. We do not have to, and it hurts understanding. Charon's point is that the purpose of social science is to generalize without stereotyping.

CATEGORIES AND GENERALIZATIONS

The Importance of Categories and Generalizations to Human Beings

Sociology is a social science, and therefore it makes generalizations about people and their social life. "The top positions in the economic and political structures are far more likely to be filled by men than by women." "The wealthier the individual, the more likely he or she will vote Republican." "In the United States the likelihood of living in poverty is greater among the African-American population than among whites." "American society is segregated." "Like other industrial societies, American society has a class system in which more than three-fourths of the population end up in approximately the same social class as they were at birth."

But such generalizations often give me a lot of trouble. I know that the sociologist must learn about people and generalize about them, but I ask myself: "Are such generalizations worthwhile? Shouldn't we simply study and treat people as individuals?" An English professor at my university was noted for explaining to his class that "you should not generalize about people—that's the same as stereotyping and everyone knows that educated people are not supposed to stereotype. Everyone is an individual." (Ironically, this is *itself* a generalization about people.)

However, the more I examine the situation, the more I realize that all human beings categorize and generalize. They do it every day in almost every situation they enter, and they almost always do it when it comes to other people. In fact, we have no choice in the matter. "Glass breaks and can be dangerous." We have learned what "glass" is, what "danger" means, and what "breaking" is. These are all categories we apply to the situations we enter so that we can understand how to act. We generalize from our past. "Human beings who have a cold are contagious, and, unless we want to catch a cold, we should not get close to them." We are here generalizing about "those with colds," "how people catch colds," and "how we should act around those with colds." In fact, every noun and verb we use is a generalization that acts as a guide for us. The reality is that we are unable to escape generalizing about our environment. That is one aspect of our essence as human beings. This is what language does to us. Sometimes our generalizations are fairly accurate; sometimes they are unfounded. However, we do in fact generalize: all of us, almost all the time! The question that introduces this chapter is a foolish one. *Should we generalize about people?* This is not a useful question simply because we have no choice. A much better question is:

How Can We Develop Accurate Generalizations About People?

The whole purpose of social science is to achieve accurate categorizations and generalizations about human beings. Indeed, the purpose of almost all academic pursuits involves learning, understanding, and developing accurate categories and generalizations.

For a moment let us consider other animals. Most are prepared by instinct or simple conditioning to respond in a certain way to a certain stimulus in their environment. So, for example, when a minnow swims in the presence of a hungry fish, then that particular minnow is immediately responded to and eaten. The fish is able to distinguish that type of stimulus from other stim-

uli, and so whenever something identical to it or close to it appears, the fish responds. The minnow is a concrete object that can be immediately sensed (seen, smelled, heard, touched), so within a certain range the fish is able to easily include objects that look like minnows and to exclude those that do not. Of course, occasionally a lure with a hook is purposely used to fool the fish, and a slight mistake in perception ends the fish's life.

Human beings are different from the fish and other animals because we have *words for objects and events* in the environment, and this allows us to *understand* that environment and not just respond to it. With words we are able to make many more distinctions, and we are able to apply knowledge from one situation to the next far more easily. We are far less dependent on immediate physical stimuli. So, for example, we come to learn what fish, turtles, and whales are, as well as what minnows, worms, lures, and boats are. We read and learn what qualities all fish have, how fish differ from whales, and what differences fish have from one another. We learn how to catch fish, and we are able to apply what we learn to some fish but not other fish. We begin to understand the actions of all fish—walleyes, big walleyes, big female walleyes. Some of us decide to study pain, and we try to determine if all fish feel pain, if some do, or if all do not. Humans do not then simply respond to the environment, but they label that environment, study and understand that environment, develop categories and subcategories for objects in that environment, and constantly try to generalize from what they learn in specific situations about those categories. Through understanding a category we are able to see important and subtle similarities and distinctions that are not available to animals who do not categorize and generalize with words.

Generalizing allows us to walk into situations and apply knowledge learned elsewhere to understanding objects there. When we enter a classroom we know what a teacher is, and we label the person at the front of the room as a teacher. We know from past experience that teachers give grades, usually know more than we do about things we are about to learn in that classroom, have more formal education than we do, and usually resort to testing us to see if we learned something they regard as important. We might have also learned that teachers are usually kind (or mean), sensitive (or not sensitive), authoritarian (or democratic); or we might have had so many diverse experiences with teachers that whether a specific teacher is any of these things will depend on that specific individual. If we do finally decide that a given teacher is, in fact, authoritarian, then we will now see an "authoritarian teacher," and we will now apply what we know about such teachers from our past.

This is a remarkable ability. We are able to figure out how to act in situations we enter because we understand many of the objects we encounter there by applying relevant knowledge about them that we learned in the past. This allows us to act intelligently in a wide diversity of situations, some of which are not even close to what we have already experienced. If we are open-minded and reflective, we can even evaluate how good or how poor our generalizations are, and we can alter what we know as we move from situation to situation.

The problem for almost all of us, however, is that many of our generalizations are not carefully arrived at or accurate, and it is sometimes difficult for us to recognize this and change them. Too often our generalizations actually stand in the way of our understanding, especially when we generalize about human beings.

To better understand what human beings do and how that sometimes gets us into trouble, let us look more closely at what "categories" and "generalizations" are.

THE MEANING OF CATEGORIZATION

Human beings categorize their environment; that is, *we isolate a chunk out of our environment, distinguish that chunk from all other parts of the environment, give it a name, and associate certain ideas with it.* Our chunks—or categories—arise in interaction; they are socially created. We discuss our environment, and we categorize it with the words we take on in our social life: "living things," "animals," "reptiles," "snakes," "poisonous snakes," "rattlers." A category is created, and once we understand it, we are able to compare objects in situations we encounter to that catego-

ry. The number of distinctions we are able to make in our environment increases manyfold. It is not only nouns that represent categories (men, boys) but also verbs (run, walk, fall), adverbs (slow, fast), and adjectives (weak, strong, intelligent, married). Much of our learning is simply aimed at understanding what various categories mean, and this involves understanding the qualities that make up those categories and the ideas associated with them.

Through learning about people (a category) we come to recognize that "all people" possess certain qualities, some of which they share with other animals (cells, brains, reproductive organs), and some of which seem unique to them (language, stereoscopic vision, conscience). We understand that people can be divided into young and old, white and black, men and women, single and married. Most of us have a pretty good idea of what a male is and a female. If asked, we could explain who belongs to the categories of homosexual and heterosexual. We do not simply recognize objects that do or do not belong; we *understand* the category by being able to describe the qualities we believe belong to objects that fit and objects that do not. We might say that a male has a penis, an old person is anyone older than 60, a teacher is someone who transmits knowledge, a human being is an animal who has a soul.

We argue over these definitions, and the more we understand, the more complex these definitions become. But categories and definitions are a necessary part of all of our lives. Armed with these, we go out and are able to cut up our environment in complex and sophisticated ways. We see an object and determine what it is (that is, what category it belongs in), and because we know something about that category, we are able to apply what we already know to that object. This allows us to act appropriately in many different situations. Simply think of all the people we meet in a given day, most of whom we know nothing about except for whatever we gather from a quick glance. We may note age, gender, dress, hairstyle, demeanor, or just a smile, and we quickly determine how to act. We are forced to place individuals into categories so we know what to do in a multitude of social situations.

It is necessary for all human beings to categorize, define, and understand their environment.

(This statement is itself a generalization about all human beings.) If we are honest with ourselves, we should recognize that each of us has created or learned thousands—even tens of thousands—of categories that we use as we look at what happens around us. The purpose of a biology class is to create useful categories of living things so that we can better understand what these things are—how they are similar, how they differ from nonliving things, and how they differ from one another. Musicians, artists, baseball players, political leaders, students, parents, scientists, con artists, and police—all of us live our lives assuming certain things about our environment based on the categories we have learned in interaction with others....

THE MEANING OF GENERALIZATION

A *category is an isolated part of our environment that we notice*. We generalize about that category by observing specific instances of objects included in it and by isolating common qualities that seem to characterize those included in that category, including other yet unobserved members we might observe in the future. We watch birds build a nest, and we assume that all birds build nests out of sticks (including birds other than the robins and sparrows we observed). We continue to observe and note instances where birds use materials other than sticks, and then we learn that some birds do not build nests but dig them out. More often, our generalizations are a mixture of observation and learning from others: We learn that wealthy people often drive Mercedes and that police officers usually carry guns. On the basis of generalizing about a category, we are able to predict future events where that category comes into play. When we see a wealthy person, we expect to see a Mercedes (or something that we learn is comparable); and when we see a police officer, we expect to see a gun. That is what a generalization is.

A *generalization describes the category. It is a statement that characterizes objects within the category and defines similarities and differences with other categories*. "This is what an educated person is!" (in contrast to an uneducated per-

son). "This is what wealthy people do to help ensure that privilege is passed down to their children." "This is what U.S. presidents have in common." "This is what Catholic people believe in."

As we shall see shortly, a generalization sometimes goes beyond just describing the category. It also explains why a particular quality develops. *That is, a generalization about a category will often be a statement of cause*. "Jewish people are liberal on social issues because of their minority position in Western societies." "U.S. presidents are male because ..." "Wealthy people send their children to private schools because ..."

Human beings, therefore, categorize their environment by using words. On the basis of observation and learning, they come to develop ideas concerning what qualities are associated with those categories. They also develop ideas as to why those qualities develop. *Ideas that describe the qualities that belong to a category and ideas that explain why those qualities exist is what we mean by generalizations*.

THE STEREOTYPE

When it comes to people, generalization is difficult to do well. The principal reason for this is that we are judgmental, and too often it is much easier for us to generalize for the purpose of evaluating (condemning or praising) others than for the purpose of understanding them. When we do this we fall into the practice of *stereotyping*.

A *stereotype is a certain kind of categorization*. It is a category and a set of generalizations characterized by the following qualities:

1. A *stereotype is judgmental*. It is not characterized by an attempt to understand, but by *an attempt to condemn or praise* the category. It makes a value judgment, and it has a strong emotional flavor. Instead of simple description of differences, there is a *moral evaluation* of those differences. People are judged good or bad because of the category. Examples: "The poor are lazy and no-good." "Students are a bunch of cheaters nowadays." "Stupid people," "crazies," "heathens," and "pigs" are some names we give to people we would have a very difficult time understanding, given the emotional names we attribute.

2. A *stereotype tends to be an absolute category.* That is, there is a *sharp distinction made between those inside and those outside the category.* There is little recognition that the category is merely a guide to understanding and that, in reality, there will be many individuals—even a majority—within a category who are exceptions to any generalization. Examples: "Men are oppressive." "Women are compassionate." "Politicians are all dishonest." "All moral people are Christian." "African Americans are poor."

3. *The stereotype tends to be a category that overshadows all others in the mind of the observer.* All other categories to which the individual belongs tend to be ignored. A stereotype treats the human being as simple and unidimensional, belonging to only one category of consequence. In fact, we are all part of a large number of categories. There is an assumption that if someone belongs to that particular category, *that is all one needs to know about the person.* A stereotype creates the human being as *simple and unidimensional.* Examples: "He is a homosexual. Therefore he lives a gay lifestyle." "She is a woman. Therefore, she must be attracted to that man." "He is a churchgoer. Therefore, he can't be guilty of theft." No matter how accurate one category is, it is very important to remember that all of us are complex mixtures of many categories. Who, after all, is the African-American divorced intelligent poet, who never finished his freshman year of college, who is a Baptist, bisexual, a father of three, and grandfather of four? Which category matters? When we stereotype, it is the category that emotionally matters to us, but not necessarily the actor.

4. *A stereotype does not change with new evidence.* When one accepts a stereotype, the category and the ideas associated with it are *rigidly accepted,* and the individual who holds it is *unwilling to alter it.* The stereotype, once accepted, becomes a filter through which evidence is accepted or rejected. Examples: "Students don't care about college anymore—I really don't care what your study shows." "I believe that people who pray together stay together. Don't confuse me with evidence that people who play together stay together too."

5. *The stereotype is not created carefully in the first place.* It is either learned culturally and simply accepted by the individual or created through *uncritical acceptance of a few concrete personal experiences.* Examples: "Politicians are bureaucrats who only care about keeping their job," "Obese people simply have no will power. My sister was obese and she just couldn't stop eating."

6. *The stereotype does not encourage a search for understanding why human beings are different from one another.* Instead of seeking to understand the cause as to why a certain quality is more in evidence in a particular category of people, a stereotype aims at exaggerating and judging differences. There is often an underlying assumption that *this is the way these people are,* it is part of their *essence,* and there seems to be little reason to try to understand the cause of differences any further than this. Examples: "Jewish people are just that way." "Poor people are just lazy." "Women don't know how to drive. That's the way they are."

Stereotypes are *highly oversimplified, exaggerated views of reality. They are especially attractive to people who are judgmental of others and who are quick to condemn people who are different from themselves.* They have been used to justify ethnic discrimination, war, and systematic murder of whole categories of people. Far from arising out of careful and systematic analysis, stereotypes *arise out of limited experience, hearsay, and culture,* and instead of aiding our understanding of the human being, *they always stand in the way of accurate understanding.*

It is not always easy to distinguish a stereotype from an accurate category. It is probably best to consider stereotypes and their opposites as extremes on a continuum. In actual fact, most categories will be neither perfectly accurate nor perfect examples of stereotypes. There are, therefore, *degrees of stereotyping* that we should recognize (see below).

Stereotype	Accurate Categorization
Judgmental	Descriptive
No exceptions	Exceptions
All-powerful category	One of many
Rejects new evidence	Changes with evidence
Not carefully created	Carefully created
Not interested in cause	Interested in cause

One final point. Stereotypes, we have emphasized, are judgmental. They are meant to simplify people so that we know which categories of people are good and which are to be avoided or condemned. This is the link between stereotypes and prejudice. Prejudice is an attitude toward a category of people that leads the actor to discriminate against individuals who are placed in that category. Always the category is a stereotype (judgmental, absolute, central, rigid, cultural, and uninterested in cause). When a prejudiced actor identifies an individual in the category, a lot is assumed to be true and disliked about that individual, and a negative response results. And once he or she acts in a negative way toward that individual, there is a ready-made justification: the stereotype ("I discriminate *because* this is the way they are!"). Stereotypes are oversimplifications of reality, and they act as both necessary elements of prejudice and rationalizations of it. Unfortunately, the stereotype also acts as a set of role expectations for those in the category, and too often people who are judged negatively are influenced to judge themselves accordingly.

SOCIAL SCIENCE: A REACTION TO STEREOTYPES

… Social science is a highly disciplined process of investigation whose purpose is to question many of our uncritically accepted stereotypes and generalizations. Social science does not always succeed. There are many instances of inaccuracies and even stereotyping that have resulted from poor science or from scientists simply not being sensitive to their own biases. It is important, however, to recognize that even though scientists make mistakes in their attempts to describe reality accurately, the whole thrust and spirit of social science is to control personal bias, to uncover unfounded assumptions about people, and to understand reality as objectively as possible. Here are some of the ways that social science (as it is supposed to work) aims at creating accurate categories and generalizations about human beings:

1. *Social science tries hard not to be judgmental about categories of people.* We recognize that generaliza-

tions and categories must not condemn or praise but must simply be guides to understanding.…

3. *Categories in social science are not assumed to be all-important for understanding the individual.* A stereotype is itself an assumption that a certain category necessarily dominates an individual's life. We might meet a young African-American single male artist. The role of each of these categories may or may not be important to the individual. For some individuals, being male or single or an artist will be most influential; for others it will be being African American. For those of us who stereotype by race, it will almost always be African American.…

4. *Social science tries to create categories and generalizations through carefully gathered evidence.* Stereotypes tend to be cultural; that is, they are taught by people around us who have generalized based on what they have simply accepted from others or what they have learned through personal experience (which is usually extremely limited in scope, unsystematic, subject to personal and social biases, and uncritically observed).…

5. *Generalizations in social science are tentative and subject to change because new evidence is constantly being examined.* Stereotypes, on the other hand, are unconditionally held. Once accepted, a stereotype causes the individual to select only that evidence that reaffirms that stereotype. A stereotype resists change.…

6. *Scientists do not categorize as an end in itself.* Instead, scientists categorize because they seek a certain kind of generalization: They seek to understand cause. In social science that means we seek to know *why* a category of people tends to have a certain quality. We generalize about categories of people *to better understand what causes* the existence of qualities that belong to a given category.…

Those of us who are *victims* of stereotyping know full well the dangers of sloppy generalization. It is one thing to stereotype plants or rocks or stars; it is quite another to stereotype people. When we stereotype people, our carelessness normally has a negative effect on individuals who are part of that particular category. We unfairly place them at a disadvantage, not giving them a chance as individuals, making judgments about them based on inaccuracies and on our own unwillingness to evaluate our generalization critically.

Even those of us who are not victims will occasionally cry out, "I am an individual! Do not categorize me." We *are* individuals. No one is ex-

actly like us. Yet, if we are honest, we must also recognize that those who do not know us will be forced to categorize us, and those who honestly want to understand humans better will have to. It is not a problem for us if the category is carefully created; and it is not a problem for us if the category is a positive one. If we apply for a job, we want the employer to categorize us as dependable, hardworking, knowledgeable, intelligent, and so on. Actually, we will even try to control how we present ourselves in situations so that we are able to influence others to place us in favorable categories: I'm cool, intelligent, sensitive, athletically talented, educated. When I write a letter of recommendation for students, I place the individual into several categories so that the reader will be able to apply what he or she knows about that category to the individual. The doctor may tell people "I am a physician" so that they will think highly of him or her as an individual. The person who announces himself as a boxer is telling us that he is tough; the rock musician is telling us that she is talented; the minister that he or she is caring—in many such cases it does not seem so bad if we are being categorized. For almost all of us, however, it is the *negative* catego-

rization that we wish to avoid. And this makes good sense: No one wants to be put into a category and negatively judged without having a chance to prove him- or herself as an individual....

But no matter how we might feel about others categorizing us and applying what they know to understanding us as a member of that category, the fact is that, except for those we know well, human beings can only be understood if we categorize and generalize. If we do this carefully, we can understand much about them, but if we are sloppy, we sacrifice understanding and end up making irrationally based value judgments about people before we have an opportunity to know them as individuals....

Social science—and sociology as a social science—is an attempt to categorize and generalize about human beings and society, but always in a careful manner. Its purpose is to reject stereotyping. It is a recognition that generalizing about people is necessary and inevitable, but stereotyping is not.

If we have to generalize, let's try to be careful. Stereotyping does not serve our own interests well because it blocks understanding; nor does it help those we stereotype.

6. THE CRAFT OF SOCIOLOGICAL INQUIRY

ROBERT R. ALFORD

[Durkheim, Weber, and Marx] each attempted in his own way to provide insight into the social totality and each made use of multiple paradigms of inquiry. While none of them had the advantage of contemporary theoretical and empirical tools, each still analyzed historical processes, patterns of structural relations, and cultural meanings to create explanations for the society being transformed around them.

Robert Alford is critical of sociologists for not connecting theory to evidence in their attempts to explain society. Here he describes the work of Karl Marx, Max Weber, and Emile Durkheim as models of good sociological explanation.

THEORY, METHODS, AND EVIDENCE IN THE CLASSIC CANON

... Durkheim, Weber, and Marx all assumed that there is a continuous interplay between theoretical assumptions and the objects of inquiry. "Theory" and "method" form moments, as it were, within the process of inquiry. To put the point another way, they assumed that theories do refer to a reality outside themselves and that the relationship between theoretical abstractions and that reality is eternally problematic.

The classic thinkers also realized the importance of understanding the conscious actions of human actors in historical situations in which actors are embedded in multiple social relations, whether defined as a community, a group, a complex organization, a class, a political party, a marriage, or a religious or ethnic group. The distinctive forms of social relations indicated by those categories are the meaningful context within which actors construct their own identities.

The three thinkers also took for granted that there are empirical regularities of human behavior, human perceptions, and human experience that it is the distinctive task of social inquiry to in-

From *Craft of Inquiry: Theories, Methods, Evidence* by Robert R. Alford, © 1998 by Robert R. Alford. Used by permission of Oxford University Press.

vestigate and explain. Recurring patterns of human experience and their association with features of social structure and history can be known. If human experiences in history were totally chaotic, random, and arbitrary, there would be nothing to investigate....

... [Their works] exemplify the interdisciplinary origins of sociology. Only Durkheim was a "sociologist," attempting to create a scholarly discipline. Weber was an economic and legal historian by training, Marx had a classical education. Both Weber and Marx ranged over the intellectual terrain, writing books that have become seminal for work in many fields. Together, Weber and Marx define the boundaries of what has come to be known as "comparative-historical sociology." That the three writers have become canonical "theorists" in sociology is a historical accident (albeit one with historical causes, of course!). Because of this complex and contradictory intellectual heritage, it is impossible to expect consensus within the field; the best that can be hoped for is a creative tension between different paradigms of inquiry.

These classic works make clear that "society" is the traditional and core unit of analysis, seen not as an aggregation of individuals, groups, communities, and organizations but as an emergent phenomenon that has its own reality independent of "lower" levels of social existence. Whether society is defined as "capitalism" and seen as polarized by class conflict or as "modern society" and seen as a differentiated congeries of groups with specialized functions ("organic solidarity") or as dominated by potentially rational bureaucratic organizations, the societal environment was always the theoretical context for the development of arguments.

Although mainstream sociological research rarely cites any of these thinkers anymore—a maturing science is supposed to forget its ancestors—the perspectives they brought to bear on society still inform our outlooks on how a society is organized and how it changes. These works are our common intellectual heritage. The paradigms of inquiry that sociologists use to construct theoretical claims and empirical generalizations were institutionalized within the discipline with the canonization of the classic nineteenth-century writings of Durkheim, Weber, and Marx. Their texts have shaped our sociological consciousness by shaping the definitions of important theoretical and empirical questions. Many of their concepts have disappeared into the assumptions that underlie contemporary work. Their impact is all the greater for having become implicit.[1]

What continues to attract scholars to the work of these classic thinkers is that each attempted in his own way to provide insight into the social totality and each made use of multiple paradigms of inquiry. While none of them had the advantage of contemporary theoretical and empirical tools, each still analyzed historical processes, patterns of structural relations, and cultural meanings to create explanations for the society being transformed around them.

SOLIDARITY, RATIONALITY, AND PRODUCTION

The classic theorists of sociology are also still relevant because—despite the profound social changes of the past century—we still live in a world that has some of the major characteristics they analyzed. Durkheim, Weber, and Marx each analyzed the simultaneously progressive and yet crisis-prone character of modern societies. Such societies exhibit enormous economic productivity, scientific progress, and technological innovation, as well as gradually expanding democratic institutions and ideals of justice and freedom. Nonetheless, racial and class inequality, injustice, lack of opportunity, political repression, and ethnic and racial violence and prejudice continue to exist. Modern societies are still subject to the crises of solidarity analyzed by Durkheim, the crises of rationality emphasized by Weber, and the crises of production that were central for Marx. And, most relevant for my argument, these crises are seen in the institutions of social science and the production of teachers, students, and knowledge. A brief sketch, focusing on how central theoretical assumptions lead to research questions, is in order.

Emile Durkheim saw modern societies as subject to crises of *solidarity:* a breakdown of the common values and sense of community needed to integrate societies faced with multiple social divisions. Racial and ethnic and religious conflict, the high incidence of divorce, the breakdown of family life, the disruption of stable jobs and careers—all these fit Durkheim's image of the pathological destruction of community and the pervasiveness of anomie: Life is no longer predictable.

Social science is one of the differentiated functions that helps integrate a complex division of labor into the "organic solidarity" envisioned by Durkheim by producing knowledge with social uses, as well as social roles (teachers, students, researchers) whose practitioners carry out the necessary functions. In normal times, students can make a series of decisions about courses and majors that will prepare them for stable careers and that enable them to count on finding a niche appropriate to their interests, talents, and skills.

But social science is not exempt from crises of solidarity, manifest in an anomic division of labor among departments, fields, and universities, as well as a forced division of labor as teaching loads increase for young scholars unable to work in their specialties. Occupational groups—such as the professoriate— are increasingly unable to provide the moral certainty of contributing to a valued social function. For students, anomie may occur if their major can no longer be counted on to prepare them for a good job.

Possible research questions might be: What are the consequences of the changing status and social role of different academic disciplines for the career choices of students? How much of a lag is there between the occurrence of changes in the labor market and a change in the self-conceptions of students? How much anomie is produced by the disruption of stable career paths?

Note that these questions are not yet empirical ones. That is, the kinds of evidence potentially available to answer them could vary tremendously. You could ask: How do private and public universities that differ in prestige compare with respect to changes in graduation rates and the proportion of students who choose particular majors? You could ask, of a sample of graduates: What was the salary of your first job? Was it in the field of your college major? You could do a historical study and ask: What have been the different sources of funding of universities (private donations, tax monies, research grants) since World War II? Has declining public funding led to pressures to reduce support for the humanities and social sciences and to increase it for work in technical fields and in the traditional professions?

These are only a few of the possible research implications of Durkheim's theory of the division of labor in modern societies and the impact of institutional crisis on academic life.

Max Weber saw industrialized societies, increasingly legitimated by bureaucratic principles of organization, as being in a crisis of rationality, and this foreboding remains relevant. Popular beliefs in public and political accountability have eroded. Opportunistic political leadership abounds. Bureaucratic organizations justify their power with ideologies of efficiency. Weber also saw the dangers of increasing militarism in a world of contending nation states mobilizing virulent ethnic loyalties for nationalist goals. Here I shall deal only with the implications of his theory of rationality for academia.

Social science is rationally organized into bureaucracies (departments, divisions, fields, public and private universities, research foundations) that produce knowledge. For students, this rational organization is manifest in sequences of re-

quired courses developed and enforced as a "major."

But social knowledge is also vulnerable to crises of rationality. "Major" requirements can inhibit a student's attempt to integrate fragmented knowledge by taking courses in many fields. Similarly, technically competent research is organized by bureaucratized "policy research" agencies that manage staffs of research assistants and generate research grants to keep the organizations going. Such research is likely to be "formally rational"—it conforms to internal criteria for "good" research. Yet, standards for theoretically coherent research on socially important problems ("substantive rationality") are all too frequently abandoned, sometimes if powerful funders object, sometimes simply because of the requirement to focus on narrow questions that can be answered by highly technical research procedures.

Some possible research questions that flow from this theoretical perspective might be: Does the rise of charismatic fundamentalist religions signify a decline in the legitimacy of science and rational bureaucratic organizations? Is being a "student" as central a personal identity for young people enrolled in college in the 1990s as it was in the 1950s? Empirically (and note the gap): Are sociology majors less religious than business majors? Has the conversation of students "hanging out" in "bull sessions" become focused more on career difficulties than on philosophical issues and politics over the past twenty years? What is the balance of perceptions among students doing research papers: Is the work only a course requirement? Is it a creative self-identified project to learn something interesting, or just a necessary part of the training for a possible social science career?

Again, these are only a few examples of ways in which Weber's theoretical perspective can be translated into research questions.

Karl Marx saw capitalist societies as in a constant crisis of *production*, resulting from a growing gap between rich and poor and an inability of many of those who produce the cornucopia of consumer goods to be able to purchase them. Marx saw market and exchange relationships based on calculation of advantage rather than on bonds of feeling as permeating more and more aspects of social life in capitalist societies. The glorification of the market, of efficient productivity, of competition (under such rubrics as "human capital") was seen as the ideology of a privileged class rather than as valid social theory. Marx's thesis that the glittering spectacle of capitalist productivity and commodity innovation masks increasing human inequalities is still relevant to an understanding of modern societies.

Social science is part of the accumulation of capital and the exploitation of labor in capitalist societies. In periods of growth and expansion, particular fields or research programs will grow, winning the competition for funds and labor power. Certain majors (law, business, computer science) will have their moment of optimistic expansion.

But, the production of social knowledge also exhibits what Marx saw as the fetishism of commodities and an anarchy of production. The contradiction between the new forces of production (computers, statistics, census data, archives) and the social relations of production (the proliferation of part-time adjunct teachers, the overproduction of Ph.D.s, the product differentiation of journals, the pressure to publish) will lead to social crises in which investment in education will shrink, academic unemployment grow, libraries lack the funds to buy books and journals. Certain majors may become almost unemployable.

Research questions flowing from Marx's theoretical perspective might include: To what extent does competition among university departments for positions, salaries, and grants mimic the model of capital accumulation and profitability in private industry? Is students' alienation from their work, from other students, from their own goals, analogous to the alienation of workers employed in factories? How necessary is the production of social science knowledge for the continuation of the core institutions of capitalist societies?

Specified empirically (again, remember the gap between theory and evidence), you might ask: What is the relationship between the status and income of a professor and the time he or she spends with students? Does this relationship vary by size of college, the college's prestige, the class background of the students? Or, to what extent are student research assistants treated as junior colleagues rather than hired labor? In conversations between professors and students, how much emphasis is placed on "training" for a career versus "liberal education" of the mind, versus simply fulfilling course and major requirements? How much change has there been in teaching loads in different types of universities, and is this change correlated with how much students have learned by graduation?

This quick attempt to show how one can restate some of Durkheim's, Weber's, and Marx's canonical theories into research questions relevant to possible contemporary trends in social science is only a background assumption for my argument here. I present this sketch only to suggest how their theories about modern society could be translated into research questions that are potentially testable with methods and evidence. Some of the questions I have posed would be answerable only with an enormous investment of time and resources, but it is important at the early stage of a research project to be playful and experimental. Push the boundaries of possible questions as far as possible before you must become concrete, realistic, and "responsible."

CONCLUSIONS

The craft of inquiry teaches you how to connect theory to evidence in order to construct valid explanations of the workings of society. Sociology needs to reunite theory, method, and evidence in a way that can be both legitimate and powerful. My core assumption is that how you define a research question and then analyze its *theoretical* context and its *empirical* implications significantly influences the trajectory and the quality of your research. Neither sophisticated theory nor high-technology statistics—not even a wealth of data—can create significance from a fuzzy research question....

Sociological inquiry cannot be converted to a set of formulas that instruct you in "research methods" in the same way that you can write down rules for baking a cake or the formula for mixing hydrogen and oxygen to produce water.

Combining theory, method, and evidence in sociology is a craft that must be learned in practice....With C. Wright Mills, my concern is to advance a theoretically informed, empirically grounded, and historically oriented social science that matters for the society outside the academy.

NOTE

1.For various of Goffman's writings, see *The Presentation of Self in Everyday Life* (New York: Doubleday Anchor Books, 1959); *Asylums* (New York: Doubleday Anchor Books, 1961); *Strategic Interactions* (Philadelphia: University of Pennsylvania Press, 1969). *Frame Analysis: An Essay on the Organization of Experience* (Boston: Northeastern University Press, 1986; Originally published 1974); and *Stigma: Notes on the Management of Spoiled Identity* (Upper Saddle River, NJ: Prentice Hall, 1963). All further references to Goffman's work are to these editions.

See the following for summaries and analyses of Goffman's work: Tom Burns, *Erving Goffman* (London and New York: Routledge, 1992), and Philip Manning, *Erving Goffman and Modern Sociology* (Stanford: Stanford University Press, 1992).

PART II

Humans as Social

What is the nature of the human being? That is, what are we, apart from what we learn?

To the sociologist, human nature cannot be understood apart from society. We are, by our very nature, social beings. It is inconceivable to have human beings in nature who are not also social beings.

Part II begins with an examination of the social nature of the human being by reminding us that we regularly act in a world populated by other people, and that their presence makes a big difference to who we are and what we do. We interact with them. In interaction, we are socialized by them; and through them, we are shaped by the society and groups that are represented by them.

The selections by Charles Cooley and Kingsley Davis focus on a central question that most people have asked in one way or another: What would we be like without some social life? Both focus on the importance of "socialization," the process by which society forms each individual and by which each of us comes to take on qualities characteristic of the human species.

Berger and Luckmann introduce us to the power of socialization. Not only does society and its representatives socialize what we become, but this socialization is one of the principal ways we are controlled by it. The individual "internalizes" society.

Erving Goffman introduces us to the importance of "social interaction," the action that people take toward one another in everyday situations. As we act back and forth, we influence others, and we are influenced by them.

Selection 11 by Richard Jenkins shows us that identity—who we are—is intimately tied to social interaction, and Herbert Blumer's selection ties social interaction to society and the human being's use of self and symbols.

Timothy Curry gives us an excellent example of how social interaction socializes us, and Berger and Luckmann's description of social interaction underlines the fact that out of social interaction arises patterns called institutions.

Part II, then, is an examination of human beings as social beings dependent on social interaction.

7. HUMAN NATURE

CHARLES COOLEY

Human functions are so numerous and intricate that no fixed mechanism could provide for them. They are also subject to radical change, not only in the life of the individual but from one generation to another.

Human beings are characterized by flexibility, plasticity, and teachability. Our nature is not commanded by what we inherit in our genes, but by our social life. Charles Cooley's description still represents well the sociological view of human nature.

… Thus the plastic, indeterminate character of human heredity involves a long and helpless infancy; and this, in turn, is the basis of the human family, because the primary and essential function of the family is the care of children. Those species of animals in which the young are adequately prepared for life by definite heredity have no family at all, while those which more or less resemble man as regards plastic heredity, resemble him also in having some rudiments, at least, of a family. Kittens, for instance, are cared for by the mother for several months and profit in some measure by her example and instruction.

More generally, this difference as regards plasticity means that the life-activities of the animal are comparatively uniform and fixed, while those of man are varied and changing. Human functions are so numerous and intricate that no fixed mechanism could provide for them. They are also subject to radical change, not only in the life of the individual but from one generation to another. The only possible hereditary basis for them is an outfit of indeterminate capacities that can be developed and guided by experience as the needs of life require.

I see a flycatcher sitting on a dead branch, where there are no leaves to interrupt his view. Presently, he darts toward a passing insect, hovers about him a few seconds, catches him, or

From *Human Nature and Social Order*, by Charles Horton Cooley, 1922, pp. 20–22, 31–34, Schocken Books, Inc. Originally published by Scribner and Sons

fails to do so, and returns to his perch. That is his way of getting a living: He has done it all his life and will go on doing it to the end. Millions of other flycatchers on millions of other dead branches are doing precisely the same thing. And this has been the life of the species for unknown thousands of years. They have, through the germ-plasm, a definite capacity for this—the keen eye, the swift, fluttering movement to follow the insect, the quick, sure action of the neck and bill to seize him—all effective with no instruction and very little practice.

Man has a natural hunger, like the flycatcher, and a natural mechanism of tasting, chewing, swallowing, and digestion; but his way of getting the food varies widely at different times of his life, is not the same with different individuals, and often changes completely from one generation to another. The great majority of us gain our food, after we have left the parental nest, through what we call a job, and a job is any activity whatever that a complex and shifting society esteems sufficiently to pay us for. It is very likely, nowadays, to last only part of our lives and to be something our ancestors never heard of. Thus whatever is most distinctively human—our adaptability, our power of growth, our arts and sciences, our social institutions and progress—is bound up with the indeterminate character of human heredity.

Of course, there is no sharp line, in this matter of teachability, between man and the other animals. The activities of the latter are not wholly predetermined, and in so far as they are not, there is a learning process based on plastic heredity. The higher animals—horses, dogs, and elephants, for example—are notably teachable, and may even participate in the changes of human society, as when dogs learn to draw carts, trail fugitives, guide the lost, or perform in a circus.

And, on the other side, those activities of man that do not require much adaptation, such as the breathing, sucking, and crying of infants, and even walking (which is learned without instruction when the legs become strong enough), are provided for by definite heredity....

8.   A CASE OF EXTREME ISOLATION

KINGSLEY DAVIS

Clearly, the history of Isabelle's development is different from that of Anna's. In both cases, there was an exceedingly low, rather blank, intellectual level to begin with. In both cases, it seemed that the girl might be congenitally feeble-minded. In both, a considerably higher level was reached later on. But the Ohio girl achieved a normal mentality within two years, whereas Anna was still marked inadequate at the end of four and a half years.

Kingsley Davis compares two cases of human isolation. The potential of both children was clearly retarded because of social isolation. However, nothing human is fixed: Isabelle got close attention, learned language, and was able to overcome early isolation. Anna did not get close attention, and her mental development did not progress very far. Interaction and the early acquisition of language seem to be central to human growth.

Early in 1940, there appeared in the *American Journal of Sociology* an account of a girl called Anna.[1] She had been deprived of normal contact and had received a minimum of human care for almost the whole of her first six years of life....

When finally found and removed from the room in the grandfather's house at the age of nearly six years, the child could not talk, walk, or do anything that showed intelligence. She was in an extremely emaciated and undernourished condition, with skeleton-like legs and a bloated abdomen. She had been fed on virtually nothing except cow's milk during the years under her mother's care.

Anna's condition when found, and her subsequent improvement, have been described in the previous report. It now remains to say what happened to her after that.

LATER HISTORY

In 1939, nearly two years after being discovered, Anna had progressed, as previously reported, to the point where she could walk, understand simple commands, feed herself, achieve some neatness, remember people, and so on. But she still did not speak, and, although she was much more like a normal infant of something over one year of age in mentality, she was far from normal for her age....

On August 30, 1939, she was taken to a private home for retarded children.... A final report

Reprinted from "Final Note on a Case of Extreme Isolation," by Kingsley Davis, in *American Journal of Sociology* 52 (1947), pp. 432–437. Used with permission from the school, made on June 22, 1942, and evidently the last report before the girl's death, pictured only a slight advance over that given above. It said that Anna could follow directions, string beads, identify a few colors, build with blocks, and differentiate between attractive and unattractive pictures. She had a good sense of rhythm and loved a doll. She talked mainly in phrases but would repeat words and try to carry on a conversation. She was clean about clothing. She habitually washed her hands and brushed her teeth. She would try to help other children. She walked well and could run fairly well, although clumsily. Although easily excited, she had a pleasant disposition.

INTERPRETATION

Such was Anna's condition just before her death. It may seem as if she had not made much progress, but one must remember the condition in which she had been found. One must recall that she had no glimmering of speech, absolutely no ability to walk, no sense of gesture, not the least capacity to feed herself even when the food was put in front of her, and no comprehension of cleanliness. She was so apathetic that it was hard to tell whether or not she could hear. And all this at the age of nearly ten years. Compared with this condition, her capacities at the time of her death seem striking indeed, although they do not amount to much more than a two-and-a-half-year mental level. One conclusion therefore seems safe, namely, that her isolation prevented a considerable amount of mental development that was undoubtedly part of her capacity. Just what her original capacity was, of course, is hard to say; but her development after her period of confinement (including the ability to walk and run, to play, dress, fit into a social situation, and, above all, to speak) shows that she had at least this much capacity—capacity that never could have been realized in her original condition of isolation.

A further question is this: What would she have been like if she had received a normal upbringing from the moment of birth? A definitive answer would have been impossible in any case,

but even an approximate answer is made difficult by her early death. If one assumes, as was tentatively surmised in the previous report, that it is "almost impossible for any child to learn to speak, think, and act like a normal person after a long period of early isolation," it seems likely that Anna might have had a normal or near-normal capacity, genetically speaking. On the other hand, it was pointed out that Anna represented "a marginal case, [because] she was discovered before she had reached six years of age," an age "young enough to allow for some plasticity."[2] While admitting, then, that Anna's isolation may have been the major cause (and was certainly a minor cause) of her lack of rapid mental progress during the four and a half years following her rescue from neglect, it is necessary to entertain the hypothesis that she was congenitally deficient....

COMPARISON WITH ANOTHER CASE

If a child could be discovered who had been isolated about the same length of time as Anna but had achieved a much quicker recovery and a greater mental development, it would be a stronger indication that Anna was deficient to start with.

Such a case does exist. It is the case of a girl found at about the same time as Anna and under strikingly similar circumstances....

Born apparently one month later than Anna, the girl in question, who has been given the pseudonym Isabelle, was discovered in November 1938, nine months after the discovery of Anna. At the time she was found, she was approximately six and a half years of age. Like Anna, she was an illegitimate child and had been kept in seclusion for that reason. Her mother was a deaf-mute, having become so at the age of two, and it appears that she and Isabelle had spent most of their time together in a dark room shut off from the rest of the mother's family. As a result, Isabelle had no chance to develop speech; when she communicated with her mother, it was by means of gestures. Lack of sunshine and inadequacy of diet had caused Isabelle to become rachitic. Her legs in particular were affected; they "were so bowed that as she stood erect, the soles of her shoes came nearly flat together, and she got about with a skittering gait."[3] Her behavior toward strangers, especially men, was almost that of a wild animal, manifesting much fear and hostility. In lieu of speech, she made only a strange croaking sound. In many ways, she acted like an infant. "She was apparently utterly unaware of relationships of any kind. When presented with a ball for the first time, she held it in the palm of her hand, then reached out and stroked my face with it. Such behavior is comparable to that of a child of six months."[4] At first, it was even hard to tell whether or not she could hear, so unused were her senses. Many of her actions resembled those of deaf children.

It is small wonder that, once it was established that she could hear, specialists working with her believed her to be feeble-minded. Even on non-verbal tests, her performance was so low as to promise little for the future. Her first score on the Stanford-Binet was 19 months, practically at the zero point of the scale. On the Vineland social maturity scale, her first score was 39, representing an age level of two and a half years.[5] "The general impression was that she was wholly uneducable and that any attempt to teach her to speak, after so long a period of silence, would meet with failure."[6]

In spite of this interpretation, the individuals in charge of Isabelle launched a systematic and skillful program of training. It seemed hopeless at first. The approach had to be through pantomime and dramatization, suitable to an infant. It required one week of intensive effort before she even made her first attempt at vocalization. Gradually she began to respond, however, and, after the first hurdles had at last been overcome, a curious thing happened. She went through the usual stages of learning characteristic of the years from one to six, not only in proper succession but far more rapidly than normal. In a little over two months after her first vocalization, she was putting sentences together. Nine months after that, she could identify words and sentences on the printed page, could write well, could add to ten, and could retell a story after hearing it. Seven months beyond this point, she had a vocabulary of 1,500 to 2,000 words and was asking compli-

cated questions. Starting from an educational level of between one and three years (depending on what aspect one considers), she had reached a normal level by the time she was eight and a half years old. In short, she covered in two years the stages of learning that ordinarily require six.[7] Or, to put it another way, her IQ trebled in a year and a half.[8] The speed with which she reached the normal level of mental development seems analogous to the recovery of body weight in a growing child after an illness, the recovery being achieved by an extra fast rate of growth for a period after the illness until normal weight for the given age is again attained.

When the writer saw Isabelle a year and a half after her discovery, she gave him the impression of being a very bright, cheerful, energetic little girl. She spoke well, walked and ran without trouble, and sang with gusto and accuracy. Today, she is over fourteen years old and has passed the sixth grade in a public school. Her teachers say that she participates in all school activities as normally as other children. Although older than her classmates, she has fortunately not physically matured too far beyond their level.[9]

Clearly, the history of Isabelle's development is different from that of Anna's. In both cases, there was an exceedingly low, rather blank, intellectual level to begin with. In both cases, it seemed that the girl might be congenitally feeble-minded. In both, a considerably higher level was reached later on. But the Ohio girl achieved a normal mentality within two years, whereas Anna was still marked inadequate at the end of four and a half years. This difference in achievement may suggest that Anna had less initial capacity. But an alternate hypothesis is possible.

One should remember that Anna never received the prolonged and expert attention that Isabelle received. The result of such attention, in the case of the Ohio girl, was to give her speech at an early stage, and her subsequent rapid development seems to have been a consequence of that. "Until Isabelle's speech and language development, she had all the characteristics of a feeble-minded child." Had Anna—who, from the standpoint of psychometric tests and early history, closely resembled this girl at the start—been given a mastery of speech at an earlier point by intensive training, her subsequent development might have been much more rapid.[10]

The hypothesis that Anna began with a sharply inferior mental capacity is therefore not established. Even if she were deficient to start with, we have no way of knowing how much so. Under ordinary conditions, she might have been a dull normal or, like her mother, a moron. Even after the blight of her isolation, if she had lived to maturity, she might have finally reached virtually the full level of her capacity, whatever it may have been. That her isolation did have a profound effect on her mentality, there can be no doubt. This is proved by the substantial degree of change during the four and a half years following her rescue.

Consideration of Isabelle's case serves to show, as Anna's case does not clearly show, that isolation up to the age of six, with failure to acquire any form of speech and hence failure to grasp nearly the whole world of cultural meaning, does not preclude the subsequent acquisition of these. Indeed, there seems to be a process of accelerated recovery in which the child goes through the mental stages at a more rapid rate than would be the case in normal development. Just what would be the maximum age at which a person could remain isolated and still retain the capacity for full cultural acquisition is hard to say. Almost certainly it would not be as high as age fifteen; it might possibly be as low as age ten. Undoubtedly, various individuals would differ considerably as to the exact age.

Anna's is not an ideal case for showing the effects of extreme isolation, partly because she was possibly deficient to begin with, partly because she did not receive the best training available, and partly because she did not live long enough.

Nevertheless, her case is instructive when placed in the record with numerous other cases of extreme isolation. This and the previous article about her are meant to place her in the record. It is to be hoped that other cases will be described in the scientific literature as they are discovered (as unfortunately they will be), for only in these rare cases of extreme isolation is it possible "to observe concretely separated two factors in the development of human personality which are always otherwise only analytically separated: the biogenic and the sociogenic factors."[11]

NOTES

1. Kingsley Davis, "Extreme Social Isolation of a Child." *American Journal of Sociology*, XLV (January 1940), pp. 554—65.
2. Ibid.
3. Francis N. Maxfield, "What Happens When the Social Environment of a Child Approaches Zero." The writer is greatly indebted to Mrs. Maxfield and to Professor Horace B. English, a colleague of Professor Maxfield, for the privilege of seeing this manuscript and other materials collected on isolated and feral individuals.
4. Marie K. Mason, "Learning To Speak after Six and One-Half Years of Silence." *Journal of Speech Disorders*, VII (1942), pp. 295—304.
5. Maxfield, unpublished manuscript.
6. Mason, *op. cit.*, p. 299.
7. Ibid., pp. 300—304.
8. Maxfield, unpublished manuscript.
9. Based on a personal letter from Dr. Mason to the writer, May 13, 1946.
10. This point is suggested in a personal letter from Dr. Mason to the writer, October 22, 1946.
11. J. A. L. Singh and Robert M. Zingg, *Wolf-Children and Feral Man* (New York: Harper & Bros., 1941), pp. 248—51.

9. SOCIALIZATION: THE INTERNALIZATION OF SOCIETY

PETER L. BERGER and THOMAS LUCKMANN

Primary socialization accomplishes what (in hindsight, of course) may be seen as the most important confidence trick that society plays on the individual—to make appear as necessity what is in fact a bundle of contingencies, and thus to make meaningful the accident of his birth.

From beginning to end, the human being is socialized. Socialization brings the external world inside the individual. Both "primary socialization" and "secondary socialization" cooperate to do this, but, as Peter Berger and Thomas Luckmann emphasize, "primary socialization is really the most important one for the individual." This selection examines primary socialization, and it is organized as follows:

1. Significant others are representatives of society and social class.
2. Significant others form the individual's identity.
3. Eventually, a generalized other is created that represents a coherent society.

... Only when he has achieved this degree of internalization is an individual a member of society. The ontogenetic process by which this is brought about is socialization, which may thus be defined as the comprehensive and consistent induction of an individual into the objective world of a society or a sector of it. Primary socialization is the first socialization an individual undergoes in childhood through which he becomes a member of society. Secondary socialization is any subsequent process that inducts an already socialized individual into new sectors of the objective world of his society....

It is at once evident that primary socialization is usually the most important one for an individual, and that the basic structure of all secondary socialization has to resemble that of primary socialization. Every individual is born into an objective social structure within which he encounters the significant others who are in charge of his socialization.[1] These significant others are imposed on him. Their definitions of his situation are posited for him as objective reality. He is thus born into not only an objective social structure but also an objective social world. The significant others who mediate this world to him modify it in the course of mediating it. They select aspects of it in accordance with their own location in the social structure, and also by virtue of their individual, biographically rooted idiosyncrasies. The social world is "filtered" to the individual through this double selectivity. Thus the lower-class child not only absorbs a lower-class perspective on the social world, he absorbs it in the idiosyncratic coloration given it by his parents (or whatever other individuals are in charge of his primary socialization). The same lower-class perspective may induce a mood of contentment, resignation, bitter resentment, or seething rebelliousness. Consequently, the lower-class child will not only come to inhabit a world greatly different from that of an upper-class child, but may do so in a manner quite different from the lower-class child next door.[2]

From *The Social Construction of Reality*, by Peter L. Berger and Thomas Luckmann. Copyright © 1966 by Peter L. Berger and Thomas Luckmann. Used with permission of Doubleday, a division of Random House, Inc.

It should hardly be necessary to add that primary socialization involves more than purely cognitive learning. It takes place under circumstances that are highly charged emotionally. Indeed, there is good reason to believe that without such emotional attachment to significant others, the learning process would be difficult if not impossible.[3] The child identifies with the significant others in a variety of emotional ways. Whatever they may be, internalization occurs only as identification occurs. The child takes on the significant others' roles and attitudes, that is, internalizes them and makes them his own. And by this identification with significant others, the child becomes capable of identifying himself, of acquiring a subjectively coherent and plausible identity. In other words, the self is a reflected entity, reflecting the attitudes first taken by significant others toward it;[4] the individual becomes what he is addressed as by his significant others. This is not a one-sided, mechanistic process. It entails a dialectic between identification by others and self-identification, between objectively assigned and subjectively appropriated identity.…

What is most important for our considerations here is the fact that the individual not only takes on the roles and attitudes of others, but in the same process takes on their world. Indeed, identity is objectively defined as location in a certain world and can be subjectively appropriated only *along with* that world. Put differently, all identifications take place within horizons that imply a specific social world. The child learns that he is what he is called. Every name implies a nomenclature, which in turn implies a designated social location.[5] To be given an identity involves being assigned a specific place in the world. Because this identity is subjectively appropriated by the child ("I *am* John Smith"), so is the world to which this identity points. Subjective appropriation of identity and subjective appropriation of the social world are merely different aspects of the *same* process of internalization, mediated by the *same* significant others.

Primary socialization creates in the child's consciousness a progressive abstraction from the roles and attitudes of specific others to roles and attitudes *in general*. For example, in the internalization of norms, there is a progression from "Mummy is angry with me now" to "Mummy is

angry with me *whenever* I spill the soup." As additional significant others (father, grandmother, older sister, and so on) support the mother's negative attitude toward soup-spilling, the generality of the norm is subjectively extended. The decisive step comes when the child recognizes that *everybody* is against soup-spilling, and the norm is generalized to "one does not spill soup"—"one" being himself as part of a generality that includes, in principle, *all* of society insofar as it is significant to the child. This abstraction from the roles and attitudes of concrete significant others is called the *generalized other*.[6] Its formation within consciousness means that the individual now identifies not only with concrete others but with a generality of others, that is, with a society. Only by virtue of this generalized identification does his own self-identification attain stability and continuity. He now has not only an identity vis-à-vis this or that significant other, but an identity *in general*, which is subjectively apprehended as remaining the same no matter what others, significant or not, are encountered. This newly coherent identity incorporates within itself all the various internalized roles and attitudes—including, among many other things, the self-identification as a non-spiller of soups.

The formation within consciousness of the generalized other marks a decisive phase in socialization. It implies the internalization of society as such and of the objective reality established therein, and, at the same time, the subjective establishment of a coherent and continuous identity. Society, identity, *and* reality are subjectively crystallized in the same process of internalization. This crystallization is concurrent with the internalization of language. Indeed, for reasons evident from the foregoing observations on language, language constitutes both the most important content and the most important instrument of socialization.

When the generalized other has been crystallized in consciousness, a symmetrical relationship is established between objective and subjective reality. What is real "outside" corresponds to what is real "within." Objective reality can readily be "translated" into subjective reality, and vice versa. Language, of course, is the principal vehicle of this ongoing translating process in both directions. It should, however, be stressed that the symmetry between objective and subjective reality cannot be complete. The two realities correspond to each other, but they are not coextensive. There is always more objective reality "available" than is actually internalized in any individual consciousness, simply because the contents of socialization are determined by the social distribution of knowledge. No individual internalizes the totality of what is objectivated as reality in his society, not even if the society and its world are relatively simple ones. On the other hand, there are always elements of subjective reality that have not originated in socialization, such as the awareness of one's own body prior to and apart from any socially learned apprehension of it. Subjective biography is not fully social. The individual apprehends himself as being both inside *and* outside society.[7] This implies that the symmetry between objective and subjective reality is never a static, once-for-all state of affairs. It must always be produced and reproduced *in actu*. In other words, the relationship between the individual and the objective social world is like an ongoing balancing act....

In primary socialization, there is no *problem* of identification. There is no choice of significant others. Society presents the candidate for socialization with a predefined set of significant others, whom he must accept as such with no possibility of opting for another arrangement. *Hic Rhodus, hic salta.* One must make do with the parents fate has regaled one with. This unfair disadvantage inherent in the situation of being a child has the obvious consequence that, although the child is not simply passive in the process of his socialization, it is the adults who set the rules of the game. The child can play the game with enthusiasm or with sullen resistance. But, alas, there is no other game around. This has an important corollary. Because the child has no choice in the selection of his significant others, his identification with them is quasi-automatic. For the same reason, his internalization of their particular reality is quasi-inevitable. The child does not internalize the world of his significant others as one of many possible worlds. He internalizes it as *the* world, the only existent and only conceivable world, the world *tout court*. It is for this reason that the world internalized in primary socialization is so much more firmly entrenched in consciousness than worlds internalized in secondary socializations. However much

the original sense of inevitability may be weakened in subsequent disenchantments, the recollection of a never-to-be-repeated certainty—the certainty of the first dawn of reality—still adheres to the first world of childhood. Primary socialization thus accomplishes what (in hindsight, of course) may be seen as the most important confidence trick that society plays on the individual—to make appear as necessity what is in fact a bundle of contingencies, and thus to make meaningful the accident of his birth.

The specific contents that are internalized in primary socialization vary, of course, from society to society. Some are found everywhere. It is language that must be internalized above all. With language, and by means of it, various motivational and interpretative schemes are internalized as institutionally defined—wanting to act like a brave little boy, for instance, and assuming that little boys are naturally divided into the brave and the cowardly. These schemes provide the child with institutionalized programs for everyday life, some immediately applicable to him, others anticipating conduct socially defined for later biographical stages—the bravery that will allow him to get through a day beset with tests of will from one's peers and from all sorts of others, and also the bravery that will be required of one later—when one is initiated as a warrior, say, or when one might be called by the god. These programs, both the immediately applicable and the anticipatory, differentiate one's identity from that of others—such as girls, slave boys, or boys from another clan. Finally, there is internalization of at least the rudiments of the legitimating apparatus; the child learns "why" the programs are what they are. One must be brave because one wants to become a real man; one must perform the rituals because otherwise the gods will be angry; one must be loyal to the chief because only if one does will the gods support one in times of danger; and so on.

In primary socialization, then, the individual's first world is constructed. Its peculiar quality of firmness is to be accounted for, at least in part, by the inevitability of the individual's relationship to his very first significant others....

Primary socialization ends when the concept of the generalized other (and all that goes with it) has been established in the consciousness of the individual. At this point, he is an effective member of society and in subjective possession of a self and a world. But this internalization of society, identity, and reality is not a matter of once and for all. Socialization is never total and never finished.

NOTES

1. Our description here, of course, leans heavily on the Meadian theory of socialization.
2. The concept of "mediation" is derived from Sartre, who lacks, however, an adequate theory of socialization.
3. The affective dimension of early learning has been especially emphasized by Freudian child psychol-ogy, although there are various findings of behav-ioristic learning theory that would tend to confirm this. We do not imply acceptance of the theoretical presuppositions of either psychological school in our argument here.
4. Our conception of the reflected character of the self is derived from both Cooley and Mead. Its roots may be found in the analysis of the "social self" by William James (*Principles of Psychology*).
5. On nomenclature, *cf.* Claude Lévi-Strauss, *La pensée sauvage*, pp. 253 *ff.*
6. The concept of the "generalized other" is used here in a fully Meadian sense.
7. Compare Georg Simmel on the self-apprehension of man as both inside and outside society. Plessner's concept of "eccentricity" is again relevant here.

10. PRESENTATION OF SELF IN EVERYDAY LIFE

ERVING GOFFMAN

When an individual appears in the presence of others, there will usually be some reason for him to mobilize his activity so that it will convey an impression to others that is in his interests to convey.

Erving Goffman approaches the human being as an actor performing on a stage. His descriptions of interaction are classic. This insightful selection is one of his most famous.

What happens when we enter the presence of others? Use this as a guide to your reading:

1. Others seek to know who we are. We control our actions to give off the picture we want to give off.
2. Others will also seek to act to control the definition of the situation.
3. A working consensus is created.
4. Ongoing interaction may question the initial picture.
5. Preventive tactics help preserve the interaction and keep actors from embarrassment.

Here, Goffman brilliantly describes something that occurs in all of our lives, every day. He gives us insight into something familiar.

When an individual enters the presence of others, they commonly seek to acquire information about him or to bring into play information about him already possessed. They will be interested in his general socio-economic status, his conception of self, his attitude toward them, his competence, his trustworthiness, and so on. Although some of this information seems to be sought almost as an end in itself, there are usually quite practical reasons for acquiring it. Information about the individual helps to define the situation, enabling others to know in advance what he will expect of them and what they may expect of him. Informed in these ways, the others will know how best to act in order to call forth a desired response from him.

For those present, many sources of information become accessible and many carriers (or "sign-vehicles") become available for conveying this information. If unacquainted with the individual, observers can glean clues from his conduct and appearance that allow them to apply their previous experience with individuals roughly similar to the one in front of them or, more important, to apply untested stereotypes to him. They can also assume from past experience that only individuals of a particular kind are likely to be found in a given social setting. They can rely on what the individual says about himself or on documentary evidence he provides as to who and what he is. If they know, or know of, the individual by virtue of experience prior to the interaction, they can rely on assumptions as to the persistence and generality of psychological traits as a way of predicting his present and future behavior.

However, during the period in which the individual is in the immediate presence of the others, few events may occur that directly provide the others with the conclusive information they will need if they are to direct wisely their own activity. Many crucial facts lie beyond the time and place of interaction or lie concealed within it. For example, the "true" or "real" attitudes, beliefs, and emotions of the individual can be ascertained only indirectly, through his avowals or through what appears to be involuntary expressive behavior. Similarly, if the individual offers the others a product or service, they will often find that, during the interaction, there will be no time and place immediately available for eating the pudding that the proof can be found in. They will be forced to accept some events as conventional or natural signs of something not directly available to the senses. In Ichheiser's terms,[1] the individual will have to act so that he intentionally or unintentionally *expresses* himself, and the others will in turn have to be *impressed* in some way by him.

The expressiveness of the individual (and therefore his capacity to give impressions) appears to involve two radically different kinds of sign activity: the expression that he *gives*, and the expression that he *gives off*. The first involves verbal symbols or their substitutes that he uses admittedly and solely to convey the information he and the others are known to attach to these symbols. This is communication in the traditional and narrow sense. The second involves a wide range of action that others can treat as symptomatic of the actor, the expectation being that the action was performed for reasons other than the information conveyed in this way. As we shall have to see, this distinction has an only initial validity. The individual does, of course, intentionally convey misinformation by means of both of these types of communication, the first involving deceit, the second feigning....

He may wish [others] to think highly of him, or to think that he thinks highly of them, or to perceive how in fact he feels toward them, or to obtain no clear-cut impression; he may wish to ensure sufficient harmony so that the interaction can be sustained, or to defraud, get rid of, confuse, mislead, antagonize, or insult them. Regardless of the particular objective the individual has in mind and of his motive for having this objective, it will be in his interest to control the conduct of the others, especially their responsive treatment of him.[2] This control is achieved largely by influencing the definition of the situation the others come to formulate, and he can influence this definition by expressing himself in such a way as to give them the kind of impression that will lead them to act voluntarily in accordance with his own plan. Thus, when an individual appears in the presence of others, there will usually be some reason for him to mobilize his activity so that it will convey an impression to others that is in his interest to convey. Because a girl's dormitory mates will glean evidence of her popularity from the calls she receives on the phone, we can suspect that some girls will arrange for calls to be made, and Willard Waller's finding can be anticipated:

> It has been reported by many observers that a girl who is called to the telephone in the dormitories will often allow herself to be called several times, in order to give all the other girls ample opportunity to hear her paged....[3]

I have said that when an individual appears before others, his actions will influence the definition of the situation they come to have. Sometimes, the individual will act in a thoroughly calculating manner, expressing himself in a given way solely to give the kind of impression to others that is likely to evoke from them a specific response he is concerned to obtain. Sometimes, the individual will be calculating in his activity but be relatively unaware that this is the case. Sometimes, he will intentionally and consciously express himself in a particular way, but chiefly because the tradition of his group or social status require this kind of expression and not because of any particular response (other than vague acceptance or approval) that is likely to be evoked from those impressed by the expression. Sometimes, the traditions of an individual's role will lead him to give a well-designed impression of a particular kind, and yet he may be neither consciously nor unconsciously disposed to create such an impression. The others, in their turn, may be suitably impressed by the individual's efforts to convey something, or may misunderstand the situation and come to conclusions that are warranted neither by the individual's intent nor by the facts. In any case, in so far as the others act *as if* the individual had conveyed a particular impression, we may take a functional or pragmatic view and say that the individual has "effectively" projected a given definition of the situation and "effectively" fostered the understanding that a given state of affairs obtains....

When we allow that the individual projects a definition of the situation when he appears before others, we must also see that the others, however passive their role may seem to be, will themselves effectively project a definition of the situation by virtue of their response to the individual and by virtue of any lines of action they

initiate to him. Ordinarily, the definitions of the situation projected by the several different participants are sufficiently attuned to one another so that open contradiction will not occur. I do not mean that there will be the kind of consensus that arises when each individual present candidly expresses what he really feels and honestly agrees with the expressed feelings of the others present. This kind of harmony is an optimistic ideal, and in any case is not necessary for the smooth working of society. Rather, each participant is expected to suppress his immediate heartfelt feelings, conveying a view of the situation he feels the others will be able to find at least temporarily acceptable. The maintenance of this surface of agreement, this veneer of consensus, is facilitated by each participant concealing his own wants behind statements that assert values to which everyone present feels obliged to give lip service. Further, there is usually a kind of division of definitional labor. Each participant is allowed to establish the tentative official ruling regarding matters that are vital to him but not immediately important to others, for example, the rationalizations and justifications by which he accounts for his past activity. In exchange for this courtesy, he remains silent or noncommittal on matters important to others but not immediately important to him. We have then a kind of interactional *modus vivendi*. Together, the participants contribute to a single overall definition of the situation that involves not so much a real agreement as to what exists but rather a real agreement as to whose claims concerning what issues will be temporarily honored. Real agreement will also exist concerning the desirability of avoiding an open conflict of definitions of the situation.[4] I will refer to this level of agreement as a "working consensus." It is to be understood that the working consensus established in one interaction setting will be quite different in content from the working consensus established in a different type of setting. Thus, between two friends at lunch, a reciprocal show of affection, respect, and concern for the other is maintained. In service occupations, on the other hand, the specialist often maintains an image of disinterested involvement in the problem of the client, while the client responds with a show of respect for the competence and integrity of the specialist. Regardless of such differences in content, however, the general form of these working arrangements is the same.

In noting the tendency for a participant to accept the definitional claims made by the others present, we can appreciate the crucial importance of the information the individual *initially* possesses or acquires concerning his fellow participants, for it is on the basis of this initial information that the individual starts to define the situation and starts to build up lines of responsive action. The individual's initial projection commits him to what he is proposing to be and requires him to drop all pretenses of being other things. As the interaction among the participants progresses, additions and modifications in this initial informational state will of course occur, but it is essential that these later developments be related without contradiction to, and even built up from, the initial positions taken by the several participants. It would seem that an individual can more easily make a choice as to what line of treatment to demand from and extend to the others present at the beginning of an encounter than he can alter the line of treatment being pursued once the interaction is underway....

Given the fact that the individual effectively projects a definition of the situation when he enters the presence of others, we can assume that events may occur within the interaction that contradict, discredit, or otherwise throw doubt on this projection. When these disruptive events occur, the interaction itself may come to a confused and embarrassed halt. Some of the assumptions on which the responses of the participants had been predicated become untenable, and the participants find themselves lodged in an interaction for which the situation has been wrongly defined and is now no longer defined. At such moments, the individual whose presentation has been discredited may feel ashamed while the others present may feel hostile, and all the participants may come to feel ill at ease, nonplussed, out of countenance, embarrassed, experiencing the kind of anomie generated when the minute social system of face-to-face interaction breaks down.

In stressing the fact that the initial definition of the situation projected by an individual tends to provide a plan for the cooperative activity that follows — in stressing this action point of view —

we must not overlook the crucial fact that any projected definition of the situation also has a distinctive moral character. It is this moral character of projections that will chiefly concern us in this report. Society is organized on the principle that any individual who possesses certain social characteristics has a moral right to expect that others will value and treat him in an appropriate way. Connected with this principle is a second, namely that an individual who implicitly or explicitly signifies that he has certain social characteristics ought, in fact, to be what he claims he is. In consequence, when an individual projects a definition of the situation and thereby makes an implicit or explicit claim to be a person of a particular kind, he automatically exerts a moral demand on the others, obliging them to value and treat him in the manner that persons of his kind have a right to expect. He also implicitly forgoes all claims to be things he does not appear to be[5] and hence forgoes the treatment that would be appropriate for such individuals. The others find, then, that the individual has informed them as to what *is*, and as to what they *ought* to see as the "is."

One cannot judge the importance of definitional disruptions by the frequency with which they occur, for apparently they would occur more frequently were not constant precautions taken. We find that preventive practices are constantly employed to avoid these embarrassments, and that corrective practices are constantly employed to compensate for discrediting occurrences that have not been successfully avoided. When the individual employs these strategies and tactics to protect his own projections, we may refer to them as "defensive practices"; when a participant employs them to save the definition of the situation projected by another, we speak of "protective practices" or "tact." Together, defensive and protective practices comprise the techniques employed to safeguard the impression fostered by an individual during his presence before others. It should be added that although we may be ready to see that no fostered impression would survive if defensive practices were not employed, we are less ready perhaps to see that few impressions could survive if those who received the impression did not exert tact in their reception of it.

In addition to the fact that precautions are taken to prevent disruption of projected definitions, we may also note that an intense interest in these disruptions comes to play a significant role in the social life of the group. Practical jokes and social games are played in which embarrassments that are to be taken unseriously are purposely engineered.[6] Fantasies are created in which devastating exposures occur. Anecdotes from the past—real, embroidered, or fictitious—are told and retold, detailing disruptions that occurred, almost occurred, or occurred and were admirably resolved. There seems to be no grouping that does not have a ready supply of these games, reveries, and cautionary tales to be used as a source of humor, a catharsis for anxieties, and a sanction for inducing individuals to be modest in their claims and reasonable in their projected expectations. The individual may tell himself through dreams of getting into impossible positions. Families tell of the time a guest got his dates mixed and arrived when neither the house nor anyone in it was ready for him. Journalists tell of times when an all-too-meaningful misprint occurred, and the paper's assumption of objectivity or decorum was humorously discredited. Public servants tell of times a client ridiculously misunderstood form instructions, giving answers that implied an unanticipated and bizarre definition of the situation.[7] Seamen, whose home away from home is rigorously heman, tell stories of coming back home and inadvertently asking mother to "pass the fucking butter."[8] Diplomats tell of the time a nearsighted queen asked a republican ambassador about the health of his king.[9]

To summarize, then, I assume that when an individual appears before others, he will have many motives for trying to control the impression they receive of the situation. This report is concerned with some of the common techniques that persons employ to sustain such impressions and with some of the common contingencies associated with the employment of these techniques. The specific content of any activity presented by the individual participant, or the role it plays in the interdependent activities of an ongoing social system, will not be at issue; I shall be concerned only with the participant's dramaturgical problems of presenting the activity before others. The issues dealt with by stagecraft and stage management are sometimes trivial, but they are quite general; they seem to occur everywhere in social life, providing a clear-cut dimension for formal sociological analysis.

NOTES

1. Gustav Ichheiser, "Misunderstandings in Human Relations," Supplement to *The American Journal of Sociology*, LV (September, 1949), pp. 6—7.
2. Here I owe much to an unpublished paper by Tom Burns of the University of Edinburgh. He presents the argument that in all interaction a basic underlying theme is the desire of each participant to guide and control the responses made by the others present. A similar argument has been advanced by Jay Haley in a recent unpublished paper, but in regard to a special kind of control, that having to do with defining the nature of the relationship of those involved in the interaction.
3. Willard Waller, "The Rating and Date Complex," *American Sociological Review*, II, p. 730.
4. An interaction can be purposely set up as a time and place for voicing differences in opinion, but in such cases, participants must be careful to agree not to disagree on the proper tone of voice, vocabulary, and degree of seriousness in which all arguments are to be phrased, and on the mutual respect that disagreeing participants must carefully continue to express toward one another. The debaters' or an academic definition of the situation may also be invoked suddenly and judiciously as a way of translating a serious conflict of views into one that can be handled within a framework acceptable to all present.
5. This role of the witness in limiting what it is the individual can be has been stressed by Existentialists, who see it as a basic threat to individual freedom. See Jean Paul Sartre, *Being and Nothingness*, trans. by Hazel E. Barnes (New York: Philosophical Library, 1956), pp. 365 *ff*.
6. E. Goffman, "Communication Conduct in an Island Community," (unpublished Ph.D. dissertation, Department of Sociology, University of Chicago, 1953).
7. Peter Blau, "Dynamics of Bureaucracy" (Ph.D. dissertation, Department of Sociology, Columbia University, forthcoming, University of Chicago Press), pp. 127—129.
8. Walter M. Beattie, Jr., "The Merchant Seaman" (unpublished M.A. report, Department of Sociology, University of Chicago, 1950), p. 35.
9. Sir Frederick Ponsonby, *Recollections of Three Reigns* (New York: Dutton, 1952), p. 46.

11. SOCIAL IDENTITY

RICHARD JENKINS

All human identities are in some sense—and usually a stronger rather than a weaker sense—social identities. It cannot be otherwise....

The title Jenkins gives this chapter in his book is "Knowing Who We Are." How do we know who we are? How do we know who other people are? Why is it important? It all relates to our everyday social interaction, the negotiation of who we are as we relate to one another in our social life.

It is a cold Friday night, and windy. You are dressed for dancing, not the weather. Finally, you reach the head of the queue outside the night club. The bouncer—although nowadays they prefer to be called doormen—raises his arm and lets your friend in. He takes one look at you and demands proof of your age. All you have in your pockets is money. That isn't enough.

You telephone the order line of a clothing catalog to buy a new jacket. The young man who answers asks for your name, address, credit card number and expiration date, your customer reference number if you have one; all in order to establish your status as someone to whom, in the absence of a face-to-face encounter, goods can be dispatched in confidence. And also, of course, to make sure that you're on the mailing list.

The immigration official asks you for your passport. She looks at your nationality, at where you were born. Your name. She checks your visa. These indicate your legitimacy as a traveler, your desirability as an entrant. She looks at the photograph, she looks at you. She asks you the purpose of your visit. She stamps the passport and wishes you a pleasant stay. Already she is looking over your shoulder at the person behind you.

On a train, the stranger in the opposite seat excuses herself. She has noticed you reading last week's newspaper from a small town several hundred miles to the east. You explain that your

From Chapter 1 of *Social Identity*, by Richard Jenkins. London: Routledge, 1996.

mother posts it to you so that you can keep up with the news from home. She recognized the newspaper because her husband is from your home town. You, it turns out, were at school with her brother-in-law. Before leaving the train she gives you her telephone number.

In everyday situations such as these, one's identity is called into question and established (or not). But the presentation or negotiation of identity is not always so ordinary or trivial: It can shake the foundations of our lives. Imagine, for example, the morning of your sixty-fifth birthday. With it, as well as birthday cards, will come retirement, a pension, a concessionary public transport pass, special rates every Tuesday at the hairdresser. Beyond that again, in the promise of free medical prescriptions and the beckoning Day Centre, hover the shades of infirmity, of dependence, of disability. Although it will be the same face you see in the bathroom mirror, you will no longer be quite the person you were yesterday. Nor can you ever be again.

Sometimes, a changed or strange situation makes the difference. An unfamiliar neighborhood, an ethnically divided city: a casual encounter can transform one's taken-for-granted identity into a dangerous liability. Something as simple as the "wrong" accent or an "ethnic" surname on your driving license can become a warrant for violence, even murder. Whether the ethnic identification is "correct" or not—in your eyes—may make no difference. Identity is often in the eye of the beholder.

Or take a different time scale, and another kind of transformation. What changes and negotiations are required by "coming out," to assume a public identification as a gay man or a lesbian? What kind of response from others is the "right" response? Which others matter? And what does such a process represent? The construction of a new identity, or the revelation of an authentic and primordial self?

Social identity is also important on a wider stage than the encounters or thresholds of individual lives. Imagine a contested border region. It might be anywhere in the world. There are different ways to settle the issue: warfare, a referendum, international arbitration. Whatever the means adopted, the outcome has implications for the identities of people on both sides. And it may not be accepted by those who find their new national identity uncongenial. Similarly, the referenda about the European Union in the early 1990s in Scandinavia were as much about the preservation and transformation of identity as anything else.

To return to gay and lesbian identity, mass public occasions such as Gay Pride in London or the Sydney Mardi Gras are affirmations that being gay or being lesbian are collective identifications. For individual participants, these occasions may (or, indeed, may not) affirm their own particular sexual identities, but these gatherings are collective rituals of identification and political mobilization before they are anything else.

These scenarios, different as they are, exemplify social identity in everyday life. It is the most mundane of things, and it can be the most extraordinary. But what does it mean to say that these situations all involve social identity? What do they have in common? How do we know who we are, and how do others identify us? How does our sense of ourselves as unique individuals square with the realization that, always and everywhere, we share aspects of our identity with many others? To what extent is it possible to become someone, or something, other than what we now are? Is it possible to "just be myself?"...

What is identity, and what is social identity? Social identity is a characteristic or property of humans as social beings. The word *identity*, however, embraces a universe of creatures, things, and substances that is wider than the limited cat-

egory of humanity. As such, its general meanings are worthy of brief attention, to provide a base line from which to begin our consideration of specifically social identity.

Consulting the Oxford English Dictionary yields a Latin root *(identitas,* from *idem,* "the same") and two basic meanings. The first is a concept of absolute sameness: "this is identical to that." The second is a concept of distinctiveness that presumes consistency or continuity over time. Approaching the idea of sameness from two different angles, the notion of identity simultaneously establishes two possible relations of comparison between persons or things: *similarity* on the one hand, and *difference* on the other.

Exploring the matter further, the verb *to identify* is a necessary accompaniment of identity: There is something active about the word that cannot be ignored. Identity is not "just there," it must always be established. This adds two further meanings to our catalog: to classify things or persons, and to associate oneself *with* something or someone else (for example, a friend, a hero, a party, or a philosophy). Each locates identity within the ebb and flow of practice and process; they are both things people do. The latter, in the context of social relations, also implies a degree of reflexivity.

We are now firmly in the realm of social identity.... All human identities are in some sense—and usually a stronger rather than a weaker sense—*social* identities. It cannot be otherwise, if only because identity is about meaning, and meaning is not an essential property of words and things. Meanings are always the outcome of agreement or disagreement, always a matter of convention and innovation, always to some extent shared, always to some extent negotiable.

Some contemporary writers about identity treat it as a basic datum that simply "is." This pays insufficient attention to how identity "works" or "is worked," to process and reflexivity, to the social construction of identity in interaction and institutionally. Understanding these processes is central to understanding what social identity is. Identity can in fact only be understood *as* process. As "being" or "becoming." One's social identity—indeed, one's social identities, for who we are is always singular and plural—is never a final or settled matter. Not even death can freeze the picture: There is always the possibility of a *post mortem* revision of identity (and some identities, that of a martyr, for example, can only be achieved beyond the grave).

So, how to define "social identity"? Minimally, the expression refers to the ways in which individuals and collectivities are distinguished in their social relations with other individuals and collectivities. It is the systematic establishment and signification, between individuals, between collectivities, and between individuals and collectivities, of relationships of similarity and difference. Taken—as they can only be—together, similarity and difference are the dynamic principles of identity, the heart of social life:

> ...The practical significance of men for one another...is determined by both similarities and differences among them. Similarity as fact or tendency is no less important than difference. In the most varied forms, both are the great principles of all internal and external development. In fact, the cultural history of mankind can be conceived as the history of the struggles and conciliatory attempts between the two.
>
> (Simmel 1950: 30)

Social identity is a game of "playing the *vis-à-vis*" (Boon 1982: 26). Social identity is our understanding of who we are and of who other people are, and, reciprocally, other people's understanding of themselves and of others (which includes us). Social identity, is, therefore, no more essential than meaning; it too is the product of agreement and disagreement, it too is negotiable.

Human social life is unimaginable without some means of knowing who others are and some sense of who we are. Because we cannot rely on our sense of smell or our animal non-verbals (although these are not insignificant in the negotiation of identity during encounters), one of the first things we do on meeting a stranger is attempt to locate them on our social maps, to identify them. And not always successfully: "Mistaken identity" is a common motif of interaction. Someone we thought was Ms. A in fact turns out to be Mrs. Q, or we take someone for French when they are Belgian.

All kinds of people other than social scientists have cause to reflect on social identity during their everyday lives. A common theme in everyday discourse, for example, is lost or confused identity, about people not knowing "who they are," about a "crisis of identity." Sometimes people talk about "social identity"; sometimes they simply talk about "identity." More often than not, however, men and women going about the business of their daily lives are concerned with *specific* social identities. We talk, for example, about whether people are born gay or become gay as a result of the way in which they were brought up. About what it means to be "grown up." About what the difference is between Canadians and Americans. We observe the family who has just moved in around the corner and shake our heads: What can you expect? They come from the wrong part of town. We watch the television news and jump to all kinds of conclusions about current events on the basis of identifications such as "Muslim," "fundamentalist Christian," or whatever.

Social change is often accompanied by rhetoric about "identity under threat." Take, for example, the public debate in the United Kingdom about the European Union. While the regulations governing sausage manufacture are presented as a threat to the "British way of life," the prospect of monetary union in Europe conjures up centuries of strife with our continental neighbors and is interpreted as another attempt to undermine British national identity. Recent debates within the Scandinavian countries about the European Union have thrown a similar barrage of concerns, albeit triggered by different issues.

Whether in the abstract or the concrete, with reference to ourselves or to others, in personal depth or during superficial casual chat, with reference to individuality, nationality, social class, gender or age (etcetera...), it seems that we cannot do without some concepts with which to think about social identity, with which to query and confirm who we are and who others are. This is probably true no matter the language or culture; it has probably always been true. Without frameworks for delineating social identity and identities, I would be the same as you and neither of us could relate to the other meaningfully or consistently. Without social identity, there is, in fact, no society.

12. THE SOCIAL INTERACTION OF HUMAN BEINGS

HERBERT BLUMER

...human society is made up of individuals who have selves (that is, make indications to themselves); that individual action is a construction and not a release, being built up by the individual through noting and interpreting features of the situations in which he acts; that group or collective action consists of the aligning of individual actions, brought about by the individuals' interpreting or taking into account each other's actions.

Human beings are social beings because we constantly engage in social interaction. No one captures the role of social interaction for our individual decisions and for the development of society as does Herbert Blumer.

The term "symbolic interaction" refers, of course, to the peculiar and distinctive character of interaction as it takes place between human beings. The peculiarity consists in the fact that human beings interpret or "define" each other's actions instead of merely reacting to each other's actions. Their "response" is not made directly to the actions of one another but instead is based on the meaning which they attach to such actions. Thus, human interaction is mediated by the use of symbols, by interpretation, or by ascertaining the meaning of one another's actions. This mediation is equivalent to inserting a process of interpretation between stimulus and response in the case of human behavior.

The simple recognition that human beings interpret each other's actions as the means of acting toward one another has permeated the thought and writings of many scholars of human conduct and of human group life. Yet few of them have endeavored to analyze what such interpretation implies about the nature of the human being or about the nature of human association. They are

Ch. 10 "Society as Symbolic Interaction" by Herbert Blumer in Arnold M. Rose (Editor), *Human Behavior and Social Processes*. Copyright © 1962 by Houghton Mifflin Company. Reprinted with permission.

usually content with a mere recognition that "interpretation" should be caught by the student, or with a simple realization that symbols, such as cultural norms or values, must be introduced into their analyses. Only G. H. Mead, in my judgment, has sought to think through what the act of interpretation implies for an understanding of the human being, human action, and human association. The essentials of his analysis are so penetrating and profound and so important for an understanding of human group life that I wish to spell them out, even though briefly.

The key feature in Mead's analysis is that the human being has a self. This idea should not be cast aside as esoteric or glossed over as something that is obvious and hence not worthy of attention. In declaring that the human being has a self, Mead had in mind chiefly that the human being can be the object of his own actions. He can act toward himself as he might act toward others. Each of us is familiar with actions of this sort in which the human being gets angry with himself, rebuffs himself, takes pride in himself, argues with himself, tries to bolster his own courage, tells himself that he should "do this" or not "do that," sets goals for himself, makes compromises with himself, and plans what he is going to do. That the human being acts toward himself in these and countless other ways is a matter of easy empirical observation. To recognize that the human being can act toward himself is no mystical conjuration.

Mead regards this ability of the human being to act toward himself as the central mechanism with which the human being faces and deals with his world. This mechanism enables the human being to make indication to himself of things in his surroundings and thus to guide his actions by what he notes. Anything of which a human being is conscious is something which he is indicating to himself—the ticking of a clock, a knock at the door, the appearance of a friend, the remark made by a companion, a recognition that he has a task to perform, or the realization that he has a cold. Conversely, anything of which he is not conscious is, *ipso facto*, something which he is not indicating to himself. The conscious life of the human being, from the time that he awakens until he falls asleep, is a continual flow of self-indications—notations of the things with which he deals and takes into account. We are given, then, a picture of the human being as an organism which confronts its world with a mechanism for making indications to itself. This is the mechanism that is involved in interpreting the actions of others. To interpret the actions of another is to point out to oneself that the action has this or that meaning or character.

Now, according to Mead, the significance of making indications to oneself is of paramount importance. The importance lies along two lines. First, to indicate something is to extricate it from its setting, to hold it apart, to give it a meaning or, in Mead's language, to make it into an object. An object—that is to say, anything that an individual indicates to himself—is different from a stimulus; instead of having an intrinsic character which acts on the individual and which can be identified apart from the individual, its character or meaning is conferred on it by the individual. The object is a product of the individual's disposition to act instead of being an antecedent stimulus which evokes the act. Instead of the individual being surrounded by an environment of pre-existing objects which play upon him and call forth his behavior, the proper picture is that he constructs his objects on the basis of his ongoing activity. In any of his countless acts—

whether minor, like dressing himself, or major, like organizing himself for a professional career—the individual is designating different objects to himself, giving them meaning, judging their suitability to his action, and making decisions on the basis of the judgment. This is what is meant by interpretation or acting on the basis of symbols.

The second important implication of the fact that the human being makes indications to himself is that his action is constructed or built up instead of being a mere release. Whatever the action in which he is engaged, the human individual proceeds by pointing out to himself the divergent things which have to be taken into account in the course of his action. He has to note what he wants to do and how he is to do it; he has to point out to himself the various conditions which may be instrumental to his action and those which may obstruct his action; he has to take account of the demands, the expectations, the prohibitions, and the threats as they may arise in the situation in which he is acting. His action is built up step by step through a process of such self-indication. The human individual pieces together and guides his action by taking account of different things and interpreting their significance for his prospective action. There is no instance of conscious action of which this is not true.

The process of constructing action through making indications to oneself cannot be swallowed up in any of the conventional psychological categories. This process is distinct from and different from what is spoken of as the "ego"—just as it is different from any other conception which conceives of the self in terms of composition or organization. Self-indication is a moving communicative process in which the individual notes things, assesses them, gives them a meaning, and decides to act on the basis of the meaning. The human being stands over against the world, or against "alters," with such a process and not with a mere ego. Further, the process of self-indication cannot be subsumed under the forces, whether from the outside or inside, which are presumed to play upon the individual to produce his behavior. Environmental pressures, external stimuli, organic drives, wishes, attitudes, feelings, ideas, and their like do not cover or explain the process of self-indication. The process of self-indication stands over against them in that the individual points out to himself and interprets the appearance or expression of such things, noting a given social demand that is made on him, recognizing a command, observing that he is hungry, realizing that he wishes to buy something, aware that he has a given feeling, conscious that he dislikes eating with someone he despises, or aware that he is thinking of doing some given thing. By virtue of indicating such things to himself, he places himself over against them and is able to act back against them, accepting them, rejecting them, or transforming them in accordance with how he defines or interprets them. His behavior, accordingly, is not a result of such things as environmental pressures, stimuli, motives, attitudes, and ideas but arises instead from how he interprets and handles these things in the action which he is constructing. The process of self-indication by means of which human action is formed cannot be accounted for by factors which precede the act. The process of self-indication exists in its own right and must be accepted and studied as such. It is through this process that the human being constructs his conscious action.

Now Mead recognizes that the formation of action by the individual through a process of self-indication always takes place in a social context.

Since this matter is so vital to an understanding of symbolic interaction it needs to be explained carefully. Fundamentally, group action takes the form of a fitting together of individual lines of action. Each individual aligns his action to the action of others by ascertaining what they are doing or what they intend to do—that is, by getting the meaning of their acts. For Mead, this is done by the individual "taking the role" of others—either the role of a specific person or the role of a group (Mead's "generalized other"). In taking such roles the individual seeks to ascertain the intention or direction of the acts of others. He forms and aligns his own action on the basis of such interpretation of the acts of others. This is the fundamental way in which group action takes place in human society.

The foregoing are the essential features, as I see them, in Mead's analysis of the bases of symbolic interaction. They presuppose the following: that human society is made up of individuals who have selves (that is, make indications to themselves); that individual action is a construction and not a release, being built up by the individual through noting and interpreting features of the situations in which he acts; that group or collective action consists of the aligning of individual actions, brought about by the individual's interpreting or taking into account each other's actions....

13. SOCIALIZATION, PAIN, AND THE NORMALIZATION OF SPORTS INJURY

TIMOTHY JON CURRY

By the time Sam had reached the elite level in sports, he had already been thoroughly socialized into the informal expectations regarding pain and injury; they had become part of his personal orientation to the sport. Athletes like Sam who pin their chances of material success on a career in sports are aware that the confirmation of their status as an athlete is both crucial and dependent on the opinions of those in the sport who adhere to the norms themselves.

This is a description of how one individual—Sam—took on the identity of "wrestler." Timothy Curry interviewed Sam extensively and tried to learn the key turning points—"epiphanies"—in his wrestling career and developing identity. We are all socialized into various identities through social interaction, and this is one example. Note that a large part of Sam's socialization into wrestling influenced Sam's definition of things within himself—pain and injury. Even such personal matters result from socialization and are part of our developing social identities.

This study describes how Sam, an elite amateur wrestler competing in a "big-time" college wrestling program, came to accept pain and injury as a normal part of his sports role-identity. Although this is a single career history, the social processes involved in the normalization of sports injury affect thousands of athletes and sports enthusiasts....

[T]he normalization of sports injury needs to be examined in a broader context than the social construction of masculinity. Furthermore, it needs to be examined over an athlete's life course, because both primary and secondary socialization is likely to contribute to the normalization of injury. By the time the elite athlete appears on the scene in college or high school, he or she may already have developed an attitude that regards even serious injury as routine.

From "A Little Pain Never Hurt Anyone: Athletic Career Socialization and the Normalization of Sports Injury," by Timothy Jon Curry. Excerpted from pp. 273–290, *Symbolic Interaction*, 16(3), 1993.

This research takes a role-identity approach that focuses on Sam's imaginative view of himself as an occupant of a social position (McCall and Simmons, 1978). Compatible with the notion of role-identity is the concept of career, defined in classic symbolic interactionist terms as having two components: an objective side, which involves moving through a sequence of social positions; and a subjective side, which involves the changes in self-conception that accompany these positional relocations (Goffman 1961; Lindesmith, Strauss, and Denzin 1991).

As a career becomes established, it serves as a "moving perspective in which the person sees his life as a whole and interprets the meaning of his various attributes, actions, and the things that happen to him" (Hughes 1958, p. 63). A career history is similar to a life history in that certain decisive moments or experiences in the respondent's life are regarded as more important than others for interpretive analysis. These turning points or experiences that the respondent recollects are termed *epiphanies*. Denzin (1989, p. 17) suggests that the types of epiphanies employed by writers such as James Joyce may be useful in constructing life histories. He identifies four: minor or illustrative, major, cumulative, and relived. Minor or illustrative epiphanies reveal underlying tensions in a situation or relationship; major epiphanies concern important turning points or moments of truth when character is revealed. The cumulative epiphany occurs as a result of a series of events, and the relived epiphany refers to the process of reliving any of the other types of epiphanies or going through them again.

PROCEDURES

This telling of Sam's career history involves one cumulative, three major, and two minor epiphanies. I gathered this history during three tape-recorded interviews, each lasting between one to two hours. The interviews were spread over several weeks....

The idea of using epiphanies to organize this material developed after the interviews themselves. There were simply too many injuries to report in detail, and a mere listing of these injuries would fail to communicate their relative significance to Sam or to his career. Several injuries—some quite severe—that Sam or I did not view as turning points have been omitted or are discussed very briefly....

ATHLETIC CAREER SOCIALIZATION

Sam's family history was such that being an athlete was virtually an ascribed identity; the only question was what type of athlete he would become and how far he would go in his career. Sam's parents assumed that Sam would participate in sports as the natural order of things, and thus an athletic identity was "bestowed" on him before he was born (Weigert, Teitge, and Teitge 1986). Sam's father was still quite active in sports when his son was born, both as a player and as an owner of a local semiprofessional football team. He had been a good athlete in high school, participating in football, basketball, track, and baseball (but not wrestling). Sam's mother was also a good high school athlete—a

runner. She was favorably disposed to having her son and his sisters participate in neighborhood sports at an early age. Her father also had been an accomplished athlete in high school; his sports including wrestling. Two of Sam's uncles on his mother's side had wrestled successfully in high school and participated in other sports. Sam's mother's youngest brother, his favorite uncle, was also very athletic, although he did not try out for high school sports. This uncle, at age sixteen, taught Sam his first wrestling moves: "When I was three, he'd come over and start tickling me. I'd run around and he'd grab my leg and take me down. He still follows my career."

Sam feels that his family's competitive spirit has influenced both him and his sisters. His elder sister, who is two years older than he, was already participating in T-ball when he was five. She and Sam continued to participate in sports together over the next six years. Sam's mother encouraged his sports participation, and his father helped organize the teams, eventually becoming a coach.

The earliest sports injury that Sam recollects occurred during his first year of T-ball:

> I was at second base when a ball was hit to the outfield, but I wasn't paying attention. I turned around, and "Whap!" the ball hit me in the eye, and my eye swelled up real big. I got a big black eye, about the size of half a softball. I think I cried right when it happened, but after that it was all right. I sat back on the bench, and then I said, "Dad, let me go back out." I was really competitive, and I liked to play. He let me go back out, but I couldn't see very well, so I had to come out and sit on the bench anyway. After the game, I had to go to the doctor. The swelling was so bad they had me sit out in the sun for a few days to make it go down.

His parents' reaction to his first sports injury established a pattern that has not varied much over the course of his sports career. His mother reacted negatively to the injury; Sam remembers that she said, "'Oh, my poor baby,' and stuff like that." She "went nuts" over his father's decision to return him to the game, and refused to talk to her husband for a week after the game. Sam comments: "Now it's a constant battle between my mom and dad when I get hurt."

Upon reflecting on his parents' behavior, Sam realized that his mother reacted in much the same way as his grandmother had reacted when her sons were injured: "My grandmother never went to watch my uncles wrestle or play football. She'd watch them play baseball and basketball, but she couldn't handle the contact sports. To this day, she hasn't seen me wrestle." His mother acts the same, especially when he wrestles tough opponents. She leaves, pretending to go to the rest room.

His father, on the other hand, shows no emotional reaction to his injuries and claims that they are not significant. His father's lack of concern about Sam's injuries are identical to his lack of concern about his own injuries:

My dad played a lot of ball, and when he'd get hurt, he'd still play. I got to see my dad playing football and baseball and getting his nose broken and stuff like that. He broke his nose ten times, even had surgery done on it...he also had five knee surgeries, and one involved major reconstruction. I'm sure he's going to have arthritis some day. He had many broken fingers and other minor injuries. Thus, he knows what he is saying when he says I have only a slight injury, and he says, "Hey, let's get up; let's get going." He believes in the rough and tough idea. I'm seeing my dad playing ball with his broken nose and all kinds of busted fingers, and I think, "I want to be like Dad and be tough like that." In wrestling, we get all kinds of minor injuries, and we "shake it out" and still compete with them, so we're doing the same thing.

Thus, Sam's attitudes toward sports injury are linked to his earliest memories of his father's sports career, and to his father's definition of sports injury as normal and to be expected. Sam's routine acceptance of injury is challenged, however, by both his mother and his grandmother. The issue of the struggle, as Sam sees it, is being "rough and tough" versus "being treated like a baby." Not surprisingly, Sam has chosen the more masculine characterization of himself as tough; in this and the following accounts, he stresses repeatedly that his behavior is similar to his father's. In this regard, Sam's career history is similar to those alluded to by researchers who have studied the development of masculinity and the male identity. Sam used

"toughness" in sports to separate himself from femininity and to develop masculinity; many other boys have used sports similarly (Connell 1990; Messner 1989).

At age seven, Sam began his socialization into what became his main career in sports. With his parents' encouragement, he became an active participant in the wrestling program at the neighborhood community center. There, he could wrestle with the older boys, and occasionally was coached by volunteers. His father orchestrated Sam's career by organizing trips and driving him to meets and tournaments: "I was in a national competition by the time I was seven, and right away my dad [was] worried about my season."

By the time Sam was eight-and-a-half or nine, he was participating in competitions sponsored by the Amateur Athletic Union (AAU); by the time he was ten, his father had organized a wrestling club. Thirty-five people joined, and they traveled to meets in Ohio and other states. Although Sam had no brothers to practice wrestling with at home, his elder sister was a good partner, and he wrestled with her. His cousin on his father's side also started wrestling when Sam was nine. Sam's sports circle, then, included family, friends, and neighbors, and, for the most part, was still considered recreational fun.

Sam views his family's involvement in sports as a special way to maintain closeness, especially with his father. To Sam, sports participation has been a means of expressing love: "We're not the kind of people who are real mushy. I don't think I've told my dad I love him, but he knows that through all the stuff we do."

The meaning of sports and sports injury is thus deeply embedded in Sam's affection towards his father. An injury not only threatens his immediate participation in sports but also threatens the relationship he and his dad have established, a relationship that apparently cannot be reestablished as easily in other domains. As a means of expressing love, however, sports become problematic at higher levels of competition, because ever greater skill demands are placed on the participants. When an athlete can no longer achieve success, he may experience difficulty in maintaining bonds with teammates, coaches, and even his father (Curry 1991).

Becoming Supermotivated

Sam's socialization into sports as a career accelerated when he began going to summer and weekend camps. His skills continued to improve, and he believed that he could excel with more training. At the national AAU tournaments, held in Lincoln, Nebraska, he learned about a wrestling camp that taught young athletes how to be "supermotivated." He and his father felt that attending this camp might give him an edge over the other boys, and this experience proved to be a major epiphany in Sam's career.

The coach of the camp had been a wrestler himself, and was well connected in the world of amateur wrestling. The camp gave Sam the idea that earning a college scholarship through wrestling was a real possibility: "There were a lot of kids from really poor families. He let them come, but he made them work for it. He'd let them know that just because they were poor they didn't have to go and be idiots."

The coach had been injured in a trampoline accident and was paralyzed from the waist down. Nonetheless, occasionally he left his wheelchair and crawled on to the mat to wrestle with the boys. Sam recollects that once he lectured the boys about being a quitter. He said, "Look at me, I didn't quit. I could have easily given up; instead I just got a million-dollar grant from the state to run this project." Sam feels that this camp taught him that hard work and discipline pay off, and that injury need not prevent success, even if it confines you to a wheelchair.

The coach stressed adherence to strict training rules and very vigorous exercise, even for his youngest students. Sam described a few of the techniques the coach used to instill discipline and motivation. On one occasion, Sam maintained the wrestler's crouch position for several hours, normally an impossible task for a preadolescent. The coach had rigged up a table top so that it could be lowered until it was a few feet from the floor, and Sam crouched underneath until the coach said it was time to quit. On another occasion, Sam was forced to run five miles with bags of sand in a knapsack on his back; the coach followed in his car to make sure that he kept moving. Such techniques were not used with all the boys, but mostly with those the coach

believed had special talent. Sam was honored by receiving such attention, and was further gratified when he was given the privilege of sleeping in the coach's house during camp. At this young age, then, the experience of pain became associated with motivation to achieve excellence in sports and with special treatment as a favored athlete. Like bodybuilders, who learn to appreciate pain because it means that muscle tissue is being torn down and rebuilt (Ewald and Jiobu 1985), Sam learned to appreciate pain because it meant that he was becoming "supermotivated."

Sam's participation in sports camps and adult-supervised competition at an early age was not unusual; many parents seek to gain an edge for their children through such practices. Abusive treatment of children is not uncommon in these camps, in part because some parents and coaches are convinced that harsh discipline will make their children more competitive (Curry and Jiobu 1984, p. 56). As athletes such as Sam come to define situations in roughly the same manner as their coaches, they acquire the key values shared by elite athletes, including "what is prized and what is disdained" (Shibutani 1986, p. 156). What is disdained is not injury or pain themselves, but allowing pain or injury to stand in the way of accomplishing a goal.

An End to Recreational Sports

From Sam's perspective, his first significant sports injury occurred when he was twelve years old. Beside the black eye described earlier, he had jammed and broken several fingers, but because those injuries healed quickly and did not incapacitate him, they did not count as real injuries. He suffered a more serious injury when he was playing basketball with his sister's friends, who were fourteen or fifteen years old. One of the players, "a guy 6'2" and 190 pounds," crashed into him and stepped heavily on his foot while trying to rebound the ball. No one believed that Sam was hurt, but he felt intense pain in his ankle and had to hop the half-mile home on one leg:

By the time I got to the edge of the grass, I could not stand on one leg anymore, so I crawled the rest of the way. My mom saw me and came running out and got me into the house. We took my shoe and sock off, and you could see the "c-o-n-v-e-r-s-e" on the heel mark on my ankle. You could still see it six weeks later. She rushed me to the hospital and got it X-rayed. Then they called my dad. His first comments are "What are you breaking your ankle for? We had to go to the tournament!" I'm thinking, "This guy must be crazy."

After reflecting further about what his father had said, however, Sam decided not to take risks in other sports and to focus on wrestling. Reluctantly, he gave up basketball, football, and other recreational sports he loved. This injury thus helped Sam define his sports career, but it also turned him away from what had been a routine and enjoyable part of his everyday life.

Sam's father was eager to narrow his choices in the hopes of creating greater opportunities for him. Coakley (1991) describes such a process as an "identity tunnel" in which young athletes are channeled into increasingly fewer activities, all of them sports related. By the time they are in their late teens, such youngsters will have few identities other than that of being a star athlete, and little experience with other roles. Now, Sam had entered the "identity tunnel."

Rendezvous with Sports Medicine

Although Sam has been encouraged constantly by his father to consider injury simply as a normal part of his sports career, he has relied on his mother to attend to his actual medical needs and take him to the doctor or the hospital. As a result, he has been subjected to her fear of sports injury and her perspective of sports as recreation — views that undercut and challenged those of his father. His next wrestling injury marked a minor epiphany; it was the first time he received care from a specialist in sports medicine whose views supported those of his father.

When Sam broke his thumb at school during wrestling practice, his father sought care from his own sports medicine physician, who was both more knowledgeable and more tolerant about sports injuries:

My dad had this sports medicine guy way back then, who always looked at his stuff and fixed him

up so he could play. Thereafter, when I would break a middle finger, I would get it taped and keep on wrestling. My mom hated my dad for this. This went on for three weeks. She hated him for taking me to this sports medicine guy. I wanted to wrestle too, but my mom couldn't understand why I would have to do this in the seventh grade. Never did make up with him over this. She finally just accepted my getting hurt all the time. When my mom got me started in sports, she said we could play, but if we got hurt we had to quit. That wasn't the way it turned out.

With a sports physician now on hand to smooth the way, the next four years involved no more than one week off at a time to treat four different broken fingers, including "a thumb and a pinky." The absence of any incapacitating injury was important because it allowed Sam to prove himself as an elite wrestler in statewide high school competition.

Success in high school is seen as crucial by ambitious athletes such as Sam because they must demonstrate superior performance if they hope to win a scholarship to college. To illustrate, fewer than 5 percent of high school football, basketball, and baseball players are accepted into college sports programs (Coakley 1990).

Becoming a Champion   When asked "at what point [he] knew [he] had it all together as a wrestler," Sam replied that as a freshman in high school, he had begun to achieve everything he wanted. At one large tournament for high school wrestlers, he set a new record for the number of persons defeated in a single weight class (128). From that moment, Sam knew that he had begun to make a reputation for himself and that he would be recognized by others as an elite wrestler. He still identifies strongly with those who have won: "All the big names, the guys that have gotten to the Olympics, they have won that tournament. I've still got things I want to achieve, but right there I knew I would be a good college wrestler."

By the time Sam was a senior in high school, he had won the state tournament three times. He had failed, however, to win the Catholic Invitational Tournament (CIT). This prestigious tournament was especially important to his teammates and coaches at the Catholic high school he attended. Although he had finished second and third in previous CITs, Sam was worried that "everybody would say I was a fluke" if he failed to finish first in his senior year. Other well-known wrestlers had won this tournament as well as the state championship in their senior year. Shortly before the tournament, however, he came home from practice with a sore knee. He thought nothing of it, but by next morning the knee was stiff.

By practice time, the knee had swollen to the size of a baseball and was very sore. ("When I banged it on the wrestling pad, it would be so painful that I just wanted to drop on my butt and hold it.") At first, Sam assumed he would have to miss the tournament, but an assistant coach persuaded him to go ahead and wrestle, even with the pain. A shot of cortisone from the local hospital reduced the pain and swelling. Both his father and a physical therapist were doubtful about the wisdom of competing and feared that he was taking things too far by risking further injury to his knee. His high school coach was also fearful, and insisted that Sam demonstrate his ability to wrestle during practice with teammates. Sam himself felt that he had a 50—50 chance of making the knee worse, but nonetheless decided it was worth the risk to win the tournament for himself and the school. Even so, he confesses now that he was "kind of scared." To make matters even more difficult, because Sam had not initially planned on entering the tournament, he had gained a few pounds and was over the weight limit. On the way to the tournament, he rode an exercise bike for several hours in the back of a recreational vehicle to lose those pounds. He arrived both dehydrated and with a swollen, sore knee. During the tournament, he wore two knee pads and continuously asked himself, "Why am I doing this?" The answer was that he believed he "was going someplace, and the college recruiters will be at the meet." As it turned out, Sam faced a freshman in the final round of the competition, and won the match easily. He felt he had lived up to other people's expectations and had proved that he was not "a fluke."

Overall, this experience with the CIT was a major epiphany in Sam's career and his developing sense of self. It was the first time he had wrestled in real pain, and against the wishes of a medical specialist and his father. In this way, he demonstrated that he was prepared to take risks and to "pay the price for success." In mastering his fear of the knee injury, Sam also became more aware of his body's vulnerabilities. In the past, he had never worn knee pads, but now, he said, "I started to take care of my knees." The implication is that Sam's identity transformation from an amateur athlete to an expert was nearly complete; he now realized that he should attempt to protect himself more adequately if he hoped to continue on this career path.

At this point in his sports career, it appears that Sam's masculinity needs and interpersonal relations with his father were becoming leitmotifs rather than dominant themes. Sam had internalized a sports role-identity sufficiently to be concerned about his reputation and was seeking athletic immortality by establishing a record that would live on in his high school after he was gone. In other words, he was concerned with his post-self—how he would be remembered by the members of the wrestling subculture in the future (Schmitt and Leonard 1986). The use of pain killers (and steroids) is a serious problem in high school athletics partly because of such pressures induced by self and others (Goldman 1992; Guttmann 1988).

Routinization of Injury at the University

Because Sam had had a stellar career in high school, he was offered scholarships to several universities. Having traveled to a number of the major wrestling schools in AAU competition, he thought he already knew what they were like. He made his selection on the basis of his personal knowledge of the coach and the assistant coach who had been hired recently to upgrade the program. Sam believed that the assistant coach would be a good wrestling partner for him, and that the head coach would provide valuable career advice. (These expectations have been met.)

Less expected, however, was the sudden increase in exposure to injuries. If Sam had thought about it, he might have wondered why the letter his parents received from the athletic director welcoming their son to the sports program stressed that all athletes were fully covered for their medical expenses during practices and competition but that the university's coverage ended at graduation. Sam soon discovered that his opponents were stronger and more experienced, and his teammates were more determined and competitive.

Moreover, the situational clues for normalizing injury were highly visible in the wrestling room. Medical trainers were present during all practices, and a sports physician was usually on call in the building. Practice seldom stopped for long when a wrestler was injured; the wrestler moved or was moved out of the way, and the coaches showed little concern or sympathy. The norm was to ignore injuries and to continue practicing. According to Sam:

> When our heavyweight got hurt and he was screaming, coach said: "Be quiet, you'll be okay. Take the pain." Some people heard it and didn't understand…he just wanted him to take it like a man.

The ambulatory injured, or "walking wounded," were still expected to come to practice; if possible, they worked out on the rowing machines or exercise bikes. These machines were positioned in plain view at the front of the room, and someone was always riding them. Experienced wrestlers hated to be seen on machines during practice because it meant that they had lost their status temporarily as team members.

The coach's philosophy was that wrestling is primarily a matter of having a winning attitude and that worrying about injury would interfere with that attitude. If a wrestler sustained what appeared to be a serious injury, it had to be documented and certified by the medical staff to be accepted by the coach. One dramatic case showed what could happen if a wrestler claimed an injury that could not be documented. In this incident, a "walk-on" wrestler suddenly began writhing and moaning on the floor during practice, covering his face with his hands. Apparently, he had received a blow to his neck or head. Because all head or spinal injuries were taken very seriously by the medical staff, he was rushed to the hospital for observation and tests. Tests, however, did not reveal any evidence of injury, and the wrestler refused to remain in the hospital

for extended observation. (He had midterm examinations to take). He never regained a position on the team because the coach suspected he was malingering, and the team physician would not clear him for practice because he refused further observation. He spent the rest of the season as an onlooker.

At the elite level, those who do not share the norms that normalize pain and injury risk being dropped from the team or placed in secondary positions, as demonstrated by the case of the unfortunate walk-on. By the time Sam had reached the elite level in sports, he had already been thoroughly socialized into the informal expectations regarding pain and injury; they had become part of his personal orientation to the sport. Athletes like Sam who pin their chances of material success on a career in sports are aware that the confirmation of their status as an athlete is both crucial and dependent on the opinions of those in the sport who adhere to the norms themselves (Donnelly and Young 1988; Hughes and Coakley 1991; McCall and Simmons 1978).

Completing the Cycle: Becoming a Role Model   We end Sam's career history at the conclusion of his junior year. When asked how the season had gone, he reported that he was 31–9–2 for the year. Still, he added, "[During the regular season] it's not like I got beat by nine guys; one guy beat me three times, one guy twice, and the other two were by two different guys. So I only got beat by four guys, and I ended up beating them during the season too … I only lost in two dual meets all season long." In an important boost to his self-esteem and career plans, he qualified for the national championships and was one of four members of the team to be designated All-American, even though his fifth-place finish was personally disappointing.

Sam has spent 14 of his 21 years working on wrestling, and his hopes that it will "pay off for [him]" depend greatly on what happens in the next few years. He wants to be a wrestling coach, perhaps combining this position with a career as a sports commentator and public speaker. In order to achieve this ambition, he believes he must become a conference and national champion, earn a spot on the Olympic team, and win a medal. Although these high aspirations may seem farfetched to others, Sam regards them as possibilities because he associates daily with people who have achieved such goals in their own careers. If these plans do not materialize, Sam has contingent career plans that he will pursue....

Because Sam's involvement in wrestling has become an important part of who he is and what he wants to become, he accepts pain and injury as part of his role-identity, rather than as a sign of bravery or macho masculinity: "I knew they [injuries] were going to happen. So yeah, I accept it. It doesn't scare me—I knew that eventually I'd hurt my knee or break my ankle. You start getting competitive, and you can be injured pretty easy."

Injury is an unavoidable part of Sam's sport. Sam's coach has been injured severely, as have all the assistant coaches. Moreover, we should not forget that Sam routinely injures others: he broke the hand of an assistant coach in practice, and he has cut his training partner's face many times ("fifty stitches' worth so far").

Moreover, as Sam's injuries have accumulated, so has his experience in dealing with them; they have given him a unique fund of professional knowledge and information. His ability to draw on these experiences provides him with considerable independence in assessing the possible risks an injury poses for his career. Thus, while Sam's attitude toward injury may seem cavalier to others, it is anything but. He has experienced and recovered from many injuries, and he realizes fully the pain and anguish they cause.

CONCLUSION

Sam's career history reveals some important insights regarding the cumulative effects of primary and secondary socialization for the normalization of the pain of injury. I conclude by reviewing key steps in the socialization process that highlight how masculinity and male identity issues became intertwined with professionalization. First, Sam's prenatal sports identity was shaped by the expectations of his immediate and extended family. By the time he was six years old, his sense of self was embedded thoroughly in sports. Second, early in childhood, Sam accepted his father's definition of sports injuries as routine and insignificant. Sam used "toughness" in sports to separate himself from femininity and to develop masculine identity; simultaneously, he also learned that athletes had to be tough if they were to be good in sports. Third, as a youth, Sam associated pain with excellence in sports and with special treatment as an athlete. He also learned that sports activity and achievement could serve as a means of expressing love between himself and his father. By the time he was twelve, Sam had entered an "identity tunnel," which focused his activities around wrestling. At this point, career concerns became as important as masculinity issues.

Fourth, as he matured, Sam developed considerable experience with pain and injury. His sense of mastery and competency was strengthened by overcoming progressively more serious injuries. As part of this secondary socialization into the normalization of pain and injury, he encountered physicians and medical trainers who kept him functional, if not healthy. Fifth, his most serious injuries came late in his career as his teammates and opponents became stronger and more skilled at dangerous techniques. Finally, as Sam's athletic career neared conclusion, he had less time to accomplish the career goals he had envisioned, and the pressure to ignore injury intensified accordingly. In sum, then, Sam's case indicates that masculinity needs or issues were of greatest importance during primary socialization, while professionalization became an increasing important factor during secondary socialization.

Sam's case offered some important insights for understanding apparent contradictions concerning masculinity, professionalization, and the meaning of injury. For example, Sam did not feel especially proud of his injuries, was initially reluctant to discuss them, and seldom referred to them as signs of masculinity. While outsiders might believe that honor and esteem were bestowed on wrestlers for withstanding pain and injury, among the athletes themselves, the occurrence of injury brought no special respect. In fact, too much attention to pain and injury lost respect because it implied a lack of focus on the primary task: competition and winning. Sam's reluctance to discuss his injuries thus reflected the status concerns of an elite athlete. On the other hand, Sam felt obligated to maintain the appearance of toughness on several occasions during his career—in the wrestling room, at the hospital, and in sports camp. Thus, while it can be said that on such occasions Sam assumed a macho identity, his most consistent concern was with maintaining or regaining peak performance.

In addition, Sam's perspective of sports injuries as normal continued after his masculinity needs were met. The persistence of such a belief, however, requires a more complex explanation than either masculinity needs or professionalization alone. Such an explanation begins by recognizing that contradictory definitions of the meaning of sports injury are gradually eliminated once an athlete has entered the identity tunnel. To illustrate, Sam's father, coaches, and physicians normalized injury to such an extent that routine occurrences such as broken fingers were not considered significant. Moreover, once Sam had internalized this orientation to injury, it was not likely to be modified. Change would require a major conversion of the self, similar in some regards to a religious conversion (Hewitt and Hewitt 1986). Indeed, such a change would threaten the social relations built up over a lifetime within an entire sports community; many sports, such as wrestling, cannot be engaged in without injury. Thus, maturity and loss of skills will not automatically bring about a change in attitude towards sports injury by former athletes. Sam, like his father, is likely to persist in believing that a little pain never hurt anybody.

REFERENCES

Coakley, Jay J. 1990. *Sport in Society*. St. Louis: Times Mirror/Mosby.

——. 1991. "Reconceptualizing 'Burnout' Among Adolescent Athletes: From a Personal Trouble to a Social Issue." Presidential address at the annual conference of the North American Society for the Sociology of Sport, Milwaukee, WI.

Connell, R. W. 1990. "An Iron Man: The Body and Some Contradictions of Hegemonic Masculinity." Pp. 83—95 in *Sport, Men, and the Gender Order*, edited by Michael A. Messner and Donald F. Sabo. Champaign, IL: Human Kinetics Books.

Curry, Timothy Jon. 1991. "Fraternal Bonding in the Locker Room: A Profeminist Analysis of Talk About Competition and Women." *Sociology of Sport Journal* 8: 119—135.

Curry, Timothy Jon and Robert M. Jiobu. 1984. *Sports: A Social Perspective*. Upper Saddle River, NJ: Prentice-Hall.

Denzin, Norman K. 1989. *Interpretive Interactionism*. Newbury Park, CA: Sage.

Donnelly, Peter and Kevin Young. 1988. "The Construction and Confirmation of Identity in Sport Subcultures." *Sociology of Sport Journal* 5: 223—240.

Ewald, Keith and Robert M. Jiobu. 1985. "Explaining Positive Deviance: Becker's Model and the Case of Runners and Body Builders." *Sociology of Sport Journal* 2: 144—156.

Goffman, Erving. 1961. "The Moral Career of the Mental Patient." Pp. 128—169 in *Asylums: Essays on the Social Situation of Mental Patients and Other Inmates*. Garden City, NY: Doubleday.

Goldman, Bob. 1992. "Retooling Your Body." *Fitness Plus* 3: 21—24.

Guttmann, Allen. 1988. *A Whole New Ball Game*. Chapel Hill: University of North Carolina Press.

Hewitt, John P. and Myrna Livingston Hewitt. 1986. *Introducing Sociology*. Upper Saddle River, NJ: Prentice-Hall.

Hughes, Everett C. 1958. *Men and Their Work*. New York: Free Press.

Hughes, Robert and Jay Coakley. 1991. "Positive Deviance Among Athletes: The Implications of Overconformity to the Sport Ethic." *Sociology of Sport Journal* 8: 307—325.

Lindesmith, Alfred R., Anselm L. Strauss, and Norman K. Denzin. 1991. *Social Psychology*, 7th ed. Upper Saddle River, NJ: Prentice-Hall.

McCall, George J. and J. L. Simmons. 1978. *Identities and Interactions*, rev. ed. New York: Free Press.

Messner, Michael A. 1989. "Masculinities and Athletic Careers." *Gender and Society* 3: 71—88.

Schmitt, Raymond L. and Wilbert M. Leonard, II. 1986. "Immortalizing the Self through Sport." *American Journal of Sociology* 91: 1088—1111.

Shibutani, Tamotsu. 1986. *Social Processes*. Berkeley: University of California Press.

Weigert, Andrew J., J. Smith Teitge, and Dennis W. Teitge. 1986. *Society and Identity*. Cambridge: Cambridge University Press.

14. THE ORIGINS OF INSTITUTIONS

PETER L. BERGER and THOMAS LUCKMANN

An institutional world, then, is experienced as an objective reality. It has a history that antedates the individual's birth and is not accessible to his biographical recollection. It was there before he was born, and it will be there after his death.

Social patterns arise in interaction. They come to be objective forces—institutions—that confront and control the individual. How do they arise? What are their qualities? Here, Peter Berger and Thomas Luckmann examine the process of "institutionalization," how social patterns become an integral part of organization, and how they acquire an independent existence from specific actors. It might be useful to keep in mind the following outline:

1. Interaction and habituation
2. Transmission and historicity
3. Objectivity
4. Legitimation
5. Social controls

...As A and B interact, in whatever manner, typifications will be produced quite quickly. A watches B perform. He attributes motives to B's actions and, seeing the actions recur, typifies the motives as recurrent. As B goes on performing, A is soon able to say to himself, "Aha! There he goes again." At the same time, A may assume that B is doing the same thing with regard to him. From the beginning, both A and B assume this reciprocity of typification. In the course of their interaction, these typifications will be expressed in specific patterns of conduct. That is, A and B will begin to play roles vis-à-vis each other. This will occur even if each continues to perform actions different from those of the other. The possibility of taking the role of the other will appear with regard to the same actions performed by both. That is, A will inwardly appropriate B's reiterated roles and make them the models for his own role-playing. For example, B's role in the activity of preparing food is not only *typified* as such by A, but enters as a constitutive element into A's own food-preparation role. Thus a collection of reciprocally typified actions will emerge, *habitualized* for each in roles, some of which will be performed separately and some in common.[1] Although this reciprocal typification is not yet institutionalization (there being only two individuals, there is no possibility of a typology of actors), it is clear that institutionalization is already present *in nucleo*.

At this stage, one may ask what gains accrue to the two individuals from this development. The most important gain is that each will be able to predict the other's actions. Concomitantly, the interaction of both becomes predictable. The "there he goes again" becomes a "there *we* go again." This relieves both individuals of a considerable amount of tension. They save time and effort, not only in whatever external tasks they might be engaged in separately or jointly, but in terms of their respective psychological economies. Their life together is now defined by a widening sphere of taken-for-granted routines....

From *The Social Construction of Reality*, by Peter L. Berger and Thomas Luckmann. Copyright © 1966 by Peter L. Berger and Thomas Luckmann. Used by permission of Doubleday, a division of Random House, Inc.

Let us push our paradigm one step further and imagine that A and B have children. At this point, the situation changes qualitatively. The appearance of a third party changes the character of the ongoing social interaction between A and B, and it will change even further as additional individuals continue to be added.[2] The institutional world, which existed *in statu nascendi* in the original situation of A and B, is now passed on to others. In this process, institutionalization perfects itself. The habitualizations and typifications undertaken in the common life of A and B—formations that until this point still had the quality of *ad hoc* conceptions of two individuals—now become historical institutions. With the acquisition of *historicity*, these formations also acquire another crucial quality, or, more accurately, perfect a quality that was incipient as soon as A and B began the reciprocal typification of their conduct: This quality is *objectivity*. This means that the institutions that have now been crystallized (for instance, the institution of paternity as it is encountered by the children) are experienced as existing over and beyond the individuals who "happen to" embody them at the moment. In other words, the institutions are now experienced as possessing a reality of their own, a reality that confronts the individual as an external and coercive fact.[3]

As long as the nascent institutions are constructed and maintained only in the interaction of A and B, their objectivity remains tenuous, easily changeable, almost playful, even while they attain a measure of objectivity by the mere fact of their formation....

A and B alone are responsible for having constructed this world. A and B remain capable of changing or abolishing it. What is more, because they themselves have shaped this world in the course of a shared biography that they can remember, the world thus shaped appears fully transparent to them. They understand the world that they themselves have made. All this changes in the process of transmission to the new generation. The objectivity of the institutional world "thickens" and "hardens," not only for the children, but (by a mirror effect) for the parents as well. The "there we go again" now becomes "this is how these things are done." A world so regarded attains a firmness in consciousness; it becomes real in an ever more massive way, and it can no longer be changed so readily. For the children, especially in the early phase of their socialization into it, it becomes *the* world. For the parents, it loses its playful quality and becomes "serious." For the children, the parentally transmitted world is not fully transparent. Because they had no part in shaping it, it confronts them as a given reality that, like nature, is opaque in places at least.

Only at this point does it become possible to speak of a social world at all, in the sense of a comprehensive and given reality confronting the individual in a manner analogous to the reality of the natural world. Only in this way, *as* an objective world, can the social formations be transmitted to a new generation....

The process of transmission simply strengthens the parents' sense of reality; ...to put it crudely, if one says, "this is how these things are done," often enough, one believes it oneself.[4]

An institutional world, then, is experienced as an objective reality. It has a history that antedates the individual's birth and is not accessible to his biographical recollection. It was there before he was born, and it will be there after his death. This history itself, as the tradition of the existing institutions, has the character of objectivity. The individual's biography is apprehended as an episode located within the objective history of the society. The institutions, as historical and objective facticities, confront the individual as undeniable facts. The institutions are *there*, external to him, persistent in their reality, whether he likes it or not. He cannot wish them away. They resist his attempts to change or evade them. They have coercive power over him, both in themselves, by the sheer force of their facticity, and through the control mechanisms that are usually attached to the most important of them. The objective reality of institutions is not diminished if the individual does not understand their purpose or their mode of operation. He may experience large sectors of the social world as incomprehensible, perhaps oppressive in their opaqueness, but real nonetheless. Because institutions exist as external reality, the individual cannot understand them by introspection. He must "go out" and learn about them, just as he must to learn about nature. This remains true even though the social world, as a humanly produced reality, is potentially understandable in a way not possible in the case of the natural world.[5]

At the same point, the institutional world requires *legitimation*, that is, ways by which it can be "explained" and justified. This is not because it appears less real. As we have seen, the reality of the social world gains in massivity in the course of its transmission. This reality, however, is a historical one that comes to the new generation as a tradition rather than as a biographical memory. In our paradigmatic example, A and B, the original creators of the social world, can always reconstruct the circumstances under which their world and any part of it was established. That is, they can arrive at the meaning of an institution by exercising their powers of recollection. A and B's children are in an altogether different situation. Their knowledge of the institutional history is by way of "hearsay." The original meaning of the institutions is inaccessible to them in terms of memory. Therefore, it becomes necessary to interpret this meaning to them in various legitimating formulas. These will have to be consistent and comprehensive in terms of the institutional order if they are to carry conviction to the new generation. The same story, so to speak, must be told to all the children. It follows that the expanding institutional order develops a corresponding canopy of legitimations, stretching over it a protective cover of both cognitive and normative interpretation. These legitimations are learned by the new generation during the same process that socializes them into the institutional order....

The development of specific mechanisms of social controls also becomes necessary with the historicization and objectivation of institutions. Deviance from the institutionally "programmed" courses of action becomes likely once the institutions have become realities divorced from their original relevance in the concrete social processes from which they arose. To put this more simply, it is more likely that one will deviate from programs set up for one by others than from programs one has helped establish oneself. The new generation posits a problem of compliance, and its socialization into the institutional order requires the establishment of sanctions. The institutions must and do claim authority over the individual, independently of the subjective meanings he may attach to any particular situation. The priority of the institutional definitions of situations must be consistently maintained over individual temptations at redefinition. The children must be "taught to behave" and, once taught, must be "kept in line." So, of course, must the adults. The more conduct is institutionalized, the more predictable and thus the more controlled it becomes. If socialization into the institutions has been effective, outright coercive measures can be applied economically and selectively. Most of the time, conduct will occur "spontaneously" within the institutionally set channels. The more (on the level of meaning) conduct is taken for granted, the more possible alternatives to the institutional "programs" will recede, and the more predictable and controlled conduct will be.

NOTES

1. The term "taking the role of the other" is taken from Mead. Here, we are taking Mead's paradigm of socialization and applying it to the broader problem of institutionalization. The argument combines key features of both Mead's and Gehlen's approaches.
2. Simmel's analysis of the expansion from the dyad to the triad is important in this connection. The following argument combines Simmel's and Durkheim's conceptions of the objectivity of social reality.
3. In Durkheim's terms, this means that, with the expansion of the dyad into a triad and beyond, the original formations become genuine "social facts," that is, they attain *choséité*.
4. For an analysis of this process in the contemporary family, *cf.* Peter L. Berger and Hansfried Kellner, "Marriage and the Construction of Reality," *Diogenes* 46 (1964), 1 ff.
5. The preceding description closely follows Durkheim's analysis of social reality. This does *not* contradict the Weberian conception of the meaningful character of society. Because social reality always originates in meaningful human actions, it continues to carry meaning even if it is opaque to the individual at a given time. The original may be *reconstructed*, precisely by means of what Weber called *Verstehen*.

PART III

Social Organization

Out of social interaction develops social organization. Groups, formal organizations, communities, and societies are all examples of organization. Part III tries to show the diversity and importance of social organization in all our lives.

There is a commonality among all types of organization: social interaction and a set of agreements—rules, ideas, and structure—that hold organization together. Dexter Dunphy and Ruth Horowitz highlight the importance of primary groups to our lives. Kai Erickson and John Freie show us the importance of living in community. Charles Lindholm describes a community that ends in self-destruction and shows us both our search for meaning in community and the dangers of losing ourselves within community.

15. THE IMPORTANCE OF PRIMARY GROUPS

DEXTER C. DUNPHY

Ideology had only an indirect effect on fighting effectiveness in both the U.S. and the German armies. The crucial variable was the degree of preservation of the cohesive primary unit.

Humans exist in a host of groups. One type of group is called the primary group, originally described by Charles Cooley. This article describes the meaning and importance of primary groups. It examines one example: the military unit.

Over our lifetime, we spend much of our time in small groups. We are born into a family. As we grow older, we venture out from our family into the play groups of childhood and later into the cliques and crowds of adolescence. We marry and establish a new family group of our own and participate in the work groups and leisure groups of adulthood. Out of the associations formed in these groups, we fashion and have fashioned in us a changing and developing conception of self; we learn ways of behaving appropriate to varied social situations, and we acquire a set of social values and attitudes that allow us to respond to the structure and pressures of the larger society about us....

For reasons that we will examine here, social scientists have devoted relatively little effort to a close and detailed study of such groups, even though these groups play a vital part in creating human personality and maintaining the integration of the secondary structures of society. We use the term *primary group* to describe groups of this kind. The term was first introduced into social science by Charles Horton Cooley in 1909. At that time, Cooley wrote in his book *Social Organization*:

By primary groups, I mean those characterized by intimate face-to-face association and cooperation. They are primary in several senses, but chiefly in that they are fundamental in forming the social nature and ideas of the individual. The result of intimate association, psychologically, is a certain fusion of individualities in a common whole, so that one's very self, for many purposes at least, is the common life and purpose of the group. Perhaps the simplest way of describing this wholeness is by saying that it is a "we," it involves the sort of sympathy and mutual identification for which "we" is the natural expression.[1]

In Cooley's definition, the word *primary* is used mainly in reference to the fundamental effect such groups have on the formation of the individual personalities of their members. Cooley makes this even clearer when he goes on to state: "The view here maintained is that human nature is not something existing separately in the individual, but a *group-nature* or *primary phase of society*, a relatively simple and general condition of the social mind."[2] Thus the term *primary* refers to the fact that such groups are the earliest kind of human association experienced by the maturing individual and also that the primary, or basic, human qualities are learned in them. Cooley's definition also makes it clear that the effect of such groups on the personalities of members derives from the internalization by them of a psychological representation or image of the group, and that such an identification is indicated by a strong emotional involvement with the group and its members.

In *Introductory Sociology*, written with Angell and Carr, Cooley specified five basic characteristics of primary groups:

- Face-to-face association
- The unspecialized character of the association
- Relative permanence
- The small number of persons involved
- The relative intimacy prevailing among the participants[3]

Cooley himself did not designate larger, more formally organized groups as *secondary groups* but the latter term is now widely used and the two kinds of groups are frequently contrasted.

Later writers dealing specifically with the concept have attempted to modify it in various ways. For instance, Shils gave explicit and thoughtful attention to Cooley's criteria in his important work on the effects of primary group membership in the army in World War II[4] and in his more recent review of primary group research.[5] Shils argues that the existence of an implicit set of group norms is another necessary aspect of the primary group:

> By "primary group" we mean a group characterized by a high degree of solidarity, informality in the code of rules that regulate the behavior of its members, and autonomy in the creation of these rules.[6]

THE STUDY OF PRIMARY GROUPS

Thus, although the primary group is a "small group" in the sense in which that term is used in the social sciences, it is a particular kind of small group. Small groups vary all the way from *ad hoc* collections of students assembled for a single experimental hour to long-term emotionally involving, highly institutionalized groups such as families. It is the latter rather than the former kind of small group to which the term *primary group* refers.

However, the concept of a primary group is better thought of as a variable than as categorical. A group is primary insofar as it is based on and sustains spontaneous participation, particularly emotional involvement and expression. It also provides intrinsic personal satisfaction, that is, personal relationships in the primary group are considered valuable in themselves and not only as means to other ends. This element of intrinsic value is often lacking in formal secondary relations that are explicitly designed to be instrumental.

We define a primary group therefore as *a small group that persists long enough to develop strong emotional attachments between members, at least a set of rudimentary, functionally differentiated roles, and a subculture of its own that includes both an image of the group as an entity and an informal normative system that controls group-relevant action of members.* For Cooley, the important general categories of such groups in our society were "groups of the family, the playground, and the neighborhood."[7] We feel it is necessary to include other kinds of groups that meet our definition but that Cooley did not recognize. As we see it, the following general classes of groups are properly referred to as primary groups:

- Families.
- Free association peer groups of childhood, adolescence, and adulthood. This category would include delinquent gangs and some small, cohesive political elites ("cabals").
- Informal groups existing in organizational settings such as classroom groups, factory work groups, small military units, and "house churches."
- Resocialization groups such as therapy groups, rehabilitation groups, and self-analytic groups....

AN EXAMPLE: PRIMARY GROUPS IN MILITARY ORGANIZATION

There is a ... tradition of organizational analysis that has centered about the problem of maintaining the morale and combat effectiveness of military personnel in armies. Morale has always been a central issue in military organizations, and military organizations have often been organized in small units. However, it was not until World War II that the crucial role of primary groups in maintaining military morale and effectiveness was seriously studied.

A number of excellent studies,[8] appearing since World War II, present information on the role of primary groups in military organizations in both the allied and German armies. However, we shall focus on Shils and Janowitz's study[9] of the Wehrmacht because their conclusions are most succinctly stated and are representative of those found in other studies.

Shils and Janowitz set out to explain the reasons why German army units continued fighting even after central command disintegrated, supplies ceased, and it was obvious that German capitulation was inevitable. During this time, there was remarkably little desertion or active surrender by individuals or groups. It had been suggested that the morale and resistance of the German forces could be attributed to the effectiveness of the Nazi propaganda machine. Shils and Janowitz reviewed the extensive studies made by the Intelligence Section of the Psychological Warfare Division of SHAEF and came to conclusions that challenge this assumption. They stated their basic hypotheses, which are confirmed by their analysis, as follows:

1. It appears that a soldier's ability to resist is a function of the capacity of his immediate primary group (his squad or section) to avoid social disintegration. When the individual's immediate group, and its supporting formations, met his basic organic needs, offered him affection and esteem from both officers and comrades, supplied him with a sense of power, and adequately regulated his relations with authority, the element of self-concern in battle, which would lead to disruption of the effective functioning of his primary group, was minimized.
2. The capacity of the primary group to resist disintegration was dependent on the acceptance of political, ideological, and cultural symbols (all secondary symbols) only to the extent that these secondary symbols became directly associated with primary gratifications.
3. Once disruption of primary group life resulted through separation, breaks in communications, loss of leadership, depletion of personnel, or major and prolonged breaks in the supply of food and medical care, such an ascendancy of preoccupation with physical survival developed that there was very little "last ditch" resistance.
4. Finally, as long as the primary group structure of the component units of the Wehrmacht persisted, attempts by the Allies to cause disaffection by the invocation of secondary and political symbols (e.g., about the ethical wrongness of the Nationalist Socialist system) were mainly unsuccessful. By contrast, where Allied propaganda dealt with primary

and personal values, particularly physical survival, it was more likely to be effective.[10]

From the point of view of the conscripted soldier, this had the following meaning:

For the ordinary German soldier, the decisive fact was that he was a member of a squad or section that maintained its structural integrity and that coincided roughly with the *social* unit that satisfied some of his major primary needs. He was likely to go on fighting, provided he had the necessary weapons, as long as the group possessed leadership with which he could identify himself, and as long as he gave affection to and received affection from the other members of his squad and platoon. In other words, as long as he felt himself to be a member of his primary group and therefore bound by the expectations and demands of its other members, his soldierly achievement was likely to be good.[11]

The authors pointed out that the German general staff instituted a replacement system that maintained the integrity of the primary groups in the army. Units that had undergone a victory were maintained as units as far as possible and when replacements were necessary, the entire personnel of a division would be withdrawn from the front as a unit. Replacements were made while the unit was out of the front line so that a unit was given time to assimilate new members before going into battle again.

Janowitz and Little also suggest[12] that the existence of cohesive primary groups does not necessarily contribute to the goals of the military organization. If this is to happen, the primary group must actively espouse the goals of the larger organization of which it is a part. Essentially the same conclusion was reached by Speien. He noted that studies of U.S. soldiers during World War II showed that they had little knowledge of and little verbalized commitment to the war.[13] He then raised the question: Why, if this were true, did they fight so well? He concluded, on reviewing the evidence available, that this was because primary group relations sustained morale and supported a generalized commitment to the military and its goals. Janowitz and Little illustrate this with the case of segregated Negro units in World War II, which were very cohesive but developed "defensive norms" that broke with the general commitment because these groups interpreted military authority as depreciating their personal dignity. Shils has also argued along the same lines, stating that "primary group solidarity functions in the corporate body to strengthen the motivation for the fulfillment of substantive prescriptions or sense of obligation…. It cannot be said that goals are set by membership in the primary group but only that efforts to achieve the legitimate, formally prescribed goals may be strengthened by such membership."[14]

A key position in terms of the integration of primary group goals and organizational goals is that of the formal leader of the unit, for example, the platoon leader. The leader occupies the classical position of middle man similar to the role of foreman of a work team in industry. He must be close enough to the men for them to identify with him and yet, at the same time, he must also represent the demands of higher authority. Shils has stressed the enlisted man's desire for a protective personal relationship with an authority figure in this kind of position, and emphasized the effectiveness of "an exemplary and protective leader" in raising morale in U.S. military units.[15]

Shils and Janowitz give evidence that indicates that the primary group in the army acts as a family surrogate, and that a man's real family loyalties were one of the most substantial threats to the solidarity of the army unit.[16] The captured German soldiers themselves identified with the family-like nature of their units with statements like: "We were a big happy family." In addition, it became clear that soldiers were most likely to desert while on furlough, or after receiving distressing news from their families. Similarly, the members of units were most likely to discuss surrendering among themselves after concretely recalling family experiences. Because of these factors, families of soldiers were instructed to avoid mentioning family deprivations in letters to the front and, as Allied bombing of the civilian population became more severe, personal messages to the front were censored to prevent distressing family news reaching the men. Thus the soldier was able to transfer his primary loyalties to his unit while physically with the unit, providing that he felt secure about his family. While actually with his family, his loyalties to them tended to be

reactivated at the expense of those to his military unit. Interestingly enough, it was those men who had the most normal identification pattern in the family who were able to identify most firmly with the military unit. This same point is also supported by evidence presented by Grinker and Spiegal.[17] It is the person with a faulty family identification pattern who is most likely to be a deviant member of a military unit and a deserter to the other side in a stress situation.

A limiting variable influencing the cohesiveness in military organizations, as in factories, is the technology with which the military unit is working. Different weapons systems require different kinds of team relationships. A submarine, for example, demands continued close contact among the crew over lengthy periods of time and virtually cuts off outside social contact. An airplane is similar but returns more quickly to base and so allows more frequent contact with non-crew members. By contrast, the members of a rifle squad in battle may readily lose contact with one another and so experience a sense of isolation from the expectations and support of other group members.

Evidence to clinch the importance of primary group cohesion as a basis for morale and effectiveness comes from those German units whose integrity was not established or adequately maintained. As the war progressed, it became increasingly difficult to maintain the integrity of primary groups. The survivors of groups suffering severe casualties were regrouped and new units of recruits were thrust directly into battle without the opportunity of solidifying primary group ties. It was in units of these kinds that desertions and active surrender occurred. In these situations, the individual seemed to readily remove his emotional ties and identifications from the group and refocus them on himself. The individual regressed to a narcissistic state and became concerned with saving his own skin—marked contrast to situations in which men in intact primary groups would fight to the bitter end.

Shils has argued that the primary group reduces a soldier's fear of death and injury by counterposing against such fear a need for approval by his comrades.[18] As evidence, he quoted the fact that replacements to U.S. combat units were more likely to say "prayer helps a lot" whereas veterans looked to concrete support from their comrades.

Thus ideology had only an indirect effect on fighting effectiveness in both the U.S. and the German armies. The crucial variable was the degree of preservation of the cohesive primary unit. The soldier fights to protect the primary group and to live up to the expectations of his fellow group members. The army in battle is the prototype of the organization under stress, and military studies illustrate most vividly the crucial role of the primary group in preserving organizational cohesiveness and goal directedness....

NOTES

1. Cooley, Charles H. 1909. *Social Organization: A Study of the Larger Mind*. New York: Scribners, p. 23.
2. Ibid., p. 29.
3. Cooley, Charles H., Robert C. Angell, and Lowell J. Carr. 1933. *Introductory Sociology*. New York: Scribners, p. 53.
4. Shils, Edward. 1950. "Primary Groups in the American Army" in Robert K. Merton and Paul F. Lazarsfeld, Eds., *Continuities in Social Research*. Glencoe, IL: Free Press, pp. 16–25.
5. Shils, Edward. 1952. "The Study of the Primary Group" in Daniel Lerner and Harold Lasswell, *The Policy Sciences*. Stanford, CA: Stanford University Press, pp. 44–69.
6. Ibid., p. 44.
7. Cooley, Charles H. *Introductory Sociology*, p. 32.
8. Shils, Edward S. and Morris Janowitz, "Cohesion and Disintegration in the Wehrmacht in World War II," *Public Opinion Quarterly*, Vol. 12 (Summer 1948), (reprinted by permission of Elsevier Science Publishing Co., Inc. Copyright © 1948 by the Trustees of Columbia University). Samuel A. Stouffer. et al., eds., *The American Soldier*, vols. 1 and 2 (Princeton, NJ: Princeton University Press, 1949); Morris Janowitz and Roger Little, Sociology and the Military Establishment, rev. ed. (New York: Russell Sage Foundation, 1965), particularly Chap. 4, "Primary Groups and Military Effectiveness," pp. 77–99; Robert K. Merton and Paul L. Lazarsfeld, eds., *Continuities in Social Research: Studies in the Scope and Method of the American Soldier* (Glencoe, IL: Free Press, 1950); Roy R. Grinker and John P. Spiegal, *Men Under Stress* (Philadelphia: Blakiston, 1945).
9. Shils and Janowitz. "Cohesion and Disintegration in the Wehrmacht," pp. 280–315.
10. Ibid., pp. 281–2.
11. Ibid., p. 284.
12. Janowitz and Little, *Sociology and the Military Establishment*, p. 78.
13. Speien in *Continuities in Social Research*.
14. Shils in *Continuities in Social Research*, op. cit., p. 22.
15. Ibid.
16. Shils and Janowitz, "Cohesion and Disintegration in the Wehrmacht."
17. Grinker and Spiegal, *Men Under Stress*, Chap. 2.
18. Shils in *Continuities in Social Research*.

16. HONOR AND REPUTATION IN THE CHICANO GANG

RUTH HOROWITZ

The gang provides a culturally acceptable peer group in which an individual can act as a member of a collectivity in the otherwise individualistic, competitive world of the streets.

This is an insightful description of life in a Chicano gang. It comes from a book-length study of the Chicago Chicano community. It underlines the fact that it is difficult for those of us outside the community to fully understand why events happen as they do in the community. Instead of explaining gang activities as examples of chaos, disorder, deviance, and lawlessness, Horowitz shows us the importance of honor and reputation in the gang and links many of the activities of gang members to these values. The gang is a *group*, and groups have rules and values to which members must conform. The gang, like all groups, establishes ways to make members *feel* important.

YOUNG MEN IN THE STREETS: HONOR AND REPUTATION

...When they were not in school, most of the male youths spent most of their time outdoors, whatever the time of the year or the weather. Even when the temperature dropped below freezing, many could be found huddled in one of the parks until eight or nine in the evening. There were few places to go indoors: their homes were too crowded, the drinking age was twenty-one, and one settlement house prohibited anyone over fourteen from entering. The only public indoor facilities were the community-run social service center; the park building (from which the Lions were often expelled); and the second settlement house, which had been taken over by local activists and sometimes stayed open late. With the limited park space and the densely populated neighborhood, there was insufficient territory for any one group to "own" much except for a bench or a single corner. Several gangs congregated at each park, and many unaffiliated youths associated with the gangs. There was little way for different groups to segregate themselves spatially and not constantly be crossing borders.

Gangs play a major role in the lives of many area males. Approximately 70 percent join one for at least a short period between the ages of twelve and seventeen, though not all tough young men join gangs. There are eight major gangs in the area, each of which is segmented by age: miniatures (ages eleven to twelve), midgets (thirteen to fourteen), littles (fifteen to seventeen), juniors (eighteen to twenty-one), and seniors (twenty-one and over). Each section has between fifteen and forty members. Not every gang has members in each category throughout its history. In addition, many short-lived gangs developed rapidly and disappeared just as fast. Although different age groups may bear the same gang name, they are not necessarily allied on all occasions. For example, in one situation, the Senior Greeks helped the Little and Junior Lions against the Junior Greeks.

It is usually possible to identify an individual as a member of a particular gang by his hangout and his official jacket sweater with the gang's emblem and its color on a stripe on the shoulder, the collar, and the belt. Sometimes they wear shoes or shirts in their colors. Neither method of identification is infallible. Many nonmembers associate with members, and members do not necessarily wear their colors all the time. Most young men in gangs wear similar clothing styles, but many other youths dress like them. Most take great care with their clothes. Len of the Lions told several other members of the gang, "I wouldn't ever wear jeans, they don't keep a crease and bag at the knees." Only those outside the street scene appear to be largely unconcerned with style and the latest fashions.

Although many youths join gangs for approximately a year, the majority of males (aged eleven to eighteen) are not in gangs at any one time. This does not mean that they can avoid interpersonal violence or even try to. In this chapter, I examine the context in which violence occurs among male youths on 32nd Street both as individuals and as members of gangs, and the different meanings of violence and its relationship to identity....

On 32nd Street, a violent response to threats to self-esteem is embedded in a code of personal honor. Honor is a normative code that stresses the inviolability of one's manhood and defines breaches of etiquette, violations of a female relative's sexual purity, and accusations of dependency on others, in an adversarial idiom. Honor sensitizes people to violations that are interpreted as derogations of fundamental properties of the self. Within a more conventional normative framework, these same actions might be appraised and evaluated as mere violations of etiquette that would be ignored or excused, or as violations of the law that would require the police. Young men tend to fluctuate between commitments to conventional and to honor-bound responses. Normative ambiguity exists when it is unclear which norms should govern interpersonal relations. The lack of commitment to either code links interaction to the marginal position of the community in the wider society, to the tension between aspiring to succeed and the limited possibility of doing so.

All male youths experience the structural position of the community, although reactions to the tensions between the excitement of street life and conventional pursuits vary. Some drift toward gangs that expressly pursue excitement and develop a strong street identity, while others prefer to pursue more conventional careers. Yet no one avoids the tension between street life and convention on 32nd Street. The meaning of violence in the construction of identity and reputation among male youths and youth groups varies from one identity orientation to another, but it is always rooted in a concern for personal honor.

INSULT, HONOR, AND VIOLENCE

Honor revolves around a person's ability to command deference in interpersonal relations. A person doubts his own efficacy or suspects that he is viewed as weak when he believes he has been publicly humiliated. This situation is particularly critical to men who do not have a history of personal accomplishments or who cannot draw on valued social roles to protect their self-esteem when they are confronted by an insulting action. In an honor-bound subculture that emphasizes manhood and defines violations of interpersonal etiquette in an adversarial manner, any action that challenges a person's right to deferential treatment in *public*—whether derogating a person, offering a favor that may be difficult to return, or demonstrating lack of respect for a female relative's sexual purity—can be interpreted as an insult and a potential threat to manhood. Honor demands that a man be able physically to back his claim to dominance and independence.

Sensitivity to Insult

A situation is defined as insulting when an actor believes another person intends to place him in a demeaning light. When he is placed in a position where he may be viewed as weak, an individual experiences a lack of self-esteem. Sensitivity to a perceived insult is particularly keen in public situations, where judgments can be made readily by others and the actor perceives himself unable to neutralize or negate the intentions of the insulter.

In a context where men believe it is important that an honorable man be in control of all situations, infringement of any rules of interpersonal etiquette may be perceived as insulting, casting doubt on a man's ability to control. How a person responds to perceived insult reflects directly on the kind of person he is and determines whether others will perceive him as admirable or contemptible. An insult is a challenge to his right to deferential treatment. His interpretation of others' intentions and his reactions to them have real consequences for his standing among his peers. Honor is not something that one has permanently; it can always be challenged and must therefore continually be reaffirmed before one's peers.

Responding to Perceived Insult

How should one respond to insult within the context of the code of honor? When actions are interpreted as insulting, honor compels an individual to take an unequivocal stand, to immediately enforce his claim to precedence no matter how small the incident may seem. Because honor concerns actions that reflect personal decisions and judgments, disputes over honor must be settled personally, not through the legal system. Direct action takes priority over legal judgments of right and wrong. One young man spent two years in jail for shooting and severely wounding the man who raped his sister. He did not even consider going to the police at the time. It was his duty, he said, to repair the affront. Some things cannot be left to the law. Dishonor is experienced as a loss of one's manhood, which is culturally defined as the ability to enforce claims to a dominant position in interpersonal relations and to resist similar claims by others. The response must be physical: violence is triggered by the norms of the code of personal honor.

The physical response must follow certain rules if this act is to contribute to an identity as an honorable man. Violence must be used only when an insult is appraised as intentional. Shooting someone in the back for fun is not following the rules, nor is beating someone while robbing him, unless the victim has failed to demonstrate sufficient deference to his captors.

Moreover, as in cowboy movies, the style violence takes is critical if others are to approve its use. Ronny, a member of the Lions gang, was chastised by another member for breaking a bottle over his opponent's head instead of beating him with his fists to win a fight. Winning a fight with an obviously weaker person is not evaluated as honorable. The bigger youth should not need to react because of his obvious superiority in strength. In certain situations, however, the inequality of sides may be justified. When a new member is being initiated into a gang, he may be jumped by three members. He will lose, and by losing, he does not change the status rankings of old members within the gang. All the new member must do is put up a good fight. Paulie's arm was broken but that was because he fought so well that the Lions "had to break it."

The importance of the style and the situational legitimacy of violence is exemplified by the reactions to movies in which personal dominance is gained through violence. Gang discussions of these movies merged directly into discussions of gang fights. Gang members saw the violence as realistic, little different in style from violence in their own lives. Young men expressed their pleasure when personal dominance was expressed through violence. In one movie, a married woman overtly flirted with another man. Her husband did nothing about it and continued to ignore his wife. The man with whom the wife had been flirting raped her, which the Lions thought was a legitimate action to maintain his honor because she was tempting him and acting as though she dominated his life. Raping her was domination of her by dishonoring her husband. Even youths who do not generally subscribe to a code of personal dominance through violence saw the rape as virtuous and honorable. The only

way her husband could regain his honor was to kill the rapist; the Lions cheered when he did so....

The Use of Guns

For the youths of 32nd Street, as for the cowboy, guns are an important symbol of a lifestyle. During the late 1960s, the number of guns obtained illegally by young people, particularly gangs on 32nd Street, increased rapidly. Using guns to gain personal domination raises several problems. First, guns change the possibilities of gaining personal dominance through violence. Unlike a good fight with physical contact, using a gun does not test real skills—a twelve-year-old or a woman can shoot a grown man. Shooting someone does little to prove real superiority. Second, using a gun increases the possibility of getting into trouble with the law. Getting caught with an unregistered gun, particularly if the person is over sixteen, is a considerably more serious offense than beating up someone in a fist fight or getting caught with a bat or chain. Third, fighting with guns increases the possibility of a life-or-death encounter. Confronted by an armed person, the other may not even get a chance to react. One slight tug at the trigger may result in death.

The ready availability of .22s, .38s, .45s, and sawed-off shotguns has changed the form of gaining dominance, particularly among the gangs. No longer are there prearranged fights, as in the 1950s, when large numbers of youths gathered to fight with bats, chains, and switchblades. Although it was possible to kill with a knife, it took much more skill, and an opponent had a much greater chance of protecting himself. Most conflicts now involve either a few armed youths who go out looking for the gang with whom they are warring or two individuals in a spur-of-the-moment fight. One young man was shot and killed by someone in a moving car. His companions could not identify the killer. Several other youths who were nearby did identify the killer, who received little approbation.

Although most youths are aware of the legal ramifications of being caught with a gun, they feel that carrying a gun is necessary because they assume (often mistakenly) that everyone else has one. Enrique was dismissed from a job that he really enjoyed when his employers learned he had been arrested on a weapons charge. Although the other Lions thought his dismissal unfair, they were well aware that the charge was serious, and that Enrique was lucky to receive probation at age nineteen. If a youth is challenged by someone with a gun and if he does not have one, he is at a disadvantage. Sam of the Lions claimed, "I never go anywhere without my heat [gun]; you aren't anyone without one. It's dangerous." The feeling of being helpless without a gun is exacerbated by the knowledge that anyone could have one. Elaborate preparations are made to carry guns secretly. Portable radios are often fitted to carry the weapons. "We saw them carry guns in dictionaries on TV but it would look funny—us carrying dictionaries," Amos, another gang member, explained as he showed me the radio.

A number of older gang members say that it is better to have the younger members kill. One Senior Greek was quick to point out that a juvenile would be much less severely punished for the offense. When a twelve- or fourteen-year-old kills someone in a gang fight, he is likely to receive a sentence of two years or less, whereas an adult might receive a life sentence.

Ambivalent feelings about the use of guns and those who use them is indicated by the fact that although gang sweaters are rarely lost, guns seem to be lost frequently. "The pigs were after me, so when I came around the alley, I threw it in the garbage. I really looked for it after the pigs cut out, but it wasn't there. Now what am I going to do without a piece [gun]? I got two dudes after my ass," Len told the Lions when they chastised him for losing another gun. Amos explained, "Like one dude has one, then when we need heats cause we expect trouble, we can't find half of them. I guess we got six heats between all of us [about thirty-five youths]."

Further indications of ambivalence toward those who use guns to defend their honor are the stories told by older gang members of "good clean" fights between gangs, by which they mean there were no guns—only chains, bats, and knives. Face-to-face combat really indicated how strong a man and his gang were, they claimed.

Now, one of the Senior Greeks told a young member of the Lions, a twelve-year-old "punk" can shoot and kill a strong and tough man. That does not change others' evaluations of the "punk." The young Lion nodded his agreement.

Yet these older men also carry and use guns. Alberto, who at twenty-five drove a public bus, was still a Senior Greek. He had responsibilities (a wife and two kids) and wanted the good things in life (a nice place to live, a stereo, a good time). He did not want to get killed; he said guns scared him. But he did fight and he did carry a gun sometimes. His sister said he punched a man who had been looking at his wife. The fight was broken up but Alberto chipped his tooth. Three weeks later, he shot at someone who kept staring at him at a bar, but no one was hit.

ETIQUETTE AND CONVENTION

There is no reason why a conventional response cannot be given in a situation that may be interpreted either as insulting or as inoffensive. Most young men have conventional social skills…. Most gang members have attended formal affairs in tuxedos and have behaved appropriately. Although they do not go to downtown restaurants frequently because of the expense, they have all been there. With their knowledge of "polite" social skills and ability to use them, most youths can respond to situations as improprieties rather than as insults.

A conventional response in this situation can best be conceived as *impression management* (Goffman 1959). Impression management implies that the actor maintains enough distance from the action to deflect any imputations of unworthiness away from himself and onto the properties of the situation. The necessary responses, then, are not violent. For example, if someone's foot is in my path and I trip, I can blame the crowded space and say "excuse me." This places the onus on the situation or the setting that happens to bring the two people together, rather than on an intention to violate another's personal space. Alternatively, I could believe the person purposely stuck out his foot so that I would fall and make a fool of myself, which would call for an honor-bound response….

"Coolness," which is much admired, may switch the onus onto the situation rather than the person. Coolness is the ability to stand back from certain situations and rationally evaluate others' actions. If, however, the offender is seen as *purposely* ignoring the other's feelings, then the victim's honor is being tampered with and the incident requires an immediate response.

NORMATIVE AMBIGUITY AND IDENTITY

Attributing meaning to others' intentions resolves a situation of normative ambiguity. Evaluating another's actions as intentionally insulting will tip this situation toward the code of honor, while evaluating the actions as unintentional will tip the situation toward convention. Both forms are considered proper modes of conduct, and young males may choose between the two responses. An ambiguous situation becomes a critical triggering event for a male youth because the manner in which he appraises and resolves the situation publicly reveals the type of person he perceives himself to be. Others' evaluations of the resolution then become part of his identity. On one extreme are those who rarely appraise situations as offenses to their honor. On the other extreme are those who frequently question others' claims to precedence in order to start a fight. Because most youths refuse to commit themselves wholeheartedly to conventional or honor-bound responses, the individual may invoke either set of norms to interpret the actions of others and to justify conduct. An individual may say on one occasion that killing is morally wrong and fighting over an infraction of the rules of etiquette is silly, and on another occasion the same person may say that it is necessary to defend one's honor, even by murder. There is a real tension between the rough-and-tumble excitement of street life and conventional behavior, and not all youths resolve it in a similar manner. Each decision made, however, can be critical to others' evaluations of a man's identity as an honorable person….

COLLECTIVE IDENTITY AS IMAGE PROMOTERS: THE LIONS

…As a member of a gang, the basic parameters of an identity are laid out by membership. Although some individual reputations extend beyond an identity as a gang member ("That's Gilberto, he's a Lion" rather than "That dude's a Lion"), many are known largely by their affiliations. As a member, one *is* a Lion, and that group has a certain reputation as a gang. It becomes each member's responsibility to uphold that reputation. The collective reputation of the gang is potentially at stake in situations of normative ambiguity if the following three conditions are satisfied:

> First, at least one party to a face-to-face encounter must feel that the presence of the other party in this setting or his behavior on this occasion endangers his safety and impugns his dignity. In light of the actor's definition of the situation as threatening and provocative, he must make a decision on the spot. If he does not assume the role of an aggressor, he may play the part of a victim. Second, the actor must respond to this emotionally charged situation in a way that visibly reveals his resolve (i.e., he feels his words, gestures or actions express a definite intention) to inflict physical injury on his antagonist or by actually doing so. Third, the actor must account for his conduct on this occasion in terms of his status as a member of a gang (Horowitz and Schwartz 1974, pp. 238–239).

… Responsibility for defending the name of the gang against collective insults becomes a criterion for continued membership.

The Construction of Gang Reputations

In seeking to protect and promote their reputations, gangs often engage in prolonged "wars," which are kept alive between larger fights by many small incidents and threats of violence. Following each incident, one gang claims precedence, which means that the other group must challenge them if they want to retain their honor and reassert their reputation. On-the-spot insults are not always necessary to provoke a fight, and claims to precedence are carried over from one incident to the next. If a group's desire to be treated with deference is not honored, the group must claim precedence. Members must also go out to claim deferential treatment and superiority by demonstrating lack of respect for their enemies. For example, the war between the Lions and Aces continued over three years with intermittent claims to precedence by each side. Expectations of affronts and small skirmishes kept up the momentum of the conflict. If either side had failed to respond publicly to the other's challenge, the challenging gang's reputation would have become increasingly formidable.

In one incident, when Rat Man thought he saw some Aces riding in a car, he shot at them but the .38 did not go off. "We are at war," he said, and that is what a gang member is supposed to do when he sees an enemy. After more incidents, several Lions borrowed a car, took two guns, and went looking for the Aces. When they returned, they claimed they had gotten off three shots but no one was hit. During this period, an Angel shot and killed an Ace, and the Lions expressed regret they had not done it. They criticized the Angel's method to avoid loss of respect in their own eyes. Later, Amos and two other Lions ran into the Ace who had thrown a brick through Amos's mother's window. Amos beat the Ace unconscious with the butt of his gun, but the Ace regained consciousness a few days later and identified Amos as his assailant. Amos claimed he would have killed him but he had no ammunition.

Several incidents in which no actual meeting occurred helped to perpetuate the war. Sometimes, some of the Senior Greeks who congregated at El Pueblo Park joined the Lions. On one occasion, I counted thirty Lions, six guns, numerous baseball bats, several chains, and many broken bottles ready for use. One of the Greeks was frightened enough to demand that another Greek leave his gun at the park when he had to leave for a few minutes. Everyone raced back and forth across the park and a lookout was posted at each corner. The darker it got, the louder and more violent the talk about the Aces became. By 9:30, people began to announce, "I've got to go home now." By 10:30 the park was almost empty. These no-show events help to maintain the fervor and momentum of the conflict.

They allowed the waiting group to assert that the others were too frightened to show up and thereby to claim precedence over them.

These were only a few of the events that occurred between the Lions and the Aces over a two-year period of their war. The Lions also took several trips into the Ace's territory and the two gangs had a big fight over a sweater. There was roughly one major incident—which may or may not have ended in conflict—each month. After each incident, someone loses and someone gains a claim to precedence over the other. The general feeling of the community in the year that most of these events occurred was that the Lions were the most violent and the least polished of any of the gangs.

When an incident is defined as a collective insult, all members must participate to ensure the continued reputation of the group or to better it. Participation also promotes group loyalty and solidarity. Members must participate even if they do not agree with a particular incident or the group is drawn into a situation by the irresponsible behavior of a member. If a person weakens the gang's right to claim deference from others by losing his sweater to another gang, someone has to get it back or the entire group suffers....

Having an identity as a Lion does not preclude membership in another type of group; however, to remain a Lion, loyalty must be demonstrated continually. Protecting the gang's claim to precedence from other gangs takes priority over any other affiliation. At one dance a Lion, Enrique, wearing a gang sweater, spoke for the Brown Berets during intermission. During the speech, Enrique talked about peace among all Latinos, but as a Lion he was arming himself against the rumored invasion of the Aces. Several of the other Lions also started associating with the Brown Berets. Nico and Ronny were the first to join. Ronny said he joined because they had helped his retarded brother over Christmas. Several of the Brown Berets started to come to the park, and several Lions drifted into the Brown Berets. They attended several meetings, and Enrique and Jim started wearing the jacket of the Berets. The Lions who did not join called the ones who did "copouts" for their dual loyalty. Several of the new Brown Berets were assigned to be armed guards, which impressed them very much. But there was too much talk and too little action, and the Lions were demanding a demonstration of loyalty. Within three months, they all dropped the Berets. The two identities were too difficult to retain. Their identities as Lions were too important to become secondary to that of the Brown Berets....

Group solidarity through commitment to the Lions' collective identity and reputation is reinforced by some sanctioned rules and regulations. These rules, however, are usually flexible, as is the organization of the group. Techniques of choosing leaders, their powers, and decision-making processes vary between groups; moreover, rules for joining and quitting and for the collection of dues are flexible. There are also differences in the way a group moves from one age segment to the next. Some groups move as a collectivity and must fight with an older group to move up. In other groups, an individual moves up when he becomes of age and the older group thinks he is good enough. In 1971, the Lions were all one group. Later they decided to divide into the Littles and the Juniors and held separate official meetings. "It just happened, we didn't hassle it, the older dudes became the Juniors and the rest, Littles. We [Juniors] don't have any real officers, we're friends, and we can have meetings when we want," explained Enrique. Most members of both groups hung out at the park, although a few did not. Only on two occasions did the Littles become involved in an incident in which the Juniors did not. Age segments of other gangs are not necessarily this close....

Friends and Partners: Gang Cohesion

Friendship, although sometimes strained, and mutual support are important factors in group solidarity. Although some studies claim that gangs have few internal cohesive mechanisms such as group goals, membership stability, and role differentiation (Klein 1971), on 32nd Street, members bolster each other and individual friendships are solidified into partners that frequently entail significant mutual sacrifices.

Examples of the social support given members can be drawn from the excuses made when a member loses a fight for his personal reputation:

the enemy did not fight fairly, he was much bigger, or he had a weapon. It is not the fault of the gang member if he seemed to end up at the bottom or sustained a larger wound. His reputation is not lowered as much by his loss as his opponent's win is deflated. There is no zero-sum game in terms of winning or losing a fight: No one loses completely. It was obvious to everyone that Sam had lost a fight. (It was not defined as a gang fight.) He had a black eye and looked terrible, but everyone had an explanation for the situation: The other man had a bottle, Sam was jumped from behind, the other man was bigger. Privately, several observers, including Lions, told me that the reason the other had a bottle was that Sam had a knife. Everyone thought Sam had fought hard and no one wanted him to feel that his esteem was lowered. His reputation was weakened outside the gang, but no one would admit this within the gang.

Most important, there is always someone around to hang out with. Meeting day after day in the same location provides a sense of continuity and social support. Even when the temperature drops below freezing, several of the Lions can be found at the park. Even the members who are going out steadily with a particular young woman usually bring her to the park for a part of the evening. She usually talks with the other women and he with the Lions. When several of the Lions joined the Brown Berets and began to spend less time at the park, the others continually bemoaned their absence.

Being a partner connotes very close ties with another man, and these relationships are generally long-standing and public. In fact, in extreme cases, a man will go to jail for his partner. Partners always stand up for each other and can say almost anything to each other. One of the Lions went to jail for a murder but never revealed the name of his accomplice (his partner).

There are, however, characteristics of this system of obtaining a reputation and maintaining honor that make trust and close ties among gang members difficult. A member's status within the gang is important in judging whether or not an incident is a collective insult and in legitimizing the absence of a member from gang action. Status within the gang is based on the evaluation of a member's reputation in the street, and that reputation is precarious. It may shift with each new attempt to assert and defend a claim to precedence. With the sensitivity of gang members to insult and the precarious nature of reputation, there is always a possibility that one gang member will judge another's behavior as not properly deferential. Although both Jim and Ham were regular members of the gang, neither was in the small inner circle. Jim was smaller than Ham but probably faster. Ham almost killed Jim one summer evening in the park. Jim called Ham, who is very dark, a "nigger" to his face. Ham interpreted this as an intended insult and started to fight. Several good punches were thrown before Ham's sister was able to separate them and drag her brother home. Because everyone is so sensitive to insult, it is possible for anyone to be perceived as an insulter, with the exception of one's partner.

This type of situation accounts for much of the fighting within the gang. Over an eighteen-month period, however, there were only three fights among the Lions that progressed further than a few teasing shoves or some verbal insults. Each time it looked as though there might be a fight, it was stopped by other members. If a fight had continued, a reordering of status relationships might have been necessary and someone might really have lost. Instead, the hierarchy remained fairly loose with attempts to build a

strong reputation focused on challenges outside the gang. A successful challenger can improve his reputation without a fellow member actually losing status. Moreover, the extensive and intensive mutual obligation system links members both existentially and symbolically and minimizes internal competition....

The gang provides a culturally acceptable peer group in which an individual can act as a member of a collectivity in the otherwise individualistic, competitive world of the streets. A youth can be a "tough warrior" and experience the solidarity of a collectivity. Membership is one way of mediating the tension between the basically competitive experience of getting a reputation and succeeding in school and the solidarity experienced within the family unit. There the collectivity is considered more important than the individual member.

REFERENCES

Goffman, Erving. 1959. *Presentation of Self in Everyday Life*. New York: Doubleday Anchor.
Horowitz, R., and G. Schwartz. 1974. "Honor, Normative Ambiguity, and Gang Violence." *American Sociological Review* 39:238–251.
Klein, Malcolm W. 1971. *Street Gangs and Street Workers*. Upper Saddle River, NJ: Prentice Hall.
Toch, Hans. 1969. *Violent Men*. Chicago: Aldine.

17. COLLECTIVE TRAUMA AT BUFFALO CREEK

KAI ERIKSON

Most of the traumatic symptoms experienced by the Buffalo Creek survivors are a reaction to the loss of communality as well as a reaction to the disaster itself; the fear, apathy, and demoralization one encounters along the entire length of the hollow are derived from the shock of being ripped out of a meaningful community setting as well as the shock of meeting that cruel black water. The line between the two phenomena is difficult to draw. But is seems clear that much of the agony experienced on Buffalo Creek is related to the fact that the hollow is quiet, devastated, without much in the way of a nourishing community life.

Humans are social beings. Their lives are embedded in social organization. They live their lives in groups, communities, and societies. Organization is something we take for granted. Really, how important is it? Sometimes it is easiest to understand something when it is no longer there for us. Here is a tragic episode in the history of West Virginia, in which several communities were wiped out by a disastrous flood. Kai Erickson studied the people along Buffalo Creek, and his book described the effects of this tragedy on their lives. In the process, Erickson tried to understand what the end to community meant to these people, creating a loss that nothing could correct. How important was their community? Read this and imagine yourself in their place.

History stopped on the day of the flood.

[*Editor's Note:* The disastrous Buffalo Creek, West Virginia, flood occurred on February 26, 1972. The sudden collapse of the Pittston Company's (the local coal company and absentee landlord's) massive refuse pile dam unleashed 132 million gallons of water and coal waste materials on the unsuspecting residents of Buffalo Creek. The rampaging wave of water and sludge traveled down the creek in waves of between twenty and thirty feet and at speeds sometimes approaching thirty miles per hour. Buffalo Creek's sixteen small towns were devastated by the deluge, over 125 people were killed, and over four thousand survivors were left homeless.]

Some 615 survivors of the Buffalo Creek flood were examined by psychiatrists one and one-half years after the event, and 570 of them, a grim 93 percent, were found to be suffering from an identifiable emotional disturbance. A skeptical neighbor from another of the behavioral sciences may want to make allowance for the fact that psychiatrists looking for mental disorder are more than apt to find it; but even so, the sheer volume of pathology is horrifying.

The medical names for the conditions observed are depression, anxiety, phobia, emotional liability, hypochondria, apathy; and the broader syndrome into which these various symptoms naturally fall is post-traumatic neurosis, or, in a few cases, post-traumatic psychosis. But the nearest

expressions in everyday English would be something like confusion, despair, and hopelessness.

Most of the survivors responded to the disaster with a deep sense of loss—a nameless feeling that something had gone grotesquely awry in the order of things, that their minds and spirits had been bruised beyond repair, that they would never again be able to find coherence, that the world as they knew it had come to an end. Now these feelings, of course, were experienced as a generalized, pervading sense of gloom, and the men and women of the hollow did not try to catalog the various strains that contributed to it. But there are recognizable themes in the stories they tell that give us some idea of what the sources of their pain might be.

ON BEING NUMBED

Almost everybody who survived the disaster did so by the thinnest of margins; and the closeness of their escapes, combined with the relentless savagery of the water, left them feeling numbed and depleted—almost as if the mad rush to safety had consumed most of their energy and the ferocity of the waves passing below them had somehow drawn off what reserves were left.

No sooner had they escaped, however, then people began to feel that they were unable to move, caught in a sluggish bank of fog, held back—as in a dream—by forces that slackened the muscles and paralyzed the will. A number of people remember having gone limp or having lost control of their limbs. Quite a few others compared their reactions to a dream state. And some simply went blank in mind as well as limp in body, as if yielding to the enormity of what was happening.

This process of retreating into a limp slump has been noted again and again in disaster research. But on Buffalo Creek, the process appears to have been somewhat exaggerated by the extraordinary power of the flood and by the helpless state in which it left its victims. To be drained of energy, to be emptied of motive and self, is to be on the verge of death itself—and that is how many of the survivors viewed their own condition later.

FACES OF DEATH

Virtually everyone on Buffalo Creek had a very close encounter with death, either because they felt doomed themselves or because they lost relatives and friends or because they came into contact with dead bodies. The upper half of the valley, where most of the serious destruction took place, was strewn with the signs of a terrible tragedy. But people who lived downstream were not spared the agony of this scene either, for the current carried it to them. So death seemed to be everywhere, overhead, underfoot, crouched in every pile of wreckage, waiting to be recognized....

SURVIVAL AND GUILT

Where one finds death on so large a scale, one also finds guilt. It is one of the ironies of human life that individuals are likely to regret their own survival when others around them are killed in what seems like a meaningless and capricious way, in part because they cannot understand by what logic they came to be spared. People who sense the hand of God in it have many hard questions to ponder, and none of them are very comforting....

THE FURNITURE OF SELF

... It is important to remember that the people of the creek had invested a great deal of time and money and pride in the process of converting the old company shacks into comfortable new dwellings. The flood cleaned out some ragged housing as it made its way down the hollow—more than the residents like to remember—but the average home had been renovated in a hundred ways. A refurbished house on Buffalo Creek served as the emblem of one's rise out of poverty. It was a measure of security, an extension of self, a source of identity. It was not only the outer shell in which one lived out one's life, but a major feature of that life.

Moreover, people lost possessions of considerable meaning to them—not only trucks and cars and appliances with an established trade-in value but mementos of no measurable worth that were highly cherished. Objects such as family Bibles or photographs, a father's favorite gun or a mother's proudest embroidery, had a place in the household almost like holy relics, and their loss was deeply mourned. They were a link with the past, and they were a link with the future.

LOSS OF FAITH IN ORDER

The disaster on Buffalo Creek had the effect of reducing people's already brittle confidence in the natural and especially in the social order....

The Buffalo Creek survivors, without saying so directly, have quite clearly lost much of their confidence in the workings of nature. They are troubled about the condition of the mountains, now scraped out inside and slashed with strip mine benches; they are troubled about the water poised over their heads in other dams both real and imaginary; they are troubled about tornadoes and avalanches, floods and rock slides, earthquakes and explosions; and they are troubled about the natural capacity of their bodies and spirits to handle all the emergencies of life.

Moreover, the people of Buffalo Creek have lost their confidence in the coal company responsible for the dam. This point may be difficult to explain, because most readers will have no difficulty at all understanding why they might resent the company. But it was part of the life of the creek. It employed hundreds of people and was represented locally by officials who lived in the area, were known by first names, and were merged into the community as individual persons. The residents knew that the company was a giant corporation with headquarters in New York, but they continued to visualize it as a kind of manorial presence at the head of the hollow that was implicated somehow in the affairs of the community. It was a proprietor, a patron—and it had obligations to fulfill.

The company violated those obligations, first by building an unworthy dam, and second by reacting to the disaster in the manner of a remote bureaucracy with holdings to protect rather than in the manner of a concerned patron with constituents to care for. The heart of the company turned out to be located a thousand miles away, and its first reflex was to treat the survivors—many of them employees with decades of loyal service—as potential adversaries in a court action.

The people who speak for the company would not come out into the light, would not take the risk of establishing eye contact, would not expose themselves even for the purposes of finding out how the residents of the hollow were faring; and if this situation provoked a gentle annoyance in some survivors, it provoked a deep indignation in others. So the prevailing feeling is one of bitterness, a bitterness so sharp that it seems to speak of betrayal as well as of personal injury.

UNIQUENESS OF BUFFALO CREEK

So these were some of the effects of the individual trauma—that first numbing moment of pain and shock and helplessness. A few paragraphs of description can scarcely begin to convey what the tragedy must have felt like to the survivors or how it has influenced their lives, but the themes noted here correspond closely to ones noted in reports of other disasters; to that extent at least, what happened on Buffalo Creek is similar to all those other floods and bombings and hurricanes and earthquakes that interrupt the flow of human life so often.

But there are differences, too. Two years after the flood, Buffalo Creek was almost as desolate as it had been the day following—the grief as intense, the fear as strong, the anxiety as sharp, the despair as dark. People still looked out at the

world with vacant eyes and drifted from one place to another with dulled and tentative movements. They rarely smiled and rarely played. They were not sure how to relate to one another. They were unsettled and deeply hurt.

Under normal circumstances, one would expect the survivors of such a disaster to convalesce gradually as the passage of time acted to dim old memories and generate new hopes. It is a standard article of psychiatric wisdom that the symptoms of trauma ought to disappear over time, and when they do not—as was generally the case on Buffalo Creek—a peculiar strain of logic is likely to follow. If one has not recovered from the effects of trauma within a reasonable span of time, or so the theory goes, it follows that the symptoms themselves must have been the result of a mental disorder predating the event itself.

Unless we are ready to entertain the possibility that virtually all the people on Buffalo Creek suffered from a palpable emotional disorder on the morning of February 26, 1972, we will have to look elsewhere for a way to explain their distress; and my argument is that a second trauma, a *collective trauma*, followed closely on the first, immobilizing recovery efforts and bringing a number of other problems into focus.

LOSS OF COMMUNALITY

The people of Buffalo Creek were wrenched out of their communities and torn away from the very human surround in which they had been so deeply enmeshed. Much of the drama is drained away when we begin to talk of such things, partly because the loss of communality seems a step removed from the vivid terror of the disaster itself and partly because the people of the hollow, so richly articulate when describing the flood and their reaction to it, do not really know how to express what their separation from the familiar tissues of home has meant to them. The closeness of communal ties is experienced on Buffalo Creek as a part of the natural order of things, and residents are no more aware of that presence than fish are aware of the water they swim in. It is simply there, the envelope in which they live, and it is taken entirely for granted.

Communality on Buffalo Creek can best be described as a state of mind shared among a particular gathering of people; and this state of mind, by definition, does not lend itself to sociological abstraction. It does not have a name or a cluster of distinguishing properties. It is a quiet set of understandings that become absorbed into the atmosphere and are thus a part of the natural order. And the key to that network of understanding is a constant readiness to look after one's neighbors—or rather, to know without being asked what needs to be done.

The difficulty is that people invest so much of themselves in that kind of social arrangement that they become absorbed by it, almost captive to it, and the larger collectivity around you becomes an extension of your own personality, an extension of your own flesh. This pattern not only means that you are diminished as a person when that surrounding tissue is stripped away, but that you are no longer able to reclaim as your own the emotional resources invested in it. To "be neighborly" is not a quality you can carry with you into a new situation like negotiable emotional currency: The old community was your niche in the classical ecological sense, and your ability to relate to that niche meaningfully is not a skill easily transferred to another setting. This situation is true whether you move into another community, or whether a new set of neighbors moves in around your old home....

In places like Buffalo Creek, the community in general can be described as the locus for activities that are normally regarded as the exclusive property of individuals. It is the *community* that cushions pain, the *community* that provides a context for intimacy, the *community* that represents morality and serves as the repository for old traditions.

Most of the traumatic symptoms experienced by the Buffalo Creek survivors are a reaction to the loss of communality as well as a reaction to the disaster itself: The fear, apathy, and demoralization one encounters along the entire length of the hollow are derived from the shock of being ripped out of a meaningful community setting as well as the shock of meeting that cruel black water. The line between the two phenomena is difficult to draw. But it seems clear that much of the agony experienced on Buffalo Creek is related to the fact that the hollow is quiet, devastated, without much in the way of a nourishing community life.

MORALE AND MORALITY

The Buffalo Creek survivors must face the post-disaster world in a state of severe demoralization, both in the sense that they have lost much of their individual morale and in the sense that they have lost (or fear they have lost) many of their moral anchors. The lack of morale is reflected in a weary apathy, a feeling that the world has more or less come to an end and that there are no longer any compelling reasons for doing anything. People are drained of energy and conviction in part because the activities that once sustained them on an everyday basis—working, caring, playing—seem to have lost their direction and purpose in the absence of a larger communal setting. They feel that the ground has gone out from under them.

The clinical name for this state of mind, of course, is *depression*; and one can hardly escape the impression that it is, at least in part, a reaction to the ambiguities of post-disaster life in the hollow. Most of the survivors never realized the extent to which they relied on the rest of the community to reflect back a sense of meaning to them, never understood the extent to which they depended on others to supply them with a point of reference. When survivors say they feel "adrift," "displaced," "uprooted," "lost," they mean that they do not seem to belong to anything and that there are no longer any familiar social landmarks to help them fix their position in time and space. They are depressed, yes, but it is a depression born of the feeling that they are suspended pointlessly in the middle of nowhere.

This failure of personal morale is accompanied by a deep suspicion that moral standards are beginning to collapse all over the hollow; and in some ways, at least, it would appear that they are. As so frequently happens in human life, the forms of misbehavior people find cropping up in their midst are exactly those about which they are most sensitive. The use of alcohol, always problematic in mountain society, has evidently increased, and there are rumors spreading throughout the trailer camps that drugs have found their way to the creek. The theft rate has risen too, and this rise has always been viewed in Appalachia as a sure index of social disorganization.

The cruelest cut of all, however, is that once close and devoted families are having trouble staying within the pale they formerly observed so carefully. Adolescent boys and girls appear to be slipping away from parental control and are becoming involved in nameless delinquencies, and there are reports from several of the trailer camps that younger wives and husbands are meeting one another in circumstances that violate all the local codes. A home is a moral sphere as well as a physical dwelling, of course, and it would seem that the boundaries of moral space began to splinter as the walls of physical space were washed down the creek.

Yet the seeming collapse of morality on Buffalo Creek differs in several important respects from the kinds of anomie sociologists think they see elsewhere in modern America. For one thing, those persons who seem to be deviating most emphatically from prevailing community norms are usually the first to judge their own behavior as unacceptable and even obnoxious. Adolescents are eager to admit that they sometimes get into trouble, and those of their elders who drink more than the rules of the hollow normally permit are likely to call themselves "alcoholics" under circumstances that seem remarkably premature to jaded strangers from the urban North. To that extent, the consensus has held: local standards as to what qualifies as deviation remain largely intact, even though a number of people see themselves as drifting away from that norm.

Moreover, there is an interesting incongruity in the reports of immorality one hears throughout the hollow. It would seem that virtually everyone in the trailer camps is now living next to persons of lower moral stature than was the case formerly, and this situation, of and by itself, is a logistical marvel. Where did all those sordid people come from? How could a community of decent souls suddenly generate so much iniquity?

It probably makes sense to suppose that quite a few of the survivors are acting more coarsely now

than they did before the disaster. But something else may be going on here, too. The relative strangers who move next door and bring their old life-styles with them may be acting improperly by some objective measure or they may not, but they are always acting in an unfamiliar way—and the fact of the matter may very well be that strangers, even if they come from the same general community, are almost by definition less "moral" than neighbors. They do not fall within the pale of local clemency and so do not qualify for the allowances neighbors make for one another on the grounds that they know the motives involved.

The old community had niches for some forms of deviation, like the role of the town drunk, and ways to absorb others into the larger tissue of communal life. But the disaster washed away the packing around those niches, leaving the occupants exposed to the frowning glances of new neighbors. So the problem has two dimensions. On the one hand, people who had not engaged in any kind of misbehavior before are now, by their own admission, doing so. On the other hand, the unfamiliar manners of a stranger seem to hint darkly of sin all by themselves, and personal habits that once passed as mild eccentricities in the old neighborhood now begin to look like brazen vices in the harsher light of the new....

LOSS OF CONNECTION

It would be stretching a point to imply that the communities strung out along Buffalo Creek were secure nests in which people had found a full measure of satisfaction and warmth, but it is wholly reasonable to insist that they were like the air people breathed—sometimes harsh, sometimes chilly, but always a basic fact of life. For better or worse, the people of the hollow were deeply enmeshed in the fabric of their community; they drew their very being from it. And when the fabric was torn away by the disaster, people found themselves exposed and alone, suddenly dependent on their own personal resources.

And the cruel fact of the matter is that many survivors, when left on their own mettle, proved to have but few resources—not because they lacked the heart or the competence, certainly, but because they had always put their abilities in the service of the larger society and did not know how to recall them for their own purposes. A good part of their personal strength turned out to be the reflected strength of the collectivity—on loan, as it were, from the communal store—and they discovered to their great discomfort that they were not good at making decisions, not good at getting along with others, not good at maintaining themselves as separate persons in the absence of a supportive surround.

Many survivors fear that they are beginning to suffer the kind of stunned disorientation and even madness that can result from prolonged stretches of isolation. One result of this fear is that people tend to draw further and further into themselves and to become even more isolated. This behavior is that of wounded animals who crawl off somewhere to nurse their hurts. It is also the behavior of people who string rough coils of barbed wire around their lonely outposts because they feel they have nothing to offer those who draw near.

So the lonesomeness increases and is reinforced. People have heavy loads of grief to deal with, strong feelings of inadequacy to overcome, blighted lives to restore—and they must do all these things without much in the way of personal resources or self-confidence. Solving problems and making decisions—those are the hard part.

The inability of people to come to terms with their own isolated selves is counterpointed by an inability to relate to others on an interpersonal, one-to-one basis. Human relations along Buffalo Creek took their shape from the expectations pressing in on them from all sides like a firm but invisible mold: They were governed by the customs of the neighborhood, the traditions of the family, the ways of the community. And when the mold was stripped away by the disaster, something began to happen to those relationships. This situation was true of everyday acquaintances, but it was doubly true of marriages....

In places like Buffalo Creek, where attachments between people are seen as a part of the natural scheme of things—inherited by birth or acquired by proximity—the idea of "forming" friendships or "building" relationships seems a little odd. These attachments are not engineered; they simply happen when the communal tone is right. So people are not sure what to do.

One result of these problems is that what remains of the community seems to have lost its most significant quality—the power it generated in people to care for each other in times of need, to console each other in times of distress, to protect each other in times of danger. Looking back, then, it does seem that the general community was stronger than the sum of its parts. When the people of the hollow were sheltered together in the embrace of a secure community, they were capable of extraordinary acts of generosity; but when they tried to relate to one another as individuals, as separate entities, they found that they could no longer mobilize whatever resources are required for caring and nurturing.

Behind this inability to care is a wholly new emotional tone on the creek—a deep distrust even of old neighbors, a fear, in fact, of those very persons on whom one once staked one's life. A disaster like the one that hammered Buffalo Creek makes everything in the world seem unreliable, even other survivors, and that base is a very fragile one on which to build a new community.

NOTE

The conclusions expressed in this article are based on personal interviews with the flood's survivors, legal depositions, psychiatric evaluations, letters from survivors to their attorneys, and answers to mail questionnaires developed and administered by the author. The excerpts have been presented without supporting documentation in the interests of space.

18. THE MEANING OF COMMUNITY

JOHN F. FREIE

Community is not formed by people who get together and agree to sign their names to a document to form a community; rather, it is created over time as people form connections with each other, develop trust and respect for each other, and create a sense of common purposes.

Freie treats community as an ideal, something that people need and work for. His book, *Counterfeit Community*, is aimed at showing us how our search for community too often attracts us to communities that are really false.

In this selection, Freie describes the qualities of what a real community should be, emphasizing human interaction, some consensus, and a feeling among members that they belong to something larger than themselves.

Community is not a place or a thing; it is a calling, a struggle, a journey.
— *Robert Booth Fowler (1991, 161)*

If we may believe the findings of archaeologists who deal with the origins of humanity, it would seem as if human beings have a need to live with other human beings. The human is "an animal with its own unique reason for living in communities" (Leakey and Lewin 1977, 157). While it is debatable whether such social behavior may be considered "natural," it seems clear that throughout human history the urge to cooperate is compelling. It is this compelling urge for sociality that makes community a reality but also makes its simulated version—counterfeit community—possible.

Community is organic, not contractual or artificial. In a sense it is a living organism that is continually changing and adapting to challenges in the environment. Just as it was impossible to impose democratic structures on Weimar Germany and expect it to become a democracy, it is not possible to impose communal structures upon

From John F. Freie. *Counterfeit Community: The Exploitation of Our Longings for Connectedness*, Rowman & Littlefield Publishers, Inc. 1998. By permission.

people and expect them to become a community. The degree to which community develops is ultimately dependent upon the nature of the social, economic, and political fabric of a group of people. Community is not formed by people who get together and agree to sign their names to a document to form a community; rather, it is created over time as people form connections with each other, develop trust and respect for each other, and create a sense of common purpose.

As a community grows, it develops a history. Bellah et al. (1985) refer to this as a "community of memory," in which the story of its past is told and retold. One important way of telling the story of the community is through rituals. Rituals transmit knowledge about the community, confirm and maintain the existence of social groups and cultural forms, justify the power of the dominant groups as well as provide legitimacy to those groups that are weaker, moderate conflict, and affirm the legitimacy of the community (Nieburg 1973). The stories and rituals create a tradition and an ethos about what constitutes good character, what represents achievement, and what ties the present to the past.

This is not to suggest that community cannot be intentionally created—it can be. In fact, at some point there must be a consciousness about the nature of community if it is to survive and prosper. But community is not characterized only by the type of structures that exist. Communal structures are necessary, but not sufficient, for the creation of community. Equally important as the structures are the feelings of community, the character of the participants, and the quality of the human interactions.

The purpose of this chapter is to define the central concept of the book: community. This is not an easy task given the multitude of definitions that have been used. In 1955 one author identified ninety-four different definitions of community being used in social science studies (Hillery 1955). Twenty-two years later an examination of definitions of community by Willis (1977) found that the same degree of nonuniformity continued to exist. Unable to establish theoretical consensus, many social scientists merely discarded the concept altogether. But the reality of life in modern America has forced a reconsideration of community, and although definitional nonuniformity continues, discussions about the decline of community and calls to action to reconstruct it have become quite popular....

COMMUNITY DEFINED

Community is *an interlocking pattern of just human relationships in which people have at least a minimal sense of consensus within a definable territory. People within a community actively participate and cooperate with others to create their own self-worth, a sense of caring about others, and a feeling for the spirit of connectedness.*

People in community interact with others in complex and intricate ways. Just as people contain within them multiple sides to their characters, community provides safe arenas in which the different dimensions of an individual's personality may be expressed. While grounding us in the supportive environment of community, genuine community also allows people to take risks so that they may further discover aspects of their own identities. It is through serious confrontation of difference that a person truly discovers what he or she believes. Thus, genuine community devoted to human growth and discovery will encourage and support a diversity of interac-

tion—diversity in terms of people as well as diversity in terms of the types of situations in which the interactions take place.

The demands of post-industrial society encourage fragmentation and specialization of our personalities. To be successful we must become experts in highly specialized areas. Community, on the other hand, buffers such tendencies and acts as an integrating force.

This process of integration is, in a sense, the building of character. By growing up in a communal environment, one learns about loyalty, commitment, and responsibility to a whole greater than oneself. In a community a person plays many different roles but, more significantly, identifies with a group that shares values and beliefs that can only be realized through cooperation and commitment. For the community to be successful, members must recognize their membership in it and develop an enlarged sense of self.

How does this process of character formation occur? Communities create a rich and varied number of public spaces and public rituals that function to involve members in common activities. At times, members may be involved in the governance of the community, at other times they may participate in entertainment rituals, and at even other times they may merely be involved in spontaneous interactions with other members. Healthy communities provide public spaces where both spontaneous and more structured gatherings may take place. Participants present themselves in different manners depending upon the audience and the environment. In doing so they reveal and express different dimensions of their personalities.

Alan Ehrenhalt (1995) describes three communities in the Chicago area in the 1950s. One of the communities he describes was the ethnically diverse St. Nick's parish on the southwest side of the city. Composed of Irish, Polish, German, Italian, and Lithuanian peoples, it was united by a web of formal and informal associations, each allowing individuals to participate in the life of the community in a different fashion. One of the most significant unifying institutions was the Catholic Church, which not only provided religious guidance but also ran the neighborhood parochial school for many children who lived in the neighborhood. But perhaps equally important for the expression of another side of one's personality was "High Mass at Hoffman's," the corner tavern where the men often drank, played cards, and entertained each other with clever stories.

While children received an education at the neighborhood school, the recreational center was the alley in the back of the house or, when adults were not around, the front stoop and front street. Thus, children played within the neighborhood, well within sight of adults who did not hesitate to help form character through the use of discipline even if the child involved was not one's own.

On summer evenings the front stoops became informal meeting places where neighbors carried on conversation well past dark. Even places of business were extensions of the web of relationships that existed in the community. Most shopping was done in the neighborhood, within walking distance of one's home. Shopping was not just an economic transaction; it was the establishment and maintenance of a relationship of trust and loyalty. Some business transactions even took on the flavor of community celebrations. Friday night at the Talman Federal Savings found hundreds of people socializing in the bank lobby as they had their quarterly dividends stamped in their books. The founder of the bank would often hire a piano player or the local church choir to entertain. The bank performed another function as well, for it held most people's mortgages. But people in the community got even more from the bank: they got a strong dose of conservative economic philosophy and psychological support. It was sometimes necessary for the bank to emphasize such values because loans were often given not on the basis of some abstract formula, but on the assessment of one's character.

Although the St. Nick's parish community was limited in some respects, it provided numerous opportunities throughout a person's life for individuals to develop aspects of their personalities. This was done within a communal context. To be sure, the community was not as racially or economically integrated as it could have been, nor was authority distributed or administered in anything approaching a democratic fashion, and, of course, the 1950s notion that a woman's place was in the kitchen prevailed here as well. But the fundamental structure for healthy psychological and moral development was present, if not fully realized.

Human interactions within communities are formal as well as informal, and both serve important functions. Formal interactions, sometimes taking the form of rituals, may take on highly structured appearances. They may be political elections, government meetings, religious holiday celebrations, school activities, sporting events, or parades. These things seem obvious. But they also include family structures, marriage, education, and patterns of work. Whatever the social arrangements, members of the community who take part link themselves to the community. Through their participation they demonstrate at least partially their role in the community. While differences in social status or rank may exist among the participants, participation in the ritual itself performs the function of cutting across such divisions and provides a source of cohesion. Furthermore, when the participants perform different roles in the rituals (in some cases high status roles, in other cases low status roles), the sense of connectedness is further enhanced.

Communities also encourage informal interactions. These may be accidental, incidental to the objectives of a formal organization, or arising from some personal desire or gregarious instinct. They may occur almost anywhere, although they are more likely to occur in "third places" (cafes, diners, bars, beauty parlors, etc.). It is in these informal interactions where friendships are formed, where attitudes and customs may form, where social skills are honed, and where one learns the habit of association. Third places provide safe arenas in which alternative ideas may be tried out, where frustrations may be vented, where authority may be harshly criticized without fear of reprisal, where cohesiveness to formal institutions may be developed, or where people may simply have fun. These informal interactions provide the community with both an additional mode to develop connectedness and a means by which change can be fostered.

Both formal and informal interactions develop as an outgrowth of the needs and interests of the members of the community; they are not imposed from outside. Organizations such as governance structures, businesses, civic organizations, entertainment events, sporting events, schools, and the like grow from and are sustained by the interests and needs of the members of the community. Because the organizations are community structures, the leaders of the organizations feel a sense of responsibility and obligation to the community that created them.

Communication within communities may include mass or secondary communication forms (e.g., newspapers, radio, perhaps even television) but, and perhaps more importantly, must include face-to-face communication (primary experiences). It is partially through direct, face-to-face communication that beliefs, values, and attitudes about the community are shared and formed as members discuss important issues or merely chat. It is through primary experiences that individuals develop skills of scrutiny and investigation and learn how to develop rapport with objects and other humans. "Perception in this sense is not merely mental; it is an act that best serves to unify mind and body; it is an achievement of the whole person who is looking, listening, scrutinizing, and discerning" (Reed 1996, 104). Secondary communication forms also help to define the community and articulate the agreed-upon beliefs within the community, although their more likely function is to inform the community about assets that are available (Jeffres, Dobos, Sweeney 1987). Both forms of communication— primary and secondary—perform the important functions of building commitment and loyalty to the community. The complex web of formal and informal interactions creates a form of social capital that nourishes and enriches community (Putnam 1995)....

Communities are not characterized merely by the nature and extent of human interaction. For members of the community there is some sense of consensus both on values, beliefs, and mores of the community as well as on the boundaries, psychological as well as physical, of the community. There exists an awareness among members that they are part of the community. In many cases the community may have a particular name with which members identify. This sense of identification goes beyond identification with any of the particular memberships in any of the subgroups that exist within the larger community.

The conscious identification with the community provides members with a sense of rootedness and illustrates a sense of caring for others. Members of a community possess a sense of trust, common purpose, common respect, and a sense of connection. It is in community that the human potential for association and growth is realized and, in so doing, a spirit of caring and trust is developed. Members of the community care for the welfare of other members of the community, even though they may not personally know each and every one of them. In this way, identification with a community provides the basis for the development of an ethical perspective. Put bluntly, community helps build character. Before a person may answer the question, "What ought I to do?" one must first be able to answer the question, "Who am I?" Individual linkages that lack an ability to richly and firmly identify with a community will be thin and fragile and subject to destructive influences.

This should not be taken, however, to suggest that conflict is not present within communities. While at least a minimum of agreement on the fundamental values of the community must exist, other differences will be present. This is inevitable because of the diversity of human beings. Because people think differently (even though they may share common experiences), it will be difficult to achieve social consensus in any community....

"Community" is, by definition, a public term. But ironically, in order to create a rich and vibrant communal environment, an equally viable private arena must exist. To an extent greater than we would like to admit, human character is forged in the dynamic relationships between the private and the public, especially when the public is represented by genuine community. If community were to be all-consuming, it would be stifling as well as potentially authoritarian. Where community is non-existent, a pervasive nihilism runs rampant. Thus, to effectively create character we must maintain a healthy tension between the public (as represented by community and mass society) and the private (as best represented by the family).

Although dimensions of character (e.g., tolerance, morality, integrity, loyalty, responsibility) are arguably best developed in public arenas, the forging of identity occurs best within the private environment of the family. It is there where one's temperament and private virtues are initially developed and where a sense of self is initially created. In the environment of community, where individuals interact with others in the workplace, at school, and in the neighborhood, character is forged. In this sense, character is seen as an interpretation of the sense of self (which was created in the private environment of the family) in the light of the atmosphere and culture of the community.

In the family a person may develop a sense of caring, but it is in community where responsibility is acted out. In the family one learns the value of morality, but it is in community where moral agency is exercised. And in the private environment of the family one develops an active orientation toward life, but it is in the community where one develops a sense of commitment to a whole greater than oneself. In Robert Putnam's words, "Dense networks of interaction probably broaden the participants' sense of self, developing the 'I' into the 'we'" (1995, 67). It is in the dynamic interplay between the private and the public where an individual most fully develops character as well as the skills needed to function effectively in society.

Traditionally, communities have existed within definable geographical boundaries, not necessarily those consistent with political boundaries. Such a sense of place continues to be an important element of community: it provides a physical location and focus for human interaction. As will be shown in the analysis that follows, the undermining of place has had devastating effects not just on our ability to create community but on other behaviors as well.

Finally, a few comments about size are in order. Some have suggested that there exists, or more appropriately, should exist a global community. Those who advocate such a position claim that it is only by becoming globalists that we will realize our interconnectedness and that we will be able to cooperate to solve global problems. For some advocating global community, it is a matter of survival. Others suggest that a global community is possible because of advances in technology (e.g., the Internet) that have allowed people from different countries and different continents to communicate almost instantaneously. These technological improvements, so goes the argument, have drawn people closer together, making a global community a foreseeable reality.

My conception of community does not include the notion of global community. There are, I believe, size limitations on the concept of community (although what they are cannot be precisely specified). The critical element in community is face-to-face human interaction. Individuals in community must possess the ability to interact physically in multiple ways over extended periods of time. Formal and informal groups, structures, rituals, celebrations, and spontaneous meetings must exist to make it physically possible for any member of the community to meet any other member of the community. This is not to say that all members actively interact with all other members, but rather that the possibility exists that they could. This dimension limits the size of community, both in terms of the size of the population that could be included and in terms of the geographical area in which community can exist.

In a like fashion, to speak of a national community is to speak only metaphorically. The kind of intensity that community requires is not possible on such a broad scale. Nonetheless, as we will see when we examine politics, the theme of national community is often used by politicians attempting to mobilize support. When the notion of a national community is not linked with localized communities, it becomes a distortion—a form of counterfeit community.

What we are left with then is an ambitious and idealistic vision of community. Striving toward its realization is the necessary action that individuals consciously and unconsciously take in an attempt to fulfill themselves. The driving force that attracts people toward community can be found in their natural desire to live in association with others and to find identity through participation in a greater whole. It is this desire to live in association with others that leads people not only toward communal life, but also, mistakenly, toward counterfeit community.

We are particularly susceptible to the lure of counterfeit community today because of the growing feelings that Americans have become too individualistic and that we are experiencing a moral crisis that can only be solved by reinventing community. Everything from crime to teenage pregnancies to personal bankruptcy has been blamed on Americans' obsession with individualism and their inability to act responsibly. In this atmosphere, virtually any claim of community will be taken seriously.

Perhaps more significantly, the concept of community has been found to be an effective marketing tool for a wide variety of purposes. It has been used to sell virtually every product imaginable, from houses to food to political candidates to religion. Claims of community have come to so permeate our society that they have become almost commonplace. Not surprisingly, upon careful examination many community claims turn out to be counterfeit....

REFERENCES

Bellah, Robert N., Richard Madsen, William M. Sullivan, Ann Swidler, and Steven M. Tipton. 1985. *Habits of the Heart*. New York: Perennial Press.

Ehrenhalt, Alan. 1995. *The Lost City: Discovering the Forgotten Virtues of Community in the Chicago of the 1950s*. New York: BasicBooks.

Hillery, George A., Jr. 1955. "Definitions of Community: Areas of Agreement." *Rural Sociology* 20: 111–23.

Jeffres, Leo W., Jean Dobos, and Mary Sweeney. 1987. "Communication and Commitment to Community." *Communication Research* 14: 619–43.

Leakey, Richard E., and Roger Lewin. 1977. *Origins*. New York: E. P. Dutton.

Nieburg, H. L. 1973. *Culture Storm: Politics and the Ritual Order*. New York: St. Martin's Press.

Putnam, Robert D. 1995. "Bowling Alone: America's Declining Social Capital." *Journal of Democracy* 6: 65–78.

Reed, Edward S. 1996. *The Necessity of Experience*. New Haven: Yale University Press.

Willis, C. L. 1977. "Definitions of Community II: An Examination of Definitions of Community Since 1950." *Southern Sociology* 9: 14–19.

19. JIM JONES AND THE PEOPLES TEMPLE

CHARLES LINDHOLM

Organized as a cooperative community, with Jim Jones as the orienting element, the Peoples Temple offered an alternative to lives of desperation, isolation, and humiliation; a new vision was not only talked about, it was lived. Middle-class whites, as well as impoverished blacks, found in the experience of the Temple something of absolute value. They chose to live in this community, and many of them chose to die rather than forgo it. That this was so is not a testament to the insanity of the Peoples Temple as much as it is an indictment of the ordinary world....

It is easy to forget that in 1978 in a community called Jonestown in Guyana hundreds of people decided to kill themselves because of their strong ties to a community that seemed threatened from the outside world.

There are many explanations given for this, but Charles Lindholm presents an insightful one highly consistent with a sociological view. His explanation is the combination of a people seeking meaning in community and a charismatic leader who understood and manipulated their yearning.

Jim Jones and his followers offer an instructive example of a charismatic movement that begins from very different premises and appealed to a different constituency than the Manson Family, but aroused in its membership the same ecstatic communal selflessness, stimulated the same paranoid intensity in the leader, and ended in a similar catastrophic bloodbath—though in the Temple the members killed themselves as well as others. It remains the most enigmatic modern cult movement, since the mass suicides at Jonestown that shocked the world in 1978 were and remain difficult to conceptualize except by postulating insanity or else the use of force.

The evidence, however, does not indicate either insanity or force to be the case. The armed guards who surrounded Jonestown drank the poison that killed their friends when they could easily have escaped, and the only shots that were fired took the lives of Jones himself and Anne Moore, one of his closest disciples, in an apparent double suicide.[1] Some converts who, through

From *Charisma*, by Charles Lindholm, B. Blackwell Press, 1990. By permission.

happenstance, were not at Jonestown killed themselves later, and others who remained alive expressed regret: "I wanted to die with my friends. I wanted to do whatever they wanted to do" (a survivor quoted in Gallagher 1979). Nor were the members of the commune "insane" in any clinical sense. In fact, as one commentator writes, "the frightening thing about most of Jones's followers is that they were amazingly normal" (Richardson 1982: 21), and even hostile witnesses testified that the Jonestown populace were "far from the robots I first expected" (Reston 1981: 229).

THE PEOPLES TEMPLE

To understand the tragedy of Jonestown, we first need to look at what it offered to those who participated. Unlike the Manson Family, the Peoples Temple (it was always written without an apostrophe) was not based on an antinomian belief system that repudiated the reality of the world. Instead, the Temple combined Pentecostal faith-healing with left-wing political activism. It opposed the divisions of modern society, and the invidious distinctions of racism, and favored instead a new communal ideology in which everyone would be treated equally and share in the common good, welded together in a loving community of healing and mutual caring under the leadership of Jim Jones.

The group itself was a much more complex and powerful organization than any of the other communes that thrived in the California atmosphere, involving about 5,000 followers at its largest. In attempting to implement his political program, Jones could mobilize his supporters in letter-writing campaigns and picket lines, giving the impression that his support base was even wider than it really was; he therefore was courted by a number of politicians, and was appointed to a city commissioner's job in San Francisco. The Temple in its prime was not a group that withdrew from the world; it was active, visible, and powerful; operating within the system to change the system.

Much of the early success of the Peoples Temple came because of the tremendous appeal Jones had for the black community, and this also differentiates the Temple sharply from most countercultural organizations, whose membership consisted of young, white, middle-class ex-students. While Jones did draw in a middle-class base of ex-political radicals and activists, as well as a cadre of white fundamentalist believers from his early evangelizing in the midwest, he was most successful at proselytizing impoverished and culturally oppressed blacks, who were impressed by the fact that the Temple was an encompassing, interracial community where people worked and lived together in harmony, without fear of hunger, loneliness, prejudice, or poverty.

Of the membership in the fully formed Peoples Temple, 80 percent were black, two-thirds of them women, many elderly, many from extremely impoverished backgrounds, many ex-drug addicts or ex-criminals. Even in his early days in Indianapolis, when his church was mostly white, Jones had had a special capacity to appeal to the outsiders and the stigmatized. As one of his followers from that era says, Jones attracted "the kind of people most folks don't want to have nothing to do with. Fat, ugly old ladies who didn't have nobody in the world. He'd pass around hugs and kisses like he really did love them, and you could see it on their faces what he meant to them" (quoted in Feinsod 1981: 17). Within the Temple the deprived, the downtrodden, the unloved found a better world, working together and united by Jim Jones's love and caring, which apparently went beyond all social boundaries. He loved them all, he would take care of them all, he would struggle tirelessly for them, he would sacrifice himself for them without any concern for material rewards. "Here's a man who says as long as I have a home, you have a home. Here's a man with only one pair of shoes and no car, one suit of clothing—I think the suit he's got on tonight was borrowed. Here's a man who works over twenty hours a day. Here's JIM JONES" (Jones's introduction at a revival meeting, quoted in Reiterman and Jacobs 1982: 307).

Indeed, this portrait was a true one as far as it went. Even though the Temple took in enormous sums of donations, and had a bankroll of about twenty million dollars in its final days, Jones, as a true charismatic in the Weberian mold, had little interest in wealth. According to one convert, "It [the money] became almost a joke with Jim. . . . We used to wonder what to do with it all. But we never spent it on much" (quoted in Kilduff and Javers 1979: 82). And Jones did devote himself completely to the church, and to his congregation, working almost around the clock to achieve his dream of an interracial socialist community.

Another appeal of the Temple, aside from its mixture of classes and races, and the loving commitment of the leader, was the fact that many whole families participated, including, in some cases, three generations. This again is very unlike other cultic groups, which generally appealed to a narrow age range of converts. In the Temple, on the other hand, one did not have to give up attachments to one's closest relatives.

Being in the Peoples Temple was therefore a far cry from membership in an isolated, powerless group living on fantasies. It was a large community with a strong socialistic ideology of sharing and activism. It had achieved real successes and had real power. Many members testified that they had faith in Jones and in his vision precisely because, as one ex-temple member recalls, it seemed that "Jim has the knowledge and ability to make this world a better place. This is the only place I've seen true integration practiced" (Mills 1979: 137). Organized as a cooperative community, with Jim Jones as the orienting element, the Peoples Temple offered an alternative to lives of desperation, isolation and humiliation; a new vision was not only talked about, it was lived. Middle-class whites, as well as impoverished blacks, found in the experience of the Temple something of absolute value. They chose to live in this community, and many of them chose to die rather than forgo it. That this was so is not a testament to the insanity of the Peoples Temple as much as it is an indictment of the ordinary world....

Consequently, as in the Hitler cult, the elite cadre not only promoted, but also actually believed strongly in their leader's charisma. They had faith that Jones did have a magical power to heal, but that using this power exhausted him unduly, so that fakery was necessary to keep him alive. They believed in his Godlike qualities, and "were convinced that Jones could foresee the future, that he had information that no one else was aware of. These members also believed that the Temple was the only antidote to all the ills of the world" (Yee and Layton 1981: 165).

This process of destabilization of the individual personality and recombination into the charismatic group was accomplished incrementally through a number of methods we have already noted: constant confrontations and public confessions, which revealed each person's weaknesses and sexual inadequacies, as well as the untrustworthiness of friends and family; the denial of all emotional bonds between individuals and a focusing of affect on Jones; obligatory participation in group rituals of emotional intensification; propaganda that played upon the corruption and evil of the outer world; forced, self-incriminating confessions of homosexuality, and so on.

Their shared deceptions about Jones's ability to heal, about his sexuality, about his omnipotence, which were originally engaged in for the sake of group solidarity, also increased commitment among the elite by eroding their own ability to distinguish between truth and falsehood. Lies constantly repeated have a transforming effect, redefining reality not only for the listener, but for the speaker as well, who sees that the delusions become reality, and that assertions of transcendent power are associated with the actual inner experience of transcendence.

Commitment was further solidified by the requirements Jones made of his disciples. All worldly goods had to be invested in the Temple; children had to be given up into the Temple. Jones continually demanded that his followers cut their ties with the past completely and move from place to place, first from Indiana to California, then to the even greater isolation of Guyana. There solidarity reached its maximum, stimulated by Jones's absolute control of information, by the near continuous group meetings, by the fatigue and hunger of the members, by the blaring of loudspeakers bringing Jones's message to the people at any hour of the day, and by the atmosphere of paranoia that Jones emanated and cultivated.[2]

This process of amalgamation into the group took place within a typically charismatic command structure in which rules were strict, rigid, and highly elaborated, as the community reflected the leader's struggle to construct a world that would contain and channel his rage and fear. At the same time, the rules could change instantaneously, according to the leader's whim. As a result, "well-intentioned people, trying to obey the rules and regulations, often committed ... crimes without realizing it" (Mills 1979: 288). The followers had to learn to live in a total universe where complete arbitrariness was combined paradoxically with obsessional regimentation. The anxieties aroused by this situation pressed the disciples to greater identification with Jones as the sole point of orientation and guidance.

Jones's charisma was also maintained by the distance he kept from actual policy implementation. The community was run on a daily basis by an administrative core of eight to ten young white women. They stood above the PC and were Jones's closest and most loyal associates and confidants. They served to deflect any hostility felt by the rank and file for the direction of the commune. When things went wrong, they were to blame, not Jones; like Hitler, he kept his pronouncements on a transcendental plane.

The identity-challenging techniques, the community structure, and the willingness of the group to participate thus all combined to create a powerful communal experience centered around the volatile personality of Jim Jones. Those who gave themselves up to the experience found themselves within a total community that they had helped to construct. And once it was built, most of them did not wish to escape it. When Jones asked them to destroy others, and then themselves, they did so....

"SPIRITUAL ENERGY": JIM JONES'S CHARISMATIC APPEAL

... As with other charismatics, this reconfiguration of personality gave Jim Jones a fantastic quality; he was the man able to walk the tightrope above nothingness, to play with the deepest human fears of death and dissolution, to express the most vivid feelings, to intuit and meet the inner desires of others, to shift and change at will, while still maintaining his control. Jim Jones became a man who could make others feel as they had never felt before, an emphatic mirror for their sufferings and desires, so that even those who later left the Temple testify that Jones seemed to have paranormal abilities to intuit their thoughts and feelings.

It was from this matrix that Jones convinced his followers of his ability to heal, to forestall death, to foretell the future, to read people's thoughts, to merge into their minds: "Twice while I was at work, I had actually felt as if Jim Jones were in my head and I was looking out at the world through his eyes" (Mills 1979: 126).

The major way Jones revealed his spiritual power was in his sermons; they were carefully constructed to heighten his immediate emotional appeal by a dramatic setting and choreography. Jones, the evangelical showman, knew how important theatricality was for creating the proper mood for achieving charismatic transference. In his earlier performances he stressed his ordinariness and his similarity to the audience in order to gain their trust, but as the congregation increased in size, as his reputation grew, and as his personal magic no longer could be applied in one-on-one confrontations, he relied more and more on trappings and effects that set him conspicuously apart from the community. The

congregation encouraged him in this. They now knew him as God, and they wanted their God to be elevated.

So, in his Californian church, infectious gospel music, often proclaiming Jim Jones as the Messiah, preceded his arrival on stage and provided an atmosphere of excitement and anticipation. He dressed in a scintillating red satin robe and sunglasses; surrounding him were his multiracial, red-shirted, black-tied aides, who merged into an indistinguishable enthusiastic chorus that echoed his sermon. Jones sat in a high chair above them all, in a setting that combined spiritual and national symbols: an American flag on one side, a framed Declaration of Independence on the other, a magnificent stained-glass window in the background....

REVOLUTIONARY SUICIDE

His techniques, coupled with the intensity of his charismatic personality and the desires of the followers for community, did indeed increase members' ties to the Temple. It was, as we have seen, a highly successful enterprise, both economically and politically. But there was a time bomb within it, since the communal dynamic demanded continued expansion; yet as the group grew, it reached its outer limits. Jones could no longer interact with everyone and fuel them with his fire; the necessities of bureaucratic planning and group maintenance meant that work was harder and less rewarding; the expansion of the group became more difficult. But most threatening were defections. In fact, withdrawal from the group paradoxically reflected the Temple's very success at giving its members improved senses of self-worth and empowerment. Some of them now felt they could deal with the world on their own terms.

But Jones and the Temple could not accept anyone growing beyond them. For Jones and the committed members, the community was everything; it provided the structure that kept them from falling into the void. Jones had spent his entire life creating relations of dependency, warding off emptiness by placing himself in the center of the worlds of others, absorbing them into his expansive fantasy. He, who had not had love, would give love completely; he, who never trusted, would command absolute trust; he, who was torn by ambivalence, would be a rock; he, who had a damaged family, would manufacture the perfect family—but it was a family no one could ever leave; it had to be eternal, and it had to engulf the world.

The community was caught in a downward spiral as Jones's paranoia and desire to maintain control created tensions that led some members to reconsider their ties to the Temple. The last straw for Jones was the effort by one apostate couple to gain custody of their child, whom Jones claimed as his heir. In response, Jones sent many of his followers to Guyana to build a refuge in the jungle which would form a nexus for a new, millennial society, and provide as well a safe place where his enemies could no longer threaten him. Of course, the demons could not be warded off; they were too deep in Jones's soul.

Furthermore, the truly heroic struggle by the emigrants to build Jonestown undercut community solidarity. Productive work in common gave many who participated an increased belief in themselves, a feeling that they were active and creative individuals. As Eric Hoffer writes, "the taste of continuous successful action is fatal to the spirit of the collectivity" (1951: 120). Jones could not countenance this challenge to the group and to his dominance. Therefore, when he arrived in Jonestown he immediately acted to erode the achievements of the pioneers who had preceded him and who had almost unbelievably managed to construct a viable enterprise in the middle of the jungle. He began to implement increasingly irrational procedures and focused on ideological indoctrination instead of farm production. And he soon talked of abandoning the commune in favor of migration to the Soviet Union. This led to resentment, to further defections, and more paranoia, in a fateful movement toward the eventual mass suicide.

The thrust toward death had long been part of Jones's character and the ideology of the Temple. Like Hitler, his fascination with death was revealed as he frightened and coerced his associates by saying he might soon give up the life he hated. He was, he said, already dead at heart, and it was only his compassion for others who depended on him that kept him alive....

When Congressman William Ryan's investigating team arrived in Jonestown from the United States to see if members were being held against their wills, Jones felt his paranoid vision was coming true. At first, he managed to keep himself under control, and even provided hospitality and entertainment for his guests. The breaking point came when a few Temple members asked to leave Jonestown with the congressional party. This meant that even in Guyana, betrayal and disintegration were possible. The social world of the Temple no longer was solid; it was being torn apart by the blandishments of Satan.

For some weeks Jones had been preparing for this moment, claiming that CIA troops were already in the jungle, and manufacturing fake attacks on the compound—just as he had manufactured attacks on his early church in Indiana. This time, however, there was no place to run. Jones burned his bridges by having the congressional party attacked. He thus took revenge on America and on those who had betrayed him. Then he told his followers that instead of succumbing to the inexorable power of the state, the Peoples Temple would destroy itself in an act of defiance.

Suicide was proclaimed a revolutionary victory, an escape from inevitable corruption, an entrance into history, and a claim for the power of the love of Jim Jones, a love that would carry the followers to their ultimate merger with him in the unity of death, which Jones typically sexualized as "the orgasm of the grave" (Jim Jones quoted in Reston 1981: 265). Jones could see this as a triumph because it matched his grandiose vision and permitted him the positive expression of his self-hatred. The fates of his individual followers were of no concern to Jones; they were nothing more than extensions of himself, poor weak beings whom he could not leave behind on his journey to death: "I did not bring you to this point to leave you without a future, without someone who loves you, who will plan and care for you" (Jim Jones quoted in Reiterman and Jacobs 1982: 451).

The only thing that could save him would be if he could have faith in something outside himself: "If I had a leader—oh, how I would love to have a leader.... If I had a God—and oh how I wish I had a God like you ... because I'm the only one there is as far as I could see. And I have searched all over heaven and earth and I certainly looked through the belly of hell" (Jim Jones quoted in Reiterman and Jacobs 1982: 226).

But Jim Jones found no escape, no matter where he looked, neither in the world, where he saw himself rejected and persecuted, nor in his heart, where the love of the Temple could no longer ward off rage and fear. Meanwhile, the community had been practicing for mass suicide for some time. The notion of death had lost its terror for them. Like their leader, they believed themselves besieged by a hostile world; the defections of their fellows solidified them all the more, and they were ready to share the ultimate emptiness with the man who had brought them together for eternity. It was not Jim Jones, but the world, that was driving them to self-destruction:

> Jim was the most honest, loving, caring concerned person whom I ever met and knew....He knew how mean the world was and he took any and every stray animal and took care of each one. His love for humans was insurmountable....Jim Jones showed us all this—that we could live together with our differences, that we are all the same human beings . . . . We died because you would not let us live in peace. (Anne Moore's last testament quoted in Moore 1986: 285–6.)

Because Jim Jones had brought them together, because they had lost themselves and been reborn in the Temple, because they could not imagine any alternative to their unity, because they believed themselves to be under attack, the members were ready and willing to give up their lives rather than lose their community or the leader who crystallized it. As one of them said, "any life outside of this collective is shit....All I want is to die a revolutionary death" (quoted in Reston 1981: 265–6). And so they killed themselves just as they killed Congressman Ryan and his party; quite willingly, and without compunction. Far from being inhuman, the suicide was a quintessentially human act; one derived from the power of the group, and the dream of transcendence.

NOTES

1. Although tape recordings make most of the sequence of the mass suicide clear, the final act remains equivocal. Jones sent some of his closest followers out of Jonestown with large sums of money before the carnage, leading some to think he may have intended to decamp, but was killed before he could escape. However, his own words seem to indicate a man very tired of living.

2. In fact, Judith Weightman (1983) has estimated that of the 26 different possible commitment mechanisms outlined by Rosabeth Kanter (1972), Jonestown used 24. It is worth mentioning here that Jones, like Hitler and many other charismatic actors, had actually studied crowd psychology and the sociology of groups, and used information in this literature to initiate new indoctrination procedures.

3. All of these women were rivals for his attention, and he was well aware how jealousy could be used to maintain their loyalty. "I tell them all I love them most," Jones said. "Actually, I love only the Cause" (Jim Jones quoted in Mills 1979: 256).

REFERENCES

Gallagher, Nora 1979: "Jonestown: The Survivors Story." *New York Times Magazine*, 18 November, 124–36.

Hoffer, Eric 1951: *The True Believer*. New York: Harper and Row.

Kilduff, Marshall and Javers, Ron 1979: *The Suicide Cult*. New York: Bantam.

Mills, Jeannie 1979: *Six Years with God: Life Inside Rev. Jim Jones's Peoples Temple*. New York: A & W Publishers.

Moore, Rebecca 1986: *The Jonestown Letters: Correspondence of the Moore Family 1970–1985*. Lewiston, MN: Edwin Mellen Press.

Reiterman, Tim with Jacobs, John 1982: *Raven: The Untold Story of the Rev. Jim Jones and his People*. New York: Dutton.

Reston, James Jr. 1981: *Our Father Who Art in Hell*. New York: Times Books.

Richardson, James T. 1982: "A Comparison Between Jonestown and Other Cults." In Ken Levi (ed.), *Violence and Religious Commitment: Implications of Jim Jones's People's Temple Movement*, University Park, PA: Pennsylvania State.

Weightman, Judith Mary 1983: *Making Sense of the Jonestown Suicides: A Sociological History of the People's Temple*. New York: Edwin Mellen Press.

Yee, Min S. and Layton, Thomas 1981: *In My Father's House*. New York: Holt, Rinehart and Winston.

PART IV

Social Structure

Social organization inevitably develops the pattern called *social structure*, the network of statuses or positions that people come to occupy in relation to one another. Students and professor are positions in a classroom; husband, wife, and children are positions in a family; upper class, middle class, and lower class are positions in society. Our position in each social structure influences much of what we *do*, what we *think*, and who we *are*. Sociologists examine human action within the context of social structure. The selections in Part IV are all attempts to understand social structure and the impact it has on the individual actor.

The first selection by William Foote Whyte examines the social structure of a friendship group. The next two selections focus on the importance of *role* in social structure. A role can most easily be understood as the set of expectations that others have for the individual in his or her position within the social structure. The idea is that role (other people's expectations) shapes what the actor does. Philip E. Zimbardo's article is an excellent example of how "mature, emotionally stable, normal, intelligent college students" are transformed when placed into dehumanizing positions. Philip Meyer describes a set of experiments by Stanley Milgram where people agree to inflict pain simply because their role demands it.

Almost all social structures are unequal. All the selections in Part IV contain elements of social power. Where positions are formal, they become "authority," and people who fill these positions claim the "legitimate right to command" some and the "obligation to obey" others. In the last selection, Herbert Kelman and V. Lee Hamilton remind us of the atrocities carried out in times of war because people claim they were ordered to do so by others who had legitimate authority within social structure.

Barbara Hisman shows us the usefulness of structural analysis applied to gender, and William M. Dugger clearly describes for us four modes of structural inequality: class, gender, race, and nation.

20. CORNER BOYS: A STUDY OF CLIQUE BEHAVIOR

WILLIAM FOOTE WHYTE

The members have clearly defined relations of subordination and superordination, and each group has a leader.

Even informal groups have social structures, and almost always the positions are unequal in power. This article discusses the relationships between leaders and followers in informal groups. As Whyte declares, "The existence of a hierarchy of personal relations in these cliques is seldom explicitly recognized by the other corner boys." Yet Whyte's analysis clearly describes such a hierarchy of positions. Group action depends on approval by the "top man." The leader in turn takes the structure into account when he or she acts. This analysis is a classic study that has influenced the study of groups in natural settings.

Here is a brief outline of topics in the article:

1. The nature of "Cornerville"
2. Inequality in groups
3. Position means the power to influence
4. The Social and Athletic Club: an analysis of structure
5. The Millers: an analysis of the leader position
6. The system of mutual obligation
7. The role of the leader

This paper presents some of the results of a study of leadership in informal groupings or gangs of corner boys in "Cornerville," a slum area of a large eastern city. The aim of the research was to develop methods whereby the position (rank or status) of the individual in his clique might be empirically determined; to study the bases of group cohesion and of the subordination and superordination of its members; and, finally, to work out means for determining the position of corner gangs in the social structure of the community....

From "Corner Boys," by William Foote Whyte, in *American Journal of Sociology*, Vol. 46. Copyright © 1941 by the University of Chicago. Reprinted by permission of the University of Chicago Press.

The population of the district is almost entirely of Italian extraction. Most of the corner boys belong to the second generation of immigrants. In general, they are men who have had little education beyond grammar school and who are unemployed, irregularly employed, or working steadily for small wages.

Their name arises from the nature of their social life. For them, "the corner" is not necessarily at a street intersection. It is any part of the sidewalk that they take for their social headquarters, and it often includes a poolroom, barroom, funeral parlor, barber shop, or clubroom. Here they may be found almost any afternoon or evening, talking and joking about sex, sports, personal relations, or politics in season. Other social activities either take place "on the corner" or are planned there.

The existence of a hierarchy of personal relations in these cliques is seldom explicitly recognized by the corner boys. Asked if they have a leader or boss, they invariably reply, "no, we're all equal." It is only through the observation of actions that the group structure becomes apparent. My problem was to apply methods that would produce an objective and reasonably exact picture of such structures.

In any group containing more than two people, there are subdivisions to be observed. No member is equally friendly with all other members. In order to understand the behavior of the individual member, it is necessary to place him not only in his group but also in his particular position in the subgroup.

My most complete study of groupings was made from observations in the rooms of the Cornerville Social and Athletic [S. and A.] Club. This was a club of corner boys, which had a membership of about 50 and was divided primarily into two cliques, which had been relatively independent of each other before the formation of the club. There were, of course, subdivisions in each clique….

As I conceive it, position in the informal group means power to influence the actions of the group. I concentrated my attention on the origination of action, to observe who proposed an action, to whom he made the proposal, and the steps that followed up to the completion of the action. I was dealing with "pair events" and "set events," to use the terminology of Arensberg and Chapple. A pair event is an event between two people. A set event is an event in which one person originates action for two or more others at the same time….

It is observation of set events that reveals the hierarchical basis of informal group organization….

At the top of the Cornerville S. and A. Club, we have Tony, Carlo, and Dom. They were the only ones who could originate action for the entire club. At the bottom were Dodo, Gus, Pop, Babe, Marco, and Bob, who never originated action in a set event involving anyone above their positions. Most of the members fell into the intermediate class. They terminated action on the part of the top men and originated action for the bottom men. Observations of the actions of the men of the intermediate class when neither top nor bottom men were present revealed that there were subdivisions or rankings within that class. This does not mean that the intermediate or bottom men never have any ideas as to what the club should do. It means that their ideas must go through the proper channels if they are to go into effect.

In one meeting of the Cornerville S. and A. Club, Dodo proposed that he be allowed to handle the sale of beer in the clubrooms in return for 75 percent of the profits. Tony spoke in favor of Dodo's suggestion but proposed giving him a somewhat smaller percentage. Dodo agreed. Then Carlo proposed to have Dodo handle the beer in quite a different way, and Tony agreed. Tony made the motion, and it was carried unanimously. In this case, Dodo's proposal was carried through, after substantial modifications, on the actions of Tony and Carlo.

In another meeting, Dodo said he had two motions to make: that the club's funds be deposited in a bank and that no officer be allowed to serve two consecutive terms. Tony was not present at this time. Dom, the president, said that only one motion should be made at a time and that, furthermore, Dodo should not make any motions until there had been opportunity for discussion. Dodo agreed. Dom then commented that it would be foolish to deposit the funds when the club had so little to deposit. Carlo expressed his agreement. The meeting passed on to other things without action on the first motion and without even a word of discussion on the second one. In the same meeting, Chris moved that a member must be in the club for a year before being allowed to hold office. Carlo said that it was a good idea, he seconded the motion, and it carried unanimously.

All my observations indicate that the idea for group action that is carried out must originate with the top man or be accepted by him so that he acts on the group. A follower may originate action for a leader in a pair event, but he does not originate action for the leader and other followers at the same time—that is, he does not originate action in a set event that includes the leader.

One may also observe that, when the leader originates action for the group, he does not act as if his followers were all of equal rank. Implicitly, he takes the structure of the group into account.

An example taken from the corner gang known as the "Millers" will illustrate this point. The Millers were a group of 20 corner boys who were divided into two subgroups. Members of both subgroups frequently acted together; but, when two activities occupied the men at the same time, the division generally fell between the subgroups. Sam was the leader of the Millers. Joe was directly below him in one subgroup. Chichi led the other subgroup. Joe as well as Sam were in positions to originate action for Chichi and his subgroup.

It was customary for the Millers to go bowling every Saturday night. On this particular Saturday night, Sam had no money, so he set out to persuade the boys to do something else. They followed his suggestion. Later, Sam explained to me how he had been able to change the established social routine of the group. He said:

> I had to show the boys that it would be in their own interests to come with me—that each one of them would benefit. But I knew I only had to convince two of the fellows. If they start to do something, the other boys will say to themselves, "If Joe does it—or if Chichi does it—it must be a good thing for us too." I told Joe and Chichi what the idea was, and I got them to come with me. I didn't pay no attention to the others. When Joe and Chichi came, all the other boys came along too.

Another example from the Millers indicates what happens when the leader and the man next to him in rank disagree on group policy. This is Sam talking again:

> One time we had a raffle to raise money to build a camp on Lake _____ [on property lent them by a local business man]. We had collected $54, and Joe and I were holding the money.... That week I knew Joe was playing pool, and he lost three or four dollars gambling. When Saturday came, I says to the boys, "Come on, we go out to Lake _____. We're gonna build that camp on the hill...." Right away Joe said "If yuz are gonna build the camp on the hill, I don't come. I want it on the other side...." All the time I knew he had lost the money, and he was only making up excuses so he wouldn't have to let anybody know.... Now the hill was really the place to build that camp. On the other side, the ground was swampy. That would have been a stupid place.... But I knew that if I tried to make them go

through with it now, the group would split up into two cliques. Some would come with me, and some would go with Joe.... So I let the whole thing drop for a while.... After, I got Joe alone, and I says to him, "Joe, I know you lost some of that money, but that's all right. You can pay up when you have it and nobody will say nothin'. But Joe, you know we shouldn't have the camp on the other side of the hill because the land is no good there. We should build it on the hill...." So he said, "All right," and we got all the boys together, and we went out to build the camp.

Under ordinary circumstances, the leader implicitly recognizes and helps to maintain the position of the man or men immediately below him, and the group functions smoothly. In this respect, the informal organization is similar to the formal organization. If the executive in a factory attempts to pass over his immediate subordinates and gives orders directly to the men on the assembly line, he creates confusion. The customary channels must be used.

The social structures vary from group to group, but each one may be represented in some form of hierarchy. The members have clearly defined relations of subordination and superordination, and each group has a leader....

Out of these interactions arises a system of mutual obligations that is fundamental to group cohesion. If the men are to carry on their activities as a unit, there are many occasions when they must do favors for one another. Frequently, one member must spend money to help another who does not have the money to participate in some of the group activities. This creates an obligation. If the situation is later reversed, the recipient is expected to help the man who gave him aid. The code of the corner boy requires him to help his friends when he can and to refrain from doing anything to harm them. When life in the group runs smoothly, the mutual obligations binding members to one another are not explicitly recognized. A corner boy, asked if he helped a fellow member because of a sense of obligation, will reply, "No, I didn't have to do it. He's my friend. That's all." It is only when the relationship breaks down that the underlying obligations are brought to light. When two members of the group have a falling-out, their actions form a familiar pattern. One tells a story something like this: "What a heel Blank turned out to be. After all I've done for him, the first time I ask him to do something for me, he won't do it." The other may say: "What does he want from me? I've done plenty for him, but he wants you to do everything." In other words, the actions that were performed explicitly for the sake of friendship are now revealed as being part of a system of mutual obligations.

Not all the corner boys live up to their obligations equally well, and this factor partly accounts for the differentiation in status among the men. The man with a low status may violate his obligations without much change in his position. His fellows know that he has failed to discharge certain obligations in the past, and his position reflects his past performances. On the other hand, the leader is depended on by all the members to meet his personal obligations. He cannot often fail to do so without causing confusion and losing his position. The relationship of status to the system of mutual obligations is most clearly revealed when we consider the use of money. Although all the men are expected to be generous, the flow of money between members can be explained only in terms of the group structure.

The Millers provide an illustration of this point. During the time I knew them, Sam, the leader, was out of work except for an occasional odd job; yet, whenever he had a little money, he spent it on Joe and Chichi, his closest friends, who were next to him in the structure of the group. When Joe or Chichi had money, which was less frequent, they reciprocated. Sam frequently paid for two members who stood close to the bottom of the structure and occasionally for others. The two men who held positions immediately below Joe and Chichi in the subgroups were considered very well off according to Cornerville standards. Sam said that he occasionally borrowed money from them, but never more than 50 cents at a time. Such loans he tried to repay at the earliest possible moment. There were four other members, with positions ranging from intermediate to the bottom, who nearly always had more money than Sam. He did not recall ever having borrowed from them. He said that the only time he had obtained a substantial sum from anyone around his corner was when he borrowed 11 dollars from a friend who was the *leader* of another corner-boy group.

The system is substantially the same for all the groups on which I have information. The leader spends more money on his followers than they on him. The farther down in the structure one looks, the fewer are the financial relations which tend to obligate the leader to a follower. This does not mean that the leader has more money than others or even that he necessarily spends more—although he must always be a free spender. It means that the financial relations must be explained in social terms. Unconsciously, and in some cases consciously, the leader refrains from putting himself under obligation to those with low status in the group....

The leader is the man who knows what to do. He is more resourceful than his followers. Past events have shown that his ideas were right. In this sense, "right" simply means satisfactory to the members. He is the most independent in judgment. Although his followers are undecided about a course of action or the character of a newcomer, the leader makes up his mind. When he gives his word to one of "his boys," he keeps it. The followers look to him for advice and encouragement, and he receives more of the confidences of the members than any other man. Consequently, he knows more about what is going on in the group than anyone else. Whenever there is a quarrel among the boys, he will hear of it almost as soon as it happens. Each party to the quarrel may appeal to him to work out a solution; and, even when the men do not want to compose their differences, each one will take his side of the story to the leader at the first opportunity. A man's standing depends partly on the leader's belief that he has been conducting himself as he should.

The leader is respected for his fairmindedness. Whereas there may be hard feelings among some of the followers, the leader cannot bear a grudge against any man in the group. He has close friends (men who stand next to him in position), and he is indifferent to some of the members; but if he is to retain his reputation for impartiality, he cannot allow personal animus to override his judgment.

The leader need not be the best baseball player, bowler, or fighter, but he must have some skill in whatever pursuits are of particular interest to the group. It is natural for him to promote activities in which he excels and to discourage those in which he is not skillful; and, insofar as he is thus able to influence the group, his competent performance is a natural consequence of his position. At the same time, his performance supports his position.

It is significant to note that the leader is better known and more respected outside of his group than is any of his followers. His social mobility is greater. One of the most important functions he performs is that of relating his group to other groups in the district. His reputation outside the group tends to support his standing within the group, and his position in the group supports his reputation among outsiders.

It should not be assumed from this discussion that the corner boys compete with one another for the purpose of gaining leadership. Leadership is a product of social interaction. The men who reach the top in informal groups are those who can perform skillfully the actions required by the situation. Most such skills are performed without long premeditation....

21. PATHOLOGY OF IMPRISONMENT

PHILIP E. ZIMBARDO

At the end of only six days, we had to close down our mock prison because what we saw was frightening.

This article needs little introduction because it truly speaks for itself. It represents the very best example of the power of social structure; how situations place people in roles, and how people subsequently become transformed, doing things they would never think of doing outside those roles.

In an attempt to understand just what it means psychologically to be a prisoner or prison guard, Craig Haney, Curt Banks, Dave Jaffe, and I created our own prison. We carefully screened over 70 volunteers who answered an ad in a Palo Alto city newspaper and ended up with about two dozen young men who were selected to be part of this study. They were mature, emotionally stable, normal, intelligent college students from middle-class homes throughout the United States and Canada. They appeared to represent the cream of the crop of this generation. None had any criminal record and all were relatively homogeneous on many dimensions initially.

From "Pathology of Imprisonment," by Philip Zimbardo, in *Society*, Vol. 9, No. 6. Copyright © 1972 by Transaction Publishers; all rights reserved. Reprinted by permission of Transaction Publishers.

Half were arbitrarily designated as prisoners by a flip of a coin, the others as guards. These were the roles they were to play in our simulated prison. The guards were made aware of the potential seriousness and danger of the situation and their own vulnerability. They made up their own formal rules for maintaining law, order, and respect, and were generally free to improvise new ones during their eight-hour, three-man shifts. The prisoners were unexpectedly picked up at their homes by a city policeman in a squad car, searched, handcuffed, fingerprinted, booked at the Palo Alto station house, and taken blindfolded to our jail. There they were stripped, deloused, put into a uniform, given a number, and put into a cell with two other prisoners where they expected to live for the next two weeks. The pay was good ($15 a day) and their motivation was to make money.

We observed and recorded on videotape the events that occurred in the prison, and we interviewed and tested the prisoners and guards at various points throughout the study. Some of the videotapes of the actual encounters between the prisoners and guards were seen on the NBC News feature "Chronolog" on November 26, 1971.

At the end of only six days, we had to close down our mock prison because what we saw was frightening. It was no longer apparent to most of the subjects (or to us) where reality ended and their roles began. The majority had indeed become prisoners or guards, no longer able to clearly differentiate between role playing and self. There were dramatic changes in virtually every aspect of their behavior, thinking, and feeling. In less than a week, the experience of imprisonment undid (temporarily) a life-time of learning; human values were suspended, self-concepts were challenged, and the ugliest, most base, pathological side of human nature surfaced. We were horrified because we saw some boys (guards) treat others as if they were despicable animals, taking pleasure in cruelty, while other boys (prisoners) became servile, dehumanized robots who thought only of escape, of their own individual survival, and of their mounting hatred for the guards.

We had to release three prisoners in the first four days because they had such acute situational traumatic reactions as hysterical crying, confusion in thinking, and severe depression. Others begged to be paroled, and all but three were willing to forfeit all the money they had earned if they could be paroled. By then (the fifth day), they had been so programmed to think of themselves as prisoners that when their request for parole was denied, they returned docilely to their cells. Now, had they been thinking as college students acting in an oppressive experiment, they would have quit once they no longer wanted the $15 a day we used as our only incentive. However, the reality was not quitting an experiment but "being paroled by the parole board from the Stanford County Jail." By the last days, the earlier solidarity among the prisoners (systematically broken by the guards) dissolved into "each man for himself." Finally, when one of their fellows was put in solitary confinement (a small closet) for refusing to eat, the prisoners were given a choice by one of the guards: give up their blankets and the incorrigible prisoner would be let out, or keep their blankets and he would be kept in all night. They voted to keep their blankets and to abandon their brother.

About a third of the guards became tyrannical in their arbitrary use of power, in enjoying their control over other people. They were corrupted by the power of their roles and became quite inventive in their techniques of breaking the spirit of the prisoners and making them feel they were worthless. Some of the guards merely did their jobs as tough but fair correctional officers, and several were good guards from the prisoners' point of view because they did them small favors and were friendly. However, no good guard ever interfered with a command by any of the bad guards; they never intervened on the side of the prisoners, they never told the others to ease off because it was only an experiment, and they never even came to me as prison superintendent or experimenter in charge to complain. In part, they were good because the others were bad; they needed the others to help establish their own egos in a positive light. In a sense, the good guards perpetuated the prison more than the other guards because their own needs to be liked prevented them from disobeying or violating the implicit guards' code. At the same time, the act of befriending the prisoners created a social reality that made the prisoners less likely to rebel.

By the end of the week, the experiment had become a reality, as if it were a Pirandello play directed by Kafka that just keeps going after the audience has left. The consultant for our prison, Carlo Prescott, an exconvict with 16 years of imprisonment in California's jails, would get so depressed and furious each time he visited our prison, because of its psychological similarity to his experiences, that he would have to leave. A Catholic priest who was a former prison chaplain in Washington, D.C., talked to our prisoners after four days and said they were just like the other first-timers he had seen.

But in the end, I called off the experiment, not because of the horror I saw out there in the prison yard, but because of the horror of realizing that *I* could have easily traded places with the most brutal guard or become the weakest prisoner full of hatred at being so powerless that I could not eat, sleep, or go to the toilet without permission of the authorities. *I* could have become Calley at My Lai, George Jackson at San Quentin, one of the men at Attica.

Individual behavior is largely under the control of social forces and environmental contingencies rather than personality traits, character, will power, or other empirically unvalidated constructs. Thus we create an illusion of freedom by attributing more internal control to ourselves, to the individual, than actually exists. We thus underestimate the power and pervasiveness of situational controls over behavior because (a) they are often nonobvious and subtle, (b) we can often avoid entering situations in which we might be so controlled, and (c) we label as "weak" or "deviant" people in those situations who do behave differently from how we believe we would.

Each of us carries around in our heads a favorable self-image in which we are essentially just, fair, humane, and understanding. For example, we could not imagine inflicting pain on others without much provocation or hurting people who had done nothing to us, who in fact were even liked by us. However, there is a growing body of social psychological research which underscores the conclusion derived from this prison study. Many people, perhaps the majority, can be made to do almost anything when put into psychologically compelling situations—regardless of their morals, ethics, values, attitudes, beliefs, or personal convictions. My colleague, Stanley Milgram, has shown that more than 60 percent of the population will deliver what they think is a series of painful electric shocks to another person even after the victim cries for mercy, begs them to stop, and then apparently passes out. The subjects complained that they did not want to inflict more pain but blindly obeyed the command of the authority figure (the experimenter) who said that they must go on. In my own research on violence, I have seen mild-mannered coeds repeatedly give shocks (which they thought were causing pain) to another girl, a stranger whom they had rated very favorably, simply by being made to feel anonymous and put in a situation in which they were expected to engage in this activity.

Observers of these and similar experimental situations never predict their outcomes and estimate that it is unlikely that they themselves would behave similarly. They can be so confident only when they are outside the situation. However, because the majority of people in these studies do act in nonrational, nonobvious ways, it follows that the majority of observers would also succumb to the social psychological forces in the situation.

With regard to prisons, we can state that the mere act of assigning labels to people and putting them into a situation in which those labels acquire validity and meaning is sufficient to elicit pathological behavior. This pathology is not predictable from any available diagnostic indicators we have in the social sciences, and it is extreme enough to modify in very significant ways fundamental attitudes and behavior. The prison situation, as presently arranged, is guaranteed to generate severe enough pathological reactions in both guards and prisoners as to debase their humanity, lower their feelings of self-worth, and make it difficult for them to be part of a society outside their prison.

22. IF HITLER ASKED YOU TO ELECTROCUTE A STRANGER, WOULD YOU? PROBABLY

PHILIP MEYER

They are somehow engaged in something from which they cannot liberate themselves. They are locked into a structure, and they do not have the skills or inner resources to disengage themselves.

No systematic study of positions and power is as clearly to the point as were the Milgram experiments done at Yale University in the 1960s. Here is an article written about Milgram's findings. The importance of social structure is made clear: In the position of experimental subject, the individual is transformed, willing to take orders from the scientist, an authority seen as having a legitimate right to command. It is easy to react to this by claiming "I would never do it," but maybe a more objective response would be, "Why do people do things like this? Why might I do something like this?" What forces are at work in social situations that lead the individual to do things he or she might not normally do?

In the beginning, Stanley Milgram was worried about the Nazi problem. He doesn't worry much about the Nazis anymore. He worries about you and me, and, perhaps, himself a little bit, too.

Stanley Milgram is a social psychologist, and when he began his career at Yale University in 1960, he had a plan to prove, scientifically, that Germans are different. The Germans-are-different hypothesis had been used by historians, such as William L. Shirer, to explain the systematic destruction of the Jews by the Third Reich. One madman could decide to destroy the Jews and even create a master plan for getting it done. But to implement it on the scale that Hitler did meant that thousands of other people had to go along with the scheme and help to do the work. The Shirer thesis, which Milgram set out to test, is that Germans have a basic character flaw that explains the whole thing, and this flaw is a readiness to obey authority without question, no matter what outrageous acts the authority commands.

The appealing thing about this theory is that it makes those of us who are not Germans feel better about the whole business. Obviously, you and I are not Hitler, and it seems equally obvious that we would never do Hitler's dirty work for him. But now, because of Stanley Milgram, we are compelled to wonder. Milgram developed a laboratory experiment that provided a systematic way to measure obedience. His plan was to try it out in New Haven on Americans and then go to Germany and try it out on Germans. He was strongly motivated by scientific curiosity, but there was also some moral content in his decision to pursue this line of research, which was in turn colored by his own Jewish background. If he could show that Germans are more obedient than Americans, he could then vary the conditions of the experiment and try to find out just what it is that makes some people more obedient than others. With this understanding, the world might, conceivably, be just a little bit better.

But he never took his experiment to Germany. He never took it any farther than Bridgeport. The first finding, also the most unexpected and disturbing finding, was that we Americans are an obedient people: not blindly obedient, and not blissfully obedient, just obedient. "I found so much obedience," says Milgram softly, a little sadly, "I hardly saw the need for taking the experiment to Germany."

There is something of the theater director in Milgram, and his technique, which he learned from one of the old masters in experimental psychology, Solomon Asch, is to stage a play with every line rehearsed, every prop carefully selected, and everybody an actor except one person. That one person is the subject of the experiment. The subject, of course, does not know he is in a play. He thinks he is in real life. The value of this technique is that the experimenter, as though he were God, can change a prop here, vary a line there, and see how the subject responds. Milgram eventually had to change a lot of the script just to get people to stop obeying. They were obeying so much that the experiment wasn't working — it was like trying to measure oven temperature with a freezer thermometer.

The experiment worked like this: If you were an innocent subject in Milgram's melodrama, you read an ad in the newspaper or received one in the mail asking for volunteers for an educational experiment. The job would take about an hour and pay $4.50. So you make an appointment and go to an old Romanesque stone structure on High Street with the imposing name of The Yale Interaction Laboratory. It looks something like a broadcasting studio. Inside, you meet a young, crew-cut man in a laboratory coat who says he is Jack Williams, the experimenter. There is another citizen, fiftyish, Irish face, an accountant, a little overweight, and very mild and harmless looking. This other citizen seems nervous and plays with his hat while the two of you sit in chairs side by side and are told that the $4.50 checks are yours no matter what happens. Then you listen to Jack Williams explain the experiment.

It is about learning, says Jack Williams in a quiet, knowledgeable way. Science does not know much about the conditions under which people learn, and this experiment is to find out about negative reinforcement. Negative rein-forcement is getting punished when you do something wrong, as opposed to positive reinforcement, which is getting rewarded when you do something right. The negative reinforcement in this case is electric shock. You notice a book on the table, titled, *The Teaching-Learning Process*, and you assume that this has something to do with the experiment.

Then Jack Williams takes two pieces of paper, puts them in a hat, and shakes them up. One piece of paper is supposed to say, "Teacher" and the other, "Learner." Draw one and you will see which you will be. The mild-looking accountant draws one, holds it close to his vest like a poker player, looks at it, and says, "Learner." You look at yours. It says, "Teacher." You do not know that the drawing is rigged, and both slips say "Teacher." The experimenter beckons to the mild-mannered "learner."

"Want to step right in here and have a seat, please?" he says. "You can leave your coat on the back of that chair...roll up your right sleeve, please. Now, what I want to do is strap down your arms to avoid excessive movement on your part during the experiment. This electrode is connected to the shock generator in the next room.

"And this electrode paste," he says, squeezing some stuff out of a plastic bottle and putting it on the man's arm, "is to provide a good contact and to avoid a blister or burn. Are there any questions now before we go into the next room?"

You don't have any, but the strapped-in "learner" does.

"I do think I should say this," says the learner. "About two years ago, I was in the veterans' hospital...they detected a heart condition. Nothing serious, but as long as I'm having these shocks, how strong are they — how dangerous are they?"

Williams, the experimenter, shakes his head casually. "Oh, no," he says. "Although they may be painful, they're not dangerous. Anything else?"

Nothing else. And so you play the game. The game is for you to read a series of word pairs: for example, *blue-girl, nice-day, fat-neck*. When you finish the list, you read just the first word in each pair and then a multiple-choice list of four other words, including the second word of the pair. The learner, from his remote, strapped-in position, pushes one of four switches to indicate which of the four answers he thinks is the right one. If he gets it right, nothing happens and you go on to the next one. If he gets it wrong, you push a switch that buzzes and gives him an electric shock. And then you go on to the next word. You start with 15 volts and increase the number of volts by 15 for each wrong answer. The control board goes from 15 volts on one end to 450 volts on the other. So that you know what you are doing, you get a test shock yourself, at 45 volts. It hurts. To further keep you aware of what you are doing to that man in there, the board has verbal descriptions of the shock levels, ranging from "Slight Shock" at the left-hand side, through "Intense Shock" in the middle, to "Danger: Severe Shock" toward the far right. Finally, at the very end, under the 435-volt and 450-volt switches, there are three ambiguous Xs. If, at any point, you hesitate, Mr. Williams calmly tells you to go on. If you still hesitate, he tells you again.

Except for some terrifying details, which will be explained in a moment, this is the experiment. The object is to find the shock level at which you disobey the experimenter and refuse to pull the switch.

When Stanley Milgram first wrote this script, he took it to 14 Yale psychology majors and asked them what they thought would happen. He put it this way: Out of one hundred persons in the teacher's predicament, how would their break-off points be distributed along the 15-volt to 450-volt scale? They thought a few would break off very early, most would quit someplace in the middle, and a few would go all the way to the end. The highest estimate of the number out of 100 who would go all the way to the end was three. Milgram then informally polled some of his fellow scholars in the psychology department. They agreed that very few would go to the end. Milgram thought so, too.

"I'll tell you quite frankly," he says, "before I began this experiment, before any shock generator was built, I thought that most people would break off at 'Strong Shock' or 'Very Strong Shock.' You would get only a very, very small proportion of people going out to the end of the shock generator, and they would constitute a pathological fringe."

In his pilot experiments, Milgram used Yale students as subjects. Each of them pushed the shock switches, one by one, all the way to the end of the board.

So he rewrote the script to include some protests from the learner. At first, they were mild, gentlemanly, Yalie protests, but "it didn't seem to have as much effect as I thought it would or should," Milgram recalls. "So we had more violent protestation on the part of the person getting the shock. All the time, of course, what we were trying to do was not to create a macabre situation, but simply to generate disobedience. And that was one of the first findings. This was not only a technical deficiency of the experiment, that we didn't get disobedience. It really was the first finding: that obedience would be much greater than we had assumed it would be and that disobedience would be much more difficult than we had assumed."

As it turned out, the situation did become rather macabre. The only meaningful way to generate disobedience was to have the victim protest with great anguish, noise, and vehemence. The protests were tape-recorded so that all the teachers ordinarily would hear the same sounds and nuances, and they started with a grunt at 75 volts, proceeded through a "Hey, that really hurts," at 125 volts, got desperate with, "I can't stand the pain, don't do that," at 180 volts, reached complaints of heart trouble at 195, an agonized scream at 285, a refusal to answer at 315, and only heart-rending, ominous silence after that.

Still, 65 percent of the subjects, 20-to-50-year-old American males, everyday, ordinary people, like you and me, obediently kept pushing those levers in the belief that they were shocking the mild-mannered learner, whose name was Mr. Wallace, and who was chosen for the role because of his innocent appearance, all the way up to 450 volts.

Milgram was now getting enough disobedience so that he had something he could measure. The next step was to vary the circumstances to see what would encourage or discourage obedience. There seemed very little left in the way of discouragement. The victim was already screaming at the top of his lungs and feigning a heart attack. So whatever new impediment to obedience reached the brain of the subject had to travel by some route other than the ear. Milgram thought of one.

He put the learner in the same room with the teacher. He stopped strapping the learner's hand down. He rewrote the script so that, at 150 volts, the learner took his hand off the shock plate and declared that he wanted out of the experiment. He rewrote the script some more so that the experimenter then told the teacher to grasp the learner's hand and physically force it down on the plate to give Mr. Wallace his unwanted electric shock.

"I had the feeling that very few people would go on at that point, if any," Milgram says. "I thought that would be the limit of obedience that you would find in the laboratory."

It wasn't.

Although seven years have now gone by, Milgram still remembers the first person to walk into the laboratory in the newly rewritten script. He was a construction worker, a very short man. "He was so small," says Milgram, "that when he sat on the chair in front of the shock generator, his feet didn't reach the floor. When the experimenter told him to push the victim's hand down and give the shock, he turned to the experimenter, and he turned to the victim, his elbow went up, he fell down on the hand of the victim, his feet kind of tugged to one side, and he said, 'Like this, boss?' Zzumph!"

The experiment was played out to its bitter end. Milgram tried it with 40 different subjects. And 30 percent of them obeyed the experimenter and kept on obeying.

"The protests of the victim were strong and vehement, he was screaming his guts out, he refused to participate, and you had to physically struggle with him in order to get his hand down on the shock generator," Milgram remembers. But 12 out of 40 did it.

Milgram took his experiment out of New Haven. Not to Germany, just 20 miles down the road to Bridgeport. Maybe, he reasoned, the people obeyed because of the prestigious setting of Yale University. If they couldn't trust a learning center that had been there for two centuries, whom could they trust? So he moved the experiment to an untrustworthy setting.

The new setting was a suite of three rooms in a run-down office building in Bridgeport. The only identification was a sign with a fictitious name: "Research Associates of Bridgeport." Questions about professional connections got only vague answers about "research for industry."

Obedience was less in Bridgeport. Forty-eight percent of the subjects stayed for the maximum shock, compared to 65 percent at Yale. But this was enough to prove that far more than Yale's prestige was behind the obedient behavior.

For more than seven years now, Stanley Milgram has been trying to figure out what makes ordinary American citizens so obedient. The most obvious answer—that people are mean, nasty, brutish, and sadistic—won't do. The subjects who gave the shocks to Mr. Wallace to the end of the board did not enjoy it. They groaned, protested, fidgeted, argued, and in some cases, were seized by fits of nervous, agitated giggling.

"They even try to get out of it," says Milgram, "but they are somehow engaged in something from which they cannot liberate themselves. They are locked into a structure, and they do not have the skills or inner resources to disengage themselves...."

"The results, as seen and felt in the laboratory," he has written, "are disturbing. They raise the possibility that human nature, or more specifically the kind of character produced in American democratic society, cannot be counted on to insulate its citizens from brutality and inhumane treatment at the direction of malevolent authority. A substantial proportion of people do what they are told to do, irrespective of the content of the act and without limitation of conscience, so long as they perceive that the command comes from a legitimate authority. If, in this study, an anonymous experimenter can successfully command adults to subdue a 50-year-old man and force on him painful electric shocks against his protest, one can only wonder what government, with its vastly greater authority and prestige, can command of its subjects...."

Stanley Milgram has his problems, too. He believes that in the laboratory situation, he would not have shocked Mr. Wallace. His professional critics reply that in his real-life situation, he has done the equivalent. He has placed innocent and naive subjects under great emotional strain and pressure in selfish obedience to his quest for knowledge. When you raise this issue with Milgram, he has an answer ready. There is, he explains patiently, a critical difference between his naive subjects and the man in the electric chair. The man in the electric chair (in the mind of the naive subject) is helpless, strapped in. But the naive subject is free to go at any time.

Immediately after he offers this distinction, Milgram anticipates the objection.

"It's quite true," he says, "that this is almost a philosophic position, because we have learned that some people are psychologically incapable of disengaging themselves. But that doesn't relieve them of the moral responsibility."

The parallel is exquisite. "The tension problem was unexpected," says Milgram in his defense. But he went on anyway. The naive subjects didn't expect the screaming protests from the strapped-in learner. But they went on.

"I had to make a judgment," says Milgram. "I had to ask myself, was this harming the person or not? My judgment is that it was not. Even in the extreme cases, I wouldn't say that permanent damage results."

Sound familiar? "The shocks may be painful," the experimenter kept saying, "but they're not dangerous."

After the series of experiments was completed, Milgram sent a report of the results to his subjects and a questionnaire, asking whether they were glad or sorry to have been in the experiment. Eighty-three and seven-tenths percent said they were glad and only 1.3 percent were sorry; 15 percent were neither sorry nor glad. However, Milgram could not be sure at the time of the experiment that only 1.3 percent would be sorry.

Kurt Vonnegut, Jr., put one paragraph in the preface to *Mother Night*, in 1966, which pretty much says it for the people with their fingers on the shock-generator switches, for you and me, and maybe even for Milgram. "If I'd been born in Germany," Vonnegut said, "I suppose I would have *been* a Nazi, bopping Jews and gypsies and Poles around, leaving boots sticking out of snowbanks, warming myself with my sweetly virtuous insides. So it goes."

Just so. One thing that happened to Milgram back in New Haven during the days of the experiment was that he kept running into people he'd watched from behind the one-way glass. It gave him a funny feeling, seeing those people going about their everyday business in New Haven and knowing what they would do to Mr. Wallace if ordered to. Now that his research results are in and you've thought about it, you can get this funny feeling too. You don't need one-way glass. A glance in your own mirror may serve just as well.

23. THE MY LAI MASSACRE: A MILITARY CRIME OF OBEDIENCE

HERBERT KELMAN and V. LEE HAMILTON

The slaughter at My Lai is an instance of a class of violent acts that can be described as sanctioned massacres.... The occurrence of sanctioned massacres cannot be adequately explained by the existence of psychological forces.... Instead, the major instigators for this class of violence derive from the policy process.... Thus it is more instructive to look not at the motives for violence but at the conditions under which the usual moral inhibitions against violence become weakened.

This selection is part of Chapter 1 in the book, *Crimes of Obedience*. The My Lai massacre is one example of a crime in which individuals claimed that they were simply following the orders of someone who had a right to command them.

The My Lai massacre took place in the midst of war. The soldier is supposed to obey—yet obedience is supposed to be tempered by "ordinary sense and understanding," by moral convictions that make disobedience an obligation and obedience a crime. How is one supposed to know? Crimes committed in the midst of authority structures are all too common, not because people are simply mean or violent, but because the nature of the structure itself makes obedience seem morally acceptable.

In their conclusion to the chapter, the authors identify three processes that encourage people to surrender moral standards to commit sanctioned massacres: authorization, routinization, and dehumanization. There is a warning here: Each of us may be moral in most situations, but we may sometimes find ourselves in positions within social structures in which we are told to do something we know is wrong. What will we do?

March 16, 1968, was a busy day in U.S. history. Stateside, Robert F. Kennedy announced his presidential candidacy, challenging a sitting president from his own party—in part out of opposition to an undeclared and disastrous war. In Vietnam, the war continued. In many ways, March 16 may have been a typical day in that war. We will probably never know. But we do know that on that day, a typical company went on a mission—which may or may not have been typical—to a village called Son (or Song) My. Most of what is remembered from that mission occurred in the subhamlet known to Americans as My Lai 4.

The My Lai massacre was investigated, and charges were brought in 1969 and 1970. Trials and disciplinary actions lasted into 1971. Entire books have been written about the army's year-long cover-up of the massacre (for example, Hersh 1972), and the cover-up was a major focus of the army's own investigation of the incident. Our central concern here is the massacre itself— a crime of obedience—and public reactions to

Excerpted from *Crimes of Obedience*, by Herbert C. Kelman and V. Lee Hamilton, pp. 1—22. Copyright © 1989, by YaleUniversity. All rights reserved. Reprinted by permission of Yale University Press.

such crimes, rather than the lengths to which many went to deny the event. Therefore this account concentrates on one day: March 16, 1968.[1]

Many verbal testimonials to the horrors that occurred at My Lai were available. More unusual was the fact that an army photographer, Ronald Haeberle, was assigned the task of documenting the anticipated military engagement at My Lai—he documented a massacre instead. Later, as the story of the massacre emerged, his photographs were widely distributed and seared the public conscience. What might have been dismissed as unreal or exaggerated was depicted in photographs of demonstrable authenticity. The dominant image appeared on the cover of *Life*: Piles of bodies jumbled together in a ditch along a trail—the dead all apparently unarmed. All were Oriental, and all appeared to be children, women, or old men. Clearly there had been a mass execution, one whose image would not quickly fade.

So many bodies (over twenty in the cover photo alone) are hard to imagine as the handiwork of one killer. These were not. They were the product of what we call a *crime of obedience*. Crimes of obedience begin with orders. But orders are often vague and rarely survive with any clarity the transition from one authority down a chain of subordinates to the ultimate actors. The operation at Son My was no exception.

"Charlie" Company, Company C, under Lt. Col. Frank Barker's command, arrived in Vietnam in December 1967. As the army's investigative unit, directed by Lt. Gen. William R. Peers, characterized the personnel, they "contained no significant deviation from the average" for the time. Seymour S. Hersh (1970) described the "average" more explicitly: "Most of the men in Charlie Company had volunteered for the draft, only a few had gone to college for even one year. Nearly half were black, with a few Mexican-Americans. Most were eighteen to twenty-two years old. The favorite reading matter of Charlie Company, like that of other line infantry units in Vietnam, was comic books" (p. 18). The action at My Lai, like that throughout Vietnam, was fought by a cross-section of those Americans who either believed in the war or lacked the social resources to avoid participating in it. Charlie

Company was indeed average for that time, that place, and that war.

Two key figures in Charlie Company were more unusual. The company's commander, Capt. Ernest Medina, was an upwardly mobile Mexican-American who wanted to make the army his career, although he feared that he might never advance beyond captain because of his lack of formal education. His eagerness had earned him a nickname among his men: "Mad Dog Medina." One of his admirers was the platoon leader, Second Lt. William L. Calley, Jr., an undistinguished, five-foot-three-inch junior-college dropout who had failed four of the seven courses in which he had enrolled his first year. Many viewed him as one of those "instant officers" made possible only by the army's then-desperate need for manpower. Whatever the cause, he was an insecure leader whose frequent claim was "I'm the boss." His nickname among some of the troops was "Surfside 5 1/2," a reference to the swashbuckling heroes of a popular television show, "Surfside 6."

The Son My operation was planned by Lieutenant Colonel Barker and his staff as a search-and-destroy mission with the objective of rooting out the Forty-Eighth Viet Cong Battalion from their base area of Son My village. Apparently, no written orders were ever issued. Barker's superior, Col. Oran Henderson, arrived at the staging point the day before. Among the issues he reviewed with the assembled officers were some of the weaknesses of prior operations by their units, including their failure to be appropriately aggressive in pursuit of the enemy. Later briefings by Lieutenant Colonel Barker and his staff asserted that no one except Viet Cong was expected to be in the village after 7 A.M. on the following day. The "innocent" would all be at the market. Those present at the briefings gave conflicting accounts of Barker's exact orders, but he conveyed at least a strong suggestion that the Son My area was to be obliterated. As the army's inquiry reported: "While there is some conflict in the testimony as to whether LTC Barker ordered the destruction of houses, dwellings, livestock, and other foodstuffs in the Song My area, the preponderance of the evidence indicates that such destruction was implied, if not specifically directed, by his orders of 15 March" (Peers Report, in Goldstein et al. 1976, p. 94).

Evidence that Barker ordered the killing of civilians is even more murky. What does seem clear, however, is that—having asserted that civilians would be away at the market—he did not specify what was to be done with any who might nevertheless be found on the scene. The Peers Report therefore considered it "reasonable to conclude that LTC Barker's minimal or nonexistent instructions concerning the handling of noncombatants created the potential for grave misunderstandings as to his intentions and for interpretation of his orders as authority to fire, without restriction, on all persons found in target area" (Goldstein et al. 1976, p. 95). Because Barker was killed in action in June 1968, his own formal version of the truth was never available.

Charlie Company's Captain Medina was briefed for the operation by Barker and his staff. He then transmitted the already vague orders to his own men. Charlie Company was spoiling for a fight, having been totally frustrated during its months in Vietnam—first by waiting for battles that never came, then by incompetent forays led by inexperienced commanders, and finally by mines and booby traps. In fact, the emotion-laden funeral of a sergeant killed by a booby trap was held on March 15, the day before My Lai. Captain Medina gave the orders for the next day's action at the close of that funeral. Many were in a mood for revenge.

It is again unclear what was ordered. Although all participants were still alive by the time of the trials for the massacre, they were either on trial or probably felt under threat of trial. Memories are often flawed and self-serving at such times. It is apparent that Medina relayed to the men at least some of Barker's general message—to expect Viet Cong resistance, to burn, and to kill livestock. It is not clear that he ordered the slaughter of the inhabitants, but some of the men who heard him thought he had. One of those who claimed to have heard such orders was Lt. William Calley.

As March 16 dawned, much was expected of the operation by those who had set it into motion. Therefore a full complement of "brass" was present in helicopters overhead, including Barker, Colonel Henderson, and their superior,

Major General Koster (who went on to become commandant of West Point before the story of My Lai broke). On the ground, the troops were to carry with them one reporter and one photographer to immortalize the anticipated battle.

The action for Company C began at 7:30 as their first wave of helicopters touched down near the subhamlet of My Lai 4. By 7:47, all of Company C was present and set to fight. But instead of the Viet Cong Forty-Eighth Battalion, My Lai was filled with the old men, women, and children who were supposed to have gone to market. By this time, in their version of the war, and with whatever orders they thought they had heard, the men from Company C were nevertheless ready to find Viet Cong everywhere. By nightfall, the official tally was 128 VC killed and three weapons captured, although later unofficial body counts ran as high as 500. The operation at Son My was over. And by nightfall, as Hersh reported: "the Viet Cong were back in My Lai 4, helping the survivors bury the dead. It took five days. Most of the funeral speeches were made by the Communist guerrillas. Nguyen Bat was not a Communist at the time of the massacre, but the incident changed his mind. 'After the shooting,' he said, 'all the villagers became Communists'" (1970, p. 74). To this day, the memory of the massacre is kept alive by markers and plaques designating the spots where groups of villagers were killed, by a large statue, and by the My Lai Museum, established in 1975 (Williams 1985).

But what could have happened to leave American troops reporting a victory over Viet Cong when in fact they had killed hundreds of noncombatants? It is not hard to explain the report of victory; that is the essence of a cover-up. It is harder to understand how the killings came to be committed in the first place, making a cover-up necessary.

MASS EXECUTIONS AND THE DEFENSE OF SUPERIOR ORDERS

Some of the atrocities on March 16, 1968, were evidently unofficial, spontaneous acts: rapes, tortures, killings. For example, Hersh (1970) describes Charlie Company's Second Platoon as entering "My Lai 4 with guns blazing" (p. 50);

more graphically, Lieutenant "Brooks and his men in the second platoon to the north had begun to systematically ransack the hamlet and slaughter the people, kill the livestock, and destroy the crops. Men poured rifle and machine-gun fire into huts without knowing—or seemingly caring—who was inside" (pp. 49–50).

Some atrocities toward the end of the action were part of an almost casual "mopping-up," much of which was the responsibility of Lieutenant LaCross's Third Platoon of Charlie Company. The Peers Report states: "The entire 3rd Platoon then began moving into the western edge of My Lai (4), for the mop-up operation.... The squad...began to burn the houses in the southwestern portion of the hamlet" (Goldstein et al. 1976, p. 133). They became mingled with other platoons during a series of rapes and killings of survivors for which it was impossible to fix responsibility. Certainly, to a Vietnamese, all GIs would by this point look alike: "Nineteen year-old Nguyen Thi Ngoc Tuyet watched a baby trying to open her slain mother's blouse to nurse. A soldier shot the infant while it was struggling with the blouse, and then slashed it with his bayonet." Tuyet also said she saw another baby hacked to death by GIs wielding their bayonets. "Le Tong, a twenty-eight-year-old rice farmer, reported seeing one woman raped after GIs killed her children. Nguyen Khoa, a thirty-seven-year-old peasant, told of a thirteen-year-old girl who was raped before being killed. GIs then attacked Khoa's wife, tearing off her clothes. Before they could rape her, however, Khoa said, their six-year-old son, riddled with bullets, fell and saturated her with blood. The GIs left her alone" (Hersh 1970, p. 72). All of Company C was implicated in a pattern of death and destruction throughout the hamlet, much of which seemingly lacked rhyme or reason.

But a substantial amount of the killing was *organized* and traceable to one authority: the First Platoon's Lt. William Calley. Calley was originally charged with 109 killings, almost all of them mass executions at the trail and other locations. He stood trial for 102 of these killings, was convicted of 22 in 1971, and at first received a life sentence. Although others—both superior and subordinate to Calley—were brought to trial, he was the only one convicted for the My Lai

crimes. Thus, the only actions of My Lai for which *anyone* was ever convicted were mass executions, ordered and committed. We suspect that there are commonsense reasons why this one type of killing was singled out. In the midst of rapidly moving events with people running about, an execution of stationary targets is literally a still life that stands out and whose participants are clearly visible. It can be proven that specific people committed specific deeds. An execution, in contrast to the shooting of someone on the run, is also more likely to meet the legal definition of an act resulting from intent—with malice aforethought. Moreover, American military law specifically forbids the killing of unarmed civilians or military prisoners, as does the Geneva Convention between nations. Thus common sense, legal standards, and explicit doctrine all made such actions the likeliest target for prosecution....

The day's quiet beginning has already been noted. Troops landed and swept unopposed into the village. The three weapons eventually reported as the haul from the operation were picked up from three apparent Viet Cong who fled the village when the troops arrived and were pursued and killed by helicopter gunships. Obviously, the Viet Cong did frequent the area. But it appears that by about 8:00 A.M., no one who met the troops was aggressive, and no one was armed. By the laws of war, Charlie Company had no argument with such people.

As they moved into the village, the soldiers began to gather its inhabitants together. Shortly after 8:00 A.M., Lieutenant Calley told Pfc. Paul Meadlo that "you know what to do with" a group of villagers Meadlo was guarding. Estimates of the numbers in the group ranged as high as eighty women, children, and old men, and Meadlo's own estimate under oath was thirty to fifty people. As Meadlo later testified, Calley returned after ten or fifteen minutes: "He [Calley] said, 'How come they're not dead?' I said, 'I didn't know we were supposed to kill them.' He said, 'I want them dead.' He backed off twenty or thirty feet and started shooting into the people—the Viet Cong—shooting automatic. He was beside me. He burned four or five magazines. I burned off a few, about three. I helped shoot 'em" (Hammer 1971, p. 155). Meadlo himself and others testified that Meadlo cried as he fired; others reported him later to be sobbing and "all broke up." It would appear that to Lieutenant Calley's subordinates, something was unusual and stressful in these orders.

At the trial, the first specification in the murder charge against Calley was for this incident; he was accused of the premeditated murder of "an unknown number, not less than thirty, Oriental human beings, males and females of various ages, whose names are unknown, occupants of the village of My Lai 4, by means of shooting them with a rifle" (Goldstein et al. 1976, p. 497).

Among the helicopters flying reconnaissance above Son My was that of CWO Hugh Thompson. By 9:00 or soon after, Thompson had noticed some horrifying events from his perch. As he spotted wounded civilians, he sent down smoke markers so that soldiers on the ground could treat them. They killed them instead. He reported to headquarters, trying to persuade someone to stop what was going on. Barker, hearing the message, called down to Captain Medina. Medina, in turn, later claimed to have told Calley that it was "enough for today." But it was not yet enough.

At Calley's orders, his men began gathering the remaining villagers—roughly seventy-five individuals, mostly women and children—and herding them toward a drainage ditch. Accompanied by three or four enlisted men, Lieutenant Calley executed several batches of civilians who had been gathered into ditches. Some of the details of the process were entered into testimony in such accounts as Pfc. Dennis Conti's: "A lot of them, the people, were trying to get up and mostly they was just screaming and pretty bad shot up.... I seen a woman tried to get up. I seen Lieutenant Calley fire. He hit the side of her head and blew it off" (Hammer 1971, p. 125).

Testimony by other soldiers presented the shooting's aftermath. Specialist Four Charles Hall, asked by Prosecutor Aubrey Daniel how he knew the people in the ditch were dead, said: "There was blood coming from them. They were just scattered all over the ground in the ditch, some in piles and some scattered out 20, 25 meters perhaps up the ditch.... They were very old

people, very young children, and mothers.... There was blood all over them" (Goldstein et al. 1976, pp. 501–02). And Pfc. Gregory Olsen corroborated the general picture of the victims: "They were—the majority were women and children, some babies. I distinctly remember one middle-aged Vietnamese male dressed in white right at my feet as I crossed. None of the bodies were mangled in any way. There was blood. Some appeared to be dead, others followed me with their eyes as I walked across the ditch" (Goldstein et al. 1976, p. 502).

The second specification in the murder charge stated that Calley did "with premeditation, murder an unknown number of Oriental human beings, not less than seventy, males and females of various ages, whose names were unknown, occupants of the village of My Lai 4, by means of shooting them with a rifle" (Goldstein et al. 1976, p. 497). Calley was also charged with and tried for shootings of individuals (an old man and a child); these charges were clearly supplemental to the main issue at trial—the mass killings and how they came about.

It is noteworthy that, during these executions, more than one enlisted man avoided carrying out Calley's orders, and more than one, by sworn oath, directly refused to obey them. For example, Pfc. James Joseph Dursi testified, when asked if he fired when Lieutenant Calley ordered him to: "No. I just stood there. Meadlo turned to me after a couple of minutes and said 'Shoot! Why don't you shoot! Why don't you fire!' He was crying and yelling. I said, 'I can't! I won't!' And the people were screaming and crying and yelling. They kept firing for a couple of minutes, mostly automatic and semi-automatic" (Hammer 1971, p. 143)....

Disobedience of Lieutenant Calley's own orders to kill represented a serious legal and moral threat to a defense *based* on superior orders, such as Calley was attempting. This defense had to assert that the orders seemed reasonable enough to carry out, that they appeared to be legal orders. Even if the orders in question were not legal, the defense had to assert that an ordinary individual could not and should not be expected to see the distinction. In short, if what happened was "business as usual," even though it might be bad business, then the defendant stood a chance of acquittal. But under direct command from "Surfside 5 1/2," some ordinary enlisted men managed to refuse, to avoid, or at least to stop doing what they were ordered to do. As "reasonable men" of "ordinary sense and understanding," they had apparently found something awry that morning; and it would have been hard for an officer to plead successfully that he was more ordinary than his men in his capacity to evaluate the reasonableness of orders.

Even those who obeyed Calley's orders showed great stress. For example, Meadlo eventually began to argue and cry directly in front of Calley. Pfc. Herbert Carter shot himself in the foot, possibly because he could no longer take what he was doing. We were not destined to hear a sworn version of the incident because neither side at the Calley trial called him to testify.

The most unusual instance of resistance to authority came from the skies. CWO Hugh Thompson, who had protested the apparent carnage of civilians, was Calley's inferior in rank but was not in his line of command. He was also watching the ditch from his helicopter and noticed some people moving after the first round of slaughter—chiefly children who had been shielded by their mothers' bodies. Landing to rescue the wounded, he also found some villagers hiding in a nearby bunker. Protecting the Vietnamese with his own body, Thompson ordered his men to train their guns on the Americans and to open fire if the Americans fired on the Vietnamese. He then radioed for additional rescue helicopters and stood between the Vietnamese and the Americans under Calley's command until the Vietnamese could be evacuated. He later returned to the ditch to unearth a child buried, unharmed, beneath layers of bodies. In October 1969, Thompson was awarded the Distinguished Flying Cross for heroism at My Lai, specifically (albeit inaccurately) for the rescue of children hiding in a bunker "between Viet Cong forces and advancing friendly forces" and for the rescue of a wounded child "caught in the intense crossfire" (Hersh 1970, p. 119). Four months earlier, at the Pentagon, Thompson had identified Calley as having been at the ditch.

By about 10:00 A.M., the massacre was winding down. The remaining actions consisted largely of isolated rapes and killings, "clean-up" shootings of the wounded, and the destruction of the village by fire. We have already seen some examples of these more indiscriminate and possibly less premeditated acts. By the 11:00 A.M. lunch break, when the exhausted men of Company C were relaxing, two young girls wandered back from a hiding place only to be invited to share lunch. This surrealist touch illustrates the extent to which the soldiers' action had become dissociated from its meaning. An hour earlier, some of these men were making sure that not even a child would escape the executioner's bullet. But now, the job was done and it was time for lunch—and in this new context, it seemed only natural to ask the children who had managed to escape execution to join them. The massacre had ended. It remained only for the Viet Cong to reap the political rewards among the survivors in hiding.

The army command in the area knew that something had gone wrong. Direct commanders, including Lieutenant Colonel Barker, had firsthand reports, such as Thompson's plaints. Others had such odd bits of evidence as the claim of 128 Viet Cong dead with a booty of only three weapons. But the cover-up of My Lai began at once. The operation was reported as a victory over a stronghold of the Viet Cong Forty-Eighth....

William Calley was not the only man tried for the events at My Lai. The actions of over thirty soldiers and civilians were scrutinized by investigators; over half of these had to face charges or disciplinary action of some sort. Targets of investigation included Captain Medina, who was tried, and various higher-ups, including General Koster. But Lieutenant Calley was the only person convicted, the only person to serve time.

The core of Lieutenant Calley's defense was superior orders. What this meant to him—in contrast to what it meant to the judge and jury—can be gleaned from his responses to a series of questions from his defense attorney, George Latimer, in which Calley sketched out his understanding of the laws of war and the actions that constitute doing one's duty within those laws:

Latimer: Did you receive any training...which had to do with the obedience to orders?

Calley: Yes, sir.

Latimer: …what were you informed [were] the principles involved in that field?

Calley: That all orders were to be assumed legal, that the soldier's job was to carry out any order given him to the best of his ability.

Latimer: …what might occur if you disobeyed an order by a senior officer?

Calley: You could be court-martialed for refusing an order and refusing an order in the face of the enemy, you could be sent to death, sir.

Latimer: [I am asking] whether you were required in any way, shape, or form to make a determination of the legality or illegality of an order?

Calley: No, sir. I was never told that I had the choice, sir.

Latimer: If you had a doubt about the order, what were you supposed to do?

Calley: …I was supposed to carry the order out and then come back and make my complaint (Hammer 1971, pp. 240–41).

Lieutenant Calley steadfastly maintained that his actions within My Lai had constituted, in his mind, carrying out orders from Captain Medina. Both his own actions and the orders he gave to others (such as the instruction to Meadlo to "waste 'em") were entirely in response to superior orders. He denied any intent to kill individuals and any but the most passing awareness of distinctions among the individuals: "I was ordered to go in there and destroy the enemy. That was my job on that day. That was the mission I was given. I did not sit down and think in terms of men, women, and children. They were all classified the same, and that was the classification that we dealt with, just as enemy soldiers." When Latimer asked if in his own opinion Calley had acted "rightly and according to your understanding of your directions and orders," Calley replied, "I felt then and I still do that I acted as I was directed, and I carried out the orders that I was given, and I do not feel wrong in doing so, sir" (Hammer 1971, p. 257).

His court-martial did not accept Calley's defense of superior orders and clearly did not share

his interpretation of his duty. The jury evidently reasoned that, even if there had been orders to destroy everything in sight and to "waste the Vietnamese," any reasonable person would have realized that such orders were illegal and should have refused to carry them out. The defense of superior orders under such conditions is inadmissible under international and military law. The U.S. Army's *Law of Land Warfare* (Dept. of the Army, 1956), for example, states that "the fact that the law of war has been violated pursuant to an order of a superior authority, whether military or civil, does not deprive the act in question of its character of a war crime, nor does it constitute a defense in the trial of an accused individual, unless he did not know and could not reasonably have been expected to know that that act was unlawful" and that "members of the armed forces are bound to obey only lawful orders" (Falk et al. 1971, pp. 71–72).

The disagreement between Calley and the court-martial seems to have revolved around the definition of the responsibilities of a subordinate to obey, on the one hand, and to evaluate, on the other…. For now, it can best be captured via the charge to the jury in the Calley court-martial, made by the trial judge, Col. Reid Kennedy. The forty-one pages of the charge include the following:

Both combatants captured by and noncombatants detained by the opposing force…have the right to be treated as prisoners…. Summary execution of detainees or prisoners is forbidden by law…. I therefore instruct you…that if unresisting human beings were killed at My Lai (4) while within the effective custody and control of our military forces, their deaths cannot be considered justified…. Thus if you find that Lieutenant Calley received an order directing him to kill unresisting Vietnamese within his control or within the control of his troops, *that order would be an illegal order.*

A determination that an order is illegal does not, of itself, assign criminal responsibility to the person following the order for acts done in compliance with it. Soldiers are taught to follow orders, and special attention is given to obedience of orders on the battlefield. Military effectiveness depends on obedience of orders. On the other hand, the obedience of a soldier is not the obedience of an automaton. A soldier is a reasoning agent, obliged to respond, not as a machine, but as a person. The law takes these factors into account in assessing criminal responsibility for acts done in compliance with illegal orders.

The acts of a subordinate done in compliance with an unlawful order given him by his superior are excused and impose no criminal liability upon him unless the superior's order is one which a man of *ordinary sense and understanding* would, under the circumstances, know to be unlawful, or if the order in question is actually known to the accused to be unlawful (Goldstein et al. 1976, pp. 525–526; emphasis added).

By this definition, subordinates take part in a balancing act, one tipped toward obedience but tempered by "ordinary sense and understanding."

A jury of combat veterans proceeded to convict William Calley of the premeditated murder of no less than twenty-two human beings. (The army, realizing some unfortunate connotations in referring to the victims as "Oriental human beings," eventually referred to them as "human beings.") Regarding the first specification in the murder charge, the bodies on the trail, he was convicted of premeditated murder of not less than one person. (Medical testimony had been able to pinpoint only one person whose wounds as revealed in Haeberle's photos were sure to be immediately fatal.) Regarding the second specification, the bodies in the ditch, Calley was convicted of the premeditated murder of not less than twenty human beings. Regarding additional specifications that he had killed an old man and a child, Calley was convicted of premeditated murder in the first case and of assault with intent to commit murder in the second.

Lieutenant Calley was initially sentenced to life imprisonment. That sentence was reduced: first to twenty years, eventually to ten (the latter by Secretary of Defense Callaway in 1974). Calley served three years before being released on bond. The time was spent under house arrest in his apartment, where he was able to receive visits from his girlfriend. He was granted parole on September 10, 1975.

SANCTIONED MASSACRES

The slaughter at My Lai is an instance of a class of violent acts that can be described as sanctioned massacres (Kelman 1973): acts of indiscriminate, ruthless, and often systematic mass violence, carried out by military or paramilitary personnel while engaged in officially sanctioned campaigns, the victims of which are defenseless and unresisting civilians, including old men, women, and children. Sanctioned massacres have occurred throughout history. Within American history, My Lai had its precursors in the Philippine war around the turn of the century (Schirmer 1971) and in the massacres of American Indians. Elsewhere in the world, one recalls the Nazis' "final solution" for European Jews, the massacres and deportations of Armenians by Turks, the liquidation of the kulaks and the great purges in the Soviet Union, and more recently the massacres in Indonesia and Bangladesh, in Biafra and Burundi, in South Africa and Mozambique, in Cambodia and Afghanistan, in Syria and Lebanon....

The occurrence of sanctioned massacres cannot be adequately explained by the existence of psychological forces—whether these be characterological dispositions to engage in murderous violence, or profound hostility against the target—so powerful that they must find expression in violent acts unhampered by moral restraints. Instead, the major instigators for this class of violence derive from the policy process. The question that really calls for psychological analysis is why so many people are willing to formulate, participate in, and condone policies that call for the mass killings of defenseless civilians. Thus it is more instructive to look not at the motives for violence but at the conditions under which the usual moral inhibitions against violence become weakened. Three social processes that tend to create such conditions can be identified: authorization, routinization, and dehumanization. Through *authorization*, the situation becomes so defined that the individual is absolved of the responsibility to make personal moral choices. Through *routinization*, the action becomes so organized that there is no opportunity for raising moral questions. Through *dehumanization*, the actors' attitudes toward the target and toward themselves become so structured that it is neither necessary nor possible for them to view the relationship in moral terms.

Authorization

Sanctioned massacres by definition occur in the context of an authority situation, a situation in which, at least for many of the participants, the moral principles that generally govern human relationships do not apply. Thus, when acts of violence are explicitly ordered, implicitly encouraged, tacitly approved, or at least permitted by legitimate authorities, people's readiness to commit or condone them is enhanced. That such acts are authorized seems to carry automatic justification for them. Behaviorally, authorization obviates the necessity of making judgments or choices. Not only do normal moral principles become inoperative, but—particularly when the actions are explicitly ordered—a different kind of morality, linked to the duty to obey superior orders, tends to take over.

In an authority situation, individuals characteristically feel obligated to obey the orders of the authorities, whether or not these orders correspond with their personal preferences. They see themselves as having no choice as long as they accept the legitimacy of the orders and of the authorities who give them. Individuals differ considerably in the degree to which—and the conditions under which—they are prepared to challenge the legitimacy of an order on the grounds that the order itself is illegal, or that those giving it have overstepped their authority, or that it stems from a policy that violates fundamental societal values. Regardless of such individual differences, however, the basic structure of a situation of legitimate authority requires subordinates to respond in terms of their role obligations rather than their personal preferences; they can openly disobey only by challenging the legitimacy of the authority. Often, people obey without question even though the behavior they engage in may entail great personal sacrifice or great harm to others.

An important corollary of the basic structure of the authority situation is that actors often do not see themselves as personally responsible for the consequences of their actions. Again, there are individual differences, depending on actors' capacity and readiness to evaluate the legitimacy of orders received. Insofar as they see themselves as having had no choice in their actions, however-

er, they do not feel personally responsible for them. They were not personal agents, but merely extensions of the authority. Thus, when their actions cause harm to others, they can feel relatively free of guilt. A similar mechanism operates when a person engages in antisocial behavior that was not ordered by the authorities but was tacitly encouraged and approved by them—even if only by making it clear that such behavior will not be punished. In this situation, behavior that was formerly illegitimate is legitimized by the authorities' acquiescence.

In the My Lai massacre, it is likely that the structure of the authority situation contributed to the massive violence in both ways—that is, by conveying the message that acts of violence against Vietnamese villagers were *required*, as well as the message that such acts, even if not ordered, were *permitted* by the authorities in charge. The actions at My Lai represented, at least in some respects, responses to explicit or implicit orders. Lieutenant Calley indicated, by orders and by example, that he wanted large numbers of villagers killed. Whether Calley himself had been ordered by his superiors to "waste" the whole area, as he claimed, remains a matter of controversy. Even if we assume, however, that he was not explicitly ordered to wipe out the village, he had reason to believe that such actions were expected by his superior officers. Indeed, the very nature of the war conveyed this expectation. The principal measure of military success was the "body count"—the number of enemy soldiers killed—and any Vietnamese killed by the U.S. military was commonly defined as a "Viet Cong." Thus, it was not totally bizarre for Calley to believe that what he was doing at My Lai was to increase his body count, as any good officer was expected to do.

Even to the extent that the actions at My Lai occurred spontaneously, without reference to superior orders, those committing them had reason to assume that such actions might be tacitly approved of by the military authorities. Not only had they failed to punish such acts in most cases, but the very strategies and tactics that the authorities consistently devised were based on the proposition that the civilian population of South Vietnam—whether "hostile" or "friendly"—was expendable. Such policies as search-and-destroy missions, the establishment of free-shooting zones, the use of antipersonnel weapons, the bombing of entire villages if they were suspected of harboring guerrillas, the forced migration of masses of the rural population, and the defoliation of vast forest areas helped legitimize acts of massive violence of the kind occurring at My Lai.

Some of the actions at My Lai suggest an orientation to authority based on unquestioning obedience to superior orders, no matter how destructive the actions these orders call for. Such obedience is specifically fostered in the course of military training and reinforced by the structure of the military authority situation. It also reflects, however, an ideological orientation that may be more widespread in the general population, as some of the data presented in this volume will demonstrate.

Routinization

Authorization processes create a situation in which people become involved in an action without considering its implications and without really making a decision. Once they have taken the initial step, they are in a new psychological and social situation in which the pressures to continue are powerful. As Lewin (1947) has pointed out, many forces that might originally have kept people out of a situation reverse direction once they have made a commitment (once they have gone through the "gate region") and now serve to keep them in the situation. For example, concern about the criminal nature of an action, which might originally have inhibited a person from becoming involved, may now lead to deeper involvement in efforts to justify the action and to avoid negative consequences.

Despite these forces, however, given the nature of the actions involved in sanctioned massacres, one might still expect moral scruples to intervene; but the likelihood of moral resistance is greatly reduced by transforming the action into routine, mechanical, highly programmed operations. Routinization fulfills two functions. First, it reduces the necessity of making decisions, thus minimizing the occasions in which moral questions may arise. Second, it makes it easier to avoid the implications of the action because the

actor focuses on the details of the job rather than on its meaning. The latter effect is more readily achieved among those who participate in sanctioned massacres from a distance—from their desks or even from the cockpits of their bombers.

Routinization operates both at the level of the individual actor and at the organizational level. Individual job performance is broken down into a series of discrete steps, most of them carried out in automatic, regularized fashion. It becomes easy to forget the nature of the product that emerges from this process. When Lieutenant Calley said of My Lai that it was "no great deal," he probably implied that it was all in a day's work. Organizationally, the task is divided among different offices, each of which has responsibility for a small portion of it. This arrangement diffuses responsibility and limits the amount and scope of decision making that is necessary. There is no expectation that the moral implications will be considered at any of these points, nor is there any opportunity to do so. The organizational processes also help further legitimize the actions of each participant. By proceeding in routine fashion—processing papers, exchanging memos, diligently carrying out their assigned tasks—the different units mutually reinforce each other in the view that what is going on must be perfectly normal, correct, and legitimate. The shared illusion that they are engaged in a legitimate enterprise helps the participants assimilate their activities to other purposes, such as the efficiency of their performance, the productivity of their unit, or the cohesiveness of their group (Janis 1972).

Normalization of atrocities is more difficult to the extent that there are constant reminders of the true meaning of the enterprise. Bureaucratic inventiveness in the use of language helps to cover up such meaning. For example, the SS had a set of *Sprachregelungen*, or "language rules," to govern descriptions of their extermination program. As Arendt (1964) points out, the term *language rule* in itself was "a code name; it meant what in ordinary language would be called a *lie*" (p. 85). The code names for killing and liquidation were "final solution," "evacuation," and "special treatment." The war in Indochina produced its own set of euphemisms, such as "protective reaction," "pacification," and "forced-draft urbanization and modernization."

The use of euphemisms allows participants in sanctioned massacres to differentiate their actions from ordinary killing and destruction and thus to avoid confronting their true meaning.

Dehumanization

Authorization processes override standard moral considerations; routinization processes reduce the likelihood that such considerations will arise. Still, the inhibitions against murdering one's fellow human beings are generally so strong that the victims must also be stripped of their human status if they are to be subjected to systematic killing. Insofar as they are dehumanized, the usual principles of morality no longer apply to them.

Sanctioned massacres become possible to the extent that the victims are deprived in the perpetrators' eyes of the two qualities essential to being perceived as fully human and included in the moral compact that governs human relationships: *identity* (standing as independent, distinctive individuals, capable of making choices and entitled to live their own lives) and *community* (fellow membership in an interconnected network of individuals who care for each other and respect each other's individuality and rights) (Kelman 1973; see also Bakan 1966 for a related distinction between "agency" and "communion"). Thus, when a group of people is defined entirely in terms of a category to which they belong, and when this category is excluded from the human family, moral restraints against killing them are more readily overcome.

Dehumanization of the enemy is a common phenomenon in any war situation. Sanctioned massacres, however, presuppose a more extreme degree of dehumanization, insofar as the killing is not in direct response to the target's threats or provocations. It is not what they have done that marks such victims for death but who they are— the category to which they happen to belong. They are the victims of policies that regard their systematic destruction as a desirable end or an acceptable means. Such extreme dehumanization becomes possible when the target group can readily be identified as a separate category of people who have historically been stigmatized and excluded by the victimizers. Often, the victims belong to a distinct racial, religious, ethnic, or political group regarded as inferior or sinister. The traditions, the habits, the images, and the vocabularies for dehumanizing such groups are already well established and can be drawn on when the groups are selected for massacre. Labels help deprive the victims of identity and community, as in the epithet "gooks" that was commonly used to refer to Vietnamese and other Indochinese peoples.

The dynamics of the massacre process itself further increase the participants' tendency to dehumanize their victims. Those who participate as part of the bureaucratic apparatus increasingly come to see their victims as bodies to be counted and entered into their reports, as faceless figures that will determine their productivity rates and promotions. Those who participate in the massacre directly—in the field, as it were—are reinforced in their perception of the victims as less than human by observing their very victimization. The only way they can justify what is being done to these people—both by others and by themselves—and the only way they can extract some degree of meaning out of the absurd events in which they find themselves participating (see Lifton 1971, 1973) is by coming to believe that the victims are subhuman and deserve to be rooted out. And thus the process of dehumanization feeds on itself.

NOTE

1. In reconstructing the events of that day, we consulted Hammer (1970), in addition to the sources cited in the text. Schell (1968) provided information on the region around My Lai. Concerning Vietnam and peasant rebellions, we consulted FitzGerald (1972), Paige (1975), Popkin (1979), and Wolf (1969).

REFERENCES

Arendt, H. (1964). *Eichmann in Jerusalem: A Report on the Banality of Evil.* New York: Viking Press.

Bakan, D. (1966). *The Duality of Human Existence.* Chicago: Rand McNally.

Department of the Army. (1956). *The Law of Land Warfare* (Field Manual, No. 27—10). Washington, DC: U.S. Government Printing Office.

Falk, R. A., G. Kolko, & R. J. Lifton (Eds.). (1971). *Crimes of War*. New York: Vintage Books.

FitzGerald, F. (1972). *Fire in the Lake: The Vietnamese and the Americans in Vietnam*. Boston: Atlantic-Little, Brown.

Goldstein, J., B. Marshall, & J. Schwartz (Eds.). (1976). *The My Lai Massacre and Its Cover-Up: Beyond the Reach of Law?* (The Peers report with a supplement and introductory essay on the limits of law). New York: Free Press.

Hammer, R. (1970). *One Morning in the War*. New York: Coward-McCann.

———. (1971). The *Court-Martial of Lt. Calley*. New York: Coward, McCann, & Geoghegan.

Hersh, S. (1970). *My Lai 4: A Report on the Massacre and Its Aftermath*. New York: Vintage Books.

———. (1972). *Cover-Up*. New York: Random House.

Janis, I. L. (1972). *Victims of Groupthink: A Psychological Study of Foreign-Policy Decisions and Fiascoes*. Boston: Houghton Mifflin.

Kelman, H. C. (1973). "Violence without Moral Restraint: Reflections on the Dehumanization of Victims and Victimizers." *Journal of Social Issues*, 29(4), 25—61.

Lewin, K. (1947). "Group Decision and Social Change." In T. M. Newcomb & E. L. Hartley (Eds.), *Readings in Social Psychology*. New York: Holt.

Lifton, R. J. (1971). "Existential Evil." In N. Sanford, C. Comstock, & Associates, *Sanctions for Evil: Sources of Social Destructiveness*. San Francisco: Jossey-Bass.

———. (1973). *Home from the War—Vietnam Veterans: Neither Victims nor Executioners*. New York: Simon & Schuster.

Paige, J. (1975). *Agrarian Revolution: Social Movements and Export Agriculture in the Underdeveloped World*. New York: Free Press.

Popkin, S. L. (1979). *The Rational Peasant: The Political Economy of Rural Society in Vietnam*. Berkeley: University of California Press.

Schell, J. (1968). *The Military Half*. New York: Vintage Books.

Schirmer, D. B. (1971, April 24). *My Lai Was Not the First Time*. New Republic, pp. 18—21.

Williams, B. (1985, April 14—15). "'I Will Never Forgive,' Says My Lai Survivor." *Jordan Times* (Amman), p. 4.

Wolf, E. (1969). *Peasant Wars of the Twentieth Century*. New York: Harper & Row.

24. GENDER AS STRUCTURE

BARBARA J. RISMAN

All structuralists presume that social structures exist outside individual desires or motives and that the structures can at least partially explain human action. All structural theorists would agree that social structure constrains human action or makes it possible.

Here is an excellent introduction of social structure applied to gender. Risman sees structure as constraint, thus affecting the individual, social interaction, and institutional control. It is on the level of interaction and institutions that makes a structural analysis complex and structure difficult to change. Risman also sees action turning against structure and even forming it, but never escaping it.

I build on this notion that gender is an entity in and of itself and has consequences at every level of analysis. And I share the concern that the very creation of difference is the foundation on which

From Barbara J. Risman, *Gender Vertigo: American Families in Transition*. Yale University Press. © 1998 by Yale University. All rights reserved.

inequality rests. In my view, it is most useful to conceptualize gender as a structure that has consequences for every aspect of society. And while the language of structure suits my purposes better than any other, it is not ideal. Despite its ubiquity in sociological discourse, no definition of the term "structure" is widely shared (see Smelser 1988 for a review of various structural traditions).

So I begin by explaining what I mean by structure and how I have derived my definition. Some consensus exists. All structuralists presume that social structures exist outside individual desires or motives and that the structures can at least partially explain human action. All structural theorists would agree that social structure constrains human action or makes it possible.

Blau's (1977) now classic definition of social structure focused solely on the constraint that collective life imposes on the individual. In their influential work, Blau and his colleagues (e.g., Rytina et al. 1988) have argued that the concept of structure is trivialized if it is located inside an individual's head in the form of internalized norms and values. Structure must be conceptualized, in this view, as a force opposing individual motivation. Structural concepts must be observable, external to the individual, and independent of individual motivation. This definition of structure imposes a clear dualism between structure and action, with structure as constraint and action as choice. I incorporate Blau's analysis of structure as constraint, but I reject the notion that structure constrains action only externally.

In order to analyze human action, we must understand not only how the social structure acts as constraint but also how and why actors choose one alternative over another. Burt (1982) suggests that actors compare themselves and their options to those in structurally similar positions. In this view, actors are purposive, rationally seeking to maximize their self-perceived well-being under social structural constraints.[1] Actions are a function of interests, but interests and ability to choose are patterned by the social structure. Burt suggests that norms develop when actors occupying similar network positions in the social structure evaluate their own options vis-à-vis the alternatives of similarly situated others. From such comparisons evolve both norms and feelings of relative deprivation or advantage. The social structure as the context of daily life creates action indirectly by shaping actors' perceptions of their interests and directly by constraining choice.

Giddens' (1984) theory adds considerable depth to the analysis of social structures as existing in a recursive relationship to individuals. That is, social structures shape individuals even as individuals are shaping their social structure. Giddens rejects a structuralism (e.g., Blau 1977) that ignores the transformative power of human action. He insists that any structural theory must be concerned with reflexivity and actors' interpretations of their own lives. When people act on structure, they do so for their own reasons. We must, therefore, be concerned with why people act as they do. Giddens insists that this concern go beyond the verbal justification easily available from actors because much of social life is so routine that actors will not articulate, or even consider, why they act. Giddens refers to this reality as practical consciousness. I refer to it as the cultural aspect of the social structure: the taken-for-granted or cognitive image rules that belong to the situational context (not only or necessarily to the actor's personality). Within this framework, we must pay considerable attention to how structure makes action possible as well as constrains it. We must bring individuals back into structural theories.

Connell (1987) applies Giddens' theory of social structure as both constraint and as created by action in his treatise on gender and power (see particularly chap. 5).[2] In his analysis, structure is assumed to specify what constrains action, and yet "since human action involves free invention … and is reflexive, practice can be turned against what constrains it; so structure can deliberately be the object of practice" (95). Action may turn against structure, but it can never escape it. An accurate analysis of any hierarchical relationship requires a focus both on how structure shapes interaction and on how human agency creates structure (Blackwelder 1993). A multilevel theory of gender as a social structure must acknowledge causality as recursive—action itself may change the immediate or future context. I build on Connell's analysis of the reflexivity of action and structure, although I return to that argument primarily in the last chapter.

Gender itself must be considered a structural property of society. It is not manifested just in our personalities, our cultural rules, or other institutions. Gender is deeply embedded as a basis for stratification, differentiating opportunities and constraints. This differentiation has consequences on three levels: (1) at the individual level, for the development of gendered selves; (2) at the interactional level, for men and women face different expectations even when they fill the identical structural position; and (3) at the institutional level, for rarely will women and men be given identical positions. Differentiation at the institutional level is based on explicit regulations or laws regarding resource distribution, whether resources be defined as access to opportunities or actual material goods. (See figure 1 for a schematic summary of the argument thus far.)

While the *gender structure* clearly affects selves, cultural rules, and institutions, far too much explanatory power is presumed to rest in the motivation of gendered selves. We live in a very individualistic society that teaches us to make our own choices and take responsibility for our own actions. What this has meant for theories about gender is that a tremendous amount of energy is spent on trying to understand why women and men "choose" to devote their life energies to such different enterprises. The distinctly socio-

logical contribution to the explanation hasn't had enough attention: even when individual women and men do *not* desire to live gendered lives or to support male dominance, they often find themselves compelled to do so by the logic of gendered choices. That is, interactional pressures and institutional design create gender and the resultant inequality, even in the absence of individual desires.

My argument and the data presented throughout this book show the strength of our gender structure at the interactional and institutional levels. Choices often assumed to be based on personalities and individual preferences (e.g., consequences of the gender structure at the individual level) are better understood as social connot that sex-role socialization or early childhood experience is trivial; gender structure creates gendered selves. But, at this point in history, sex-role socialization itself is ambivalent. In addition, it is clear that even women with feminist worldviews and substantial incomes are constrained by gender structures.

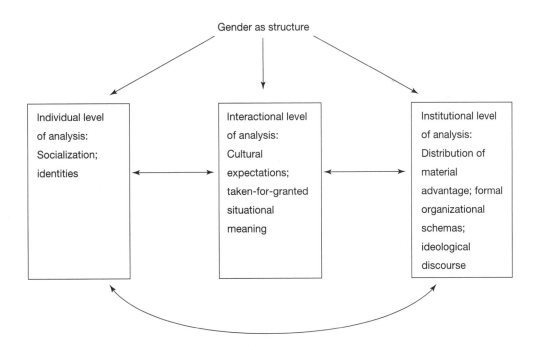

Gender as structure

| Individual level of analysis: Socialization; identities | Interactional level of analysis: Cultural expectations; taken-for-granted situational meaning | Institutional level of analysis: Distribution of material advantage; formal organizational schemas; ideological discourse |

Figure 1. Gender as Structure

In spite of the removal of some gender discrimination in both law and organizations, gender stratification remains. That is, formal access to opportunities may be gender neutral, yet equality of results may not ensue. Therefore, neither the individual-level explanations nor those based solely on institutional discrimination can explain continued gender stratification in families. Instead, the cognitive images to which we must respond during interaction are the engines that drive continued gender stratification when individuals desire egalitarian relationships and the law allows them (cf. Ridgeway 1997)....

The reconceptualization of gender as a social structure at every level helps us to understand stability and change in contemporary American marriage. Gender rules and cognitive expectations operate as interactional constraints that often create gender hierarchy even among heterosexual feminist couples who bring equivalent external material resources to their relationship. We find that the few heterosexual couples who can repudiate internalized gendered selves and overcome many of the barriers to equality in the workplace still often fail to find equality in marriage. Alternatives are so constrained within our gender structure that even those who consciously reject inequality based on gender may be contributing to the re-creation of gender stratified marriages and to a social structure that disadvantages women. The re-creation of a gender-stratified society is an unintended consequence of institutionally constrained actions—even of those committed to gender equality, and even in a society where laws are at least nominally gender-neutral. Gender structure at the interactional and institutional levels so thoroughly organizes our work, family, and community lives that even those who reject gender inequality in principle sometimes end up being compelled by the "logic" of gendered situations and cognitive images to choose gendered strategies.[3]

I do not mean to suggest that we do not all own gendered selves, or that institutional sexism has disappeared. Rather, I am simply suggesting that even if we overcame our gendered predispositions and were lucky enough to overcome most of the barriers of institutional sexism, the consequences of gender at the interactional level would still constrain our attempts at social change.

FEMINIST MARRIAGE: CONFLICT AMONG IMAGES, INSTITUTIONS, AND NEW SELVES

Traditional marriage is male dominated. The very terminology used to describe the husband—"the head of the household"—says it clearly. Yet it would be hard to isolate how gender structure *constrains* individuals when individual ideologies, cultural cognitive images, and the institutional force of law are all consistent and interdependent. The consequences of gender structure at the interactional and institutional levels are most easily illustrated when the structure operates in opposition to internalized normative desires. It is currently possible to analyze the effects of gender structure at the interactional and institutional levels despite individual-level opposition to stratification. That is, it is possible to imagine and locate couples committed to gender equality and to analyze how contextual and institutional levels of gender structure affect them. I argue that our gender structure pushes even committed feminists toward a gendered division of labor and toward male-dominated relationships.

On the cultural level, the consequences of gender structure clearly exist beyond the individuals involved. The normative expectations attached to gender in marriage (one aspect of the "rules") are very strong. Gender remains a "master status" (e.g., Hughes 1945), an organizing principle of marriage; expectations imputed to actors nearly always differ by sex. For example, men are not expected to assume a reflective identity (e.g., to become a Mr. Her) upon marriage. Because a reflective identity is based on association with someone else, it is a subordinate identity. Similarly, routine marital rituals are gender stratified. Bridal showers are based on the assumption that women will shoulder the responsibility for domestic labor. Fathers give away brides to the bridegrooms. Not all couples follow these rituals, of course. But when they do not, they are seen as making a choice that requires explanation. No choice is perceived, no explanations are needed, if rituals are followed. Most young couples, at least those without strong ideological commitments, follow the routine path without considering the unintended consequences: creating yet another stratified marriage.

Marriage is only one institution in which gender stratification is manifested, and it may not even be the most oppressive institution, softened as it can be by warm feelings. Yet marriage is one of the linchpins of inequality in American society. In what other institution are social roles, rights, and responsibilities based—even ideologically—on ascribed characteristics? When life options are tied to racial categories we call it racism at best and apartheid at worst. When life options are tied to gender categories we call it marriage.

The social structure clearly constrains gendered action even as it makes it possible. Wives, even those who have no motivation to provide domestic service to their husbands, are constrained to do so by social expectations. A husband who has a disheveled appearance reflects poorly on his wife's domestic abilities (in real life as well as "ring around the collar" commercials). A wife will be sanctioned by friends and family for keeping a cluttered and dusty home; a husband will not be. Husbands' behaviors are constrained as well. A husband who is content with a relatively low-wage, low-stress occupation may be pressured (by his wife, among others) to provide more for his family. Few wives, however, are pressured into higher-stress, higher-wage occupations by their families. The expectations we face during ongoing interaction often push us to behave as others want us to (Heiss 1981).

Cultural images within marriage also make gendered action possible. Husbands are not free to work long hours in order to climb the career ladder or increase income unless they are superordinate partners in a system in which wives provide them the "leisure" (i.e., freedom from responsibility for self-care or family care) to do so. Some married women may leave jobs they dislike because the position of domestic wife is open to them. A husband and father unable to keep a job has few other options for gaining self-esteem and identity.

Individuals often act in a structurally patterned fashion, without much thought. Routine is taken for granted even when the action re-creates the inequitable social structure. A woman may choose to change her name upon marriage simply because it seems easier. (Some women may not even know they are making a choice, as name change is so routine in their social circle.) Yet by changing her name a woman implicitly supports and re-creates a reflective definition of wifehood. She does gender. Similarly, when a woman assents to her children carrying her husband's surname (even when she herself has retained her own), she is re-creating a patrilineal system by which family identity is traced primarily through the male line. In both these examples a couple's intention may be to create a nuclear family identity and to avoid the awkwardness of hyphenated names for children. Whatever the intention, the structure has constrained the possible choices available to them. Their purposive actions may provide them with both the desired consequences (one family name) and the unintended consequence of re-creating a gender structure based on reflective female identity and patrilineal family names....

SUMMARY

I have argued that gender is a social structure. It organizes our entire world. At the individual level we learn who we are and want to be within a world where boys and girls are treated almost as though they were different kinds of creatures. At the interactional level our expectations for others' behaviors are filtered through a gender lens (Howard et al. 1996). The cultural rules and cognitive images that give shape and substance to our daily lives—especially those rules and images that surround our most intimate relationships—are profoundly attached to our biological sex. As the twentieth century closes, much of the formal, legalized, institutional sex discrimination has been eliminated, at least in Western societies. But the formal institutions to which we must all adapt—our workplaces, in particular—were built on assumptions both of gender difference and sexual inequality. Industrial capitalism could never have been organized as it now exists unless there was an implicit belief that paid workers were not, or should not be, responsible for the weak, the infirm, the aged, or the young.

The gender structure so pervades our lives that we often do not even see it. We fail to recognize that these differential expectations for men and women, for husbands and wives, are how sexual difference is transformed into gender stratification. I have argued that our gender structure at the interactional level is at the core of the male privilege still obvious in marriage and the family and that the structure of our interactional encounters re-creates gender stratification even when the people involved are committed to equality.

But does this theoretical perspective mean that we are doomed forever to re-create gender inequality? In the next three chapters I hope to convince the reader that gender is a social structure that we can get beyond. Gender need not organize our family systems, even if it always has done so.

NOTES

1. Burt's notion of purposive and rational action differs from that of more atomistic theorists because he does not assume that actors necessarily have enough information to act effectively in their own best interest. Nor does he assume that the consequences of actions are necessarily intended.
2. Connell refers to action as "practice."
3. Choosing the best of bad alternatives is clearly not a free choice at all. Still, I use the language of choice to remind readers that individual actors wrestle with alternatives and make decisions.

REFERENCES

Blackwelder, Stephen P. 1993. "Duality of Structure in the Reproduction of Race, Class, and Gender Inequality." Paper presented at the Society for the Study of Social Problems Meetings, Miami.

Blau, Peter M. 1977. *Inequality and Heterogenity*. New York: Free Press.

Burt, Ronald S. 1982. *Toward a Structural Theory of Action*. New York: Academic Press.

Connell, Robert W. 1987. *Gender and Power: Society, the Person, and Sexual Politics*. Stanford, CA: Stanford University Press,

Giddens, Anthony. 1979. *Central Problems in Social Theory*. Berkeley: University of California Press.

Heiss, Jerold. 1981. "Social Rules." In *Social Psychology: Sociological Perspectives*, edited by Morris Rosenberg and Ralph H. Turner. New York: Basic Books.

Howard, Judith, Barbara Risman, Mary Romero, and Joey Sprague. 1996.

Hughes, Everett C. 1945. "Dilemmas and Contradictions of Status." *American Journal of Sociology* 50: 353–359.

Ridgeway, Cecilia. 1997. "Interaction and the Conservation of Gender Inequality: Considering Employment." *American Sociological Review* 62: 218–235.

Rytina, Steve, Peter Blau, Jenny Blum, and Joseph Schwartz. 1988. "Inequality and Intermarriage: Paradox of Motive and Constraint." *Social Forces* 66:645–675.

Smelser, Neil J. 1988. ""Social Structure." In *Handbook of Sociology*, edited by Neil J. Smelser. Beverly Hills, CA: Sage.

25. FOUR MODES OF INEQUALITY

WILLIAM M. DUGGER

Gender inequality is the domination of one gender by another....Race inequality is practiced by one race discriminating against another....Class inequality in capitalism is practiced through the exploitation of the workers by the capitalists....Nation inequality is practiced through the predation of powerful nations on weak nations....The groups are separate and unequal. Individuals do not choose to join one group or the other, but rather are assigned to a particular group by the operation of law, tradition, and myth. Culture and coercion, not individual preference and choice, are the operative factors.

William M. Dugger describes the meaning of structure related to gender, race, class, and nation. Structure is inequality, and inequality is practiced through domination, discrimination, exploitation, and predation. Dugger describes the myths that support inequality, and shows us how myths and practices are mutually supportive. He also criticizes the myths.

THE INEQUALITY TABLEAU

A mode of inequality is a social process whereby a powerful group of humans (top dogs) reaps benefits for itself at the expense of a less powerful group (underdogs). The process involves an institutionalized struggle over power, status, and wealth. Four modes of inequality will be discussed: (1) gender, (2) race, (3) class, and (4) nation. These do not include all of the ways in which humans take advantage of each other, but they do cover much of the ground. Moreover, the four modes overlap and reinforce each other.

Corresponding to each mode is a set of practices whereby the top dogs take advantage of the underdogs. These practices ensure that the top dogs win. Corresponding to each mode of inequality is also a set of enabling myths that culturally enforce the practices and "make the game seem fair" to both the top dogs and the underdogs. A focal point also exists for each mode of inequality. The focal point is a particular institution where the inequality resides—where the myths justifying it are learned and the practices realizing it actually take place. These focal points frequently change as the particular mode of inequality evolves. Moreover, corresponding to each mode is an antidote—a set of values, meanings, and beliefs—that can debunk the enabling myths. Inequality, then, is a whole complex of modes, practices, enabling myths, focal points, and antidotes. This complex does not reach a balance of forces. It is not an equilibrium system, but an interacting process of cumulative causation in which inequality either gets worse or better. Seldom, if ever, does it stay the same.

From William M. Dugger, "Four Modes of Inequality," pp. 21–38 in *Inequality: Radical Institutionalist Views on Race, Gender, Class, and Nation*, ed. William M. Dugger, Greenwood Press, 1996. By permission.

Values are central to inequality. They either rationalize it by making it seem fair and true, or they debunk it by pointing out its injustice and falsehood. We can pretend to be value neutral about inequality, but we never are.

Four Modes of Inequality Defined

Gender inequality is the domination of one gender by another. In our time and place (the twentieth century in the Western Hemisphere), men dominate women through a whole series of gendered practices. These practices are supported and justified by myths about female inferiority and male superiority. These myths are the substance of sexism. Sexist myths enable men to dominate women without feeling guilty and also enable women to be dominated without mass rebellion or suicide. The antidote to gender inequality is feminism.

Race inequality is practiced by one race discriminating against another. In our time and place, the most significant form is the discrimination of white Europeans against black Africans or other people of color. It is justified by myths about African, Asian, and Latin American inferiority and about European superiority. These myths are the substance of today's racism. Racist myths enable white Europeans to discriminate against non-European people of color without feeling guilty and also enable those people of color to adjust to their unfair treatment without fully realizing that it is unfair. The antidote to discrimination is civil rights.

Class inequality in capitalism is practiced through the exploitation of the workers by the capitalists. In Soviet communism, the workers were exploited by the nomenklatura. Class exploitation is supported by its own myths. In the West, the myths are about market efficiency, while in the East, the myths were formerly about the dictatorship of the proletariate. Class myths enable a powerful class to exploit a powerless class and are comparable to racist and sexist myths in terms of effect, if not in terms of content. The antidote to exploitation is economic democracy (see Dugger 1984).

Nation inequality is practiced through the predation of powerful nations on weak nations and is supported by jingoistic myths about national honor and foreign treachery. Jingoistic myths allow the members of powerful nations to take pride in the killing of the members of weak nations rather than feel shame. The antidote to national predation is internationalism. Table 1 summarizes all the modes, practices, myths, and antidotes.

Table 1 The Inequality Tableau

Modes	Practices	Myths	Antidotes
Gender	Domination	Sexism	Feminism
Race	Discrimination	Racism	Civil Rights
Class	Exploitation	Classism	Economic Democracy
Nation	Predation	Jingoism	Internationalism

FOUR MODES OF INEQUALITY EXPLAINED INSTITUTIONALLY

Mode of inequality refers to the way in which people are grouped for giving offense and for receiving it. The groups are separate and unequal. Individuals do not choose to join one group or the other, but rather are assigned to a particular group by the operation of law, tradition, and myth. Culture and coercion, not individual preference and choice, are the operative factors.

Grouping (1): The Class Mode of Inequality

When individuals are grouped into classes, the boundaries are based mainly on how they appropriate their incomes, but also on how large the incomes are. The upper class is composed of capitalists and people who have managed to appropriate large incomes for themselves. An exact number cannot be placed on just how large that income has to be, but the inexact nature of its boundary does not mean an upper class does not exist. It exists because its members have acquired and used differential economic advantages and have kept the lower strata from doing the same. The appropriation of large incomes can be done through the control of wealth or important services. Those who own or control industrial and financial capital—wealthy families, corporate executives, investment bankers, and the like—can use their capitalist position to enlarge their income. Such capitalists are the most powerful members of the upper class; they set its ideological tone and make it essentially a capitalist class. Those who control the delivery of financially important services—corporate lawyers, lobbyists, politicians, and the like—can also appropriate large incomes. The middle class is composed of the "wannabe" groups—those who want to appropriate large incomes but lack the differential advantage needed to do so. They are contenders but were born to the wrong parents; they were sent to the wrong schools, had access to the wrong social connections, or were steered into the wrong professions. Members of the lower class are not in contention, whether they themselves realize it or not. Enough class overlap and circulation between classes exists to allow a limited role for individual choice, merit, and luck. Nonetheless, membership in a particular class is determined primarily by what class a person is born into rather than that individual person's rise or fall (see Osberg 1984).

Although class is an economic category, it is also strongly influenced by cultural factors. The kind of school attended and the kind of learning that takes place there vary by class, as do family structures, religions, beliefs, values, and meanings. (For a conservative view of cultural factors and class, see Berger and Berger 1983. For a liberal view, see Jencks et al., 1972, 1979. For a radical view, see Green 1981; Harrington 1983.) All the basic institutions teach the youth of each class the values, beliefs, and meanings appropriate to their economic station in life. When the class role has been learned and accepted, the person will be well adjusted, perhaps even happy. When the class role is rejected, unhappiness and maladjustment result, and either a change in class will be attempted or a rebel will be made. (For further discussion see Moore 1978.)

Grouping (2): The Race Mode of Inequality

When individuals are grouped into races, the boundary between discriminating and discriminated groups is based on race, but race itself is as much a cultural heritage as it is a biological endowment. The particular form that the race mode of inequality takes in the United States will illustrate the point. (The classic work is Myrdal 1962.) "African American" is as much a cultural as a biological grouping. It does not necessarily include all people whose skin is black. Many people from India, Melanesia, and Sri Lanka are black, as are Native Australians. Many have their own problems and face their own injustices, but they are not in the racially discriminated group of African Americans. Even though the group of African Americans excludes many people whose skin is black, it also includes some people whose skin is white. People with white skins are African Americans if their ancestors were seized for slaves in Africa and forcibly transported to the Americas, where miscegenation and a whole myriad of laws, traditions, and myths forced generation after generation of, not only the dark-skinned, but also the fair-skinned, members of the group into an inferior position relative to "white" Europeans. Cultural learning, not genetics, was the principal factor operating throughout the period.

Grouping (3): The Gender Mode of Inequality

Females (those with ovaries) are assigned to the group called women and males (those with testicles) are assigned to the group called men. However, gender, like race, is as much cultural as it is biological. Female humans are taught to be women by their culture; male humans are taught to be men by their culture as well. What the assignees learn to become is determined by what the culture teaches them, not by their gonads. Humans with ovaries are expected to learn to be women. Humans with testicles are expected to learn to be men. That is, they learn how they are expected to behave in their assigned roles. Their genitals do not teach them; their culture does.

(The classic is Mead 1949.) The males of today are expected to be superior to the females, and the females are expected to be inferior to the males.

Grouping (4): The Nation Mode of Inequality

When people are grouped into nations, arbitrary geopolitical boundaries separate the groups into the chosen people and the foreigners. Such groupings are also based on ethnic differences within individual nations, and can produce a considerable degree of inequality. However, when ethnic differences are combined with the power of the nation-state, an even more effective mode of inequality is formed. (Religion plays a role as well but will not be discussed in this chapter.) A nation is an area controlled by one state, where allegiance is to that state rather than another. Cultural and language differences may further differentiate the people in one state from those in another. Moreover, the controlling states may accentuate the differences through state education, state religion, and other forms of propoganda. The individuals who happen to find themselves identified as French, German, Italian, or Russian are not so by nature. They must be taught these identities. Since the nation mode of grouping people is particularly arbitrary, it relies very heavily on the teaching of alleged group differences. People must be taught that foreigners are untrustworthy, ignorant, brutal, and inferior. Only then can national leaders use their jingoism for supporting attacks against other nations or for mounting a defense against (imagined) attacks. Those members of the underlying population who do not accept their assigned roles in these jingoistic activities are exiled, ridiculed, imprisoned, or executed. A complex system of passports and identification papers keeps track of people and makes sure they are assigned to the "correct" national group—whether they want to be or not. Formidable security agencies are created by each nation to implement the groupings. Security agencies such as the former Soviet State Security Committee (KGB) and the U.S. Central Intelligence Agency (CIA) and Federal Bureau of Investigation (FBI) become focal points of nationalism.

FOUR PRACTICES OF INEQUALITY

The practices of inequality are interrelated forms of parasitic collective action. They cannot be reduced down to just one abstract practice without doing great damage to the multifaceted reality of inequality. The domination of women by men is really not the same as the exploitation of workers by capitalists, nor is the discrimination against African Americans by European Americans the same as the German invasion of Poland. Consequently, each practice will be discussed separately.

Practice (1): Domination

The domination of women by men has an institutionalized focal point in patriarchal societies—the family. An institution—and the family is no exception—is made up of people performing activities according to a set of rules that are justified by a set of values, beliefs, and meanings. As people perform their activities according to the rules, they internalize the values, beliefs, and meanings that justify the rules. Domination within the patriarchal family involves the male parent telling the female parent and her offspring (if any) how to conduct family activities. The patriarch exercises power over the other family members, assigning them most of the burdens and appropriating for himself most of the benefits of the family's activities. The patriarch enjoys liberties, and the other family members suffer exposure to the liberties. The patriarch appropriates most of the family status, wealth, and power. In full-blown patriarchy, the family becomes the extension of the patriarch's will. The other family members cannot own property or appropriate income in their own names; they cannot display status on their own behalves, nor exercise power to serve their own authentic wills.

Following the path of least resistance, as most of us do, the members of the family accept the rules that support the male parent's practices because they accept the values, beliefs, and meanings that support them. Male parents come to believe that they are the best judges of what is best for the other members of the family and that resistance to their will is not just inconvenient to them, but harmful for the family and immoral as well. Female parents come to believe that *family* means the patriarchal family only, and that no other types of families or meanings are possible. The female parent also learns to value her subservient role in patriarchy and to feel a real loss if deprived of it.

The values, beliefs, and meanings that support male domination within the family also spread to other social institutions. The acceptance of the subservient wife/mother role generalizes to the acceptance of a subservient worker role—including the acceptance of low-paid occupations or of lower pay for the same kind of work that males do. In the twentieth century, domination originating in the family has been picked up by a new and rising social control mechanism—bureaucracy. As women have moved into paid work outside the home, they have partially escaped the practices of domination within the home only to become enmeshed in the practices of domination within the modern bureaucracy, which now controls the workplace in both capitalist enterprises and government agencies. Access to the highest-paying jobs is controlled by a web of rules and traditions favoring males over females; so, too, is access to status and power within the workplace. Furthermore, if women turn from the family to the welfare agency instead of the workplace, the story is largely the same. State and federal welfare agencies control access to the welfare system through a web of rules and regulations formulated by males and based on the traditional roles of the patriarchal family.

Practice (2): Discrimination

I will focus on discrimination against African Americans. While the focal point for patriarchy begins with the family and the process of procreation, the focal point for discrimination began with slavery and the process of production. Although slavery varied from state to state and even from region to region within the same state, it always was supported by a racist culture in which Europeans were considered to be the superiors and Africans, the inferiors. The racist culture dehumanized Africans, turning them into property that could be bought and sold at will.

Although the brutality of slavery varied, it always was coercive. Although the frequency of selling slaves varied, the owner's right to sell a human being as a commodity always was retained.

Agitation by whites for reform and resistance from slaves generally hardened the attitudes of slave owners and increased their coercive hold over their slaves. Neither the slaves' resistance nor the abolitionists' moral outrage led to reform. Slavery was an either/or institution. It could not be reformed; it could only be abolished. It was not amenable to institutional adjustment. In this lies a lesson: incremental institutional adjustment, though desirable on its own merits, can lead to a hardening of inequality. Incremental institutional adjustment can act more like a vaccine against progress toward equality than a means of actually attaining equality. The Civil War finally ended slavery. (For further discussion, see Fogel and Engerman 1974; Genovese 1965, 1969; Hirshson 1962; Mellon 1988; Oates 1975; Stampp 1956; Low and Clift 1981, 756–96.)

Racism did not end with slavery; it has continued for 130 years. After reconstruction in the South, Jim Crow laws and sharecropping replaced slave codes and slavery itself. Now, however, instead of supporting slavery or sharecropping, racism supports a whole series of discriminatory practices diffused throughout the economy, society, and polity. In developments similar to those that are moving male domination over females out of the old focal point in the family and into the larger arena of the modern bureaucracy, the focal point for discrimination has moved, first out of slavery into sharecropping, and now out of sharecropping into bureaucracy. Now, educational bureaucracies control access to good education and training, while corporate and government bureaucracies control access to good jobs. Zoning laws, public housing bureaucracies, lending agent bureaucracies, and municipalities all control access to good housing. The bureaucratic rules and regulations are stacked against the African American in favor of the European American. The practice of discrimination has become institutionalized in the bureaucratic life of modern society. It has moved out of the production processes of the old agrarian South into the whole of society, where it is joined by male domination over females, upper class exploitation of the lower class, and the predation of the chosen people on foreigners.

Practice (3): Exploitation

The practice of class inequality is exploitation. Its focal point in capitalism is the hierarchical workplace, where owners hire workers and use them for producing commodities for a profit. The owners try to enlarge the flow of income that goes to them after all contractual costs are paid and after all costs that can be avoided are avoided (externalities). As in gender and race inequality, the practice of class inequality has become bureaucratized, and far more so than in the other modes of inequality. The production and sale of commodities for a profit is now organized by corporate bureaucracies. The income appropriated by the wage workers, middle managers, engineers, equity owners, and debt owners (rentier capital) is now the subject of bureaucratic rules, state regulations, court decisions, and continual struggle between different organizations and different hierarchical levels within organizations. The struggle is to obtain a differential economic advantage that will allow the appropriation of more income at the expense of those who have no such advantages. Such advantages are usually obtained through property ownership, but physicians, hospital administrators, lawyers, lobbyists, politicians, and even celebrities are also involved in the acquisition and use of differential economic advantages. The practices of exploitation are quite varied. Owners enlarge their incomes by pushing down wages and pushing up the prices of their products and by paying out higher dividends, interest, and rent to themselves. Chief executive officers of corporations enlarge their incomes by downsizing their companies and upsizing their own compensation packages. Physicians and hospital administrators charge exorbitant fees, perform unneeded services, and reap their rewards. Celebrities in the sports and entertainment fields push up their fees and salaries, endorsements, and such. We pay the higher ticket prices and wish that we could raise our "rates" as well. Lobbyists and politicians work out agreements between conflicting factions and pass new legislation that affects us all. Then they collect their fees for service rendered or leave public service for more lucrative private service, hoping the rest of us will not come to see whom they really serve.

Practice (4): Predation

The nation state is the focal point for predation, which is practiced through war and diplomacy. Favorable treatment is sought for the nation's elite groups of capitalist corporations and state bureaucracies (military or civilian). Successful predator nations build empires by forming shifting alliances with other predators, occupying opposing nations, subjecting opposing nations to unfavorable trade relations, or setting up puppet regimes within opposing nations.

Predation also allows the predatory apparatus of each state to extract status, power, and wealth from the underlying population of that state. The underlying population is induced to grant the state's predatory apparatus exceptional power in the name of defending the homeland. The liberties of citizens are reduced in the name of national security, and their exposure to arbitrary action by security officials is increased. Dissent becomes treason. Power is concentrated in the internal security apparatus and the external predatory apparatus. The status of the nation's predatory apparatus is increased by instilling in the underlying population the great importance of defending the homeland and of honoring those who do. Numerous medals and awards are granted to the national heroes as they fill up the cemeteries, hospitals, and prisons. The wealth of the nation's predatory apparatus is increased by inducing the underlying population to grant it exemplary taxing authority. (For further discussion see Melman 1983; Dumas 1986.)

Opposing predatory nations are busy doing the same thing. The activities of the one predatory apparatus gives the other predators stronger motivation to step up their own war preparations to a more feverish pitch. Each nation's predatory apparatus comes to serve as the reason for each other nation's predatory apparatus to expand itself. They are as much allies in their predation of their underlying populations as they are adversaries in their struggle against each other.

ENABLING MYTHS: THE CULTURAL SUPPORT OF INEQUALITY

Enabling myths are composed primarily of the stereotypes men believe about women, European Americans believe about African Americans, the upper class believes about the lower class, and the chosen people believe about foreigners. However, enabling myths are more than the stereotypes believed by the beneficiaries of inequality. Inequality must be justified, in the minds of both its victims and its beneficiaries. To avoid unrest among the victims, they must be taught that their treatment is not really unfair. To avoid guilty consciences among the beneficiaries—which is not nearly as important nor as difficult as avoiding unrest among the victims—the beneficiaries must be taught that their advantages are due them. Such learning is not resisted. It is easy to be convinced that one deserves all the good things that come one's way. Teaching acceptance to the victims is much harder and more important than teaching it to the beneficiaries, so it is the primary function of enabling myths. It is not easy to be convinced that one deserves all the bad things that come one's way.

Enabling myths also create "otherness" and this involves more than just instilling superiority in the top dogs and inferiority in the underdogs but also centrality and marginality For one to be superior, an "other" must be inferior. For one to be the center of things, an "other" must be on the margin. The enabling myths of sexism, for example, put males at the center of humanity and females on the margin. Simone de Beauvoir explained;

> Thus humanity is male and man defines woman not in herself but as relative to him; she is not regarded as an autonomous being. ... She is defined and differentiated with respect to man and not he with reference to her; she is the incidental, the inessential as opposed to the essential. He is the Subject, he is the Absolute—she is the Other. (Beauvoir [1952] 1989, xxii–xxiii)

(1) Sexism: The Myths Supporting Gender Inequality

Sexist myths begin with the category of "otherness." Males are the ones; they are the center. Females are the others; they are the margin.

Thus, when categorizing the human species we say "mankind" or "man." However, when we say "womankind" or "woman," we do not mean the human species. We mean women, the margin. Men are the categorically human; women are other. The justification for males dominating females begins here. Then it ranges far and wide. Public activities—those that yield wealth, status, and power—are the realm of men. Private activities—those that do not yield wealth, status, and power—are the realm of women. Men can speak better than women in public. Men are more intelligent and articulate. Men make better bosses. They are less emotional than women, more straightforward and honest in the pursuit of goals. Women are too emotional and intuitive, less straightforward. Their place is in the home. Man's place is in the world. Women who internalize these myths find it easier to accept their narrowed role in life. Men who internalize these myths find it easier to keep women in their narrowed role, to exclude them with no regrets. Well-adjusted men and women may even succeed in putting the confined role of women on a pedestal, and idealizing it as the embodiment of feminine truth and beauty.

This feminine mystique is a myth about the proper role of woman (Friedan [1963] 1983). It contains positive inducements to reward women for accepting it—they are put on a pedestal, and raised to the height of feminine truth and beauty. The myth also contains negative sanctions (taboos) to punish women for violating it—they are put in the pit, and accused of being untrue to their femininity and ugly to boot. (Just three centuries ago, we burned such women as witches.)

(2) Racism: The Myths Supporting Race Discrimination

Like sexist myths, racist myths also begin with "otherness." In the United States, literature refers to the writings of white Europeans; art means the works of white Europeans; culture, in short, means Greco-Roman culture. African writings are other; African art is other. Some exceptions exist: blues and jazz in music, and Pablo Picasso's adaptations of African art in painting and sculp-

ture are notable. Nonetheless, in the United States, the African American is still *the other*, and the European is still *the one*.

From the foundation of otherness, the myths of racism spring forth. Racist beliefs, like the other enabling myths, are opportunistic. They serve a purpose, even though their propogation and acceptance need not be consciously opportunistic. Racial myths are resistant to evidence contradicting them. They exist in the realm of magic and superstition, not that of fact and experience (Myrdal 1962, 100). They are related directly to the otherness of the African American in the mind of the European American. Racial myths are rational in the sense that they serve the purpose of enabling "whites" to take advantage of "blacks." However, racial myths are also profoundly irrational in the sense that they are psychologically grounded in magic and in superstitious dread of the unknown, of the other.

(3) Classism: The Myths Supporting Class Exploitation

Classist myths are the most sophisticated of all, as they are layered. The first layer of class myths supports the denial of class exploitation, while the second layer of myths supports the belief that the capitalist/Western world is a free market system. The third layer supports the belief that a free market system is neutral with respect to class, and that it involves no class exploitation, but only individual competition, which results in benefits for all.

We are constantly aware of class and of our own class standing relative to others. However, while we constantly think in terms of class, we do not think in terms of class exploitation. One of the most profound discoveries of Thorstein Veblen was that Americans in the lower strata seldom think of the upper strata in the bitter terms of exploitation. Rather than feel resentment, those in the lower strata feel envy. They do not want to overthrow their exploiters. They want to move up into the higher strata themselves (Veblen [1899] 1975). Americans do not think straight when it comes to class because they do not think of it in terms of exploitation. (For further discussion, see DeMott 1991.)

The denial of class exploitation is supported by the belief that ours is a free market system. Beneficial market competition, not differential economic advantage, is believed to be the way in which our economy distributes income. Milton Friedman's two works for the general reader, *Capitalism and Freedom* (1962) and *Free to Choose* (with Rose Friedman; 1980), are the most popular representations of the myth of the market system. In the mythical world of these two popular books, free markets are those that are unfettered by government interference. In such markets, monopolies cannot exist for long, and so the freedom of the market becomes the foundation for the freedom of the polity and the society. Furthermore, in these free markets, individuals are "free to choose," not only what they will buy and what they will sell, but also how prosperous they will become. If they are thrifty, innovative, willing to take risks, and hard working, they can rise very far. No barriers hold them back, unless government interferes with their efforts or unions either keep them out of lucrative employment or take away their profits with exorbitant wages.

The Friedmans do qualify their market utopia. They add in a central bank that provides a framework of monetary stability by following a growth rate rule for the money stock, if we could just agree how to measure the money stock. They also add in a negative income tax to help the poor and maybe also an educational voucher, allegedly to help poor children. They even recognize the need for a limited court system—one that enforces the rules and makes sure that contracts are performed. Nonetheless, the market utopia they describe will benefit us all, provided we keep government interference at a minimum.

There is no class exploitation in the Friedmans' world; no gender domination, racial discrimination, or national predation—unless it is instigated by government interference. The Friedmans' utopia sounds very much like the utopia of Adam Smith, with his system of natural liberty. However, a major difference destroys the similarity. Smith's utopia was used to attack the tyranny of the monarchy's mercantilism. It was used by the underdogs of the time to push their way through the barriers erected by the top dogs of the time. It was used by the upstart merchants and mechanics to rise up against the resistance of the landed aristocracy and against the power of the great, royally-chartered, monopoly-granted, trading companies (Smith 1937; Dugger 1990). While Smith's utopia was used to defend the efforts of the upstarts, the Friedmans' utopia is used to attack the efforts of the upstarts. The upstarts of Smith's time were the merchants and mechanics, but they have grown rich and become established. They are no longer the underdogs but rather the top dogs. The upstarts of the Friedmans' time now must push against the former merchants and mechanics, who have become great retailing corporations, giant industrial conglomerates, and entrenched managerial and professional groups.

The upstarts of the Friedmans' time are women dominated by men, African Americans discriminated against by European Americans, workers and communities exploited by corporate capital, and foreign devils preyed upon by the predatory apparatus of powerful nations. Moreover, the way they push up against the top dogs is to call upon the state, particularly the welfare state, to aid them in their struggle. However, the Friedmans insist that the underdogs should not call for help, or try to improve their position through state aid. Instead, they should simply aid themselves by working harder, being smarter, and saving more. If they do not thrive, it is their own fault. They were not talented enough or did not work hard enough. If the victims of domination, discrimination, exploitation, and predation actually believe that, the top dogs are safe.

What a powerful enabling myth this is. It not only enables class inequality, it enables all the other forms of inequality as well. The wretched of the earth have only themselves to blame for their wretchedness. Here is another important intersection of the different modes of inequality. They are all enabled by the market utopian myth. In fact, the market utopian myth is so powerful that its pull became irresistible to even the former Soviet nomenklatura, who abandoned the myth of the dictatorship of the proletariat for the myth of the utopian market. No longer able to keep the former Soviet masses in their subservient places with the old myth, the nomenklatura adopted a new myth. The new propaganda is for free markets, while the reality involves reconstructed centers of differential economic advantage hidden by a new cover of darkness.

(4) Jingoism: The Myths Supporting National Predation

Jingoism supports national predation. In the United States, jingoism means that "Americans" are "the one" and foreigners, "the other." We are the ones with the manifest destiny. This belief has been with us for a very long time and needs little further discussion here (see Baritz 1985; Slotkin, 1985). Jingoism also involves denial and projection, which form an effective mechanism to justify attack and this requires further elaboration.

When the predatory apparatus of the United States attacks another nation, the attack is accompanied by a denial of our own hostile intentions and by projection of hostile intentions onto the nation being attacked. The best recent example of the denial-projection mechanism involved stories circulated in the United States about Libyan hit squads infiltrating the country with instructions to assasinate important U.S. leaders. We subsequently learned that the stories and other alleged hostilities were not true, but they did provide us with the opportunity to justify an air raid against Libya by projecting our own hostile intentions onto the Libyans (see Woodward 1987).

The denial and projection mechanism also allowed us to take a number of hostile actions against the Sandinista government in Nicaragua. It is the foundation of our great fear of international terrorism. We see Saddam Hussein of Iraq as being at the center of a vast network of terrorists who are poised for a myriad of attacks against the United States, both at home and abroad. (For further discussion of the "terrorism terror" see Perdue 1989; Herman and O'Sullivan 1990.)

Jingoism differs from the other enabling myths in a very important and tragic way. In gender, class, and race inequality the enabling myths of sexism, classism, and racism can be inculcated in their negative forms in the underdog groups. However, this is far less possible in nation inequality. Leaders of one nation are hard-pressed to convince the people of the opposing nation that they are inferior foreign devils, which makes the nation mode of inequality a particularly unstable and violent form. With the underdog groups harder to fool, inequality between nations requires more violence to enforce. Husbands have killed their wayward wives in patriarchal societies. European Americans have killed disrespectful African Americans, and capitalists have killed revolting workers. However, such killing does not occur on the same vast scale as it does in nation inequality. Indeed, "chosen peoples" (nations) have killed tens of millions of foreigners in the last century alone. It seems easier to kill foreigners than to pacify them with myths.

Enabling myths do four related things simultaneously: (1) they provide an opportunistic rationalization of privilege, (2) they create a superstitious dread of the unknown in the minds of the top dogs, (3) they create the otherness of the victim, and (4) they make it possible to deny that injustice occurs by encouraging the underdogs to blame themselves.

THE ANTIDOTES FOR INEQUALITY

Means of debunking myths are readily available. However, debunking specific myths is not enough because as long as the practices of inequality persist, innovative minds will create new myths to support them. The practices of inequality must be changed, and doing so will take more than just a change of heart. It takes collective action to change social practices. The adage that "you cannot legislate morality" is exactly wrong. In fact, you cannot change morality unless you legislate change in practices. Change the practices and the morals will follow. What people come to believe derives, in large part, from what they do (see Veblen 1919, 1–31, 32–55). Then, however, they use some of their beliefs to justify what they do. In the first instance, their beliefs come from their habits of life; beliefs are largely habitual constructs. Thus, to change the beliefs, the myths that support inequality, the practices of inequality must also be changed.

Inequality, then, must be attacked from two directions simultaneously. First, the irrational myths that support inequality must be debunked. This is the responsibility of the churches, the schools, the sciences, the arts, and the social movements. Second, the actual practices of inequality must be transformed through collective action. This is the responsibility of the unions, the professional associations, the corporate boards, the courts, the legislatures, and, again, the social movements. The following remarks deal with debunking the myths rather than changing the practices.

Debunking the Myths

Unfortunately, rumors of evil foreign intentions spring up eternally, so they must continually be investigated and the truth or falsehood of them exposed on a case-by-case basis. The only way to deal with them as they arise is to have faith and insist upon an open society, an aggressive press, and an informed citizenry. Racist, sexist, and classist myths already have been debunked at length by numerous researchers. For my purposes here, only a brief discussion of the highlights of these debunking efforts is necessary.

With social Darwinism, enabling myths became "scientific." Biological differences between the races and sexes were measured and listed by researchers of high standing in scientific circles. One of the most infamous "scientific" myths supporting racism and sexism had to do with the allegedly biologically determined mental superiority of men over women and of the "white" race over the "black" race. The biological determinists were avid bone collectors and skull measurers—rigorously mathematical and objective. They created the "science" of craniometry. The craniometricians "proved" that the white race was mentally superior to the black race and that men were mentally superior to women because the craniums of men were larger than those of women and the craniums of whites were larger than those of blacks. Of course, many of their measurements were inaccurate and their samples biased. Nevertheless, their findings were accepted in wide university and scientific circles. However, when cranium size was finally related to body size, the results took a dramatic turn. Women were found to have larger craniums relative to their body size than men! Thus, the craniometricians lost heart, and face. How could they admit that women were actually more mentally

advanced than men? Of course, the craniometricians were men, and white ones at that. Moreover (needless to say), no evidence of any kind exists that can link mental ability to the size of the cranium of a healthy human of any color or sex (see Gould 1981; Montagu 1974; Ayres [1927] 1973). These first biological determinists, who were supporters of racism and sexism, were eventually debunked by other, better scientists. However, a new crop of biological determinists has stepped into the cultural vacuum to conjure up deceptive bell curves in place of cranium sizes.

Although the keepers of the sacred truths of classism behave much like the biological determinists before them, the myths of classism have a very different origin. The market myth goes back to Adam Smith, in whose hands it was not an enabling myth. It did not justify the inequality of the status quo; instead, it attacked that inequality. The market myth now defends inequality, but it did not start out that way. The market myth's origin is noble, not base, so debunking it is much harder.

THE DYNAMICS OF INEQUALITY: CIRCULAR PROCESS

Inequality is not an equilibrium state but a circular process. Inequality either gets worse or better, but it does not reach an equilibrium. The continued practice of inequality strengthens the myths that support it, and the stronger myths then lend even greater support to the practice. The resulting circular process is not characterized by offsetting forces that reach a balance but by cumulative causation that continues to move an inegalitarian society toward more inequality or continues to move an egalitarian society toward more equality. The inequality process is a vicious circle, but the equality process is a virtuous circle. Both processes are cumulative, not offsetting.

The Vicious Circle

Collective action of the top dogs against the underdogs establishes the practices of inequality. White Europeans established the great Atlantic slave trade. Males established patriarchy; state leaders established the system of nation-states; and property holders established capitalism. They all did so through collective action. Then, the myths of each form of inequality strengthened the practices of inequality. White Europeans came to believe themselves racially superior to black Africans. Black Africans, who were trapped in slavery, were taught that they must adjust to it or perish. The practice of patriarchy strengthened sexist myths, and the sexist myths then strengthened the sexist practices. State leaders established nation-states. We learned that we were English or French or German and that the foreigners were plotting against us. This strengthened the hands of the state leaders as they extracted more income, status, and power from the underlying populations. They used their gains in foreign plots, teaching us the truth in jingoism. Feudal property holders pushed us off the commons and taught us to value their private property. We believed them and worked ever harder for them, hoping that we could save enough to get some property for ourselves. In each mode of inequality, parasitic practices are established through collective action, and then enabling myths make the practices seem legitimate. The practices then become more entrenched because of the myths, and the myths begin to seem like truths because of the practices. The process is circular.

The Virtuous Circle

If the vicious circle were all there is to the story, we humans would probably have destroyed ourselves long ago. However, there is more. Just as there is a vicious circle of inequality, there is a virtuous circle of equality. Collective action of the underdogs against the top dogs can put an end to the practices of inequality, albeit perhaps only to establish another set of parasitic practices whereby the old underdogs attack the old top dogs. The first become last and the last become first; the meek inherit the earth. Perhaps however, the practices of inequality can be replaced with the practices of equality. The possibility of a virtuous circle replacing the vicious circle is not that remote. The religious leaders of the

American civil rights movement did not seek to replace white racism with black racism. Malcolm X became an enlightened antiracist, an egalitarian. Setting the example for the rest of us to follow, African-American collective action took the high road. African Americans took collective action against inequality and made considerable progress in eliminating racist practices and myths. Of course, much more needs to be done. Nevertheless, as racist practices were resisted by collective action and as racist myths were debunked, it became harder for white people to believe the myths and continue the practices. Thus, a virtuous circle was begun. Then, however, racial progress was interrupted, and then reversed by the Ronald Reagan administration and retrenchment. The vicious circle has replaced the virtuous, once again.

CONCLUDING REMARKS

This chapter supplied a simple vocabulary for describing inequality and suggested a dynamic framework of circular and cumulative causation for showing how the forces of inequality move in a reinforcing, rather than offsetting, fashion. The vocabulary includes the modes, practices, myths, focal points, and antidotes for inequality. A few examples and a bit of institutional context were provided to illustrate the concepts. The overall purpose was to help elucidate inequality and the different forms it takes, and to put the forms in an appropriate context. The treatment was introductory and exploratory, not exhaustive or definitive.

REFERENCES

Ayres, Clarence E. [1927] 1973. *Science: The False Messiah*. Clifton, NJ: Augustus M. Kelley.
Baritz, Loren. 1985. *Backfire*. New York: William Morrow.
Beauvoir, Simone de. [1952] 1989. *The Second Sex*. Translated and edited by H. M. Parshley. New York: Random House.
Becker, Gary S. 1971. *The Economics of Discrimination*. 2d ed. Chicago: University of Chicago Press.
___. 1981. *A Treatise on the Family*. Cambridge: Harvard University Press.

Berger, Brigitte, and Peter L. Berger. 1983. *The War over the Family*. Garden City, NY: Anchor Press/Doubleday.

Braverman, Harry. 1974. *Labor and Monopoly Capital*. New York: Monthly Review Press.

Coleman, Richard P., and Lee Rainwater, with Kent A. McClelland. 1978. *Social Standing in America*. New York: Basic Books.

DeMott, Benjamin. 1991. *The Imperial Middle*. New York: William Morrow.

Dugger, William M. 1984. "The Nature of Capital Accumulation and Technological Progress in the Modern Economy." *Journal of Economic Issues*, 18 (Sept.): 799–823.

___. 1989a. *Corporate Hegemony*. Westport, CT: Greenwood Press.

___. 1989b. "Instituted Process and Enabling Myth: The Two Faces of the Market." *Journal of Economic Issues*, 23 (June): 606–15.

___. ed. 1989c. *Radical Institutionalism*. Westport, CT: Greenwood Press.

___. 1990. "From Utopian Capitalism to the Dismal Science: The Effect of the French Revolution on Classical Economics." In Warren J. Samuels, ed., *Research in the History of Economic Thought and Methodology*. Vol. 8. Greenwich, CT.: JAI Press, pp. 153–73.

Dumas, Lloyd Jeffry. 1986. *The Overburdened Economy*. Berkeley: University of California Press.

Fogel, Robert William, and Stanley L. Engerman. 1974. *Time on the Cross*. Boston: Little, Brown and Company.

Friedan, Betty. [1963] 1983. *The Feminine Mystique*. New York: Dell Publishing.

Friedman, Milton. 1962. *Capitalism and Freedom*. Chicago: University of Chicago Press.

Friedman, Milton, and Rose Friedman, 1980. *Free to Choose*. New York: Avon Books.

Genovese, Eugene D. 1965. *The Political Economy of Slavery*. New York: Pantheon.

___. 1969. *The World the Slaveholders Made*. New York: Vintage Books.

Gould, Stephen Jay. 1981. *The Mismeasure of Man*. New York: W. W. Norton.

Green, Philip, 1981. *The Pursuit of Inequality*. New York: Pantheon.

Hacker, Andrew. 1995. *Two Nations*. New York: Ballantine Books.

Harrington, Michael. 1983. *The Politics at God's Funeral*. New York: Holt, Rinehart and Winston.

Herman, Edward S., and Gerry O'Sullivan. 1990. *The "Terrorism" Network*. New York: Pantheon.

Hirshson, Stanley P. 1962. *Farewell to the Bloody Shirt*. Chicago: Quadrangle Books.

Jencks, Christopher, and Marshall Smith, Henry Acland, Mary Jo Bane, David Cohen, Herbert Gintis, Barbara Heyns, Stephan Michelson. 1972. *Inequality*. New York: Basic Books.

Jencks, Christopher, and Susan Bartlett, Mary Corcoran, James Crouse, David Eaglesfield, Gregory Jackson, Kent McClelland, Peter Mueser, Michael Olneck, Joseph Schwartz, Sherry Ward, Jill Williams. 1979. *Who Gets Ahead?* New York: Basic Books.

Low, W. Augustus, and Virgil A. Clift. 1981. *Encyclopedia of Black America*. New York: Da Capo Press.

Mead, Margaret. 1949. *Male and Female*. New York: Dell Publishing.

Mellon, James, ed. 1988. *Bullwhip Days*. New York: Avon Books.

Melman, Seymour. 1983. *Profits without Production*. New York: Alfred A. Knopf.

Montagu, Ashley. 1974. *The Natural Superiority of Women*. Rev. ed. New York: Macmillan Publishing Company.

Moore, Barrington, Jr. 1978. *Injustice: The Social Bases of Obedience and Revolt*. White Plains, NY: M.E. Sharpe.

Myrdal, Gunnar. 1962. *An American Dilemma*. New York: Harper and Row.

Oates, Stephen B. 1975. *The Fires of Jubilee*. New York: Harper and Row.

Osberg, Lars. 1984. *Economic Inequality in the United States*. Armonk, NY: M. E. Sharpe.

Perdue, William D. 1989. *Terrorism and the State*. New York: Praeger.

Slotkin, Richard. 1985. *The Fatal Environment*. New York: Atheneum.

Smith, Adam. 1937. *The Wealth of Nations*. Edited by Edwin Canaan. New York: Modern Library.

Stampp, Kenneth M. 1956. *The Peculiar Institution*. New York: Vintage Books.

Stanfield, J. Ron. 1982. "Toward a New Value Standard in Economics." *Economic Forum*, 13 (Fall): 67–85.

Veblen, Thorstein. [1899] 1975. *The Theory of the Leisure Class*. New York: Augustus M. Kelley.

___. 1919. *The Place of Science in Modern Civilization and Other Essays*. New York: B. W. Huebsch.

Woodward, Bob. 1987. *Veil*. New York: Simon and Schuster.

PART V

Social Class

Social class is probably the most obvious way people are structured in society. Before the 1960s, most Americans believed that the United States was indeed a land of opportunity where each individual had an equal chance to make it to the top. Since then, most of us have come to realize that some people are born into poverty and find it very difficult to escape, while others are born into luxury with almost no chance to become poor. Many people do change their class to some extent, but the amount of change is usually small. No matter how we might try to deny its importance, class remains an important part of people's lives. It affects their "life chances" (their opportunities in life), and their "lifestyle" (how they live their lives) in very direct and indirect ways.

What is the meaning of democracy in a society characterized by a class system that excludes large numbers of people from participating, and that seems to be getting more extreme and less mobile? Is there any way to limit the riches of the few and the poverty of so many? What is the future of our society if present trends continue?

Sociologists tend to see class as an economic rank in society that makes a big difference in everyone's life. Almost always, class is considered in studies that sociologists perform and in theories they develop.

Four selections discuss class in Part V of this book. If you examine closely the rest of the book, you will note that there are a number of selections relevant to class.

Robert Purrucci and Earl Wysong examine what they describe as the new American class structure: not a diamond, not a pyramid, but a double diamond. Robert Coles describes to us the socialization of children of affluence in the United States, and Herbert Gans examines why it is so difficult to rid society of poverty. Finally, Bernard Rosen describes the blue-collar working class, both its decline in and anger toward recent economic developments.

26. THE NEW AMERICAN CLASS STRUCTURE

ROBERT PURRUCCI and EARL WYSONG

...although there may be 130 million Americans involved in occupations and jobs for which they are compensated, their amount of compensation varies widely according to how they are related to the production process.... The groups are distinguished as (1)those who own capital and business, (2) those who control corporations and the workers in those corporations, (3) those who possess credentialed knowledge, which provides a protected place in the labor market, (4) the self-employed, small-business owners who operate as solo entrepreneurs with limited capital, and (5) those with varying skills who have little to offer in the labor market but their capacity to work.

Here is an interesting and insightful analysis of class structure in America today. There are many ways to divide people into classes, but Purrucci and Wysong focus our attention on people's relationships to one another in the economic order rather than simply on income or wealth. They arrive at what they call a double-diamond diagram of class structure rather than the usual pyramid or single diamond. This emphasizes two major classes: a privileged class and a new working class.

In our society, the occupational structure as embedded in organizations is the key to understanding the class structure, and a person's occupation is one aspect of class position. But how do the hundreds of different occupations combine to create a structure of distinct classes with different amounts of economic, political, and social power? What aspects of occupations determine their position in the class structure?

People often speak of their occupation or their job as what they do for a living. An occupation or job describes how a person is related to the economy in a society or what one does in the process of the production of goods and services. An occupation or job provides people with the means to sustain life ("to make a living"); and the sum total of the work done by people in their occupations or jobs is the wealth generated by the economic

From Robert Perrucci and Earl Wysong, *The New Class Society*, Rowman & Littlefield Publishers, Inc., 1999. By permission.

system. In one sense there is a parallel or symmetric relation between the availability of jobs and the amount of wealth that is generated. The more people in a society are working at making a living, the better the economic health of the total society. But there is also sense in which there is an asymmetric relationship between the well-being of working people ("how much of a living they make") and the total wealth that is generated. Some people contribute more to the total wealth than they receive for their work, as in the case of some workers whose wages are a fraction of the value of their products when they are sold. And some people may receive ten or twenty times more in income for their work than that received by others. So although there may be 130 million Americans involved in occupations and jobs for which they are compensated, their amount of compensation varies widely according to how they related to the production process. There are a variety of ways in which people are related to the production process in today's economy.

The Privileged Class

The activity of some people in the system of production is focused on their role as owners of investment capital. Such a person may be referred to colloquially as the "boss" or, in more respectful circles, as a "captain of industry," an "entrepreneur," or a "creator of wealth," but in the language of class analysis they are all owner-employers. The owner may actually be the sole proprietor of the XYZ Corporation and be involved in the day-to-day decisions of running that corporation. But ownership may also consist in the possession of a large number of shares of stock in one or several corporations in which many other persons may also own stock. However, the ownership of stock is only socially and economically meaningful when (1) the value of shares owned is sufficient to constitute "making a living," or (2) the percentage of shares of stock owned relative to all shares is large enough to permit the owner of said shares to have some say in how the company is run. Members of this group (along with the managers and professionals) control most of the wealth in America. The point of this discussion is to distinguish owners of investment capital from the millions of Americans who own shares of stock in companies, who own mutual funds, or whose pension funds are invested in the stock market. The typical American stock owner does not make a living from that ownership and has nothing to say about the activities of the companies he or she "owns."

On the lower rungs of the owner-employer group are the proprietors of small but growing high-tech firms that bring together venture capital and specialized knowledge in areas involving biomedical products or services and computer software forms. These are "small" businesses only in Department of Commerce classifications (less than $500,000 in sales), for they bear no resemblance to the Korean grocer, the Mexican restaurant owner, or the African American hair salon found in many American cities. They are more typically spin-off firms created by technical specialists who have accumulated some capital from years of employment in an industrial lab or a university and have obtained other investment capital from friends, family, or private investors.

A second activity in the system of production is that of manager, the person who makes the day-to-day decisions involved in running a corporation, a firm, a division of a corporation, or a section within a company. Increasingly, managers have educational credentials and degrees in business, management, economics, or finance. Managers make decisions about how to use the millions of dollars of investment capital made available to them by the owners of investment capital.

The upper levels of the managerial group include the top management of the largest manufacturing, financial, and commercial firms in the United States. These managers receive substantial salaries and bonuses, along with additional opportunities to accumulate wealth. Table 1 presents a typical pattern of "modest" compensation for the officers of a large firm. We refer to this compensation as "modest" because it is far below the multimillion-dollar packages of compensation for CEOs at IBM, AT&T, Disney, and Coca-Cola (which range from $20

Table 1 Compensation for Corporate Executives

Position	Annual Compensation	Bonus	Stock Options
President and chief executive officer	$608,846	$325,000	$2,159,916
Executive vice pres. and financial officer	376,769	142,000	732,493
Senior vice president	267,861	146,000	390,663
Vice president	292,577	86,000	488,324
Vice president	262,500	67,000	488,329

Source: Based on data from the Annual Report and Proxy Statements, Great Lakes Chemical Corporation, 1997, West Lafayette, IN.

million to $50 million). But such distinctions are probably pointless, because we are describing executives whose wealth is enormous in comparison with others not in their class. For example, the top CEO in the listing above also owns 102,772 shares of stock in the corporation he heads. The value of these shares is $8,220,000. The executive vice president owns 166,488 shares, and the other VPs own "only" 25,000 to 75,000 shares.

Lower levels of the managerial group carry out the important function of supervising the work done by millions of workers who produce goods and services in the economy. The success of these managers, and their level of rewards, is determined by their ability to get workers to be more productive, which means to produce more at a lower cost.

Professionals carry out a third activity in the economic system. This group's power is based on the possession of credentialed knowledge or skill, such as an engineering degree, a teaching degree, or a degree in public relations. Some may work as "free professionals," providing service for a fee, such as doctors, dentists, or lawyers. But most professionals work for corporations, providing their specialized knowledge to enhance the profit-making potential of their firm or of firms that buy their services. The professional group is made up of university graduates with degrees in the professional schools of medicine, law, business, and engineering and in a variety of newly emerging fields (e.g., computer sciences) that serve the corporate sector. The possession of credentialed knowledge unifies an otherwise diverse group, which includes doctors who may earn $500,000 a year and computer specialists who earn $50,000 a year.

The potential to accumulate wealth is very great among certain segments of professionals. Median net salary in 1995 for all doctors was $160,000, ranging from a high median salary of $240,000 in radiology to $125,000 in family practice. Unfortunately, these averages hide the salaries of graduates from elite medical schools and those affiliated with the most prestigious hospitals. Also absent is information about doctor's entrepreneurial activities such as ownership of nursing homes or pharmaceutical firms.

Similar opportunities for high income exist among lawyers, where partners at the nation's elite law firms average $335,000 and associates average $80,000 (1988). Even law professors at prestigious law schools have a chance to amass a small fortune while teaching and practicing law or consulting. A recent *New York Times* story reported that a professor at Harvard Law School gave the school a bequest of $5 million.[1] The *Times* reported that the professor is "not one of the school's prominent moonlighters" and is "unlike Prof. Alan M. Dershowitz, the courtroom deity who has defended Leona Helmsley and Mike Tyson and is on the O.J. Simpson defense team." So how did the professor do it? By "writing and consulting."

Professors at elite universities who are in selected fields like law, medicine, business, biomedical engineering, or electrical engineering have opportunities to start high-tech firms and to consult for industry in ways that can significantly enhance income. Even "modest" activities, like becoming an outside director for a bank or industrial firm, can be very rewarding. A colleague in a business school at a Big Ten university who is a professor of management has been on the board of directors of a chemical corporation for twenty years. His annual retainer is $26,000. He gets an additional $1,000 a day for attending meetings of the board or committee meetings and $500 a day for participating in telephone conference meetings (the board meets six times a year, and committees from one to six times a year). Each non-employee director gets a $50,000 term life insurance policy and a $200,000 accidental death and dismemberment insurance policy. After serving on the board for a minimum of five years, directors are eligible for retirement benefits equal to the amount of the annual retainer at the time of retirement. Retirement benefits begin at the time of the director's retirement from the board and continue for life.

Why does the president of this university, or its Board of Trustees, allow a professor to engage in such lucrative "outside activities"? Maybe it's because the president, whose annual salary is $200,000, holds four director positions that give him more than $100,000 a year in additional income.

Professionals in elite settings not only make six-figure salaries, but they have enough "discretionary time" to pursue a second line of activity that may double or triple their basic salaries. Not a bad deal for the professional class.

Not everyone with a credentialed skill is in the privileged professional class. We exclude from this group workers like teachers, social workers, nurses, and most university professors at nonelite schools. They are excluded because of where they obtained their degrees, where they are employed, and the market for their skills. Each of these factors limits job security and provides very modest levels of income (i.e., consumption capital) and little investment capital. Thus, we distinguish between elite and marginal professional groups, with only the former being in the privileged class.

The New Working Class

Finally, there is the large majority of Americans: employees who sell their capacity to work to an employer in return for wages. This group typically carries out its daily work activities under the supervision of the managerial group. They have limited skills and limited job security. Such workers can see their jobs terminated with virtually no notice. The exception to this rule is the approximately 14 percent of workers who are unionized; but even union members are vulnerable to having their jobs eliminated by new technology, restructuring and downsizing, or the movement of production to overseas firms.

This working group also consists of the many thousands of very small businesses that include self-employed persons and family stores based on little more than "sweat equity." Many of these people have been "driven" to try self-employment as a protection against limited opportunities in the general labor market. But many are attracted to the idea of owning their own business, an idea that has a special place in the American value system: it means freedom from the insecurity and subservience of being an employee. For the wage worker, the opportunities for starting a business are severely limited by the absence of capital. Aspirations may be directed at a family

business in a neighborhood where one has lived, such as a dry-cleaning store, a beauty shop, a gas station, or a convenience store. Prospects for such businesses may depend upon an ethnic "niche" where the service, the customer, and the entrepreneur are tied together in a common cultural system relating to food or some personal service. The failure rate of these small businesses is very high, making self-employment a vulnerable, high-risk activity.

Another sizable segment of wage earners, perhaps 10–15 percent, has very weak links to the labor market. For these workers, working for wages takes place between long stretches of unemployment, when there may be shifts to welfare benefits or unemployment compensation. This latter group typically falls well below official poverty levels and should not be considered as part of the "working poor." The working poor consists of persons who are working full-time at low wages, with earnings of about $12,000 a year—what you get for working full-time at $6.00 an hour.

Table 2 provides a summary of these major segments of Americans with different standing in the current economy. The groups are distinguished as (1) those who own capital and business, (2) those who control corporations and the workers in those corporations, (3) those who possess credentialed knowledge, which provides a protected place in the labor market, (4) the self-employed, small-business owners who operate as solo entrepreneurs with limited capital, and (5) those with varying skills who have little to offer in the labor market but their capacity to work.

These segments of the class structure are defined by their access to essential life-sustaining resources and the stability of those resources over time. As discussed earlier, these resources include consumption capital, investment capital, skill capital, and social capital. The class segments differ in their access to stable resources over time, and they represent what is, for all practical purposes, a two-class structure, represented by a double diamond (see figure 1). The top diamond represents the privileged class, composed of those who have stable and secure resources that they can expect will be available to them over time. This privileged class can be subdivided into the superclass of owners, employers, and CEOs, who directly or indirectly control enormous economic resources, and the credentialed class of managers and professionals with the knowledge and expertise that is essential to major industrial, financial, commercial, and media corporations and key agencies of government. The bottom diamond is the new working class, composed of those who have unstable and insecure resources over time. One segment of this class has a level of consumption capital that provides income sufficient for home ownership and for consumption patterns that suggest they are "comfortable." Thus, we label this segment the comfort class, represented by school teachers, civil servants, social workers, nurses, some small-business owners, and skilled unionized carpenters, machin-ists, or electricians. Despite their relatively "high" incomes ($35,000–$50,000), the comfort class is vulnerable to major economic downturns or unforeseen crises (e.g., health problems) and has limited investment capital to buffer such crises.

The largest segment of the new working class is composed of the wage earners with modest skills and unpredictable job security. This group includes the machine operators in a manufacturing plant, bank clerks, and the supervisors who could be displaced by new production technology, computerized information systems, or other "smart" machines. Their job insecurity is similar to that of the growing segment of temporary and part-time workers, thereby making them the contingent class.

Table 2   Class Structure in America

Class Position	Class Characteristics	Percentage of Population
Privileged Class		
Superclass	Owners and employers. Make a living from investments or business ownership; incomes at six- to seven-figure level, yielding sizable consumption and investment capital.	1–2%
Credentialed Class		
Managers	Mid- and upper-level managers and CEOs of corporations and public organizations. Incomes for upper-level CEOs in seven-figure range, others, six-figures.	13–15%
Professionals	Possess credentialed skill in form of college and professional degrees. Use of social capital and organizational ties to advance interests. Wide range of incomes, from $75K to upper-six figures.	4–5%
New Working Class		
Comfort Class	Nurses, teachers, civil servants, very-small-business owners, and skilled and union carpenters machinists, or electricians. Incomes in the $35–50K range but little investment capital.	10%
Contingent Class		
Wage earners	Work for wages in clerical and sales jobs, personal services, and transportation and as skilled craft workers, machine operators, and assemblers. Members of this group are often college graduates. Incomes at $30K and lower.	50%
Self-employed	Usually self-employed with no employees, or family workers. Very modest incomes, with high potential for failure.	3–4%
Excluded class	In and out of the labor force in a variety of unskilled, temporary jobs.	10–15%

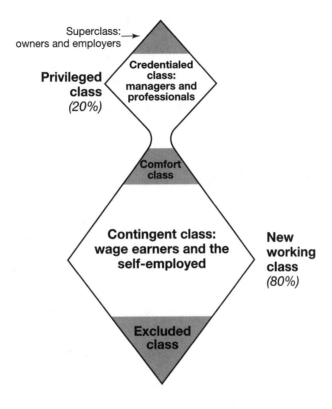

Figure 1 Double-diamond Diagram of Class Structure and Class

At the bottom of the new working class are those without marketable skills who move in and out of the labor force in temporary jobs or in seasonal employment. They are the excluded class, who either are treated as "waste," because they are no longer needed as either cheap labor or as consumers, or fill the most undesirable jobs in restaurant kitchens or as nighttime cleaners of downtown buildings.

It is important to keep in mind that a person's location in the double-diamond class structure is related to his or her occupation but not determined by that occupation (as is the case in the production and functionalist models of class, discussed earlier in this chapter). Some lawyers are in the top diamond, and some in the bottom. Some engineers, scientists, and professors are in the privileged class, and some in the new working class. It is not occupation that determines class position but access to generative capital—stable, secure resources over time.

THE NEW AMERICAN CLASS STRUCTURE DEFINED

Figure 1 provides a picture of the new American class structure as a "double diamond," divided between the privileged and those lacking the privileges that come with money, elite credentials, and social connections. This two-class structure is composed of approximately 20 percent privileged Americans and 80 percent nonprivileged Americans. Members of the employer, managerial, and professional classes have a stable income flow, employment stability, savings, pensions, and insurance. Their positions in the economy enable them to use their resources to accumulate more resources and to insure their stability over time. The new working class has little in the way of secure resources. Their jobs are unstable, as they can be eliminated by labor-replacing technology or corporate moves to offshore production. Only marginal professionals and craft workers possess some skills that provide short-term security, but even their skills are being eroded by new technology, the reorganization of work, and the decline of union power.[2]

This image of class structure in American society is based on three important principles that define the new American class structure and how it works in practice.

Class Structure Is Intergenerationally Permanent

One of the most significant aspects of class structures is their persistence over time. The inequality that a person experiences today provides the conditions that determine the future. This aspect of class structure is rarely discussed by the media or even by scholars devoted to the layer-cake image of inequality. In fact, most discussion of class structure views that structure, and one's place in it, as temporary and ever changing. The belief in equality of opportunity states that regardless of where a person starts out in life it is possible to move up through hard work, motivation, and education. Similarly, the overall structure is viewed as changing, as revealed in statistics on the median income, the expanding middle class, or the declining percentage of the population living below the poverty line. In short, the popular image of class differences is that they are temporary and constantly changing. But in fact, nothing could be further from the truth when it comes to the new class system in the United States.

The "rules of the game" that shape the class structure are designed to reproduce that structure. Let's consider a few of those "rules" and how they work.

First, our legal system gives corporations the right to close down a plant and move the operation overseas, but it does not give workers a right to their jobs. Owners and employers have property rights that permit wide latitude in making decisions that impact on workers and communities. But workers' jobs are not viewed as a property right in the law. The protected right to a secure job would provide workers with a stable resource over time and modify their vulnerable situation in the class system.

Second, people in privileged classes have unrestricted opportunities to accumulate wealth (i.e., extensive consumption capital and investment capital). The accumulation process is based on tax laws that favor the rich, a variety of loopholes to avoid taxes, and an investment climate that enables the rich to get richer. The share of net worth and financial wealth going to the top 20 percent of the population is staggering (see figure 1). One out of five Americans owns almost everything, while the other four are on the outside looking in.[3]

This extraordinary disparity in wealth not only provides a clear picture of the polarized two-class structure, it also provides the basis for persistence of that structure. Because inheritance and estate laws make it possible to do so, wealth is transmitted across generations, and privilege is thereby transmitted to each succeeding generation.

Another feature of the American class structure that contributes to its permanence is the sheer size of the privileged class. It consists of approximately twenty million households, or between forty million and fifty million people. A class of this numerical size, with its associated wealth, is able to fill all the top positions across the institutional spectrum. Moreover, it is able to fill vacant positions or newly created positions from among its own members. Thus, recruitment of talented women and men from the nonprivileged class will become increasingly rare.

Third, the so-called equality of opportunity in America is supposed to be provided by its system of public education. Yet anyone who has looked at the quality of education at the primary and secondary levels knows that it is linked to the class position of parents. Spending-per-pupil in public schools is tied to property taxes, and therefore the incomes of people in school districts. Schools in poor districts have the poorest physical facilities, libraries, laboratories, academic programs, and teachers.[4] Some of the children who survive this class-based public education are able to think about some sort of post-secondary education. But even here the game is stacked against them.

Going to college is based on the ability to pay the costs of tuition and, unless the student lives at home, room and board. Even at low-cost city colleges and state universities the expenses exceed what many working-class families can afford. On the other hand, even if college attendance were not tied to the ability to pay, it is not likely that many youngsters from low-income families would think of college as a realistic goal, given the low quality of their educational experience in primary and secondary grades.

Thus, the "rules of the game" that are the foundation for the class structure are designed primarily to transmit advantage and disadvantage across generations. This persistence of structure exists even when there are instances of upward social mobility—the sons and daughters of working-class families who move into the professional classes. This upward mobility occurs in a very selective way and without changing the rules of the game. For example, when the birthrates among the privileged class fail to produce enough children to fill all the jobs for doctors, lawyers, engineers, computer specialists, and managers, it is necessary to recruit the most talented young men and women from the working class. The most talented are identified through special testing programs and curriculum tracking and are encouraged to consider advanced education. "Elite" colleges and universities develop special financial and academic programs for talented working-class students, and a variety of fellowship programs support those with financial need. Upward mobility is made possible not by changing the rules of the game but by "creaming" the most talented members of the working class. The "creaming" process has the dual effect of siphoning off potential leaders from the working class and supporting the belief in equality of opportunity and upward mobility.

There Is No Middle Class

Most views of class structure, as noted earlier, present a "layer-cake" image of class differences. There are six or eight classes made up of groups of occupations that differ in prestige, education level, or income. These differences between classes are not sharp and discontinuous but gradual shadings of difference between one class and another. The layer-cake image encourages a belief in a "center" or a "middle class" that is large and stands between the upper and lower classes. The different groups in the middle may think of

themselves as being "better off" than those below them and may see opportunities to move up the "ladder" by improving education, job skills, or income.

This image of class structure is stabilizing, in that it encourages the acceptance of enormous material inequality in American society because of the belief that anyone can improve his or her situation and become one of the "rich and famous." It also encourages greater attention to the small differences between groups and tends to ignore the large differences. For example, many Americans are hardworking men and women who often work two jobs to make ends meet but are limited by these low-wage and no-benefit jobs. These people are often most hostile to the welfare benefits provided for people who are just below them in income. A working poor person gets $12,000 a year for full-time work, whereas a welfare family may get the same amount in total benefits without working. However, these same working poor rarely have their hostility shaped and directed toward the rich, who may be more responsible for the low wages, limited benefits, and inadequate pensions of the working poor.

The belief in a middle class also allows politicians to proclaim their support for tax breaks for what they call the middle class while debating whether the middle class includes those with incomes up to $150,000 a year or only those earning up to $100,000.

In our conception of class structure, there can be no middle class. Either you have stable, secure resources over time, or you do not. Either you have a stable job and income, or you do not. Either you have secure health insurance and pensions that provide adequate income, or you do not.

Classes Have Conflicting Interests

In the layer-cake theory of class structure, each class is viewed as having more or less of some valued quality or commodity such as education, occupational skill, or income. Members of each class may aspire to become members of classes above them, and they may harbor negative opinions and prejudices of those in classes below them. But classes, in this theory, are not fundamentally opposed to one another. Of course, there is often discussion of why members of certain classes might support or oppose particular political candidates because of their social or economic policies. But these alliances or oppositional views are seen as linked to shifting issues and are not tied to class interests.

In our view, the two large classes of privileged and working-class Americans have fundamentally different and opposed objective interests, so that when one class improves its situation the other class loses. The advantages of the privileged class, expressed in its consumption capital, investment capital, skill capital, and social capital, are enjoyed at the expense of the working class. Any action to make the resources of the working class more stable, by improving job security or increasing wages and pensions, for example, would result in some loss of capital or advantage for the privileged.

Consider the most extreme test of the existence of oppositional interests between the privileged and exploited classes. One might expect that the highest unifying symbol of the country—the presidency—might be above the taint of class interests. However, a recent unauthorized disclosure of a transcript of President Bill Clinton's meeting with President Boris Yeltsin of Russia sounds like two "petty professionals" trying to make the best deal for their services. "Collusion was recently exposed in a classified transcript of the Presidents' private meeting at the anti-terrorism summit in February [1996]. According to the leaked memorandum, Clinton promised Yeltsin support for his reelection bid with 'positive' U.S. policies toward Russia. In exchange, Clinton asked Yeltsin to lift trade barriers on imports of U.S. chicken parts (40 percent of which come from Arkansas—specifically, a large portion from Tyson Foods, a heavy contributor to Clinton's campaign)."[5] "Pimping" for chicken parts! If this is what goes on at the level of presidential discourse, what might be discussed at meetings of corporate executives, doctors, lawyers, and other credentialed elites? How do the sons, daughters, nephews, nieces, and probably even cousins of the elites get their jobs in the media, foundations, and other plush appointments in the nation's institutions? Slim chance that some bright graduate of a regional college (one with a direction in its name) who submits a resumé believing that the potential employer wants "the best person for the job" will ever be considered.

Given the existence of oppositional interests, it is expected that members of the privileged class will work to advance their interests. As employers they will seek to minimize worker wages and benefits and to fight efforts by workers to organize. As media owners, filmmakers, and writers they will produce cultural products and information that undermine efforts by the working class to organize and advance their interests. Think, for example, about how the media and opinion makers are quick to cry "class warfare" whenever someone points to the wealth of the privileged. Think also about how the opinion makers reacted to the role of Nation of Islam leader Louis Farrakhan in the Million-Man March on the Capitol mall in October of 1995. Every effort was made to discredit Farrakhan and to separate him from the march. The integrationist ideology of the slain civil rights leader Martin Luther King Jr. was resurrected over and over again, as if to say that the privileged class supports the legitimate aspirations of African Americans but not their efforts to develop their own social and economic communities and to ignore white society while doing so.

These three principles—Class structure has intergenerational permanence, There is no middle class, and Classes have conflicting interests—provide a basis for understanding the central defining features of the American class structure. We have, in effect, tried to answer the question, What is class inequality? In the next chapter we address the question, How does class inequality work?

NOTES

1. David Herzenhorn, "The Story Behind a Generous Gift to Harvard Law School," *New York Times*, April 7, 1995.
2. Harley Shaiken, *Work Transformed: Automation and Labor in the Computer Age* (New York: Holt, Rinehart and Winston, 1985); David F. Noble, *Forces of Production: A Social History of Industrial Automation* (New York: Knopf, 1984).
3. Edward N. Wolff, *Top Heavy* (New York: Twentieth Century Fund, 1996).
4. Jonathan Kozol, *Savage Inequalities: Children in America's Schools* (New York: Harper, 1991).
5. "Chicken on Chechnya?" *Nation*, April 29, 1996, 3.

27. THE CHILDREN OF AFFLUENCE

ROBERT COLES

There is, I think, a message that virtually all quite well-off American families transmit to their children—an emotional expression of those familiar, classbound prerogatives—money, and power. I use the word entitlement to describe that message.

Robert Coles has done a number of studies concerning class in the United States, focusing especially on the ideas and lives of children of poverty. This article is about the children of the affluent—those whom Coles describes as possessing a state of mind called *entitlement*, which claims as rights that which others regard as luxuries. This analysis goes far in showing how one's class influences what one expects from life, how those expectations are claimed as a matter of right, and how they influence what the child actually "chooses" to do in life.

Dramatic and secluded; old, historic, and architecturally interesting; large and with good grounds; private and palatial; beautifully restored; big, interesting, high up, and with an uninterrupted view; so the real-estate descriptions go. In the cities, it is a town house or luxury apartment on Nob Hill, Beacon Hill, the Near North Side, the Garden District. Outside the major cities, the house is in a town, township, village, station, even crossing. Anything to make it clear that one does not live simply "in the suburbs," that one is outside or away—well outside or well away, as it is so often put. The houses vary: imitation English castles; French provincial; nineteenth-century American; contemporary one-levels in the tradition of Gropius or Neutra. Sometimes the setting is formal, sometimes it is a farm—animals, rail fences, pastureland, a barn, maybe a shed or two, a flower garden, and more recently, a few rows of vegetables. Sometimes there is a swimming pool, a tennis court, a greenhouse. Sometimes the house stands on a hill, affords a view for miles around. Sometimes trees stand close guard; and beyond them, thick brush and more trees, a jumble of them: no view, but complete privacy. Sometimes there is a paved road leading from a street up to the house's entrance. Sometimes the road is a dusty path or a trail—the casual countrified scene, prized and jealously guarded.

The trees matter; so do the grass and the shrubbery. These are not houses in a row, with patches of new grass, fledgling trees, and a bush or two. These are homes surrounded by spacious lawns and announced by tall, sturdy trees. Hedges are common, carefully arranged. And often there is a brook running through the land.

In Texas or in New Mexico, the architecture of the houses changes, as do to a degree the flora and fauna. Now the homes are ranches, big sprawling ones, many rooms in many wings. Acres and acres of land are given over to horse trails, gardens, large swimming pools, even airplane strips for private planes. In New Mexico, the large adobe houses boast nearby cacti, corrals, and so often, stunning views: across a valley, over toward mountains miles and miles away.

In such settings are a small group of America's children raised. I have for years visited the homes of boys and girls whose parents are well-to-do indeed, and sometimes quite wealthy. They are parents whose decisions have affected, in one way or another, the working-class and poor families I have worked with—growers,

From *The Atlantic Monthly*, September 1977. By permission of Robert Coles.

mine owners, other prominent businessmen, lawyers, and bankers, or real estate operators. I have wanted to know how their children grew up, how their children see themselves—and how they see their much more humble age-mates, with whom they share American citizenship, if nothing else. Put differently, I have wanted to know how the extremes of class, poverty, and wealth variously affect the psychological and moral development of a particular nation's particular century's children.

"Comfortable, comfortable places" was the way one girl described her three homes: an enormous duplex apartment in Chicago, a ski lodge in Aspen, and a lovely old New England clapboard home by the ocean toward the end of Cape Cod. She was not bragging; she knew a pleasurable, cozy, even luxurious life when she saw one (had one), and was at ease describing its many, consistent comforts. She happened to be sitting on a large sofa as she offered her observation. She touched a nearby pillow, also rather large, then moved it a bit closer to herself. In a rather uncharacteristic burst of proprietary assertiveness, the girl said: "I'd like to keep this pillow for my own house, when I'm grown up."

Children like her have a lot to look after and, sometimes, feel attached to. At the same time, they may often be overwhelmed with toys, gadgets, presents. These are children who have to contend with, as well as to enjoy, enormous couches, pillows virtually as big as chairs, rugs that were meant to be in the palaces of the Middle East, dining room tables bigger than the rooms many American children share with brothers or sisters. Always they are aware of the importance and fragility of objects: a vase, a dish, a tray, a painting or lithograph or pencil sketch, a lamp. How much of that world can the child even comprehend? Sometimes, in a brave attempt to bring everything under control, a young child will enumerate (for the benefit of a teacher or a friend) all that is his or hers, the background against which a life is carried on.

Finally, the child may grow weary, abandon the spoken catalog and think of one part of his or her life that means *everything*: a snake that can reliably be seen in a certain stretch of mixed grass and shrubbery along the driveway; a pair of pheasants who come every morning to the lawn

and appear remarkably relaxed as they find food; a dog or a cat or a pony or a pet bird; a friend who lives near a summer home, or the son or daughter of a Caribbean cook or maid; a visit to an amusement park—a visit which, for the child, meant more than dozens of toys, some virtually untouched since they arrived; or a country remembered above all others—Ireland or England, France or Switzerland.

These are children who learn to live with *choices*: more clothes, a wider range of food, a greater number of games, toys, hobbies, than other boys and girls may ever be able to imagine for themselves. They learn also to assume instruction—not only at school, but at home—for tennis, swimming, dancing, horseback riding. And they learn, often enough, to feel competent at those sports, in control of themselves while playing them, and not least, able to move smoothly from one to the other rather than driven to excel. It is as if the various outdoor sports are like suits of clothing, to be put on, enjoyed, then casually slipped off.

Something else many of these children learn: The newspapers, the radio, the television offer news not merely about "others" but about neighbors, friends, acquaintances of one's parents—or about issues one's parents take seriously, talk about, sometimes get quite involved in. These are children who have discovered that the "news" may well be affected, if not crucially molded, by their parents as individuals or as members of a particular segment of society. Similarly, parental authority wielded in the world is matched by parental authority exerted at home. Servants are called in, are given instructions or, indeed, even replaced summarily. In a way, those servants—by whatever name or names they are called—are for these American children a microcosm of the larger world, as they will experience it. They are the people who provide convenience and comfort. They are the people who, by and large, aim to please. Not all of them "live in"; there are cleaning women, delivery people, caretakers, town inspectors, plumbers and carpenters and electricians, carriers of telegrams, of flowers, of special delivery letters. Far more than their parents, the children observe the coming and going, the back-door bustle, the front-door activity of the "staff."

It is a complicated world, a world that others watch with envy and with curiosity, with awe, anger, bitterness, resentment. It is a world, rather often, of action, of talk believed by the talkers to have meaning and importance, of schedules or timetables. It is a world in motion—yet, at times, one utterly still: a child in a garden, surrounded by the silence that acres of lawn or woods can provide. It is a world of excitement and achievement. It is an intensely private world that can suddenly become vulnerable to the notice of others. It is, obviously, a world of money and power—a twentieth-century American version of both. It is also a world in which children grow up, come to terms with their ample surroundings, take to them gladly, deal with them anxiously, and show themselves boys and girls who have their own special circumstances to master—a particular way of life to understand and become a part of.

ENTITLED

It won't do to talk of *the* affluent in America. It won't do to say that in our upper-middle-class suburbs, or among our wealthy, one observes clear-cut, consistent psychological or cultural characteristics. Even in relatively homogeneous places, there are substantial differences in home-life, in values taught, hobbies encouraged, beliefs advocated or sometimes virtually instilled.

But it is the obligation of a psychological observer like me, who wants to know how children make sense of a certain kind of life, to document as faithfully as possible the way a common heritage of money and power affects the assumptions of particular boys and girls. Each child, of course, is also influenced by certain social, racial, cultural, or religious traditions, or thoroughly idiosyncratic ones—a given family's tastes, sentiments, ideals. And yet, the sheer fact of class affiliation has enormous power over a child's inner life….

Wealth does not corrupt nor does it ennoble. But wealth does govern the minds of privileged children, gives them a peculiar kind of identity that they never lose, whether they grow up to be stockbrokers or communards, and whether they lead healthy or unstable lives. There is, I think, a message that virtually all quite well-off American families transmit to their children—an emotional expression of those familiar, classbound prerogatives, money and power. I use the word *entitlement* to describe that message.

The word was given to me by the rather rich parents of a child I began to talk with almost two decades ago, in 1959. I have watched those parents become grandparents, and have seen what they described as "the responsibilities of entitlement" handed down to a new generation. When the father, a lawyer and stockbroker from a prominent and quietly influential family, referred to the "entitlement" his children were growing up to know, he had in mind a social rather than a psychological phenomenon: the various juries or committees that select the Mardi Gras participants in New Orleans's annual parade and celebration. He knew that his daughter was "entitled" to be invited.

He wanted, however, to go beyond that social fact. He talked about what he had received from his parents and what he would give to his children, "automatically, without any thought," and what they too would pass on. The father was careful to distinguish between the social entitlement and "something else," a "something else" he couldn't quite define but knew he had to try to evoke if he was to be psychologically candid:

> Our children have a good life ahead of them; and I think they know it now. I think they did when they were three or four, too. It's *entitlement*, that's what I call it. My wife didn't know what I was talking about when I first used the word. She thought it had something to do with our ancestry. Maybe it does. I don't mean to be snide. I just think our children grow up taking a lot for granted, and it can be good that they do, and it can be bad. It's like anything else; it all depends. I mean, you can have spoiled brats for children, or you can have kids who want to share what they have. I don't mean give away all their money. I mean be responsible, and try to live up to their ideals, and not just sit around wondering which island in the Caribbean to visit this year, and where to go next summer to get away from the heat and humidity here in New Orleans.

At the time, he said no more; at the time, I wasn't especially interested in pursuing the subject. But as months became years, I came back to that word *entitlement*. There is, as it happens, a psychiatric term that closely connects with it.

Narcissistic entitlement is the phrase, when referring to a particular kind of "disturbed" child. The term could be used in place of the more conventional, blunter ones: a smug, self-satisfied child; or a child who thinks he owns the world, or will one day. It is an affliction that strikes particularly the wealthy child....

If narcissism is something a migrant child or a ghetto child has to contend with, it will take on one flavor (narcissistic despair, for instance), whereas for a child of wealth, narcissistic entitlement is the likely possibility. The child has much, but wants and expects more, all assumed to be his or hers by right—at once a psychological and material inheritance that the world will provide. One's parents will oblige, will be intermediaries, will go back and forth—bringing from stores or banks or wherever those various offerings that serve to gratify the mind's sense of its own importance, its own *due*.

This syndrome is one that wealthy parents recognize instinctively, often wordlessly—and fear. When their children are four, five, and six, parents able to offer them virtually anything sometimes begin to pull back, in concern if not in outright horror. Not only has a son become increasingly demanding or petulant; even when he is quiet, he seems to be sitting on a throne of sorts—expecting things to happen, wondering with annoyance why they don't, reassuring himself and others that they will or, if they don't, shrugging his shoulders and waiting for the next splendid moment.

It was just such an impasse—not dramatic, but quite definite and worrisome—that prompted the New Orleans father quoted earlier to use the word *entitlement*. He had himself been born to wealth, as will be the case for generations of his family to come, unless the American economic system changes drastically in the future. But he was worried about what a lot of money can do to a personality. When his young daughter, during a Mardi Gras season, kept *assuming* she would one day receive this honor and that honor—indeed, become a Mardi Gras queen— he realized that his notion of "entitlement" was

not quite hers. *Noblesse oblige* requires a gesture toward others.

He was not the only parent to express such a concern to me in the course of my work. In homes where mothers and fathers profess no explicit reformist persuasions, they nevertheless worry about what happens to children who grow up surrounded by just about everything they want, virtually on demand. "When they're like that, they've gone from spoiled to spoiled rotten—and beyond, to some state I don't know how to describe."

Obviously, it is possible for parents to have a lot of money yet avoid bringing up their children in such a way that they feel like members of a royal family. But even parents determined not to spoil their children often recognize what might be called the existential (as opposed to strictly psychological) aspects of their situation. A father may begin rather early on lecturing his children about the meaning of money; a mother may do her share by saying *no*, even when *yes* is so easy to say. Such a child, by the age of five or six, has very definite notions of what is possible, even if it is not always permitted. That child, in conversation, and without embarrassment or the kind of reticence and secretiveness that come later, may reveal a substantial knowledge of economic affairs. A six-year-old girl I spoke to knew that she would, at twenty-one, inherit half a million dollars. She also knew that her father "only" gave her twenty-five cents a week, whereas some friends of hers received as much as a dollar. She was vexed; she asked her parents why they were so "strict." One friend had even used the word "stingy" for the parents. The father, in a matter-of-fact way, pointed out to the daughter that she did, after all, get "anything she really wants." Why, then, the need for an extravagant allowance? The girl was won over. But admonitions don't always modify the quite realistic appraisal children make of what they are heir to; and they don't diminish their sense of entitlement—a state of mind that pervades their view of the world....

28. THE USES OF POVERTY: THE POOR PAY ALL

HERBERT J. GANS

Many of the functions served by the poor could be replaced if poverty were eliminated, but almost always at higher costs to others, particularly more affluent others.

This article examines the poor in America and shows how they are used in society and how they function for the rest of us. Herbert J. Gans is saying: Let's face it, you and I benefit from having the poor. Do not think that Gans is saying there must be a class of poor; instead he is arguing that, in capitalism, the poor are exploited in a number of ways. Eliminating the poor will be costly to the affluent. Poverty is then tied to the structure of society: People are kept in low positions in large part for the benefit of those in high positions. Those in high positions, because they benefit, refuse to make real changes that deal with ending poverty.

Associating poverty with positive functions seems at first glance to be unimaginable. Of course, the slumlord and the loan shark are commonly known to profit from the existence of poverty, but they are viewed as evil men, so their activities are classified among the dysfunctions of poverty. However, what is less often recognized, at least by the conventional wisdom, is that poverty also makes possible the existence or expansion of respectable professions and occupations, for example, penology, criminology, social work, and public health. More recently, the poor have provided jobs for professional and paraprofessional "poverty warriors," and for journalists and social scientists, this author included, who have supplied the information demanded by the revival of public interest in poverty.

Clearly, then, poverty and the poor may well satisfy a number of positive functions for many nonpoor groups in American society. I shall describe thirteen such functions—economic, social, and political—that seem to me most significant.

THE FUNCTIONS OF POVERTY

First, the existence of poverty ensures that society's "dirty work" will be done. Every society has such work: physically dirty or dangerous, temporary, dead-end and underpaid, undignified and menial jobs. Society can fill these jobs by paying higher wages than for "clean" work, or it can force people who have no other choice to do the dirty work—and at low wages. For America, poverty functions to provide a low-wage labor pool that is willing—or, rather, unable to be unwilling—to perform dirty work at low cost. Indeed, this function of the poor is so important that in some southern states, welfare payments have been cut off during the summer months when the poor are needed to work in the fields. Moreover, much of the debate about the negative income tax and the family assistance plan has concerned their impact on the work incentive, by which is actually meant the incentive of the poor to do the needed dirty work if the wages therefrom are no larger than the income grant. Many economic activities that involve dirty work depend on the poor for their existence: restaurants, hospitals, parts of the garment industry, and "truck farming,"

159

among others, could not persist in their present form without the poor.

Second, because the poor are required to work at low wages, they subsidize a variety of economic activities that benefit the affluent. For example, domestics subsidize the upper-middle and upper classes, making life easier for their employers and freeing affluent women for a variety of professional, cultural, civic, and partying activities. Similarly, because the poor pay a higher proportion of their income in property and sales taxes, among others, they subsidize many state and local governmental services that benefit more affluent groups. In addition, the poor support innovation in medical practice as patients in teaching and research hospitals and as guinea pigs in medical experiments.

Third, poverty creates jobs for a number of occupations and professions that serve or "service" the poor, or protect the rest of society from them. As already noted, penology would be minuscule without the poor, as would the need for police. Other activities and groups that flourish because of the existence of poverty are the numbers game, the sale of heroin and cheap wines and liquors, Pentecostal ministers, faith healers, prostitutes, pawn shops, and the peacetime army, which recruits its enlisted men mainly from among the poor.

Fourth, the poor buy goods others do not want and thus prolong the economic usefulness of such goods—day-old bread, fruit and vegetables that would otherwise have to be thrown out, secondhand clothes, and deteriorating automobiles and buildings. They also provide incomes for doctors, lawyers, teachers, and others who are too old, poorly trained, or incompetent to attract more affluent clients.

In addition to economic functions, the poor perform a number of social functions.

Fifth, the poor can be identified and punished as alleged or real deviants in order to uphold the legitimacy of conventional norms. To justify the desirability of hard work, thrift, honesty, and monogamy, for example, the defenders of these norms must be able to find people who can be accused of being lazy, spendthrift, dishonest, and promiscuous. Although there is some evidence that the poor are about as moral and law-abiding as anyone else, they are more likely than middle-class transgressors to be caught and punished when they participate in deviant acts. Moreover, they lack the political and cultural power to correct the stereotypes that other people hold of them and thus continue to be thought of as lazy, spendthrift, and so on, by those who need living proof that moral deviance does not pay.

Sixth, and conversely, the poor offer vicarious participation to the rest of the population in the uninhibited sexual, alcoholic, and narcotic behavior in which they are alleged to participate and which, being freed from the constraints of affluence, they are often thought to enjoy more than the middle classes. Thus many people, some social scientists included, believe that the poor not only are more given to uninhibited behavior (which may be true, although it is often motivated by despair more than by lack of inhibition) but derive more pleasure from it than affluent people (a finding that research by Lee Rainwater, Walter Miller, and others shows to be patently untrue). However, whether the poor actually have more sex and enjoy it more is irrelevant; as long as middle-class people believe this to be true, they can participate in it vicariously when instances are reported in factual or fictional form.

Seventh, the poor also serve a direct cultural function when culture created by or for them is adopted by the more affluent. The rich often collect artifacts from extinct folk cultures of poor people; and almost all Americans listen to the blues, Negro spirituals, and country music, which originated among the southern poor. Recently, they have enjoyed the rock styles that were born, like the Beatles, in the slums, and in the last year, poetry written by ghetto children has become popular in literary circles. The poor also serve as culture heroes, particularly, of course, to the left; but the hobo, the cowboy, the hipster, and the mythical prostitute with a heart of gold have performed this function for a variety of groups.

Eighth, poverty helps guarantee the status of those who are not poor. In every hierarchical society, someone has to be at the bottom; but in American society, in which social mobility is an important goal for many and people need to know where they stand, the poor function as a reliable and relatively permanent measuring rod for status comparisons. This is particularly true for the working class, whose politics is influenced by the need to maintain status distinctions between themselves and the poor, much as the aristocracy must find ways of distinguishing itself from the *nouveaux riches*.

Ninth, the poor also aid the upward mobility of groups just above them in the class hierarchy. Thus a goodly number of Americans have entered the middle class through the profits earned from the provision of goods and services in the slums, including illegal or nonrespectable ones that upper-class and upper-middle-class businessmen shun because of their low prestige. As a result, members of almost every immigrant group have financed their upward mobility by providing slum housing, entertainment, gambling, narcotics, and the like to later arrivals—most recently to blacks and Puerto Ricans.

Tenth, the poor help to keep the aristocracy busy, thus justifying its continued existence. "Society" uses the poor as clients of settlement houses and beneficiaries of charity affairs; indeed, the aristocracy must have the poor to demonstrate its superiority over other elites who devote themselves to earning money.

Eleventh, the poor, being powerless, can be made to absorb the costs of change and growth in American society. During the nineteenth century, they did the backbreaking work that built the cities; today, they are pushed out of their neighborhoods to make room for "progress." Urban renewal projects to hold middle-class taxpayers in the city and expressways to enable suburbanites to commute downtown have typically been located in poor neighborhoods because no other group will allow itself to be displaced. For the same reason, universities, hospitals, and civic centers also expand into land occupied by the poor. The major costs of the industrialization of agriculture have been borne by the poor, who are pushed off the land without recompense; and they have paid a large share of the human cost of the growth of American power overseas, for they have provided many of the foot soldiers for Vietnam and other wars.

Twelfth, the poor facilitate and stabilize the American political process. Because they vote and participate in politics less than other groups, the political system is often free to ignore them.

Moreover, because they can rarely support Republicans, they often provide the Democrats with a captive constituency that has no other place to go. As a result, the Democrats can count on their votes, and be more responsive to voters—for example, the white working class—who might otherwise switch to the Republicans.

Thirteenth, the role of the poor in upholding conventional norms (see the fifth point, earlier) also has a significant political function. An economy based on the ideology of *laissez faire* requires a deprived population that is allegedly unwilling to work or that can be considered inferior because it must accept charity or welfare in order to survive. Not only does the alleged moral deviancy of the poor reduce the moral pressure on the present political economy to eliminate poverty, but socialist alternatives can be made to look quite unattractive if those who will benefit most from them can be described as lazy, spendthrift, dishonest, and promiscuous.

THE ALTERNATIVES

I have described thirteen of the more important functions poverty and the poor satisfy in American society, enough to support the functionalist thesis that poverty, like any other social phenomenon, survives in part because it is useful to society or some of its parts. This analysis is not intended to suggest that because it is often functional, poverty *should* exist, or that it *must* exist. For one thing, poverty has many more dysfunctions than functions; for another, it is possible to suggest functional alternatives.

For example, society's dirty work could be done without poverty, either by automation or by paying "dirty workers" decent wages. Nor is it necessary for the poor to subsidize the many activities they support through their low-wage jobs. This would, however, drive up the costs of these activities, which would result in higher prices to their customers and clients. Similarly, many of the professionals who flourish because of the poor could be given other roles. Social workers could provide counseling to the affluent, as they prefer to do anyway; and the police could devote themselves to traffic and organized crime. Other roles would have to be found for badly trained or incompetent professionals now relegated to serving the poor, and someone else would have to pay their salaries. Fewer penologists would be employable, however. And Pentecostal religion could probably not survive without the poor—nor would parts of the second-hand and third-hand goods market. And in many cities, "used" housing that no one else wants would have to be torn down at public expense.

Alternatives for the cultural functions of the poor could be found more easily and cheaply. Indeed, entertainers, hippies, and adolescents are already serving as the deviants needed to uphold traditional morality and as devotees of orgies to "staff" the fantasies of vicarious participation.

The status functions of the poor are another matter. In a hierarchical society, some people must be defined as inferior to everyone else with respect to a variety of attributes, but they need not be poor in the absolute sense. One could conceive of a society in which the "lower class," though last in the pecking order, received 75 percent of the median income, rather than 15 to 40 percent, as is now the case. Needless to say, this would require considerable income redistribution.

The contribution the poor make to the upward mobility of the groups that provide them with goods and services could also be maintained without the poor's having such low incomes. However, it is true that if the poor were more affluent, they would have access to enough capital to take over the provider role, thus competing with, and perhaps rejecting, the "outsiders." (Indeed, owing in part to antipoverty programs, this is already happening in a number of ghettos, where white storeowners are being replaced by blacks.) Similarly, if the poor were more affluent, they would make less willing clients for upper-class philanthropy, although some would still use settlement houses to achieve upward mobility, as they do now. Thus "society" could continue to run its philanthropic activities.

The political functions of the poor would be more difficult to replace. With increased affluence, the poor would probably obtain more political power and be more active politically. With higher incomes and more political power, the poor would be likely to resist paying the costs of growth and change. Of course, it is possible to imagine urban renewal and highway projects that properly reimbursed the displaced people, but such projects would then become considerably more expensive, and many might never be built. This, in turn, would reduce the comfort and convenience of those who now benefit from urban renewal and expressways. Finally, hippies could serve also as more deviants to justify the existing political economy—as they already do. Presumably, however, if poverty were eliminated, there would be fewer attacks on that economy.

In sum, then, many of the functions served by the poor could be replaced if poverty were eliminated, but almost always at higher costs to others, particularly more affluent others. Consequently, a functional analysis must conclude that poverty persists not only because it fulfills a number of positive functions but also because many of the functional alternatives to poverty would be quite dysfunctional for the affluent members of society. A functional analysis thus ultimately arrives at much the same conclusion as radical sociology, except that radical thinkers treat as manifest what I describe as latent: That social phenomena that are functional for affluent or powerful groups and dysfunctional for poor or powerless ones persist; that when the elimination of such phenomena through functional alternatives would generate dysfunctions for the affluent or powerful, they will continue to persist; and that phenomena like poverty can be eliminated only when they become dysfunctional for the affluent or powerful, or when the powerless can obtain enough power to change society.

29. BLUE COLLAR BLUES

BERNARD CARL ROSEN

[The working class] have suffered the cruelist fate that can befall a social class: they have lost a social revolution. Through no fault of their own they have been grievously hurt by the techno-service system's triumph over manufacturing. They have become losers, and losing is hard to take. What is even sadder, they still do not fully understand what is going on.

Bernard Rosen examines how the economy has changed dramatically in the past twenty years and with it the increasing decline of importance and power of the blue collar worker. He describes a "new elite" surfacing in the American economy, which ignores and even is hostile toward the working class, causing the latter to lose the security and self confidence they once had before the "information revolution."

No group feels more badly treated than the working class. No group feels more keenly that its interests are being neglected, that its status is in freefall, that its economic security is in jeopardy. And perhaps no group feels more worried and angry. To sympathetic observers the reason for the workers' discontent seems obvious enough: the techno-service society has treated them shabbily. How can anyone doubt this? Haven't their wages been slashed, their claim to a job ignored, perhaps the job itself eliminated? Is not their condition dire? Haven't they, as one newsmagazine put it, been shafted?[1] And isn't this the cause of their disgruntled mood?

It is not that simple. Economic factors alone do not explain working-class discontent. It is true that many factory workers feel pinched. Some have lost their jobs; others have taken pay cuts; most find pay increases harder to come by. This is painful and no doubt contributes to blue-collar anxiety. But it is not the only cause of their discontent, not even the most important one. In fact, on average, objective conditions have not deteriorated to the extent workers think they

have. In many cases they have remained the same; in some cases they have improved.

General opinion notwithstanding, it is not only economic deprivation, a state of the pocketbook, from which some workers suffer; it is also relative social deprivation, a state of the mind. What has in truth declined for almost all blue-collar workers is their satisfaction with their social position. When they contrast their position with what they think it should be, they feel a distinct sense of loss. But it is less a loss of dollars than a loss of respect.

Many workers are angry because they believe they have been cheated out of what is rightly theirs: an honored place in society. They feel unwelcome and ridiculed, like an old suit, out-of-fashion and shabby, ready for the trash can. The skills and muscles that once assured them an honored place in society have declined in value, and as a result so have they. Their values are being replaced by new values and their needs and those of society no longer mesh harmoniously. A new social order now calls the tune, and blue-collar workers, like musicians in a strange orchestra playing an unfamiliar tune, are now minor performers—off key and getting little applause.

Blue-collar workers feel powerless to protect themselves against forces they don't understand,

From Bernard Carl Rosen, *Winners and Losers of the Information Revolution: Psychosocial Change and Its Discontents*, Praeger, 1998. By permission.

and vulnerable to the scorn and slander of people they despise and fear. They are becoming deracinated. Their roots are in a world that is rapidly losing influence and, as a result, so are they. The old manufacturing economy in which they played an important role no longer rules the economic roost. Its place has been taken by a new system, the information society produced by the Second Great Transformation—a system to which they are ill-adapted and in which they feel poorly rewarded.

Their place in this world is not the one they expected and feel they rightly deserve. As they see it, their contributions to society are undervalued and taken for granted. Unfortunately society no longer sees it their way, and they are having difficulty accepting this sad fact. In truth, they have suffered the cruelest fate that can befall a social class: they have lost a social revolution. Through no fault of their own they have been grievously hurt by the techno-service system's triumph over manufacturing. They have become losers, and losing is hard to take. What is even sadder, they still do not fully understand what is going on....

Mostly, factory workers produce objects for unknown customers, whose personality needs they need never consider. No one asks the production worker to greet the customer with a smile and an offer to be of service. Nor is the workplace as competitive for blue-collar workers as it is for knowledge creators and information processors. Competition exists, of course, on the factory floor, but it tends to be controlled by company and union rules. Also, the production worker has less opportunity to threaten others or be threatened by them, and thus less reason to adopt the chameleon's disguise.

On those occasions when they try to play the chameleon's game, dealing in intangible images rather than material objects, the factory worker's relative lack of the verbal and interpersonal skills intrinsic to the Chameleon Complex is a distinct liability. The Chameleon Complex may be an asset to middle-class men and women; its absence can be a handicap for blue-collar workers trying to get ahead in situations where impression management counts a lot. Perhaps for all these reasons, chameleonism strikes blue-collar workers as downright dishonest. And they feel awkward and out of place in a society that tacitly accepts chameleonism as the norm.

THE END OF AN ERA

Even though . . . the economy remains strong, it would be foolish to deny that some workers have experienced severe economic loss and that this has contributed to their anxiety. Massive economic change—the Second Great Transformation—is costing some workers their jobs. This has caused pain and it deserves discussion, even though, as I believe, it is only one of several factors contributing to the current mood of discontent among blue-collar workers.

Workers are learning that lean and mean corporations are hard to live with, that job security is something their parents may have known but which is no longer certain for them. They are learning that improved productivity and economic growth do not necessarily create jobs for everyone, and that a continually rising standard of living can no longer be taken for granted. In brief, they are learning an old, if obvious, lesson—that slim wallets depress the spirit and joblessness can lead to despair. Unfortunately, Americans are ill-prepared for the school of economic hard knocks. They have grown accustomed to more work benefits, greater job security, and larger paychecks than workers have ever known before.

The current plight of workers mauled by economic change is particularly excruciating because for a brief period, from the end of World War II to the early 1970s, blue-collar workers enjoyed an astounding improvement in social position and living standard. During that period the economy became significantly more productive, enriching the lives of people in almost every station in life. Never before had the material condition of so many Americans changed so much for the better in so short a time with such far-reaching consequences.

The extraordinary growth of the American economy after 1945 created a wealth of good-paying jobs that was unprecedented anywhere in the world. Skilled workers, and even those with few if any skills, enjoyed incomes never dreamed of by previous generations. Real earnings of the typical worker were twice as high around 1972 than they had been in the late 1940s.[2] Automatically, almost magically, the children of the working class, many of them factory workers like their parents, stepped on the escalator that is the American Dream, moved into well-paying jobs, bought houses in the suburbs, and took on the title and accoutrements of the middle class. Ambitious war veterans from every social stratum equipped themselves with college degrees bought with money provided by the GI Bill, and buoyed by a burgeoning economy became managers, entrepreneurs, and professionals, joining the ranks of the upper-middle class.

But this period of exuberant economic growth and fabulous social mobility did not last. In mid-1973, the bright days of seemingly endless and effortless growth came to an end. The economy, which had been growing at a brisk average rate of 3.9 percent during the period 1950 to 1970, slowed to a modest growth rate of 1 or 2 percent. Jobs became scarcer and real wages increased slowly; the upward movement of average family income slowed to a crawl.[3]

Among the first to feel the pinch of the slowdown were factory workers doing routine, repetitive work. Many of them began to live in fear of the ax. Across the nation, workers who once felt secure started to churn with anxiety about their future in companies for which they had worked for many years and to which they had given, as the saying goes, the best years of their lives. Looking about them or following the news in the media, they discovered that workers were losing their jobs. Many companies began reacting to grim economic news: they were losing money. Profit margins had slipped disastrously. Pretax profits, which had averaged 16.9 percent in the 1950s, fell to 10.7 percent in the 1970s and to 8.7 percent in the 1980s. Companies had to respond to this progressive decline or go under. Some in fact became bankrupt, others were taken over by competitors, but many survived.

Stung by foreign competition, desperate to survive in a fiercely competitive global market, eager to fend off angry stockholders and keep their own jobs, corporate managers undertook a number of draconian measures to return their companies to profitability. For one thing, some of them began moving production abroad to locations where routine work could be quickly

learned and efficiently performed, where workers could make things comparable in quality to that obtained from more highly-paid Americans.

Consider these sobering statistics. It costs about $16 an hour to employ a production worker in the United States, as compared with $2.40 in Mexico, $1.50 in Poland, and 50 cents or less in China, India, Malaysia, and Indonesia. Auto manufacturing highlights the extent of international wage differentials. Mexican workers producing 1993 Ford Escorts earned $2.38 an hour; Americans working on the same car earned $17.50 an hour. With wage differentials this large it does not take a rocket scientist to figure out how the *Fortune* 500 firms across America were able to cut their American payroll from 16.2 million in 1990 to 11.8 million in 1993 and still keep production high. Many of them had transferred some of their production to low-cost countries.

Employers in poor countries often force their workers to accept wages Americans would not tolerate. Some workers in Shenzhen, China, earn as little as one yuan (12 American cents) an hour, and work 12 to 13 hour days, seven days a week. In India millions of children, some as young as seven years of age, weave carpets for a pittance. Factory conditions are often Dickensian—dark and dismal and dangerous. Hundreds of workers die needlessly in factory fires, trapped in buildings that lack the simplest precautions against accidental conflagration or provisions for escape once a fire breaks out. Industrial accidents are common; the risk of being accidentally killed in a factory is six times higher in South Korea and fifteen times higher in Pakistan than in the United States. Competition for manufacturing jobs with workers willing to work under such conditions seems hopelessly unfair to many Americans.[4]

Transferring some of their production to low-wage countries was only one of the strategies companies employed to stay afloat in turbulent economic waters. There were others. Where possible manufacturers began employing robots and computers, increasing productivity but also putting people out of work. Like the Luddites (1811–16), who smashed machines in the textile mills of industrializing England in a futile effort to save their jobs, few workers have difficulty comprehending the connection between technology and unemployment. In 1930, John Maynard Keynes saw it too. "We are being afflicted with a new disease . . . technological unemployment," he explained to policy makers worried by a sinking economy that, as time would show, was slowly slipping into the worst depression of modern times.[5] And even more recently, economist Paul Krugman reminded us that machine-driven efficiency inevitably hurts some workers. The gain in long term riches must be paid for in the short run by production workers whose jobs and skills are being swallowed up by technological progress. This is regrettable but unavoidable, he concluded. There is no gain without pain.

In addition to transferring production abroad and introducing advanced technologies, managers began to reduce their workforces. In some industries, appreciable numbers of production workers were laid off or forced into retirement. In one year alone, 1993, the top 100 American electronic companies eliminated 480,000 jobs. For example, Compaq Computer Corporation, the world's biggest maker of computers, laid off 20 percent of its staff. In a different field, Caterpillar, the manufacturer of construction and mining machinery, took an even harsher step: it slashed its work force 31 percent. U.S. West, a Baby Bell telephone company headquartered in Englewood, Colorado, began phasing out 9,000 jobs, about one-seventh of its work force. American Telephone and Telegraph, mother of phone companies, announced in 1996 that it would lay off no less than 40,000 of its employees. Albert J. Dunlap ("Chainsaw Al" to his critics), chairman of the Sunbeam Corporation, announced in 1997 that he would slash Sunbeam's overall workforce in half, having previously lopped off one-third of the workforce at the Scott Paper Company in just 28 months.[6]

Rather than lay off employees, some corporations seek to reduce expenses by simply not filling vacant slots, forcing the remaining employees to carry the workload of their former co-workers. At the General Motors Fisher Body plant in Flint, Michigan, employees gripe that they are being asked to do what used to be several different jobs. "If somebody retires, all they do is take the work and give it to other people," said one worker. That complaint is echoed by others in many industries across the country. Said one employee of Gamma, a large photo lab in Chicago, which had dismissed 16 percent of the staff the year before: "Everyone has to do everyone's job in addition to their own."[7] When the workload becomes too burdensome and the complaints of workers too noisy to be ignored, some companies fill full-time positions with part-time or temporary hired hands, who receive no expensive benefits, health insurance, unemployment payments, and paid vacations, and can be laid off at a moment's notice.

Another tactic is to pile on the overtime. Some companies use overtime to wring the most out of their facilities without having to hire new people or expand the plant. The factory workweek in 1994, a robust year when the economy grew at a 4 percent annual rate, averaged a near record 42 hours, including 4.6 hours of overtime. The big-three auto makers pushed this figure to ten hours a week overtime. "We are the workingest people in the world," says Audrey Freedman, a labor economist.[8] But workers complain of exhaustion. One worker even welcomed a brief strike just to get a few days off. Still, notwithstanding bone-weariness and the loss of precious time with family and friends, overtime pay is welcome to most workers and princely to some. Many autoworkers are earning $65,000 to $70,000 a year, and electricians on plant-maintenance crews working seven-day weeks can push their income to as much as $100,000 annually.[9] Paying overtime is expensive to the company, of course, but it is cheaper than building new plants and hiring new workers.

Some companies sought to increase production without cutting the work force or substantially increasing overtime. The Birmingham Steel Corporation took this route. As recently as 1987, it had produced 167,000 tons of steel with 184 workers, an average of 912 tons per worker. Six years later, after tightening production procedures and strictly controlling new hiring, it produced 276,000 tons with 207 workers, an average of 1,335 per person, which works out to an 8 percent increase in productivity per year, a remarkable figure by any standard. Many other industries have also become more productive, bringing down costs and boosting production. In the entire country, over all industrial production was 40 percent higher in 1994 and four times higher than in 1950. In effect, more was being made with fewer people....

THE WAR AGAINST THE WORKING CLASS

... Whom then do they blame for their unhappy condition? Who are the people who make them feel unappreciated and insecure? The villain is the New Elite, the upwardly-mobile, bright, hardworking, eager for power and wealth, information processors who dominate the techno-service society.

Elitists rub blue-collar workers the wrong way. For one thing, the Elite's wealth and power are too new, too different, too offensive to working-class sensibilities to have won the acceptance given to the inheritors of old money and to the possessors of valued talent and quirky good fortune. For another thing, the masters of the information society make no bones about their own moral and intellectual superiority. With grating hauteur, they have announced to the world that their special mission is to save America and make it atone for its sins. Such pretensions to superiority stick in the worker's craw. Worse yet, as a demonstration of its moral superiority the Elite is pushing affirmative action policies that undermine the workers' sense of security and confidence in themselves. It is this loss of security and self-confidence, this feeling of having lost status respect, at least as much as anything else, that accounts for blue-collar disaffection.

The hostility many workers feel for the New Elite surfaced during the debates about the wisdom of enlarging the free trade pact with Canada to include Mexico. Elitists generally supported the North American Free Trade Agreement. Said one young lawyer, interviewed as she was catching a train bound for a Chicago suburb, "We've got to keep up with the world. It's just smart economic policy." Other lawyers, stockbrokers, and accountants catching the same train also enthusiastically supported the treaty. It was, as one man put it, a "no brainer."

As he saw it, the United States has everything to gain and nothing to lose by opening its gates to trade with Mexico.

But to many workers the issue looked entirely different. To Sharon Jones, a 36-year-old union worker who cleans train cars for $8 an hour, the treaty presented a threat to her livelihood. "It's going to take our jobs away," she said. And then she added, in angry tones that revealed the blue-collar suspicion of the credentialed class, "I know the rich people say it won't. But what do they care about working people? The only ones looking to protect people like us is the A.F.L.-C.I.O. And if the union says it's bad, I trust them. Got no reason to trust those other folks." And to another worker, a Chicago truck driver named Dennis McGue, the treaty looked like the work of "fancy-pants elites" who cared nothing for the workers. "I guess when you live up on a hill," he said, "you just don't see the people in the valley."[10]

The "people on the hill" generally know little about the "people in the valley" and care little that the blue-collar class has had to endure a steady deterioration in status. Nor are they impressed when factory workers point to the importance of their work. Quite the reverse. For one thing, many arts and skills are in decline. Ancient crafts have been broken into simple operations, routinized and robbed of intrinsic merit. Old skills, painfully acquired through long years of apprenticeship, have fallen into disuse, replaced by robots and computers. And for another thing, even granted that workers still make things that move on roads and fly through the air, that clothe and house the nation, that arm the military and win wars, these are the products of an old regime, the manufacturing system, now in relative decline. A new system, the information economy, is in ascendance, and its masters take for granted the goods the old system still builds. As the New Elite sees it, building bridges and roads, making cars and airplanes, count for less in the national scheme of things than building pyramids of words. Possessing and processing information are what really matter; manual work can be delegated to lesser breeds.

This attitude baffles and infuriates most blue-collar workers. It is not what they had expected. In the past, society understood their importance and visibly showed its respect. Organized in powerful labor unions, as many of them were, blue-collar workers were people to whom politicians and employers paid heed. They lobbied for legislation to protect their interests; they demanded wage increases that appreciably lifted their pay. And if their demands were not met they tied a company up in strikes that in time would bring it to its knees. Taken all in all, with its voice in the councils of government, its contributions to political parties and the clout that resulted from judiciously placed money, organized labor had won a place at the table of power. It negotiated as equals with employers and politicians over its share of the nation's economic pie. And as labor's influence grew, the worker enjoyed the esteem that power always brings.

Needless to say, much has changed since the glory days of working-class influence. Blue-collar clout has declined as the unions, particularly in manufacturing industries, have lost members. In the 1950s about a quarter of all workers in the private sector belonged to labor unions. Today, only 11 percent are union members, about the same as in the 1930s. And in a marked change with the past, while blue-collar membership declined service sector membership grew: today service workers are the most rapidly growing segment of unionized labor.

As though economic disappointment and declining influence were not trouble enough, workers must also contend with attacks upon their values and personal worth. At times the media portray them, especially the white males, as louts, beer-sodden inebriates, mindless television addicts, coarse boors oblivious to the needs of women, lesbians, and gays, to the sensibilities of the crippled, the old, the fat, the ugly, and other fashionable minorities. Their lives are ridiculed as shallow and crude, wasted years spent in the pursuit of tawdry pleasure, without commitment to ideas, to the joys of self-discovery, and to the advancement of high culture. They feel under attack from all sides. Call this paranoia if you like. Say it will go away when times get better, when factory jobs once again become well paid and secure, when the golden past is somehow recaptured. But remember that working class anxiety persists in these relatively good times, that it

hangs on even as the gross national product grows briskly, employment goes up and inflation down....

Perhaps most damaging is the charge that factory workers are dumb. Social researchers, psychometricians, and other elite members of the information society bluntly question the blue-collar worker's ability to cope with the demands of the information age. They assert that the average blue-collar worker lacks the intelligence to cope with the technical requirements of the information system. Blue-collar IQ scores, researchers report, tend to fall on the wrong side of the bell curve, below the median. In the judgment of Richard Herrnstein and Charles Murray, authors of *The Bell Curve*, blue-collar workers tend to be deficient in "cognitive ability," the capacity to handle abstractions and process information.[11] Many of them cannot puzzle out the instructions in work manuals or understand complex job processes, and for these reasons are doomed to stay in the lower reaches of the workforce. Rattled by this low assessment of their intelligence, some workers wonder whether the elite may not be right. Certainly, the jabberwocky jargon of computer technology leaves most of them at sea, adrift and bewildered. Worse than that, they feel diminished.

But it is not the assessment of their IQ that most troubles blue-collar workers. What troubles them even more is the feeling that they no longer fit into the economy in the comfortable, reassuring way they once did, that they no longer mesh neatly with the rest of society—and that no one cares. In this conclusion they are entirely correct. They are, in fact, out-of-synch with the new system. They had been educated to work in harmony with other parts of a complex machine called the manufacturing system. But since this system has been downgraded by the techno-service economy, which needs a different kind of workforce, they sense, quite accurately, that they have been relegated to second place, along with the system they were trained to fit.

In a manufacturing system the factory is the major trainer of workers. The factory is a forceful school: its spirit enters the mind and marrow of the worker. It is in the factory that workers acquire many of the traits that define their character: respect for authority and tradition, a need for order and predictability, an admiration for technical competence. The rhythm of its machines, the constant insistence on efficiency and reliability, these attributes of the factory subtly shape workers in ways that make them suitable for life in an industrial society. Day in and day out, by example and direct instruction, the modern factory teaches him how to function in a formally organized, deeply hierarchical system, characterized by a complex division of labor, an emphasis on specialization and technical skill, a devotion to competence and efficiency. . . .

When workers complain about workforce reductions and plant shutdowns, they are told this drastic action had to be taken, even though it meant throwing people out of work and shattering their lives. The plant had to be closed because it was losing money. People had to be laid off because meticulously conducted studies showed the work force was bloated and the work shoddy. That these actions caused some people pain was regrettable, but it was for the greater good of the company and the country. Workers often find these arguments hard to refute. Sheepishly, they admit the workforce had become too large and the work may have been sloppy. Why else were Americans buying Japanese cars in preference to American ones?

Blue-collar workers cannot hope to beat the Elite at its own game. Elite arguments were fashioned by people who are extremely skilled in the use of language, expert at using words to confuse as well as to enlighten, weaving a web of verbiage to trap the unwary. Words make workers uncomfortable. They are accustomed to making tangible objects and tend to judge the value of things by their obvious utility. They are suspicious of the tools Elitists use to ply their trades: words and images, mysterious devices of dubious value. But without words and the skill to use them, workers lack the right weapons to deal with the Elite. And so, when told that their anger is not justified and must not be expressed, that it must be swallowed, bottled up, reasoned away, and treated with scorn for the selfish, ugly thing it is, they are dumbstruck, literally at a loss for words.

Though baffled and beaten into silence by abstruse argument and softened by appeals to their better nature, many workers nevertheless remain angry. Occasionally, their anger erupts in bursts of sporadic violence or electoral revolt. The abrupt dismissal of many Democratic party politicians in the 1994 midterm elections was said to have been due to the revolt of blue-collar voters furious at the way elite politicians had been treating them. At other times blue-collar anger has taken the form of nativist outbursts at immigrants, sporadic bombings of government buildings, and attempts to set up sovereign enclaves in isolated areas—for example, an Aryan nation in the Northwest or a separate republic in Texas.

But usually the rage is hidden, buried beneath a mountain of denial, repressed from consciousness. Nonetheless, the anger is still there. It can be denied, but it can't be eliminated by denial. Boiling beneath the surface and unable to find an acceptable outlet, repressed rage takes a terrible revenge on people who will not admit its existence. For rage will be heard from, whether its possessor likes it or not. Repressed anger surfaces in feelings of irrational fear and restlessness and in a sense of drift and alienation. Its effects can be seen in the pervasive anxiety that afflicts blue-collar losers. . . .

NOTES

1. Cover of *U.S. News and World Report*, January 22, 1996.
2. The growth rate in income was part of a long-term process. From 1839 to 1886 real income doubled, and between 1913 and 1950 the Gross Domestic Product grew an average of 1.6 percent annually, which is striking considering that this period included the Great Depression. See Paul Krugman, *Peddling Prosperity* (New York: W. W. Norton, 1994), p. 3; see also *The Economist*, June 5, 1993, p. 22.
3. Steven Ratner, *New York Times Magazine*, September 19, 1993, p. 96. See also Robert J. Samuelson, *The Good Life and Its Discontents* (New York: Times Books, 1995), p. 114.
4. Data on the effects of foreign competition on American workers were taken from "Global Survey," *The Economist*, October 1, 1994, p. 32.
5. Steven Ratner, *New York Times Magazine*, September 19, 1993, p. 96.
6. For data on downsizing, see *The Economist*, July 31, 1993, p. 59; and Jon D. Hull, "The State of the Union," *Time*, January 30, 1995, pp. 53–75. For a

description of its often cruel and demoralizing effects, see William Hoffman et al., "Impact of Plant Closings on Automobile Workers and Their Families," *Journal of Contemporary Human Services*, February 1991, pp. 103–107; Barry Bluestone and Bennett Harrison, *The Deindustrialization of America* (New York: Basic Books, 1982), p. 32; and Kevin Kelly, *Business Week* (Industrial Technology Edition), March 9, 1992, p. 33.

7.The quotations on downsizing are taken from George J. Church, "We're No. 1," *Time*, October 24, 1994, pp. 51–56.

8.Quoted in ibid.

9.Ibid.

10.Dirk Johnson, "Chicago on Trade Accord: A Split Along Class Lines," *New York Times*, November 14, 1993. Quotations on the trade accord are taken from this article.

11.Richard J. Herrstein and Charles Murray, *The Bell Curve* (New York: Free Press, 1994).

PART VI

Ethnic and Racial Inequality

Society is not only structured by class, but also by race and ethnic-group membership.

To many Americans, diversity is a quality that makes us a unique and great society. To others, diversity is regarded as a basic cause for many of our problems. In either case, diversity has been and remains a way that power, privilege, and prestige is distributed in society. Nonwhites and Hispanics are systematically placed in low positions in relation to whites and Anglos. Hence, sociologists often will label such groups "minorities."

It is difficult to adequately describe all the various ethnic and racial minorities in the United States and all aspects of inequality, so it is important to treat these as a place to begin. Also note that several other selections in this reader also focus on issues related to ethnic and racial inequality.

The first three articles in Part VI focus on African Americans. Steven Steinberg examines occupational opportunities, Clarence Page race and middle class identity, and Andrew Hacker gives an insightful description of the world in which African Americans exist.

The fourth selection by John Farley describes the origins of the structure between Anglos and Mexicans in American society, and Robert G. Lee gives us a picture of how Americans generally define Asian Americans.

30. OCCUPATIONAL OPPORTUNITIES AND RACE

STEPHEN STEINBERG

This job crisis is the single-most important factor behind the familiar tangle of problems that beset black communities. Without jobs, nuclear families become unglued or are never formed. Without jobs, or husbands with jobs, women with young children are forced onto the welfare rolls. Without jobs, many ghetto youth resort to the drug trade or other illicit ways of making money.... In short, there is no exit from the racial quagmire unless there is a national commitment to address the job crisis in black America.

The real source of the oppression of African Americans in the United States lies in our occupational structure. In the world of work, we are segregated and we always have been. Where opportunities to correct this have arisen, we have not committed ourselves to correcting this. Stephen Steinberg looks at the history of slavery and immigration and how both have produced and maintained this segregation. Then he examines the "myth of the black middle class" and points out that instead of bringing about true integration of the work force, middle-class occupations have continued to perpetuate a society of occupational segregation. Finally, he examines job discrimination in relation to the black working class and poor. Without solving the problem of work, according to Steinberg, "the legacy of slavery," American racism in all areas of life, will continue.

The essence of racial oppression is not the distorted and malicious stereotypes that whites have of blacks. These constitute the *culture* of oppression, not to be confused with the thing itself. Nor is the essence of racism epitomized by sitting in the back of a bus. In South Africa, this was called "petty apartheid" as opposed to "grand apartheid," the latter referring to political disfranchisement and the banishment of millions of blacks to isolated and impoverished "homelands." In the United States, the essence of racial oppression—*our* grand apartheid—is a racial division of labor, a system of occupational segregation that relegates most blacks to work in

the least desirable job sectors or that excludes them from job markets altogether.[1]

The racial division of labor had its origins in slavery when some 650,000 Africans were imported to provide cheap labor for the South's evolving plantation economy. During the century after the abolition of slavery, the nation had the perfect opportunity to integrate blacks into the North's burgeoning industries. It was not Southern racism but its Northern variant that prevented this outcome. This is worth emphasizing because it has become customary—part of America's liberal mythology on race—to place the blame for the nation's racist past wholly on the South. But it was not Southern segregationists and lynch mobs who excluded blacks from participating in the critical early phases of industrialization. Rather, it was an invisible color line across *Northern* industry that barred blacks categorically from employment in the vast manufacturing sector, except for a few menial and low-paying jobs that white workers spurned. Nor can the blame be placed solely on the doorstep of greedy capitalists, those other villains of liberal iconography. Workers themselves and their unions were equally implicated in maintaining a system of occupational apartheid that reserved industrial jobs for whites and that relegated blacks to the preindustrial sector of the national economy. The long-term effects were incalculable because this closed off the only major channel of escape from racial oppression in the South. Indeed, had the industrial revolution not been "for whites only," it might have obviated the need for a civil rights revolution a century later.

The exclusion of blacks from the industrial sector was possible only because the North had access to an inexhaustible supply of immigrant labor. Some 24 million immigrants arrived between 1880 and 1930. A 1910 survey of twenty principal mining and manufacturing industries conducted by the United States Immigration Commission found that 58 percent of workers were foreign born. When the Commission asked whether the new immigration resulted in "racial displacement," it did not have blacks in mind, but rather whites who were native born or from old immigrant stock. Except for a cursory examination of the competition between Italian and black agricultural workers in Louisiana, nothing in the forty-volume report so much as hints at the possibility that mass immigration might have deleterious consequences for blacks, even though black leaders had long complained that immigrants were taking jobs that, they insisted, rightfully belonged to blacks.[2]

If blacks were superfluous so far as Northern industry was concerned, the opposite was true in the South, where black labor was indispensable to the entire regional economy. Furthermore, given the interdependence between the regional economies of the South and the North, occupational apartheid had indirect advantages for the North as well. Remember that the cotton fiber that Irish, Italian, and Jewish immigrants worked with in mills and sweatshops throughout the North was supplied by black workers in the South. In effect, a system of labor deployment

had evolved whereby blacks provided the necessary labor for Southern agriculture, and European immigrants provided the necessary labor for Northern industry.

This regional and racial division of labor cast the mold for generations more of racial inequality and conflict. Not until the First World War were blacks given significant access to Northern labor markets. In a single year—1914—the volume of immigration plummeted from 1.2 million immigrant arrivals to only 327,000. The cutoff of immigration in the midst of an economic expansion triggered the Great Migration, as it was called, of Southern blacks to the urban North. Industries not only employed blacks in large numbers but even sent labor agents to the South to recruit black workers. Between 1910 and 1920, there was a net migration of 454,000 Southern blacks to the North, a figure that exceeded the volume of the previous forty years combined. Here is historical proof that blacks were just as willing as Europe's peasants to uproot themselves and migrate to cities that offered the opportunity for industrial employment. To suggest that blacks "were not ready to compete with immigrants," as the author of a recent volume on immigration does, is a flagrant distortion of history.[3] The simple truth is that Northern industry was open to immigrants and closed to blacks. Whatever opprobrium was heaped on these immigrants for their cultural and religious difference, they were still beneficiaries of racial preference.

It is generally assumed that the Second World War provided a similar demand for black labor, but initially this was not the case. Because the war came on the heels of the Depression, there was a surfeit of white labor and no compelling need to hire blacks.[4] Indeed, it was blacks' frustration with their exclusion from wartime industries that prompted A. Philip Randolph and his followers to threaten a march on Washington in 1941 until Roosevelt issued his executive order banning discrimination in federal employment and defense contracts. The opening up of Northern labor markets triggered another mass migration of Southern blacks—1.6 million migrated between 1940 and 1950; by the end of the war, 1.5 million black workers were part of the war-production work force. This represented an unprecedented breach in the nation's system of occupational apartheid—one that set the stage for future change as well.

Still, as recently as 1950, two-thirds of the nation's blacks lived in the South, half of them in rural areas. It was not the Civil War, but the mechanization of agriculture a century later that finally liberated blacks from their historic role as agricultural laborers in the South's feudal economy. By the mid-fifties, even the harvest of cotton became mechanized with the mass production of International Harvester's automatic cotton picking machine. The number of man-hours required to produce a bale of cotton was reduced from 438 in 1940, to 26 in 1960, to only 6 in 1980.[5] Agricultural technology had effectively rendered black labor obsolete, and with it the caste system whose underlying function had been to regulate and exploit black labor.[6] Thus it was that in one century, white planters went all the way to Africa to import black laborers; in the next century, the descendants of Southern planters gave the descendants of African slaves one-way bus tickets to Chicago and New York.

When blacks finally arrived in Northern cities, they encountered a far less favorable structure of opportunity than had existed for immigrants decades earlier.[7] For one thing, these labor markets had been captured by immigrant groups who engaged in a combination of ethnic nepotism and unabashed racism. For another, the occupational structures were themselves changing. Not only were droves of manufacturing jobs being automated out of existence, but a reorganization of the global economy resulted in the export of millions of manufacturing jobs to less developed parts of the world.

Thus the fact that the technological revolution in agriculture lagged nearly a half-century behind the technological revolution in industry had fateful consequences for blacks at both junctures. First, blacks were restricted to the agricultural sector during the most expansive periods of the industrial revolution. Then, they were evicted from rural America and arrived in Northern cities at a time when manufacturing was beginning a steep and irreversible decline. Yet...the fact that more blacks were not integrated into Northern labor markets cannot be explained only in terms of the operation of color-blind econom-ic forces. At least as important was the pervasive racism that restricted the access of black workers not only to jobs in declining industries, but also to new jobs in the expanding service sector.

THE IMMIGRATION DILEMMA

The economic fortunes of African-Americans have always been linked to immigration. Suppose that Europe's "huddled masses" had been flocking to the New World in the seventeenth century. Then Southern planters would not have been impelled to go all the way to Africa to find laborers, and the nation would have been spared the ignominy of slavery. Suppose, on the other hand, that the huddled masses of Europe had *not* flocked to America's cities during the century after slavery. Then Northern industrialists would have had to put aside their racist predilections and tapped the pool of black laborers in the South who were desperate to escape the yoke of Southern oppression. Indeed, this is precisely what happened during both World Wars when the cutoff of immigration led to the absorption of blacks into Northern labor markets. The two brief intervals in the twentieth century when immigration was at low ebb marked the two major periods of economic and social advancement for African-Americans.

The post-civil rights era presented yet another opportunity to integrate blacks into the occupational mainstream, especially given the sharp decline of the white birth rate and the improved climate of tolerance toward blacks. But once again, African-Americans have had to cope with an enormous influx of immigrants, this time from Asia, Latin America, and the Caribbean. Ironically, it was the civil rights movement that led to the passage of the 1965 Hart-Celler Act, which abolished the national origins quotas that had restricted immigration outside of Europe. In the two ensuing decades, there have been some 15 million immigrant arrivals, not to mention millions more who are undocumented.[8]

This massive volume of immigration amounts to a double whammy as far as African-Americans are concerned: Not only has there been an erosion of job structures in cities with high concentrations of blacks, but black workers must compete with increasing numbers of immigrants for scarce jobs. William Julius Wilson's whole emphasis is that the United States has been exporting millions of jobs to the Third World. However, the nation is also importing workers from these same countries at an even faster rate. The availability of large numbers of foreign workers allows employers to exercise their racial preferences when it comes to hiring new workers. As the last hired, blacks often find themselves in the hiring queue even behind recent immigrants....

To be sure, immigration may on balance be beneficial for the economy as a whole, as the apostles of immigration contend. There is obvious validity in the claim that immigrants do not just take jobs, they create them as well. This is especially evident when one examines the thriving ethnic economies in "gateway cities" like Los Angeles, New York, San Francisco, and Miami. On the other hand, as Jacqueline Jackson has pointed out, "too often the jobs created are not for domestic minorities but for the next wave of immigrants recruited through ethnic networks."[9] Besides, what is at issue here is not whether immigration is generally beneficial to the American economy, but whether it is specifically detrimental to the interests of African-Americans and other marginal workers....

While demographers, economists, and sociologists debate the effects of immigration, a groundswell of resentment has built up within the black community itself. Public opinion polls indicate that a solid majority of blacks see immigrants as competitors for jobs and would favor lowering the ceiling on immigration.[10] Yet most black leaders have been reluctant to speak out against immigration policy. For one thing, many blacks sympathize with these struggling minorities, some of whom are also of African descent. For another, black leaders do not want to feed the forces of xenophobia and reaction that are behind the recent upsurge of nativism. Finally, black leaders have been wary about jeopardizing their coalition with Hispanics in Congress and elsewhere, even though public opinion polls indicate that most rank-and-file Hispanics also would support a lower ceiling on immigration.[11]...

Here we arrive at the critical question. If the rationale behind immigration has to do with declining fertility rates and an anticipated decline in new labor force entrants, why is policy not directed at addressing the scandalously high rates of black unemployment? Why is there no crash program to provide job training for minority youth whose detachment from the job market has so many deleterious consequences for themselves as well as the rest of the society? Why is there no serious effort to enforce antidiscrimination laws and to tear down racist barriers in major occupational structures, including the so-called "ethnic economy" in which racial discrimination is virtually endemic? Why are there no incentives or mandates to induce employers to hire and train unemployed youths?

It is difficult to escape the conclusion that political and economic leaders have given up on black youth and opted to rely on immigrants to make up for any labor deficits....

The immigration of some 15 million documented immigrants over the past several decades represents another missed opportunity in American history. The nation could have taken advantage of a secular decline in its working-age population to integrate blacks and other marginal groups into the occupational mainstream. More is involved here than achieving parity and justice for blacks. This was the nation's chance to attack the structures of inequality that rend the society, undermining the stability of political institutions and compromising the quality of life.

Why was the opportunity missed? To have acted otherwise would have required a level of commitment to racial equality that was lacking. It would also have required programs and expenditures for which there was no political will. In the final analysis, the nation succumbed once again to its endemic racism and to its collective indifference to the plight of its black citizens. Although immigration has produced a more racially diverse population, paradoxically, this new diversity has reinforced the preexisting structure of occupational apartheid.[12]

THE MYTH OF THE BLACK MIDDLE CLASS

At first blush, the existence of a large black middle class would suggest that racist barriers in occupations are no longer insurmountable—in other words, that occupational apartheid is not the problem it was in times past. To be sure, the existence of this middle class signifies a historic breakthrough. Never before have so many blacks been represented at the higher echelons of the occupational world—in the professions and in corporate management. Never before have so many blacks found employment in core industries, in both the white-collar and blue-collar sectors. Nor can this new black middle class, given its size, be dismissed as "window dressing" or "tokenism." Yet there are other grounds for doubting that the existence of this large black middle class signifies the demise of occupational apartheid.

In the first place, insofar as this black middle class is an artifact of affirmative action policy, it cannot be said to be the result of the autonomous workings of market forces. In other words, the black middle class does not reflect a lowering of racist barriers in occupations so much as the opposite: Racism is so entrenched that without government intervention there would be little "progress" to boast about.

Second, although a substantial segment of the new black middle class is found in corporate management, there is a pattern of racial segregation *within* these structures (similar to what happens in many "integrated" schools). Studies have found that many black managers work in personnel functions, often administering affirmative action programs. Others function as intermediaries between white corporations and the black community or the black consumer.[13] Cut off from the corporate mainstream, these black executives often find themselves in dead-end jobs with little job security. By outward appearances, they have "made it" in the white corporate world, but their positions and roles are still defined and circumscribed by race.

Much the same thing can be said about the black business sector. In an incisive analysis of "The Making of the Black Middle Class," Sharon Collins provides the following account:

> Black entrepreneurs are concentrated in segregated rather than generalized services. In 1979, 68 percent of black-owned businesses were in retail and selected services that marketed their wares almost exclusively to black consumers. In 1979, 99 percent of all minority business was based on federal procurement or sales to the minority consumers.[14]

In her analysis of data on Chicago-based minority professional service firms, Collins found a similar pattern of racial segmentation, even with firms doing business with the government:

> Personnel service firms provided workers for units with racial concerns, such as the Office of Manpower. Black law firms were hired for contact compliance and labor-management issues in segregated services such as Housing and Urban Development. Certified public accountant firms performed pre-grant and general audits for segregated sites such as Cook County Hospital. Management consulting firms provided technical assistance primarily to agencies such as Chicago's Department of Human Services or the Federal Office of Minority Business Development. Engineers provided professional services to predominantly black sites such as Chicago's Northshore Sanitary District.[15]

In short, the much ballyhooed growth of black-owned business has generally occurred within the framework of a racially segregated economy.[16]

Finally, there is the double-edged sword associated with public sector employment. On the one hand, the fact that government employment has opened up to blacks marks another change of historic dimensions. For two decades after the Second World War, black representation in government was largely restricted to the Postal Service and to low-level clerical and service positions. As noted earlier, today some 1.6 million blacks, constituting one-fourth of the entire black labor force, are employed by government. Indeed, this is the source of much of the "progress" we celebrate.

On the other hand, it shows once again that racial progress has depended on the intervention of government, in this instance as a direct employer. Furthermore, within the ranks of government, there is a great deal of internal segregation. For the most part, blacks employed in government are social welfare providers in such areas as education, welfare, health, employment security, and public housing. Essentially, they function as intermediaries and as a buffer between white America and the black underclass. As Michael Brown and Steven Erie have argued, "the principal economic legacy of the Great Society for the black community has been the creation of a large-scale social welfare economy of publicly funded middle-income service providers and low-income service and cash transfer recipients."[17]

To conclude, as Collins does, that "the growth of a black middle class is *not* evidence of a decline in racial inequality in the United States" is perhaps an overstatement.[18] After all, the sheer existence of a large black middle class means that blacks are no longer a uniformly downtrodden people. On the other hand, it may signify not the *dissolution* so much as an *artful reconfiguration* of caste boundaries in the occupational world. To control the disorder emanating from the ghettos of America, a new class of "Negro jobs" has been created. They are not the dirty, menial, and backbreaking jobs of the past. On the contrary, they are coveted jobs that offer decent wages and job security. Nevertheless, they are jobs that are pegged for blacks and that function within the context of racial hierarchy and division.

Precisely because the new black middle class is largely a product of government policy, its future is subject to the vagaries of politics. Already it is apparent, as two economists have concluded, that "the epoch of rapid black relative economic advance ended sometime in the late 1970s and early 1980s and…some of the earlier gains eroded in the 1980s."[19] Court decisions restricting minority set-asides have already had a severe impact on black businesses.[20] The current attack on affirmative action will inevitably lead to a further erosion of black socioeconomic gains. Finally, just as blacks benefited disproportionately from the growth of government, they will certainly be severely affected by the current movement to cut the size of the government and the scope of government services. Black public-sector workers are especially vulnerable to layoffs because they are disproportionately found in positions that are heavily dependent on federal subsidies.[21]

THE JOB CRISIS IN BLACK AMERICA

If the new black middle class does not signify a fundamental decline in racial inequality, then what are we to conclude about the persistence and growth of the black underclass? In *Poor*

People's Movements, written in 1979, Piven and Cloward provided an apt description of the current situation when they wrote: "In effect, the black poor progressed from slave labor to cheap labor to (for many) no labor at all."[22] Indeed, a job crisis of the magnitude that existed in the society at large during the Great Depression afflicts black America today. In the Depression, the crisis was defined as such, and extraordinary programs were developed to overhaul basic economic institutions and to create jobs for the unemployed. In the case of the black job crisis, however, social policy has been predicated on the assumption that black unemployment stems from the deficiencies of black workers, and social policy has rarely advanced beyond some meager job training programs.[23]

A few statistics will suffice to convey the dimensions of this job crisis. In 1994, the unemployment rate was 11.5 percent for blacks and 5.3 percent for whites.[24] According to one estimate, blacks would need 1.6 million jobs to achieve parity with whites. The job deficit for black men over 20 is 736,000 jobs; for black women over 20, it is 150,000 jobs; and for black teenagers it is 500,000 jobs.[25]

As is often pointed out, the government's measure of unemployment is only the tip of the iceberg because it leaves out "discouraged workers" who have given up looking for work, as well as "involuntary part-time workers" who want full-time employment. The National Urban League has developed its own measure of "hidden unemployment" that includes these two groups. In 1992, the League's hidden unemployment rate was 13.3 percent for whites and 25.5 percent for blacks. Thus, one-quarter of the black population, involving roughly 3 million workers, are effectively jobless.[26] Even this figure does not sufficiently reflect the depth of the problem because it leaves out the working poor—those who are employed full time, but whose wages leave them below the poverty line.

This job crisis is the single-most important factor behind the familiar tangle of problems that beset black communities. Without jobs, nuclear families become unglued or are never formed. Without jobs, or husbands with jobs, women with young children are forced onto the welfare rolls. Without jobs, many ghetto youth resort to the drug trade or other illicit ways of making money. Ironically, those who end up in prison do find work—in prison shops that typically pay fifty cents or less an hour—only to find themselves jobless on the outside. Given this fact, the high rate of recidivism should come as no surprise. For different reasons, schools are generally ineffective in teaching children whose parents lack stable jobs and incomes. In short, there is no exit from the racial quagmire unless there is a national commitment to address the job crisis in black America.

Tragically, this nation does not have the political will to confront its legacy of slavery, even if this means nothing more than providing jobs at decent wages for blacks who continue to be relegated to the fringes of the job market. Instead, a mythology has been constructed that, in ways reminiscent of slavery itself, alleges that blacks are inefficient and unproductive workers, deficient in the work habits and moral qualities that delivered other groups from poverty....

What would be involved in restoring racial justice to the national agenda? We must begin where the civil rights revolution ended—by attacking the deep-seated institutionalized inequalities that exist between the white and black citizens of this nation. The historic achievement of the civil rights revolution was to tear down the walls of segregation. The challenge today is to erect the structures of racial equality. If occupational apartheid is the essence of American racism, as has been argued here, then the keystone of remedial social policy must be a concerted attack on occupational apartheid....

Any serious effort to resume the unfinished racial agenda must begin with the detailed policy agenda laid out by the Kerner Commission in 1968. At the top of this agenda was a series of proposals dealing with employment, consistent with the promise of the Employment Act of 1946 to provide "a useful job at a reasonable wage for all who wish to work." Specific proposals included beefing up the enforcement powers of the Equal Employment Opportunities Commission, creating new jobs in both the public and private sectors, providing subsidies to employers to hire and train the hard-core unemployed, and launching programs of economic development and social reconstruction targeted for poverty areas and racial ghettos.

Another policy initiative follows from the analysis in this chapter:

Immigration policy must take into account the legitimate interests of native workers, especially those on the economic margin. After all, the meaning of citizenship is diminished if it does not include the right to a job at decent wages.[27] For African-Americans who have toiled on American soil for centuries, and whose sons and daughters have died in the nation's wars, the case for national action is especially urgent. Today we are confronted with the spectacle of these oldest of Americans again being passed over by new waves of immigrants. It is difficult to escape the conclusion that present immigration policy not only subverts the cause of racial justice, but, given the immense human and social costs of the racial status quo, is also antithetical to the national interest.

To be sure, other principles weigh on the formulation of immigrant policy. Many immigrants—especially Mexicans who are migrating to territory once possessed by Mexico—have historical and moral claim for access to American labor markets. Also to be considered is the proud liberal tradition of America as an asylum for the dispossessed. Like the immigrants of yore, the new immigrants contribute immeasurably to "the building of America," its culture as well as its economy. These factors, however, must be balanced against the deleterious effects that the continuing volume of immigration has on groups on the economic margin—not only African-Americans but on the immigrants themselves and their children....

We need a renewed national commitment to dealing with the job crisis that afflicts black America. This would begin with vigorous enforcement of antidiscrimination laws. However, the lesson of the post-civil-rights era is that antidiscrimination laws are minimally effective unless they are backed up with compliance checks and other enforcement mechanisms—in short, affirmative action. The significance of affirmative action is that it amounts to a frontal assault on the racial division of labor. Whatever its limitations, affirmative action has produced the most significant departure from the occupational caste system that has existed since slavery. If racial progress is to continue, affirmative action must be extended to wider segments of the work force.

Again, it may seem gratuitous to say this at a time when racism and reaction are feeding on one another, and there is a tidal wave of opposition against affirmative action. However, there is a maddening illogic to the current crusade against welfare, crime, out-of-wedlock births, and the other "pathologies" associated in the popular mind with the ghetto population. Unless jobs and opportunities are targeted for black youth and young adults, punitive legislation and the withdrawal of public assistance will only produce more desperation and even greater disorder....

The job crisis in black America is allowed to fester for one basic reason: Because the power elites of this nation regard these black communities as politically and economically expendable. They can afford to do so as long as they are not under great countervailing pressure, either from a mobilized black protest movement or from spontaneous ghetto uprisings. This is a situation of politics-as-usual so long as poverty and joblessness manifest themselves as "quiet riots"—that is, as crime and violence that can be contained through a criminal justice system that currently has a prison population exceeding one million people.

On the other hand, when these communities do finally erupt in full-scale riots, as South Central Los Angeles did in the aftermath of the Rodney King episode, suddenly race is back on the national agenda. Even the mainstream media resisted the temptation merely to resort to moral platitudes. *Newsweek* proclaimed that "This Was No Riot, It Was a Revolt," and described "the siege of LA" as a "bloody wake-up call" to reverse the neglect of America's inner cities.[28]

NOTES

1. For an excellent analysis of the historical relationship between race and occupational structures, see Harold M. Baron, "The Demand for Black Labor," *Radical America* 5 (March-April 1971); and idem, "The Web of Urban Racism," in *Institutional Racism in America*, ed. Louis L. Knowles and Kenneth Prewitt (Upper Saddle River, NJ: Prentice Hall, 1969), pp. 134–76.
2. See Lawrence H. Fuchs, "The Reactions of Black Americans to Immigration," in *Immigration Reconsidered*, ed. Virginia Yans-McLaughlin (New York: Oxford University Press, 1990), especially pp.

295–97, and David J. Hellwig, "Patterns of Black Nativism," *American Studies* 23 (Spring 1982).
3. Muller, Thomas. 1993. *Immigrants and the American City*. New York: New York University Press, p. 91.
4. Myrdal, Gunnar. 1994. *An American Dilemma: The Negro Problem and Modern Democracy*. New York: Harper & Row, p. 1005.
5. Government Printing Office. 1975. *Historical Statistics of the United States*. Washington, DC: Government Printing Office, p. 500. Jaynes, Gerald David and Robin M. Williams, Jr. 1989. A *Common Destiny*. Washington, D.C.: National Academy Press, p. 273.
6. Piven, Frances Fox and Richard A. Cloward. 1979. *Poor People's Movements*. New York: Vintage Books, Chapter 4.
7. In a paper written for the National Advisory Commission on Civil Disorders in 1968, Herbert Gans debunked the notion that blacks arriving in Northern cities were following in the footsteps of earlier immigrants and could therefore anticipate the same beneficial outcomes. "Escaping from Poverty: A Comparison of the Immigrant and Black Experience," in *People, Plans, and Policies* (New York: Columbia University Press, 1991), Chapter 18.
8. For a recent demographic analysis of the new immigration, see Reuben C. Rumbaut, "Origins and Destinies: Immigration to the United States Since World War II," *Sociological Forum* 9 (December 1994), pp. 583–621.
9. Jackson, "Seeking Common Ground for Blacks and Immigrants," p. 95.
10. For example, a 1983 national poll found that 69 percent of black respondents agreed that "illegal immigrants are a major harm to U.S. jobless," and 73 percent said that "the U.S. should admit fewer or a lot fewer legal immigrants." Jackson, "Seeking Common Ground for Blacks and Immigrants," p. 96. For a comprehensive review of poll findings on the immigration issue, see Muller, *Immigrants and the American City*, pp. 161–66.

A recent New York Times/CBS News Poll found that the percentage of Americans who favored a decrease in immigration had risen to 61 percent, up from 49 percent when the question was last asked in 1986. Compared to whites, black Americans were nine percentage points more likely to see immigrants taking jobs away, but nine percentage points less likely to prefer a decrease in immigration. Seth Mydans, "Poll Finds Tide of Immigration Brings Hostility," *New York Times*, June 27, 1993.
11. For an informative discussion of the role that black organizations and the Congressional Black Caucus played in the debate over the Simpson-Mazzoli bill in 1983 and 1984, see Muller, *Immigrants and the American City*, pp. 52–67.
12. A note on the politics of immigration. As Otis L. Graham, Jr., suggests, it is a mistake to equate im-

migration restriction with xenophobia or reaction; "Illegal Immigration and the Left," *Dissent* 29 (Summer 1980). Historically, elements of organized labor, including unions made up largely of immigrants, have favored restrictive immigration policies because they feared that unlimited immigration depressed wages and standards, created a bottom tier of immigrant workers, and prevented changes in the structure of the secondary labor market. For Graham's more recent statements on this issue, see "Immigration and the National Interest," in *U.S. Immigration in the 1980s: Reappraisal and Reform*, ed. David Simcox, pp. 124—36; and "Uses and Misuses of History in the Debate Over Immigration Reform," *The Public Historian*, 8, no. 2 (Spring 1986), pp. 41—64.

Although working-class opposition to immigration often stemmed from xenophobia and racism, other legitimate interests were also involved. This has been acknowledged by John Higham, author of *Strangers in the Land*—the classic history of nativism—in the preface to the book's second edition. In the revised edition of *Send These to Me: Immigrants in Urban America* (Baltimore: Johns Hopkins University Press, 1984), Higham writes sympathetically of the Simpson-Mazzoli bill, which included sanctions on employers who hired undocumented workers. The commission that led to the passage of this legislation was headed by a prominent liberal, Father Theodore Hesburgh.

On the other hand, free-market economists and business interests have championed the cause of expanded immigration. See, for example, M. S. Forbes, Jr., "We Need More People," *Forbes* (February 9, 1987); "The Rekindled Flame," Editorial, *Wall Street Journal*, July 3, 1989; Michael J. Mandel and Christopher Farrell, "The Immigrant: How They're Helping to Revitalize the U.S. Economy," *Business Week* (July 13, 1992); Wattenberg and Zinsmeister, "The Case for More Immigration," pp. 19—25; and Simon, "The Case for Greatly Increased Immigration," pp. 89—103.

13. Heidrick and Stuggles, Inc., "Chief Personnel Executives Look at Blacks in Business," cited in Sharon M. Collins, "The Making of the Black Middle Class," *Social Problems* 30 (April 1983), p. 379. See also Sharon M. Collins, "The Marginalization of Black Executives," *Social Problems* 36 (October 1989), pp. 317—29; and idem, "Blacks on the Bubble: The Vulnerability of Black Executives in White Corporations," *Sociological Quarterly* 34 (August 1993), pp. 429—47.

14. Collins, "The Making of the Black Middle Class," p. 377.

15. Ibid. p. 379.

16. Also to be considered are the many and subtle ways in which old-fashioned racism afflicts even the black middle class. For two recent works, see Joe E. Feagin and Melvin P Sikes, *Living with Racism* (Boston: Beacon Press, 1994); and David Wellman,

Portraits of White Racism (Cambridge: Cambridge University Press, 1993).

17. Brown, Michael K. and Steven P. Erie. "Blacks and the Legacy of the Great Society: The Economic and Political Impact of Federal Social Policy," *Public Policy* 29 (Summer 1981), pp. 301.

18. Collins, "The Making of the Black Middle Class," p. 379.

19. Bound, John and Richard B. Freeman. "Black Economic Progress: Erosion of the Post-1965 Gains in the 1980s," in *The Question of Discrimination*, Shulman and Darity (eds.), p. 47.

20. de Courcy Hinds, Michael. "Minority Business Set Back Sharply by Courts' Rulings," *New York Times*, December 23, 1991.

21. For example, when the Reagan administration reduced social spending between 1980 and 1981, 76 percent of the 400 employees laid off in Chicago's Department of Human Services were black, as were 40 percent of the 186 workers laid off in the Department of Health. In contrast, the federal cutbacks barely affected the predominantly white work force in Chicago's Streets and Sanitation Department, which is funded with local revenues. Collins, "The Making of the Black Middle Class," p. 377.

22. Piven and Cloward, *Poor People's Movements*, p. 184.

23. As Margaret Weir points out with respect to the 1960s: "This decade of intellectual ferment and policy experimentation left a surprisingly meager legacy for employment policy. Labor market policy became subsumed into the poverty program, offering job preparation to those on the fringes on the labor market, and to the black poor in particular." *Politics and Jobs* (Princeton, NJ: Princeton University Press, 1992). For an incisive analysis of the political functions of job training programs, see Gordon Lafer, "Minority Unemployment, Labor Market Segmentation, and the Failure of Job Training Policy in New York City," *Urban Affairs Quarterly* 28 (December 1992).

24. U.S. Department of Labor, Bureau of Labor Statistics. *Employment and Earnings, January 1995*. Washington, DC: Government Printing Office.

25. Swinton, David H. "The Economic Status of African-Americans: 'Permanent' Poverty and Inequality," in *The State of Black America* (Washington, DC: National Urban League, 1991), p. 53. Swinton states that the remainder of the overall shortage is caused by demographic factors.

26. "Quarterly Economic Report on the African-American Worker," National Urban League, Report No. 32 (September 1992). Jim Sleeper writes: "…what kinds of hard work and moral discipline may people who envision a democratic and just society demand even of the poorest and most oppressed; what, indeed, would it be condescending and worse not to demand of 'the least among us'?" *The Closest of Strangers* (New York: W. W. Norton, 1990), p. 37. Regarding the scarcity of jobs,

see George James, "The Job Is Picking Up Garbage; 100,000 Want It," *New York Times,* September 21, 1990.

27. At least in principle, this has been government policy over the past half-century. With the passage of the Employment Act of 1946, a large bipartisan majority in Congress endorsed the principle that "it is the continuing policy and responsibility of the Federal Government" to bring about "conditions under which there will be afforded useful employment opportunities…for those able, willing, and seeking work." This principle was affirmed in the 1978 Humphrey-Hawkins Act. Except for a few sporadic attempts at government job creation programs, however, the mechanisms to achieve full employment have never been put into place. On the contrary, government fiscal policy is commonly used to engineer unemployment in order to contain inflation. For an astute analysis of "the political collapse of full employment," see Weir, *Politics and Jobs,* Chapter 5.

28. Hackworth, David H. "This Was No Riot, It Was a Revolt." *Newsweek* (May 11, 1992), p. 30; and ibid., (May 25, 1992), p. 33.

31. RACE AND MIDDLE CLASS IDENTITY IN AMERICA

CLARENCE PAGE

Today I live a well-integrated life in the suburbs. Black folks still tell me how to be "black" when I stray from the racial party lines, while white folks tell me how to be "color-blind." I still feel as frustrated in my attempts to transcend race as a reluctant lemming must feel while being rushed over the brink by its herd. But I find I have plenty of company in my frustration. Integration has not been a simple task for upwardly mobile African-Americans, especially for those of us who happen also to be parents.

Here is the perspective of a commentator, essayist, journalist, African American, who has become middle class and "integrated." Yet he expresses uneasiness about his identity in American society. Color always was and continues to be an important part of American society, he writes. Although choices abound for black people ("if they can afford them"), we are not a colorblind society, and we need to be honest about that. Change is taking place, but serious questions remain about "who I am" and what kind of society we should become. Page describes the importance of living in a diverse society, but a diverse society should not allow race to matter for purposes of discrimination and oppression of people.

The message in this essay is not an easy one to understand because it shows the complexities of racial and ethnic differences: the desire to claim an identity for oneself, yet the discrimination that others use to exclude those who claim it; the opportunities that exist for many African Americans, yet the continued denial of opportunity for large numbers; the integration that is at the surface, the sharp division underneath.

Race has long had a rude presence in my life. While visiting relatives in Alabama as a child in the 1950s, I first saw water fountains marked "white" and "colored." I vaguely recall being excited. I rushed over to the one marked "colored" and turned it on, only to find, to my deep disappointment, that the water came out clear, just like the water back home in Ohio.

"Segregation," my dad said. I'd never heard the word before. My southern-born parents explained that it was something the white folks "down home" practiced. Some "home." Yet unpleasant experiences in the North already had taught me a more genteel, yet no less limiting, version.

"There are places white people don't want colored to go," my elders told me in their soft southern accents, "and white people make the rules."

We had plenty of segregation like that in the North. We just didn't have the signs, which made it cheaper and easier to deny. We could look out of my schoolhouse window to see a public swimming pool closed to nonwhites. We had to go across town to the separate-but-equal "pool for colored." The steel mill that was our town's biggest employer held separate picnics for colored and white employees, which seemed to be just fine with the employees. Everyone had a good time, separately and unequally. I think the colored folks, who today would be called the "black community," were just happy to have something to call their own.

When I was about six years old, I saw a television commercial for an amusement park near the southern Ohio factory town where I grew up.

I chose to go. I told my parents. They looked at each other sadly and informed me that "little colored kids can't go there." I was crushed.

"I wish I was white," I told my parents.

"No, you don't!" Mom snapped. She gave me a look terrible enough to persuade me instantly that no, I didn't.

"Well, maybe for a few minutes, anyway?" I asked. "Just long enough for me to get past the front gate?" Then I could show them, I thought. I remember I wanted to show them what a terrific kid I was. I felt sorry for the little white children who would be deprived of getting to know me.

Throughout our childhood years, my friendships with white schoolchildren (and with Pancho from the only Latino family in the neighborhood) proceeded without interruption. Except for the occasional tiff over some injudicious use of the N-word or some other slur we had picked up from our elders, we played in each other's backyards as congenially as Spanky, Buckwheat, and the rest of the gang on the old Hal Roach Our Gang comedies we used to watch on television.

Yet it quickly became apparent to me that my white friends were growing up in a different reality from the one to which I was accustomed. I could tell from the way one white friend happily discussed his weekend at LeSourdesville Lake that he did not have a clue of my reality.

"Have you been?" he asked.

"Colored can't go there," I said, somewhat astonished that he had not noticed.

"Oh, that can't be," he said.

For a moment, I perked up, wondering if the park's policy had changed. "Have you seen any colored people there?" I asked.

My white friend thought for a moment, then realized that he had not. He expressed surprise. I was surprised that he was surprised.

By the time I reached high school in the early 1960s, LeSourdesville Lake would relax its racial prohibitions. But the lessons of it stuck with me. It taught me how easily white people could ignore the segregation problem because, from their vantage point, it was not necessarily a problem. It was not necessarily an advantage to them, either, although some undoubtedly thought so. White people of low income, high insecurity, or fragile ego could always say that, no matter how badly off they felt, at least they were not black. Segregation helped them uphold and maintain this illusion of superiority. Even those white people who considered themselves to have a well-developed sense of social conscience could easily rationalize segregation as something that was good for both races. We played unwittingly into this illusion, I thought, when my friends and I began junior high school and, suddenly thrust into the edgy, high hormonal world of adolescence, quickly gravitated into social cliques according to tastes and race.

It became even more apparent to me that my white friends and I were growing up in *parallel realities*, not unlike the parallel universes described in the science fiction novels and comic books I adored—or the "parallel realities" experienced by Serbs, Bosnians, and Croatians as described years later by feminist writer Slavenka Drakulic in *The Balkan Express*. Even as the evil walls of legal segregation were tumbling down, thanks to the hard-fought struggles of the civil rights movement, it occurred to me that my reality might never be quite the same as that experienced by my white friends. We were doomed, I felt, to dwell in our parallel realities. Separated by thick walls of prejudice, we would view each other through windows of stained-glass perceptions, colored by our personal experiences. My parents had taught me well.

"Don't be showin' yo' color," my parents would admonish me in my youth, before we would go out in public, especially among white folks. The phrase had special meaning in Negro conversations. Imbued with many subtle meanings and nuances, the showing of one's "color" could be an expression of chastisement or warning, admonishment or adulation, satire or self-hatred, anger or celebration. It could mean acting out or showing anger in a loud and uncivilized way.

Its cultural origins could be traced to the Africa-rooted tradition of "signifying," a form of witty, deliberately provocative, occasionally combative word play. The thrill of the game comes from taking one's opponent close to the edge of tolerable insult. Few subjects—except perhaps sex itself—could be a more sensitive matter between black people than talk about someone else's "color." The showing of one's "color," then, connoted the display of the very worst stereotypes anyone ever dreamed up about how black people behaved. "White people are not really white," James Baldwin wrote in 1961, "but colored people can sometimes be extremely colored."

Sometimes you can still hear black people say, in the heat of frustration, "I almost showed my color today," which is a way of saying they almost lost their "cool," "dropped the mask," or "went off." Losing one's cool can be a capital offense by black standards, for it shows weakness in a world in which spiritual rigor is one of the few things we can call our own. Those who keep their cool repress their "color." It is cool, in other words, to be colorless.

The title of [the volume from which this chapter is taken], *Showing My Color*, emerged from my fuming discontent with the current fashions of *racial denial*, steadfast repudiations of the difference race continues to make in American life. Old liberals, particularly white liberals who have become new conservatives, charge that racial pride and color consciousness threaten to "Balkanize" American life, as if it ever was a model of unity. Many demand that we "get past race." But denials of a cancer, no matter how vigorous they may be, will not make the malignancy go away.

No less august a voice than the Supreme Court's conservative majority has taken to arguing in the 1990s for a "colorblind" approach to civil rights law, the area of American society in which color and gender consciousness have made the most dramatic improvement in equalizing opportunities.

The words of the Reverend Martin Luther King, Jr., have been perverted to support this view. Most frequently quoted is his oft-stated dream of the day when everyone would "not be judged by the color of their skin but by the content of their character." I would argue that King never intended for us to forget *all* about color. Even in his historic "I Have a Dream" speech, from which this line most often is lifted, he also pressed the less-often quoted but piquantly salient point about "the promissory note" America gave freed slaves, which, when they presented it, was returned to them marked "insufficient funds."

• • •

I would argue that too much has been made of the virtue of "color-blindness." I don't want Americans to be blind to my color as long as color continues to make a profound difference in determining life chances and opportunities. Nor do I wish to see so significant a part of my identity denied. "Ethnic differences are the very essence of cultural diversity and national creativity," black social critic Albert Murray wrote in *The*

Omni-Americans (1970). "The problem is not the existence of ethnic differences, as is so often assumed, but the intrusion of such differences into areas where they do not belong."

Where, then, *do* they belong? Diversity is enriching, but race intrudes rudely on the individual's attempts to define his or her own identity. I used to be "colored." Then I was "Negro." Then I became "black." Then I became "African-American." Today I am a "person of color." In three decades, I have been transformed from a "colored person" to a "person of color." Are you keeping up with me?

Changes in what we black people call ourselves are quite annoying to some white people, which is its own reward to some black people. But if white people are confused, so are quite a few black people. There is no one way to be black. We are a diverse people amid a nation of diverse people. Some black people are nationalists who don't want anything to do with white people. Some black people are assimilationists who don't want anything to do with other black people. Some black people are integrationists who move in and out of various groups with remarkable ease. Some of us can be any of the three at any given time, depending on when you happen to run into us.

Growing up as part of a minority can expose the individual to horrible bouts of identity confusion. I used to think of myself as something of a *transracial man*, a figure no less frustrated than a transsexual who feels trapped in the body of something unfamiliar and inappropriate to his or her inner self.

These bouts were most torturous during adolescence, the period of life when, trembling with the shock of nascent independence from the ways of one's elders, the budding individual stitches together the fragile garments of an identity to be worn into adulthood. Stuttering and uncooperative motor skills left me severely challenged in dancing, basket shooting, and various social applications; I felt woefully inadequate to the task of being "popular" in the hot centers of black social activity at my integrated high school and college. "Are you black?" an arbiter of campus militancy demanded one day, when he "caught" me dining too many times with white friends. I had the skin pass, sure enough,

but my inclinations fell well short of his standards. But I was not satisfied with the standards of his counterparts in the white world, either. If I was not "black" enough to please some blacks, I would never be "white" enough to please all whites.

Times have changed. Choices abound for black people, if we can afford them. Black people can now go anywhere they choose, as long as they can pay the bill when they get there. If anyone tries to stop them or any other minorities just because of their color, the full weight of the federal government will step in on the side of the minorities. I thank God and the hard-won gains of the civil rights revolution for my ability to have more choices. But the old rules of race have been replaced in many ways by new ones.

• • •

Today, I live a well-integrated life in the suburbs. Black folks still tell me how to be "black" when I stray from the racial party lines, while white folks tell me how to be "color-blind." I still feel as frustrated in my attempts to transcend race as a reluctant lemming must feel while being rushed over the brink by its herd. But I find I have plenty of company in my frustration. Integration has not been a simple task for upwardly mobile African-Americans, especially for those of us who happen also to be parents.

A few years ago, after talking to black friends who were raising teenage boys, I realized that I was about to face dilemmas not unlike those my parents faced. My son was turning three years old. Everyone was telling me that he was quite cute, and because he was the spitting image of his dad, I was the last to argue.

But it occurred to me that in another decade he would be not three but thirteen. If all goes well, somewhere along the way he is going to turn almost overnight from someone who is perceived as cute and innocent into someone who is perceived as a menace, the most feared creature on America's urban streets today, a *young black male*. Before he, like me when I was barred from a childhood amusement park, would have a chance to let others get to know him, he would be judged not by the content of his character, but by the color of his skin....

• • •

My mom is gone now, after helping set me up with the sort of education that has freed me to make choices. I have chosen to move my father to a nice, predominantly white, antiseptically tidy retirement village near me in Maryland with large golf courses and swimming pools. It is the sort of place he might have scrubbed floors in but certainly not have lived in back in the old days. It has taken him a while to get used to having so many well-off white people behaving so nicely and neighborly to him, but he has made the adjustment well.

Still the ugly specter of racism does not easily vanish. He and the other hundred or so African-American residents decided to form a social club like the other ethnically or religiously based social clubs in the village. One night during their meeting in the main social room, someone scrawled *KKK* on little sheets of paper and slipped them under the windshields of some of their cars in the parking lot. "We think maybe some of the white people wanted the blacks to socialize with the whites, not in a separate group," one lady of the club told me. If so, they showed an unusual method for extending the arms of brotherhood.

I live in a community that worships diversity like a state religion, although individuals sometimes get tripped up by it. The excellent Spanish "immersion" program that one of the county's "magnet" schools installed to encourage middle-class parents to stay put has itself become a cover for "white flight" by disgruntled white parents. Many of them, despite a lack of empirical evidence, perceive the school's regular English program as inferior, simply because it is 90 percent minority and mostly composed of children who come from a less-fortunate socioeconomic background. So the Spanish immersion classes designed to encourage diversity have become almost exclusively white and Asian America, while the English classes have become almost exclusively—irony of ironies—black and Latino, with many of the children learning English as a second language. Statistically, the school is "diverse" and "integrated." In reality, its student body is divided by an indelible wall, separate but supposedly equal....

Despite all these color-conscious efforts to educate the county's children in a color-blind ideal of racial equality, many of our children seem to be catching on to race codes anyway, although with a twist suitable to the hip-hop generation. One local junior high school teacher, when he heard his black students referring to themselves as "bad," had the facts of racial life explained to him like this: They were not talking about the "bad means good" slang popularized by Michael Jackson's *Bad* album. They meant "bad" in the sense of misbehaving and poorly motivated. The black kids are "bad," the students explained, and the white kids are "good." The Asian kids are "like white," and the Latino kids "try to be bad, like the blacks." Anyone who tried to break out of those stereotypes was trying to break the code, meaning that a black or Latino who tried to make good grades was "trying to be white."

It is enough, as Marvin Gaye famously sang, to make you want to holler and throw up both your hands. Yet my neighbors and I hate to complain too loudly because, unlike other critics you may read or hear about, we happen to be a liberal community that not only believes in the dream of integration and true diversity, but actually is trying to live it.

We reside in Montgomery County, Maryland, the most prosperous suburban county per capita in the Washington, D.C., area. Each of the above-mentioned controversies has been reported in the pages of the *Washington Post* and other local media, right under the noses and, in some cases, within the families of some of the nation's top policy makers....

We see icons of black success—Colin Powell, Douglas Wilder, Bill Cosby, Oprah Winfrey, Bryant Gumbel, the two Michaels: Jordan and Jackson—not only accepted but adored by whites in ways far removed from the arm's-length way white America regarded Jackie Robinson, Willie Mays, Lena Horne, and Marian Anderson.

Yet, although the media show happy images of blacks, whites, Asians, and Hispanics getting along, amicably consuming the good life, a fog of false contentment conceals menacing fissures cracking the national racial landscape.

Despite the growth of the black middle class, most blacks and whites live largely separate lives. School integration actually peaked in 1967, according to a Harvard study, and has declined ever since. Economic segregation has proceeded without interruption, distancing poor blacks not only from whites but also from upwardly mobile blacks, making the isolation and misery of poor blacks worse. One out of every two black children lives below the poverty line, compared to one out of every seven white children. Black infants in America die at twice the rate of white infants. A record-setting million inmates crowd the nation's prisons, half of them black. The black out-of-wedlock birth rate has grown from about 25 percent in 1965 to more than 60 percent (more than 90 percent in the South Bronx and other areas of concentrated black poverty) in 1990.

The good news is very good, but the bad news has become steadily worse. Economically, we are still playing catch-up. In 1865, newly freed from slavery, African Americans controlled 3 percent of the wealth in America, United States Civil Rights Commissioner Arthur Fletcher tells me. Today, we still control just 3 percent of the wealth. After all this time, we have become free, more often than not, to make other people wealthier. The decline of industrial America, along with low-skill, high-pay jobs, has left much of black America split in two along lines of class, culture, opportunity and hope. The "prepared" join the new black middle class, which grew rapidly in the 1970s and early 1980s. The unprepared populate a new culture, directly opposed not only to the predominantly white mainstream, but also to any blacks who aspire to practice the values of hard work, good English, and family loyalty that would help them to join the white mainstream. The results of this spiritual decline, along with economic decline, have been devastating. Although more black women go to college than ever before, it has become a commonplace to refer to young black males as an endangered species. New anti-black stereotypes replace the old. Prosperous, well-dressed African Americans still complain of suffering indignities when they try to hail a taxicab. The fact that the taxi that just passed them by was driven by a black cabby, native born or immigrant, makes no difference....

Behind our questions of race lurk larger questions of identity, our sense of who we are, where we belong, and where we are going. Our sense of place and peoplehood within groups is a perpetu-

al challenge in some lives, particularly lives in America, a land where identity bubbles quite often out of nothing more than a weird alchemy of history and choice. "When I discover who I am, I'll be free," Ralph Ellison once wrote.

I reject the melting pot metaphor. People don't melt. Americans prove it on their ethnic holidays, in the ways they dance, in the ways they sing, in the culturally connected ways they worship. Displaced peoples long to celebrate their ethnic roots many generations and intermarriages after their ancestors arrived in their new land. Irish-American celebrations of St. Patrick's Day in Boston, Chicago, and New York City are far more lavish than anything seen on that day in Dublin or Belfast. Mexican-American celebrations of Cinco de Mayo, the Fifth of May, are far more lavish in Los Angeles and San Antonio than anything seen that day in Mexico City. It is as if holidays give us permission to expose our former selves as we imagine them to be. Americans of European descent love to show their ethnic cultural backgrounds. Why do they get nervous only when black people show their love for theirs? Is it that black people on such occasions suddenly remind white people of vulnerabilities black people feel quite routinely as a minority in a majority white society? Is it that white people, by and large, do not like this feeling, that they want nothing more than to cleanse themselves of it and make sure that it does not come bubbling up again? Attempts by Americans to claim some ephemeral, all-inclusive "all-American" identity reminds me of Samuel Johnson's observation: "Sir, a man may be so much of everything, that he is nothing of anything."

Instead of the melting pot metaphor, I prefer the mulligan stew, a concoction my parents tell me they used to fix during the Great Depression, when there was not a lot of food around the house and they "made do" with whatever meats, vegetables, and spices they had on hand. Everything went into the pot and was stirred. up, but the pieces didn't melt. Peas were easily distinguished from carrots or potatoes. Each maintained its distinctive character. Yet each loaned its special flavor to the whole, and each absorbed some of the flavor from the others. That flavor, always unique, always changing, is the beauty of America to me, even when the pot occasionally boils over....

African Americans are as diverse as other Americans. Some become nationalistic and ethnocentric. Others become pluralistic or multicultural, fitting their black identity into a comfortable niche among other aspects of themselves and their daily lives. Whichever they choose, a comfortable identity serves to provide not only a sense of belonging and protection for the individual against the abuses of racism, but also, ultimately, a sturdy foundation from which the individual can interact effectively with other people, cultures, and situations beyond the world of blackness.

"Identity would seem to be the garment with which one covers the nakedness of the self," James Baldwin wrote in *The Devil Finds Work* (1976), "in which case, it is best that the garment be loose, a little like the robes of the desert, through which one's nakedness can always be felt, and, sometimes, discerned. This trust in one's nakedness is all that gives one the power to change one's robes."

The cloak of proud black identity has provided a therapeutical warmth for my naked self after the chilly cocoon of inferiority imposed early in my life by a white-exalting society. But it is best worn loosely, lest it become as constricting and isolating for the famished individual soul as the garment it replaced.

The ancestral desire of my ethnic people to be "just American" resonates in me. But I cannot forget how persistently the rudeness of race continues to intrude between me and that dream. I can defy it, but I cannot deny it....

32. BLACKS IN AMERICA

ANDREW HACKER

In the eyes of white Americans, being black encapsulates your identity. No other racial or national origin is seen as having so pervasive a personality or character. Even if you write a book on Euclidean algorithms or Renaissance sculpture, you will still be described as a "black author." Although you are a native American, with a longer lineage than most, you will never be accorded full membership in the nation or society. More than that, you learn early that this nation feels no need or desire for your physical presence.

This is a powerful chapter from a very enlightening book, *Two Nations*. The purpose of this book is to show that the unique position of African Americans makes it difficult to create a society of equal opportunity.

Andrew Hacker claims that race matters—and it matters a lot. It matters because our society has always regarded race as a basis for oppression and discrimination. Hacker is especially sensitive to the position of the African American, and this chapter captures their situation like no other selection I have ever read.

Hacker makes a single point in this chapter: Being black in America has consequences—in the areas of wealth, identity, raising children, occupational opportunities, place of residence, and treatment in the criminal justice system. Being black influences how one is viewed, how one discusses one's life and achievements, and how one sees society, whites, and police. Being black influences what one says to people, what they say, and what happens in day-to-day interactions with whites. And, finally, being black has consequences for the strain and rage one feels toward one's own position in society.

Hacker is beckoning us to understand all this by trying to place ourselves in the position of blacks in American society.

Most white Americans will say that, all things considered, things aren't so bad for black people in the United States. Of course, they will grant that many problems remain. Still, whites feel there has been steady improvement, bringing blacks closer to parity, especially when compared with conditions in the past. Some have even been heard to muse that it's better to be black because affirmative action policies make it a disadvantage to be white.

What white people seldom stop to ask is how they may benefit from belonging to their race. Nor is this surprising. People who can see do not regard their vision as a gift for which they should offer thanks. It may also be replied that having a white skin does not immunize a person from misfortune or failure. Yet even for those who fall to the bottom, being white has a worth. What could that value be?

Let us try to find out by means of a parable: Suspend disbelief for a moment, and assume that what follows might actually happen:

> You will be visited tonight by an official you have never met. He begins by telling you that he is extremely embarrassed. The organization he represents has made a mistake, something that hardly ever happens.
>
> According to their records, he goes on, you were to have been born black: to another set of parents, far from where you were raised.
>
> However, the rules being what they are, this error must be rectified, and as soon as possible. So at midnight tonight, you will become black. And this will mean not simply a darker skin, but the bodily and facial features associated with African ancestry. However, inside you will be the person you always were. Your knowledge and ideas will remain intact. But outwardly you will not be recognizable to anyone you now know.
>
> Your visitor emphasizes that being born to the wrong parents was in no way your fault. Consequently, his organization is prepared to offer you some reasonable recompense. Would you, he asks, care to name a sum of money you might consider appropriate? He adds that his group is by no means poor. It can be quite generous when the cir-
> cumstances warrant, as they seem to in your case. He finishes by saying that their records show you are scheduled to live another fifty years—as a black man or woman in America.
>
> How much financial recompense would you request?

When this parable has been put to white students, most seemed to feel that it would not be out of place to ask for $50 million, or $1 million for each coming black year. And this calculation conveys, as well as anything, the value that white people place on their own skins. Indeed, to be white is to possess a gift whose value can be appreciated only after it has been taken away. And why ask so large a sum? Surely this needs no detailing. The money would be used, as best it could, to buy protection from the discriminations and dangers white people know they would face once they were perceived to be black.

Of course, no one who is white can understand what it is like to be black in America. Still, were they to spend time in a black body, here are some of the things they would learn.

In the eyes of white Americans, being black encapsulates your identity. No other racial or national origin is seen as having so pervasive a personality or character. Even if you write a book on Euclidean algorithms or Renaissance sculpture, you will still be described as a "black author." Although you are a native American, with a longer lineage than most, you will never be accorded full membership in the nation of society. More than that, you learn early that this nation feels no need or desire for your physical presence. (Indeed, your people are no longer in demand as cheap labor.) You sense that most white citizens would heave a sigh of relief were you simply to disappear. While few openly propose that you return to Africa, they would be greatly pleased were you to make that decision for yourself.

Your people originated in Africa, and you want to feel pride in your homeland. After all, it was where humanity began. Hence your desire to know more of its peoples and their history, their culture and achievements, and how they endure within yourself. W. E. B. Du Bois said it best: "two thoughts, two unrecognizable stirrings, two warring ideals in one black body."

Yet there is also your awareness that not only America, but also much of the rest of the world, regards Africa as the primal continent— the most backward, the least developed—by almost every modern measure. Equally unsettling, Africa is regarded as barely worth the world's attention, a region no longer expected to improve in condition or status. During its periodic misfortunes—usually famine or slaughter—Africa may evoke compassion and pity. Yet the message persists that it must receive outside help because there is little likelihood that it will set things right by itself.

Then there are the personal choices you must make about your identity. Unless you want to stress a Caribbean connection, you are an American and it is the only citizenship you have. At the same time, you realize that this is a white country, which expects its inhabitants to think and act in white ways. How far do you wish to adapt, adjust, assimilate, to a civilization so at variance with your people's past? For example, there is the not-so-simple matter of deciding on your diction. You know how white people talk and what they like to hear. Should you conform to those expectations, even if it demands denying or concealing much of your self? After all, white America gives out most of the rewards and prizes associated with success. Your decisions are rendered all the more painful by the hypocrisy of it all because you are aware that, even if you make every effort to conform, whites will still not accept you as one of their own.

So to a far greater degree than for immigrants from other lands, it rests on you to create your own identity. But it is still not easy to follow the counsel of Zora Neale Hurston: "Be as black as you want to be." For one thing, that choice is not always left to you. By citizenship and birth, you may count as an American, yet you find yourself agreeing with August Wilson when he says, "we're a different people." Why else can you refer to your people as "folks" and "family," to one another as "sisters" and "brothers," in ways whites never can?

There are moments when you understand Toni Morrison's riposte, "At no moment in my life have I ever felt as though I were an American." This in turn gives rise to feelings of sympathy with figures like Cassius Clay, H. Rap Brown, Lew Alcindor, and Stokely Carmichael, who decided to repatriate themselves as Muhammad Ali, Jamil Abdullah al-Amin, Kareem Abdul-Jabbar, and Kwame Touré.

Those choices are not just for yourself. There will be the perplexing—and equally painful—task of having to explain to your children why they will not be treated as other Americans: that they will never be altogether accepted, that they will always be regarded warily, if not with suspicion or hostility. When they ask whether this happens because of anything they have done, you must find ways of conveying that, no, it is not because of any fault of their own. Further, for reasons you can barely explain yourself, you must tell them that much of the world has decided that you are not and cannot be their equals; that this world wishes to keep you apart, a caste it will neither absorb nor assimilate.

You will tell your children this world is wrong. But, because that world is there, they will have to struggle to survive, with scales weighted against them. They will have to work harder and do better, yet the result may be less recognition and reward. We all know life can be unfair. For black people, this knowledge is not an academic theory but a fact of daily life.

You find yourself granting that there are more black faces in places where they were never seen before. Within living memory, your people were barred from major league teams; now they command the highest salaries in most professional sports. In the movies, your people had to settle for roles as servants or buffoons. Now at least some of them are cast as physicians, business executives, and police officials. But are things truly different? When everything is added up, white America still prefers its black people to be performers who divert them as athletes and musicians and comedians.

Yet where you yourself are concerned, you sense that in mainstream occupations, your prospects are quite limited. In most areas of employment, even after playing by the rules, you find yourself hitting a not-so-invisible ceiling. You wonder if you are simply corporate wallpaper, a protective coloration they find it prudent to display. You begin to suspect that a "qualification" you will always lack is white pigmentation.

In theory, all Americans with financial means and a respectable demeanor can choose where they want to live. For over a generation, courts across the country have decreed that a person's race cannot be a reason for refusing to rent or sell a residence. However, the law seems to have had little impact on practice because almost all residential areas are entirely black or white. Most whites prefer it that way. Some will say they would like a black family nearby, if only to be able to report that their area is integrated. But not many do. Most white Americans do not move in circles where racial integration wins social or moral credit.

This does not mean it is absolutely impossible for a black family to find a home in a white area. Some have, and others undoubtedly will. Even so, black Americans have no illusions about the hurdles they will face. If you look outside your designated areas, you can expect chilly receptions, evasive responses, and outright lies: a humiliating experience, rendered all the more enraging because it is so repeated and prolonged. After a while, it becomes too draining to continue the search. Still, if you have the income, you will find an area to your liking; but it will probably be all black. In various suburbs and at the outer edges of cities, one can see well-kept homes, outwardly like other such settings. But a closer view shows all the householders to be black.

This is the place to consider residential apartheid—and that is what it is—in its full perspective. Black segregation differs markedly from that imposed on any other group. Even newly arrived immigrants are more readily accepted in white neighborhoods.

Nor should it be assumed that most black householders prefer the racial ratios in areas where they currently reside. Successive surveys have shown that, on average, only about one in eight say they prefer a neighborhood that is all or mostly black, which is the condition most presently confront. The vast majority—some 85 percent—state they would like an equal mixture of black and white neighbors. Unfortunately, this degree of racial balance has virtually no chance of being realized. The reason, very simply, is that hardly any whites will live in a neighborhood or community where half the residents are black. So directly or indirectly, white Americans have the power to decide the racial composition of communities and neighborhoods. Most egregious have been instances in

which acts of arson or vandalism force black families to leave. But such methods are exceptional. There are other, less blatant, ways to prevent residential integration from passing a certain "tipping" point.

Here we have no shortage of studies. By and large, this research agrees that white residents will stay—and some new ones may move in—if black arrivals do not exceed 8 percent. But once the black proportion passes that point, whites begin to leave the neighborhood and no new ones will move in. The vacated houses or apartments will be bought or rented by blacks, and the area will be on its way to becoming all black....

Americans have extraordinarily sensitive antennae for the colorations of neighborhoods. In virtually every metropolitan area, white householders can rank each enclave by the racial makeup of the residents. Given this knowledge, where a family lives becomes an index of its social standing. Although this is largely an economic matter, proximity to blacks compounds this assessment. For a white family to be seen as living in a mixed—or changing—neighborhood can be construed as a symptom of surrender, indeed as evidence that they are on a downward spiral.

If you are black, these white reactions brand you as a carrier of contamination. No matter what your talents or attainments, you are seen as infecting a neighborhood simply because of your race. This is the ultimate insult of segregation. It opens wounds that never really heal and leaves scars to remind you how far you stand from full citizenship.

• • •

Except when you are in your own neighborhood, you feel always on display. On many occasions, you find you are the only person of your race present. You may be the only black student in a college classroom, the only black on a jury, the sole black at a corporate meeting, the only one at a social gathering. With luck, there may be one or two others. You feel every eye is on you, and you are not clear what posture to present. You realize that your presence makes whites uncomfortable; most of them probably wish you were not there at all. But because you are, they want to see you smile so that they can believe you are being treated well. Not only is an upbeat air expected, but you must never show exasperation or anger, let alone anything that could look like a chip on your shoulder. Not everyone can keep such tight control. You don't find it surprising that so many black athletes and entertainers seek relief from those tensions.

Even when not in white company, you know that you are forever in their conversations. Ralph Ellison once said that, to whites, you are an "invisible man." You know what he meant. Yet for all that, you and your people have been studied and scrutinized and dissected, caricatured, and pitied or deplored, as no other group ever has. You see yourself reduced to data in research, statistics in reports. Each year, the nation asks how many of your teenagers have become pregnant, how many of your young men are in prison. Not only are you continually on view, you are always on trial.

What we have come to call "the media" looms large in the lives of almost all Americans. Television and films, newspapers and magazines, books and advertising, all serve as windows on a wider world, providing real and fantasized images of the human experience. The media also help us to fill out our own identities, telling us about ourselves, or the selves we might like to be.

If you are black, most of what is available for you to read and watch and hear depicts the activities of white people, with only rare and incidental allusions to persons like yourself. Black topics and authors and performers appear even less than your share of the population, not least because the rest of America doesn't care to know about you. Whites will be quick to point out that there have been successful "black" programs on radio and television, as well as popular black entertainers and best-selling authors. Yet in these and other instances, it is whites who decide which people and productions will be underwritten, which almost always means that "black" projects have to appeal to whites as well. You sometimes sense that much that is "black" is missing in artists like Jessye Norman and Toni Morrison, Paul Robeson, and Bill Cosby, who you sense must tailor their talents to white audiences. You often find yourself wishing they could just be themselves, among their own people.

At the same time, you feel frustration and disgust when white America appropriates your music, your styles, indeed your speech and sexuality. At times, white audiences will laud the originality of black artists and performers and athletes. But in the end, they feel more comfortable when white musicians and designers and writers and athletic coaches adapt black talents to white sensibilities.

Add to this your bemusement when movies and television series cast more blacks as physicians and attorneys and executives than one will ever find in actual hospitals or law firms or corporations. True, these depictions can serve as role models for your children, encouraging their aspirations. At the same time, you do not want white audiences to conclude that since so many of your people seem to be doing well, little more needs to be done.

Then there are those advertisements showing groups of people. Yes, one of them may be black, although not too black, and always looking happy to be in white company. Still, these blacks are seldom in the front row, or close to the center. Even worse, you think you have detected a recent trend: In advertisements that include a person of color, you see Asians being used instead of blacks....

Well, what about assimilation? Here you receive the same message given immigrants: If you wish to succeed, or simply survive, adapt to the diction and demeanor of the Anglo-American model. But even if you opt for that path, you will never receive the acceptance accorded to other groups, including newcomers arriving from as far away as Asia and the Middle East. In the view of those who set the rules, if you are of African origin, you will never fully fit the image of a true American. Notice how even blacks who espouse conservative opinions are regarded more as curiosities than as serious citizens.

Whether you would like to know more white people is not an easy question to answer. So many of the contacts you have with them are stiff and uneasy, hardly worth the effort. If you are a woman, you may have developed some cordial acquaintances among white women at your place of work because women tend to be more relaxed when among themselves. Still, very few black men and women can say that they have white "friends," if by that is meant people they confide in or entertain in their homes.

Of course, friendships often grow out of shared experiences. People with similar backgrounds can take certain things for granted when with one another. In this respect, you and white people may not have very much in common. At the same time, by no means all your outlooks and interests relate to your race. There probably are at least a few white people you would like to know better. It just might be that some of them would like to know you. But as matters now stand, the chances that these barriers will be broken do not appear to be very great.

Societies create vocabularies, devising new terms when they are needed, and retaining old ones when they serve a purpose. Dictionaries list words as obsolete or archaic, denoting that they are no longer used or heard. But one epithet survives, because people want it to. Your vulnerability to humiliation can be summed up in a single word. That word, of course, is *nigger.*

When a white person voices it, it becomes a knife with a whetted edge. No black person can hear it with equanimity or ignore it as "simply a word." This word has the force to pierce, to wound, to penetrate, as no other has. There have, of course, been terms like *kike* and *spic* and *chink*. But these are less frequently heard today, and they lack the same emotional impact. Some nonethnic terms come closer, such as *slut* and *fag* and *cripple*. Yet, *nigger* stands alone with its power to tear at one's insides. It is revealing that whites have never created so wrenching an epithet for even the most benighted members of their own race.

Black people may use *nigger* among themselves, but with a tone and intention that is known and understood. Even so, if you are black, you know that white society devised this word and keeps it available for use. (Not officially, of course, or even in print; but you know it continues to be uttered behind closed doors.) Its persistence reminds you that you are still perceived as a degraded species of humanity, a level to which whites can never descend.

You and your people have problems, far more than your share. And it is not as if you are ignorant of them, or wish to sweep them under a rug. But how to frame your opinions is not an easy matter. For example, what should you say about black crime or addiction or out-of-wedlock pregnancies? Of course, you have much to say on these and other topics, and you certainly express your ideas when you are among your own people. And you can be critical—very critical—of a lot of behavior you agree has become common among blacks.

However, the white world also asks that black people conduct these discussions in public. In particular, they want to hear you condemn black figures they regard as outrageous or irresponsible. This cannot help but annoy you. For one thing, you have never asked for white advice. Yet whites seem to feel that you stand in need of their tutelage, as if you lack the insight to understand your own interests. Moreover, it makes sense for members of a minority to stand together, especially because so many whites delight in magnifying differences among blacks. Your people have had a long history of being divided and conquered. At the same time, you have no desire to be held responsible for what every person of your color thinks or does. You cannot count how many times you have been asked to atone for some utterances of Louis Farrakhan, or simply to assert that he does not speak for you. You want to retort that you will choose your own causes and laments. Like other Americans, you have no obligation to follow agendas set by others....

You may, by a combination of brains and luck and perseverance, make it into the middle class. And like all middle-class Americans, you will want to enjoy the comforts and pleasures that come with that status. One downside is that you will find many white people asking why you aren't doing more to help members of your race whom you have supposedly left behind. There is even the suggestion that, by moving to a safer or more spacious area, you have callously deserted your own people.

Yet hardly ever do middle-class whites reflect on the fact that they, too, have moved to better neighborhoods, usually far from poorer and less equable persons of their own race or ethnic origins. There is little evidence that middle-class whites are prepared to give much of themselves in aid of fellow whites who have fallen on misfortune. Indeed, the majority of white Americans have chosen to live in sequestered suburbs, where they are insulated from the nation's losers and failures.

Compounding these expectations, you find yourself continually subjected to comparisons with other minorities or even members of your own race. For example, you are informed that blacks who have emigrated from the Caribbean earn higher incomes than those born in the United States. Here the message seems to be that color by itself is not an insurmountable barrier. Most stinging of all are contrasts with recent immigrants. You hear people just off the boat (or, nowadays, a plane) extolled for building businesses and becoming productive citizens. Which is another way of asking why you haven't matched their achievements, considering how long your people have been here.

Moreover, immigrants are praised for being willing to start at the bottom. The fact that so many of them manage to find jobs is taken as evidence that the economy still has ample opportunities for employment. You want to reply that you are not an immigrant, but as much a citizen as any white person born here. Perhaps you can't match the mathematical skills of a teenager from Korea, but then neither can most white kids at suburban high schools. You feel much like a child being chided because she has not done as well as a precocious sister. However, you are an adult, and do not find such scolding helpful or welcome.

No law of humanity or nature posits a precise format for the family. Throughout history and even in our day, households have had many shapes and structures. The same strictures apply to marriage and parental relationships. All this requires some emphasis, given concerns expressed about "the black family" and its presumed disintegration. In fact, the last several decades have seen a weakening of domestic ties in all classes and races.

Black Americans are fully aware of what is happening in this sphere. They know that most black children are being born out of wedlock and that these youngsters will spend most of their growing years with a single parent. They understand that a majority of their marriages will dissolve in separation or divorce, and that many black men and women will never marry at all. Black Americans also realize that tensions between men and women sometimes bear a violence and bitterness that can take an awful toll.

If you are black, you soon learn it is safest to make peace with reality: to acknowledge that the conditions of your time can undercut dreams of enduring romance and "happily ever after." This is especially true if you are a black woman because you may find yourself spending many of your years without a man in your life. Of course, you will survive and adapt, as your people always have. Central in this effort will be joining and sustaining a community of women—another form of a family—on whom you can rely for love and strength and support.

If you are a black woman, you can expect to live five fewer years than your white counterpart. Among men, the gap is seven years. Indeed, a man living in New York's Harlem is less likely to reach sixty-five than is a resident of Bangladesh. Black men have a three-times-greater chance of dying of AIDS, and outnumber whites as murder victims by a factor of seven. According to studies, you get less sleep, are more likely to be overweight and to develop hypertension. This is not simply caused by poverty. Your shorter and more painful life results, in considerable measure, from the anxieties that come with being black in America.

If you are a black young man, life can be an interlude with an early demise. Black youths do what they must to survive in a hostile world, with the prospect of violence and death on its battlefields. Attitudes can turn fatalistic, even suicidal: gladiators without even the cheers of an audience.

When white people hear the cry, "the police are coming!" it almost always means, "help is on the way." Black citizens cannot make the same assumption. If you have been the victim of a crime, you cannot presume that the police will actually show up; or, if they do, that they will take much note of your losses or suffering. You sense police officials feel that blacks should accept being robbed or raped as one of life's everyday risks. It seems to you obvious that more detectives are assigned to a case when a white person is murdered.

If you are black and young and a man, the arrival of the police does not usually signify help but something very different. If you are a teenager simply socializing with some friends, the police may order you to disperse and get off the streets. They may turn on a searchlight, order you against a wall. Then comes the command to spread your legs and empty out your pockets, and stand splayed there while they call in your identity over their radio. You may be a college student and sing in a church choir, but that will not overcome the police presumption that you have probably done something they can arrest you for.

If you find yourself caught up in the system, it will seem like alien terrain. Usually your judge and prosecutor will be white, as will most members of the jury as well as your attorney. In short, your fate will be decided by a white world.

This may help to explain why you have so many harsh words for the police, even though you want and need their protection more than white people do. After all, there tends to be more crime in areas where you live, not to mention drug dealing and all that comes in its wake. Black citizens are at least twice as likely as whites to become victims of violent crimes. Moreover, in almost all these cases, the person who attacks you will be black. Because this is so, whites want to know, why don't black people speak out against the members of their race who are causing so much grief? The reason is partly that you do not want to attack other blacks while whites are listening. At least equally important is that, although you obviously have no taste for violence, you are also wary of measures that might come with a campaign to stamp out "black crime...." At this point, you might simply say that you are not sure that you want a more vigorous police presence if those enforcers are unable to distinguish between law-abiding citizens and local predators. Of course, you want to be protected. But not if it means that you and your friends and relatives end up included among those the police harass or arrest....

As you look back on the way this nation has treated your people, you wonder how so many have managed to persevere amid so much adversity. About slavery, of course, too much cannot be said. Yet even within living memory, there were beaches and parks—in the North as well as in the South—where black Americans simply could not set foot. Segregation meant separation without even a pretense of equal facilities. In Southern

communities that had only a single public library or swimming pool, black residents and taxpayers could never borrow a book or go for a swim. Indeed, black youths were even forbidden to stroll past the pool, lest they catch a glimpse of white girls in their bathing costumes.

How did they endure the endless insults and humiliations? Grown people being called by their first names, having to avert their eyes when addressed by white people, even being expected to step off a sidewalk when whites walked by. Overarching it all was the terror, with white police and prosecutors and judges possessing all but total power over black lives. Not to mention the lynchings by white mobs, with victims even chosen at random, to remind all blacks of what could happen to them if they did not remain compliant and submissive.

You wonder how much that has changed. Suppose that you find yourself having to drive across the country, stopping at gasoline stations and restaurants and motels. As you travel across the heart of white America, you can never be sure how you will be received. Although the odds are that you will reach your destination alive, you cannot be so sure that you will not be stopped by the police or spend a night in a cell. So you would be well advised to keep to the speed limit and not exceed it by a single mile. Of course, white people are pulled over by state troopers; but how often are their cars searched? Or if a motel clerk cannot "find" your reservation, is it because she has now seen you in person? And are all the toilet facilities at this service station really out of order?

The day-to-day aggravations and humiliations add up bit by bitter bit. To take a depressingly familiar example, you stroll into a shop to look at the merchandise, and it soon becomes clear that the clerks are keeping a watchful eye on you. Too quickly, one of them comes over to inquire what it is you might want, and then remains conspicuously close as you continue your search. It also seems that they take an unusually long time verifying your credit card. And then you and a black friend enter a restaurant and find yourselves greeted warily, with what is obviously a more anxious reception than that given to white guests. Yes, you will be served, and your table will not necessarily be next to the kitchen. Still, you sense that they would rather you had chosen some other eating place. Or has this sort of thing happened so often that you are growing paranoid?

So there is the sheer strain of living in a white world, the rage you must suppress almost every day. No wonder black Americans, especially black men, suffer so much from hypertension. (If ever an illness had social causes, this is certainly one.) To be black in America means reining in your opinions and emotions as no whites ever have to do. Not to mention the forced and false smiles you are expected to contrive to assure white Americans that you harbor no grievances against them.

Along with the tension and the strain and the rage, there come those moments of despair. At times, the conclusion seems all but self-evident that white America has no desire for your presence or any need for your people. Can this nation have an unstated strategy for annihilating your people? How else, you ask yourself, can one explain the incidence of death and debilitation from drugs and disease; the incarceration of a whole generation of your men; the consignment of millions of women and children to half-lives of poverty and dependency?[1] Each of these debilities has its causes; indeed,

analyzing them has become a minor industry. Yet with so much about these conditions that is so closely related to race, they say something about the larger society that has allowed them to happen.

This is not to say that white officials sit in secret rooms, plotting the genocide of black America. You understand as well as anyone that politics and history seldom operate that way. Nor do you think of yourself as unduly suspicious. Still, you cannot rid yourself of some lingering mistrust. Just as your people were once made to serve silently as slaves, could it be that if white America begins to conclude that you are becoming too much trouble, it will find itself contemplating more lasting solutions?

NOTE

1.In 1990, when a sample of black Americans were asked if they thought that the government was deliberately encouraging drug use among black people, 64 percent felt that this might be true. When asked if they suspected that AIDS had been purposely created by scientists to infect black people, 32 percent believed there might be some truth in this view.

33. MEXICAN AMERICANS

JOHN FARLEY

By 1900, even the largest and wealthiest Mexican landowners had generally been deprived of their land.... The Chicano agricultural laborer was in a position only marginally better than slavery.... [Most] found themselves in a caste system with little chance of advancement.

To understand dominant-minority relations, it is important to know the historical background. Here, John Farley concisely describes the relationships between Anglos and Mexican-Americans in Texas and the Southwest. The themes in this history are similar to those of other minorities: conflict, power, economic exploitation, and the emergence of a relatively permanent social structure. Chicanos differ from other minorities, however, in one important way: Economic exploitation involved first their land, then their labor.

EARLY CONTACTS

The first contact between Mexicans and Americans came about in what is now the southwestern United States. This contact increased to a sizable scale in the early 1800s, as the Mexican population expanded northward and the American population expanded westward. This Mexican population was mostly mestizo, a mixture of Spanish and Indian, which was by that time the overwhelming majority of the Mexican population. There were also, however, some recent white immigrants from Spain, who preferred to think of themselves as Spanish rather than Mexican and were generally so recognized. At this time, the present-day states of Texas, California, New Mexico, Arizona, and Utah were all part of Mexico, as were most of Colorado and small parts of three other states. The relationship between white Americans, or Anglos, and Mexicans during this period might best be described as having elements of both cooperation and competition. There was a certain amount of competition, but there was little ethnic stratification between Mexicans and Anglos. Both groups were landowners, farmers, and ranchers; Mexicans were operating ranches on a large scale in Texas by the late eighteenth century, and later in California, especially after Mexico became independent from Spain in 1822 (Meier and Rivera 1972, Chapter 3). In addition to the general absence of ethnic inequality, the competition between Anglos and Mexicans was limited and—as we have indicated—was counterbalanced by significant elements of cooperation....

To summarize, then, Mexican and Anglo residents in the early stages of southwestern settlement lived side by side in relatively equal status, with relatively cooperative relationships. In each of the three major areas (Texas, California, and Nuevo Mexico, which largely comprised present-day Arizona and New Mexico), the life style and mode of production was somewhat different, but in all three, the pattern was one of relative equality with substantial elements of cooperation. Of

From *Majority-Minority Relations*, pp. 116–123, by John E. Farley. Copyright © 1982. Reprinted by permission of Prentice Hall, Upper Saddle River, NJ.

course, both groups in different ways oppressed the southwestern Indian people, but they treated and regarded one another as relative equals.

ORIGINS OF ETHNIC STRATIFICATION

Texas

During the 1830s, a chain of events began that was to prove disastrous for Mexicans living in Aztlan, as the region of Mexico that became part of the United States is sometimes called. By the early 1830s, conflict had arisen in Mexico over the role of that country's national government. Some Mexicans, the centralists, wanted a strong national government that would exercise close administrative control over all of Mexico. Others, the federalists, wanted a looser confederation with greater local autonomy, not unlike the system of the United States. Most Texans—both Mexican and Anglo—favored the latter approach and sided with the federalists. Ultimately, centralists came to control Mexico's national government. The army came to Texas to control the dissident federalists, but in the process spilled so much blood that a revolution was started and Texas ended up—for a short time—as an independent nation (Alvarez 1973). This chain of events upset the power balance, creating new demands for land among whites in Texas in a way that resulted almost overnight in gross social inequality between Anglos and Mexicans. Why did this happen? First, Texas's independence from Mexico accelerated the influx of white immigrants, mostly from the United States South. Before long, Anglos outnumbered Mexicans in Texas by a ratio of five to one (Grebler et al. 1970, 40). These immigrants brought with them the prejudices of the South as well as a tremendous demand for land. Many sought to set up a plantation system for raising cotton, similar to the pattern in the South. Outnumbering the Mexicans as they did, they soon appealed for admission to the United States, and in 1845, Texas was annexed. The situation now was totally changed, and the past cooperation of the Mexicans with the Anglos was forgotten. Most Mexicans were quickly deprived of their land, either by force or by American law (backed by force), which consistently served Anglo, not Mexican, interests. By 1900, even the largest and wealthiest Mexican landowners had generally been deprived of their land (Alvarez 1973).

During this period, there was also a great upsurge in anti-Mexican prejudice, which further contributed to the subordination of the now Mexican-American people in Texas. Alvarez (1973) cites three major reasons for this upsurge in prejudice. First, the warfare with Mexico had led most Anglos to view *all* Mexicans as former enemies, even though most of them had also opposed Mexico's centralist government and many had fought for Texas's independence from Mexico. Second, as noted, many had learned intense race prejudice in the United States South and readily applied notions of racial inferiority to Mexicans. Finally, racist ideology served an economic purpose in supporting and rationalizing the Anglos' actions of taking land from the Mexicans.

California and Nuevo Mexico

Most of the rest of the Southwest—California and Nuevo Mexico—became part of the United States in 1848 as a result of the Treaty of Guadelupe Hidalgo, which ended the Mexican War. This war was the result of a number of factors, particularly Mexican objections to the annexation of Texas by the United States, American desire to expand westward into Nuevo Mexico and California, and border disputes all along the U.S.-Mexican border (Meier and Rivera 1972, Chapter 4). During this war, Nuevo Mexico surrendered itself to the United States without a fight, in part because of opposition to the centralist government of Mexico. In California, the situation was somewhat different. The cooperation between Anglos and *Californios* (Mexican settlers in California) during the 1820s and 1830s increasingly turned to conflict during the 1840s as more and more Anglo settlers came to northern California over the Oregon trail. Here, too, opposition to the centralists among both Anglos

and Mexicans was strong enough that California declared its independence from Mexico in 1836. In 1840, however, California returned to Mexican control. But increasingly, the influx of white settlers caused Anglo-*Californio* conflicts which ended any cooperation between the two, even though both had opposed the centralists in Mexico. In 1846, a new independence movement known as the Bear Flag Revolt took place. This movement came to be pretty much controlled by Anglos, who soon antagonized *Californios* in Los Angeles so strongly that they rebelled against the Anglos, who by now were openly proclaiming California to be United States territory. This led to the only serious fighting in the part of the Mexican War that occurred in what is now the United States, and led to effective American control of California by 1847. Meanwhile, the major fighting of the war was taking place in Mexico, which had been invaded by U.S. troops. In 1847, Mexico City was captured; a year later, the Treaty of Guadelupe Hidalgo was signed and ratified. This treaty ceded most of California and Nuevo Mexico to the United States, formally recognized American sovereignty over Texas, and resolved the border disputes along the Texas-Mexico boundary in favor of the United States. In protocol accompanying the treaty, the United States agreed in writing to recognize the land ownership of Mexicans in the ceded territories. The 80,000 Mexicans living in the ceded territories also were given U.S. citizenship rights, and most became citizens.[1] A few years later, the present United States-Mexican border was established when the Gadsden Purchase (1853) ceded the southern parts of present-day Arizona and New Mexico to the United States.

As was the case a few years earlier in Texas, the annexation of Nuevo Mexico and California caused a critical change in the power structure, which sooner or later proved disastrous for the Mexican people living in these two territories. The familiar pattern was repeated: Once there was a sizable influx of Anglos into an area, the Anglos and Mexican-Americans came into competition over land. Once this happened, the Mexican-Americans were nearly always deprived of their land, despite the international agreement (and numerous verbal promises) that this would not happen. Sometimes the land was simply taken by force. At other times, the legal system accomplished the same result. This was possible because the Mexican and American concepts of land ownership were different, as were the methods for legally proving a land claim (Meier and Rivera 1972). Thus, many Mexicans who could easily have proven their claims in Mexican courts could not do so in American courts. It is also true, of course, that judges and magistrates were usually Anglo and protected Anglo interests, and that Anglo landowners were often better able to afford quality lawyers. Furthermore, even when Mexican-Americans did eventually win their claims, they were so deeply in debt from the cost of the legal battle—some dragged on for as long as seventeen years—that they often lost part or all of their land because of the debt (Meier and Rivera 1972, 80). Put simply, the balance of power was totally on the side of the Anglo-Americans....

Cause of Anglo-Chicano Inequality

This brief discussion of the early history of Anglo-Chicano relations is sufficient to confirm that Noel's (1968) theory about the origins of ethnic stratification can be applied to Mexican-Americans as well as to other U.S. minorities.[2] Only in the presence of all three elements cited by Noel—ethnocentrism, competition, and unequal power—did patterns of near-total domination of Chicanos by Anglos emerge. Early competition for land and the whites' superior power and numbers brought this about first in Texas. The Treaty of Guadelupe Hidalgo gave political and legal power to whites throughout the Southwest, but this did not immediately cause great ethnic inequality except in northern California, where the Gold Rush began almost immediately after the treaty. In other areas, subordination of the Mexican-American population tended to come when there was a sizable influx of whites—in the 1870s and 1880s in southern California, and later in New Mexico. This influx added the element of competition as whites wanting land deprived Mexican-Americans of

their land claims. It also increased both white ethnocentrism and the inequality of the power balance.

As with blacks and Indians, racist stereotypes developed and were used to justify mistreatment of Chicanos. Another form of ethnocentrism was the concept of "manifest destiny," which was used to justify annexation of Mexican territory and to displace both Mexican-Americans and Indians from their lands. This view was that the white man's supernaturally willed destiny was to rule and "civilize" all of North America, from coast to coast. Thus, the conquest of indigenous Indian and Mexican-American populations and the taking of their lands could be justified—it was God's will. The other factor, unequal power, was also increased with a large influx of whites. Whites became a numerical majority, which augmented the legal and political power they already held. For all these reasons, there was a close association between the numerical balance of Anglos and Chicanos and the amount of inequality between the two groups in various times and places throughout the Southwest.

In some regards, the history of Chicanos is very different from that of blacks and Native Americans. Only Chicano history involves the conquest by force of a sovereign, internationally recognized nation-state and the abrogation of rights accorded to its citizens by that nation. In spite of this and other differences, however, the origin of Anglo-Chicano inequality seems to involve the same three elements as [with]…Afro-Americans and Native Americans.

Exploitation of Chicanos for Labor

Another way in which Mexican-Americans are unique among the three groups…is that only they were exploited on a large scale for *both* their land and their labor in this country. Blacks had no land here because they were not indigenous: They were brought here under a system of forced migration to be exploited for their labor. Indians…were never enslaved on a large scale, and their resistance to forced assimilation, as well as their forced isolation on the reservation, generally kept white employers from seeing them as an easy source of cheap labor. Mexican-Americans, however, soon came to be exploited for their labor as well as their land. We have already discussed at length the exploitation of Chicanos for their land and the reasons behind it. In the remainder of this section, we shall examine the ways in which Anglos took advantage of Mexican-Americans as a source of cheap labor.

As Mexican-Americans were being displaced from their land by whites during the 1850—1900 period, whites in the Southwest were developing an economic system largely built around mining, large-scale agriculture, and railroad transportation. These types of economic activity, especially mining and large-scale agriculture, are highly labor-intensive and are most profitable when there is a large labor supply. The owners of the ranches and mines accordingly sought a supply of laborers willing to do hard, dirty work for low wages (Grebler et al. 1970, 51). Although bonded laborers from Asia were brought to the west to do some of this work, Mexican-Americans became the most important source of such labor....

By the early twentieth century, the Chicano agricultural laborer was in a position only marginally better than slavery, in a system that in some ways resembled the paternalistic pattern of race relations. To a large degree, Mexican-Americans were restricted to certain low-paying, low-status jobs, so that ethnicity largely determined one's status and economic position. Frequently, the total control over minority group life associated with paternalistic systems was present for farm and mine workers, who were required to buy their goods at inflated prices at the company or ranch store and were closely supervised by labor contractors. Frequently, too, the system of labor was more unfree than free, because workers were often bound to their employers to work off the debts incurred at these company stores. Finally, there was the paternalism—the constant assertion by ranch, farm, and mine owners that their Mexican-American workers were happy, that the owners had their best interests at heart, and that the workers needed "close super-

vision" because they were incapable of functioning on their own. And, of course, there was the oft-repeated claim that Mexican-Americans were incapable of work other than unskilled farm or labor work and that they were especially suited to this type of work....

The situation was highly exploitative. Hours were long, pay exceedingly low, food and housing were poor, and education was practically nonexistent. Especially in the rural areas, few Chicanos were permitted to rise above this status so that the system of stratification closely fit the caste model: One's status was pretty well determined by one's ethnic group.... Most Mexican-Americans in the latter nineteenth and early twentieth centuries found themselves in a caste system with little chance of advancement....

NOTES

1. Although Indians in the ceded territories previously had the right of Mexican citizenship, they did not receive the right of U.S. citizenship (Meier and Rivera 1972, 70).
2. For more complete discussions of Chicano history, see the previously cited publications as well as McWilliams, 1949, which is considered by some to be the best general work on Mexican-American history in the southwest.

REFERENCES

Alvarez, Rodolfo. 1973. "The Psycho-Historical and Socioeconomic Development of the Chicano Community in the United States." *Social Science Quarterly* 53:920—942. Reprinted in Norman R. Yetman and C. Hoy Steele (eds.), *Majority and Minority: The Dynamics of Racial and Ethnic Relations.* Boston: Allyn and Bacon, 1975.

Grebler, Leo, Joan W. Moore, and Ralph C. Guzman. 1970. *The Mexican-American People.* New York: The Free Press.

Meier, Matt S., and Felicano Rivera. 1972. *The Chicanos: A History of Mexican Americans.* New York: Hill and Wang.

Noel, Donald L. 1968. "A Theory of the Origin of Ethnic Stratification." *Social Problems* 16: 157—172.

34. YELLOW FACE: ASIAN AMERICANS IN POPULAR CULTURE

ROBERT G. LEE

Not until 1952, after more than a century in the United States, were Asian immigrants finally granted the right to become naturalized citizens. Even so, long after the legal status of "alien" has been shed, the "common understanding" that Asians are an alien presence in America, no matter how long they may have resided in the United States nor how assimilated they are, is still prevalent in American culture.

One of my best friends, an English professor born and raised in Singapore, made me sensitive to the fact that for many people the word "oriental" is derogatory. It denotes strangeness, foreign, alien, mysterious, and even noncivilized. It was with surprise that I discovered a book by Robert G. Lee called *Orientals*, and as I read the book I saw the wisdom of my friend's criticism of the label.

What Lee does in his book is to show the racist stereotypes associated with Asian Americans, especially the tendency for white Americans to think of Asian American as permanent aliens in America. Lee shows us that in popular culture Asians are defined as a "foreign racial category" which makes them threats to the "American national familiy."

MARKING THE ORIENTAL

In March 1997, the cover of *National Review* featured President William Jefferson Clinton, first lady Hillary Rodham Clinton, and Vice President Al Gore, all in yellowface. The president, portrayed as a Chinese houseboy—buck-toothed, squinty-eyed and pigtailed, wearing a straw "coolie" hat—serves coffee. The first lady, similarly buck-toothed and squinty-eyed, outfitted as a Maoist Red Guard, brandishes a "Little Red Book," while the vice president, robed as Buddhist priest, beatifically proffers a begging bowl already stuffed with money.

In using the yellowface cartoon to illustrate a story about alleged political corruption, the editors of *National Review* simultaneously emphasized their racial point and revived a tradition of

racial grotesques that had illustrated broadsides, editorials, and diatribes against Asians in America since the mid-nineteenth century. The cover story summarized allegations that the Clinton administration had solicited campaign donations from Asian contributors in exchange for policy favors. These allegations virtually ignored the much larger illegal campaign contributions of non-Asians and focused almost exclusively on Asian and Asian American contributors.[1] Like most of the mainstream media, *National Review* was silent on the broader questions: the impact of multinational corporations on American politics and the baleful influence of big money on big politics. *National Review* instead played the race card. Focusing only on the Asian and Asian American campaign contributions, *National Review* made it clear that it was not corporate money, or even foreign money generally, but specifically Asian money that polluted the American political process. In the eyes of the *National Review* editors, the nation's first family (with Al Gore as po-

From Robert G. Lee, *Orientals: Asian Americans in Popular Culture*. Reprinted by permission of Temple University Press. © 1999 by Temple University. All Rights Reserved.

tential heir) had been so polluted by Asian money that they had literally turned yellow.

Yellowface marks the Asian body as unmistakably Oriental; it sharply defines the Oriental in a racial opposition to whiteness. Yellowface exaggerates "racial" features that have been designated "Oriental," such as "slanted" eyes, overbite, and mustard-yellow skin color. Only the racialized Oriental is yellow; Asians are not. Asia is not a biological fact but a geographic designation. Asians come in the broadest range of skin color and hue.

Because the organizing principle behind the idea of race is "common ancestry," it is concerned with the physical, the biological, and the reproductive. But race is not a category of nature; it is an ideology through which unequal distributions of wealth and power are naturalized—justified in the language of biology and genealogy. Physiognomy is relevant to race only insofar as certain physical characteristics, such as skin color or hue, eye color or shape, shape of the nose, color or texture of the hair, over- or underbite, etc., are *socially defined* as markers of racial difference.

The designation of yellow as the racial color of the Oriental is a prime example of this social constructedness of race. In 1922, the U.S. Supreme Court denied Takao Ozawa, an immigrant from Japan, the right to become a naturalized citizen. In its ruling, the court recognized the fact that some Asians, including Ozawa, were of a paler hue than many European immigrants already accepted into the nation as "white." Race, the court concluded, was not a matter of actual color but of "blood" or ancestry, and Ozawa, being of Japanese "blood," could not claim to be white, no matter how white his skin.[2]

What does Yellowface signify? Race is a mode of placing cultural meaning on the body. Yellowface marks the Oriental as indelibly alien. Constructed as a race of aliens, Orientals represent a present danger of pollution. An analysis of the Oriental as a racial category must begin with the concept of the alien as a polluting body.

The cultural anthropologist Mary Douglas argues that fears of pollution arise when things are out of place. Soil, she observes, is fertile earth when on the ground with tomatoes growing in it; it is polluting dirt when on the kitchen table.

Pollutants are objects, or persons, perceived to be out of place. They create a sense of disorder and anomaly in the symbolic structure of society. Douglas observes that pollution is not a conscious act. Mere presence in the wrong place, the inadvertent crossing of a boundary, may constitute pollution.[3] Aliens, outsiders who are inside, disrupt the internal structure of a cultural formation as it defines itself vis-à-vis the Other; their presence constitutes a boundary crisis. Aliens are always a source of pollution.

Not all foreign objects, however, are aliens—only objects or persons whose presence disrupts the narrative structure of the community. It is useful here to distinguish between the alien and the merely foreign. Although the two terms are sometimes used interchangeably, they carry different connotations. "Foreign" refers to that which is outside or distant, while "alien" describes things that are immediate and present yet have a foreign nature or allegiance. The difference is political. According to the *Oxford English Dictionary*, as early as the sixteenth century "alien" referred to things whose allegiance lay outside the realm in which they resided, as in "alien priories"—monasteries in England whose loyalty was to Rome. This early definition of "alien" emphasized the unalterable nature of the foreign object and its threatening presence.

Only when the foreign is present does it become alien. The alien is always out of place, therefore disturbing and dangerous. The difference between the alien and the merely foreign is exemplified by the difference between the immigrant and the tourist. Outsiders who declare their intention of leaving may be accorded the status of guest, visitor, tourist, traveler, or foreign student. Such foreigners, whose presence is defined as temporary, are seen as innocuous and even desirable. On the other hand, if the arriving outsiders declare no intention to leave (or if such a declared intention is suspect), they are accorded the status of alien, with considerably different and sometimes dire consequences. Only when aliens exit or are "naturalized" (cleansed of their foreignness and remade) can they shed their status as pollutants.

Alienness is both a formal political or legal status and an informal, but by no means less powerful, cultural status. The two states are hardly synonymous or congruent. Alien legal status and the procedures by which it can be shed often depend on the cultural definitions of difference. In 1923, a year after it denied Takao Ozawa the right to naturalize, the Supreme Court stripped Bhagat Singh Thind, an Indian immigrant who was already an American through naturalization, of his U.S. citizenship.[4] In *Ozawa v. United States*, the court had ruled that no matter what the actual color of his skin, nor how much he could prove himself culturally assimilated, Ozawa's Japanese "blood" made him "unamalgamable" by marriage into the American national family. In *United States v. Thind*, despite the ethnological evidence presented by Thind that he, a high-caste Hindu, was a descendent of Aryans and hence white by "blood," the court ruled that he was not, holding that race was not a scientific category but a social one, and upheld the revocation of Thind's citizenship.

In both *Ozawa* and *Thind*, the Supreme Court tacitly recognized race to be a product of popular ideology. In both cases, Chief Justice Sutherland, writing for the court, cited the existence of a "common understanding" of racial difference which color, culture, and science could not surmount. The important thing about race, the Supreme Court held, was not what social or physical scientists at the time may have had to say about it, but rather how it was "popularly" defined.

Not until 1952, after more than a century of settlement in the United States, were Asian immigrants finally granted the right to become naturalized citizens. Even so, long after the legal status of "alien" has been shed, the "common understanding" that Asians are an alien presence in America, no matter how long they may have resided in the United States nor how assimilated they are, is still prevalent in American culture. In 1996, the immediate response of the Democratic National Committee to allegations that it had accepted illegal campaign donations from foreigners was to call Asian American contributors to the party's coffers and demand that they verify their status as citizens or permanent residents. One such donor, Suzanne Ahn, a prominent Houston physician and civic leader, reported to the U.S. Commission on Civil Rights that DNC auditors threatened to turn her name over to the news

media as "uncooperative" if she did not release personal financial information to them. Ahn concluded that she had been investigated by the DNC, the FBI, and the news media simply because she had contributed to the DNC and was Asian American. Even public figures do not escape the assumption that Asian Americans are really foreigners in disguise. When Matthew Fong, a fourth-generation Californian, ran as a Republican candidate for Secretary of State in California—a position his mother March Fong Yu had held for the better part of two decades—he was asked by news reporters whether his loyalties were divided between the U.S. and China.[5]

In the run-up to the 1996 presidential elections, a cartoon by syndicated cartoonist Pat Oliphant played on the persistent "common understanding" of Asian Americans as permanent aliens in America. It showed a befuddled poll watcher confronted with a long line of identically short Oriental men with identical black hair, slit eyes behind glasses, and buck teeth, all wearing identical suits and waving ballots. Referring to the Asian American DNC official who was made the poster boy of the fund-raising scandal, the caption reads, "The 3,367th John Huang is now voting." Echoing the public comment of presidential candidate Ross Perot that none of the Asian names brought out in the campaign finance scandal thus far sounded like they belonged to "real" Americans, one of Oliphant's signature nebbishes asks from the margin, "Just how many John Huangs are there? How many you want?"[6] The cartoon plays on the "common understanding" that Orientals are indistinguishable as individuals and thus ultimately fail as "real" Americans. How could Oliphant's poll watcher, the yeoman guardian of the American political process and embodiment of "common understanding," possibly hope to distinguish among all the Orientals flooding into the nation's body politic?

POPULAR CULTURE AND RACE

The Oriental as a racial category is never isolated from struggles over race, ethnicity, sexuality, gender, and national identity. The Supreme Court's "common understanding" is a legal fiction. It gives popular convention, the common sense of "real" Americans, the power to define race. The "common understanding" of the Oriental as racialized alien therefore originates in the realm of popular culture, where struggles over who is or who can become a "real American" take place and where the categories, representations, distinctions, and markers of race are defined. Some studies attribute hostility toward Asian immigrants directly to economic competition and the creation of an ethnically defined segmented labor market. They provide us with an economic framework for understanding the dynamics of class and race and a map of the economic terrain on which anti-Asian hostility has been built. By themselves, however, those studies do not account for the development or functioning of specific racial images of Asians in American culture.[7]

This book takes up popular culture as a process, a set of cultural practices that define American nationality—who "real Americans" are in any given historical moment. American citizenship and American nationality are not synonymous; citizenship carries with it an implicit assumption or promise of equality, at least in political and legal terms, while nationality contains and manages the contradictions of the hierarchies and inequalities of a social formation. Nationality is a constantly shifting and contested terrain that organizes the ideological struggle over hierarchies and inequalities.

The nature of popular culture is the subject of much debate.[8] Popular culture is most often identified as having its roots in the organic culture of the common folk or peasant life, in opposition to court or bourgeois culture. Popular culture, then, is often characterized by politically resistant, if often nostalgic, qualities. Ever since the rise of industrial capitalism in the early nineteenth century, popular culture has been in reality complex, increasingly shaped by the capitalist processes of its production and circulation. Nevertheless, popular culture, albeit sometimes reconstituted as co-opted or deracinated mass culture, continues to be identified with subordinated groups, as opposed to the dominant ruling class.

The mobilization of national identity under the sign "American" has never been a simple matter of imposing elite interests and values on the social formation, but is always a matter of negotiation between the dominant and the dominated. Subordinated groups offer resistance to the hegemony of elite culture; they create subaltern popular cultures and contest for a voice in the dominant public sphere.[9] The saloon vies with the salon, the boardwalk with the cafe, and the minstrel theater with the opera house as an arena for public debate and political ideas.[10]

Although it mobilizes legitimacy, the cultural hegemony of dominant groups is never complete; it can render fundamental social contradictions invisible, explain them away, or ameliorate them, but it cannot resolve them.[11] However deracinated, whether co-opted, utopian, nostalgic, or nihilist, popular culture is always contested terrain. The practices that make up popular culture are negotiations, in the public sphere, between and among dominant and subaltern groups around the questions of national identity: What constitutes America? Who gets to participate and on what grounds? Who are "real Americans"?

Since popular culture is a significant arena in which the struggle over defining American nationality occurs, it also plays a critical role in defining race. Race is a principal signifier of social differences in America. It is deployed in assigning differential political rights and capital and social privilege, in distinguishes between citizens presumed to have equal rights and privileges and inherently unequal, subordinated subjects.[12] Although race is often camouflaged or rendered invisible, once produced as a category of social difference it is present everywhere in the social formation and deeply imbedded in the popular culture. The Oriental as a racial category is produced, not only in popular discourse about race *per se* but also in discourses having to do with class, gender and sexuality, family, and nation. Once produced in those discourses, the Oriental becomes a participant in the production and reproduction of those social identities.[13]...

THE SIX FACES OF THE ORIENTAL

Six images—the pollutant, the coolie, the deviant, the yellow peril, the model minority, and the gook—portray the Oriental as an alien body and a threat to the American national family. From each of these racial paradigms emerges a wide array of specific images. Each of these representations was constructed in a specific historical moment, marked by a shift in class relations accompanied by cultural crisis. At such times American nationality—who the "real Americans" are—is redefined in terms of class, gender, race, and sexuality.

The representation of the Asian as pollutant originated in mid-nineteenth-century California. For white settlers from the East, Chinese settlers from the West disrupted the mythic narrative of westward expansion. The Chinese constituted an alien presence and a threat of pollution which earlier fantasies of exotic but distant Asia could not contain. In the popular imagination, California was a free-soil Eden, a place where small producers, artisans, farmers, and craftsmen might have a second chance to build a white republic, unstained by chattel slavery or proletarian labor.[14] In this prelapsarian imagery, the Chinese were both identified with the moral chaos of the Gold Rush and portrayed as the harbingers of industrial wage slavery. As the national debate over slavery, abolition, and statehood came to a boiling point in the late 1860s, the ideal of establishing California as both free and racially pure demanded the removal, or at least the exclusion, of both Chinese and African Americans.

The representation of the Chinese immigrant worker as a coolie came about as the U.S. working class was formed in the 1870s and 1880s. Although they had come to America as free (albeit highly proletarianized) workers, Chinese immigrants found themselves segregated into a racially defined state of subordination as "coolie labor." The Chinese "coolie" was portrayed as unfree and servile, a threat to the white working man's family, which in turn was the principal symbol of an emergent working-class identity that fused class consciousness with gendered national and racial identity. The coolie representation not only allowed the nascent labor movement, dominated by its skilled trades, to exclude Chinese from the working class; it also enabled the skilled trades to ignore the needs of common labor, which it racialized as "coolie labor" or "nigger

work."[15] Irish immigrants who were in the process of consolidating their own claim to Americanness and a white racial identity led the popular anti-Chinese movement.

The Oriental as deviant, in the person of the Chinese household servant, is a figure of forbidden desire. The deviant represents the possibility of alternative desire in a period during which middle-class gender roles and sexual behavior were being codified and naturalized into a rigid heterosexual cult of domesticity. In the West, the Chinese immigrant played a central role in the transition from a male-dominated, frontier culture shaped by the rituals of male bonding to a rigidly codified heterosexual Victorian culture. In the 1860s and early 1870s, hundreds of Chinese women were brought to San Francisco and forced into prostitution. By the end of the decade, thousands of Chinese immigrant men were driven out of the mines and off farms and ranches and were hired into middle-class households as domestic servants. Both of these situations opened up possibilities of interracial sex and intimacy. Middle-class whites regarded the Chinese with ambivalence. On the one hand, the Chinese were indispensable as domestic labor; on the other, they represented a threat of racial pollution within the household. A representation of the Oriental as both seductively childlike and threateningly sexual allowed for both sympathy and repulsion. The representation of the Oriental as deviant justified a taboo against intimacy through which racial and class stability could be preserved.

By the turn of the century, Asian immigrants were represented as the yellow peril, a threat to nation, race, and family. The acquisition of territories and colonies brought with it a renewed threat of "Asiatic" immigration, an invasion of "yellow men" and "little brown brothers." At the moment when the United States prepared to pick up "the white man's burden" in the Caribbean and the Pacific, "Asiatic immigration" was said to pose "the greatest threat to Western civilization and the White Race."[16] Domestically, the triumph of corporatism, the homogenization or deskilling of industrial labor, urbanization, and immigration had all contributed to massive changes in both middle-and working-class families. These changes contributed to the construction of a culture of consumption, reflected in new gender roles as well as new sexual attitudes and behavior among men and women of both classes. In the aftermath of the First World War and the Bolshevik Revolution, these domestic social and cultural transformations were accompanied by deep anxieties about racial suicide and class struggle.[17] Through its supposed subversion of the family, the yellow peril threatened to undermine what Lothrop Stoddard, a popular advocate of eugenics and racial geopolitics, called the "inner dikes" of the white race.

The representation of Asian Americans as a model minority, although popularly identified with the late 1960s and 1970s, originated in the racial logic of Cold War liberalism of the 1950s. The image of Asian Americans as a successful case of "ethnic" assimilation helped to contain three spectres that haunted Cold War America: the red menace of communism, the black menace of racial integration, and the white menace of homosexuality. In place of a radical critique calling for structural changes in American political economy, the model minority mythology substituted a narrative of national modernization and ethnic assimilation through heterosexuality, familialism, and consumption. By the late 1960s, an image of "successful" Asian American assimilation could be held up to African Americans and Latinos as a model for nonmilitant, nonpolitical upward mobility.

Since the 1970s, the model minority image has coexisted with and reinforced a representation of the Asian American as the gook. The shift in the U.S. economy from large-scale industrial production to flexible accumulation and the global realignment of capital and labor have brought about new crises of class, race, and national identity. In the context of these contemporary crises, the "intact" and "traditional" Asian American family is promoted as a model of productivity, savings, and mobility, not just for African America or Latino families but now for all American families, including those of the white middle class. Simultaneously, however, in post-Vietnam and post-liberal American popular culture, the Asian American is represented as the invisible enemy and the embodiment of inauthentic racial and national identities—the gook. The Vietnam War is replayed in popular culture

as the narrative of American decline in the post-industrial era. The received wisdom of the Vietnam War narrative is that America's defeat in Southeast Asia was brought about by a faceless and invisible Asian enemy, aided and abetted by an American counterculture. The rapid growth of the Asian American population and its apparent success render the model minority, like the now-mythic Viet Cong, everywhere invisible and powerful. In the narrative of American decline, Asian Americans are represented as the agents of foreign or multinational capital. In this narrative of national decline, Asian American success is seen as camouflage for subversion. The model minority is revealed to be a simulacrum, a copy for which no original exists, and thus a false model of the American family. In the dystopic narrative of American national decline, the model minority resembles the replicants in the science fiction book and film *Blade Runner*—a cyborg, perfectly efficient but inauthentically human, the perfect gook.

The cultural crises in American society that give rise to these representations of the Oriental come in the wake of economic change, particularly in what economic historians Gordon and Reich call transformations of the structure of accumulation.[18] The transformation of the social relations of production and the organization of work and segmentation of the labor market have profound effects on the structures, relations, and meaning of families, gender, and race. At each stage of capitalist development, new "emergent" public spheres are constituted and new demands arise for participation in the dominant public sphere.[19] The popular discourse of race in which these constructions of the Oriental were produced and deployed is not a transparent or unmediated reflection of the economy, but rather an expression of social contradictions drawing on images of the present, visions of the future, and memories of the past....

NOTES

1. Non-Asians fined by the Federal Election Commission for illegal contributions to the Clinton-Gore re-election campaign included Simon Fireman, who was fined $6 million (the largest such fine ever levied), and Thomas Kramer,

a German national who was fined $323,000. See "Petition of the National Asian Pacific American Legal Consortium et al. to the United State Commission on Civil Rights," September 10, 1997, reprinted at http://www2.ari.net/oca/camp/complain.html.

2. *Takao Ozawa v. United States*, 260 U.S. 178 (1922).

3. Mary Douglas, Purity and Danger: *An Analysis of the Concepts of Pollution and Taboo* (London and New York: Ark Paperbacks, 1966), 54.

4. *Ozawa*, and *United States v. Bhagat Singh Thind*, 261 U.S. 204 (1923). For an analysis of these cases, see Philip Tajitsu Nash in Hyung Chan Kim, ed., *Asian Americans and the Supreme Court* (Hamden, Conn.: Greenwood Press, 1993), and Jeff H. Lesser, "Always Outsiders: Asians, Naturalization and the Supreme Court: 1740–1944," *Amerasia Journal* 12 (1985):83–100.

5. See "Petition of the National Asian Pacific American Legal Consortium et al. to the United States Commission on Civil Rights."

6. For a detailed analysis of the media coverage of the John Huang affair, see Frank Wu and May Nicholson, "Racial Aspects of Media Coverage of the John Huang Matter," *Asian American Policy Review* 7(1997):1–37.

7. An alternative view, which locates the image of the Chinese immigrant in America in the constellation of racial images in nineteenth-century American culture, is Ronald Takaki, *Iron Cages: Race and Culture in Nineteenth-Century America* (Seattle: University of Washington Press, 1979). Takaki's view, like Alexander Saxton's in *The Rise and Fall of the White Republic* (London and New York: Verso, 1990), is a Gramscian class analysis.

8. For a succinct review of these debates, see John Storey, *An Introductory Guide to Cultural Theory and Popular Culture* (Athens, GA.: University of Georgia Press, 1993).

9. Jurgen Habermas argues that the idea of the citizen came into being in the public sphere that emerged in the seventeenth and eighteenth centuries in bourgeois drawing rooms, salons, and cafes. This public sphere was a social space between the realm of the state and the realm of civil society (composed of the private family sphere and the sphere of commodity exchange and social labor). The public sphere is the realm in which the individual is constituted as public citizen and where he (the bourgeois male, in Habermas's historical account) makes his interests heard by the state. See Jurgen Habermas, *The Structural Transformation of the Public Sphere: An Inquiry into a Category of Bourgeois Society*, translated by Thomas Burger (Cambridge: Massachusetts Institute of Technology Press, 1989). Habermas's focus on a single public sphere defined by the political emancipation of the bourgeois male has been challenged by Nancy Fraser and others, who argue for the existence of multiple public spheres whose participants include the disenfranchised and the marginalized: women,

racial minorities, and the working class. See Nancy Fraser, *Power, Discourse, and Gender in Contemporary Social Theory* (Minneapolis: University of Minnesota Press, 1989), and "What's Critical about Critical Theory? The Case of Gender," in *Unruly Practices* (Minneapolis: University of Minnesota Press, 1990); and Craig Calhoun, "Populist Politics, Communications Media, and Large Scale Societal Integration," *Sociological Theory* 6 (no. 2, 1988):219–241.

10. On the significance of saloon, boardwalks, and popular theater see, respectively, Roy Rosenzweig, *Eight Hours for What We Will: Workers and Leisure in an Industrial City, 1870-1920* (New York: Cambridge University Press, 1983); Kathy Peiss, *Cheap Amusements: Working Women and Leisure in Turn-of-the-Century* New York (Philadelphia: Temple University Press, 1986); and Sean Wilentz, *Chants Democratic: New York City & the Rise of the American Working Class, 1788–1850* (New York: Oxford University Press, 1984).

11. The notion of hegemony comes, of course, from Gramsci. For a critique that emphasizes the incomplete and contested nature of hegemony, see James Scott, *Domination and the Arts of Resistance: Hidden Transcripts* (New Haven: Yale University Press, 1990).

12. The thesis that sovereignty rests in the privatized body is John Locke's. See the chapter "On Property" in *The Second Treatise of Government*, edited by Thomas P. Reardon (Indianapolis: Bobbs-Merrill, 1952), 16–30. On the "abstract citizen," see also Lisa Lowe, *Immigrant Acts: On Asian American Cultural Politics* (Durham, NC: Duke University Press, 1996), 2.

13. Sociologists Michael Omi and Howard Winant argue that race cannot be explained as simply a subcategory or an epiphenomenon of another single social dynamic such as class formation or ethnicity, but instead exists as a separate category of social difference. They argue that the production and reproduction of race is historically contingent, decentered, and contested. Michael Omi and Howard Winant, *Racial Formation in the United States: From the 1960s to the 1990s*, 2nd ed. (New York and London: Routledge, 1994), 53–76 passim.

14. See David Roediger, The Wages of Whiteness: *Race and the Making of the American Working Class* (London and New York: Verso, 1991).

15. Alexander Saxton, *The Indispensable Enemy: Labor and the Anti-Chinese Movement in California* (Berkeley, University of California Press, 1971).

16. Lothrop Stoddard, *The Rising Tide of Color Against White World-Supremacy* (New York: Charles Scribner's Sons, 1920).

17. See, for example, T.J. Jackson Lears, *No Place of Grace: Antimodernism and the Transformation of American Culture, 1880–1920* (New York: Pantheon Books, 1981).

18. Of the many and varied periodizations of American economic history, the one I have found must useful

for this study is the analysis of changes in the labor market and the social structure of accumulation by David M. Gordon, Richard Edwards, and Michael Reich, *Segmented Work, Divided Workers: The Historical Transformation of Labor in the United States* (New York: Cambridge University Press, 1982). They examine the relationship between long cycles of economic activity and the social structure of accumulation. They outline three periods in the development of American capitalism with regard to labor:

- Initial proletarianization, from the 1820s to the 1890s.
- Homogenization, from the 1870s to the onset of World War I, during which the labor markets became more competitive and the dominance of skilled crafts positions was diminished by the large-scale introduction of semiskilled labor.
- Segmentation, from the 1920s to the present, during which political and economic forces have produced qualitative differences in the organization of work and three distinct labor markets: a secondary labor market, plus a primary labor market divided into independent and subordinate sectors.

Gordon et al. link these broad periods to long swings (on the order of twenty-five years) in global economic activity, each associated with a distinct social structure of accumulation, the institutional environment in which capital accumulation takes place. For a periodization shaped by both economy and culture, see Herbert Gutman, *Work, Culture, and Society in Industrializing America: Essays in American Working-Class and Social History* (New York: Knopf, 1976), 1–78.

19. use "emergent" here in the same counterhegemonic sense that Raymond Williams uses the term in *Culture and Society* (London: Penguin, 1971).

PART VII

Gender Inequality

Probably all societies are structured by gender. Men and women are differentiated, categorized, and assigned roles, identities, and differing levels of power, prestige, and privilege. Although numerically a majority in society, women still constitute a minority in American society in terms of position in relation to men.

Judith Howard and Jocelyen Hollander are interested in examining the differences and similarities between men and women, showing us the strong role that the social definition of gender place. The second selection by Andrew Hacker examines economic inequality and the final selection by Martin and Hummer ask important questions about our views of women in society as they play themselves out in one institution, the fraternity. Their main question is: To what extent does violence against women, including rape, exist because of how we define what it means to be a man or woman in society?

35. THE MEANING OF GENDER

JUDITH HOWARD and JOCELYN A. HOLLANDER

...although gender differences may exist, they are not the same as sex differences. In other words, just because women and men may appear to behave or think differently does not mean that they have different innate characteristics or abilities. Instead, these differences may be (and, we believe, generally are) constructed through social processes.

What exactly are the differences between men and women, and are they important? Judith Howard and Jocelyn Hollander carefully define several words associated with this issue and try to show that whatever real differences exist—and these tend ot be exaggerated by most people—are gender related, meaning socially constructed. They conclude that sex differences are exaggerated, and gender differences are important only because society regards them as so.

Over the last 30 years, social psychologists (and others) have become more and more interested in gender. But what exactly is "gender"? When we talk about gender, do we mean the biological characteristics of females and males, such as genes or genitals? Do we mean the social roles that men and women play—mother, father, breadwinner, caretaker? Or are we talking about personal characteristics, such as aggressiveness or nurturance?

Another source of confusion is that the relationship between *gender* and other terms is poorly defined. Some writers use the term *gender*, some discuss *sex*, and some examine *sex roles* or *gender roles*. Moreover, some authors use these words interchangeably, whereas others distinguish carefully between them. Our goal in the rest of this chapter is to untangle these confusions and spell out exactly what we mean—and do not mean—by the term gender. In this section, we define gender and compare it with related terms: *sex, gender role, gender stereotype, gender identity, sexuality,* and *sexual orientation*. We

From Judith A. Howard and Jocelyn A. Hollander, *Gendered Situations, Gendered Selves: A Gender Lens on Social Psychology*, Sage Publications, 1996. By permission.

also define two other terms, *race* and *social class*, that we use throughout this book. Our discussion will help to illuminate precisely what we mean by a gender lens.

SEX

What is sex? When we fill out official forms, whether applying for a job, a driver's license, admission to college, or a credit card, we are usually asked to declare our sex by checking the box marked "male" or the box marked "female." How do we know which box to check?

The definition of sex seems straightforward: The term is generally used to refer to the biological characteristics that distinguish males and females, such as reproductive organs or chromosomes. Most people in this society think of sex as dichotomous and unchangeable. That is, they assume that there are only two boxes one can check, female and male, and that everyone falls into one (and only one) of these categories. Moreover, they assume that one always falls into the same category: Someone who checks the "female" box at age 20 will have checked the same box at age 10, and will check it at ages 50 and 85 as well.

However, these assumptions are not always correct. *Hermaphrodites*, for example, are people who are not easily classified as male or female: Their reproductive organs and chromosomal structures are ambiguous (Money and Ehrhardt 1972). For example, a child may be born with both male and female genitalia. Which box would this person check on official forms? Specialists estimate that up to 4% of the population may be intersexed in this way. In fact, Fausto-Sterling (1993) suggests that a more logical categorization scheme would actually include five sexes: males, females, and three types of hermaphrodites. *Transsexuals*, on the other hand, are people who have literally changed their sex—they have been surgically and hormonally altered so that they appear to be a sex different from that as which they were born. A well-known example is Jan Morris, a writer who began life as a boy, James, but who now lives as a woman, Jan. (Transsexuals are distinct from *transvestites*, who wear the clothes associated with the other sex.) Because transsexuals have the genetic structure of one sex but the physical appearance of another, they are also not easily classified as one or the other sex.

The belief in two sexes is an example of what Mehan and Wood (1975) have called an "incorrigible proposition": an unquestioned belief that cannot be proven wrong, even in the face of contradictory evidence. In this society, we believe that there are two, and only two, sexes, and when we encounter a situation that challenges this belief, such as a person who doesn't fit neatly into one of these two categories, we adjust the situation to fit our beliefs rather than adjusting our beliefs to fit the situation. In the case of hermaphroditism, for example, we "correct" the ambiguity by surgical or hormonal means and assign the person to one of our two categories rather than admitting the possibility of more than two categories.

How do we determine someone's sex? Most people would answer this question by appealing to biology: Males have penises and XY chromosomes, whereas females have vaginas, more prominently developed breasts, and XX chromosomes. In everyday life, however, we do not normally use these criteria to distinguish between males and females. Yet we rarely have trouble classifying those we meet as male or female:

> When encountering older children or adults for the first time, most of us do not usually examine their genitals to label their sex! Instead, we use their attire, movements, sex-related characteristics such as height or musculature, and their general style of self-presentation as cues to their sex. (Unger and Crawford 1992:17–18)

Thus assigning someone to a sex category is as much a social process as the application of physiological criteria. As we shall see in the next section, the way we ascribe sex is deeply intertwined with gender.

GENDER

Gender is a slippery term. Most scholars would agree with the statement that gender has something to do with the social behaviors and characteristics associated with biological sex; however, there is substantially less agreement on exactly what this statement means.

Social scientists use the term gender in two different ways. Some use gender interchangeably with sex, suggesting that sex and gender are essentially the same thing. (Indeed, some argue that the term gender is meaningless and should be abandoned, because everything, they believe, reduces to sex.) These researchers might assume, for example, that women care for children (and are nurturing in general) because of their biological ability to bear children. This perspective sees gender as somehow essential to males and females; it is believed to be both innate and unchanging. For this reason, this approach is sometimes called the *essentialist perspective* on gender. Biology is believed to determine the social behaviors and characteristics of males and females.

Other scholars distinguish between sex and gender, using sex to refer to biological characteristics as we have described above but using gender to mean the culturally determined behaviors and personality characteristics that are associated with, but not determined by, biological sex. These writers do not assume that the relationship between sex and gender is direct or automatic. Rather, they believe that some mediating process, such as socialization, leads individuals to behave in gendered ways.[1] Thus different cultures may develop distinct notions of gender, which seem natural because they are associated with sex but that are socially, rather than biologically, driven. In contrast with the essentialist perspective described above, this nonessentialist perspective does not see gendered characteristics and behaviors as innate or unchangeable. It is this perspective that we adopt in this book, for reasons we detail below.

What does it mean to say that something is *gendered*? In this book, we use this phrase to mean that ideas about gender—assumptions and beliefs on both individual and societal levels—affect the thoughts, feelings, behaviors, resources, or treatment of women and men. Thus, to the extent that women and men dress, talk, or act differently because of societal expectations, their behavior is gendered. To the extent that an organization assigns some jobs to women and others to men on the basis of their assumed abilities, that organization is gendered. And to the extent that a professor treats a student differently because that student is a man or a woman, their interaction is gendered.

There are a number of variations on the nonessentialist perspective, which we discuss at greater length in Chapter 2. For now, we simply note that essentialist and nonessentialist positions are often at loggerheads. This is true not only in scholarly analyses but in the nonacademic world as well. For example, these perspectives were hotly debated at the United Nations Fourth World Conference on Women in Beijing, China, in 1995. At a preparatory meeting in New York City, former U.S. Representative Bella Abzug read the following statement:

> The current attempt by several Member States to expunge the word "gender" from the Platform for Action and to replace it with the word "sex" is an insulting and demeaning attempt to reverse the gains made by women, to intimidate us and to block further progress. We will not be forced back into the "biology is destiny" concept that seeks to define, confine, and reduce women and girls to their physical sexual characteristics....

> The meaning of the word "gender" has evolved as differentiated from the word "sex" to express the reality that women's and men's roles and status are socially constructed and subject to change. In the present context, "gender" recognizes the multiple roles [filled] throughout our life cycles, the diversity of our needs, concerns, abilities, life experiences, and aspirations—as individuals, as members of families and households, and in society as a whole. The concept of "gender" is embedded in contemporary social, political, and legal discourse.... The infusion of gender perspectives into all aspects of UN activities is a major commitment approved at past conferences and it must be reaffirmed and strengthened at the Fourth World Conference on Women. (Abzug 1995)

As Abzug notes, the choice of perspective (here symbolized by the choice between the terms sex and gender) can have real consequences for women—and for men as well—when those perspectives are used to guide public policy.

GENDER AS DIFFERENCE

In practice, research on gender—from any perspective—has tended to focus on differences between women and men. This tendency persists despite the fact that research shows very few significant sex differences (e.g., Maccoby and Jacklin 1974; Fausto-Sterling 1985). In fact, the distributions of women and men on most characteristics tend to be overlapping rather than separate. Nonetheless, many researchers continue to focus on differences rather than on the extensive similarities between the sexes or even on the extensive variations within each sex. This pattern of research reinforces the essentialist belief that there are large, stable, innate differences between the sexes and encourages biological explanations for those few differences that are resilient. Thorne, Kramarae, and Henley (1983) write that these studies mistake "description ... for explanation" (p. 15) and warn that just because studies find differences between males and females does not mean that sex is the *cause* of the differences. For example, one analysis of gender differences in conversational patterns concluded that power, not sex per se, was the source of those differences (Kollock, Blumstein, and Schwartz 1985).

There are a number of reasons why researchers continue to prioritize sex differences. One of these reflects a pattern typical of human cognition. As we noted in the discussion of cognition above, human beings have a tendency to categorize information wherever possible. As an ostensibly dichotomous characteristic with highly visible social trappings (e.g., hairstyle and apparel), sex is a prime basis for cognitive categorization. The pervasive tendency to focus on sex differences rather than on similarities thus may derive partly from cognitive processes.]

The persistent belief in sex difference in the face of contradictory evidence is also tied in part to the human quest for self-identity; we want to know who we are. This quest has a peculiar character, at least in Western culture: Knowing who we are implies knowing who we are not. Gender is one fundamental source of identity. Although there are several contradictory theories of how gender identity is created, most social psychologists concur that children learn at a very young age to adopt gender as a basic organizing principle for themselves and the social worlds they are learning about. In particular, children tend to regard gender as bipolar. "Children regard a broad range of activities as exclusively appropriate for only one sex or the other, and ... they strongly prefer same-sex playmates ... and gender-appropriate toys, clothes, and activities" (Bem 1993:111). As studies of gender stereotypes among adults reveal, gender polarization does not wane as children grow older. The cultural centrality of gender, together with the susceptibility of gender to a bipolar model, defines the contemporary social psychological approach to gender.

Perhaps as a result of these tendencies, researchers often expect to find sex differences. Social psychologists are not immune from popular essentialist beliefs about gender. These expectations often act as self-fulfilling prophecies, predisposing the researchers to focus on or even to elicit information that confirms their beliefs. Many studies have shown that experimenters' hypotheses affect research findings. According to Weisstein (1970),

These studies are enormously important when assessing the validity of psychological studies of women. Since it is beyond doubt that most of us start with notions as to the nature of men and women, the validity of a number of observations of sex differences is questionable, even when these observations have been made under carefully controlled conditions. Second, and more important, [these studies] point quite clearly to the influence of social expectation. In some extremely important ways, people are what you expect them to be or at least they behave as you expect them to behave. (p. 215)

The biases that have plagued social psychology were apparent as early as 1910, when psychologist Helen Thompson Wooley commented, "There is perhaps no field aspiring to be scientific where flagrant personal bias, logic martyred in the cause of supporting a prejudice, unfounded assertions, and even sentimental rot and drivel, have run riot to such an extent as here" (Wooley 1910:340).

Another reason for social psychology's focus on sex differences has to do with the structure of the field itself. Over the past century, psychology and sociology (like other sciences) have become more and more reliant on statistical tests. These tests are designed to identify significant differences between groups and therefore shape a search for differences rather than similarities (Unger and Crawford 1992:12). Moreover, even if a difference is *statistically* significant (i.e., unlikely to have occurred by chance), it may not be *substantively* significant (i.e., meaningful). For example, Eagly and Carli's (1981) review of the literature on social influence found that even though sex differences were often statistically significant, they explained less than 1% of the variance in influenceability and thus contributed very little to understanding influenceability. Reviews of other sex differences have found similar patterns of statistically, but not substantively, significant effects (Deaux 1984).

Researchers may also have a difficult time disseminating the results of studies that find no evidence of sex differences. Findings of similarity are not "newsworthy"; academic journals are much less likely to publish such studies. Newspapers and other media are similarly disposed: Whereas reports of sex differences in math abilities garner headlines and newsmagazine cover stories, reports of similarity are relegated to short, unobtrusive articles, if indeed they are reported at all (Eccles and Jacobs 1986). Thus, even if the majority of research projects were to find no significant differences between women and men, *published* research might actually consist of only those few studies that do find differences.

Sex differences research also tends to ignore the fact that *different* often means *unequal*. In other words, such research tends to ignore power relationships. Carrigan and his colleagues write that in the study of gender, "relations have been interpreted as differences. The greater social power of men and the sexual division of labor are interpreted as 'sexual dimorphism' in behavior. With this, the whole question of social structure is spirited away" (Carrigan, Connell, and Lee 1987, pp. 75–76). Even when research considers power differences between genders, it rarely looks at power differences within genders—that is, it ignores very real differences among women and among men, homogenizing each category as though gender is the most important differentiating feature (Fine and Gordon 1989).

Research on gender differences also ignores the fact that behavior is specific to situations, depending on factors such as the structure of the social context or the attitudes and expectations of others in that context. For example, one study found that women's behavior in a simulated job interview depended on the perceived gender stereotypes of the interviewer. When the research participants believed the interviewer to hold traditional views of women, they behaved in a more stereotypically feminine manner (von Baeyer, Sherk, and Zanna 1981). These women altered the femininity of their behavior to best achieve their goals in the interview. Individuals' behavior may change significantly from one situation to the next, and the results of a psychological study may depend on which situation is examined.

Indeed, the experimental laboratory itself affects the expression of gender. Although it purportedly allows scientists to study gender in an objective context, the laboratory is in fact a specific social setting that affects the respondent as do all social contexts. The laboratory is no more neutral than any other situation.

Thus it is important to exercise caution when interpreting research reports of sex difference.

Findings of difference may be due not so much to meaningful differences in the abilities or behavior of women and men as to a host of other factors, including the norms of publishing and research and the biases of researchers. On the other hand, just because these reports of sex differences may be misleading does not mean that they should be ignored. The belief that males and females are fundamentally different is widely shared among Americans and, indeed, among most peoples of the world. These beliefs, regardless of their validity, influence our identities, thoughts, and behaviors and may cause men and women to behave differently (gender difference) even if no underlying difference in ability (sex difference) exists. In other words, these beliefs have material consequences regardless of their basis in fact. Thus we contend that sex differences research must be taken seriously—if only to understand how essentialist beliefs shape social psychological research and social life. We suggest that readers keep these issues in mind as they proceed through the next chapters. For now, however, we return to our definitions of key terms.

GENDER ROLE

Another common term in social psychology is gender role, which is often used interchangeably with sex role. Sociologists use the term *role* to refer to "a set of prescriptions and proscriptions for behavior—expectations about what behaviors are appropriate for a person holding a particular position within a particular social context" (Kessler and McKenna 1978:11). The term gender role, then, refers to the characteristics and behaviors believed to be appropriate for men or for women. People expect that others will behave in accord with their gender role, and they punish those who violate these expectations.

The concept of gender role has been strongly criticized, however. For example, some note that these roles are based on the theorist's ideas of what people should be like rather than on what people really are like (Carrigan et al. 1987). Most people's lives, in fact, do not conform to what gender roles prescribe. Moreover, talking about "the male gender role" and "the female gender role" also ignores the very real variation among women and among men, and overlooks the substantial overlap in the characteristics and behaviors of males and females.

Perhaps more important, the concept of gender roles ignores issues of power and inequality. Gender role theory describes the relationship between women and men as one of difference and complementarity: The sexes are "separate but equal," and both roles serve important functions in society. But in fact male and female "roles" are not equally valued and are not necessarily "functional" for everyone. The concept of roles masks, for example, that women have traditionally been legally subservient to men in the family. Until relatively recently in the United States, women could not own property or enter into a contract, and men were (and still are in some states) legally allowed to rape and beat their wives. These are not the hallmarks of an equal relationship, a fact that is hidden by role terminology (Carrigan et al. 1987; Lopata and Thorne 1978). As a result of these critiques, many scholars have discarded the terms sex role and gender role. However, we discuss these terms here because they are still very much a part of both popular and social psychological discourse.

GENDER STEREOTYPE

Stereotypes are "strongly held overgeneralizations about people in some designated social category" (Basow 1992:3). For example, many Americans have stereotypes about athletes, professors, or police officers. These beliefs are "not necessarily based on fact or personal experience, but applied to each role occupant regardless of particular circumstance" (Kessler and McKenna 1978:12). Unlike roles, stereotypes do not imply that individuals should conform to particular expectations for behavior. Nor do they suggest that these beliefs are useful, either for individuals or for societies. Because stereotypes are oversimplifications, they may be inaccurate for a group as a whole, as well as for any particular member of that group.

Gender stereotypes, then, are beliefs about the characteristics of women and men, including their physical characteristics, typical behaviors, occupational positions, or personality traits. Reflecting the assumption that sex is dichotomous, stereotypes for women and men often involve polar opposites. For example, "Traits related to instrumentality, dominance, and assertiveness ... are believed more characteristic of men, while such traits as warmth, expressiveness, and concern for other people are thought more characteristic of women" (Deaux and Major 1990:95; see also Rosenkrantz et al. 1968). Such polarizations serve to increase the perception of difference between women and men, and mask the ways in which they are similar.

This does not mean that stereotypes paint all women or all men as the same. Indeed, stereotypes for certain subgroups of men and women, such as businesswomen, homemakers, or blue-collar working men, are common. Stereotypes may also vary by race, ethnicity, or class.... However, these variations are accommodated as subtypes subsumed under the more general stereotypes of women and men. The fact that we create subtypes rather than modifying our dichotomous view of gender suggests our deep investment in the idea of gender differences.

GENDER IDENTITY

The term gender identity refers to one's inner sense of oneself as female or male; it is a major part of one's self-concept. Gender identity develops during very early childhood, and once established, it is quite resistant to change (Kessler and McKenna 1978:9). Gender identity tends to be dichotomous—people generally think of themselves as male or female, not something in between. This is probably due to our "incorrigible proposition" that there are two, and only two, sexes. Kate Bornstein (1994), a male-to-female transsexual, writes that

> I know I'm not a man—about that much I'm very clear, and I've come to the conclusion that I'm probably not a woman either, at least not according to a lot of people's rules on this sort of thing. The trouble is, we're living in a world that insists we be one or the other—a world that doesn't bother to tell us exactly what one or the other is." (p. 8)

Gender identity is a subjective feeling; it cannot be determined without asking a person directly. Gender identity may or may not be congruent with someone's sex or gender, and it is unrelated to sexual orientation. Transsexuals, for example, generally go through sex-change operations because they feel that they do not "fit" their biological sex. Jan Morris (1974) describes her gender identity in this way: "I was born with the wrong body, being feminine by gender but male by sex, and I could achieve completeness only when the one was adjusted to the other" (p. 26). Like many other transsexuals, however, Morris ultimately found that it was easier to change her body than her social identity.

Although everyone has a gender identity, the salience of this identity may vary among people. For example, women are more likely than men to spontaneously mention gender when asked to describe themselves (Deaux and Major 1990:93). The salience of gender identity may also vary between situations: A woman alone in a group of men, for example, is likely to find her gender to be more salient than when she is in a group of other women (Cota and Dion 1986). Indeed, group identity is generally more salient for those in any kind of subordinate position, indicating the relevance of social position and power to identity.

SEXUALITY

Sexuality is a fuzzy term, often used to refer to a group of related concepts, including sexual behavior (what you do), eroticism (what turns you on), sexual orientation (who turns you on), or desire to engage in sexual activity. A discussion of sexuality may seem out of place in a book focusing on gender and social psychology. Nonetheless, sexuality is often associated with gender, although the two are not equivalent. This association probably results from the popular essentialist belief that gender is the natural outgrowth of biological sex. Because sexuality is also believed to be biologically driven, gender and sexuality are often thought to be directly related (Schwartz and Rutter, forthcoming).

As with gender, however, there are other perspectives on sexuality. Like other activities, sexual behavior has a social and symbolic component. Consider the activity of a woman baring her breasts. Now vary the social context: How would this action be interpreted if the woman is in her lover's bedroom, her doctor's consulting room, or a public place? Now take the last location, a public place, and vary the reasons for her action: She is participating in a public demonstration, performing at a strip joint, or breast-feeding her baby. It is the social context, not the activity itself, that leads us to impute meaning to the woman's action as being erotic, clinical, political, exhibitionist, or maternal. The meaning of sexual behaviors varies by situation, and we evaluate behavior on the basis of goals and motivations. Meaning also varies by culture: In some societies, women's breasts are always bare and thus do not elicit the charged interpretations that they do in our own culture. Sexual meanings are thus socially constructed, not inherent in an activity.

Similarly, sexuality is not innate in individuals. For evidence, we can point to the fact that expectations for the sexual behavior of men and women vary historically and cross-culturally. Traditional Western dating scripts, for example, expected men to be more physical and aggressive and women to be more passive and emotional in sexual situations. Although it might appear that these expectations have changed (and they have, to varying extents among different social groups and regions), they have not entirely disappeared. Men, for example, are still expected to take the lead in sexual situations, and women who violate gender expectations by being sexually assertive risk being labeled "pushy," "aggressive," or worse. However, other cultures have very different expectations for women and men. For example, Ford and Beach (1951) report that women are expected to be the sexual aggressors among societies such as the Maoris and the Trobriand Islanders. Sexual behavior is thus guided by social factors as much as by biology.

What, then, is the relationship between sexuality and gender? Expectations for "appropriate" sexual behavior and characteristics differ by gender; sexuality becomes a way of expressing gender. For example, Lillian Rubin's (1976) study of U.S. working-class families found that women were expected to be sexually passive and inexperienced, whereas men were expected to be more dominant, experienced, and adventurous. And as the next section points out, there are also expectations about whom we perform sexual behaviors with. An important point, however, is that this society's construction of sexuality helps maintain the existing gender hierarchy. The definition of men as aggressive and women as passive reinforces men's power over women and women's dependence on men. Popular culture's ideology of love and romance also reinforces gender inequality: For example, Cantor (1987) found that in popular media "women are usually depicted as subordinate to men and passive-dependent. . . . The basic message is that sexual relationships are all-important in women's lives" (1987:190). Thus, when women attempt to meet cultural expectations about heterosexual relationships, they contribute to their own subordination. However, the examples provided by other cultures show us that this pattern is not innate in human beings.

SEXUAL ORIENTATION

Sexual orientation, the match between one's sex and the sex of one's (desired or actual) sexual partners, is one component of sexuality. Like sexuality more generally, sexual orientation is part of gender expectations. For example, the expectations for a "real man" include heterosexuality. Think of male icons such as James Bond, Indiana Jones, or Rocky: Besides being strong and daring, these characters were all attracted and attractive to beautiful women. Thus, in this society, "Mainstream masculinity is heterosexual masculinity" (Carrigan et al. 1987:83; see also Connell 1987, 1995). This version of masculinity is a yardstick against which all men are measured: "The homosexual-heterosexual dichotomy acts as a central symbol in all rankings of masculinity. Any kind of powerlessness, or refusal to compete among men readily becomes involved with the imagery of homosexuality" (Carrigan et al. 1987:86). A similar argument can be made for women: Mainstream femininity entails heterosexuality, and any deviation from feminine norms risks "accusations" of lesbianism (Rich 1980), a status to which many people attach stigma. Thus sexual orientation is integrally related to gender. Sexual orientation is one of the ways in which gender is performed,

while at the same time, gender incorporates and depends on sexual orientation.

Like sex and gender, people tend to think of sexual orientation as dichotomous: One is either heterosexual or homosexual. But sexual orientation is better described as a continuum, with many possible variations between the two poles. Some people (bisexuals) are attracted to people of both sexes. Some people are attracted to people of one sex but maintain relationships with people of another; these people cannot be easily classified. Many people who define themselves as heterosexual, in fact, have had some sort of homosexual experiences (Blumstein and Schwartz 1983:43). It should be noted that sexual orientation is distinct from gender identity. Although some people think that those who prefer same-sex partners must be "confused" ... about their own gender identity, this is not the case. In fact "most gay men and lesbian women have no confusion about their gender identity; they simply prefer sexual partners of the same sex" (Vander Zanden 1990:358).

What is the source of sexual orientation? Debate rages in the scientific community and the popular press about whether sexual orientation is genetically or environmentally determined; at the moment, there is no consensus on the answer. One thing is certain, however: Like sexuality, the meaning of sexual orientation is socially constructed. Homosexuality is not everywhere as stigmatized as it is in the United States: Many past and present societies of the world, including the ancient Greeks and the modern Sambia of New Guinea, condone and practice both heterosexuality and homosexuality in some forms (Ford and Beach 1951). Moreover, the meanings of homosexuality and heterosexuality vary depending on the social context, even within the United States. Childhood sexual play, for example, is interpreted very differently from adult relationships. Or to give another example, the same man who might never consider engaging in homosexual activity in everyday life might practice it within an all-male prison context. Like the meaning of sexuality more broadly, the meaning of sexual orientation varies depending on context, goals, and motivations....

To conclude this chapter, we return to the metaphor of the *gender lens*. What do we mean by this term? What can we see through the gender lens that we cannot see without it?

Throughout this book, we emphasize two points. First, we argue that social psychology has simultaneously ignored and been deeply influenced by gender. Social psychologists have assumed that situations and behavior are gender neutral; yet they have nonetheless allowed prevailing cultural assumptions about gender to affect the questions they have posed and the answers they have provided. Most obviously, as we discussed earlier, social psychologists have focused on gender differences in personality and behavior and have often assumed that these difference are fixed, stable, and rooted in biological sex.

Our second argument in this book is that although gender differences may exist, they are not the same as sex differences. In other words, just because women and men may appear to behave or think differently does not mean that they have different innate characteristics or abilities. Instead, these differences may be (and, we believe, generally are) constructed through social processes. Thus, in a sense, we are arguing that these differences are not as meaningful as people—both social psychologists and laypeople—believe they are.

This does not mean that we should ignore these differences, however. If that were the case, there would be no reason to write (or read) this book. On the contrary, these ideas about gender deeply affect people's thoughts and behaviors and are central to the ways in which resources, power, and status are distributed in most (if not all) societies. In other words, despite its lack of grounding in sex, gender has real, material consequences for people's lives. For this reason, it is crucial to understand gender and the role it plays in the social world. Only through such an understanding can we hope to address the pervasive and deeply damaging social problems (discrimination, violence, injustice, and so on) that continue to plague our society.

Looking at the world through a gender lens, then, means recognizing and analyzing the central role that gender plays in social life. More concretely, it implies two seemingly contradictory tasks. First, it means unpacking the taken-for-granted assumptions about gender that pervade social psychology and, more generally, social life.

We must show how the terms we use to discuss gender (such as gender role) naturalize inequality and perpetuate gender difference. We must question the truth of these assumptions and, where warranted, reveal them as the illusions they are.

At the same time, looking through the gender lens means showing just how central these assumptions about gender continue to be to the perception and interpretation of the world, regardless of their grounding in reality. We must show how our unquestioned ideas about gender affect the world we see, the questions we ask, and the answers we can envision. In other words, we must show how deeply the social world is gendered and how far-reaching the consequences are. Looking at social life through the gender lens means asking where gender is overemphasized and where it is ignored; it means making the invisible visible and questioning the reality of what we see.

NOTE

1. Indeed, some authors also argue that sex itself is a social construction (Kessler and McKenna 1978; Scott 1988). According to this view,

Society not only shapes personality and behavior, it also shapes the ways in which the body appears. But if the body is itself always seen through social interpretation, then sex is not something that is separate from gender but is, rather, that which is subsumable under it. (Nicholson 1994:79)

REFERENCES

Abzug, Bella. 1995. "A Message from NGO Women to U.N. Member States, the Secretariat, and the Commission on the Status of Women." Speech delivered at the Final Preparatory Meeting for the Fourth World Conference on Women, April 3. (Press release from the Women's Environment and Development Organization [WEDO], 212-759-7982).

Basow, Susan A. 1992. *Gender: Stereotypes and Roles.* Pacific Grove, CA: Brooks/Cole.

Bem, Sandra L. *The Lenses of Gender: Transforming the Debate on Sexual Inequality.* New Haven, CT: Yale University Press.

Blumstein, Philip and Pepper Schwartz. 1983. *American Couples: Money, Work, and Sex.* New York: Morrow.

Bornstein, Kate. 1994. *Gender Outlaw: On Men, Women, and the Rest of Us.* New York: Vintage.

Carrigan, Tim, R. W. Connell, and John Lee. 1985. "Toward a New Sociology of Masculinity." *Theory and Society* 14:551–604.

———. 1987. *Toward a New Sociology of Masculinity.* Boston: Allen & Unwin.

Connell, R. W. 1987. *Gender and Power: Society, the Person, and Sexual Politics.* Stanford, CA: Stanford University Press.

Deaux, Kay. 1976. *The Behavior of Women and Men.* Monterey, CA: Brooks/Cole.

——— 1984. "From Individual Differences to Social Categories: Analysis of a Decade's Research on Gender." *American Psychologist* 39:105–16.

Deaux, Kay and Brenda Major. 1990. *A Social-Psychological Model of Gender.* New Haven, CT: Yale University Press.

Eagly, Alice H. and Linda L. Carli. 1981. "Sex of Researchers and Sex-Typed Communications as Determinants of Sex Differences in Influenceability: A Meta-Analysis of Social Influence Studies." *Psychological Bulletin* 90:1–20.

Eccles, Jacquelynne S. and Janis E. Jacobs. 1986. "Social Forces Shape Math Attitudes and Performance." *Signs: Journal of Women in Culture and Society* 11:367–89.

Fausto-Sterling, Anne. 1985. *Myths of Gender: Biological Theories About Women and Men.* New York: Basic Books.

Fine, Michelle and Susan M. Gordon. 1989. "Feminist Transformations Of/Despite Psychology." Pp. 147–74 in *Gender and Thought: Psychological Perspectives*, edited by M. Crawford and M. Gentry. New York: Springer-Verlag.

Ford, Clellan S. and Frank A. Beach. 1951. *Patterns of Sexual Behavior.* New York: Harper.

Kessler, Susan J. and Wendy McKenna. 1978. *Gender: An Ethnomethodological Approach.* New York: John Wiley.

Kollock, Peter, Philip Blumstein, and Pepper Schwartz. 1985. "Sex and Power in Interaction: Conversational Privileges and Duties." *American Sociological Review* 50:34–46.

Lopata, Helen Z. and Barrie Thorne. 1978. "On the Term 'Sex Roles.' " *Signs: Journal of Women in Culture and Society* 3:718–21.

Maccoby, Eleanor E. and Carol Jacklin. 1974. *The Psychology of Sex Differences.* Stanford, CA: Stanford University Press.

Mehan, Hugh M. and Houston W. Wood. 1975. *The Reality of Ethnomethodology.* New York: John Wiley.

Money, J. and Anke Ehrhardt. 1972. *Man and Woman, Boy and Girl.* Baltimore: Johns Hopkins University Press.

Morris, Jan. 1974. *Conundrum.* New York: Harcourt Brace Jovanovich.

Rich, Adrienne. 1980. "Compulsory Heterosexuality and Lesbian Existence." *Signs: Journal of Women in Culture and Society* 5:631–60.

Rosenkrantz, Paul S., Susan R. Vogel, H. Bee, Inge K. Broverman, and Donald M. Broverman. 1968. "Sex-Role Stereotypes and Self Concepts among College Students." *Journal of Consulting and Clinical Psychology* 32:287–95.

Rubin, Lillian. 1976. *Worlds of Pain: Life in the Working Class Family.* New York: Basic Books.

Schwartz, Pepper and Virginia Rutter. Forthcoming. *Gender, Sex, and Society.* Thousand Oaks, CA: Sage.

Thorne, Barrie, Cheris Kramarae, and Nancy Henley. 1983. *Language, Gender, and Society.* Rowley, MA: Newbury House.

Unger, Rhoda and Mary Crawford. 1992. *Women and Gender: A Feminist Psychology.* New York: McGraw-Hill.

Vander Zanden, James W. 1990. *The Social Experience: An Introduction to Sociology.* New York: McGraw-Hill.

Visher, Christy A. 1983. "Gender, Police Arrest Decisions, and Notions of Chivalry." *Criminology* 21(1):5–28.

von Baeyer, Carl L., Debbie L. Sherk, and Mark P. Zanna. 1981. "Impression Management in the Job Interview: When the Female Applicant Meets the Male (Chauvinist) Interviewer." *Personality and Social Psychology Bulletin* 7:45–51.

Weisstein, Naomi. 1970. " 'Kinder, Kuche, Kirche' as Scientific Law: Psychology Constructs the Female." Pp. 205–20 in *Sisterhood Is Powerful*, edited by R. Morgan. New York: Vintage.

Wooley, Helen Thompson. 1910. "Psychological Literature: A Review of the Most Recent Literature on the Psychology of Sex." *Psychological Bulletin* 7:335–42.

36. THE GENDER GAP: CONTOURS AND CAUSES

ANDREW HACKER

Although the typical woman's wallet is fuller than ever before, it is still measurably thinner than the typical American man's. And although it is now true that when men and women hold the same jobs, they tend to be paid the same wage, women still have less chance of reaching the highest earnings levels. What's more, even though more women are entering occupations traditionally held by men, once they get there, the positions start to decline in prestige and pay.

What is nice about this selection is its simplicity. It very carefully lays out the relative position of women and men in the economic world. It focuses on the income differences between them, and emphasizes that although there have been gains in equity, there are also some disturbing trends. Hacker also investigates segregation in the workplace and emphasizes the many ways in which women are excluded from top jobs in society, and ultimately, get less money and power.

American women are still far from economic parity. In some spheres, progress has been made, and those gains will be documented here. There can be no denying that these advances are long overdue and far from sufficient. Yet the story is not wholly one of improvement. An unhappy fact of our times is that in some ways women are worse off than they were in the past.

Although the typical woman's wallet is fuller than ever before, it is still measurably thinner than the typical American man's. And although it is now true that when men and women hold the same jobs, they tend to be paid the same wage, women still have less chance of reaching the highest earnings levels. What's more, even though more women are entering occupations traditionally held by men, once they get there, the positions start to decline in prestige and pay.

But the world of work offers only a partial view of the economic disparities between the sexes. So

Reprinted with the permission of Scribner, a Division of Simon and Schuster. *Money: Who Has How Much and Why?*, by Andrew Hacker. Copyright © 1997 by Andrew Hacker.

it makes sense to look at the population as a whole. In 1995, the median income for the 92.1 million adult men was $22,562, while the midpoint for the 96.0 million women was $12,130. This means women receive $538 for every $1,000 going to men. This is not an auspicious ratio. Indeed, it could be construed as society's verdict that women's needs and contributions amount to half of those of men. But even that figure can be viewed as evidence of progress: As recently as 1975, American women received a paltry $382 for each $1,000 received by men.

However, this aggregate comparison has limited meaning because most men hold full-time jobs, whereas the majority of women have no earnings from employment or work only part-time. Indeed, almost 10 million women told the Census Bureau in 1995 that they had no incomes at all, or at least none that came to them in their own names. Most of these women are nonworking wives, ranging from blue-collar homemakers to the spouses of top executives. Their lack of a personal income pulls down the gender ratio. And when we examine marriages where both partners work, the typical wife emerges earning only $418 for each $1,000 made by her husband. (Few wives have investments of their own that yield them comfortable independent incomes.)

So marriage is the chief cause of the income gap and will remain so as long as it relegates more women than men to tending to the home and caring for the children. In fact, over 40 percent of at-home wives either have no children or all of their youngsters are grown...most of these women never developed careers, and few have shown much interest in entering the work force. There are still husbands who declare that they do not want their wives to work, and not all are affluent executives who want their mates available to pack their suitcases and entertain business clients. In the households where only the husband brings home a paycheck, his earnings are often quite modest. Over a third of these breadwinners make less than $30,000 a year. Thus many families still rank what they see as domestic values ahead of whatever material benefits additional earnings would produce....

...Although the fact that more women are working has increased their income relative to men, the fact that more are on their own has had a countervailing effect. Today, over one-fifth of all families are headed by single women. And in more than a third of these households, the mother has never been married. Some of the single women heading families receive public assistance, which is intended to keep them alive but below the poverty line. And although over half find work, their median income is only $17,170, and fewer than a third have incomes that exceed $25,000 a year.

PROGRESS TOWARD PARITY?

Interestingly enough, the first signs of progress toward economic parity between men and women came during the still-traditional 1950s. This was supposed to be a period when women eschewed paid employment and instead opted for early marriage and a procession of children. Yet as Table 1 shows, the pay ratio of women who were working rose by 25 percent, from $486 to $607, the largest increase of any postwar decade. Several reasons for this stand out. To start, women were abandoning what had been one of

TABLE 1   Cause for Applause?

Year	Percent Working	Pay Ratio to Men
1950	31.4%	$486
1960	34.8%	$607
1970	42.6%	$594
1980	51.5%	$602
1990	57.5%	$716
1995	58.7%	$714

their principal occupations, and an ill-paid one at that: domestic service. Back in 1940, 2.4 million women cleaned and cooked and cared for children in other people's homes; by 1970, only half that number were so employed. It appears that the women who chose to work were expecting more from their jobs, including better pay. Even if many women were still secretaries, the corporate world was remaking its own image. The sassy gum chewers of Hollywood such as Joan Blondell would not fit in with the new carpeted corridors. At this time, also, two other major occupations for women began to pay more, for the classic economic reasons. Nurses and schoolteachers were in short supply because so many women were staying at home. In the suburbs, the future-oriented middle class was willing to pay for quality education and health care. Starting in the world of "women's" work, a ripple effect caused women's expectations to rise even in the domesticated Eisenhower era.

But progress came to a halt. The pay ratio reached by 1960 remained essentially the same in 1970 and 1980. Hence, the slogan *59 Cents!* that was emblazoned on protest placards in the early days of the women's movement, often accompanied by a popular ballad of the time: "Fifty-nine cents for every man's dollar; fifty-nine cents, it's a low-down deal!" These laments were not unavailing; during the 1980s the ratio rose from $602 to $716. One stimulus was that lawyers and judges began applying the hitherto somnolent Equal Pay Act of 1963, which said that at jobs that called for "equal skill, effort, and responsibility," there could be no gap in "wages to employees of the opposite sex." Also significant was that fewer women were becoming secretaries and nurses or teachers, just as an earlier generation had abandoned domestic service. If we total up these traditionally "female" occupations, in

1970 they had absorbed 28 percent of all employed women, but by 1995, only 18 percent. Indeed, in 1995, the work force had 700,000 fewer secretaries than in 1980. An obvious reason is the advent of word-processing equipment, which facilitates copying and correcting. Also, in many organizations, the position has been retitled "assistant." And, as a further sign of our times, just as women were less willing to do routine typing, men were adapting to the keyboard because it was the only way to communicate with a computer. And in a reverse twist, the number of household workers began to rise in the 1980s, reflecting a demand for nannies in two-career families.

Statistics also indicate that women have been investing their time and effort in ways that augment their economic value. Postponing marriage and children is one route to a higher income; additional education is another. In 1994, the most recent figures at this writing, women accounted for well over half—54 percent—of those awarded bachelor's degrees, compared to 43 percent in 1970 and 35 percent in 1960. Even more graphic has been their entry into professional programs. As Table 2 shows, in 1964 they were barely visible in engineering, dentistry, and business administration, and received well under 10 percent of degrees awarded in architecture, law, and medicine. Today, apart from engineering, women have made substantial strides in most professional programs. In the 1995 entering classes at Yale, Stanford, and Johns Hopkins medical schools, they outnumbered men.

TABLE 2   Proportion of Degrees Awarded to Women

Professional Programs	1964	1994
Architecture	4.0%	36.6%
Engineering	0.4%	16.4%
Business (MBA level)	2.7%	36.5%
Dentistry	0.7%	38.5%
Medicine	6.5%	37.9%
Law	3.1%	43.0%
Pharmacy	13.9%	66.8%
Academic doctorates	10.6%	44.1%*

* American citizens only.

But an increased presence in many occupations and professions does not necessarily lead to greater equity in earnings for women. Table 3 presents a mixed picture. The Bureau of Labor Statistics only began releasing pay differentials in 1983, but that at least allows comparisons across a twelve-year period. Although some occupations have witnessed modest progress, in none have women's earnings breached the 90 percent mark, and in many they are still below 70 percent. Even more disturbing is the finding that, in some fields, women's remuneration has actually dropped relative to men's. Among salaried lawyers and physicians and high-school teachers, women comprise a large share of those recently entering those professions, which may account for their lower wages. But among health technicians and electronic assemblers, the proportion of women has actually been dropping, which means another explanation is needed....

TABLE 3   Women's Earnings (per $1,000 Received by Men)

Occupation	1983	1995
More Than 10 Percent Improvement		
Chefs and cooks	$711	$885
Realtors	$683	$794
Production inspectors	$563	$649
Waiters and waitresses	$721	$822
Public administrators	$701	$786
Computer analysts	$773	$860
Less Than 10 Percent Improvement		
Journalists	$782	$855
Retail sales	$636	$693
Insurance adjusters	$651	$691
Financial managers	$638	$674
Education administrators	$671	$708
Janitors and cleaners	$810	$844
Engineers	$828	$862
Accountants	$706	$734
College faculty	$773	$781
Deterioration		
High school teachers	$886	$881
Health technicians	$839	$813
Electronic assemblers	$857	$808
Lawyers	$890	$818
Physicians	$816	$649

SEXUAL SEGREGATION

By most measures, the last quarter century has seen steady moves by women into positions traditionally reserved for men. As Table 4 shows, the advances have been real in fields as varied as medicine and meat cutting and bartending. But in some cases, progress may be less than it first appears. In 1970, insurance adjusters were mainly men, and in their well-paid work they examined burnt-out buildings and wrecked cars. Today, insurance adjusters are mainly women, who sit at computer terminals entering insurance claims. Many are part-time employees, with few or no benefits. And some…even do their jobs from their homes. Or, to cite another example, in 1970, the typical typesetter was a well-paid union worker who set hot lead for a newspaper in a printing plant. Today, type is generally keyed in electronically by women who are paid a fraction of what their male forerunners received. Many of the new women pharmacists count out pills for mail-order services and never see a customer. Few of the incoming female physicians will have practices of their own, but will be employed—or subject to scrutiny—by health-maintenance organizations.

Indeed, it has been argued that occupations start to admit women just when a field is beginning to decline in prestige and economic standing. That happened many years ago, when men ceased being bank tellers. Sometimes, as with typesetting, new technologies reconfigure the job. Moreover, women entering law and university teaching are finding that the ground rules have been changed. Until recently, most law partners and college professors enjoyed lifetime tenure. But now fewer attorneys can expect to become partners; and those who do can now be dismissed. Colleges, after years of being overstaffed in their top ranks, are tending to replace more of their retiring faculty members with discardable adjuncts. What may be added, although it hardly provides solace, is that young men who are also entering these and other professions will encounter the same barriers and rebuffs.

A smaller but still discernible pattern of change within the workforce has been the decision by some men to enter fields traditionally associated with women. The development began

TABLE 4 Women's Shares Within Occupations

	1970	1995
Total workforce	38.0%	46.1%
Considerable Change		
Insurance adjustors	29.6%	73.9%
Typesetters	16.8%	67.3%
Educational administrators	27.8%	58.7%
Publicists	26.6%	57.9%
Bartenders	21.0%	53.5%
Government administrators	21.7%	49.8%
College faculty	29.1%	45.2%
Insurance agents	12.9%	37.1%
Pharmacists	12.1%	36.2%
Photographers	14.8%	27.1%
Lawyers	4.9%	26.4%
Physicians	9.7%	24.4%
Butchers and meatcutters	11.4%	21.6%
Architects	4.0%	19.8%
Telephone installers	2.8%	16.0%
Dentists	3.5%	13.4%
Police officers	3.7%	12.9%
Clergy	2.9%	11.1%
Engineers	1.7%	8.4%
Sheet-metalworkers	1.9%	7.5%
Modest Change		
Hotel receptionists	51.4%	75.2%
Social workers	63.3%	67.9%
High-school teachers	49.6%	57.0%
Journalists	41.6%	53.2%
Realtors	31.2%	50.7%
Computer programmers	24.2%	29.5%
Essentially No Change		
Dental hygienists	94.0%	99.4%
Secretaries	97.8%	98.5%
Registered nurses	97.3%	93.1%
Elementary-school teachers	83.9%	84.1%
Librarians	82.1%	83.2%.
Men Replacing Women		
Telephone operators	94.0%	88.4%
Data entry keyers	93.7%	82.9%
Waiters and waitresses	90.8%	77.7%
Cooks and chefs	67.2%	44.5%

with flight attendants and then extended to nursing. By and large, these tend to be younger men who feel comfortable working with women. One has only to observe a plane's cabin crew to appreciate the symbiosis. And we are now accustomed to a male voice answering our requests for telephone numbers. The country has more restaurants with stylish pretensions than ever before, and one validation of that status is to have male waiters. Of course, many of these men view what they are doing as temporary or transitional. They may be deferring career decisions or waiting for openings in their chosen fields. Indeed, much of our service economy is predicated on the inclination of young people to remain single, to manage on modest pay, and to live and share expenses with other persons of their age.

Does the arrival of women really spell economic decline for an occupation or a profession? The task is to find whether gender is the operative factor or whether other forces are at work. Between 1970 and 1995, for example, women rose from being 4.9 percent of the country's lawyers to an impressive 26.4 percent. Yet what also happened was that the head count of lawyers more than tripled, rising from 288,000 to 894,000. So a growing glut of lawyers was the principal reason for the overall decline in pay for that profession. Moreover, of some 600,000 new lawyers, only about a third were women; so they should not be blamed for a falling wage scale.

Still, because so many of them are newcomers, relatively more women will be in an occupation's lower levels. In fact, earnings for younger people of both genders have become quite comparable. Among full-time workers under the age of twenty-five, women make $950 for every $1,000 paid to men. This approach to parity is even more revealing because she is still more likely to be starting out as a teacher while he is more apt to be a better-paid engineer. And if they are both beginning engineers, today their pay will usually be identical. In fact, the *National Law Journal* found that among law school students graduating in 1994, for men the median starting salary was $48,000, while the typical woman graduate began at $50,000.

It is certainly true that more women take part-time jobs, frequently because they must be—or want to be—available for family obligations. Yet it is hard to find figures to support the presumption that women give less of themselves. We do have a few measures that fill in parts of the story. For example, it might be assumed that women will choose jobs that are closer to their homes so that they can attend to domestic duties or because they are less disposed to look farther afield for a better job. As it happens, the Census can provide an answer because it collates the "travel time to work" for all employed Americans. Its most recent published study showed that the one-way journey for men averaged 23.7 minutes, while the jobs that women chose called for a 20.3 minute trip. A difference of 3.4 minutes does not suggest that women are markedly less adventuresome.

One way to hold home-life factors constant is to confine the comparison to workers who have never been married. Of course, most of these workers are younger people. It is still assumed that some single women are marking time at their jobs and have no aspirations for lifetime careers. Yet we all know older women who never married, and almost all of them have made their jobs a major part of their lives. Indeed...the Census analysis of "never married" workers on full-time schedules found that women ended up earning $1,005 for every $1,000 made by men. So when it comes to dedication, the women are actually ahead. Moreover, current demographic data suggests that in the years ahead, more women will be foregoing marriage, which will expand the pool of women who will be able to compete with men on an equal footing.

Ascending an occupation's ladder generally requires years of experience, either within a single organization or in the field as a whole. No one will be surprised to learn that women as a group do not have as many years on their resumes. Lester Thurow stressed this point several years ago when he said that ages twenty-five to thirty-five are the takeoff years for careers, when one gets seasoned on the job and noticed for promotion. "But the decade between twenty-five and thirty-five," he said, "is precisely the decade when women are most apt to leave the labor force or become part-time workers." Thurow is about half right. In the time period he says is crucial, 73 percent of the men are fully employed, compared with only 51 percent of the women. But there is another way to look at work experience. By focusing on age distributions within the workforce, we find that women who are twenty-five to thirty-five account for 29 percent of all fully employed women, which turns out to be exactly the proportion for men in the same age range. As Thurow says, some men may be slated for success in this "takeoff" decade. The question is why so many fewer women are put on the promotion lists.

EQUAL PAY FOR EQUAL WORK?

Of course, two people doing the same job should receive the same wage. But it isn't always easy to agree on whether identical work is being done. Nor is it easy to find statistics that assess the relative competence of men and women workers. But one way to start might be by limiting ourselves to all full-time workers who are in their early thirties, from thirty to thirty-four, a group that currently contains about 8 million men and 5 million women. The women in this cohort deserve to be taken seriously. Fully 20 percent have not yet been married, in most cases by their own decision, which suggests they have other aspirations. Another 17 percent are divorced or separated or widowed, which in most cases means they must now support themselves. And the remaining 63 percent who are married are combining full-time employment with domestic obligations. Also, at this age, about the same proportions of women and men have completed college, so the two genders look quite similar in their commitment to careers and their investments in education.

Of course, Table 5 cannot tell us whether the men and women are performing "equal" tasks. What we do see is that the women's median earnings stand at $825 per $1,000 for the men, a relatively high ratio as current comparisons go, but still far from parity. This age group is important because it contains what should be the most promising echelon of women. Yet they are not even half as likely to have $50,000 jobs, and they are a third less apt to be in the $35,000 to $50,000 tier. In contrast, men are a third less

likely to be found in the bottom bracket. The bottom line is that employers have shown much less inclination to promote accomplished women to $50,000 positions, while they seem to feel that as few men as possible should be made to take jobs paying less than $20,000. Another factor is that, thus far, women have been more likely than men to choose lower-paying professions: for example, in museums and galleries (average earnings: $18,928) or book publishing ($35,204), rather than, say, petroleum refining ($57,616) or as security and commodity brokers ($81,796).

A double standard for incomes persists not only on earth, but in the galaxies of stars. Over the years, the top moneymakers in the music industry have been all-male groups such as the Beatles, the Rolling Stones, the Eagles, Pink Floyd, and the Grateful Dead. Individual performers such as Michael Jackson, Garth Brooks, Billy Joel, and Elton John have made measurably more than the top female performers. Among authors, Stephen King, John Grisham, Tom Clancy, and Michael Crichton command larger advances than do such blockbusting novelists as Judith Krantz, Jackie Collins, and Patricia Cornwell. The men's books are then made into big-budget movies, while the women must settle for seeing theirs prepared as four-part specials for the small screen.

There is no shortage of theories to explain why this is the case. One certainly is that men have always put their stamp on art and entertainment, at the same time making sure that enough of what they produce will appeal to women. Many more women bought novels by Anthony Trollope and Charles Dickens compared with the number of men attracted to Jane Austen and the Brontës. True, women have contributed their movie dollars and television watching to Barbra Streisand and Roseanne and Oprah Winfrey. Yet, although these performers have become extremely rich, they still comprise a relatively short list. Of course, plays and movies and television series all have women stars, and most men do like seeing female faces and figures. But not always for their acting abilities. Indeed, men tend to shy away from entertainment in which women have too dominant a role. Recall how every episode of Mary Tyler Moore's long-running program had her surrounded by men with

TABLE 5　Earnings of Full-Time Workers, Age 30 to 34

7,905,000 Men		5,013,000 Women
15.7%	Over $50,000	6.7%
20.1%	$35,000 to $50,000	14.6%
39.4%	$20,000 to $35,000	41.4%
24.8%	Under $20,000	37.3%
$28,449	Median Earnings	$23,479
($1,000)	(Ratio)	($825)

strongly written scripts. And with Roseanne, one suspects that insofar as men were watching her show, it was mainly because the women in their lives insisted having the program on.

It was not always this way. Table 6 shows two sets of rankings: on the left, Hollywood's best-paid stars in 1934, and on the right, the biggest moneymakers sixty years later in 1994. Most apparent, of course, is that a majority of the 1934 group were women.

It is interesting to ponder why female movie stars were popular and highly paid in the 1930s. There may be lessons worth resurrecting from that distant era of Janet Gaynor and Norma Shearer.

TABLE 6 The Top Ten: Hollywood's Best-Paid Stars Then and Now

1934		1994
Will Rogers	#1	Harrison Ford
Clark Gable	#2	Sylvester Stallone
Janet Gaynor	#3	Bruce Willis
Wallace Beery	#4	Tom Hanks
Mae West	#5	Kevin Costner
Joan Crawford	#6	Clint Eastwood
Bing Crosby	#7	Arnold Schwarzenegger
Shirley Temple	#8	Michael Douglas
Marie Dressier	#9	Jim Carrey
Norma Shearer	#10	Robin Williams

37. FRATERNITIES AND RAPE ON CAMPUS

PATRICIA YANCEY MARTIN and ROBERT A. HUMMER

Our examination of men's social fraternities on college and university campuses as groups and organizations led us to conclude that fraternities are a physical and socio-cultural context that encourages the sexual coercion of women. We make no claims that all fraternities are 'bad' or that all fraternity men are rapists. Our observations indicated, however, that rape is especially probable in fraternities because of the kinds of organizations they are, the kinds of members they have, the practices their members engage in, and a virtual absence of university or community oversight.

This article is about fraternities. Its aim is to show how the culture of the fraternity encourages values, ideas, and activities that lead to the sexual exploitation of women and even rape. Martin and Hummer began their investigation with a case of gang rape at Florida State University. They examined newspaper articles, interviewed students, administrators, alumni advisers to Greek organizations, judges, attorneys, rape-victim advocates, and state prosecutors. The research was supplemented by reports from other authors and agencies. Individuals embedded in fraternity life are influenced by a view of women that causes actions that would probably not occur outside that organization. The social patterns themselves encourage rape—"the fraternity as a group and organization is at issue."

From "Fraternities and Rape on Campus," by Patricia Yancey Martin and Robert A. Hummer, in *Gender and Society* (3:4), pp. 474–497. Copyright © 1989 by *Gender and Society*. Reprinted by permission of Sage Publications, Inc.

Rapes are perpetrated on dates, at parties, in chance encounters, and in specially planned circumstances. That group structure and processes, rather than individual values or characteristics, are the impetus for many rape episodes was documented by Blanchard (1959) 30 years ago (also see Geis 1971), yet sociologists have failed to pursue this theme (for an exception, see Chancer 1987). A recent review of research (Muehlenhard and Linton 1987) on sexual violence, or rape, devotes only a few pages to the situational contexts of rape events, and these are conceptualized as potential risk factors for individuals rather than qualities of rape-prone social contexts.

Many rapes, far more than come to the public's attention, occur in fraternity houses on college and university campuses, yet little research has analyzed fraternities at American colleges and universities as rape-prone contexts (cf. Ehrhart and Sandler 1985). Most of the research on fraternities reports on samples of individual fraternity men. One group of studies compares the values, attitudes, perceptions, family socioeconomic status, psychological traits (aggressiveness, dependence), and so on, of fraternity and nonfraternity men (Bohrnstedt 1969; Fox, Hodge, and Ward 1987; Kanin 1967; Lemire 1979; Miller 1973). A second group attempts to identify the effects of fraternity membership over time on the values, attitudes, beliefs, or moral precepts of members (Hughes and Winston 1987; Marlowe and Auvenshine 1982; Miller 1973; Wilder, Hoyt, Doren, Hauck, and Zettle 1978; Wilder, Hoyt, Surbeck, Wilder, and Carney 1986). With minor exceptions, little research addresses the group and organizational context of fraternities or the social construction of fraternity life (for exceptions, see Letchworth 1969; Longino and Kart 1973; Smith 1964).

Gary Tash, writing as an alumnus and trial attorney in his fraternity's magazine, claims that over 90 percent of all gang rapes on college campuses involve fraternity men (1988, p. 2). Tash provides no evidence to substantiate this claim, but students of violence against women have been concerned with fraternity men's frequently reported involvement in rape episodes (Adams and Abarbanel 1988). Ehrhart and Sandler (1985) identify over 50 cases of gang rapes on campus perpetrated by fraternity men, and their analysis points to many of the conditions that we discuss here. Their analysis is unique in focusing on conditions in fraternities that make gang rapes of women by fraternity men both feasible and probable. They identify excessive alcohol use, isolation from external monitoring, treatment of women as prey, use of pornography, approval of violence, and excessive concern with competition as precipitating conditions to gang rape (also see Merton 1985; Roark 1987).

The study reported here confirmed and complemented these findings by focusing on both conditions and processes. We examined dynamics associated with the social construction of fraternity life, with a focus on processes that foster the use of coercion, including rape, in fraternity men's relations with women. Our examination of men's social fraternities on college and university campuses as groups and organizations led us to conclude that fraternities are a physical and socio-cultural context that encourages the sexual coercion of women. We make no claims that all fraternities are "bad" or that all fraternity men are rapists. Our observations indicated, however, that rape is especially probable in fraternities because of the kinds of organizations they are, the kinds of members they have, the practices their members engage in, and a virtual absence of university or community oversight. Analyses that lay blame for rapes by fraternity men on "peer pressure" are, we feel, overly simplistic (cf. Burkhart 1989; Walsh 1989). We suggest, rather, that fraternities create a socio-cultural context in which the use of coercion in sexual relations with women is normative and in which the mechanisms to keep this pattern of behavior in check are minimal at best and absent at worst. We conclude that unless fraternities change in fundamental ways, little improvement can be expected.

METHODOLOGY

Our goal was to analyze the group and organizational practices and conditions that create in fraternities an abusive social context for women. We developed a conceptual framework from an initial case study of an alleged gang rape at Florida

State University that involved four fraternity men and an 18—year-old coed. The group rape took place on the third floor of a fraternity house and ended with the "dumping" of the woman in the hallway of a neighboring fraternity house. According to newspaper accounts, the victim's blood-alcohol concentration, when she was discovered, was .349 percent, more than three times the legal limit for automobile driving and an almost lethal amount. One law enforcement officer reported that sexual intercourse occurred during the time the victim was unconscious: "She was in a life-threatening situation" (*Tallahassee Democrat*, 1988b). When the victim was found, she was comatose and had suffered multiple scratches and abrasions. Crude words and a fraternity symbol had been written on her thighs (*Tampa Tribune*, 1988). When law enforcement officials tried to investigate the case, fraternity members refused to cooperate. This led, eventually, to a five-year ban of the fraternity from campus by the university and by the fraternity's national organization.

In trying to understand how such an event could have occurred, and how a group of over 150 members (exact figures are unknown because the fraternity refused to provide a membership roster) could hold rank, deny knowledge of the event, and allegedly lie to a grand jury, we analyzed newspaper articles about the case and conducted open-ended interviews with a variety of respondents about the case and about fraternities, rapes, alcohol use, gender relations, and sexual activities on campus. Our data included over 100 newspaper articles on the initial gang rape case; open-ended interviews with Greek (social fraternity and sorority) and non-Greek (independent) students (N = 20); university administrators (N = 8, five men, three women); and alumni advisers to Greek organizations (N = 6). Open-ended interviews were held also with judges, public and private defense attorneys, victim advocates, and state prosecutors regarding the processing of sexual assault cases. Data were analyzed using the grounded theory method (Glaser 1978; Martin and Turner 1986). In the following analysis, concepts generated from the data analysis are integrated with the literature on men's social fraternities, sexual coercion, and related issues.

FRATERNITIES AND THE SOCIAL CONSTRUCTION OF MEN AND MASCULINITY

Our research indicated that fraternities are vitally concerned—more than with anything else—with masculinity (cf. Kanin 1967). They work hard to create a macho image and context and try to avoid any suggestion of "wimpishness," effeminacy, and homosexuality. Valued members display, or are willing to go along with, a narrow conception of masculinity that stresses competition, athleticism, dominance, winning, conflict, wealth, material possessions, willingness to drink alcohol, and sexual prowess vis-a-vis women.

Valued Qualities of Members

When fraternity members talked about the kind of pledges they prefer, a litany of stereotypical and narrowly masculine attributes and behaviors was recited, and feminine or woman-associated qualities and behaviors were expressly denounced (cf. Merton 1985). Fraternities seek men who are "athletic," "big guys," good in intramural competition, "who can talk college sports." Males "who are willing to drink alcohol," "who drink socially," or "who can hold their liquor" are sought. Alcohol and activities associated with the recreational use of alcohol are cornerstones of fraternity social life. Nondrinkers are viewed with skepticism and rarely selected for membership.[1]

Fraternities try to avoid "geeks," nerds, and men said to give the fraternity a "wimpy" or "gay" reputation. Art, music, and humanities majors, majors in traditional women's fields (nursing, home economics, social work, education), men with long hair, and those whose appearance or dress violate current norms are rejected. Clean-cut, handsome men who dress well (are clean, neat, conforming, fashionable) are preferred. One sorority woman commented that "the top-ranking fraternities have the best-looking guys."

One fraternity man, a senior, said his fraternity recruited "some big guys, very athletic" over a two-year period to help overcome its image of wimpiness. His fraternity had won the interfraternity competition for highest grade-point average several years running but was looked down on as "wimpy, dancy, even gay." With their bigger, more athletic recruits, "our reputation improved; we're a much more recognized fraternity now." Thus a fraternity's reputation and status depends on members' possession of stereotypically masculine qualities. Good grades, campus leadership, and community service are "nice" but masculinity dominance—for example, in athletic events, physical size of members, athleticism of members—counts most.

Certain social skills are valued. Men are sought who "have good personalities," are friendly, and "have the ability to relate to girls" (cf. Longino and Kart 1973). One fraternity man, a junior, said: "We watch a guy [a potential pledge] talk to women…. [W]e want guys who can relate to girls." Assessing a pledge's ability to talk to women is, in part, a preoccupation with homosexuality and a conscious avoidance of men who seem to have effeminate manners or qualities. If a member is suspected of being gay, he is ostracized and informally drummed out of the fraternity. A fraternity with a reputation as wimpy or tolerant of gays is ridiculed and shunned by other fraternities. Militant heterosexuality is frequently used by men as a strategy to keep each other in line (Kimmel 1987).

Financial affluence or wealth, a male-associated value in American culture, is highly valued by fraternities. In accounting for why the fraternity involved in the gang rape that precipitated our research project had been recognized recently as "the best fraternity chapter in the United States," a university official said: "They were good-looking, a big fraternity, had lots of BMWs [expensive, German-made automobiles]." After the rape, newspaper stories described the fraternity members' affluence, noting the high number of members who owned expensive cars (*St. Petersburg Times*, 1988).

The Status and Norms of Pledgeship

A *pledge* (sometimes called an *associate member*) is a new recruit who occupies a trial membership status for a specific period of time. The pledge period (typically ranging from 10 to 15 weeks) gives fraternity brothers an opportunity to assess and socialize new recruits. Pledges evaluate the fraternity also and decide whether they want to become brothers. The socialization experience is structured partly through assignment of a Big Brother to each pledge. Big Brothers are expected to teach pledges how to become a brother and to support them as they progress through the trial membership period. Some pledges are repelled by the pledging experience, which can entail physical abuse; harsh discipline; and demands to be subordinate, follow orders, and engage in demeaning routines and activities, similar to those used by the military to "make men out of boys" during boot camp.

Characteristics of the pledge experience are rationalized by fraternity members as necessary to help pledges unite into a group, rely on each other, and join together against outsiders. The process is highly masculinist in execution as well as conception. A willingness to submit to authority, follow orders, and do as one is told is viewed as a sign of loyalty, togetherness, and unity. Fraternity pledges who find the pledge process offensive often drop out. Some do this by openly quitting, which can subject them to ridicule by brothers and other pledges, or they may deliberately fail to make the grades necessary for initiation or transfer schools and decline to reaffiliate with the fraternity on the new campus. One fraternity pledge who quit the fraternity he had pledged described an experience during pledgeship as follows:

> This one guy was always picking on me. No matter what I did, I was wrong. One night after dinner, he and two other guys called me and two other pledges into the chapter room. He said, "Here, X, hold this 25 pound bag of ice at arms' length 'til I tell you to stop." I did it even though my arms and hands were killing me. When I asked if I could stop, he grabbed me around the throat and lifted me off the floor. I thought he would choke me to death. He cussed me and called me all kinds of names. He took one of my fingers and twisted it until it nearly broke…. I stayed in the fraternity for a few more days, but then I decided to quit. I hated it. Those guys are sick. They like seeing you suffer.

Fraternities' emphasis on toughness, withstanding pain and humiliation, obedience to superiors, and using physical force to obtain compliance contributes to an interpersonal style that de-emphasizes caring and sensitivity but fosters intragroup trust and loyalty. If the least macho or most critical pledges drop out, those who remain may be more receptive to, and influenced by, masculinist values and practices that encourage the use of force in sexual relations with women and the covering up of such behavior (cf. Kanin 1967).

Norms and Dynamics of Brotherhood

Brother is the status occupied by fraternity men to indicate their relations to each other and their membership in a particular fraternity organization or group. Brother is a male-specific status; only males can become brothers, although women can become "Little Sisters," a form of pseudomembership. "Becoming a brother" is a rite of passage that follows the consistent and often lengthy display by pledges of appropriately masculine qualities and behaviors. Brothers have a quasi-familial relationship with each other, are normatively said to share bonds of closeness and support, and are sharply set off from nonmembers. *Brotherhood* is a loosely defined term used to represent the bonds that develop among fraternity members and the obligations and expectations incumbent on them (cf. Marlowe and Auvenshine [1982] on fraternities' failure to encourage "moral development" in freshman pledges).

Some of our respondents talked about brotherhood in almost reverential terms, viewing it as the most valuable benefit of fraternity membership. One senior, a business-school major who had been affiliated with a fairly high-status fraternity throughout four years on campus, said:

> Brotherhood spurs friendship for life, which I consider its best aspect, although I didn't see it that way when I joined. Brotherhood bonds and unites. It instills values of caring about one another, caring about community, caring about ourselves. The values and bonds [or brotherhood] continually develop over the four years [in college] while normal friendships come and go.

Despite this idealization, most aspects of fraternity practice and conception are more mundane. Brotherhood often plays itself out as an overriding concern with masculinity and, by extension, femininity. As a consequence, fraternities comprise collectivities of highly masculinized men with attitudinal qualities and behavioral norms that predispose them to sexual coercion of women (cf. Kanin 1967; Merton 1985; Rapaport and Burkhart 1984). The norms of masculinity are complemented by conceptions of women and femininity that are equally distorted and stereotyped and that may enhance the probability of women's exploitation (cf. Ehrhart and Sandler 1985; Sanday 1981, 1986).

Practices of Brotherhood

Practices associated with fraternity brotherhood that contribute to the sexual coercion of women include a preoccupation with loyalty, group protection and secrecy, use of alcohol as a weapon, involvement in violence and physical force, and an emphasis on competition and superiority.

Loyalty, Group Protection, and Secrecy Loyalty is a fraternity preoccupation. Members are reminded constantly to be loyal to the fraternity and to their brothers. Among other ways, loyalty is played out in the practices of group protection and secrecy. The fraternity must be shielded from criticism. Members are admonished to avoid getting the fraternity in trouble and to bring all problems "to the chapter" (the local branch of a national social fraternity) rather than to outsiders. Fraternities try to protect themselves from close scrutiny and criticism by the Interfraternity Council (a quasi-governing body composed of representatives from all social fraternities on campus), their fraternity's national office, university officials, law enforcement, the media, and the public. Protection of the fraternity often takes precedence over what is procedurally, ethically, or legally correct. Numerous examples were related to us of fraternity brothers' lying to outsiders to "protect the fraternity."

Group protection was observed in the alleged gang rape case with which we began our study. Except for one brother, a rapist who turned state's evidence, the entire remaining fraternity membership was accused by university and criminal justice officials of lying to protect the fraternity.

Members consistently failed to cooperate even though the alleged crimes were felonies, involved only four men (two of whom were not even members of the local chapter), and the victim of the crime nearly died. According to a grand jury's findings, fraternity officers repeatedly broke appointments with law enforcement officials, refused to provide police with a list of members, and refused to cooperate with police and prosecutors investigating the case (*Florida Flambeau*, 1988).

Secrecy is a priority value and practice in fraternities, partly because full-fledged membership is premised on it (for confirmation, see Ehrhart and Sandler 1985; Longino and Kart 1973; Roark 1987). Secrecy is also a boundary-maintaining mechanism, demarcating in-group from out-group, us from them. Secret rituals, handshakes, and mottoes are revealed to pledge brothers as they are initiated into full brotherhood. Because only brothers are supposed to know a fraternity's secrets, such knowledge affirms membership in the fraternity and separates a brother from others. Extending secrecy tactics from protection of private knowledge to protection of the fraternity from criticism is a predictable development. Our interviews indicated that individual members knew the difference between right and wrong, but fraternity norms that emphasize loyalty, group protection, and secrecy often overrode standards of ethical correctness.

Alcohol as Weapon   Alcohol use by fraternity men is normative. They use it on weekdays to relax after class and on weekends to "get drunk," "get crazy," and "get laid." The use of alcohol to obtain sex from women is pervasive—in other words, it is used as a weapon against sexual reluctance. According to several fraternity men whom we interviewed, alcohol is the major tool used to gain sexual mastery over women (cf. Adams and Abarbanel 1988; Ehrhart and Sandler 1985). One fraternity man, a 21—year-old senior, described alcohol use to gain sex as follows: "There are girls that you know will fuck, then some you have to put some effort into it…. You have to buy them drinks or find out if she's drunk enough…."

A similar strategy is used collectively. A fraternity man said that at parties with Little Sisters: "We provide them with 'hunch punch' and

things get wild. We get them drunk and most of the guys end up with one." "'Hunch punch,'" he said, "is a girls' drink made up of overproof alcohol and powdered Kool-Aid, no water or anything, just ice. It's very strong. Two cups will do a number on a female." He had plans in the next academic term to surreptitiously give hunch punch to women in a "prim and proper" sorority because "having sex with prim and proper sorority girls is definitely a goal." These women are a challenge because they "won't openly consume alcohol and won't get openly drunk as hell." Their sororities have "standards committees" that forbid heavy drinking and easy sex.

In the gang rape case, our sources said that many fraternity men on campus believed the victim had a drinking problem and was thus an "easy make." According to newspaper accounts, she had been drinking alcohol on the evening she was raped; the lead assailant is alleged to have given her a bottle of wine after she arrived at his fraternity house. Portions of the rape occurred in a shower, and the victim was reportedly so drunk that her assailants had difficulty holding her in a standing position (*Tallahassee Democrat*, 1988a). While raping her, her assailants repeatedly told her they were members of another fraternity under the apparent belief that she was too drunk to know the difference. Of course, if she was too drunk to know who they were, she was too drunk to consent to sex (cf. Allgeier 1986; Tash 1988).

One respondent told us that gang rapes are wrong and can get one expelled, but he seemed to see nothing wrong in sexual coercion one-on-one. He seemed unaware that the use of alcohol to obtain sex from a woman is grounds for a claim that a rape occurred (cf. Tash 1988). Few women on campus (who also may not know these grounds) report date rapes, however; so the odds of detection and punishment are slim for fraternity men who use alcohol for "seduction" purposes (cf. Byington and Keeter 1988; Merton 1985).

Violence and Physical Force   Fraternity men have a history of violence (Ehrhart and Sandler 1985; Roark 1987). Their record of hazing, fighting, property destruction, and rape has caused them problems with insurance companies (Bradford 1986; Pressley 1987). Two university officials told us that fraternities "are the third riskiest property to insure behind toxic waste dumps and amusement parks." Fraternities are increasingly defendants in legal actions brought by pledges subjected to hazing (Meyer 1986; Pressley 1987) and by women who were raped by one or more members. In a recent alleged gang rape incident at another Florida university, prosecutors failed to file charges but the victim filed a civil suit against the fraternity nevertheless (Tallahassee Democrat, 1989).

Competition and Superiority   Interfraternity rivalry fosters in-group identification and out-group hostility. Fraternities stress pride of membership and superiority over other fraternities as major goals. Interfraternity rivalries take many forms, including competition for desirable pledges, size of pledge class, size of membership, size and appearance of fraternity house, superiority in intramural sports, highest grade-point averages, giving the best parties, gaining the best or most campus leadership roles, and, of great importance, attracting and displaying "good looking women." Rivalry is particularly intense over members, intramural sports, and women (cf. Messner 1989).

FRATERNITIES' COMMODIFICATION OF WOMEN

In claiming that women are treated by fraternities as commodities, we mean that fraternities knowingly, and intentionally, *use* women for their benefit. Fraternities use women as bait for new members, as servers of brothers' needs, and as sexual prey.

Women as Bait

Fashionably attractive women help a fraternity attract new members. As one fraternity man, a junior, said, "They are good bait." Beautiful, sociable women are believed to impress the right kind of pledges and give the impression that the fraternity can deliver this type of woman to its members. Photographs of shapely, attractive coeds are printed in fraternity brochures and

videotapes that are distributed and shown to potential pledges. The women pictured are often dressed in bikinis, at the beach, and are pictured hugging the brothers of the fraternity. One university official says such recruitment materials give the message: "Hey, they're here for you, you can have whatever you want," and, "we have the best looking women. Join us and you can have them too." Another commented: "Something's wrong when males join an all-male organization as the best place to meet women. It's so illogical."

Fraternities compete in promising access to beautiful women. One fraternity man, a senior, commented that "the attraction of girls [i.e., a fraternity's success in attracting women] is a big status symbol for fraternities." One university official commented that the use of women as a recruiting tool is so well entrenched that fraternities that might be willing to forgo it say they cannot afford to unless other fraternities do so as well. One fraternity man said, "Look, if we don't have Little Sisters, the fraternities that do will get all the good pledges." Another said, "We won't have as good a rush [the period during which new members are assessed and selected] if we don't have these women around."

In displaying good-looking, attractive, skimpily dressed, nubile women to potential members, fraternities implicitly, and sometimes explicitly, promise sexual access to women. One fraternity man commented that "part of what being in a fraternity is all about is the sex" and explained how his fraternity uses Little Sisters to recruit new members:

> We'll tell the sweetheart [the fraternity's term for Little Sister], "You're gorgeous; you can get him." We'll tell her to fake a scam and she'll go hang all over him during a rush party, kiss him, and he thinks he's done wonderful and wants to join. The girls think it's great too. It's flattering for them.

Women as Servers

The use of women as servers is exemplified in the Little Sister program. Little Sisters are undergraduate women who are rushed and selected in a manner parallel to the recruitment of fraternity men. They are affiliated with the fraternity in a formal but unofficial way and are able, indeed required, to wear the fraternity's Greek letters. Little Sisters are not full-fledged fraternity members, however; and fraternity national offices and most universities do not register or regulate them. Each fraternity has an officer called Little Sister chairman who oversees their organization and activities. The Little Sisters elect officers among themselves, pay monthly dues to the fraternity, and have well-defined roles. Their dues are used to pay for the fraternity's social events, and Little Sisters are expected to attend and hostess fraternity parties and hang around the house to make it a "nice place to be." One fraternity man, a senior, described Little Sisters this way: "They are very social girls, willing to join in, be affiliated with the group, devoted to the fraternity." Another member, a sophomore, said: "Their sole purpose is social—attend parties, attract new members, and 'take care' of the guys."

Our observations and interviews suggested that women selected by fraternities as Little Sisters are physically attractive, possess good social skills, and are willing to devote time and energy to the fraternity and its members. One undergraduate woman gave the following job description for Little Sisters to a campus newspaper:

> It's not just making appearances at all the parties but entails many more responsibilities. You're going to be expected to go to all the intramural games to cheer the brothers on, support and encourage the pledges, and just be around to bring some extra life to the house. [As a Little Sister] you have to agree to take on a new responsibility other than studying to maintain your grades and managing to keep your checkbook from bouncing. You have to make time to be a part of the fraternity and support the brothers in all they do. (The *Tomahawk*, 1988)

The title of *Little Sister* reflects women's subordinate status; fraternity men in a parallel role are called *Big Brothers*. Big Brothers assist a sorority primarily with the physical work of sorority rushes, which, compared to fraternity rushes, are more formal, structured, and intensive. Sorority rushes take place in the daytime and fraternity rushes at night, so fraternity men are free to help. According to one fraternity member, Little Sister status is a benefit to women because it gives them a social outlet and "the protection of the brothers." The gender-stereotypic conceptions and obligations of these Little Sister and Big Brother statuses indicate that fraternities and sororities promote a gender hierarchy on campus that fosters subordination and dependence in women, thus encouraging sexual exploitation and the belief that it is acceptable.

Women as Sexual Prey

Little Sisters are a sexual utility. Many Little Sisters do not belong to sororities and lack peer support for refraining from unwanted sexual relations. One fraternity man (whose fraternity has 65 members and 85 Little Sisters) told us they had recruited "wholesale" in the prior year to "get lots of new women." The structural access to women that the Little Sister program provides and the absence of normative supports for refusing fraternity members' sexual advances may make women in this program particularly susceptible to coerced sexual encounters with fraternity men.

Access to women for sexual gratification is a presumed benefit of fraternity membership, promised in recruitment materials and strategies and through brothers' conversations with new recruits. One fraternity man said: "We always tell the guys that you get sex all the time, there's always new girls.... After I became a Greek, I found out I could be with females at will." A university official told us that, based on his observations, "no one [i.e., fraternity men] on this campus wants to have 'relationships.' They just want to have fun [i.e., sex]." Fraternity men plan and execute strategies aimed at obtaining sexual gratification, and this occurs at both individual and collective levels.

Individual strategies include getting a woman drunk and spending a great deal of money on her. As for collective strategies, most of our undergraduate interviewees agreed that fraternity parties often culminate in sex and that this outcome is planned. One fraternity man said fraternity parties often involve sex and nudity and can "turn into orgies." Orgies may be planned in advance, such as the Bowery Ball party held by one fraternity. A former fraternity member said of this party:

The entire idea behind this is sex. Both men and women come to the party wearing little or nothing. There are pornographic pinups on the walls and usually porno movies playing on the TV. The music carries sexual overtones.... They just get schnockered [drunk] and, in most cases, they also get laid.

When asked about the women who come to such a party, he said: "Some Little Sisters just won't go.... The girls who do are looking for a good time, girls who don't know what it is, things like that."

Other respondents denied that fraternity parties are orgies but said that sex is always talked about among the brothers and they all know "who each other is doing it with." One member said that most of the time, guys have sex with their girlfriends "but with socials, girlfriends aren't allowed to come and it's their [members'] big chance [to have sex with other women]." The use of alcohol to help them get women into bed is a routine strategy at fraternity parties.

CONCLUSIONS

In general, our research indicated that the organization and membership of fraternities contribute heavily to coercive and often violent sex. Fraternity houses are occupied by same-sex (all men) and same-age (late teens, early twenties) peers whose maturity and judgment is often less than ideal. Yet fraternity houses are private dwellings that are mostly off-limits to, and away from the scrutiny of, university and community representatives, with the result that fraternity house events seldom come to the attention of outsiders. Practices associated with the social construction of fraternity brotherhood emphasize a macho conception of men and masculinity, a narrow, stereotyped conception of women and femininity, and the treatment of women as commodities. Other practices contributing to coercive sexual relations and the cover-up of rapes include excessive alcohol use, competitiveness, and normative support for deviance and secrecy (cf. Bogal-Allbritten and Allbritten 1985; Kanin 1967).

Some fraternity practices exacerbate others. Brotherhood norms require "sticking together"

regardless of right or wrong; thus rape episodes are unlikely to be stopped or reported to outsiders, even when witnesses disapprove. The ability to use alcohol without scrutiny by authorities and alcohol's frequent association with violence, including sexual coercion, facilitates rape in fraternity houses. Fraternity norms that emphasize the value of maleness and masculinity over femaleness and femininity and that elevate the status of men and lower the status of women in members' eyes undermine perceptions and treatment of women as persons who deserve consideration and care (cf. Ehrhart and Sandler 1985; Merton 1985).

Androgynous men and men with a broad range of interests and attributes are lost to fraternities through their recruitment practices. Masculinity of a narrow and stereotypical type helps create attitudes, norms, and practices that predispose fraternity men to coerce women sexually, both individually and collectively (Allgeier 1986; Hood 1989; Sanday 1981, 1986). Male athletes on campus may be similarly disposed for the same reasons (Kirshenbaum 1989; Telander and Sullivan 1989).

Research into the social contexts in which rape crimes occur and the social constructions associated with these contexts illumine rape dynamics on campus. Blanchard (1959) found that group rapes almost always have a leader who pushes others into the crime. He also found that the leader's latent homosexuality, desire to show off to his peers, or fear of failing to prove himself a man are frequently an impetus. Fraternity norms and practices contribute to the approval and use of sexual coercion as an accepted tactic in relations with women. Alcohol-induced compliance is normative, whereas, presumably, use of a knife, gun, or threat of bodily harm would not be because the woman who "drinks too much" is viewed as "causing her own rape" (cf. Ehrhart and Sandler 1985).

Our research led us to conclude that fraternity norms and practices influence members to view the sexual coercion of women, which is a felony crime, as sport, a contest, or a game (cf. Sato 1988). This sport is played not between men and women but between men and men. Women are the pawns or prey in the interfraternity rivalry game; they prove that a fraternity is successful or prestigious. The use of women in this way encourages fraternity men to see women as objects and sexual coercion as sport. Today's societal norms support young women's right to engage in sex at their discretion, and coercion is unnecessary in a mutually desired encounter. However, nubile young women say they prefer to be "in a relationship" to have sex, while young men say they prefer to "get laid" without a commitment (Muehlenhard and Linton 1987). These differences may reflect, in part, American puritanism and men's fears of sexual intimacy or perhaps intimacy of any kind. In a fraternity context, getting sex without giving emotionally demonstrates "cool" masculinity. More important, it poses no threat to the bonding and loyalty of the fraternity brotherhood (cf. Farr 1988). Drinking large quantities of alcohol before having sex suggests that "scoring" rather than intrinsic sexual pleasure is a primary concern of fraternity men.

Unless fraternities' composition, goals, structures, and practices change in fundamental ways, women on campus will continue to be sexual prey for fraternity men. As do all male enclaves dedicated to opposing faculty and administration and to cementing group ties, fraternity members eschew any hint of homosexuality. Their version of masculinity transforms women, and men with womanly characteristics, into the out-group. "Womanly men" are ostracized; feminine women are used to demonstrate members' masculinity. Encouraging renewed emphasis on their founding values (Longino and Kart 1973), service orientation and activities (Lemire 1979), or members' moral development (Marlowe and Auvenshine 1982) will have little effect on fraternities' treatment of women. A case for or against fraternities cannot be made by studying individual members. The fraternity as a group and organization is at issue. Located on campus along with many vulnerable women, embedded in a sexist society, and caught up in masculinist goals, practices, and values, fraternities' violation of women—including forcible rape—should come as no surprise.

NOTE

1. Recent bans by some universities on open-keg parties at fraternity houses have resulted in heavy drinking before coming to a party and an increase in drunkenness among those who attend. This may aggravate, rather than improve, the treatment of women by fraternity men at parties.

REFERENCES

Allgeier, Elizabeth. 1986. "Coercive Versus Consensual Sexual Interactions." G. Stanley Hall Lecture to American Psychological Association Annual Meeting. Washington, DC, August.

Adams, Aileen and Gail Abarbanel. 1988. *Sexual Assault on Campus: What Colleges Can Do.* Santa Monica, CA: Rape Treatment Center.

Blanchard, W. H. 1959. "The Group Process in Gang Rape." *Journal of Social Psychology* 49:259–66.

Bogal-Allbritten, Rosemarie B. and William L. Allbritten. 1985. "The Hidden Victims: Courtship Violence Among College Students." *Journal of College Student Personnel* 43:201–4.

Bohrnstedt, George W. 1969 "Conservatism, Authoritarianism and Religiosity of Fraternity Pledges." *Journal of College Student Personnel* 27:36–43.

Bradford, Michael. 1986. "Tight Market Dries Up Nightlife at University." *Business Insurance* (March 2):2, 6.

Burkhart, Barry. 1989. Comments in Seminar on Acquaintance/Date Rape Prevention: A National Video Teleconference, February 2.

Burkhart, Barry R. and Annette L. Stanton. 1985. "Sexual Aggression in Acquaintance Relationships." Pp. 43–65 in *Violence in Intimate Relationships,* edited by G. Russell. Englewood Cliffs, NJ: Spectrum.

Byington, Diane B. and Karen W. Keeter. 1988. "Assessing Needs of Sexual Assault Victims on a University Campus." Pp. 23–31 in *Student Service: Responding to Issues and Challenges.* Chapel Hill: University of North Carolina Press.

Chancer, Lynn S. 1987. "New Bedford, Massachusetts, March 6, 1983–March 22, 1984: The 'Before and After' of a Group Rape." *Gender & Society* 1:239–60.

Ehrhart, Julie K. and Bernice R. Sandler. 1985. *Campus Gang Rape: Party Games?* Washington, DC: Association of American Colleges.

Farr, K. A. 1988. "Dominance Bonding Through the Good Old Boys Sociability Network." *Sex Roles* 18:259–77.

Florida Flambeau. 1988. "Pike Members Indicted in Rape." (May 19):1, 5.

Fox, Elaine, Charles Hodge, and Walter Ward. 1987. "A Comparison of Attitudes Held by Black and White Fraternity Members." *Journal of Negro Education* 56:521–34.

Geis, Gilbert. 1971. "Group Sexual Assaults." *Medical Aspects of Human Sexuality* 5:101–13.

Glaser, Barney G. 1978. *Theoretical Sensitivity: Advances in the Methodology of Grounded Theory.* Mill Valley, CA: Sociology Press.

Hood, Jane. 1989. "Why Our Society Is Rape-Prone." *New York Times*, May 16.

Hughes, Michael J. and Roger B. Winston, Jr. 1987. "Effects of Fraternity Membership on Interpersonal Values." *Journal of College Student Personnel* 45:405—11.

Kanin, Eugene J. 1967. "Reference Groups and Sex Conduct Norm Violations." *The Sociological Quarterly* 8:495—504.

Kimmel, Michael, ed. 1987. *Changing Men: New Directions in Research on Men and Masculinity*. Newbury Park, CA: Sage.

Kirshenbaum, Jerry. 1989. "Special Report, An American Disgrace: A Violent and Unprecedented Lawlessness Has Arisen Among College Athletes in All Parts of the Country." *Sports Illustrated* (February 27):16—19.

Lemire, David. 1979. "One Investigation of the Stereotypes Associated with Fraternities and Sororities." *Journal of College Student Personnel* 37:54—57.

Letchworth, G. E. 1969. "Fraternities Now and in the Future." *Journal of College Student Personnel* 10:118—22.

Longino, Charles F., Jr., and Gary S. Kart. 1973. "The College Fraternity: An Assessment of Theory and Research." *Journal of College Student Personnel* 31:118—25.

Marlowe, Anne F. and Dwight C. Auvenshine. 1982. "Greek Membership: Its Impact on the Moral Development of College Freshmen." *Journal of College Student Personnel* 40:53—57.

Martin, Patricia Yancey and Barry A. Turner. 1986. "Grounded Theory and Organizational Research." *Journal of Applied Behavioral Science* 22:141—57.

Merton, Andrew. 1985. "On Competition and Class: Return to Brotherhood." *Ms.* (September):60—65, 121—22.

Messner, Michael. 1989. "Masculinities and Athletic Careers," *Gender & Society* 3:71—88.

Meyer, T. J. 1986. "Fight Against Hazing Rituals Rages on Campuses." *Chronicle of Higher Education* (March 12):34—36.

Miller, Leonard D. 1973. "Distinctive Characteristics of Fraternity Members." *Journal of College Student Personnel* 31:126—28.

Muehlenhard, Charlene L. and Melaney A. Linton. 1987. "Date Rape and Sexual Aggression in Dating Situations: Incidence and Risk Factors." *Journal of Counselling Psychology* 34:186—96.

Pressley, Sue Anne. 1987. "Fraternity Hell Night Still Endures." *Washington Post* (August 11):B1.

Rapaport, Karen and Barry R. Burkhart. 1984. "Personality and Attitudinal Characteristics of Sexually Coercive College Males." *Journal of Abnormal Psychology* 93:216—21.

Roark, Mary L. 1987. "Preventing Violence on College Campuses." *Journal of Counselling and Development* 65:367—70.

Sanday, Peggy Reeves. 1981. "The Socio-Cultural Context of Rape: A Cross-Cultural Study." *Journal of Social Issues* 37:5—27.

——. 1986. "Rape and the Silencing of the Feminine." Pp. 84—101 in *Rape*, edited by S. Tomaselli and R. Porter. Oxford: Basil Blackwell.

St. Petersburg Times, 1988. "A Greek Tragedy." (May 19):1F, 6F.

Sato, Ikuya. 1988. "Play Theory of Delinquency: Toward a General Theory of 'Action.'" *Symbolic Interaction* 11:191—212.

Smith, T. 1964. "Emergence and Maintenance of Fraternal Solidarity." *Pacific Sociological Review* 7:29—37.

Tallahassee Democrat. 1988a. "FSU Fraternity Brothers Charged." (April 27):1A, 12A.

——. 1988b. "FSU Interviewing Students About Alleged Rape." (April 24):1D.

——. 1989. "Woman Sues Stetson in Alleged Rape." (March 19):3B.

Tampa Tribune. 1988. "Fraternity Brothers Charged in Sexual Assault of FSU Coed." (April 27):6B.

Tash, Gary B. 1988. "Date Rape." *The Emerald of Sigma Pi Fraternity* 75(4):1—2.

Telander, Rick and Robert Sullivan. 1989. "Special Report, You Reap What You Sow." *Sports Illustrated* (February 27):20—34.

The Tomahawk. 1988. "A Look Back at Rush, A Mixture of Hard Work and Fun." (April/May):3D.

Walsh, Claire. 1989. Comments in Seminar on Acquaintance/ Date Rape Prevention: A National Video Teleconference, February 2.

Wilder, David H., Arlyne E. Hoyt, Dennis M. Doren, William E. Hauck, and Robert D. Zettle. 1978. "The Impact of Fraternity and Sorority Membership on Values and Attitudes," *Journal of College Student Personnel* 36:445—49.

Wilder, David H., Arlyne E. Hoyt, Beth Shuster Surbeck, Janet C. Wilder, and Patricia Imperatrice Carney. 1986. "Greek Affiliation and Attitude Change in College Students." *Journal of College Student Personnel* 44:510—19.

PART VIII

Culture

As people interact over time, they come to develop a shared reality; a perspective; a common definition of what is true, moral, and worthwhile. This, to most sociologists, is the meaning of culture. Americans share a culture. Most of us take that culture for granted, and we come to judge others (and one another) according to the qualities of that culture. Within the United States, there are many communities, formal organizations, and groups developing their own culture to an extent. Therefore, for example, Harvard University will have a different culture from Princeton University, General Motors, and Los Angeles County Hospital. Some organizations in the United States will not only develop a radically different culture from that shared by most Americans, but those organizations will sometimes challenge and eventually alter the general culture.

Four selections are included in Part VIII. Howard S. Becker introduces the meaning of culture in an excellent, interesting, and clear manner, drawing on his experience as a jazz musician. Gini and Sullivan's analysis of work shows us the importance of culture on people's view of work, as well as their willingness to do work. Arnold Goldstein challenges us to face the major role that violence plays in American culture from its beginning to the present day. Finally Elijah Anderson describes the culture of the street and shows us the power of this culture when it is in conflict with the culture of the home.

38. CULTURE: A SOCIOLOGICAL VIEW

HOWARD S. BECKER

On the one hand, culture persists and antedates the participation of particular people in it. Indeed, culture can be said to shape the outlooks of people who participate in it. But cultural understandings, on the other hand, have to be reviewed and remade continually, and in the remaking, they change.

This article is an attempt to describe the meaning of *culture* and to show its subtleties and importance. The following questions might be a good guide through Becker's analysis:

1. What is culture?
2. How does culture aid collective action?
3. How does culture arise?
4. Why does culture stay the same and why does it change?
5. How does culture guide public behavior?
6. How does culture socialize the individual?
7. Why does culture make it easier for people to plan their lives?

I was for some years what is called a Saturday night musician, making myself available to whoever called and hired me to play for dances and parties in groups of varying sizes, playing everything from polkas through mambos, jazz, and imitations of Wayne King. Whoever called would tell me where the job was, what time it began, and usually would tell me to wear a dark suit and a bow tie, thus ensuring that the collection of strangers he was hiring would at least look like a band because they would all be dressed more or less alike. When we arrived at work, we would introduce ourselves—the chances were, in a city the size of Chicago (where I did much of my playing), that we were in fact strangers—and see who we knew in common and whether our paths had ever crossed before. The drummer would assemble his drums, the others would put together their instruments and tune up, and when it was time to start, the leader would announce the

Becker, Howard S., "Culture: A Sociological View," *Yale Review*, September 2 1982. 71:513-527. Copyright Yale University.

name of a song and a key—"Exactly Like You" in B flat, for instance—and we would begin to play. We not only began at the same time, but also played background figures that fit the melody someone else was playing and, perhaps most miraculously, ended together. No one in the audience ever guessed that we had never met until twenty minutes earlier. And we kept that up all night, as though we had rehearsed often and played together for years. In a place like Chicago, that scene might be repeated hundreds of times during a weekend.

What I have just described embodies the phenomenon that sociologists have made the core problem of their discipline. The social sciences are such a contentious bunch of disciplines that it makes trouble to say what I think is true, that they all in fact concern themselves with one or another version of this issue—the problem of collective action, of how people manage to act together. I will not attempt a rigorous definition of collective action here, but the story of the Saturday night musicians can serve as an example of it. The example might have concerned a larger group—the employees of a factory who turn out several hundred automobiles in the course of a day, say. Or it might have been about so small a group as a family. It needn't have dealt with a casual collection of strangers, although the ability of strangers to perform together that way makes clear the nature of the problem. How do they do it? How do people act together so as to get anything done without a great deal of trouble, without missteps and conflict?

We can approach the meaning of a concept by seeing how it is used, what work it is called on to do. Sociologists use the concept of culture as one of a family of explanations for the phenomenon of concerted activity.... Robert Redfield defined culture as "conventional understandings made manifest in act and artifact." The notion is that the people involved have a similar idea of things, understand them in the same way, as having the same character and the same potential, capable of being dealt with in the same way; they also know that this idea is shared, that the people they are dealing with know, just as they do, what these things are and how they can be used. Because all of them have roughly the same idea, they can all act in ways that are roughly the same, and their activities will, as a result, mesh and be coordinated. Thus, because all those musicians understood what a Saturday night job at a country club consisted of and acted accordingly, because they all knew the melody and harmony of "Exactly Like You" and hundreds of similar songs, because they knew that the others knew this as they knew it, they could play that job successfully. The concept of culture, in short, has its use for sociologists as an explanation of those musicians and all the other forms of concerted action for which they stand....

Culture, however, explains how people act in concert when they *do* share understandings. It is thus a consequence (in this kind of sociological thinking) of the existence of a group of acting people. It has its meaning as one of the resources people draw on in order to coordinate their activities. In this it differs from most anthropological thinking in which the order of importance is reversed, culture leading a kind of independent existence as a system of patterns that make the existence of larger groups possible.

Most conceptions of culture include a great deal more than the spare definition I have just offered. But I think, for reasons made clear later, that it is better to begin with a minimal definition and then to add other conditions when that is helpful....

How does culture—shared understanding—help people to act collectively? People have ideas about how a certain kind of activity might be carried on. They believe others share these ideas and will act on them if they understand the situation in the same way. They believe further that the people they are interacting with believe that they share these ideas too, so that everyone thinks that everyone else has the same idea about how to do things. Given such circumstances, if everyone does what seems appropriate, action will be sufficiently coordinated for practical purposes. Whatever was under way will get done—the meal served, the child dealt with, the job finished—well enough that life can proceed.

The cultural process, then, consists of people doing something in line with their understanding of what one might best do under the given circumstances. Others, recognizing what was done as appropriate, will then consult their notions of what might be done and do something that seems right to them, to which others in return will respond similarly, and so on. If everyone has the same general ideas in mind, and does something congruent with that image or collection of ideas, then what people do will fit together. If we all know the melody and harmony of "Exactly Like You," and improvise accordingly, whatever comes out will sound reasonable to the players and listeners, and a group of perfect strangers will sound like they know what they are doing.

Consider another common situation. A man and woman meet and find each other interesting. At some stage of their relationship, they may consider any of a variety of ways of organizing their joint activities. Early on, one or the other might propose that they "have a date." Later, one or the other might subtly or forthrightly suggest that they spend the night together. Still later, they might try "living together." Finally, they might decide to "get married." They might skip some of these stages and they might not follow that progression, which in contemporary America is a progression of increasingly formal commitment.

In other societies and at other times, of course, the stages and the relationships would differ. But, whatever their variety, insofar as there are names for those relationships and stages, and insofar as most or all of the people in a society know those names and have an idea of what they imply as far as continuing patterns of joint activity are concerned, then the man and woman involved will be able to organize what they do by referring to those guideposts. When one or the other suggests one of these possibilities, the partner will know, more or less, what is being suggested without requiring that every item be spelled out in detail, and the pair can then organize their daily lives, more or less, around the patterns suggested by these cultural images.

What they do from day to day will of course not be completely covered by the details of that imagery, although they will be able to decide many details by consulting it together and adapting what it suggests to the problem at hand. None of these images, for example, really establishes who takes the garbage out or what the details of their sexual activity may be, but the images do, in general, suggest the kind of commitments and obligations involved on both sides in a wide range of practical matters.

That is not the end of the matter, however. Consider a likely contemporary complication: The woman, divorced, has small children who live with her. In this case, the couple's freedom of action is constrained, and no cultural model suggests what they ought to do about the resulting difficulties. The models for pairing and for rearing children suggest incompatible solutions, and the partners have to invent something. They have to improvise.

This raises a major problem in the theory of culture I am propounding. Where does culture come from? The typical cultural explanation of behavior takes the culture as given, as preexisting the particular encounter in which it comes into play. That makes sense. Most of the cultural understandings we use to organize our daily behavior are there before we get there and we do not propose to change them or negotiate their details with the people we encounter. We do not propose a new economic system every time we go to the grocery store. But those understandings and ways of doing things have not always been there.

Most of us buy our food in supermarkets today, and that requires a different way of shopping from the corner grocery stores of a generation ago. How did the new culture of supermarkets arise?

One answer is that the new culture was imposed by the inventors of the concept, the owners of the new stores that embodied it. They created the conditions under which change was more or less inevitable. People might have decided not to shop in supermarkets and chain stores, but changing conditions of urban life caused so many of them to use the new markets that the corner grocery, the butcher shop, the poultry and fish stores disappeared in all but a few areas. Once that happened, supermarkets became the only practical possibility left, and people had to invent new ways of serving themselves.

So, given new conditions, people invent culture. The way they do it was suggested by William Graham Sumner a century ago in *Folkways*. We can paraphrase him in this way. A group finds itself sharing a common situation and common problems. Various members of the group experiment with possible solutions to those problems and report their experiences to their fellows. In the course of their collective discussion, the members of the group arrive at a definition of the situation, its problems and possibilities, and develop a consensus as to the most appropriate and efficient ways of behaving. This consensus thenceforth constrains the activities of individual members of the group, who will probably act on it, given the opportunity. In other words, new situations provoke new behavior. But people generally find themselves in company when dealing with these new situations, and because they arrive at their solutions collectively, each assumes that the others share them. The beginnings of a new shared understanding thus come into play quickly and easily.

The ease with which new cultural understandings arise and persist varies. It makes a difference, for one thing, how large a group is involved in making the new understandings. At one extreme, as I have noted, every mating couple, every new family, has to devise its own culture to cover the contingencies of daily interaction. At the other, consider what happens during industrialization when hundreds of thousands—per-

Constant creation of culture [handwritten note in top margin]

haps millions—of people are brought from elsewhere to work in the new factories. They have to come from elsewhere because the area could not support that many people before industrialization. As a result, the newcomers differ in culture from the people already there, and they differ as well in the role they play in the new industries, usually coming in at the bottom. When industrialization takes place on a large scale, not only does a new culture of the workplace have to be devised, but also a new culture of the cities in which they all end up living—a new experience for everyone involved.

The range of examples suggests, as I mean it to, that people create culture continuously. Because no two situations are alike, the cultural solutions available to them are only approximate. Even in the simplest societies, no two people learn quite the same cultural material; the chance encounters of daily life provide sufficient variation to ensure that. No set of cultural understandings, then, provides a perfectly applicable solution to any problem people have to solve in the course of their day, and they therefore must remake those solutions, adapt their understandings to the new situation in the light of what is different about it. Even the most conscious and determined effort to keep things as they are would necessarily involve strenuous efforts to remake and reinforce understandings so as to keep them intact in the face of what was changing.

There is an apparent paradox here. On the one hand, culture persists and antedates the participation of particular people in it. Indeed, culture can be said to shape the outlooks of people who participate in it. But cultural understandings, on the other hand, have to be reviewed and remade continually, and in the remaking, they change.

This is not a true paradox, however: The understandings last *because* they change to deal with new situations. People continually refine them, changing some here and some there but never changing all of them at once. The emphasis on basic values and coherence in the definition of culture arises because of this process. In making the new versions of the old understandings, people naturally rely on what they already have available, so that consciously planned innovations and revolutions seem, in

historical perspective, only small variations on what came before.

To summarize, how culture works as a guide in organizing collective action and how it comes into being are really the same process. In both cases, people pay attention to what other people are doing and, in an attempt to mesh what they do with those others, refer to what they know (or think they know) in common. So culture is always being made, changing more or less, acting as a point of reference for people engaged in interaction.

What difference does it make that people continually make culture in the way I have described? The most important consequence is that they can, as a result, cooperate easily and efficiently in the daily business of life, without necessarily knowing each other very well.

Most occupations, for example, operate on the premise that the people who work in them all know certain procedures and certain ways of thinking about and responding to typical situations and problems, and that such knowledge will make it possible to assemble them to work on a common project without prior team training. Most professional schools operate on the theory that the education they offer provides a basis for work cooperation among people properly trained anywhere. In fact, people probably learn the culture that makes occupational cooperation possible in the workplace itself. It presents them with problems to solve that are common to people in their line of work, and provides a group of more experienced workers who can suggest solutions. In some occupations, workers change jobs often and move from workplace to workplace often (as do the weekend musicians), and they carry what they have learned elsewhere with them. That makes it easy for them to refine and update their solutions frequently, and thus to develop and maintain an occupational culture. Workers who do not move but spend their work lives in one place may develop a more idiosyncratic work culture, peculiar to that place and its local problems—a culture of IBM or Texas Instruments or (because the process is not limited to large firms) Joe's Diner.

At a different level of cooperative action, Goffman has described cultural understandings that characterize people's behavior in public. For

As much as culture shapes people, people are also constantly revising culture. [handwritten note in bottom margin]

instance, people obey a norm of "civil inattention," allowing each other a privacy that the material circumstances of, say, waiting for a bus, do not provide. Because this kind of privacy is what Americans and many others find necessary before they can feel comfortable and safe in public (Hall has shown how these rules differ in other cultures), these understandings make it possible for urban Americans to occupy crowded public spaces without making each other uneasy. The point is not trivial, because violations of these rules are at least in part responsible for the currently common fear that some public areas are "not safe," quite apart from whatever assaults have taken place in them. Most people have no personal knowledge of the alleged assaults, but they experience violation of what might be called the "Goffman rules" of public order as the prelude to danger and do not go to places that make them feel that way.

Cultural understandings, if they are to be effective in the organization of public behavior, must be very widely held. That means that people of otherwise varying class, ethnic, and regional cultures must learn them routinely and must learn them quite young, because even small children can disrupt public order very effectively. That requires, in turn, substantial agreement among people of all segments of the society on how children should be brought up. If no such agreement exists, or if some of the people who agree in principle do not manage to teach their children the necessary things, public order breaks down, as it often does.

In another direction, cultural understandings affect and "socialize" the internal experiences people have. By applying understandings they know to be widely accepted to their own perhaps inchoate private experiences, people learn to define those internal experiences in ways that allow them to mesh their activities relevant to those topics with those of others with whom they are involved. Consider the familiar example of falling in love. It is remarkable that one of the experiences we usually consider private and unique—falling in love—actually has the same character for most people who experience it. That is not to say that the experience is superficial, but rather that when people try to understand their emotional responses to others, one

available explanation of what they feel is the idea, common in Western culture, of romantic love. They learn that idea from a variety of sources, ranging from the mass media to discussion with their peers, and they learn to see their own experiences as embodiments of it. Because most people within a given culture learn to experience love in the same way from the same sources, two people can become acquainted and successfully fall in love with each other—not an easy trick.

Because shared cultural understandings make it easy to do things in certain ways, moreover, their existence favors those ways of doing things and makes other ways of achieving the same end, which might be just as satisfactory to everyone involved, correspondingly less likely. Random events, which might produce innovations desirable to participants, occur infrequently. In fact, even when the familiar line of activity is not exactly to anyone's liking, people continue it simply because it is what everyone knows and knows that everyone else knows, and thus is what offers the greatest likelihood of successful collective action. Everyone knows, for instance, that it would be better to standardize the enormous variety of screw threads in this country, or to convert the United States to the metric system. But the old ways are the ones we know, and, of course, in this instance, they are built into tools and machines that would be difficult and costly to change. Many activities exhibit that inertia, and they pose a problem that sociologists have been interested in for many years: Which elements of a society or culture are most likely to change? William Fielding Ogburn, for instance, proposed sixty years ago that material culture (screw threads) changed more quickly than social organization, and that the resultant "lag" could be problematic for human society.

A final consequence: The existence of culture makes it possible for people to plan their own lives. We can plan most easily for a known future, in which the major organizational features of society turn out to be what we expected them to be and what we made allowances for in our planning. We need, most importantly, to predict the actions of other people and of the organizations that consist of their collective actions. Culture makes those actions, individual and collective, more predictable than they would otherwise be.

People in traditional societies may not obey in every detail the complex marriage rules held out to them, but those rules supply a sufficiently clear guide for men and women to envision more or less accurately when they will marry, what resources will be available to them when they do, and how the course of their married life will proceed....

In modern industrial societies, workers can plan their careers better when they know what kinds of work situations they will find themselves in and what their rights and obligations at various ages and career stages will be. Few people can make those predictions successfully in this country any more, which indicates that cultural understandings do not always last the twenty or thirty years necessary for such predictability to be

possible. When that happens, people do not know how to prepare themselves for their work lives and do not receive the benefits of their earlier investments in hard work. People who seemed to be goofing off or acting irrationally, for example, sometimes make windfall profits as the work world comes to need just those combinations of skills and experiences that they acquired while not following a "sensible" career path. As technical and organizational innovations make new skills more desirable, new career lines open up that were not and could not have been predicted ten years earlier. The first generation of computer programmers benefited from that kind of good luck, as did the first generation of drug researchers, among others.

39. CULTURE AND THE DEFINITION OF WORK

A. R. GINI and T. J. SULLIVAN

The work ethic in all its various formulations contains elements of both myth and reality.... [I]t helps perpetuate a certain perspective on reality that might not otherwise exist....

Gini and Sullivan introduce us to the idea of culture by focusing on the meaning of work. Western culture before the sixteenth century generally regarded work as a necessary but unattractive task. Protestantism eventually changed that view, and by the nineteenth century, the culture of America was one that regarded work as moral, as a good end in and of itself. Yet, not everyone accepted this view, and indeed there is evidence that this view was generally accepted only by the middle class, who, in turn, tried to control the laboring class through accepting its definition. The last part of this selection focuses on post—World War II America and our attempts to define work as noble despite its drudgery.

From Chapter 1 of *It Comes with the Territory: An Inquiry Concerning Work and the Person*, by A.R. Gini and T.J. Sullivan. New York: Random House. Reprinted by permission.

Folk wisdom has it that the main problem with work is that so few people are able to avoid it. For the vast majority, work is an inescapable and irreducible fact of existence. Work is a necessary evil, an activity that is required to sustain and justify the hours between sleeping, eating, and attempting to enjoy ourselves. It is, for most of us, like Larkin's toad: We cannot "drive the brute off." In its very worst light, work is seen as "something evil, a punishment, the great and grindingly inevitable burden of toil and mortality laid upon the human situation."[1] Studs Terkel's book *Working* has become the bible for those who feel that work is by definition degrading, debilitating, and dehumanizing. True believers need only open this text at random to find documented proof that work is one, if not the major, cause of "economic unfreedom," "physical debasement," "personal alienation," and "social ennui." At best, work looms so large and problematic in the lives of most of us that we tend to take it for granted and either calmly forget about it or actively suppress the full significance of its effect on our lives. It is simply *there*, as illness, death, taxes, and mortgage payments are there, something to be endured.[2] From this perspective, such statements as "Work is love made visible" (Kahlil Gibran) and "To work is to pray" (St. Benedict) are saccharine palliatives that in no way reflect the reality of the situation. The cynical response to such platitudes is, "If work has so many benefits, why is it that so many people spent so much of their lives trying to avoid it?" *Chicago Tribune* columnist Mike Royko accurately encapsulates the spirit of the "common man's" feelings about work when his alter ego in the column, Slats, says:

> …[W]hy do you think the lottery is so popular? Do you think anybody would play if the super payoff was a job on the night shift in a meat packing plant? People play it so that if they win they can be rich and idle… like I told you years ago—if work is so good, how come they have to pay us to do it?[3]

The data being generated in academic circles support this commonsense portrait of work. Since the mid-1950s, a horde of sociologists and industrial psychologists have descended on the workplace in a frenetic attempt to probe, measure, and analyze how workers relate to work, what they feel about work, and how it affects personal values, private lives, and general world views. The reports from these investigations are not far removed from the "bar-room grumblings" most of us are familiar with. The surveys indicate that when asked the question, "Are Americans less motivated to work now?" employees answer both yes and no. The results indicate that some workers are satisfied with certain aspects of their work and others are not. The important point to keep in mind, however, is that for most people, the critical issue is not, "Do I still want to work?" as much as "Does my job turn me off?" Surveys show a consistently strong reaffirmation of the value of work for three-quarters of the population. Even more surprising, when asked if they would choose to continue to work even if they could live comfortably for the rest of their lives without doing so, most people say they would choose to work. A seeming contradiction appears when workers are asked: "If you were free to go into any type of job you wanted, what would your choice be?"

The job he or she now has:	38.1
Retire and not work at all:	1.9
Prefer some other job to the job he or she has now:	60.4[4]

The paradox here is that, in general, people want to work but dislike their present jobs; they do not find the work fulfilling or expansive. Perhaps one of the characters in Studs Terkel's book most eloquently stated is the predicament in which many workers find themselves:

> I think most are looking for a calling, not a job. Most of us, like the assembly line worker, have jobs that are not big enough for people.[5]

I believe that work is the means by which we become and complete ourselves as persons; we create ourselves in our work. To restate the old Italian proverb "You are what you eat," in regard to work "You are the work you do." We must be very careful, therefore, in the work we choose. Work is a necessary and defining activity in the development of the human personality. Work is the mark of man, and work molds man, or, as Gregory Baum has stated, "labor [work] is the axis of human self-making."[6] All of us need work, work that ennobles the product and ennobles the

[handwritten margin notes:]
People want a fulfilling occupation (not to be idle)

Common sense idea of work: don't want to do it.

Work allows people to define themselves as individuals.

producer as well. This is what E. F. Schumacher has called "good work."

Although many people do not like their work, they need it to help them focus on reality, find a creative outlet, and define themselves as individuals. Finances aside, the main reason people don't like their work is that their jobs don't match their skills, interests, or talents. It isn't that all work is bad; it is rather that some work is bad for some people at some times. Ideally, the goal of work should be analogous to the Greek definition of happiness: "The use of all of one's powers to achieve excellence...."

For most of us, working is an entirely nondiscretionary activity. We must work in order to survive, certainly to survive with a modicum of security and comfort.[7] Historically, work has carried with it a certain coercive quality; one is forced to work, to do something in order to carry on. In primitive, subsistence societies, there was no distinction between working and not working. To be awake was to be working. A person was born, worked, and died....

I take it to be the case, however, that the common laments against work are not simply based on the fact that most of us are part of the captive work force and hence accept work as inevitable. In well over one hundred studies in the last twenty-five years, workers have regularly depicted their jobs as physically exhausting, boring, psychologically diminishing, or personally humiliating and unimportant.[8] In the opening lines of *Working*, Terkel compellingly exemplifies this point of view:

> This book, being about work, is, by its very nature, about violence—to the spirit as well as to the body. It is about ulcers as well as accidents, about shouting matches as well as fist fights, about nervous breakdowns as well as kicking the dog around. It is above all (or beneath all) about daily humiliations. To survive the day is triumph enough for the walking wounded among the great many of us.[9]

The poor reputation that work currently enjoys has a long and convoluted history. The image of the "negative necessity" of work seems to have partial origins in the various etymologies of the word itself. The Greek word for "labor" (work), *ponos*, also means "sorrow."[10] In Latin, the word *labor* also means "extreme effort associated with pain." According to Hannah Arendt, "labor" has the same etymological root as *labare* ("to stumble under a burden"), signifying "trouble, distress, difficulty." The French word *travail* connotes "a heavy, burdensome task." It likewise is of Latin origin and originally denoted the *tripalium*, a three-pronged instrument of torture used by the Roman legionnaires, hence the suggestion of "sorrow and pain." In medieval German, the word *Arbeit* ("to labor") can also be translated to signify "tribulation, persecution, adversity, or bad times." Finally, the word "occupation" emerges from the Latin *occupare*, connoting the adversarial posture "of seizing hold of or grappling with a task." Clearly, these etymologies leave little doubt about antiquity's association of work with pain or irksomeness.[11]

The common perception of work as a "negative and ignoble" activity can also be traced to classical sources. The Bible tells us that originally there was no work to be done in the Garden of Eden; toil was described as a curse imposed by God to symbolize humankind's banishment. After the Fall, work became a necessary activity. For Milton, "man's first disobedience" resulted in the curse of work.[12] Genesis graphically expresses the curse that sin brought with it: "Cursed is the ground because of you; in toil you shall eat of it all the days of your life.... In the sweat of your face you shall eat bread till you return to the ground, for out of it you were taken."[13] One interpretation of the Jewish tradition perceives work as "painful drudgery" to which we are condemned by sin. It is accepted as an expiation through which one can atone for sin and prepare for the arrival of the Messiah. Work is a "heavy yoke" that is "hard to bear," and Ecclesiastes can be heard to sigh: "The labor of man does not satisfy the soul."[14] Primitive Christianity, like Judaism, regarded work as a punishment from God. But work was not only seen as a result of original sin, but also as a means to redemption by sharing the goods of one's labor with those who were in greater need. Thus work, as a means of charity, was a source of grace. Yet work is never exalted as anything in itself, but only as an instrument of purification, charity, or expiation.

By the time of Thomas Aquinas in the thirteenth century, work was being considered a necessity of nature. According to Aquinas, each of

[handwritten margin notes:]
Likewise in the Bible, work was a punishment.

Work has originally been seen as painful.

Work was seen as a way of redemption.

us must use our God-given talents ("steward-ship") in the service of both ourselves and others. In fulfilling the duty of work, we acquire skill, fulfill our obligations of charity, and pay homage to our creator. With the Scholastic synthesis, work became a natural right and duty, the sole legitimate basis for society, the foundation for property and profit, as well as the means for personal salvation.[15] Nonetheless, the work of this life was still thought to be of little consequence compared to the spiritual work of preparing to face God. By itself, work had no purpose, for only the contemplation of God could redeem life.[16]

To the ancient Greeks, whose physical labor was done by slaves, work brutalized the mind and made men unfit for the practice of the gentlemanly virtues. The Greeks regarded work as a curse, a drudgery, and a heavy-hearted activity. Plutarch in his chapter on Pericles remarks that no well-born man would want to be the craftsman Phidias. Because while a gentleman enjoys the contemplation of the sculptor's masterpieces, he himself would never consider using a hammer and chisel and being covered with dust, sweat, and grime.[17] The Greeks felt that work enslaved the worker, chained him to the will of others, and corrupted his soul. Work by its very nature inhibited the use of reason and thereby impeded the search for the ultimate ends of life. Work was accepted not as an end in itself but as a means by which some might be freed to pursue higher goals. Aristotle declared that just as the goal of war was peace, so the object of work was leisure. Leisure meant activity pursued free of compulsion or desire for gain, free for the contemplation of philosophical issues and truths. Aristotle saw work as a burden he had no duty to bear. He himself never worked, accepting the slavery of others because it freed him for leisure.[18]

Work both as a private activity and as a way of life began to take on a less onerous nature during the Renaissance and the Reformation. It was during this period that work, no matter how high or low the actual task, began to develop—at least at the theoretical level—a positive ethos of its own. Most historians credit the origin of the work ethic to Martin Luther. According to Luther, one was summoned by God to a secular "calling" that today we would call a job.[19] Luther stressed that all callings were necessary to life; no one calling

was to be recognized as more necessary or blessed than another, and, therefore, all callings had equal worth in the sight of God. For Luther, work was a form of serving God: "There is just one best way to serve God—to do most perfectly the work of one's profession." Thus the only way to live acceptably before God was through devotion to one's calling. However, God demanded more than occasional good works. He demanded a methodical life of good works in a unified pattern of work and worship.[20]

With John Calvin in the sixteenth century, we find Luther's ideas extended, systematized, and institutionalized. Work was divine, a way of serving God. Work was the will of God, and even ceaseless "dumb toil" sufficed to please Him. Calvin preached the "predestination of the elect." He believed that the elect could be recognized by certain outward signs, which included self-denial and devotion to duty, and that God caused the elect to prosper. "To prosper" or "to succeed" meant to enjoy not only wealth and happiness on earth, but eternal salvation. "Success" was the symbol of "selective salvation." Calvin managed, no matter how indirectly, to provide a rationale linking work and the Divine with material success and comfort.

In *The Protestant Ethic and the Spirit of Capitalism* (1905), Max Weber observed that the rise of Protestantism and the rise of capitalism generally coincided in England and throughout most European countries. Weber's explanation was that many basic Protestant ideas encouraged capitalistic activities. For example, the Reformation taught that each person would be individually judged by God, and that judgment would be based on one's whole life's work or "calling." The reformers also taught that the fruits of one's "calling"—money—should not be spent frivolously or unnecessarily. According to Weber, these ideas led to a life of hard work, self-discipline, asceticism, and concern with achievement. This ethic helped advance the rise of the private entrepreneur in that it led to the accumulation of money that could not be spent on luxuries, but that could and should be put into one's own business.[21]

Labor analyst Michael Cherrington maintains that the work ethic typically embraces one or more of the following beliefs:

1. People have a moral and religious obligation to fill their lives with heavy physical toil. For some, this means that hard work, effort, and drudgery are to be valued for their own sake; physical pleasures and enjoyments are to be shunned; and an ascetic existence of methodical rigor is the only acceptable way to live.
2. Men and women are expected to spend long hours at work, with little or no time for personal recreation and leisure.
3. A worker should have a dependable attendance record, with low absenteeism and tardiness.
4. Workers should take pride in their work and do their jobs well.
5. Workers should be highly productive and produce a large quantity of goods or services.
6. Employees should have feelings of commitment and loyalty to their profession, their company, and their work group.
7. Workers should be achievement oriented and constantly strive for promotions and advancement. High-status jobs with prestige and the respect of others are important indicators of a "good" person.
8. People should acquire wealth through honest labor and retain it through thrift and wise investments. Frugality is desirable; extravagance and waste should be avoided.[22]

For Weber, the work ethic seems to mean a commitment to work beyond its utility in providing a living. It is "a conviction that work is a worthwhile activity in its own right, not merely...the means to material comfort or wealth."[23]

The direct theological descendants of the Reformation, and of John Calvin in particular, were the dour Puritans who migrated to New England. Citing the parable of the talents (Matthew 25), Calvin urged the Puritans to prosper: "You may labor to be rich for God, though not for the flesh or sin."[24] The gospel of work in America was preached from many other pulpits: William Penn constantly reminded the Quakers of Philadelphia that "diligence is a virtue useful and laudable among men.... Frugality is a virtue too, and not of little use in life.... It is proverbial, 'A Penny sav'd is a Penny got.'"[25] Perhaps the real solidification of the work ethic in America occurred with its practical translation and secularization by Benjamin Franklin. In his various publications, Franklin taught that wealth was the result of virtue and the proper display of character. In his *Autobiography*, he defines the work

ethic in his list of ideal traits: "Temperance, Silence, Order, Resolution, Frugality, Industry, Sincerity, Justice, Moderation, Cleanliness, Tranquillity, Chastity, Humility."[26] With Franklin, the work ethic shifted from a direct form of worshipping God to an indirect way of rendering service to God by developing one's character and doing good to others.[27] Unlike the Puritans, Franklin's craftsman no longer worked for God's glory, but for himself. He maintained that "God helps those who help themselves." Nevertheless, hard work remained the only standard for private success and social usefulness.

By the nineteenth century, the Protestant ethic in America had changed its name at least three times, but its essential focus had not changed at all. Whether it was called the *Protestant ethic*, the *Puritan ethic*, the *work ethic*, or the *immigrant ethic*, hard work was seen as good in and of itself, the only ticket to survival and the possibility of success. According to the noted labor historian Daniel T. Rogers, the central premise of the work ethic is that work is the core of the moral life. "Work made men useful in a world of economic scarcity. It staved off the doubts and temptations that preyed on idleness; it opened the way to deserved wealth and status; it allowed one to put the impress of mind and skill on the material world."[28] In many ways, the work ethic posited one's very right to existence; one achieved worth through work.

During the nineteenth century, we see the first stirrings of dissatisfaction with this ethic. These came not from churches, employers, or even workers themselves, but from artists. The popularity of Dickens's novels and of plays such as Gerhart Hauptmann's 1893 drama about cottage industries, *The Weavers*, were foreshadowings of a discontent that would manifest itself only in the mid-twentieth century. Until that time, the moral preeminence of work stood essentially unchallenged as an accepted social value. C. Wright Mills pointed out that "the gospel of work has been central to the historic tradition of America, to its image of itself, and to the images the rest of the world have of America."[29] There can be little question that this reverence for work, along with an abundance of natural resources and human capital, was an important determinant of America's material success.[30]

Moreover, because of this need for a pool of diligent laborers, every agent of authority and education proclaimed the merits of work. From Luther to Franklin to Horatio Alger, workers received a steady diet of exhortation and incantation from press, pulpit, and primer. All work was worthwhile and laudable; work well done would inevitably bring reward, and work avoided led to degradation and ruin.[31]

It is, however, important to keep in mind that tracing the idea of work through history is difficult, and the record is inconsistently one-sided. As Barbara Tuchman pointed out in *A Distant Mirror* (1978), the history of an ancient society is usually limited to the record keeping of the nobility and the intelligentsia. Few or no records are to be found depicting what the lower classes actually thought or felt about any momentous occurrence of their age. For example, we have no record of what a Greek slave, a medieval peasant, a Reformation craftsman, or a New England Puritan farmer had to say about the day-to-day experiences of work. We do however have the philosophical speculations of Aristotle, Aquinas, Calvin, and Jonathan Edwards.[32] We infer, therefore, that the proposition of the "nobility of work" is not a working-class concept but a middle-class one. We do not, however, embrace the cynical view that has labeled the Protestant work ethic as pure "ideological subterfuge" geared to maximizing the workers' efforts and thereby increasing the owners' pool of capital. Rather, we maintain that the Protestant work ethic has often been used as a means of masking the drudgery and necessity of work. We accept the notion that true believers were in fact theologically motivated in their actions and achieved a great deal of personal solace as well as material reward and comfort from their work. Moreover, we take it to be the case that those who subscribed to the more secularized version of the work ethic did so with the faithful expectation that their efforts would reap personal and social gain. Nonetheless, part of the overall effect of the work ethic was to acclimate the individual worker to the inevitable. We want to contend that the tradition of the work ethic glorified and legitimized work and gave it a teleological orientation—a sense of purpose or design—that helped to both sustain individual effort and ameliorate its temporal brutishness.

Perhaps former President Richard Nixon's often quoted 1971 Labor Day speech best exemplifies our point. He said: "Scrubbing floors and emptying bedpans have just as much dignity as there is in any work done in this country—including my own…." We suggest that while both jobs must be done and done well, these jobs are too disparate in their impact and import to warrant serious comparison.

Daniel Yankelovich, in *New Rules: Searching for Self-Fulfillment in a World Turned Upside Down*, contends that the post-World War II formulation of the "work ethic myth" is the "giving/getting compact":

- Even though we no longer had anything in common, we stayed together. We didn't break up our marriage even when the children were grown.
- We lived on his salary even though I was making good money at the time. He said he would not feel right if we spent the money I earned for food and rent.
- I never felt I could do enough for my parents, especially my mother. She sacrificed a promising career as a singer to take care of us. I realize now that she must have been miserable most of the time. (Why?) Because she said so. She kept reminding us what she was giving up, but we didn't take her seriously.
- It never occurred to me not to have children. Now I realize I'd have felt less put upon if I had freely chosen that destiny and not had it chosen for me.
- I've worked hard all my life, and I've made a success out of it for myself and my family. We have a nice home. We have everything it takes to be comfortable. I've been able to send my kids to good schools, and my wife and I can afford to go anywhere we want. Yes, I have a real sense of accomplishment.
- Sure it was a rotten job. But what the hell. I made a good living, I took care of my wife and kids. What more do you expect?

The old giving/getting compact might be paraphrased this way:

I give hard work, loyalty, and steadfastness. I swallow my frustrations and suppress my impulse to do what I would enjoy, and do what is expected of me instead. I do not put myself first; I put the needs of others ahead of my own. I give a lot, but what I get in return is worth it. I receive an ever-growing standard of living and my family life with a devoted spouse and decent kids. Our children will take care of us in our old age if we really need it, which thank goodness we will not. I have a nice home, a good job, the respect of my friends and neighbors, a sense of accomplishment at having made something of my life. Last but not least, as an American, I am proud to be a citizen of the finest country in the world.[33]

For Yankelovich, no matter what the source or accuracy of this compact, it is difficult to exaggerate how important it has been in supporting the goals of American society in the postwar period. It lies at the very heart of what we mean by the "American dream." Right or wrong, the "giving/getting compact" has helped to sustain and direct the efforts of millions over the years.

The work ethic in all its various formulations contains elements of both myth and reality. In essence, it is a view of the world that promotes and helps to perpetuate a certain perspective on reality that might not otherwise exist. The work ethic is a myth in the sense that nineteenth-century philosopher Georges Sorel used the word; that is, that the truth of the myth is relatively unimportant as long as it furthers the end in view.[34] In general, it must be remembered that the work ethic is a product of an era of scarcity and deprivation, when one either worked or starved. It made the negative aspects of work bearable by giving work a moral quality. The conclusion remains that the work ethic was and is an ideology propagated by the middle classes for the working classes with just enough plausibility to make it credible....[5]

For all its glorification, and no matter how many honorifics we attach to it, work remains, in the eye of the common man, a task to be endured. As trade unionist Gus Tyler has stated, "There are at least two work ethics: that of the overseer and that of the overseen." He claims that workers are not opposed to the work ethic in any literal sense. "But work *per se* as an ethical imperative gets little, if any, attention because, to union people, work is such a necessity that it is almost unnecessary to construct a system of values, with theological overtones, to justify labor. If American unionists have an ethic, it is probably best summed up in the old slogan: 'a fair day's pay for a fair day's work.'"[36] From the unionist point of view, therefore, the proper and only response possible to Max Weber's question "Do we

work to live or live to work?" is "We work to live." Most unionists are not so much guilty of working to live as they are guilty of being asked a question to which the answer is moot. If they are *compelled* to work in order to live, why bother asking? Recent appraisals of work and the worker by such scholars as Daniel Bell, Clark Kerr, Robert Strauss, and Daniel Yankelovich have confirmed the suspicion long held by most workers that dull, hard work is not necessarily ennobling and does not produce cultural heroes and role models. Working hard is a basic dimension of human existence; it is a duty. From this point of view, working is obligatory and, although it may at times well warrant a gray—if not red—badge of courage, it is basically a requirement of existence and only a means toward an end. As a character in a popular series of detective mysteries has put it: "If work was [such] a good thing, the rich would have it all and not let you do it."[37] Unquestionably, my favorite anecdote on this topic is the story of the rich man's response to his daughter's question "Is sex fun or work?" "Sex must be fun for women," he replied, "because if it were work, your mother would have the maid do it."

Nonetheless, the country's classic work ethic is by no means dead. The mythology lingers on and is perpetuated by diverse sources. The good word on work can now be heard from Jesse Jackson, Lee Iacocca, George Gilder, Ronald Reagan, and certain prime-time television beer commercials.

Jesse Jackson's interpretation of the work ethic stays, perhaps, closest to one of the original tenets of the doctrine; that is, "how to get more and do better." For Jackson, "black power" is economic success, as this is achieved by getting a piece of the action, working hard, saving, starting one's own business, being innovative, and/or constantly extending the scope and market of one's business. For Jackson, the black community will only achieve equality with the white community when it successfully emulates Benjamin Franklin's model. He has spent the last fifteen years exhorting blacks to take pride in who they are, to finish school, to work hard, to be, in short, Puritan. In many ways, his message and that of Operation PUSH is a restatement of immigrant work ethic exhortations to get a job, do well, work hard, and things will necessarily be better than they were before.

In recent years, Lee Iacocca has emerged not only as the chief spokesman for Chrysler but also, indirectly, as the spokesman for the entire American automobile industry and the sanctity of the American worker's ability. Iacocca's commercial presentations have the emotional punch of a Knute Rockne half-time pep talk. In general, the commercials deliver a message that can be paraphrased as follows: So the foreign cars have been made better! So they have given you better value! So they have on percentage outsold us in the last seven years! OK, we were wrong! We weren't listening to what you wanted! But we hear you now! We're sorry, we forgot what got us to where we are today! Americans can outbuild any car maker in the world! We can build cars that out-perform, outlast and out-distance all our competitors! American "know-how" created the auto industry! We've proven our abilities in the past, we'll prove them to you again! American ingenuity is based on the American worker! I believe in the American worker and so do you! Buy our cars, I personally guarantee them for five years and/or 50,000 miles! Buy American!

On a more academic level, George Gilder, former economist and Nixon White House speech writer, has put together a series of books and articles on the entrepreneurial ethic as the cornerstone of capitalistic prosperity.[38] For Gilder, it is the entrepreneur who creates the "trickle-down effect," which in turn stimulates the "invisible hard mechanism," thereby creating "the greatest possible good for the greatest possible number." For Gilder, the farsighted, risk-taking, hardworking, self-sacrificing businessman is the catalyst propelling the entire laissez-faire economic system.

Ronald Reagan consciously attempted to resuscitate the Jeffersonian model of the "rugged individual." This classic model is the individual who is able, by hard work, individual know-how, and personal ingenuity, to create and maintain most if not all the necessities of life. This is the model of the self-sufficient "agrarian atomist" who first conquered this country by farming the shores of the East Coast and then proceeded during the next 200 years to follow the challenge of our Western expansion. It is not altogether surprising that Reagan's image of the "rugged individual" closely resembles many of the main characters in novelist Louis L'Amour's Western sagas. L'Amour's heroes are self-directed individuals who came into a new region, pacified it, cultivated it, and made it a safe place to rear a family. For Reagan, this country's "manifest destiny" became a fact and not a slogan because of the vision, courage, and hard work of our pioneer ancestors. These are, he believes, the virtues that have made us strong and prosperous and that must be maintained and fostered if the dream of America is to be continued and fulfilled for those who come after us. And these are virtues strongly embodied in the traditional Protestant work ethic.

Prime-time beer commercials are mythic playlets, romanticizing and idealizing the Herculean efforts of men at work.[39] They depict men pouring molten ingots in factories, spanning huge chasms with cables of steel, cutting down tall trees in the mist of a rain forest, blasting tunnels through mountains of solid granite, sailing ancient square-riggers through tempestuous seas, skiing the Tetons to check for avalanche faults, and staging a multi-vehicle highway crash for the concluding scene of a Clint Eastwood film. And through all the grit of these various scenarios, the participants are, to a man, grinning from ear to ear at both their accomplishments and their camaraderie. After all of this, the worker-warriors retire to a local saloon where they consume large quantities of iced beer and debrief one another in a warm sundown glow of work well done and worth doing.

For all of the hoopla and popular promotion, we feel that the general work force remains unconvinced and unmoved. No matter what the gimmicks, slogans, and logos, too much of the work of life remains uninteresting, unenjoyable, and without obvious purpose and distinction. For too many of us, work is the "curse of Adam," and to be relieved of it would be counted a boon and a blessing. The term "Protestant work ethic," which began as an explanation for the economic behavior of an historical people, exists today almost solely as a pejorative phrase.[40] According to social critic Michael Harrington, whatever value it may have had, the Protestant work ethic has devolved to the notion that "a man establishes his worth in the eyes of his neighbor and his God ... by doing drudgery and engaging in savings."[41]

NOTES

1."What Is the Point of Working?" *Time*, May 11, 1981. pp. 93—94.
2.Lee Braude, *Work and Workers: A Sociological Analysis* (New York: Praeger Publications, 1975), p. 3.
3.Mike Royko, "Silver Spoon Fits, Why Not Wear It?" *Chicago Tribune*, November 11, 1985, Sec. 1, p. 3.
4.Michael Maccoby and Katherine A. Terzi, "What Happened to the Work Ethic?" in W. Michael Hoffman and Thomas J. Wyly (eds.), *The Work Ethic in Business* (Cambridge, MA: Oelgeschlager, Gunn, and Hain, Publishers, 1981), pp. 31—34.
5.Studs Terkel, *Working* (New York: Pantheon Books, 1974), p. 521.
6.Gregory Baum, *The Priority of Labor* (New York: Paulist Press, 1982), p. 10.
7.Jay B. Rurlich, *Work and Love: The Crucial Balance* (New York: Summit Books, 1980), p. 29.
8.*Work in America: Report of a Special Task Force to the Secretary of Health, Education and Welfare* (Cambridge, MA: MIT Press, 1980), p. 13.
9.Terkel, *Working*, p. xi.
10.Hannah Arendt points out that the words *labor* and *work* are really two different words; for Arendt, they connote two different but not disparate meanings. The Latin work is *ponos*, the French *travail*, and the German *Arbeit*. The word *work* has different etymological roots. In Latin, "to work" is *facere* or *fabricari*; in Greek, it is *ergazesthai*; in French, it is *ouvrer*; and in German, *werken*. For Arendt, *labor* is the "toil of life," that "drudgery" that must be done to minister to the necessities of existence. To labor is to use one's body to achieve a task. *Work*, she feels, has a higher significance. It connotes "to make," "to do with intention," "to accomplish as task"; it refers to craftsmanship. Granting Professor Arendt these real and implied differences, we shall nevertheless use these terms as if they were synonymous.
11.Hannah Arendt, *The Human Condition* (Chicago: University of Chicago Press, 1958), pp. 48 n., 80 n., 110 n.
12.Braude, *Work and Workers*, p. 5.
13.*The New Oxford Annotated Bible* (New York: Oxford University Press), Gen. 3:17b—19.
14.Adriand Tilgher, *Homo Faber: Work Through the Ages*, trans. Dorothy Canfield Fisher (Chicago: Henry Regnery, 1965), pp. 11—12.
15.Ibid., pp. 29—40.
16.Sar A. Levitan and Wm. B. Johnston, *Work Is Here to Stay, Alas* (Salt Lake City: Olympian Publishing Co., 1973), p. 28.
17.*Plutarch's Lives* (New York: Modern Library, 1932), p. 183.
18.Levitan and Johnston, *Work Is Here to Stay, Alas*, p. 28.
19.Tilgher, *Homo Faber*, p. 49.
20.Michael Cherrington, *The Work Ethic: Working Values and Values that Work* (New York: AMACOM, 1980), pp. 20—33.
21.Michael Argyle, *The Social Psychology of Work* (New York: Taplinger Publishing, 1972), pp. 22—23.
22.Cherrington, *The Work Ethic*, p. 20.
23.Gerhard E. Lewski, *The Religious Factor: A Sociological Study of Religious Impact on Politics, Economics and Family Life* (New York: Doubleday, 1961), pp. 4—5.
24.Maccoby and Terzi, "What Happened to the Work Ethic?" p. 22.
25.Cherrington, *The Work Ethic*, p. 35.
26.Jesse L. Lemisch, *Benjamin Franklin: 'The Autobiography' and Other Writings* (New York: New American Library, 1961), p. 95.
27.Cherrington, *The Work Ethic*, p. 35.
28.Daniel T. Rodgers, *The Work Ethic in Industrial America, 1850—1920* (Chicago: University of Chicago Press, 1978), p. 14.
29.C. Wright Mills, "The Meaning of Work Throughout History," in Fred Best (ed.), *The Future of Work* (Upper Saddle River, NJ: Prentice Hall, 1973), p. 6.
30.Joseph F. Quinn, "The Work Ethic and Retirement," in *The Work Ethic—A Critical Analysis* (Madison, WI: Industrial Relations Research Association, 1983), p. 87.
31.Levitan and Johnston, *Work Is Here to Stay, Alas*, p. 31.
32.Ibid., p. 27.
33.Daniel Yankelovich, *New Rules: Searching for Self-Fulfillment in a World Turned Upside Down* (New York: Bantam Books, 1982), p. 7.
34.Jack Barbash, "Which Work Ethic?" in *The Work Ethic—A Critical Analysis*, p. 258.
35.Ibid., p. 232.
36.Gus Tyler, "The Work Ethic: A Union View," in *The Work Ethic—A Critical Analysis*, pp. 197—198.
37.Elmore Leonard, *Split Images* (New York: Avon, 1981), p. 13.
38.George Gilden, *Wealth and Poverty* (New York: Bantam Books, 1982); also *The Spirit of Enterprise* (New York: Simon and Schuster, 1984).
39."What Is the Point of Working?" pp. 93—94.
40.Joseph Epstein, "Work and Its Contents," *The American Scholar*, Summer 1983, p. 307.
41.Eric Larrabee, "Time to Kill: Automation, Leisure, and Jobs," in Robert V. Guthrie (ed.), *Psychology in the World Today* (Reading, MA: Addison-Wesley, 1968), p. 312.

40. CULTURE AND VIOLENCE IN AMERICA

ARNOLD GOLDSTEIN

So America's history is contradictory.... We are a free, democratic, progressive, creative country.... [We] have insulted, injured, assaulted, abused, raped, and murdered one another at levels that are dismayingly high....

This selection sketches our history by focusing on the theme of violence. How central is violence to our culture?

HOW DID WE GET HERE?

The United States was born in a spirit of freedom and democracy, yet also with a strong belief in the use of individual and group violence. The Revolutionary War lasted seven years and succeeded in its goal of a new and independent nation. It also began our two-century-long love affair with the gun, as four hundred thousand victorious citizen-soldiers helped proclaim the right to bear arms.

The new nation lay along the Eastern coast of a three-thousand-mile wide unexplored continent of buffalo and other game to kill, of Native Americans to displace, of a frontier to conquer. As our citizens began moving westward in the late 1700s, a frontier mentality went with them. Self-reliance, independence, and impatience with the poorly developed laws and law enforcement of the day were also part of this mentality. Justice often meant "frontier justice," in which groups of local citizenry took the law into their own hands: Hanging horse thieves or riding undesirables out of town were among the ways such early criminal sentencing was handled.

Although our mass media have long glamorized it, frontier living was rarely as easy and romantic as usually portrayed. Often, it was very

Modified and reproduced by special permission of the Publisher, Consulting Psychologists Press, Inc., Palo Alto, CA 94305 from *Violence in America*, by Arnold Goldstein. Copyright 1996 by Davies-Black. All rights reserved. Further reproduction is prohibited without the Publisher's written consent.

difficult economically, which helped give rise to outlaw gangs, bank robbers, counterfeiters, and other criminal behavior. A tide of immigration to the United States commenced in earnest in the early 1800s, and grew to a flood of newcomers of diverse backgrounds to our shores as the twentieth century unfolded. The ingredients in this great, human melting pot often mixed poorly and often resulted in high levels of individual and group violence directed at these migrants, especially in the cities.

The Civil War, 1861 to 1865, pitted Northerner against Southerner and, at times, neighbor against neighbor, even cousin against cousin in bitter, lethal combat. Its price was high—well beyond the actual war casualties of 617,000 dead and 375,000 injured soldiers. Out of the war grew forces that yielded new and virulent forms of aggression throughout the country. Often stemming from war-related animosities, feuding, lynching, and high levels of vigilante activity erupted. The feud, primarily developing in Southern mountain states, was a kind of interfamily guerrilla warfare. Much more deadly in its effects was lynching, in which unorganized mobs captured and hung usually guiltless black persons. It is the shame of America that 3,209 recorded lynchings occurred during the years 1889 to 1918.

Vigilante aggression also became more organized during this post-Civil War period, with the Ku Klux Klan, the Bald Knobbers, the White Cappers, and many more such groups targeting not just blacks but several other minority groups as well. Also at this time, the much-romanticized cowboy gang became prominent. Their specialties—stagecoach, train, and bank robberies—to this day portrayed as exciting and heroic events, were plain and simple acts of criminal violence.

Much of the recorded violence in America in the late 1800s and early 1900s was group violence associated with the industrialization of our country. There were violent labor strikes in the mining, railroad, and auto industries as well as violent government response to the strikers. Although there are numerous accounts of violence by individuals during these years, actual numbers are largely unavailable because the FBI did not begin compiling crime statistics for murder, assault, rape, and similar violent crimes until 1933. Nevertheless, it is clear that during the years in which Prohibition was the law of the land (1920 to 1933), murder and mayhem between and among bootleggers and liquor hijackers in their rivalry for market control was at a level of often lethal intensity. During the two world wars and the economic depression in the 1930s, there was less violence here for individuals and groups. The same was true in other countries. Perhaps when citizens feel joined together against a common enemy, there is less motivation to attack each other.

As the twentieth century moved along, feuding, vigilante groups, lynching, and labor violence all receded, but aggression in seemingly new and more serious individual forms appeared. Spouse and child abuse has been with us all along, but was in a sense "discovered" as it became a matter for more public discussion and concern in the mid-1960s. It has since become recognized as widely practiced in our homes and severely damaging to many of our citizens. So too for the crime of rape, as the women's movement of this same period called our collective attention to its nature, its frequency, and its serious consequences. As is widely known, in this period, America's homicide rate far exceeded that of all other modern nations—and still does today.

Since the 1970s, the levels of murder, rape, abuse, and assault by adults are a continuing serious concern, but our main worry seems to be the flourishing of juvenile crime. Aided by the massive influx of drugs into our country, armed by our arsenal of weaponry, encouraged by its unremitting portrayal in the media, and in imitation of many of their heroes, our sons and daughters have reached new peaks of aggression in their lives, both as individuals and in growing numbers of gangs.

So America's history is contradictory. We are a free, democratic, progressive, creative country of protected citizen rights, rule by law, legal transfer of power, economic opportunity for at least most of our citizens, and much more that is good. We are also a country in which, for more than two hundred years, our people have insulted, injured, assaulted, abused, raped, and murdered one another at levels that are dismayingly high and seem to be growing. That is where we are and, briefly, how we got here.

41. THE CODE OF THE STREET

ELIJAH ANDERSON

The hard reality of the world of the street can be traced to the profound sense of alienation from mainstream society and its institutions felt by many poor inner-city black people, particularly the young. The code of the street is actually a cultural adaptation to a profound lack of faith in the police and the judicial system—and in others who would champion one's personal security.

Elijah Anderson distinguishes between two opposing cultures in the poor black community: the "decent" and the "street." He shows how this conflict pulls at the individual, making individual directions unpredictable to some extent.

Of all the problems besetting the poor inner-city black community, none is more pressing than that of interpersonal violence and aggression. This phenomenon wreaks havoc daily on the lives of community residents and increasingly spills over into downtown and residential middle-class areas. Muggings, burglaries, carjackings, and drug-related shootings, all of which may leave their victims or innocent bystanders dead, are now common enough to concern all urban and many suburban residents.

The inclination to violence springs from the circumstances of life among the ghetto poor—the lack of jobs that pay a living wage, limited basic public services (police response in emergencies, building maintenance, trash pickup, lighting, and other services that middle-class neighborhoods take for granted), the stigma of race, the fallout from rampant drug use and drug trafficking, and the resulting alienation and absence of hope for the future. Simply living in such an environment places young people at special risk of falling victim to aggressive behavior. Although there are often forces in the community that can counteract the negative influences—by far the most powerful is a strong, loving, "decent" (as inner-city residents put

From Elijah Anderson, *Code of the Street: Decency, Violence, and the Moral Life of the Inner City.* Copyright © 1999 by Elijah Anderson. Used by permission of W.W. Norton & Company.

it) family that is committed to middle-class values—the despair is pervasive enough to have spawned an oppositional culture, that of "the street," whose norms are often consciously opposed to those of mainstream society. These two orientations—decent and street—organize the community socially, and the way they coexist and interact has important consequences for its residents, particularly for children growing up in the inner city. Above all, this environment means that even youngsters whose home lives reflect mainstream values—and most of the homes in the community do—must be able to handle themselves in a street-oriented environment.

This is because the street culture has evolved a "code of the street," which amounts to a set of informal rules governing interpersonal public behavior, particularly violence.[1] The rules prescribe both proper comportment and the proper way to respond if challenged. They regulate the use of violence and so supply a rationale allowing those who are inclined to aggression to precipitate violent encounters in an approved way. The rules have been established and are enforced mainly by the street-oriented; but on the streets the distinction between street and decent is often irrelevant. Everybody knows that if the rules are violated, there are penalties. Knowledge of the code is thus largely defensive, and it is literally necessary for operating in public. Therefore, though families with a decency orientation are usually opposed to the values of the code, they often reluctantly encourage their children's familiarity with it in order to enable them to negotiate the inner-city environment.

At the heart of the code is the issue of respect—loosely defined as being treated "right" or being granted one's "props" (or proper due) or the deference one deserves. However, in the troublesome public environment of the inner city, as people increasingly feel buffeted by forces beyond their control, what one deserves in the way of respect becomes ever more problematic and uncertain. This situation in turn further opens up the issue of respect to sometimes intense interpersonal negotiation, at times resulting in altercations. In the street culture, especially among young people, respect is viewed as almost an external entity, one that is hard-won but easily lost—and so must constantly be guarded. The rules of the code in fact provide a framework for negotiating respect. With the right amount of respect, individuals can avoid being bothered in public. This security is important, for if they are bothered, not only may they face physical danger, but they will have been disgraced or "dissed" (disrespected). Many of the forms dissing can take may seem petty to middle-class people (maintaining eye contact for too long, for example), but to those invested in the street code, these actions, a virtual slap in the face, become serious indications of the other person's intentions. Consequently, such people become very sensitive to advances and slights, which could well serve as a warning of imminent physical attack or confrontation.

The hard reality of the world of the street can be traced to the profound sense of alienation from mainstream society and its institutions felt by many poor inner-city black people, particularly the young. The code of the street is actually a cultural adaptation to a profound lack of faith in the police and the judicial system—and in others who would champion one's personal security. The police, for instance, are most often viewed as representing the dominant white society and as not caring to protect inner-city residents. When called, they may not respond, which is one reason many residents feel they must be prepared to take extraordinary measures to defend themselves and their loved ones against those who are inclined to aggression. Lack of police accountability has in fact been incorporated into the local status system: the person who is believed capable of "taking care of himself" is accorded a certain deference and regard, which translates into a sense of physical and psychological control. The code of the street thus emerges where the influence of the police ends and where personal responsibility for one's safety is felt to begin. Exacerbated by the proliferation of drugs and easy access to guns, this volatile situation results in the ability of the street-oriented minority (or those who effectively "go for bad") to dominate the public spaces.

NOTE

1. For a plausible description tracing the tradition and evolution of this code, with its implications for violence on the streets of urban America, see Fox Butterfield, *All God's Children* (New York: Knopf, 1995).

PART IX

Social Control and Social Deviance

Social control refers to all the various ways a society and its representatives attempt to ensure ongoing conformity and cooperation. The easiest way of exercising social control is to have people "willingly" obey the rules and accept both the structure and the culture. This is attempted through socialization, the process by which various representatives of society form the human being by teaching him or her the social patterns of society.

Other than socialization, representatives of society attempt to ensure conformity by punishing nonconformity. In the first selection, Peter Berger shows us the wide range of methods used. Who ends up being punished? Those we define as "deviant." In fact, the labeling of people as deviant is one attempt to punish them for actions we dislike. Erich Goode's first selection is an excellent introduction to why certain acts and people are labeled deviant. Goode's second selection, "The Social Creation of Stigma," is a very thoughtful and challenging examination of how and why people stigmatize others and what the implications are for those who are stigmatized. Stigmatization is a reflection of the values held by those of us who point fingers—and it is too easy for us to point fingers without carefully examining both society and our own motivations.

The selection by William J. Chambliss, "The Saints and the Roughnecks," has become a classic in sociology because it highlights how deviance is always subjective and very often class-biased. A classic statement by Emile Durkheim describes the role of crime and punishment in society, and the final selection by Walker, Moen, and Dempster-McClain questions the idea that diversity causes inequality, and asks whether both diversity and inequality make social order difficult.

42. THE MEANING OF SOCIAL CONTROLS

PETER L. BERGER

No society can exist without social control. Even a small group of people meeting but occasionally will have to develop their mechanisms of control if the group is not to dissolve in a very short time.

Social control is the "mechanism" used to "eliminate undesirable personnel and...'to encourage the others.'" It is the "means used by a society to bring its recalcitrant members back into line.... It is the negative sanctions or punishments that await those who attempt to stray from the fold." Peter Berger does two things in this article: (1) He describes the various kinds of controls, from violence to economic pressure to "ridicule, gossip, and opprobrium" (rejection). (2) He describes the many "systems" that exercise such controls, including the political system, employers, colleagues, various "social involvements," and finally "the circle of one's family and personal friends."

This is a fascinating description, but it is also a nightmare of sorts. "The individual who, thinking consecutively of all the people he is in a position to have to please, from the collector of the Internal Revenue Service to his mother-in-law, gets the idea that all of society sits right on top of him." But Berger tells us only half of the social control story. There is also a whole host of rewards that operate to encourage conformity, from getting an "A" on an exam to a promotion on the job. These things also constitute social controls.

Social control is one of the most generally used concepts in sociology. It refers to the various means used by a society to bring its recalcitrant members back into line. No society can exist without social control. Even a small group of people meeting but occasionally will have to develop their mechanisms of control if the group is not to dissolve in a very short time. It goes without saying that the instrumentalities of social control vary greatly from one social situation to another. Opposition to the line in a business organization may mean what personnel directors call a *terminal interview* and what those in a criminal syndicate call a *terminal automobile ride*. Methods of control vary with the purpose and character of the group in question. In either case,

control mechanisms function to eliminate undesirable personnel and (as it was put classically by King Christopher of Haiti when he had every tenth man in his forced-labor battalion executed) "to encourage the others."

The ultimate and, no doubt, the oldest means of social control is physical violence. In the savage society of children, it is still the major one. But even in the politely operated societies of modern democracies, the ultimate argument is violence. No state can exist without a police force or its equivalent in armed might. This ultimate violence may not be used frequently. There may be innumerable steps before its application, in the way of warnings and reprimands. But if all the warnings are disregarded, even in so slight a matter as paying a traffic ticket, the last thing that will happen is that a couple of cops show up at the door with handcuffs and a Black Maria. Even the moderately courteous cop who hands out the

From *An Invitation to Sociology*, by Peter L. Berger. Copyright © 1963 by Peter L. Berger. Used by permission of Doubleday, a division of Random House, Inc.

initial traffic ticket is likely to wear a gun — just in case. And even in England, where he does not in the normal course of events, he will be issued one if the need arises....

In any functioning society, violence is used economically and as a last resort, with the mere threat of this ultimate violence sufficing for the day-to-day exercise of social control. For our purposes in this argument, the most important matter to underline is that nearly all men live in social situations in which, if all other means of coercion fail, violence may be officially and legally used against them....

Next in line after the political and legal controls, one should probably place economic pressure. Few means of coercion are as effective as those that threaten one's livelihood or profit. Both management and labor effectively use this threat as an instrument of control in our society. But economic means of control are just as effective outside the institutions properly called the economy. Universities or churches use economic sanctions just as effectively in restraining their personnel from engaging in deviant behavior deemed by the respective authorities to go beyond the limits of the acceptable. It may not be actually illegal for a minister to seduce his organist, but the threat of being barred forever from the exercise of his profession will be a much more effective control over this temptation than the possible threat of going to jail. It is undoubtedly not illegal for a minister to speak his mind on issues that the ecclesiastical bureaucracy would rather have buried in silence, but the chance of spending the rest of his life in minimally paid rural parishes is a very powerful argument indeed. Naturally such arguments are employed more openly in economic institutions proper, but the administration of economic sanctions in churches or universities is not very different in its end results from that used in the business world.

Where human beings live or work in compact groups, in which they are personally known and to which they are tied by feelings of personal loyalty (the kind that sociologists call *primary groups*), very potent and simultaneously very subtle mechanisms of control are constantly brought to bear on the actual or potential deviant. These are the mechanisms of persuasion, ridicule, gossip, and opprobrium. It has been discovered that in group discussions going on over a period of time, individuals modify their originally held opinions to conform to the group norm, which corresponds to a kind of arithmetic mean of all the opinions represented in the group. Where this norm lies obviously depends on the constituency of the group. For example, if you have a group of twenty cannibals arguing over cannibalism with one noncannibal, the chances are that in the end he will come to see their point and, with just a few face-saving reservations (concerning, say, the consumption of close relatives), will go over completely to the majority's point of view. But if you have a group discussion between ten cannibals who regard human flesh aged over sixty years as too tough for a cultivated palate and ten other cannibals who fastidiously draw the line at fifty, the chances are that the group will eventually agree on fifty-five as the age that divides the *déjeuner* from the *débris* when it comes to sorting out prisoners. Such are the wonders of group dynamics. What lies at the bottom of this apparently inevitable pressure toward consensus is probably a profound human desire to be accepted, presumably by whatever group is around to do the accepting. This desire can be manipulated most effectively — as is well known by group therapists, demagogues, and other specialists in the field of consensus engineering.

Ridicule and gossip are potent instruments of social control in primary groups of all sorts. Many societies use ridicule as one of the main controls over children — the child conforms not for fear of punishment but in order not to be laughed at. Within our own larger culture, "kidding" in this way has been an important disciplinary measure among southern Negroes. But most men have experienced the freezing fear of making oneself ridiculous in some social situation. Gossip, as hardly needs elaboration, is especially effective in small communities, where most people live their lives in a high degree of social visibility and inspectability by their neighbors. In such communities, gossip is one of the principal channels of communication, essential for the maintenance of the social fabric. Both ridicule and gossip can be manipulated deliberately by any intelligent person with access to their lines of transmission.

Finally, one of the most devastating means of punishment at the disposal of a human community is to subject one of its members to systematic opprobrium and ostracism. It is somewhat ironic to reflect that this is a favorite control mechanism with groups opposed on principle to the use of violence. An example of this would be "shunning" among the Amish and Mennonites. An individual who breaks one of the principal taboos of the group (for example, by getting sexually involved with an outsider) is "shunned." This means that, while permitted to continue to work and live in the community, not a single person will speak to him—ever. It is hard to imagine a more cruel punishment. But such are the wonders of pacifism....

It is possible, then, to perceive oneself as standing at the center (that is, at the point of maximum pressure) of a set of concentric circles, each representing a system of social control. The outer ring might well represent the legal and political system under which one is obligated to live. This is the system that, quite against one's will, will tax one, draft one into the military, make one obey its innumerable rules and regulations, if need be put one in prison, and in the last resort will kill one. One does not have to be a right-wing Republican to be perturbed by the ever-increasing expansion of this system's power into every conceivable aspect of one's life. A salutary exercise would be to note down for the span of a single week all the occasions, including fiscal ones, in which one came up against the demands of the politico-legal system. The exercise can be concluded by adding up the sum total of fines and/or terms of imprisonment that disobedience to the system might lead to. The consolation, incidentally, with which one might recover from this exercise would consist of the recollection that law-enforcement agencies are normally corrupt and of only limited efficiency.

Another system of social control that exerts its pressures towards the solitary figure in the center is that of morality, custom, and manners. Only the most urgent-seeming (to the authorities, that is) aspects of this system are endowed with legal sanctions. This does not mean, however, that one can safely be immoral, eccentric, or unmannered. At this point, all the other instrumentalities of social control go into action. Immorality is punished by loss of one's job, eccentricity by the loss of one's chances of finding a new one, bad

manners by remaining uninvited and uninvitable in the groups that respect what they consider good manners. Unemployment and loneliness may be minor penalties compared to being dragged away by the cops, but they may not actually appear so to the individuals thus punished. Extreme defiance against the mores of our particular society, which is quite sophisticated in its control apparatus, may lead to yet another consequence—that of being defined, by common consent, as "sick."

Enlightened bureaucratic management (such as, for example, the ecclesiastical authorities of some Protestant denominations) no longer throws its deviant employees out on the street, but instead compels them to undergo treatment by its consulting psychiatrists. In this way, the deviant individual (that is, the one who does not meet the criteria of normality set up by management or by his bishop) is still threatened with unemployment and with the loss of his social ties, but in addition, he is also stigmatized as one who might very well fall outside the pale of responsible men altogether, unless he can give evidence of remorse ("insight") and resignation ("response to treatment"). Thus, the innumerable "counseling," "guidance," and "therapy" programs developed in many sectors of contemporary institutional life greatly strengthen the control apparatus of the society as a whole and especially those parts of it where the sanctions of the politico-legal system cannot be invoked.

But in addition to those broad coercive systems that every individual shares with vast numbers of fellow controllees, there are other and less extensive circles of control to which he is subjected. His choice of an occupation (or, often more accurately, the occupation in which he happens to end up) inevitably subordinates the individual to a variety of controls, often stringent ones. These are the formal controls of licensing boards, professional organizations, and trade unions—in addition, of course, to the formal requirements set by his particular employers. Equally important are the informal controls imposed by colleagues and coworkers. Again, it is hardly necessary to elaborate overly on this point. The reader can construct his own examples—the physician who participates in a prepaid comprehensive health insurance program, the undertaker who advertises inexpensive funerals, the engineer in industry who does not allow for planned obsolescence in his calculations, the minister who says that he is not interested in the size of the membership of his church (or rather, the one who acts accordingly—they nearly all say so), the government bureaucrat who consistently spends less than his allotted budget, the assembly-line worker who exceeds the norms regarded as acceptable by his colleagues, and so on. Economic sanctions are, of course, the most frequent and effective ones in these instances—the physician finds himself barred from all available hospitals, the undertaker may be expelled from his professional organization for "unethical conduct," the engineer may have to volunteer for the Peace Corps, as may the minister and the bureaucrat (in, say, New Guinea, where there is as yet no planned obsolescence, where Christians are few and far between, and where the governmental machinery is small enough to be relatively rational), and the assembly-line worker may find that all the defective parts of machinery in the entire plant have a way of congregating on his workbench. But the sanctions of social exclusion, contempt, and ridicule may be almost as hard to bear. Each occupational role in society, even in very humble jobs, carries with it a code of conduct that is very hard indeed to defy. Adherence to this code is normally just as essential for one's career in the occupation as technical competence or training.

The social control of one's occupational system is so important because the job decides what one may do in most of the rest of one's life—which voluntary associations one will be allowed to join, who will be one's friends, where one will be able to live. However, quite apart from the pressures of one's occupation, one's other social involvements also entail control systems, many of them less unbending than the occupational one, but some even more so. The codes governing admission to and continued membership in many clubs and fraternal organizations are just as stringent as those that decide who can become an executive at IBM (sometimes, luckily for the harassed candidate, the requirements may actually be the same). In less exclusive associations, the rules may be more lax and one may only rarely get thrown out, but life can be so thoroughly unpleasant for the persistent nonconformist to the local folkways that continued participation becomes humanly impossible. The items covered by such unwritten codes will, naturally, vary greatly. They may include ways of dressing, language, aesthetic taste, political or religious convictions, or simply table manners. In all these cases, however, they constitute control circles that effectively circumscribe the range of the individual's possible actions in the particular situation.

Finally, the human group in which one's so-called private life occurs, that is the circle of one's family and personal friends, also constitutes a control system. It would be a grave error to assume that this is necessarily the weakest of them all just because it does not possess the formal means of coercion of some of the other control systems. It is in this circle that an individual normally has his most important social ties. Disapproval, loss of prestige, ridicule, or contempt in this intimate group has far more serious psychological weight than the same reactions encountered elsewhere. It may be economically disastrous if one's boss finally concludes that one is a worthless nobody, but the psychological effect of such a judgment is incomparably more devastating if one discovers that one's wife has arrived at the same conclusion. What is more, the pressures of this most intimate control system can be applied at those times when one is least prepared for them. At one's job, one is usually in a better position to brace oneself, to be on one's guard, and to pretend than one is at home. Contemporary American "familism," a set of values that strongly emphasizes the home as a place of refuge from the tensions of the world and of personal fulfillment, contributes effectively to this control system. The man who is at least relatively prepared psychologically to give battle in his office is willing to do almost anything to preserve the precarious harmony of his family life. Last but not least, the social control of what German sociologists have called the "sphere of the intimate" is particularly powerful because of the very factors that have gone into its construction in the individual's biography. A man chooses a wife and a good friend in acts of essential self-definition. His most intimate relationships are those he must count on to sustain the most important elements of his self-image. To risk, therefore, the disintegration of these relationships means to risk losing himself in a total way. It is no wonder then that many an office despot promptly obeys his wife and cringes before the raised eyebrows of his friends.

If we return once more to the picture of an individual located at the center of a set of concentric circles, each one representing a system of social control, we can understand a little better that location in society means to locate oneself with regard to many forces that constrain and coerce one. The individual who, thinking consecutively of all the people he is in a position to have to please, from the Collector of Internal Revenue to his mother-in-law, gets the idea that all of society sits right on top of him — and had better not dismiss that idea as a momentary neurotic derangement. The sociologist, at any rate, is likely to strengthen him in this conception, no matter [how much] other counselors may tell him to snap out of it....

43. AN INTRODUCTION TO DEVIANCE

ERICH GOODE

In all societies, large and small, industrialized or agrarian, some degree of individuality among members exists.... And in all societies, there is a point at which 'individuality' becomes deviance.

Erich Goode's introduction to his textbook provides an understanding of the nature of deviance and how sociologists examine that subject. The study of deviance, Goode maintains, has focused not so much on why people commit deviant acts, but more on "how others condemn and punish them" and on what deviant behavior is really like.

Society is on shaky ground, in a way. What is taught as "the right way" is not the only way, and it is necessary to try to establish and reestablish the rules on a more than casual basis. Authorities establish fictions to protect the rules. Goode points out, "The fact is, we are not always successfully socialized into believing that our society is always right in everything it teaches. We are not robots." Some people will question the rules and even the social order itself. Goode, therefore, introduces the human being who fails to assume the positions in structure waiting for him or her, who questions the culture, who seems to assume "that the rules are a lie, a hoax, and are invalid or ineffective." To be labeled "deviant" is to represent to the defenders of society "a heresy against the said order."

Throughout this selection, Goode looks at why some people are labeled deviant and condemned. Although he does not really show why some people are able to reject the game of society, he does introduce two important points about individuality:

1. Societies punish individuals in order to discourage what are perceived as threats to the moral order. Individuality is not something that is safe for the actor.
2. Despite all of society's attempts to control, to socialize, to gain commitment, to get the individual to accept the culture and the structure, some people, for reasons not explained, escape and become individuals or join with others into groups that also do not accept society's rules.

Goode describes the human as more alive, more active, and more challenging than do the authors of earlier selections in this book: Norms are not as exact as other sociologists describe; humans are not as conformist; society is not so much the puppet theater. Yet Goode does not try to analyze where individuality comes from. Are we naturally rebellious? Is individuality an accident? Or can we trace individuality, like most other things, to socialization and social structure?

On October 13, 1972, 45 Uruguayans, including 15 members of an amateur rugby team, took off from Mendoza, Argentina, in a Fairchild F—227 across the Andes Mountains toward Santiago, Chile. At 3:30 in the afternoon, the aircraft crashed, ploughing into a desolate region of the snowy range at an altitude of 11,500 feet. The crash left 17 dead and a number of others mortally wounded. A dozen more were to die before the party was rescued 72 days later. There were only 16 survivors. On the eighth day after the crash, word came over their transistor radio that the search party looking for them had been called off. Their food supplies consisted of some candy, jam, dates and plums, one packet of crackers, and a can of salted almonds. By the tenth day, even these skimpy supplies, although parsimoniously rationed, were gone. There was no living creature within miles of them—not even a blade of grass. They were in the center of the Andes, in one of the most inaccessible and inhospitable regions of the earth. Without food, death was absolutely certain.

For some days, several of the boys had realized that if they were to survive they would have to eat the bodies of those who had died in the crash. It was a ghastly prospect. The corpses lay around in the snow, preserved by the intense cold…. While the thought of cutting flesh from those who had been their friends was deeply repugnant to them all, a lucid appreciation of their predicament led them to consider it…. Most of the bodies were covered by the snow, but the buttocks of one protruded…. With no exchange of words, Canessa knelt, bared the skin, and cut into the flesh with a piece of broken glass. It was frozen hard and difficult to cut, but he persisted until he had cut away twenty slivers the size of matchsticks…. He

prayed to God to help him do what he knew to be right and then took a piece of meat in his hand. He hesitated. Even with his mind so firmly made up, the horror of the act paralyzed him. His hand would neither rise to his mouth nor fall to his side while the revulsion that possessed him struggled with his stubborn will. The will prevailed. The hand rose and pushed the meat into his mouth. He swallowed it. He felt triumphant. His conscience had overcome a primitive, irrational taboo. He was going to survive (Read 1974: 82, 85–86).

When they emerged into the world of civilization, many of their parents were horrified by the revelation of how they had survived. One mother "could not control the aghast expression on her face" when her son told her "of the extremes to which they had gone" to keep alive. Another mother "gave an involuntary grimace of horror" when her son informed her what their source of nourishment had been. "Like many of the other mothers who still had faith in their sons' survival, she had not thought, in detail, of how this miracle might be achieved; she assumed that there would be woods to shelter them, with rabbits running over the pine needles and fish swimming in the streams" (Read 1974: 312—313). Later, when the world had gotten used to the idea that cannibalism was absolutely necessary for survival, the young men were treated everywhere they went as heroes.

On June 26, 1968, a New York City policeman, Frank Serpico, began testifying in a series of appearances before a grand jury inquiry investigating the acceptance of payoffs by gamblers to police officers. By January 1969, the grand jury had completed its hearings. Theoretically, these hearings were secret, but word leaked out that Serpico had been testifying against his fellow officers. Transferred to another borough, "Serpico was elaborately ignored. No one said anything to him or even looked at him. And then it happened":

As Serpico stood alone, a plainclothesman...walked up to him. He stopped about three feet from Serpico, and reached into his pocket and took out a knife.... The others in the room fell silent. Out of the corner of his eye, Serpico could see some of them smirking. The plainclothesman with the knife said, "We know how to handle guys like you." He extended his right hand, the one with the knife in it, pressed a button in the handle with his thumb, and five inches of steel blade leaped out, pointing up. "I ought to cut your tongue out," the plainclothesman said (Maas 1974: 227).

After disarming him, Serpico pulled out a nine-millimeter Browning automatic and trained it on his assailant as the other men watched in horror. "How many rounds does it hold?" one of them asked, mesmerized by the enormous size of the weapon. "Fourteen," Serpico replied. "Fourteen? What do you need fourteen rounds for?" "How many guys you got in this office?" (1974: 228).

After his confrontation with the officer with the switchblade, "everyone figuratively tiptoed around" Serpico, but "he remained completely ostracized" (1974: 235).

James Morris served five years in one of Britain's most elite and military-minded cavalry regiments, including a stint in World War II. At 26, in 1953, he climbed three-quarters of the way up the world's highest mountain and scooped all other reporters on the story that Edmund Hillary and Tenzing Norkay had conquered Mount Everest. His entire life was like that: flamboyant, adventurous, romantic. While in Cairo as a reporter for *The Times* of London, Morris lived in a houseboat on the Nile. He had married at 22 and eventually fathered five children. Once, after quitting a reporting job, he bought an old Rolls-Royce and "moved his growing family in stately progress across the southern counties of England, and into France, Italy, and Spain, renting houses along the way that seemed to possess some vaguely superior quality of age or distinction."

Neither in life nor work did he shirk risks or plead caution, and in his writing he always responded sympathetically to the most manly images. Soldiers and adventurers brought out the best in him, and in his own way he seemed to belong to their brotherhood, displaying the discipline of the one and the carefree spirit of the other (Holden 1974: 19).

There was only one thing wrong: During his entire life, James Morris wanted to be a woman. "Please God, make me a girl," he would plead night after night in his childhood. This desire grew stronger as he grew older. "In the end, I couldn't go on as a man any longer because I really believed I *was* a woman, anyway—so I was living a lie, wasn't I?" In the early 1960s, Morris consulted with Dr. Harry Benjamin, an endocrinologist who conducted a pioneering research on (and first gave a name to) transsexuals. In 1963, Morris began taking female hormones. His body and face began to change; he acquired softer, more rounded features. He began to appear on the streets of Oxford, where he had a country home, dressed in women's clothing. He registered for research at one of Oxford's libraries under the name of a woman. Morris was, in fact, experimenting with passing as a woman. At first, only his wife knew; then a few close friends; eventually it became public knowledge. By 1972, James Morris began writing book reviews under the "suitably androgynous" name of Jan Morris. That year, he flew to Casablanca and underwent a sex change operation. The transition from James Morris, the man, to Jan Morris, the woman, was complete. His prayers had been answered (Morris 1974).

In the early morning hours just after midnight on Saturday, August 9, 1969, four young Charles Manson followers—Susan Atkins, Patricia Krenwinkel, Linda Kasabian, and Charles Watson—drove up a hill in a fashionable neighborhood of Beverly Hills, stopping in front of a residence located at 10050 Cielo Drive. Watson cut the telephone wires to the house, and the group climbed the fence surrounding the house. While they were hiding a change of clothes in the bushes, the headlights of a car in the driveway attracted their attention. Watson went to the car, ordered the driver, Steven Parent, 18 years old, to halt. Over the young man's pleas for mercy, Watson shot Parent four times. Watson then returned to the three young women and, together, they pushed Parent's Rambler back up the driveway away from the gate.

The party then walked down the driveway toward the house. Watson crawled into the dining room window and opened the front door, letting two of the women inside; Kasabian remained outside. There were four occupants of the house at the time—Voytek Frykowski, Abigail Folger, Jay Sebring, and Sharon Tate. Watson, Atkins, and Krenwinkel brutally murdered all four and wrote the word PIG on the front door with Sharon Tate's blood. Then they rejoined the waiting Kasabian, left by the front gate, and hurried down the hill to the car. The three killers changed their bloody clothes and drove off.

These four, it turns out, lived in a kind of commune headed by 34—year-old Charles Manson, who believed himself to be Jesus Christ. Manson had spent half of his life behind prison bars. Released in 1967, Manson gravitated to the Haight-Ashbury area of San Francisco and quickly established himself as something of a prophet among the area's young and often homeless street people. He developed a philosophy, "Helter Skelter," which was to be launched by the murder of affluent whites and to be climaxed by Manson becoming the "ruler of the world." The Tate-Frykowski-Folger-Sebring murders were simply part of a large but undetermined number of killings engineered or actually performed by Manson (Bugliosi, with Gentry, 1974, 1975).

What do cannibalism, testifying against one's fellow police officers, changing one's sex, and mass murder have in common? We would search in vain for similarities if we tried to understand the motives of the people involved, if we tried to determine the causes of their actions. We would also search in vain for some sort of internal consistency in these actions—if they all harmed others, if they were uniformly self-destructive, or if they broke some religious or natural law. The only thing that they have in common, really, is that they are all examples of deviant behavior….

THE SOCIAL CONSTRUCTION OF REALITY

If, by "instincts," we mean behavioral impulses that are with us at birth, that do not have to be learned, humans have some instincts that "wire" us for some forms of behavior. Infants grasp and suckle. When presented with a smiling face, they smile back. Harlow showed that infant monkeys deprived of tactile nurturance do not grow up to do the sorts of things that other monkeys do.

Humans, probably much more than monkeys, "need" warmth and affection; this, too, might be considered analogous to an instinct.

However, these few instincts do not take us very far. They do not dictate any specific or complex forms of behavior. We could not survive, at birth, on our instincts alone. In order to survive, we need one another. All the peoples of the world depend on, and have to devise, a culture—a system of rules and regulations that takes the place of instincts. Our world, then, has to be *humanly constructed*. This necessitates a social construction of reality (Berger and Luckmann 1966). Our relationship with our physical environment, unlike that of animals, is not fixed. The necessity for invention is almost absolute. Luckily, our capacity for invention is equally prodigious.

Not only must humans create a social order that protects its members from annihilation, but we must also infuse the world with meaning. We have to convince ourselves that certain things matter. No civilization could continue if large numbers of its members saw life and everything in it as a matter of emotional indifference. It would be impossible for a society to exist if all people met every situation with a shrug of the shoulders and a grunt that said, "What's the difference?"

Thus, it is the job of all societies to convince their members—large numbers of them at any rate—that there *is* meaning in life and in the universe. Consequently, we are, as existentialist philosopher Merleau-Ponty puts it, "*condemned to meaning.*"

Although we are *theoretically* capable of creating a multiplicity of worlds, still, as a people, we are "compelled to impose a meaningful order on reality" (Berger 1967: 22). Every socially constructed universe "is an area of meaning carved out of a vast mass of meaninglessness, a small clearing of lucidity in a formless, dark, always ominous jungle" (Berger 1967: 29). "*All* societies are constructed in the face of chaos" (Berger and Luckmann 1966: 103). One major job of every civilization, then, is *universe maintenance* (Berger and Luckmann 1966: 105). A culture offers a kind of "protective cocoon" against chaos and death.

To be effective, these social constructions we call a society have to appear to be "natural," inevitable, and God-given—not artificially, symbolically, and humanly constructed. Members of the society have to be convinced of the ultimate reality of their culture, and have to remain ignorant of their mere expediency, their artificiality. We have to "forget" our own role in the creation of meaning. We have to see the rules of society as "something other than a human product" (Berger and Luckmann 1966: 61). We have to believe that they are right in some larger sense. The humanly made rules of society "are given a cosmic status" (Berger 1967: 36). We have to accept the social world, its views of right and wrong, of true and false, of good and bad, as taken for granted, as self-evident. Successful socialization is the internalization of society's rules such that they are not questioned, but rather seen as inevitable, in the nature of things. "The humanly-made world is explained in terms that deny its human production;" a kind of "fictitious inexorability" is placed on the rules of a culture (Berger 1967: 89, 95). This means that the "socially created" aspect of human existence has an authoritarian side to it as well as a side that inclines us toward freedom.

Once large numbers of the members of a society begin questioning the validity and the legitimacy of the social order and its rules, their foundation and their grip on people becomes shaky. The fact is, we are not always successfully socialized into believing that our society is always right in everything it teaches. We are not robots. We are not sponges that simply "soak up" rules. There will always be a certain number of people who question the rules, even the entire social order. In fact, it is often difficult to determine just what "the rules of society" are because there may be many competing sets of rules that are believed by different sets of people in that society. However, it is often the case that a majority believes in the validity of one set of rules. And those who believe otherwise, or who do things that seem to contradict these rules, will be regarded with suspicion. These people are often seen as troublemakers who threaten the social order. They seem to offer an alternative way of looking at reality, at the world, at the rules. They are engaged (or so some think) in an active denial of the social order.

Deviance is often seen as a kind of alternative world view. It announces that the rules are a lie, a hoax, and are invalid or ineffective. Hostility is directed at deviants in large part because they challenge the very basis of what most of us have been taught from the cradle. Once a set of rules is historically institutionalized and legitimated, many members of that society have a great emotional investment in protecting the status quo from any onslaught from those whom they consider barbarians. Because the rules have taken on a kind of semi-sacred status, deviance is a heresy against the social order. Hostility toward the deviant, relegating deviants to the status of inferior beings, is an outgrowth of the need to protect the symbolic universe that one sees as protective and nurturant.

> [The roots of this hostility, then] may lie in the extremely significant function that the symbolic universe serves in making social life possible.... [Human] life is by its nature disorderly and the symbolic universe helps to create for us a kind of certainty and anchorage. Anything that threatens to strip us of this protective cocoon will inevitably be seen as evil.... [The] deviant is a person whose existence does threaten to inundate with chaos the symbolic system by which order and meaning are given to human existence (Scott 1972: 30, 31).

Probably the classic case of this perceived threat to the social universe created by conventional society is the world view ascribed to witches in the Middle Ages, and the deviant image they acquired. Hostility and outrage seemed at that time to be the only reasonable reaction to such heresy. There existed, writes Norman Cohn, author of *Europe's Inner Demons*, "somewhere in the midst of the great society, another society, small and clandestine, which not only threatened the existence of the great society but was also addicted to practices that were felt to be wholly abominable in the literal sense of anti-human." There was, consequently, an "urge to purify the world through the annihilation of some category of human beings imagined as agents of corruption and incarnation of evil" (Cohn 1975: xiv).

There are, of course, different types of deviants and different reasons for conventional people to condemn them. Clearly, one major type are deviants who deny or challenge (or seem to) the validity of the institutional order with which we are comfortable. Communists and political revolutionaries fit this description for many conventionals. So do atheists, "swingers," users of illegal drugs, and women's liberationists. Many members of our society denounce them because they fear what they stand for, they fear the contamination of their world, they fear that the basis of their own reality will be undermined.

Sometimes people do not fear the specific threat that the deviant's world view offers to theirs; they even may feel smugly superior and righteous face to face with certain deviants. But they may fear that people around them — or even they themselves — will become, or secretly *are*, the deviant they see, interact with, or imagine. Certainly, many "straight" men react in a hostile way to homosexuals for this reason: Their own sense of security in being heterosexual (what they see as their own "masculinity") is shaky. Many men look down on prostitutes (even though they may make use of their services) because they fear that their wives, daughters (or even mothers) are, were, or could become prostitutes. Conventional people are contemptuous of many deviants because they are seen as pitiable. They do not so much challenge the legitimacy of the social order as demonstrate that its downfall is entirely possible. We, too, and those we care about, in fact *anyone*, could become a poor, unfortunate creature — an alcoholic, a suicide, a drug addict, an insane person.

In addition, people fear and hate deviants because they threaten our well-being, perhaps our very physical existence. They are thought, actually or potentially, to visit violence on us, or on those we are close to, or on the social body as a whole. Many "criminals" would fit this description. So would juvenile delinquents. On the other hand, there are perpetrators of damage and violence that conventional people rarely condemn — politicians who start wars for patriotic reasons, for instance. Most deviants commit no damage of any kind on conventional people, ever. This "damage" reason is usually cited for a society's opposition to deviance and deviants; it is, in fact, the weakest reason of all. People see deviants as dangerous because they are already condemned; they do not condemn deviants because they are dangerous.

Many deviants also threaten powerful, established interests. Hostility toward deviance does not arise spontaneously out of society's "culture." In every society, certain members have more power to shape public opinion and the legal structure than others do. These more influential members may see in certain behavior a potential threat to what they have. It often happens that what they have was obtained at the expense of less powerful members of their society. The powerful want to maintain the status quo — and try to convince the less advantaged that this is for the best. When the behavior of a threatening group comes too close for comfort, adverse public opinion alone is not sufficient; the powerful have their ideology translated into the criminal code. Thus, deviant behavior often becomes illegal behavior as well. Deviants may divert attention from the sources of inequality in a society — they may serve a kind of "scapegoating" function. Or the social control and punishment of deviance may serve to isolate and immobilize those who are too threatening (or are perceived as too threatening) to the most affluent and powerful members of society. This does not account for hostility toward all deviant behavior, but it does illuminate a great deal of the condemnation of deviance.

More general than the threat to powerful established interests is the fact that deviant behavior is widely seen as a challenge to the established hierarchical order — the ranking system of a society. The moral order (notions of right and wrong) rests on making invidious comparisons between people. Some are elevated and others lowered by what they do. When people do things we disapprove of, our sense of our own position in this stratificational system is threatened. Conventional people feel that they deserve a higher position in the moral hierarchy because they have followed the rules, and that others should be placed lower because they have not. Deviance may be seen as an "attack on an existing arrangement of ranked statuses." "Anyone who successfully promotes a new convention in which he is skilled and I am not attacks...my position in the world.... When new people successfully create a new world that defines other conventions as embodying ... value, all the participants in the old world who cannot make a place in the new lose out" (Becker 1974: 774).[1] Deviance, in short, is seen by many members of a society as challenging a moral order that is the basis for a ranking system. People fear that a new moral order will be one in which their own ranking will be low. Consequently, they wish to punish those who seem to be trying to take their existing privileges and position away. They need not even rank very high in the existing system. All that is necessary is that they feel that their position will be lowered. This may be enough to generate fear, insecurity, and hostility toward the offending party.

THE UNIVERSALITY OF DEVIANCE

Deviance is universal. Not only do people everywhere set rules detailing what constitutes appropriate and inappropriate—or conventional and deviant—behavior, but groups of people everywhere experience deviance in their midst. And everywhere, some sort of punishment is meted out for nonconformity. No society experiences absolute conformity from all its members. *Deviance is implicit in social organization.* In order to render human existence viable and workable, rules have to be set. And when rules are set, it is inevitable that they will be broken by some people at some time. The social organization of the condemnation of deviant behavior is universal. And the behavior itself—that is, some sort of behavior that touches off condemnation— is also universal. *The only universal in deviance is its very existence.* There are no actions that are literally condemned everywhere, but the condemnation of some actions does exist everywhere. Exactly what it is that upsets people is enormously variable. And exactly how flexible "the rules" are is also highly variable. But the fact that large numbers of the members of a society will and do become upset at something others do is everywhere the case.

It has been claimed that socially disapproved or "deviant" behavior is only characteristic of (or widespread in) complex, industrialized, urbanized societies—that illiterate, tribal folk societies experience little or no significant deviance. They are perceived as homogeneous, with everyone living in harmony and conformity. People in these societies, some say, tend to act pretty much alike, to believe more or less the same things. It

turns out that these claims are grossly exaggerated. In fact, "troublesome behavior is frequent and varied in the world's small and simple societies" (Edgerton 1973: 25). In all societies, large and small, industrialized or agrarian, some degree of individuality among members exists. It is, of course, measurably greater in some societies than others; but it may not be *experienced* as lesser in the small societies, where small differences may take on greater subjective importance. And in all societies, there is a point at which "individuality" becomes deviance....

NOTE

1. Becker's argument here applies specifically to artistic convention, and it is based on an unpublished paper by Everett C. Hughes, who in turn borrowed the idea from William Graham Sumner's *Folkways.*

REFERENCES

Becker, Howard S. "Art as Collective Action." *American Sociological Review*, Vol. 39 (December 1974): 767—776.

Berger, Peter L. *The Sacred Canopy.* Garden City, NY: Doubleday, 1967.

———— and Thomas Luckmann. *The Social Construction of Reality.* Garden City, NY: Doubleday, 1966.

Bugliosi, Vincent, with Curt Gentry. *Helter Skelter.* New York: Norton, 1974; New York: Bantam, 1975.

Cohn, Norman. *Europe's Inner Demons: An Enquiry Inspired by the Great Witch Hunt.* New York: Basic Books, 1975.

Edgerton, Robert B. "Deviant Behavior and Cultural Theory." Reading, MA: Addison-Wesley, *Module in Anthropology* no. 37, 1973.

Holden, David. "James and Jan." *The New York Times Magazine*, March 17, 1974: 18—19, 78ff. Reprinted by permission, New York Times Company.

Maas, Peter. *Serpico.* New York: Bantam. 1974.

Morris, Jan. *Conundrum.* New York: New American Library, 1975.

Read, Piers Paul. *Alive: The Story of the Andes Survivors.* Philadelphia: Lippincott, 1974. Reprinted by permission of J. B. Lippincott Company.

Scott, Robert A. "A Proposed Framework for Analyzing Deviance as a Property of Social Order." In Robert A. Scott and Jack D. Douglas (eds.), *Theoretical Perspectives on Deviance.* New York: Basic Books, 1972.

44. THE SOCIAL CREATION OF STIGMA

ERICH GOODE

In contemporary America, obesity is stigmatized. Fat people are considered less worthy human beings than thin people are…. Men and women of average weight tend to look down on the obese, feel superior to them, reward them less, punish them, make fun of them…. What is more, thin people will feel that this treatment is just….

By examining our reaction to obesity, Erich Goode illustrates very well what stigma means and why it occurs. He challenges all of us to examine our reactions to other people, and to ask ourselves how we have come to believe what we do.

Bertha was a massive woman. She weighed well over 400 pounds. Still, people enjoyed her company, and she had an active social life. One Friday night, Bertha and several of her friends stopped in a local Burger and Shake for a quick snack. Bertha disliked fast-food restaurants with good reason: Their seats were inadequate for her size. But she was a good sport and wanted to be agreeable, so she raised no objection to the choice of an eating establishment. Bertha squeezed her huge body into the booth and enjoyed a shake and burger. A typical Friday night crowd stood waiting for tables, so Bertha and her companions finished their snack and began to vacate the booth so that others could dine. But Bertha's worst fears were realized: She was so tightly jammed in between the table and the chair that she was stuck.

Bertha began struggling to get out of the booth, without success. Her friends pulled her, pushed her, and twisted her—all to no avail. She was trapped. Soon, all eyes in the Burger and Shake were focused on the hapless Bertha and her plight. Onlookers began laughing at her. Snickers escalated to belly laughs, and the restaurant fairly rocked with raucous laughter and

cruel, taunting remarks, "Christ, is she fat." "What's the matter, honey—one burger too many?" "Look at the trapped whale!" "How could anyone get that fat!" Bertha's struggles became frenzied; she began sweating profusely. Every movement became an act of desperation to free herself from her deeply humiliating situation. Finally, in a mighty heave, Bertha tore the entire booth from its bolts and she stood in the middle of the floor of the Burger and Shake, locked into the booth as if it had been a barrel. The crowd loved it, and shrieked with laughter that intensified in volume and stridency, as Bertha staggered helplessly, squatting in the center of the room.

One of Bertha's friends ran to his car, grabbed a hammer and a wrench, came back in, and began smashing at the booth. He broke it into pieces that fell to the floor, freeing the woman from her torture chamber. Bertha lumbered and pushed her way through the laughing, leering crowd, and ran to her car, hot tears in her eyes and burning shame in her throat. The friend who freed her limply placed the pieces of the chair and table onto the counter. The employees, now irritated, demanded that he pay for the damaged booth, but he and Bertha's other companions simply left the restaurant.

After that incident, Bertha rarely left her house. Two months later, she died of heart failure. She was 31 years old.

In contemporary America, obesity is stigmatized. Fat people are considered less worthy human beings than thin people are. They receive less of the good things that life has to offer, and more of the bad. Men and women of average weight tend to look down on the obese, feel superior to them, reward them less, punish them, make fun of them. The obese are often an object of derision and harassment for their weight. What is more, thin people will feel that this treatment is just, that the obese deserve it, indeed, that it is even something of a humanitarian gesture because such humiliation will supposedly inspire them to lose weight. The stigma of obesity is so intense and so persuasive that eventually the obese will come to see themselves as deserving of it, too.

The obese, in the words of one observer, "are a genuine minority, with all the attributes that a corrosive social atmosphere lends to such groups: poor self-image, heightened sensitivity, passivity, withdrawal, a sense of isolation and rejection." They are subject to relentless discrimination, they are the butt of denigrating jokes, they suffer from persecution; it would not be an exaggeration to say that they attract cruelty from the thin majority. Moreover, their friends and family rarely give the kind of support and understanding they need to deal with this cruelty; in fact, it is often friends and family who are themselves meting out the cruel treatment. The social climate has become "so completely permeated with anti-fat prejudice that the fat themselves have been infected by it. They hate other fat people, hate themselves when they are fat, and will risk anything—even their lives—in an attempt to get thin…. Anti-fat bigotry … is a psychic net in which the overweight are entangled every moment of their lives" (Louderback 1970, pp. v, vi, vii). The obese typically accept the denigration thin society dishes out to them because they feel, for the most part, that they deserve it. And they do not defend other fat people who are being criticized because they are a mirror of themselves; they mirror their own defects—the very defects that are so repugnant to them. Unlike the members of most other minorities, they don't fight back; in fact, they feel that they can't fight back. Racial, ethnic and religious minorities can isolate themselves to a degree from majority prejudices;

the obese cannot. The chances are, most of the people they meet will be average size, and they live in a physical world built for individuals with much smaller bodies. The only possibilities seem to be to brace themselves—to cower under the onslaught of abuse—or to retreat and attempt to minimize the day-to-day disgrace.

Our hostility toward the overweight runs up and down the scale, from the grossly obese to men and women of average weight. If the hugely obese are persecuted mightily for their weight, the slightly overweight are simply persecuted proportionally less—they are not exempt. We live in a weight-obsessed society. It is impossible to escape nagging reminders of our ideal weight. Standing at the checkout counter in a supermarket, we are confronted by an array of magazines, each with its own special diet designed to eliminate those flabby pounds. Television programs (and advertising even more so) display actresses and models who are considerably slimmer than average, setting up an almost impossibly thin ideal for the viewing public. If we were to gain ten pounds, our friends would all notice it, view the gain with negative feelings, and only the most tactful would not comment on it.

These exacting weight standards not surprisingly fall more severely on the shoulders of women than on men. In a survey of the 33, 000 readers of *Glamour* who responded to a questionnaire placed in the August 1983 issue of the magazine, 75 percent said that they were "too fat," even though only one-quarter were overweight according to the stringent 1959 Metropolitan Life Insurance Company's height-weight tables. (According to Metropolitan's current standards, even fewer of *Glamour*'s readers are deemed overweight.) Still more surprising, 45 percent who were *under*weight according to Metropolitan's figures felt that they were "too fat." Only 6 percent of the respondents felt "very happy" about their bodies; only 15 percent described their bodies as "just right." When looking at their nude bodies in the mirror, 32 percent said that they felt "anxious," 12 percent felt "depressed," and 5 percent felt "repulsed."

Commenting on the *Glamour* survey, one of the researchers who analyzed its results, Susan Wooley, professor of psychiatry at the University of Cincinnati's medical school, stated, "What we see is a steadily growing cultural bias—almost no woman of whatever size feels she's thin enough" (*Glamour* 1984, p. 199). When asked which of the following would make them happiest, 22 percent chose success at work, 21 percent said having a date with a man they admired, and 13 percent said hearing from an old friend. However, the alternative that attracted the highest proportion of the sample was losing weight—42 percent. The overwhelming majority (80 percent) said that they have to be slim to be attractive to men. A substantial proportion had "sometimes" or "often" used the potentially dangerous weight-loss methods of diet pills (50 percent), liquid formula diets (27 percent), diuretics (18 percent), laxatives (15 percent), fasting or starving (45 percent), and self-induced vomiting (15 percent). Judging from the results of this survey, it is safe to say that the readers of *Glamour* who responded to it are obsessed about being thin.

Evidence suggests that the standards for the ideal female form have gotten slimmer over the years. Women whose figures would have been comfortably embraced by the norm a generation or more ago are now regarded as overweight, even fat. The model for the White Rock Girl, inspired by the ancient Greek goddess Psyche, was 5'4" tall in 1894 and she weighed 140; her measurements were 37"-27"-38". Over the years, the woman who was selected to depict the White Rock Girl has gotten taller, slimmer, and has weighed less. In 1947, she was 5'6", weighed 125 pounds. and measured 35"-25"-35". And today, she's 5'8", weighs 118, and measures 35"-24"-34". Commenting on this trend in an advertising flyer, the executives of White Rock explain: "Over the years the Psyche image has become longer legged, slimmer hipped, and streamlined. Today—when purity is so important—she continues to symbolize the purity of all White Rock products." The equation of slenderness with purity is a revealing comment on today's obsession with thinness: Weighing a few pounds over some mythical ideal is to live in an "impure" condition. Interestingly, today's American woman averages 5'4" and weighs 140 pounds, the same as 1894's White Rock Girl.

Advertising models represent one kind of ideal; they tend to be extremely thin. They are not, however, the only representation of the ideal female form depicted by the media. There are, it may be said, several ideals, not only one. Photographs appear to add between five and ten pounds to the subject; clothes add a few more in seeming bulk. (White Rock's Psyche, however, wears very little in the way of clothes.) Consequently, fashion models typically border on the anorexic, and women who take them as role models to be emulated are subjecting themselves to an almost unattainable standard. It would be inaccurate to argue that all American women aspire to look like a fashion model, and it would be inaccurate to assert that women in all media are emaciated. Still, it is entirely accurate to say that the ideal woman's figure as depicted in the media is growing slimmer over the years. Even in settings where women were once fairly voluptuous, today's version has slimmed them down significantly.

Before 1970, contestants in Miss America pageants weighed 88 percent of the average for American women their age; after 1970, this declined somewhat to 85 percent. More important, before 1970, pageant *winners* weighed the same as the other contestants; after 1970, however, winners weighed significantly *less* than the contestants who didn't win—82.5 percent of the average for American women as a whole. Similarly, the weight of women who posed for *Playboy* centerfolds also declined between 1959 and 1978. Centerfolds for 1959 were 91 percent of the weight for an average American woman in her 20s; this declined to 84 percent in 1978. The measurements of the 1959 *Playboy* were 37"-22"-36". In 1978, they were 35"-24"-34 1/2" indicating a growing preference for a less voluptuous, and a slimmer and more angular, or "tubular" ideal appearance. Interestingly, during this same period, the American woman under 30 *gained* an average of five pounds (which was entirely caused by an increase in height during this time, not an increase in bulk). The number of diet articles published in six popular women's magazines nearly doubled between 1959 and 1979 (Garner et al. 1980). Thus, American women suffer from what might be described as a triple whammy—they are evaluated more severely on the basis of looks than is true of men, the standards of ideal weight for them falls within a far narrower range than it does for men, and these standards are becoming more rigid over time.

The increasingly slim standards of feminine beauty represent the most desirable point on a scale. The opposite end of this scale represents undesirable territory—obesity. If American women have been evaluated by standards of physical desirability that have shifted from slim to slimmer over the years, it is reasonable to assume that, during this same period, it has become less and less socially acceptable to be fat. In tribal and peasant societies, corpulence was associated with affluence. An abundant body represented a corresponding material abundance. In a society in which having enough to eat is a mark of distinction, heaviness will draw a measure of respect. This is true not only for oneself but also for one's spouse or spouses, and one's children as well. With the coming of mature industrialization, however, nutritional adequacy becomes sufficiently widespread as to cease being a sign of distinction; slenderness rather than corpulence comes to be adopted as the prevailing esthetic standard among the affluent (Powdermaker 1960; Cahnman 1968, pp. 287—288). In fact, what we have seen is a gradual adoption of the slim standard of attractiveness in all economic classes for both men and women, but much more strongly and stringently for women. And although it is more firmly entrenched in the upper socioeconomic classes, the slim ideal has permeated all levels of society.

Not only is obesity unfashionable and considered unesthetic to the thin majority, it is also regarded as "morally reprehensible," a "social disgrace" (Cahnman 1968, p. 283). Fat people are *set apart* from men and women of average size; they are isolated from "normal" society (Millman 1980). Today, being obese bears something of a *stigma*. In the words of sociologist Erving Goffman, the stigmatized are "disqualified from full social acceptance." They have been reduced "from a whole and usual person to a tainted, discounted one." The bearer of stigma is a "blemished person…to be avoided, especially in public places." The individual with a stigma is seen as "not quite human" (Goffman 1963, pp. i. 1, 3, 5).

Over the centuries, the word *stigma* has hidden two meanings—one good and the second, very bad. Among the ancient Greeks, a stigma was a brand on the body of a person, symbolizing that the bearer was in the service of the temple. In medieval Christianity, *stigmata* were marks resembling the wounds and scars on the body of Jesus, indicating that the bearer was an especially holy individual. It is, however, the negative meaning of the word that is dominant today. In ancient times, criminals and slaves were branded to identify their inferior status; the brand was a stigma. Lepers were said to bear the stigma of their loathsome disease. As it is currently used, stigma refers to a stain or reproach on one's character or reputation, or a symbol or sign of this inferiority or defect. Anything that causes someone to look down on, condemn, denigrate, or ignore another can be said to be *stigmatizing*.

A stigmatizing trait is rarely isolated. Hardly anyone who possesses one such characteristic is thought to have only one. A single sin will be regarded as housing a multitude of others as well, to be the "tip of the iceberg." The one stigmatizing trait is presumed to hide "a wide range of imperfections" (Goffman 1963, p.5). To be guilty of one sin automatically means to be thought of as being guilty of a host of others along with it. The one negative trait is a *master status*—everything about the individual is interpreted in light of the single trait. "Possession of one deviant trait may have a generalized symbolic value, so that people automatically assume that its bearer possesses other undesirable traits allegedly associated with it." Thus, the question is raised when confronting someone with a stigma: "What kind of person would break such an important rule?" The answer that is offered is typically: "One who is different from the rest of us, who cannot or will not act as a moral human being and therefore might break other important rules." In short, the stigmatizing characteristic "becomes the controlling one" (Becker 1963, pp. 33, 34).

To be stigmatized is to possess a *contaminated* identity. Interaction with nonstigmatized individuals will be strained, tainted, awkward, inhibited. Although the nonstigmatized may, because of the dictates of polite sociability, attempt to hide their negative feelings toward the stigmatized trait specifically, or the stigmatized individual as a whole, and act normally, they are, nonetheless, intensely *aware* of the other's blemish. Likewise, the stigmatized individual remains self-conscious about his or her relations with "normals," believing (often correctly) that the stigma is the exclusive focus of the interaction.

> I am always worried about how Jane judges me because she is the real beauty queen and the main gang leader. When I am with her, I hold my breath hard so my tummy doesn't bulge and I pull my skirt down so my fat thighs don't show. I tuck in my rear end. I try to look as thin as possible for her. I get so preoccupied with looking good enough to get into her gang that I forget what she's talking to me about.... I am so worried about how my body is going over that I can hardly concentrate on what she's saying. She asks me about math and all I am thinking about is how fat I am (Allon 1976, p. 18).

Highly stigmatized individuals, in the face of hostility on the part of the majority to their traits and to themselves as bearers of those traits, walk along one of two paths in reacting to stigma. One is to fight back by forming subcultures or groups of individuals who share the characteristics the majority rejects, and to treat this difference from the majority as a badge of honor—or at least, as no cause for shame. Clearly, the homosexual subculture provides an example of the tendency to ward off majority prejudices and oppression. This path is trod by those who feel that the majority's opinion of them and of the characteristic the majority disvalues is illegitimate or invalid—just plain wrong. Here, the legitimacy of the stigma is rejected. A trait, characteristic, a form of behavior that others look down on, they say, is no cause for invidiousness. You may put us down, those who travel this path say, but you have no right to do so. What we are or do is every bit as blameless, indeed, honorable, as what you are or do.

The second path the stigmatized take in reacting to stigma from the majority is *internalization*. Here, stigmatized individuals hold the same negative attitudes toward themselves as the majority does. The stigmatized individual is dominated by feelings of self-hatred and self-derogation. Thus, those who are discriminated against are made to understand that they *deserve* it; they come to accept their negative treatment as just (Cahnman 1968, p. 294). They feel that the majority has a right to stigmatize them. They may despise themselves for being who or what they are, for doing

what they do or have done. As we see in testimony from fat people themselves, there is a great deal of evidence to suggest that the obese are more likely to follow the second path than the first. In fact, it might be said that in comparison with the possessors of all stigmatized characteristics or behavior, the obese most strongly agree with the majority's negative judgment of who they are....

Overweight individuals are "stigmatized because they are held responsible for their deviant status, presumably lacking self-control and will power. They are not merely physically deviant as are physically disabled or disfigured persons, but they [also] seem to possess characterological stigma. Fat people are viewed as 'bad' or 'immoral'; supposedly, they do not want to change the error of their ways" (Allon 1982, p. 131):

> The obese are presumed to hold their fate in their own hands; if they were only a little less greedy or lazy or yielding to impulse or oblivious of advice, they would restrict excessive food intake, resort to strenuous exercise, and as a consequence of such deliberate action, they would reduce.... While blindness is considered a misfortune, obesity is branded as a defect.... A blind girl will be helped by her agemates, but a heavy girl will be derided. A paraplegic boy will be supported by other boys, but a fat boy will be pushed around. The embarrassing and not infrequently harassing treatment that is meted out to obese teenagers by those around them will not elicit sympathy from onlookers, but a sense of gratification; the idea is that they have got what was coming to them (Cahnman 1968, p. 294).

The obese are overweight, according to the popular view, because they eat immodestly and to excess. They have succumbed to temptation and hedonistic pleasure seeking, where other, more virtuous and less self-indulgent individuals have resisted. It is, as with behavioral deviance, a matter of a struggle between vice and virtue. The obese must therefore pay for the sin of overindulgence by attracting well-deserved stigma (Cahnman 1968; Maddox et al. 1968). The obese suffer from what the public sees as "self-inflicted damnation" (Allon 1973, 1982). In one study of the public's rejection of individuals with certain traits and characteristics, it was found that the stigma of obesity was in between that of physical handicaps such as blindness, and behavioral deviance such as homosexuality (Hiller 1981, 1982). In other words, the public stigmatized the obese *more* than possessors of involuntarily acquired undesirable traits but *less* than individuals who engage in unpopular, unconventional behavior.

This introduces a *moral* dimension to obesity that is lacking in other physical characteristics. The stigma of obesity entails three elements or aspects: (1) The overweight attract public scorn; (2) they are told that this scorn is deserved; (3) they come to accept this negative treatment as just (Cahnman 1968, p. 293). A clear-cut indication that the obese are derogated because of their presumed character defects can be seen in the fact that if obesity is seen to be caused strictly by a physical abnormality, such as hormonal imbalance, the individual is condemned by the public almost not at all, whereas if the etiology of the obesity is left unexplained (and therefore is presumed to be a result of a lack of self-control, resulting in overeating), the individual is, indeed, severely stigmatized (DeJong 1980). A trait that is seen as beyond the individual's control, for which he or she is held to be not responsible, is seen as a misfortune. In contrast, character flaws are regarded in a much harsher light. Obesity is seen as the outward manifestation of an undesirable character; it therefore invites retribution, in much of the public's eyes.

So powerfully stigmatized has obesity become that, in a *New York Times* editorial (Rosenthal 1981), one observer argues that obesity has replaced sex and death as our "contemporary pornography." We attach some degree of shame and guilt to eating. Our society is made up of "modern puritans" who tell one another how "*repugnant* it is to be fat"; "what's really disgusting," we feel, "is not sex, but fat." We are all so humorless, "so relentless, so determined to punish the overweight.... Not only are the overweight the most stigmatized group in the United States, but fat people are expected to participate in their own degradation by agreeing with others who taunt them."

REFERENCES

Allon, Natalie. 1976. *Urban Life Styles.* Dubuque, IA: W. C. Brown.

Becker, Howard S. 1963. *Outsiders: Studies in the Sociology of Deviance.* New York: Free Press.

Cahnman, Weiner J. 1968. "The Stigma of Obesity." *The Sociological Quarterly,* 9 (Summer), 283–299.

DeJong, William. 1980. "The Stigma of Obesity: The Consequences of Naive Assumptions Concerning the Causes of Physical Deviance." *Journal of Health and Social Behavior,* 21, 75–87.

Garner, David M., Paul E. Garfinkel, D. Schwartz, and M. Thompson. 1980. "Cultural Expectations of Thinness in Women." *Psychological Reports,* 47, 483-491.

Goffman, Erving. 1963. *Stigma: Notes on the Management of Spoiled Identity.* Upper Saddle River, NJ: Prentice-Hall/Spectrum.

Louderback, Llewellyn. 1970. *Fat Power: Whatever You Weigh Is Right.* New York: Hawthorn Books.

Maddox, George L., Kurt W. Back, and Veronica Liederman. 1968. "Overweight as Social Deviance and Disability." *Journal of Health and Social Behavior,* 9 (December 1968), 287–298.

Millman, Marxia. 1980. *Such a Pretty Face: Being Fat in America.* New York: W. W. Norton.

Powdermaker, Hortense. 1960. "An Anthropological Approach to the Problem of Obesity." *Bulletin of the New York Academy of Medicine,* 36, 286–295.

45. THE SAINTS AND THE ROUGHNECKS

WILLIAM J. CHAMBLISS

Selective perception and labeling—finding, processing, and punishing some kinds of criminality and not others—means that visible, poor, nonmobile, outspoken, undiplomatic, "tough" kids will be noticed, whether their actions are seriously delinquent or not. Other kids, who have established a reputation for being bright (even though underachieving), disciplined, and involved in respectable activities, who are mobile and moneyed, will be invisible when they deviate from sanctioned activities.

This article is fascinating. It is, on the one hand, about deviance—more specifically, how deviance is defined. Deviance always exists in a social context: Other people define it; other people punish it.

It is, on the other hand, about social class. It is a comparison of two groups of boys: One group is working class, and the other is middle class. It shows how class influences behavior, but more important, how class influences adult perception of that behavior.

The point of the author is simple: Deviance defined by middle-class people is biased against those who are working class. Perceptions are selective. A further point is also important here: Labeling someone as deviant may in fact encourage further deviance.

Eight promising young men—children of good, stable, white, upper-middle-class families, active in school affairs, good pre-college students—were some of the most delinquent boys at Hanibal High School. Although community residents and parents knew that these boys occasionally sowed a few wild oats, they were totally unaware that sowing wild oats completely occupied the daily routine of these young men. The Saints were constantly occupied with truancy, drinking, wild driving, petty theft, and vandalism. Yet not one was officially arrested for any misdeed during the two years I observed them.

This record was particularly surprising in light of my observations during the same two years of another gang of Hanibal High School students, six lower-class white boys known as the

From "The Saints and the Roughnecks," by William Chambliss, in *Society*, Vol. II, No. 1. Copyright © 1973 by Transaction Publishers, all rights reserved. Reprinted by permission of Transaction Publishers.

Roughnecks. The Roughnecks were constantly in trouble with police and community even though their rate of delinquency was about equal with that of the Saints. What was the cause of this disparity? The result? The following consideration of the activities, social class, and community perceptions of both gangs may provide some answers.

THE SAINTS FROM MONDAY TO FRIDAY

The Saints' principal daily concern was with getting out of school as early as possible. The boys managed to get out of school with minimum danger that they would be accused of playing hookey through an elaborate procedure for obtaining "legitimate" release from class. The most common procedure was for one boy to obtain the release of another by fabricating a meeting of some committee, program or recognized club. Charles might raise his hand in his 9:00 chemistry class and ask to be excused—a euphemism for going to the bathroom. Charles would go to Ed's math class and inform the teacher that Ed was needed for a 9:30 rehearsal of the drama club play. The math teacher would recognize Ed and Charles as "good students" involved in numerous school activities and would permit Ed to leave at 9:30. Charles would return to his class, and Ed would go to Tom's English class to obtain his release. Tom would engineer Charles' escape. The strategy would continue until as many of the Saints as possible were freed. After a stealthy trip to the car (which had been parked in a strategic spot), the boys were off for a day of fun.

Over the two years I observed the Saints, this pattern was repeated nearly every day. There were variations on the theme, but in one form or another, the boys used this procedure for getting out of class and then off the school grounds. Rarely did all eight of the Saints manage to leave school at the same time. The average number avoiding school on the days I observed them was five.

Having escaped from the concrete corridors, the boys usually went either to a pool hall on the other (lower-class) side of town or to a cafe in the suburbs. Both places were out of the way of people the boys were likely to know (family or school officials), and both provided a source of entertainment. The pool hall entertainment was the generally rough atmosphere, the occasional hustler, the sometimes drunk proprietor and, of course, the game of pool. The cafe's entertainment was provided by the owner. The boys would "accidentally" knock a glass on the floor or spill cola on the counter—not all the time, but enough to be sporting. They would also bend spoons, put salt in sugar bowls, and generally tease whoever was working in the cafe. The owner had opened the cafe recently and was dependent on the boys' business, which was, in fact, substantial because in between the horsing around and the teasing, they bought food and drinks.

THE SAINTS ON WEEKENDS

On weekends, the automobile was even more critical than during the week, for on weekends the Saints went to Big Town—a large city with a population of over a million 25 miles from Hanibal. Every Friday and Saturday night, most of the Saints would meet between 8:00 and 8:30 and would go into Big Town. Big Town activities included drinking heavily in taverns or nightclubs, driving drunkenly through the streets, and committing acts of vandalism and playing pranks.

By midnight on Fridays and Saturdays, the Saints were usually thoroughly high, and one or two of them were often so drunk they had to be carried to the car. Then the boys drove around town, calling obscenities to women and girls; occasionally trying (unsuccessfully so far as I could tell) to pick girls up; and driving recklessly through red lights and at high speeds with their lights out. Occasionally they played "chicken." One boy would climb out the back window of the car and across the roof to the driver's side of the car while the car was moving at high speed (between 40 and 50 miles an hour); then the driver would move over and the boy who had just crawled across the car roof would take the driver's seat.

Searching for "fair game" for a prank was the boys' principal activity after they left the tavern. The boys would drive alongside a foot patrolman and ask directions to some street. If the policeman leaned on the car in the course of answering the question, the driver would speed away, causing him to lose his balance. The Saints were careful to play this prank only in an area where they were not going to spend much time and where they could quickly disappear around a corner to avoid having their license plate number taken.

Construction sites and road repair areas were the special province of the Saints' mischief. A soon-to-be-repaired hole in the road inevitably invited the Saints to remove lanterns and wooden barricades and put them in the car, leaving the hole unprotected. The boys would find a safe vantage point and wait for an unsuspecting motorist to drive into the hole. Often, although not always, the boys would go up to the motorist and commiserate with him about the dreadful way the city protected its citizenry.

Leaving the scene of the open hole and the motorist, the boys would then go searching for an appropriate place to erect the stolen barricade. An "appropriate place" was often a spot on a highway near a curve in the road where the barricade would not be seen by an oncoming motorist. The boys would wait to watch an unsuspecting motorist attempt to stop and (usually) crash into the wooden barricade. With saintly bearing, the boys might offer help and understanding.

A stolen lantern might well find its way onto the back of a police car or hang from a street lamp. Once a lantern served as a prop for a reenactment of the "midnight ride of Paul Revere" until the "play," which was taking place at 2:00 A.M. in the center of a main street of Big Town, was interrupted by a police car several blocks away. The boys ran, leaving the lanterns on the street, and managed to avoid being apprehended.

Abandoned houses, especially if they were located in out-of-the-way places, were fair game for destruction and spontaneous vandalism. The boys would break windows, remove furniture to the yard and tear it apart, urinate on the walls, and scrawl obscenities inside.

Through all the pranks, drinking, and reckless driving, the boys managed miraculously to avoid being stopped by police. Only twice in two years was I aware that they had been stopped by a Big Town policeman. Once was for speeding (which they did every time they drove, whether they were drunk or sober), and the driver managed to convince the policeman that it was simply an error. The second time they were stopped they had just left a nightclub and were walking through an alley. Aaron stopped to urinate and the boys began making obscene remarks. A foot patrolman came into the alley, lectured the boys, and sent them home. Before the boys got to the car, one began talking in a loud voice again. The policeman, who had followed them down the alley, arrested this boy for disturbing the peace and took him to the police station where the other Saints gathered. After paying a $5.00 fine, and with the assurance that there would be no permanent record of the arrest, the boy was released.

The boys had a spirit of frivolity and fun about their escapades. They did not view what they were engaged in as "delinquency," although it surely was by any reasonable definition of that word. They simply viewed themselves as having a little fun and who, they would ask, was really hurt by it? The answer had to be no one, although this fact remains one of the most difficult things to explain about the gang's behavior. Unlikely though

it seems, in two years of drinking, driving, carousing, and vandalism, no one was seriously injured as a result of the Saints' activities.

THE SAINTS IN SCHOOL

The Saints were highly successful in school. The average grade for the group was B, with two of the boys having close to a straight A average. Almost all the boys were popular, and many of them held offices in the school. One of the boys was vice-president of the student body one year. Six of the boys played on athletic teams.

At the end of their senior year, the student body selected ten seniors for special recognition as the "school wheels"; four of the ten were Saints. Teachers and school officials saw no problem with any of these boys and anticipated that they would all "make something of themselves."

How the boys managed to maintain this impression is surprising in view of their actual behavior while in school. Their technique for covering truancy was so successful that teachers did not even realize that the boys were absent from school much of the time. Occasionally, of course, the system would backfire and then the boy was on his own. A boy who was caught would be most contrite, would plead guilty and ask for mercy. He inevitably got the mercy he sought.

Cheating on examinations was rampant, even to the point of orally communicating answers to exams as well as looking at one another's papers. Because none of the group studied and because they were primarily dependent on one another for help, it is surprising that grades were so high. Teachers contributed to the deception in their admitted inclination to give these boys (and presumably others like them) the benefit of the doubt. When asked how the boys did in school, and when pressed on specific examinations, teachers might admit that they were disappointed in John's performance, but would quickly add that they "knew that he was capable of doing better," so John was given a higher grade than he had actually earned. How often this happened is impossible to know. During the time I observed the group, I never saw any of the boys take homework home. Teachers may have been "understanding" very regularly....

THE POLICE AND THE SAINTS

The local police saw the Saints as good boys who were among the leaders of the youth in the community. Rarely, the boys might be stopped in town for speeding or for running a stop sign. When this happened, the boys were always polite, contrite, and pled for mercy. As in school, they received the mercy they asked for. None ever received a ticket or was taken into the precinct by the local police.

The situation in Big Town, where the boys engaged in most of their delinquency, was only slightly different. The police there did not know the boys at all, although occasionally the boys were stopped by a patrolman. Once they were caught taking a lantern from a construction site. Another time they were stopped for running a stop sign, and on several occasions they were stopped for speeding. Their behavior was as before: contrite, polite, and penitent. The urban police, like the local police, accepted their demeanor as sincere. More important, the urban police were convinced that these were good boys just out for a lark.

THE ROUGHNECKS

Hanibal townspeople never perceived the Saints' high level of delinquency. The Saints were good boys who just went in for an occasional prank. After all, they were well dressed, well mannered, and had nice cars. The Roughnecks were a different story. Although the two gangs of boys were the same age, and both groups engaged in an equal amount of wild-oat sowing, everyone agreed that the not-so-well-dressed, not-so-well-mannered, not-so-rich boys were heading for trouble. Townspeople would say, "You can see the gang members at the drugstore, night after night, leaning against the storefront (sometimes drunk) or slouching around inside buying cokes, reading magazines, and probably stealing old Mr. Wall blind. When they are outside and girls walk by, even respectable girls, these boys make suggestive remarks. Sometimes their remarks are downright lewd."

From the community's viewpoint, the real indication that these kids were in for trouble was that they were constantly involved with the police. Some of them had been picked up for stealing, mostly small stuff, of course, "but still, it's stealing small stuff that leads to big-time crimes." "Too bad," people said. "Too bad that these boys couldn't behave like the other kids in town; stay out of trouble, be polite to adults, and look to their future."

The community's impression of the degree to which this group of six boys (ranging in age from 16 to 19) engaged in delinquency was somewhat distorted. In some ways, the gang was more delinquent than the community thought; in other ways, they were less.

The fighting activities of the group were fairly readily and accurately perceived by almost everyone. At least once a month, the boys would get into some sort of fight, although most fights were scraps between members of the group or involved only one member of the group and some peripheral hanger-on. Only three times in the period of observation did the group fight together: once against a gang from across town, once against two blacks, and once against a group of boys from another school. For the first two fights, the group went out "looking for trouble"—and they found it both times. The third fight followed a football game and began spontaneously with an argument on the football field between one of the Roughnecks and a member of the opposition's football team.

Jack had a particular propensity for fighting and was involved in most of the brawls. He was a prime mover of the escalation of arguments into fights.

More serious than fighting, had the community been aware of it, was theft. Although almost everyone was aware that the boys occasionally stole things, they did not realize the extent of the activity. Petty stealing was a frequent event for the Roughnecks. Sometimes they stole as a group and coordinated their efforts; other times they stole in pairs. Rarely did they steal alone.

The thefts ranged from very small things like paperback books, comics, and ballpoint pens to expensive items like watches. The nature of the thefts varied from time to time. The gang would go through a period of systematically shoplifting items from automobiles or school lockers. Types of thievery varied with the whim of the gang.

Some forms of thievery were more profitable than others, but all thefts were for profit, not just thrills.

Roughnecks siphoned gasoline from cars as often as they had access to an automobile, which was not very often. Unlike the Saints, who owned their own cars, the Roughnecks would have to borrow their parents' cars, an event which occurred only eight or nine times a year. The boys claimed to have stolen cars for joy rides from time to time....

The Roughnecks, then, engaged mainly in three types of delinquency: theft, drinking, and fighting. Although community members perceived that this gang of kids was delinquent, they mistakenly believed that their illegal activities were primarily drinking, fighting, and being a nuisance to passersby. Drinking was limited among the gang members, although it did occur, and theft was much more prevalent than anyone realized.

Drinking would doubtless have been more prevalent had the boys had ready access to liquor. Because they rarely had automobiles at their disposal, they could not travel very far, and the bars in town would not serve them. Most of the boys had little money, and this, too, inhibited their purchase of alcohol. Their major source of liquor was a local drunk who would buy them a fifth if they would give him enough extra to buy himself a pint of whiskey or a bottle of wine.

The community's perception of drinking as prevalent stemmed from the fact that it was the most obvious delinquency the boys engaged in. When one of the boys had been drinking, even a casual observer seeing him on the corner would suspect that he was high.

There was a high level of mutual distrust and dislike between the Roughnecks and the police. The boys felt very strongly that the police were unfair and corrupt. Some evidence existed that the boys were correct in their perception.

The main source of the boys' dislike for the police undoubtedly stemmed from the fact that the police would sporadically harass the group. From the standpoint of the boys, these acts of occasional enforcement of the law were whimsical and uncalled for. It made no sense to them, for example, that the police would come to the corner occasionally and threaten them with arrest for loitering when the night before the boys had been out siphoning gasoline from cars and the police had been nowhere in sight. To the boys, the police were stupid on the one hand, for not being where they should have been and catching the boys in a serious offense, and unfair on the other hand, for trumping up "loitering" charges against them.

From the viewpoint of the police, the situation was quite different. They knew, with all the confidence necessary to be a policeman, that these boys were engaged in criminal activities. They knew this partly from occasionally catching them, mostly from circumstantial evidence ("the boys were around when those tires were slashed"), and partly because the police shared the view of the community in general that this was a bad bunch of boys. The best the police could hope to do was to be sensitive to the fact that these boys were engaged in illegal acts and arrest them whenever there was some evidence that they had been involved. Whether or not the boys had in fact committed a particular act in a particular way was not especially important. The police had a broader view: Their job was to stamp out these kids' crimes; the tactics were not as important as the end result.

Over the period that the group was under observation, each member was arrested at least once. Several of the boys were arrested a number of times and spent at least one night in jail. Although most were never taken to court, two of the boys were sentenced to six months' incarceration in boys' schools.

THE ROUGHNECKS IN SCHOOL

The Roughnecks' behavior in school was not particularly disruptive. During school hours, they did not all hang around together, but tended instead to spend most of their time with one or two other members of the gang who were their special buddies. Although every member of the gang attempted to avoid school as much as possible, they were not particularly successful, and most of them attended school with surprising regularity. They considered school a burden—something to be gotten through with a minimum of conflict. If they were "bugged" by a particular teacher, it could lead to trouble. One of the boys, Al, once threatened to beat up a teacher and, according to the other boys, the teacher hid under a desk to escape him.

Teachers saw the boys the way the general community did, as heading for trouble, as being uninterested in making something of themselves. Some were also seen as being incapable of meeting the academic standards of the school. Most of the teachers expressed concern for this group of boys and were willing to pass them despite poor performance, in the belief that failing them would only aggravate the problem.

The group of boys had a grade point average just slightly above C. No one in the group failed either grade, and no one had better than a C average. They were very consistent in their achievement or, at least, the teachers were consistent in their perception of the boys' achievement.

Two of the boys were good football players. Herb was acknowledged to be the best player in the school, and Jack was almost as good. Both boys were criticized for their failure to abide by training rules, for refusing to come to practice as often as they should, and for not playing their best during practice. What they lacked in sportsmanship they made up for in skill, apparently, and played every game no matter how poorly they had performed in practice or how many practice sessions they had missed.

TWO QUESTIONS

Why did the community, the school, and the police react to the Saints as though they were good, upstanding, nondelinquent youths with bright futures but to the Roughnecks as though they were tough, young criminals who were headed for trouble? Why did the Roughnecks and the Saints in fact have quite different careers after high school—careers which, by and large, lived up to the expectations of the community?

The most obvious explanation for the differences in the community's and law enforcement agencies' reactions to the two gangs is that one group of boys was "more delinquent" than the other. Which group *was* more delinquent? The answer to this question will determine in part how we explain the differential responses to these

groups by the members of the community and, particularly, by law enforcement and school officials.

In sheer number of illegal acts, the Saints were the more delinquent. They were truant from school for at least part of the day almost every day of the week. In addition, their drinking and vandalism occurred with surprising regularity. The Roughnecks, in contrast, engaged sporadically in delinquent episodes. Although these episodes were frequent, they certainly did not occur on a daily or even a weekly basis.

The difference in frequency of offenses was probably caused by the Roughnecks' inability to obtain liquor and to manipulate legitimate excuses from school. Because the Roughnecks had less money than the Saints, and teachers carefully supervised their school activities, the Roughnecks' hearts may have been as [evil] as the Saints', but their misdeeds were not nearly as frequent.

There are really no clear-cut criteria by which to measure qualitative differences in antisocial behavior. The most important dimension of the difference is generally referred to as the "seriousness" of the offenses.

If seriousness encompasses the relative economic costs of delinquent acts, then some assessment can be made. The Roughnecks probably stole an average of about $5.00 worth of goods a week. Some weeks, the figure was considerably higher, but these times must be balanced against long periods when almost nothing was stolen.

The Saints were more continuously engaged in delinquency, but their acts were not for the most part costly to property. Only their vandalism and occasional theft of gasoline would so qualify. Perhaps once or twice a month, they would siphon a tankful of gas. The other costly items were street signs, construction lanterns, and the like. All these acts combined probably did not quite average $5.00 a week, partly because much of the stolen equipment was abandoned and presumably could be recovered. The difference in cost of stolen property between the two groups was trivial, but the Roughnecks probably had a slightly more expensive set of activities than did the Saints.

Another meaning of seriousness is the potential threat of physical harm to members of the community and to the boys themselves. The

Roughnecks were more prone to physical violence; they not only welcomed an opportunity to fight, they went seeking it. In addition, they fought among themselves frequently. Although the fighting never included deadly weapons, it was still a menace, however minor, to the physical safety of those involved.

The Saints never fought. They avoided physical conflict both inside and outside the group. At the same time, however, the Saints frequently endangered their own and other people's lives. They did so almost every time they drove a car, especially if they had been drinking. Sober, their driving was risky; under the influence of alcohol, it was horrendous. In addition, the Saints endangered the lives of others with their pranks. Street excavations left unmarked were a very serious hazard.

Evaluating the relative seriousness of the two gangs' activities is difficult. The community reacted as though the behavior of the Roughnecks was a problem, and they reacted as though the behavior of the Saints was not. But the members of the community were ignorant of the array of delinquent acts that characterized the Saints' behavior. Although concerned citizens were unaware of much of the Roughnecks' behavior as well, they were much better informed about the Roughnecks' involvement in delinquency than they were about the Saints'.

VISIBILITY

Differential treatment of the two gangs resulted in part because one gang was infinitely more visible than the other. This differential visibility was a direct function of the economic standing of the families. The Saints had access to automobiles and were able to remove themselves from the sight of the community. In as routine a decision as to where to go to have a milkshake after school, the Saints stayed away from the mainstream of community life. Lacking transportation, the Roughnecks could not make it to the edge of town. The center of town was the only practical place for them to meet because their homes were scattered throughout the town and any noncentral meeting place put an undue hardship on some members. Through necessity, the

Roughnecks congregated in a crowded area where everyone in the community passed frequently, including teachers and law enforcement officers. They could easily see the Roughnecks hanging around the drugstore.

The Roughnecks, of course, made themselves even more visible by making remarks to passersby and by occasionally getting into fights on the corner. Meanwhile, just as regularly, the Saints were either at the cafe on one edge of town or in the pool hall at the other edge of town. Without any particular realization that they were making themselves inconspicuous, the Saints were able to hide their time-wasting. Not only were they removed from the mainstream of traffic, but they were almost always inside a building.

On their escapades, the Saints were also relatively invisible because they left Hanibal and traveled to Big Town. Here, too, they were mobile, roaming the city, rarely going to the same area twice.

DEMEANOR

To the notion of visibility must be added the difference in the responses of group members to outside intervention with their activities. If one of the Saints was confronted with an accusing policeman, even if he felt he was truly innocent of a wrongdoing, his demeanor was apologetic and penitent. A Roughneck's attitude was almost the polar opposite. When confronted with a threatening adult authority, even one who tried to be pleasant, the Roughneck's hostility and disdain were clearly observable. Sometimes he might attempt to put up a veneer of respect, but it was thin and was not accepted as sincere by the authority.

School was no different from the community at large. The Saints could manipulate the system by reigning compliance with the school norms. The availability of cars at school meant that once free from the immediate sight of the teacher, the boys could disappear rapidly. And this escape was well-enough planned that no administrator or teacher was nearby when the boys left. A Roughneck who wished to escape for a few hours was in a bind. If it were possible to get free from class, downtown was still a mile away, and even if he arrived there, he was still very visible. Truancy for the Roughnecks meant almost certain detection, while the Saints enjoyed almost complete immunity from sanctions.

BIAS

Community members were not aware of the transgressions of the Saints. Even if the Saints had been less discreet, their favorite delinquencies would have been perceived as less serious than those of the Roughnecks.

In the eyes of the police and school officials, a boy who drinks in an alley and stands intoxicated on the street corner is committing a more serious offense than is a boy who drinks to inebriation in a nightclub or a tavern and drives around afterwards in a car. Similarly, a boy who steals a wallet from a store will be viewed as having committed a more serious offense than a boy who steals a lantern from a construction site.

Perceptual bias also operates with respect to the demeanor of the boys in the two groups when they are confronted by adults. It is not simply that adults dislike the posture affected by boys of the Roughneck ilk; more important is the conviction that the posture adopted by the Roughnecks is an indication of their devotion and commitment to deviance as a way of life. The posture becomes a cue, just as the type of the offense is a cue, to the degree to which the known transgressions are indicators of the youths' potential for other problems.

Visibility, demeanor, and bias are surface variables that explain the day-to-day operations of the police. Why do these surface variables operate as they do? Why did the police choose to disregard the Saints' delinquencies while breathing down the backs of the Roughnecks?

The answer lies in the class structure of American society and the control of legal institutions by those at the top of the class structure. Obviously, no representative of the upper class drew up the operational chart for the police that led them to look in the ghettoes and on street corners—which led them to see the demeanor of lower-class youth as troublesome and that of upper-middle-class youth as tolerable. Rather, the procedures simply developed from experience—experience with irate and influential upper-middle-class parents insisting that their

son's vandalism was simply a prank and his drunkenness only a momentary "sowing of wild oats"—experience with cooperative or indifferent, powerless, lower-class parents who acquiesced to the laws' definition of their son's behavior.

ADULT CAREERS OF THE SAINTS AND THE ROUGHNECKS

The community's confidence in the potential of the Saints and the Roughnecks apparently was justified. If anything, the community members underestimated the degree to which these youngsters would turn out "good" or "bad."

Seven of the eight members of the Saints went on to college immediately after high school. Five of the boys graduated from college in four years. The sixth one finished college after two years in the army, and the seventh spent four years in the air force before returning to college and receiving a B.A. degree. Of these seven college graduates, three went on for advanced degrees: One finished law school and is now active in state politics, one finished medical school and is practicing near Hanibal, and one boy is now working for a Ph.D. The other four college graduates entered submanagerial, managerial, or executive training positions with larger firms.

The only Saint who did not complete college was Jerry. Jerry had failed to graduate from high school with the other Saints. During his second senior year, after the other Saints had gone on to college, Jerry began to hang around with what several teachers described as a "rough crowd"—the gang that was heir apparent to the Roughnecks. At the end of his second senior year, when he did graduate from high school, Jerry took a job as a used car salesman, got married, and quickly had a child. Although he made several abortive attempts to go to college by attending night school, when I last saw him (ten years after high school), Jerry was unemployed and had been living on unemployment for almost a year. His wife worked as a waitress.

Some of the Roughnecks have lived up to community expectations. A number of them were headed for trouble. A few were not.

Jack and Herb were the athletes among the Roughnecks, and their athletic prowess paid off handsomely. Both boys received unsolicited athletic scholarships to college. After Herb received his scholarship (near the end of his senior year), he apparently did an about-face. His demeanor became very similar to that of the Saints. Although he remained a member in good standing of the Roughnecks, he stopped participating in most activities and did not hang on the corner as often.

Jack did not change. If anything, he became more prone to fighting. He even made excuses for accepting the scholarship. He told the other gang members that the school had guaranteed him a C average if he would come to play football—an idea that seems far-fetched, even in this day of highly competitive recruiting.

During the summer after graduation from high school, Jack attempted suicide by jumping from a tall building. The jump would certainly have killed most people trying it, but Jack survived. He entered college in the fall and played four years of football. He and Herb graduated in four years, and both are teaching and coaching in high schools. They are married and have stable families. If anything, Jack appears to have a more prestigious position in the community than does Herb, though both are well respected and secure in their positions.

Two of the boys never finished high school. Tommy left at the end of his junior year and went to another state. That summer he was arrested and placed on probation on a manslaughter charge. Three years later, he was arrested for murder; he pleaded guilty to second-degree murder and is serving a 30—year sentence in the state penitentiary.

Al, the other boy who did not finish high school, also left the state in his senior year. He is serving a life sentence in a state penitentiary for first-degree murder.

Wes is a small-time gambler. He finished high school and "bummed around." After several years, he made contact with a bookmaker who employed him as a runner. Later he acquired his own area and has been working it ever since. His position among the bookmakers is almost identical to the position he had in the gang; he is always around, but no one is really aware of him. He makes no trouble, and he does not get into any. Steady, reliable, capable of keeping his mouth closed, he plays the game by the rules, even though the game is an illegal one.

That leaves only Ron. Some of his former friends reported that they had heard he was "driving a truck up north," but no one could provide any concrete information.

REINFORCEMENT

The community responded to the Roughnecks as boys in trouble, and the boys agreed with that perception. Their pattern of deviancy was reinforced, and breaking away from it became increasingly unlikely. Once the boys acquired an image of themselves as deviants, they selected new friends who affirmed that self-image. As that self-conception became more firmly entrenched, they also became willing to try new and more extreme deviances. With their growing alienation came freer expression of disrespect and hostility for representatives of the legitimate society. This disrespect increased the community's negativism, perpetuating the entire process of commitment to deviance. Lack of a commitment to deviance works the same way. In either case, the process will perpetuate itself unless some event (like a scholarship to college or a sudden failure) external to the established relationship intervenes. For two of the Roughnecks (Herb and Jack), receiving college athletic scholarships created new relations and culminated in a break with the established pattern of deviance. In the case of one of the Saints (Jerry), his parents' divorce and his failing to graduate from high school changed some of his other relations. Being held back in school for a year and losing his place among the Saints had sufficient impact on Jerry to alter his self-image and virtually ensure that he would not go on to college as his peers did. Although the experiments of life can rarely be reversed, it seems likely in view of the behavior of the other boys who did not enjoy this special treatment by the school that Jerry, too, would have "become something" had he graduated as anticipated. For Herb and Jack, outside intervention worked to their advantage; for Jerry it was his undoing.

Selective perception and labeling—finding, processing, and punishing some kinds of criminality and not others—means that visible, poor, nonmobile, outspoken, undiplomatic, "tough" kids will be noticed, whether their actions are seriously delinquent or not. Other kids, who have established a reputation for being bright (even though underachieving), disciplined, and involved in respectable activities, who are mobile and moneyed, will be invisible when they deviate from sanctioned activities. They'll sow their wild oats—perhaps even wider and thicker than their lower-class cohorts—but they won't be noticed.

When it's time to leave adolescence, most will follow the expected path, settling into the ways of the middle class, remembering fondly the delinquent but unnoticed fling of their youth. The Roughnecks and others like them may turn around, too. [But] it is more likely that their noticeable deviance will have been so reinforced by police and community that their lives will be effectively channeled into careers consistent with their adolescent background.

46. SOCIETY, CRIME, AND PUNISHMENT

EMILE DURKHEIM

...since there cannot be a society in which the individuals do not differ more or less from the collective type, it is also inevitable that, among these divergences, there are some with a criminal character. What confers this character upon them is not the instrinsic quality of a given act but that definition which the collective conscience leads them.

Durkheim makes the case that crime is an integral part of society as long as there are rules. Crime may even contribute to change in society, and give the criminal a definite positive role in society.

Crime is present not only in the majority of societies of one particular species but in all societies of all types. There is no society that is not confronted with the problem of criminality. Its form changes; the acts thus characterized are not the same everywhere; but, everywhere and always, there have been men who have behaved in such a way as to draw upon themselves penal repression....

No doubt it is possible that crime itself will have abnormal forms, as, for example, when its rate is unusually high. This excess is, indeed, undoubtedly morbid in nature. What is normal, simply, is the existence of criminality, provided that it attains and does not exceed, for each social type, a certain level, which it is perhaps not impossible to fix in conformity with the preceding rules.[1]

Here we are, then, in the presence of a conclusion in appearance quite paradoxical. Let us make no mistake. To classify crime among the phenomena of normal sociology is not to say merely that it is an inevitable, although regrettable phenomenon, due to the incorrigible wickedness of men; it is to affirm that it is a factor in public health, an integral part of all healthy societies. This result is, at first glance, surprising enough to have puzzled even ourselves for a long time. Once this first surprise has been overcome, however, it is not difficult to find reasons explaining this normality and at the same time confirming it.

In the first place crime is normal because a society exempt from it is utterly impossible. Crime, we have shown elsewhere, consists of an act that offends certain very strong collective sentiments. In a society in which criminal acts are no longer committed, the sentiments they offend would have to be found without exception in all individual consciousnesses, and they must be found to exist with the same degree as sentiments contrary to them. Assuming that this condition could actually be realized, crime would not thereby disappear; it would only change its form, for the very cause which would thus dry up the sources of criminality would immediately open up new ones....

Imagine a society of saints, a perfect cloister of exemplary individuals. Crimes, properly so called, will there be unknown; but faults which appear venial to the layman will create there the same scandal that the ordinary offense does in ordinary consciousness. If, then, this society has the power to judge and punish, it will define these acts as criminal and will treat them as such. For the same reason, the perfect and upright man judges his smallest failings with a severity that the majority reserve for acts more truly in the nature of an offense. Formerly, acts of violence against persons were more frequent than they are today, because respect for individual dignity was less strong. As this has increased, these crimes have become more rare; and also, many acts violating this sentiment have been introduced into the penal law which were not included there in primitive times.[2]

In order to exhaust all the hypotheses logically possible, it will perhaps be asked why this unanimity does not extend to all collective sentiments without exception. Why should not even the most feeble sentiment gather enough energy to prevent all dissent? The moral consciousness of the society would be present in its entirety in all the individuals, with a vitality sufficient to prevent all acts offending it—the purely conventional faults as well as the crimes. But a uniformity so universal and absolute is utterly impossible; for the immediate physical milieu in which each one of us is placed, the hereditary antecedents, and the social influences vary from one individual to the next, and consequently diversify consciousnesses. It is impossible for all to be alike, if

only because each one has his own organism and that these organisms occupy different areas in space. That is why, even among the lower peoples, where individual originality is very little developed, it nevertheless does exist.

Thus, since there cannot be a society in which the individuals do not differ more or less from the collective type, it is also inevitable that, among these divergences, there are some with a criminal character. What confers this character upon them is not the intrinsic quality of a given act but that definition which the collective conscience lends them. If the collective conscience is stronger, if it has enough authority practically to suppress these divergences, it will also be more sensitive, more exacting; and, reacting against the slightest deviations with the energy it otherwise displays only against more considerable infractions, it will attribute to them the same gravity as formerly to crimes. In other words, it will designate them as criminal.

Crime is, then, necessary; it is bound up with fundamental conditions of all social life, and by that very fact it is useful, because these conditions of which it is part are themselves indispensable to the normal evolution of morality and law.... Every pattern is an obstacle to new patterns, to the extent that the first pattern is inflexible. The better a structure is articulated, the more it offers a healthy resistance to all modification; and this is equally true of functional, as of anatomical, organization. If there were no crimes, this condition could not have been fulfilled; for such a hypothesis presupposes that collective sentiments have arrived at a degree of intensity unexampled in history. Nothing is good indefinitely and to an unlimited extent. The authority which the moral conscience enjoys must not be excessive; otherwise no one would dare criticize it, and it would too easily congeal into an immutable form. To make progress, individual originality must be able to express itself. In order that the originality of the idealist whose dreams transcend his century may find expression, it is necessary that the originality of the criminal, who is below the level of his time, shall also be possible. One does not occur without the other.

Nor is this all. Aside from this indirect utility, it happens that crime itself plays a useful role in this evolution. Crime implies not only that the way remains open to necessary changes but that in certain cases it directly prepares these changes. Where crime exists, collective sentiments are sufficiently flexible to take on a new form, and crime sometimes helps to determine the form they will take. How many times, indeed, it is only an anticipation of future morality—a step toward what will be! According to Athenian law, Socrates was a criminal, and his condemnation was no more that just. However, his crime, namely, the independence of his thought, rendered a service not only to humanity but to his country. It served to prepare a new morality and faith which the Athenians needed, since the traditions by which they had lived until then were no longer in harmony with the current conditions of life. Nor is the case of Socrates unique; it is reproduced periodically in history. It would never have been possible to establish the freedom of thought we now enjoy if the regulations prohibiting it had not been violated before being solemnly abrogated. At that time, however, the violation was a crime, since it was an offense against sentiments still very keen in the average conscience. And yet this crime was useful as a prelude to reforms which daily became more necessary. Liberal philosophy had as its precursors the heretics of all kinds who were justly punished by secular authorities during the entire course of the Middle Ages and until the eve of modern times.

From this point of view the fundamental facts of criminality present themselves to us in an entirely new light. Contrary to current ideas, the criminal no longer seems a totally unsociable being, a sort of parasitic element, a strange and unassimilable body, introduced into the midst of society.[3] On the contrary, he plays a definite role in social life. Crime, for its part, must no longer be conceived as an evil that cannot be too much suppressed. There is no occasion for self-congratulation when the crime rate drops noticeably below the average level, for we may be certain that this apparent progress is associated with some social disorder. Thus, the number of assault cases never falls so low as in times of want.[4] With the drop in the crime rate, and as a reaction to it, comes a revision, or the need of a revision in the theory of punishment. If, indeed, crime is a disease, its punishment is its remedy and cannot be otherwise conceived; thus, all the discussions it arouses bear on the point of determining what the punishment must be in order to fulfill this role of remedy. If crime is not pathological at all, the object of punishment cannot be to cure it, and its true function must be sought elsewhere.

NOTES

1. From the fact that crime is a phenomenon of normal sociology, it does not follow that the criminal is an individual normally constituted from the biological and psychological points of view. The two questions are independent of each other. This independence will be better understood when we have shown, later on, the difference between psychological and sociological facts.
2. Calumny, insults, slander, fraud, etc.
3. We have ourselves committed the error of speaking thus of the criminal, because of a failure to apply our rule (*Division du travail social*, pp. 395–96).
4. Although crime is a fact of normal sociology, it does not follow that we must not abhor it. Pain itself has nothing desirable about it; the individual dislikes it as society does crime, and yet it is a function of normal physiology. Not only is it necessarily derived from the very constitution of every living organism, but it plays a useful role in life, for which reason it cannot be replaced. It would, then, be a singular distortion of our thought to present it as an apology for crime. We would not even think of protesting against such an interpretation, did we not know to what strange accusations and misunderstandings one exposes oneself when one undertakes to study moral facts objectively and to speak of them in a different language from that of the layman.

47. DIVERSITY, INEQUALITY AND SOCIAL ORDER

HENRY A. WALKER, PHYLLIS MOEN,
and DONNA DEMPSTER-MCCLAIN

Diversity and equality are uncomfortable bedfellows. Social and economic inequalities regularly accompany—and are interwoven with—categorical differences among people.... [The question confronting the United States is]: Can a nation in which inequality is enmeshed with diversity maintain and/or establish a sense of community?

The authors show us diversity among people in society usually brings about inequality, and both diversity and inequality may work against a sense of a community. The United States is a society of diversity, inequality, and division. To some thinkers—assimilationists—the solution is the erasing of group differences. To others—the pluralists—there must be respect for differences without inequality. This disagreement characterizes much of the ongoing debates that characterize American society today.

America is a nation of uncommon racial, ethnic, and cultural *diversity*. It is also characterized by substantial social and economic *inequality*. This book, in an effort to provide a fresh look at diversity, inequality, and community in American society, offers a sociological perspective on the challenges that contemporary intergroup relations pose for life in the twenty-first century.[1]

Diversity and inequality stand at the center of contemporary public policy debates. Can we have one without the other? Will greater diversity accompanying recent changes in the pace and character of immigration benefit or harm the nation? Before the immigration reforms of the 1960s, the overwhelming majority of newcomers were white and European. Today, 80 percent of immigrants come from Asian or Latin American countries. Many Americans express concern that the "new" immigrants will not "fit in." Some even argue that they will disrupt and eventually destroy "the American way of life." This pessimistic view is countered by others who claim that continued immigration is not only beneficial but essential to the nation's vitality.[2]

On the economic front, will rising inequalities further divide and destabilize American society? The evolution of a global marketplace has had paradoxical effects on American society, with the rich getting richer and the poor getting poorer. These developments, along with the concerted efforts of many public officials to reduce social welfare costs, have widened the chasm between those on the lower rungs of the economic ladder and those at the top. Many fear that growing economic disparity divides the national community, fostering not only greater economic inequality but also fueling social unrest and instability.

From Henry A. Walker, Phyllis Moen, and Donna Dempster-McClain, eds. "Introduction," in *A Nation Divided: Diversity, Inequality, and Community in American Society.* Copyright © 1999 by Cornell University. Used by permission of the publisher, Cornell University Press.

287

Diversity and equality are uncomfortable bed-fellows. Social and economic inequalities regularly accompany—and are interwoven with—categorical differences among people. Wherever people differ on nominal characteristics (e.g., race, gender), they also possess different amounts of the things societies value. As an example, members of ethnic group A get more or less education, more or less income than those in group B. Charles Tilly (1999) calls patterns of this sort *durable inequalities*. Durable inequalities have important effects on life chances and choices, as well as on the prospect for national cohesion and community....

AMERICA: DIFFERENT BY DESIGN?

Can a nation in which inequality is enmeshed with diversity maintain and/or establish a sense of community? The American founders struggled mightily with this question. Their vantage point was the world they had fled—a world in which substantial economic and social inequalities were endemic. Much of the strife that typified European nations in the seventeenth and eighteenth centuries was grounded in ethnic, religious, and class differences.

The founders took two bold steps to ensure that they would live in a far different world. First, they created a society based on a unique set of organizing principles. Its founding documents proclaimed the "natural" equality of its members, possessing "unalienable rights to life, liberty, and the pursuit of happiness." The founders' second initiative was even bolder. They held that the new nation would shelter and nurture a new "race" of people—the Americans—drawing its members from every corner of the globe. In America, every *man* would be free—free to express himself, free of religious favoritism and persecution—and equal. We retain the language of the founders to emphasize a cardinal point: the founders equated Americans with "men," defined as white, free, property owners, aged twenty-one or older. These definitions were disputed *before* they were included in the founding documents and have been subjected since to continuing revision. *Every* debate about admitting new

categories of persons to citizenship is a debate about who is to be regarded as an American (see also Bem 1999).

The founders established the legal equality of (some, but not all) diverse peoples. Any person admitted to citizenship expected—and had the right to demand—civil, social, and political rights (Marshall 1949) equal to those held by any other citizen. Whether the founders took those steps to reduce the potential for intergroup friction and discord is unclear. Obviously, their actions did not eliminate or prevent—and in some case even ensured—the development of durable inequalities across race, class, and gender lines.

As a consequence, the American people are both diverse *and* divided. They differ along common divisions such as race, ethnic heritage, religion, and gender. They differ as well on dimensions that have always existed but have only recently entered the public discourse, dimensions such as sexual orientation and patterns of family life. Many of these categorical differences are linked to durable social and economic inequalities, thus fostering divisiveness. Groups of Americans who have less of some socially valued good than their fellows—whether income or respect—express discontent with their position and, increasingly, disaffection with the American ideal. Their disenchantment has been translated into political action with increasing frequency.[3] This is not to say that American society is coming apart at the seams, but the national fabric may well be in need of repair.

Current divisions exist in part because the founders did not extend legal equality to *all* persons. The denial of legal equality to some categories of persons (e.g., blacks, women, and American Indians) ensured the privileged position of white males as a "protected class." Since its founding, the American nation has come to extend civil, social, and political rights to many groups that were initially denied them. Impetus for the extension of rights lay in the tension between the national ethos and the practical, moral, and legal realities of life in American society. The presence of "Americans" without legal equality created a legitimization crisis—an American dilemma (Myrdal 1944) that called the American creed into question. How does a nation proclaim the "natural" equality of all its members but deny legal equality to some?

The extension of legal rights to groups that were initially denied them resolved one source of tension in American society. However, the acquisition of full rights of citizenship did not—indeed could not—ensure the elimination of durable inequalities that were a product of that initial legal inequality. Durable inequalities, once established, are difficult to eliminate. As a consequence, some durable inequalities persist despite the legal equality of races, ethnic groups, and women and men.[4]

American society, then, as both diverse and unequal, faces the challenge of fostering a sense of community. Most Americans subscribe to the dictum of *"e pluribus unum"* but differ on how to achieve it. Some presume that reducing or eliminating diversity is the key to establishing social harmony (Schlesinger 1992).[5] Others argue that governments can (and should) encourage *diversity* but eliminate *durable inequality*, thereby creating the conditions for a communal society (e.g., Takaki 1993).

GENERALIZING ACROSS TIME AND SPACE

The challenges created by the dynamic tensions between diversity, inequality, and community in American society are not new. Neither are they unique; a number of other nations face these same challenges. Moreover, as globalization proceeds and national and cultural systems converge (Inkeles 1998), the number of nations that face such problems will surely increase....

World historical patterns presage a global society in which durable inequalities based on race and cultural differences are likely to spread to societies that have had largely homogeneous populations. Immigration may trigger the development of durable inequalities, but it is not the sole determinant of the patterns of culturally or racially based inequalities found in contemporary America. As a consequence, whether American society can establish or maintain community also has implications for increasingly diverse societies across the globe.

THE PROBLEM OF SOCIAL INTEGRATION

Concerns about the effects of diversity and inequality on social stability illuminate a general sociological issue—the problem of *social integration* (Parsons 1951; Williams 1970). How is society possible (Simmel [1908] 1971)? How can a collection of individuals with different skills, abilities, and interests create an enduring collective life? How does a society achieve social integration (Parsons 1951)? These questions motivated the founders of modern sociology and intrigued their philosopher ancestors.

The first generation of sociologists did not agree about the processes that establish or maintain integrated communities, but they had clear ideas about the forms they take. Early sociologists identified two ideal-typical patterns of cohesive social relationships or societies. Durkheim ([1893] 1964) described them as systems of mechanical and organic solidarity; Tönnies (1957) called them *Gemeinschaft* and *Gesellschaft*. Weber (1968) used the terms "communal and associative relationships." Societies that exhibit mechanical solidarity (*Gemeinschaft* or communal societies) are generally small and made up of individuals who share a number of personal characteristics, attitudes, beliefs, and so on. Shared interests, beliefs, and actions are presumed to provide the social glue that holds such societies together. Societies characterized by organic solidarity (*Gesellschaft* or associative societies) are larger and contain more complex combinations of persons who differ with respect to a variety of individual characteristics, normative systems, attitudes, and so on. These more complex societies are held together by the *interdependence* of the individuals, groups, and institutions within them.

Those early ideas may have overstated the differences in the processes that hold societies (of any type) together. For example, it is clear that interdependence is an important source of cohesion for groups and societies of any size. It is also clear that similarities among group members on a variety of characteristics contribute (either directly or indirectly) to integration (i.e., communality) within groups or societies. Current ideas about how societies composed of diverse (and unequal) peoples can create community are based in, and consistent with, long-standing sociological analyses. Theory and research on ethnic and gender relations illustrate those ideas.

Ethnic Differences and Social Integration

Durable inequalities organized around ethnic differences are the rule in ethnically (or racially) diverse societies. Such inequalities are also correlated with ethnic tensions and conflicts. Sociologists and political scientists offer a number of arguments to explain the relationship between ethnic inequality and social conflict and disruption (Hannan 1979; Hechter 1975; Lipset and Rokkan 1967; Olzak 1992). Others suggest how ethnic harmony can be created or restored in culturally diverse societies (see also Williams, 1999). The *assimilationist* and *pluralist* models are especially germane to our discussion.

Social scientists use the term "assimilation" to describe both a process and its outcomes. Following Horowitz (1975), we define "assimilation" as a social process that results in the "erasing of group boundaries."[6] *Amalgamation* and *incorporation* are two distinct outcomes of assimilation processes (Horowitz 1975; Park and Burgess [1921] 1969). A nation or society that achieves amalgamation is one in which there exists a complete blending of dissimilar groups. The product of amalgamation may contain elements of each constituent group, but the amalgam is unlike any of the groups that entered the process. The "melting pot" ideal reflects the idea of amalgamation. On the other hand, societies that undergo incorporation are marked by a result that closely resembles (but may not be identical to) one of the constituent groups. The dominance of Anglo cultural forms in the United States is an example of incorporation. Neither differences in power nor invidious discrimination are necessary to produce incorporation, but discrimination and substantial differences in the relative power of assimilating groups can ensure it (see also Walker's arguments 1999).

The pluralist model describes societies in which distinct (racial or cultural) elements maintain their unique character but have equal civil, social, and political rights. As an example, distinct subcultural groups may share governmental institutions including national parliaments, universal taxing authorities, and common military services. However, each subcultural group may also maintain separate cultural, political, and economic institutions (e.g., ethnic religions, political parties, or occupational niches).

Gender Differences and Social Integration

The concepts and models used to describe ethnic differences can also be applied to the distinctive life course experiences of women and men. Consider, for example, occupational career paths, typically reflecting men's, not women's, experiences (Bem 1993; Moen 1998). The very notion of a "career," of moving through a series of related jobs over the life course, reflects a typically male biography.

As growing numbers of women (from every race, ethnic, age, and class category) began to enter, remain in, or reenter the work force, they were expected to become "like men," that is, to downplay family or other nonwork interests or obligations. Women were expected to follow an *assimilative* and, specifically, *incorporative* model of career development and progression. Sandra Lipsitz Bem (1999) raises questions about the social integration of both women and sexual minorities. She questions the incorporative form of assimilation and suggests alternative models. C. Wright Mills (1959) pointed out that a different arrangement existed in the past. Before the industrial revolution most people worked in either agriculture or other family businesses. Though there were divisions by age and gender, everyone in the household was engaged in productive work.

With industrialization, the new work career became synonymous with the male breadwinner template, although young women (and women of all ages in financial need) were also in the labor force. *Unpaid work*—domestic household labor, family caregiving, community volunteer participation—was rendered marginal to the "business" of society and, consequently, the business of mainstream social science. Such unpaid work has been disproportionately accomplished by women, perpetuating both women's marginal status and durable gender inequalities.

The heterogeneity embodied in women's life experiences (e.g., Moen, Dempster-McClain, and Williams 1989, 1992) and the distinctiveness of women's life paths compared with men's (e.g., Han and Moen 1999) demonstrate the difficulty of assimilating women into male templates. It also reframes the central question of this volume: shall we continue (or return to) an incorporative model of occupational careers or open ourselves to multiple patterns consistent with a pluralist model? The issue is how to integrate occupational, family, and community role pathways (for men as well as women) without perpetuating durable economic, status, and time inequalities based on gender.

IMPLICATIONS

The ongoing debates about managing diversity and "multiculturalism" can be described in assimilationist and pluralist terms. One side presumes that achieving social integration and harmony depends on eliminating as many differences as possible (i.e., creating similarity, see Parsons 1951; Schlesinger 1992). "Real" Americans are those who conform to some set of shared (but constrained) personal characteristics, beliefs, values, and behaviors. The alternative "valuing diversity" argument espouses pluralism. Its proponents presume that social harmony rests on recognizing and "privileging" the unique beliefs, values, and so on, of distinct cultural (or racial) groups.

Under the assimilationist model, social integration and a sense of community depend on minimizing differences. Individual inequalities (e.g., in income and social status) can be tolerated because they do not function as bases for social conflict among groups organized around nominal differences. On the other hand, the pluralist model permits—indeed requires by definition—group differences. Under this model, social integration depends on the elimination of *inequality* but not *difference*. But in practice, pluralism implies differences in beliefs, values, motivations, and behaviors that are typically reflected in concrete inequalities such as income or edu-

cational attainments. Consequently, the central issue that both assimilationists and pluralists must address is the persistent diversity of the American people and the inequalities that accompany it....

NOTES

1. Following Weber (1968), we use the term community to describe a collection of diverse peoples who believe they belong together.
2. The general populace expresses considerable ambivalence about the role of immigrants in American society. More than three-fourths (77.2%) of respondents to a recent survey agreed that the United States should take stronger measures to stop the inflow of immigrants. On the other hand, more than three-fifths (62.1%) agreed that the presence of immigrants makes Americans more open to (new) ideas and cultures (Davis and Smith 1996).
3. The persistence and intensity of ethnic politics (e.g., black, Hispanic, or Jewish activism) is extensively documented. More recently, activists who represent other clusters of "different" people (e.g., immigrants and homosexuals but also disenchanted whites like the "Freemen") have appeared on the national scene.
4. Legal equality has not been extended to all groups. Religious groups are a notable exception. We live in an age of great debate about the meaning of religious freedom and about the proper role of religion in politics (Carter 1993). Yet, members of some established religions must restrict their religious practices. As an example, an orthodox Muslim man must restrict himself to one wife in the United States.
5. Isolation of people by social category (e.g., race) and assimilation satisfy the objective of reducing diversity. It has become fashionable to dismiss those who promote either solution as "racist." Clearly, forced or voluntary separation expresses distaste and intolerance for out-groups. However, categorical discrimination is not required to produce assimilation, as we point out below.
6. See Milton M. Gordon (1964) for a thorough discussion of assimilation and the complexity of assimilation processes.

REFERENCES

Bem, Sandra L. 1993. *The Lenses of Gender: Transforming the Debate on Sexual Inequality.* New Haven, CT: Yale University Press.
——. 1999. "Gender, Sexuality, and Inequality: When Many Become One, Who Is the One and What Happens to the Others?," pp. 70–86 in *A Nation Divided: Diversity, Inequality, and Community in*

American Society, ed. Phyllis Moen, Donna Dempster-McClain, and Henry A. Walker. Ithaca: Cornell University Press.

Durkheim, Emile. [1893] 1964. *The Division of Labor in Society*. Glencoe, IL: Free Press.

Han, Shin-Kap, and Phyllis Moen. 1999. "Clocking Out: Temporal Patterning of Retirement." *American Journal of Sociology* 105(1): In press.

Han, Shin-Kap, and Phyllis Moen. 1999. "Work and Family in Temporal Context: A Life Course Approach." *The Annals of the American Academy of Political and Social Science* March:98–110.

Hannan, Michael T. 1979. "The Dynamics of Ethnic Boundaries in Modern States." In *National Development and the World System*, edited by M. T. Hannan and J. W. Meyer, 253–75. Chicago: University of Chicago Press.

Hechter, Michael. 1975. *Internal Colonialism*. London: Routledge & Kegan Paul.

Horowitz, Donald L. 1975. "Ethnic Identity." In *Ethnicity: Theory and Experience*, edited by N. Glazer and D. P. Moynihan, 111–40. Cambridge, MA: Harvard University Press.

Inkeles, Alex. 1998. *One World Emerging?: Convergence and Divergence in Industrial Societies*. Boulder, CO: Westview.

Lipset, Seymour Martin, and Stein Rokkan. 1967. *Party Systems and Voter Alignments*. New York: Free Press.

Marshall, T. H. 1949. *Citizenship and Social Class*. Cambridge, U.K.: Cambridge University Press.

Moen, Phyllis, Donna Dempster-McClain, and Robin M. Williams, Jr. 1989. "Social Integration and Longevity: An Event History Analysis of Women's Roles and Resilience." *American Sociological Review* 54 (August):635–47.

Myrdal, Gunnar. 1944. *An American Dilemma*. New York: Harper & Row.

Olzak, Susan. 1992. *The Dynamics of Ethnic Competition and Conflict*. Stanford: Stanford University Press.

Park, Robert E., and Ernest Burgess, eds. [1921] 1969. *Introduction to the Science of Sociology*. Chicago: University of Chicago Press.

Parsons, Talcott. 1951. *The Social System*. Glencoe, IL: Free Press.

Schlesinger, Arthur M., Jr. 1992. *The Disuniting of America*. New York: Norton.

Simmel, Georg. [1908] 1971. "How Is Society Possible?" In *Georg Simmel: On Individuality and Social Forms*, edited by D. N. Levine, 6–22. Chicago: University of Chicago Press.

Takaki, Ronald. 1993. *A Different Mirror*. Boston: Little, Brown.

Tilly, Charles. 1999. "Durable Inequality," pp. 15–33 in *A Nation Divided: Diversity, Inequality, and Community in American Society*, ed. Phyllis Moen, Donna Dempster-McClain, and Henry A. Walker. Ithaca: Cornell University Press.

Toennics, Ferdinand. 1957. *Community and Society*. Translated and edited by Charles P. Loomis. East Lansing, MI: Michigan State University.

Walker, Henry A. 1999. "Two Faces of Diversity: Recreating the Stranger Next Door?," pp. 52–69 in *A Nation Divided: Diversity, Inequality, and Community in American Society*, ed. Phyllis Moen, Donna Dempster-McClain, and Henry A. Walker. Ithaca: Cornell University Press.

Weber, Max. 1968. *Economy and Society*, edited by G. Roth and C. Wittich. Berkeley: University of California Press.

Williams Robin M. [1947] 1999. "The Reduction of Intergroup Tensions," pp. 277–295 in *A Nation Divided: Diversity, Inequality, and Community in American Society*, ed. Phyllis Moen, Donna Dempster-McClain, and Henry A. Walker. Ithaca: Cornell University Press.

———. 1970. *American Society: A Sociological Interpretation*. New York: Alfred A. Knopf.

PART X

Social Institutions: Political and Economic

Institutions are the various accepted means by which society is able to operate. They are the patterns by which we solve ongoing problems. For society to continue, institutions must work. If they do not, services will not be adequately provided for people, social problems will become increasingly serious, and problems of order will arise more regularly.

Part X focuses on economic and political institutions. Economic institutions are those patterns created in society that deal with producing, distributing, and consuming goods and services. Political institutions are those patterns that deal with governing society. Both types of institutions have a lot to do with social power; in sociology, there almost always are attempts to show how political and economic institutions are linked.

The first selection by John Kenneth Galbraith ties economics to politics by examining the politics of the affluent and how those politics perpetuate great inequalities in society. Krujit and Koonings show us the role that violence and fear play in the politics of Latin America.

The last three selections examine three economic institutions in the United States: capitalism, the corporation, and a highly technological economic system. To Michael Zweig, capitalism is an institution which works against community and cooperation. To Carl Boggs, real social power is no longer in government; it is in the dominance of the corporation. To Aronowitz and DiFazio, the revolution in our society is the scientific-technological revolution which is not in the interests of those who seek secure and challenging work. All three selections should cause all of us to examine more critically the economic institutions that many of us too often take for granted.

48. THE POLITICS OF THE CONTENTED

JOHN KENNETH GALBRAITH

[The Contented Majority] rule under the rich cloak of democracy, a democracy in which the less fortunate do not participate … they are [not] silent in their contentment. They can be…very angry and very articulate about what seems to invade their state of self-satisfaction.

Americans pride themselves on a set of political institutions they call democracy. However, can a democracy exist when large numbers of people are excluded from the process (or exclude themselves from the process), especially if they are the most discontented and the most disadvantaged in the society? In this critique of American democracy, Galbraith describes the views of those who are active in and have come to control our political system. They are not a few rich people, but instead a large diversity of contented people who work together to keep what they have and protect themselves through action and through a set of principles they claim to be democratic. Galbraith's book describes these contented people, and this selection is an analysis worth serious attention if we are to understand the working of our political institutions.

…In past times, the economically and socially fortunate were, as we know, a small minority—characteristically a dominant and ruling handful. They are now a majority, though…a majority not of all citizens but of those who actually vote. A convenient reference is needed for those so situated and who so respond at the polls. They will be called the *Contented Majority*, the *Contented Electoral Majority*, or more spaciously, the *Culture of Contentment*. There will be adequate reiteration that this does not mean they are a majority of all those eligible to vote. They rule under the rich cloak of democracy, a democracy in which the less fortunate do not participate. Nor does it mean—a most important point—that they are silent in their contentment. They can be, as when this book goes to press, very angry and very articulate about what seems to invade their state of self-satisfaction.

• • •

Although income broadly defines the contented majority, no one should suppose that that majority is occupationally or socially homogeneous. It includes the people who manage or otherwise staff the middle and upper reaches of the great financial and industrial firms, independent businessmen and women, and those in lesser employments whose compensation is more or less guaranteed. Also the large population—lawyers, doctors, engineers, scientists, accountants and many others, not excluding journalists and professors—who make up the modern professional class. Included also are a certain, if diminishing, number who once were called *proletarians*—those with diverse skills whose wages are now, with some frequency, supplemented by those of a diligent wife. They, like others in families with dual paychecks, find life reasonably secure.

Further, although they were once a strongly discontented community, there are the farmers, who, when buttressed by government price supports, are now amply rewarded.[1] Here, too, there is a dominant, if not universal, mood of satisfaction. Finally, there is the rapidly increasing num-

ber of the aged who live on pensions or other retirement allowance and for whose remaining
years of life there is adequate or, on occasion,
ample financial provision.

None of this suggests an absence of continuing personal aspiration or a unanimity of political
view. Doing well, many wish to do better. Having
enough, many wish for more. Being comfortable,
many raise vigorous objection to that which in-
vades comfort. What is important is that there is
no self-doubt in their present situation. The future for the contented majority is thought effectively within their personal command. Their
anger is evident—and, indeed, can be strongly
evident—only when there is a threat or possible
threat to present well-being and future
prospect—when government and the seemingly
less deserving intrude or threaten to intrude their
needs or demands. This is especially so if such
action suggests higher taxes.

As to political attitude, there is a minority, not
small in number, who do look beyond personal
contentment to a concern for those who do not
share in the comparative well-being. Or they see
the more distant dangers that will result from a
short-run preoccupation with individual comfort.
Idealism and foresight are not dead; on the contrary, their expression is the most reputable form
of social discourse. Although self-interest, as we
shall see, does frequently operate under a formal
cover of social concern, much social concern is
genuinely and generously motivated.

Nonetheless, self-regard is, predictably, the
dominant—indeed the controlling—mood of the
Contented Majority. This becomes wholly evident when public action on behalf of those outside this electoral majority is the issue. If it is to
be effective, such action is invariably at public
cost. Accordingly, it is regularly resisted as a matter of high, if sometimes rather visibly contrived,
principle. Of this, more later.

• • •

In the recent past, much has been held wrong
with the performance of the United States government as regards both domestic and foreign
policy. This has been widely attributed to the inadequacy, incompetence, or generally perverse
performance of individual politicians and political leaders. Mr. Reagan and his now accepted intellectual and administrative detachment, and

Mr. Bush, his love of travel and his belief in ora-
tory as the prime instrument of domestic action,
have been often cited. Similarly criticized have
been leaders and members of the Congress, and,
if less stridently, governors and other politicians
throughout the Republic.

This criticism, or much of it, is mistaken or, at
best, politically superficial. The government of
the United States in recent years has been a valid
reflection of the economic and social preferences
of the majority of those voting—the electoral majority. In defense of Ronald Reagan and George
[H.] Bush as Presidents, it must be said and emphasized that both were, or are, faithful representatives of the constituency that elected them. We
attribute to politicians what should be attributed
to the community they serve.

• • •

The first and most general expression of the
Contented Majority is its affirmation that those
who compose it are receiving their just deserts.
What the individual member aspires to have and
enjoy is the product of his or her personal virtue,
intelligence, and effort. Good fortune being
earned or the reward of merit, there is no equi-
table justification for any action that impairs it—
that subtracts from what is enjoyed or might be
enjoyed. The normal response to such action is
indignation or, as suggested, anger at anything in-
fringing on what is so clearly deserved.

There will be, as noted, individuals—on frequent occasion in the past, some who have inherited what they have—who will be less certain
that they merit their comparative good fortune.
And more numerous will be those scholars, journalists, professional dissidents, and other voices
who will express sympathy for the excluded and
concern for the future, often from positions of
relative personal comfort. The result will be political effort and agitation in conflict with the
aims and preferences of the contented. The
number so motivated is, to repeat, not small, but
they are not a serious threat to the electoral majority. On the contrary, by their dissent, they give
a gracing aspect of democracy to the ruling position of the fortunate. They show in their articulate way that "democracy is working." Liberals in
the United States, Labour politicians and spokes-
men in Britain, are, indeed, vital in this regard.
Their writing and rhetoric give hope to the ex-

cluded and, at a minimum, ensure that they are not both excluded *and* ignored.

Highly convenient social and economic doctrine also emerges in defense of contentment, some of which is modern and some ancient. As will be seen, what once justified the favored position of the few—a handful of aristocrats or capitalists—has now become the favoring defense of the comfortable many.

• • •

The second, less conscious but extremely important characteristic of the Contented Majority, one already noted, is its attitude toward time. In the briefest word, short-run public inaction, even if held to be alarming as to consequence, is always preferred to protective long-run action. The reason is readily evident. The long run may not arrive; that is the frequent and comfortable belief. More decisively important, the cost of today's action falls or could fall on the favored community; taxes could be increased. The benefits in the longer run may well be for others to enjoy. In any case, the quiet theology of laissez faire holds that all will work out for the best in the end.

Here, too, there will be contrary voices. These will be heard, and often with respect, but not to the point of action. For the Contented Majority, the logic of inaction is inescapable. For many years, for example, there has been grave concern in the northeastern United States and extending up to Canada over acid rain caused by sulphurous emissions from the power plants of the Midwest. The long-run effects will, it is known, be extremely adverse—on the environment, the recreational industries, the forest industry, maple sugar producers, and on the general benignity of local life and scene. The cost of corrective measures to the electric power plants and their consumers will be immediate and specific; the longer-term conservation reward will, in contrast, be diffuse, uncertain, and debatable as to specific incidence. From this comes the policy avowed by the contented. It does not deny the problem, this not being possible; rather, it delays action. Notably, it proposes more research, which very often provides a comforting, intellectually reputable gloss over inaction. At the worst, it suggests impaneling a commission, the purpose of which would be to discuss and recommend action or perhaps postponement thereof. At the very worst, there is limited, perhaps symbolic, ac-

tion, as in recent times. Other long-run environmental dangers—global warming and the dissipation of the ozone layer—invite a similar response.

Another example of the role of time is seen in attitudes toward what is called, rather formidably, the *economic infrastructure of the United States*—its highways, bridges, airports, mass transportation facilities, and other public structures. These are now widely perceived as falling far below future need and even present standards of safety. Nonetheless, expenditure and new investment in this area are powerfully and effectively resisted. Again the very plausible reason: Present cost and taxation are specific; future advantage is dispersed. Later and different individuals will benefit; why pay for persons unknown? So again the readily understandable insistence on inaction and the resulting freedom from present cost. Contentment is here revealed to be of growing social influence, more decisive than in the past. The interstate highway system, the parkways, the airports, even perhaps the hospitals and schools of an earlier and financially far more astringent time but one when the favored voters were far fewer, could not be built today.

In the 1980s, the preference for short-run advantage was dramatically evident, as will later be noted, in the continued deficits in the budget of the United States and in the related and resulting deficits in the international trade accounts. Here, the potential cost to the favored voting community, the Contented Electoral Majority, was highly specific. To reduce the deficit meant more taxation or a reduction in expenditures, including those important to the comfortable. The distant benefits seemed, predictably, diffuse and uncertain as to impact. Again, no one can doubt that Presidents Reagan and Bush were or are in highly sympathetic response to their constituency on this matter. Although criticism of their action or inaction has been inevitable, their instinct as to what their politically decisive supporters wanted has been impeccable.

• • •

A third commitment of the comfortably situated is to a highly selective view of the role of the state—of government. Broadly and superficially speaking, the state is seen as a burden; no political avowal of modern times has been so often reiterated and so warmly applauded as the need "to get government off the backs of the people." The albatross was not hung more oppressively by his shipmates around the neck of the Mariner. The need to lighten or remove this burden and therewith, agreeably, the supporting taxes is an article of high faith for the comfortable or Contented Majority.

But although government in general has been viewed as a burden, there have been, as will be seen, significant and costly exceptions from this broad condemnation. Excluded from criticism, needless to say, have been Social Security, medical care at higher income levels, farm income supports, and financial guarantees to depositors in ill-fated banks and savings and loan enterprises. These are strong supports to the comfort and security of the Contented Majority. No one would dream of attacking them, even marginally, in any electoral contest.

Specifically favored also have been military expenditures, their scale and fiscally oppressive effect notwithstanding. This has been for three reasons. These expenditures, as they are reflected in the economy in wages, salaries, profits, and assorted subsidies to research and other institutions, serve to sustain or enhance the income of a considerable segment of the Contented Electoral Majority. Weapons expenditure (unlike, for example, spending for the urban poor) rewards a very comfortable constituency.

More important, perhaps, [is that] military expenditures—and those for the associated operations of the CIA and (to a diminishing extent) the Department of State—have been seen in the past as vital protection against the gravest perceived threat to continued comfort and contentment. That threat was from Communism, with its clear and overt, even if remote, endangerment of the economic life and rewards of the comfortable. This fear, in turn, extending on occasion to clinical paranoia, ensured support to the military establishment. And American liberals, no less than conservatives, felt obliged, given their personal commitment to liberty and human rights, to show by their support of defense spending that they were not "soft on Communism."

The natural focus of concern was the Soviet Union and its once seemingly stalwart satellites in Eastern Europe. Fear of the not-inconsiderable competence of the Soviets in military tech-

nology and production provided the main pillar of support for American military spending. However, the alarm was geographically comprehensive. It supported expenditure and military action against such improbable threats as those from Angola, Afghanistan, Ethiopia, Grenada, El Salvador, Nicaragua, Laos, Cambodia, and, massively, tragically, and at great cost, from Vietnam. From being considered a source of fear and concern, only Communist China was, from the early 1970s on, exempt. Turning against the Soviet Union and forgiven for its earlier role in Korea and Vietnam, it became an honorary bastion of democracy and free enterprise, which, later repressive actions notwithstanding, it rather substantially remains.

The final reason that military expenditures have continued to be favored is the self-perpetuating power of the military and weapons establishment itself—its control of the weaponry it is to produce, the missions for which it is to be prepared, and in substantial measure the funds that it receives and dispenses.

Until World War II, the fortunately situated in the United States, the Republican Party in particular, resisted military expenditures, as they then resisted all government spending. In the years since, the presumed worldwide Communist menace, as frequently it was designated, brought a major reversal: Those with a comfortable concern for their own economic position became the most powerful advocates of the most prodigal of military outlays. With the collapse of Communism, an interesting question arises as to what the attitude of the contented will now be. That the military establishment, public and private, will continue on its own authority to claim a large share of its past financial support is not, however, seriously in doubt.

• • •

Such are the exceptions that the Contented Majority makes to its general condemnation of government as a burden. Social expenditure favorable to the fortunate, financial rescue, military spending and, of course, interest payments—these constitute in the aggregate by far the largest part of the federal budget and that which in recent times has shown by far the greatest increase. What remains—expenditures for welfare, low-cost housing, health care for those otherwise unprotected, public education, and the diverse needs of the great urban slums—is what is now viewed as the burden of government. It is uniquely that which serves the interests of those outside the Contented Electoral Majority; it is, and inescapably, what serves the poor. Here again, Mr. Reagan and now Mr. Bush showed or now show a keen sense of their constituency. So also they do with regard to one further tendency of the Contented Majority.

• • •

The final characteristic here to be cited and stressed is the tolerance shown by the contented of great differences in income. These differences have already been noted, as has the fact that the disparity is not a matter that occasions serious dispute. A general and quite plausible convention is here observed: The price of prevention of any aggression against one's own income is tolerance of the greater amount for others. Indignation at, and advocacy of, redistribution of income from the very rich, inevitably by taxes, opens the door for consideration of higher taxes for the comfortable but less endowed. This is especially a threat given the position and possible claims of the least favored part of the population. Any outcry from the fortunate half could only focus attention on the far inferior position of the lower half. The plush advantage of the very rich is the price the Contented Electoral Majority pays for being able to retain what is less but what is still very good. And, it is averred, there could be solid social advantage in this tolerance of the very fortunate: "To help the poor and middle classes, one must cut the taxes on the rich."[2]

Ronald Reagan's single-most celebrated economic action (the acceptance of the related budget deficit possibly apart) was his tax relief for the very affluent. Marginal rates on the very rich were reduced from a partly nominal 70 percent to 50 percent in 1981; then, with tax reform, the rate on the richest fell to 28 percent in 1986, although this was partly offset by other tax changes. The result was a generous increase in the after-tax income in the higher income brackets. That part of Mr. Reagan's motivation was his memory of the presumptively painful tax demands on his Hollywood pay seems not in doubt. He was also influenced by the economic ideas that had been adapted to serve tax reduction on the rich— broadly, the doctrine that if the horse is fed amply with oats, some will pass through to the road for

the sparrows. But once again there was also the sense of what served his larger constituency, as well as that of the concurring Congress. This constituency accepted the favor to the very rich in return for protection for itself.

• • •

In summary, we see that much that has been attributed in these past years to ideology, idiosyncrasy, or error of political leadership has deep roots in the American polity. It has been said, and often, in praise of Ronald Reagan as President that he gave the American people a good feeling about themselves This acclaim is fully justified as regards the people who voted for him, and even perhaps as regards that not inconsiderable number who, voting otherwise, found themselves in silent approval of the very tangible personal effect of his tax policies.

In past times in the United States, under government by either of the major parties, many experienced a certain sense of unease, of troubled conscience and associated discomfort when contemplating those who did not share the good fortune of the fortunate. No such feeling emanated from Ronald Reagan; Americans were being rewarded as they so richly deserved. If some did not participate, it was because of their inability or by their choice. As it was once the privilege of Frenchmen, both the rich and the poor, to sleep under bridges, so any American had the undoubted right to sleep on street grates. This might not be the reality, but it was the presidentially ordained script. And this script was tested by Ronald Reagan, out of his long and notable theatrical training, not for its reality, not for its truth, but, as if it were a motion picture or a television commercial: for its appeal. That appeal was widespread; it allowed Americans to escape their consciences and their social concerns and thus to feel a glow of self-approval.

Not all, of course, could so feel, nor, necessarily, could a majority of all citizens of voting age. And there was a further and socially rather bitter circumstance, one that has been conveniently, neglected: the comfort and economic well-being of the Contented Majority was being supported and enhanced by the presence in the modern economy of a large, highly useful, even essential class that does not share in the agreeable existence of the favored community.

NOTES

1. "The average 1988 income of farm operator households was $33,535, compared with $34,017 for all U.S. households. However, 5 percent of farm operator households had incomes above $100,000, compared to 3.2 percent of all U.S. households." *Agricultural Income and Finance: Situation and Outlook Report* (Washington, D.C.: U.S. Department of Agriculture Economic Research Service, May 1990), p. 26.

2. George Gilder, *Wealth and Poverty* (New York: Basic Books, 1981), p. 188. He is quoted by Kevin Phillips in *The Politics of Rich and Poor: Wealth and the American Electorate in the Reagan Aftermath* (New York: Random House, 1990), p. 62.

49. VIOLENCE AND FEAR IN LATIN AMERICA

DIRK KRUIJT and KEES KOONINGS

It is not easy to overcome the legacy of violence and fear in post-authoritarian Latin America. Not only is this due to the continuing stiuation of political instability and institutional uncertainty, which continues to make the threat of the resurrection of violent and arbitrary regimes a real one; the current civil and democratic governments also find it difficult to remove the legacy of institutionalized and arbitrary violence embedded in the state. Furthermore, the deepening of social inequalities, and the appearance of new governance voids with respect to maintaining a peaceful social order and the rule of law, provide new fuel to the long-lasting fire of violence and fear in Latin America.

Violence in Latin America is a central part of the political order and difficult to work against as nations attempt to build a real democracy. Sometimes the threat is because the state no longer monopolizes the legitimate use of violence; more often the state turns to the use of violence and creates order through the use of fear.

In September 1989, one of the authors, acting as a member of a negotiating mission to the Christian Democratic government of Guatemala, participated in a lengthy dialogue with the then vice-president of the country, Lic.

From Dirk Kruijt and Kees Koonings. "Introduction: Violence and Fear in Latin America," pp. 1–30 in *Societies of Fear: The Legacy of Civil War, Violence and Terror in Latin America*, ed. Kees Koonings and Dirk Kruijt. Zed books, 1999. By permission.

Roberto Carpio Nicolle. The national government, the first civilian one after a long period of military rule, was trying to attract technical and financial support from European donor countries. Guatemala had become eligible for European aid, not only because the country needed to be rebuilt after the gruesome civil war and the crisis of the 1980s, but also because it had become a politically fashionable recipient, after all those years of pariah status within the international community. Mr. Carpio had been the president of the constitutional reform committee during the transition period from military rule to a civilian government. As the constitutional vice-president, he was the head of the national public sector, and, at the very moment of the interview, the acting president as well. At the end of the last negotiating session—the topic was a support project for his ambitious national antipoverty and micro-enterprise programme—the delicate theme of human rights was touched upon. When the delegation leader insisted upon guarantees against paramilitary forces and death squads while executing the agreed project, the Guatemalan vice-president turned red and, with his face flushed, began to argue in the following way:

> You are asking for specific guarantees and I cannot give you an adequate response. It is not in my power to promise you a clear-cut solution in your fine European terms. I have been a leading journalist during the years of the military and the repression. I have been threatened and had to go abroad to be safe. Now I am the vice-president, even the acting president of this country. I have written the essential parts of the constitution. Apparently I am invested with all political power. But in fact, my friends, I have to share power with a lot of players, some of them invisible. In this country, the military are still in command. This is Guatemala, my friends, you cannot implement a government programme without their implicit permission. Then, of course, there are the paramilitary forces, the death squads, as you said. OK, can you suggest something I can do with them? They are present and absent at the same time. They are nowhere and everywhere; and they ask for their share. Then there are the drug dealers, the mafias. Of course, I should negate their very existence, as I should with the military, the police, the criminals and the drug lords. But we are here in Guatemala and their presence is a reality. And then there is the problem of CACIF.[1] They consider a small increase of taxation by 2 or 3 per cent as communism, and the military believe them! CACIF controls the entire national economy. So, reconsidering these facts, what kind of guarantees are you asking for?

Thus he expressed in a nutshell the problem under study. Latin America has a legacy of terror, of violence, of fear. Of all the countries on the continent, Guatemala is one of the most significant examples of a 'society of fear'. The constitu-tion of this kind of society and the persistence of its characteristics—in other words, the long-term consequences of violence, repression and arbitrariness—are recurrent features of the Latin American political landscape. Unfortunately, these problems have not vanished from the continent's social and political scene despite almost two decades of efforts to end authoritarianism and civil war and to rebuild democracy and legitimate civil governance....

It is our assertion that social and political violence has been an endemic and permanent feature of the pattern of nation-building in Latin America and the conflicts generated by this process. We will suggest a typological distinction between three kinds of violence in the history of Latin America: violence related to maintaining the traditional rural and oligarchic social order; violence related to the problem of the modernization of the state and the incorporation of the masses in politics; and, finally, violence related to the present-day difficulties of consolidating democratic stability, economic progress and social inclusion. We then proceed to discuss two enduring background features that underly, in our understanding, the tenacity of social and political violence in Latin America. In the first place, it is nurtured by long-lasting patterns of social exclusion of large parts of the population. It has been observed that Latin America has experienced relatively few fundamental social revolutions despite the almost permanent 'pre-revolutionary' nature of the profound social cleavages within the region's social fabric.[2] It may be true that current social inequalities seldom lead to massive violent reactions by the poor and excluded; violent protests seem to be localized, focused and of short duration.[3] Still, as we will argue, these cleavages lead to what we call the "informalization" of society and the subsequent erosion of the notion of citizenship. We feel that this tendency runs counter to the prospect of institutionalizing and pacifying political life. Second, we point at the legacy of violence engrained in the dynamics of the state and politics. We especially refer to the institutionalization of arbitrary violence within the state and the effects this has, in terms of generalized fear, on politics and on social life in general....

... Violence has historically been a central feature in the evolution of inequality and deprivation, ethnic discrimination, criminal violence, death squads, kidnapping and so on, can be mentioned alongside the stereotyped *pronunciamientos, cuartelazos* and *golpes* perpetrated by the military, with their accompanying political assassinations, repression, torture and disappearances, revolutionary armed struggle, and outside interventions frequently associated with politics in Latin America. Together, these forms present a broad array of threats to what can be called "livelihood security". A consistent lack of the basic parameters of such security leads to the creation of fear as an endemic condition. Fear related to livelihood insecurity is an often latent but at times manifest phenomenon affecting a large part of the population up till the present day. Here we deal, however, not so much with these kinds of what some would call "structural violence", but with violence and fear that are more directly related to the way political power has been used. In fact, we would suggest that three broad types, or cycles, of violence can be discerned in the social and political history of Latin America since the mid-nineteenth century. These cycles are characterized not only by the nature of the violence involved, but especially by the way it is related to patterns of social and political domination and interaction. These patterns are historical as well, but it is not easy to set them in a chronological order, as we will see below.

VIOLENCE IN THE TRADITIONAL ORDER

The first cycle refers to the kind of violence that underlies, almost as if it were taken for granted, the social and political domination of rather closed and restricted elites predicated upon the systematic exclusion of the "masses, castes, and classes." This type of violence, with certain roots in colonial history, came to the fore in the course of the nineteenth century. As such, it was imbued with a basic ambivalence that remained a distinctive feature of Latin American societies up till the present. On the one hand, we see elite adherence to European civility, progress, liberalism, bourgeois society; on the other hand, this civility was founded upon extreme social hierarchies led by the logic of exclusion....

Nevertheless, this order was a violent one. Force and coercion were manifest on different levels and in various forms. The interaction between patrons and clients across hierarchical class divisions usually combined loyalty, based on the extension of resources, with allegiance produced by coercion. Clientelism has been analysed as being one important mechanism in reproducing class hierarchies in Latin America.[4] Labour systems, especially in the countryside, often involved coercive recruitment methods, such as forced or indentured field labour. Strikes carried out by the nascent urban working classes and their organizations were generally met with repressive action.[5] The popular adage among politicians in Brazil's Old Republic was: 'the social problem is a police problem'....

MASS POLITICS, POLITICAL VIOLENCE AND 'INTERNAL WARFARE'

The second cycle of violence we would like to distinguish was brought about by what Weffort calls the "problem of the incorporation of the masses" into the Latin American political process.[6] The rise of anti-oligarchic counter-elites and the growing pressure from organized popular sectors to take part in power arrangements challenged the prevailing oligarchic order.[7] The transition—sometimes abrupt, sometimes gradual—to wider (popular) political participation generally led to the emergence of populist regimes marked by corporatism and limited formal democracy.[8] But whatever the manner in which populist regimes came to power or their subsequent characteristics, some degree of violence was almost always involved. Violence was generated not only to overthrow the so-called old order, but also, as in Argentina or Peru in the 1930s, to fend off populist or reformist intrusions into the political arena. What is important for our discussion, however, is that social violence became more politicized, and even ideologically charged, concomitant with the opening up of the political domain....

Regardless of the differences between the various bureaucratic-authoritarian "projects" (there are, for instance, basic differences between the

Brazilian and the Chilean variety), they had in common a certain conservative notion of the "national interest" or "permanent national objectives", that were seen as threatened by radical (communist) internal enemies. These enemies (the former populists and the newly arriving radical leftists inspired by the Cuban revolution) were confronted with the logic of internal warfare, regardless of the actual strength of left-wing armed struggle.[9] From Guatemala to Argentina, the dictatorships declared war on their populations in the name of freedom and the preservation of western-Christian civilization.[10] This violence was based on clear doctrinal guidelines and strategic notions, as in a genuine war, but its perverse effects were inevitable in the sense that internal warfare led to state terrorism. One of the key characteristics of systematic state terrorism is the proliferation of arbitrariness. No national security doctrine or "strong democracy" concept will ever manage to restrain the perpetrators of state violence on the level of the day-to-day practices of the *guerra sucia*.... consolidating the institutional framework for democratic politics, and the basic consensus among political forces that is necessary to sustain it. Still, this does not mean that all conditions for effective governance are now progressively met.[11] Governance is jeopardized by a number of problems. The persistence of violence and social conflicts is one of them.

VIOLENCE IN POST-AUTHORITARIAN LATIN AMERICA

The advent of democracy, now formally prevailing everywhere except Cuba, did not mean the end of violence as a social and political problem. On the contrary, one might cynically state that violence is being democratized in Latin America. It ceased to be the resource of only the traditionally powerful or of the grim uniformed guardians of the nation. Violence increasingly appears as an option for a multitude of actors in pursuit of all kind of goals.

The textbook example of this trend is, of course, Colombia. The deployment of violence has become so customary that to a certain extent the Colombian state has ceased to exist in its

Weberian quality of the monopolizer of the legitimate use of violence. Not only the military, the paramilitaries, the guerrillas, and the drug cartels use violence as a matter of course; also at lower levels of society, violence can mean a career or an instrument for social mobility, or even an instrument for reversing traditional social hierarchies. For instance, in the city of Medellin, the spread of violence not only enabled the ascent of "marginal" youngsters from the *tugurios* (the shantytowns), but also created new spaces for neighbourhood associations to confront a traditionally conservative municipal administration.[12] Further illustrations can be derived from the case of Brazil. Brazil presents the ambivalent situation of a country in which, on the one hand, formal redemocratization has proceeded considerably and enjoys widespread support and legitimacy. During the past decades, Brazilian society has been thoroughly politicized and a lively civil society has been mushrooming. At the same time, however, violence and arbitrariness remain prominent features of national life.

These forms of violence in Brazil and elsewhere are not new, but apprehension has clearly been rising over the past ten years or so. In addition, it nurtures an overall climate in which (especially on the level of daily law enforcement) random and arbitrary violence persists in spite of the demise of authoritarian rule. This kind of violence is not only directed at common criminals, but also at social activists such as landless peasants occupying an estate, metal-workers on strike, or gold miners (*garimpeiros*) being expelled from their site. Especially on Brazil's Amazon frontier, daily violence is endemic and testifies to the incapacity of the state to uphold a legitimate and peaceful internal order. This may well contribute to a general climate (as a matter of fact to a large extent created by the introduction of everyday arbitrariness during the dictatorship) in which violence is seen as a normal option with which to pursue interests, attain power or resolve conflicts.

The "new violence" in Latin America pits the repressive instincts of the traditional elites and the security forces against an increasingly wide variety of actors who also have recourse to violence, despite the establishment of formal democratic rule. This new kind of social and political insecurity is, in the first place, exacerbated by the continuation and even deepening of social cleavages in virtually every Latin American country during the past two decades. In the second place, the end of military rule did not abolish the prerogatives and the self-appointed role of the armed forces to deal with "threats", as has been systematically demonstrated by Lovemann.[13] This means that violent backlashes in response to social mobilization or "upheavals" remain a common feature of post-authoritarian Latin America. In addition, years or decades of arbitrary rule contributed to an overall climate of impunity among incumbents of the security forces (most notably the police and the special anti-subversive units) which very often gave law enforcement under the new democracies a grim and, in fact, criminal overtone. We witness state representatives who resort to arbitrary violence despite the installation of democracy and the adoption of pro-active human rights policies by central governments. We see the mushrooming of (organized) criminal violence at the same time as grassroots civic organizations with peaceful agendas proliferate. The perilous trend seems to be that the basic ambiguity of Latin America we mentioned earlier is being reproduced: progress towards democratization and citizens' empowerment goes hand in hand with the erosion of state legitimacy due to the state's failure to promote social participation and the rule of law. This leaves what could be called "governance voids", which are inevitably occupied by actors who obey the law of the jungle. In turn, new authoritarian backlashes, or the perversion of civil governance, may eventually result. In the next two sections, we will discuss both components of present-day "societies of fear" in more detail.

THREATENING A PEACEFUL SOCIAL ORDER: POVERTY, INFORMALITY AND EXCLUSION

Pauperization, mass poverty, informality and social exclusion became increasingly intense phenomena during the aftermath of the military dictatorships in the early 1980s. They sprang up as the result of the economic crisis, aggravated in the short term by the structural adjustment packages in most Latin American countries. Already historically characterized by endemic poverty and extreme patterns of inequality. Latin America saw the numbers of those living in misery swelled by the "new poor", the lower middle and formal working classes that recently fell victim to the economic crisis and the adjustment policies carried out in the mid- and late 1980s. The new poor are the members of what used to be the working class and the urban middle classes, together with former rural smallholders and peasants.

Since the 1970s, poverty in Latin America has become an increasingly urban phenomenon, which increases its potential to provoke social conflict, disturbances of order and political radicalization. However, if one thing stands out with regard to the strategies employed by the urban poor, it is the peaceful and inventive nature of their strategies for daily survival. Poverty is identified largely with the "informal sector", a social and economic complex within the national economy and society. From Monterrey in Mexico to Puerto Mont in Chile, the informal sector has been growing, reflected in the multitude of small-scale activities of all kinds which have taken the capital cities and other urban localities by storm. Half of the inhabitants of the capital cities of Mexico, Central America and most Andean countries describe themselves as "informal". Seen from the inside, "informality" operates separately from the formal economic and social institutions, and from the elementary civil rights associated with them: employment, a regular income, labour unions, social legislation, and access to the social institutions that provide such basic needs as health services, education and housing. Seen from the outside, the Latin American "private sector of the poor" (the domain of social exclusion and poverty) is growing at an astonishing rate: and it is now challenging national governments, whatever the ideology of the president or the composition of the cabinet.

Although not directly conducive to violence, the social and political consequence of this long-term process of informalization and social exclusion is the erosion of the legitimacy of the formal civil, political and public order....

It is perhaps cynical to argue that a certain "democratization of violence" has been under way in Latin America. Formerly the use of violence was restricted to certain sectors: the aristocracy, the elite, the army, the police. Nowadays most of Latin America's urban society (and part of rural society) has access to small arms equipment. The proliferation of violence, even in its more anomic forms, has reached the stage of mass production and mass consumption.

SOCIETIES OF FEAR: THEIR CAUSES AND CONSEQUENCES

Fear is the institutional, cultural and psychological repercussion of violence. Fear is a response to institutional destabilization, social exclusion, individual ambiguity and uncertainty. In Latin America, a latent though sometimes open "culture of fear" has obtained institutional characteristics, induced by systematic yet at the same time arbitrary violence, often organized from above by the state apparatus or by central authorities and reproduced within the *fuerzas del orden*. Then, as is argued by Edelberto Torres-Rivas in the final chapter of this volume, the culture of fear is embedded in a generalized climate marked by the "trivialization of horror". The second cycle of political violence and internal warfare mentioned above was marked by the perfecting of state terrorism and the proliferation of arbitrary repression with systemic logic. Without the supporting doctrines of low-intensity warfare against the internal enemies of the state, Latin America could not have developed its "harvest of violence"[14] and its "psychoanalysis of violence."[15] The near-anomic environment of anxiety, characteristic of the third cycle of violence we distinguished above, would be much less pronounced without Latin America's heyday of armoured repression, terror and torture....

The creation of an apparatus of systematic repression and a concomitant climate of fear, sanctioned by the armed forces, but permitted to exist by civil governments and the justice apparatus, was the result of a combination of explicit policies and implicit routines. Although rooted in the process of state formation during the second half of the nineteenth century, the principles of a police state, where the forces of law and order are transformed into the battalions of brutality and repression, were fully elaborated during the cycle

of authoritarianism from the 1960s to the 1980s. This formed the backbone of "societies of fear" in which a climate of insecurity, anxiety and suspense overshadowed all other feelings. Ultimately, the power centre of the terror machinery was localized in the legitimized (and sometimes legalized) independent working of the armed forces and their more sinister extended arms and legs: the intelligence community, the security forces, the paramilitary organizations, the different, subordinated local police bodies and sometimes even the death squads.[16] After transitions to formal democratic government, substantial parts of this apparatus remained untouched. Lovemann rightly stresses the threat to strengthening democracy posed by the continuing supervision of social and political life by the military, based upon their guardianship of "permanent national objectives" and anchored in exceptional legislation: "Maintaining the essential features of national security legislation ... has significantly altered the meaning of democracy in Latin America by imposing severe constraints, both psychological and legal, on the extent to which public life can be carried out, whether in areas of public contestation, electoral competition, and/or opposition to the incumbent government.[17]"...

The problem of fear at the societal and individual level has only recently begun to be addressed. The present state of scholarly research is that of comparative case studies. In some cases, the build-up of the specialized instruments and routines of state terrorism are described in detail, as well as the responses of individual victims.[18] The traumatic consequences of violent experiences, such as torture and intimidation, disappearances, executions, and arbitrary arrests, and the minute description of ethnographical experiences of violent situations, contribute mainly to the phenomenology of individual responses to collective violence.[19] However, the subjective and initially individual responses are, during the next stages of state terrorism, collective answers that take on, in the long run, the shape of societal characteristics.[20] House searches and arrests, followed by lack of information about the prisoner's whereabouts and by apparently random accusations, torture and the widespread knowledge of indiscriminate torturing of captured victims, contribute to a generalized climate of individual weakness, of permanent alertness without the possibility of escape, of collective powerlessness, of lack of control over daily life and the near future, and of a distorted perception of reality. Facts and certainties become blurred, all news is threatening, and the boundaries between good and evil are veiled. Felicity and hope are substituted by fantasies of suffering, feelings of vulnerability, worries and phobias, and self-blame. Self-blame is followed by self-censorship and the culture of silence, an avoidance of discussion, and secrecy about trivialities. Horror becomes a routine social phenomenon.

A recently published anthropological description of daily life in war-torn Guatemala describes explicitly how the routinization of terror and the socialization of violence determine daily life in Indian *municipios* in the department of Chimaltenango.[21] Routinization, as the author remarks, allows people to live in a chronic state of fear with a façade of normality. Fear surfaces in dreams and chronic illness. Whisperings, innuendos and rumours of death lists circulate. Ambiguity becomes institutionalized. The people live under constant surveillance. The military encampment, camouflaged, is situated on a nearby hillside. Spies, military commissioners and civil patrollers provide the backbone of military scrutiny. Traditional village authorities are subordinated to the local military commander. Terror becomes defused through subtle messages. Language and symbols are utilized to mitigate military vigilance and presence. The militarization of the mind affects the children: the use of camouflage cloth for civilian clothing, military wallets, key chains, belts, caps and toy helicopters reproduces the intertwining of military and civilian life. Former enforced recruits, having left as Maya Indians, return home to become the military commissioners, paid informers or heads of the civil patrols. Families' loyalties are divided; a fragile integrity of village life is apparently maintained. Silence and secrecy serve as a protective shield, and the villages have been transformed into a kind of micro-cosmos of fear.

It is not easy to overcome the legacy of violence and fear in post-authoritarian Latin America. Not only is this due to the continuing situation of political instability and institutional uncertainty, which continues to make the threat of the resurrection of violent and arbitrary regimes a real one; the current civil and democratic governments also find it difficult to remove the legacy of institutionalized and arbitrary violence embedded in the state. Furthermore, the deepening of social inequalities, and the appearance of new governance voids with respect to maintaining a peaceful social order and the rule of law, provide new fuel to the long-lasting fire of violence and fear in Latin America.

NOTES

1. CACIF is the national Chamber of Commerce and Industry, unifying the land owning, financial and commercial bourgeoisie.
2. See Touraine, *America Latina*.
3. One could think of the so-called bread riots against structural adjustment policies that took place in countries such as Argentina, Brazil and Venezuela during the 1980s and early 1990s. Other examples may be the indigenous uprisings in Ecuador in the early 1990s, or the landless movement in Brazil. It is debatable to what extent the movement of the Ejercito Zapatista de Liberación Nacional (Zapatista Army of National Liberation, EZLN) in Chiapas, Mexico, can be seen as a limited and focused violent reaction, since they not only advocate the specific demands of the Chiapas (and other) indigenous populations, but have also called for a reform of the Mexican political system. Only the guerilla wars fought in Central America, Peru and, to a lesser degree, Colombia in the 1980s were closer to constituting "revolutionary projects."
4. See Flynn, "Class, clientelism and coercion."
5. See Koonings, Kruijt and Wils, "Very long march."
6. See Weffort, *Populismo*.
7. One of the original formulations of this issue was given by Tella. "Populism and reform."
8. For an illuminating distinction between democratic and authoritarian varieties of Latin American populism see Dix. "Populism."
9. See Wickham-Crowley, *Guerillas and Revolution*, for a detailed analysis of armed rebellions during the second half of the twentieth century. The armed struggle of the Latin American Left was largely unsuccessful and contributed to the incorporation of the Left in the pro-democracy forces in many countries after 1980. Also see Angell, "Incorporating the left."
10. In this book emphasis is placed on the domestic dimensions of the authoritarian and repressive regimes of the 1960s, 1970s and 1980s. This does not mean, however, that external influences were not relevant for the rise and consolidation of these regimes and the shaping of their repressive practices. During the 1960s and 1970s, it was common

usage to stress the pervasive influence of the United States in putting into power a long list of military dictatorships and also in staging counter-insurgency campaigns. There is no doubt that the USA gave various forms of support to the Latin American military through military assistance programmes, development cooperation and diplomatic and intelligence liaisons. However, Rouquié argues that this does not mean that the Latin American military regimes were merely "the sixth side of the Pentagon" (see Rouquié, *Military*). Especially in Brazil and the southern cone countries, the USA basically offered a *nihil obstat* kind of support to the militarization of politics that was well founded in nationally developed geopolitical thinking and related doctrines on the role of the military in politics (see Child, "Geopolitical thinking"). On the other hand, the hand of the USA can be clearly seen in Central America and the Caribbean. From the adventures of William Walker in nineteenth-century Nicaragua to the interventions in Panama and Haiti in the early 1990s, the USA has followed a constant and systematic practice of direct interference with politics and civil wars. Finally, since the 1980s, the Pentagon and the CIA have been gradually superseded by the US Drug Enforcement Agency (DEA) whose high-profile activities include involving the military of a number of countries (especially in the Andean region) in its "war on drugs."

11. We refer to governance not only in the strict sense used by, among others, the World Bank (meaning the ability to carry out sensible adjustment programmes and creating the long-term conditions for market-led growth) but also in terms of deepening democratic participation, accountability and legitimacy.

12. Argued by Roldán, "Citizenship, class and violence."

13. See Lovemann, "'Protected democracies."

14. *Harvest of Violence* is the title of Carmack's splendid reader on the Guatemalan tragedy.

15. See Rodriguez Rabal, *Violencia*.

16. See Garretón. "Fear in military regimes"; also Alves, *Estado e oposição*, pp. 166ff.

17. See Lovemann, "Protected democracies", p. 141.

18. See Weiss Fagen, "Repression"; also Rial, "Makers and guardians of fear."

19. See Nordstrom and Robben, *Fieldwork under Fire.*

20. As remarked by Salimovich, Lira and Weinstein. "Victims of fear," p. 72, in reference to their analysis of experiences in authoritarian and post-authoritarian Chile.

21. See Green, "Living in a state of fear."

REFERENCES

Alves, Maria Helena Moreira, *Estado e oposição no Brasil, 1964–1984.* Petrópolis, RJ: Vozes, 1985.

Angell, Alan, "Chile since 1958," in Leslie Bethell (ed.), *Chile since Independence.* Cambridge: Cambridge University Press, 1993, pp. 129–202.

——"Incorporating the left in democratic politics." In Jorge I. Domínguez and Abraham F. Lowenthal (eds.) *Constructing Democratic Governance—Themes and Issues.* Baltimore; Johns Hopkins University Press 1996. pp 3–25.

Carmack, Robert M., "El impacto de la Revolución y la reforma en las culturas indígenas de los Altos: una reseña crítica de obras recientes." *Mesoamerica* 10 (18). 1989. pp. 401–25.

Child, John, "Geopolitical thinking in Latin America," *Latin American Research Review* 14(2), 1979, pp. 89–111.

Dix, "Populism: authoritarian and democratic", *Latin American Research Review* 20(2), 1985, pp. 29–52.

Flynn, Peter, "Class, clientelism, and coercion: some mechanisms of internal dependency and control", Paper for the CEDLA workshop on Dependency in Latin America. Amsterdam, 1973.

Garretón, Manuel Antonio, "The political evolution of the Chilean military regime and problems in the transition to democracy," in Guillermo O'Donnell, Philippe C. Schmitter and Lawrence Whitehead (eds), *Transitions from Authoritarian Rule: Latin America.* Baltimore: Johns Hopkins University Press, 1986, pp. 95–122.

——"Fear in military regimes: an overview," in Juan F. Corradi, Patricia Weiss Fagen and Manuel Antonio Garretón (eds), *Fear at the Edge. State Terror and Resistance in Latin America.* Berkeley: University of California Press, 1992, pp. 13–25.

Green, Lina, "Living in a state of fear," in Caroline Nordstrom and Antonius C. G. M. Robben (eds), *Fieldwork under Fire. Contemporary Studies of Violence and Survival.* Berkeley: University of California Press, 1995, pp. 105–27.

Koonings, Kees, Dirk Kruijt and Frits Wils, "The very long march of history," in Henk Thomas (ed.), *Globalization and Third World Trade Unions.* London: Zed, 1995, pp. 99–129.

Lovemann, Brian, "Protected democracies and military guardianship: political transitions in Latin America, 1978–1993". *Journal of Interamerican Studies and World Affairs* 36(2), 1994, pp. 105–90.

Nordstrom, Caroline and Antonius C. G. M. Robben (eds), *Fieldwork under Fire. Contemporary Studies of Violence and Survival.* Berkeley: University of California Press, 1995.

Rial, Juan, "The armed forces and the question of democracy in Latin America", in Louis W. Goodman, Johanna S. R. Mendelson and Juan Rial (eds). *The Military and Democracy. The Future of Civil-Military Relations in Latin America.* Lexington, MA, and Toronto: Lexington Books, 1990, pp. 3–21.

——"Makers and guardians of fear," In Juan F. Corradi, Patricia Weiss Fagen and Manuel Antonio Garretón (eds), *Fear at the Edge. State Terror and Resistance in Latin America.* Berkeley: University of California Press, 1992, pp. 90–103.

Rodríguez Rabal, César, *La violencia de las horas. Un estudio psicoanalitico sobre la violencia en el Peru.* Caracas: Nueva Sociedad, 1995.

Roldán, Mary, "Citizenship, class and violence in historical perspective: the Colombian case". Paper for the LASA 20th International Conference, Guadalajara, 1997.

Rouquié, Alain, *The Military and the State in Latin America.* Berkeley: University of California Press, 1989.

Salimovich, Sofia, Elizabeth Lira and Eugenia Weinstein, "Victims of fear: the social psychology of repression." In Juan F. Corradi, Patricia Weiss Fagen and Manuel Antonio Garretón (eds), *Fear at the Edge. State Terror and Resistance in Latin America.* Berkeley: University of California Press, 1992, pp. 147–73.

Tella, Torcuato di, "Populism and reform in Latin America," in Claudio Véliz (ed.), *Obstacle to Change in Latin America.* Oxford: Oxford University Press, 1972.

Touraine, Alain, *America Latina: Politica y Sociedad.* Madrid: Espasa-Calpe, 1989.

Wickham-Crowley, Timothy P., "Terror and guerrilla warfare in Latin America, 1956–1970." *Comparative Studies in Society and History* 32(2). 1990, pp. 201–37.

——.*Guerrillas and Revolution in Latin America. A Comparative Study of Insurgents and Regimes since 1956.* Princeton, NJ: Princeton University Press, 1992.

50. THE INSTITUTION OF CAPITALISM

MICHAEL ZWEIG

The "capitalists'" sense of entitlement is out of touch with reality because it denies the social foundation of their wealth. Poor people's claims to society's help with the provision of basic needs, or to common courtesy and respect, are more in tune with the realities of our mutual responsibilities.

For many of us, capitalism is the key to America's economic success in the world. For Michael Zweig, capitalism as it is practiced sacrifices community and cooperation for individualism and self-interest. Zweig argues that capitalism ignores community responsibility, refuses to recognize the role of luck in economic success, and unfairly assumes the moral superiority of those who become wealthy.

The search for the proper balance between self-interest and service to others suggests the basis of an ethical evaluation of the market economy and capitalism, because capitalism poses the very same problem: What is the connection between self-interest and service to the community? The pursuit of self-interest may be an essential life pri-

From Michael Zweig, *The Working Class Majority: America's Best Kept Secret.* © 2000 by Michael Zweig. Used by permission of the publisher, Cornell University Press.

ority, but when does following self-interest stop being a legitimate priority of business and keep companies from serving the larger community? What happens when self-interest becomes the whole point of economic activity?

It's fine to pursue narrow self-interest, except when it cuts us off from or disrespects the social connections and responsibilities that help to define us as we participate in the larger society. Just as a firefighter pursues self-interest as a priority, but not as an end, self-interested economic activity needs to be understood as a priority, perhaps, but not as an end. The end is playing a constructive part in the larger society, not out of a misty sense of altruism, but to nourish the relationships that give us our character, place, and meaning in the world.…

SELF-INTEREST IS NOT ENOUGH

The conservative agenda asserts the superiority of the capitalist market system. In this view, self-interest is the dominant motive for economic activity, and private ownership of business with minimum restrictions is necessary to allow people to capture for themselves the benefits that come from their economic activity.

It is no mystery that this view should appeal to capitalists, who are the core supporters of the conservative cause. But the implications of such a market society for ethics and values are grim indeed. Let's look at three ways the exaggerated assertion of individualism and self-interest breaks away from reality: it disregards the connections among us; it ignores the role of luck; and it denies the social origin of wealth.

Connectedness

Seeing the world in terms solely of the market ignores the complex interconnectedness of human beings. Even Adam Smith, the great original champion of early capitalism, wrote of the conflict between market exchange and morality. Over two hundred years ago Smith described how the capitalist division of labor ended self-sufficiency and the market brought people together to coordinate their activities. He pointed out:

> It is not from the benevolence of the butcher, the brewer, or the baker, that we expect our dinner, but from their regard to their own interest. We address ourselves, not to their humanity but to their self-love, and never talk to them of our own necessities but of their advantages.[1]

Smith, a professor of moral philosophy when he founded the modern study of economics, tells us here that self-love and humanity are in opposition. He tells us that, in a market economy, each of us acts without concern for others, with a concern only for ourselves. Each person appeals to others' self-interest, but actually only as a means to serve his or her own ends.

This approach defeats "humanity," as Smith calls it, or community responsibility, as I have called it, because it undermines and denies true mutual concern. The point of ethics and morality in social conduct is to find ways to guide our responsibility toward others. If the only thing that counts is me, there is no place for ethics of any sort as a guide to my behavior, because social ethics are about relationships between people, the terms of mutual responsibility, a guide to each of us about our obligations to others.

An overriding belief in the market and reliance on self-interest defeat morality. They trivialize ethics by making true concern for others irrelevant or, worse, self-defeating, as in "nice guys finish last." Even the idea of "enlightened self-interest"—in which we appear to behave altruistically now only as a means to a longer-term self-interest that would be undermined by immediate selfishness—doesn't solve the problem. In the world of "enlightened self-interest," we still see ourselves as isolated individuals in a sea of other isolated individuals. This way of thinking about society fails to recognize the ways that individuals are also social, created and sustained in a network of other people. It cannot guide us to a recognition of our interdependence and of the moral emptiness of individualism.

We are social beings. But the usual way we think about the social nature of human beings doesn't fully capture what is going on. Everyone knows that "no man is an island," that we live in groups, that we need one another to survive. As Adam Smith put it: "In civilized society, [a person] stands at all times in need of the cooperation and assistance of great multitudes, while his whole life is scarce sufficient to gain the friendship of a few persons."[2] The strength Adam Smith found in the market was exactly its ability to coordinate the economic connections among us so that, through buying and selling in the market, we could get what we need from one another without knowing one another. Through the market, we can reach beyond the personal connections and personal obligations that were the limits of earlier societies—a positive result of the growth of markets.

The Institution of Capitalism 309

But people are social in different and more complicated ways. We are each distinctive beings, but each of us is also a set of relationships. We are created in relationships; our ideas and values and needs arise in our connections with others, not solely out of our minds and bodies fully distinct from others. We are social because we are, in part but literally, the connections we have with others.

Adam Smith was right to point out that in the modern, capitalist world, these connections extend beyond the immediate circle of family, friends, and co-workers we know directly. These are the people who immediately come to mind when we think of the communities that have shaped us. But in the modern world, our very nature as people and the very content of our individuality is also created in an extensive and impersonal network of relationships. Our life chances and experiences are not just our own doing; they are not just the making of our family's influence; they are also the product of the entire structure of society as it bears on each of us.

This is why we cannot protect ourselves individually by referring only to our immediate self-interest. We have to be concerned with the relationships we have to the broader community as well. To protect ourselves, we need to protect and nurture and make healthy and look after the interests of all those in society with whom we jointly make a life on this planet. Their lives literally are our own....

Individuality, privacy, and self-interested behavior are essential ingredients of Western life. No political or ethical system that denies them can be effective. We wouldn't want the stifling eradication of individual initiative that so often characterized collectivist societies in the twentieth century. But neither can the kind of individualism that capitalism fosters play a positive role. By separating the individual from social connections, raw individualism becomes dysfunctional because it is false to the reality of our mutual dependence and mutual responsibilities....

In short, any discussion of values in society has to include the terms on which we limit the activity of private business. Of course, many owners oppose limits on what they can do with their businesses and resist the idea that business has any purpose beyond making money. They are only too happy to welcome the recent emphasis on family values, because it lets them off the hook and puts greedy, predatory business practices beyond the reach of moral review.

Luck

"There but for the grace of God go I." Whether you take life's chances as the work of God, or as the effect of social and natural processes beyond our powers to control, or as the result of random events, it remains a fact that we do not fully control our destiny. Luck of all sorts plays an enormous role. Successful athletes and artists often talk about luck. Successful business leaders also acknowledge it on occasion. As one mutual fund manager put it, "When you're younger, you are more inclined to believe that the profits you make in the market are due to your own wit or talent. When you get older, maybe you get a little wiser and discover that it's exogenous [external] forces that are making you all that money."[3] We saw in Chapter 2 that even Horatio Alger put luck at the heart of many rags-to-riches tales that became icons of the American Dream.

Of course, being in the right place at the right time does not guarantee success. A person has to be able to make something out of a lucky break, and that ability comes from the successful person's own skills and talents. But the central place of luck in our lives cannot be denied. It requires humility from the successful, as well as compassion for those who fail. And it certainly rules out any conclusions about the relative moral worth of those who succeed compared with those who fail.

The place of luck in our lives has other ethical consequences. The Golden Rule, "do unto others as you would have others do unto you," is not a call for tit-for-tat reciprocity, like "an eye for an eye and a tooth for a tooth." It involves a recognition that you might well *become* the other. Social ethics need to reflect the risky reality we all face. Laws and regulations need to be acceptable no matter who you are, no matter who you might become.[4]

A philosophy of individualism that ignores the place of luck and the shaping power of social relationships beyond the individual accentuates the hubris of those who succeed and intensifies the sense of worthlessness of those who fail. The widespread lack of self-esteem among poor and other working class children and young adults is a serious problem, reaching almost epidemic proportions. It holds back their learning and their productivity, as well as causing deep personal suffering. But the successful can also suffer from the effects of extreme individualism. Their often overblown sense of self-importance has its own unreality, which leads to the self-doubts that gnaw at many of the rich and powerful, and to the personal despair that follows the fall from power many of them experience at one time or another.

The Origins of Wealth

A third problem with market individualism that leads it to moral bankruptcy is its failure to acknowledge that private wealth is socially created. Here again it helps to look at the problem through the lens of class....

To see how this is true, it may help to take the discussion away from capitalism for a moment, with all the controversies that a frank discussion of it brings, and look instead at slavery. No one doubts any longer that the wealth of the slave owner originated in the work of the slave. Whatever the slave received in the way of sustenance came from the work of the slaves themselves, given back to the slave only after the owner took it from the slaves who had produced it in the first place. In fact, the slave owner took everything the slaves produced as his own, by right of ownership over the slaves themselves. What the slave owner did not return to the slave, he kept, and this was the basis of his wealth.

Likewise, feudal kings and other nobility drew their wealth from the work of the serfs and other producers who were forced to give up a share of what they made. The specific mechanisms that accomplished this transfer of wealth from those who created it to those who took it as their right were different under feudalism than under slavery. But the two systems shared a common fundamental fact: the wealth of the property owners was the fruit of the labor of others.

Although slave owners and feudal lords developed different arguments to justify their right to take the wealth created by others, their justifications shared a common theme. They routinely asserted the moral weakness and personal and intellectual inferiority of the producer, whether slave or serf, and, by contrast, the moral superiority and natural goodness and intelligence of the owners and rulers themselves.

This is not to say that the slave owner and the feudal aristocrat didn't do a full day's work. They had a lot to do, organizing and enforcing the everyday operations of their societies and dealing with the many levels of intrigue and conflict that challenged their power. But, looking back, the work that occupied them was not like the work of those from whom they took their wealth. The self-righteous claims to moral authority advanced by the slaveholding and aristocratic elites of earlier times look quaint and ignorant by modern, capitalist standards.

Now capitalism dominates the world economy and has established the new standards of political and economic life. Since the end of the Cold War, the capitalist way has been virtually unchallenged. It appears natural, and its standards and justifications are conventional wisdom widely accepted as self-evident. But, if we look more closely, we can see remarkable similarities between capitalism and earlier societies.

Adam Smith, the first person to take a serious look at wealth in capitalist society, had this to say about where wealth comes from when it is capitalist profit:

> The value which the workmen add to the materials, therefore, resolves itself ... into two parts, of which the one pays their wages, the other the profits of their employer. . . . He would have no interest to employ them unless he expected from the sale of their work something more than what was sufficient to replace his stock....[5]

In other words, profits come from the value workers add when they make new products. Not only do the workers' wages come from what they have produced; all that the capitalist claims as his own as the profit of his enterprise *also* comes from what the workers have produced, and these words of wisdom are from the man whose face decorated neckties proudly worn by the free market economists of the Reagan administration! In fact, Adam Smith tells us, the only reason a capitalist employs anyone at all is the expectation that the employee will generate a profit for the owner through his labor. In short, you are employed to make your employer rich, which comes as no surprise to employers and employees alike, even today.

Most executives of the capitalist class probably put in full days at work, as much or more than the slave owner or the feudal lord. Again, the work of modern executives is different from the work of their employees. It is the work of control, of strategic planning, the work of managing intrigue and challenges to their control, whether from their workforce or from other businesses, or the government, or foreign competition. It is the work necessary to organize and maintain the structures that allow them to become and remain rich through the taking Adam Smith described.

Capitalists work hard at what they do. Theirs is not a life of leisure. But it isn't true, as the popular wisdom so often holds, that workers have an easy life by comparison. We often hear that the lucky worker goes home at five o'clock to an evening of beer and television, while the boss stays back to worry about all the details required to keep the business running. Even when the worker doesn't go off to a second job and the boss does work longer hours, the popular wisdom misses the fact that work stress comes less from the number of hours worked than from lack of control on the job. For all the pressures and tough decisions managers and executives face, workers experience more stress and, as a result, have a much higher incidence of ulcers, high blood pressure, heart disease, and other stress-related disorders compared with the managers, professionals, and executives above them.[6]

Capitalists like to say they are the risk takers in society, and this is why they should be richly rewarded. But workers are at constant risk for their jobs and livelihood. Workers risk their health and safety at work and in their neighborhoods to a far greater extent than their employers do. And in every aspect of life, workers face their risks with far less cushion in case of hard times or bad breaks than do the capitalists. . . .

Here we come back to the reality of individual success and failure. In some important ways, success comes from the work of the individual, of course. But there are limits to what an individual

can claim as his or her own accomplishment (or failure). As we saw earlier in this chapter, each of us is not just an individual, isolated from others, making it, or not, on our own. Each of us is also a set of relationships with others, near and far, who help create us and shape what we can and cannot accomplish as individuals, to whom we owe much that cannot be repaid directly in the market. The capitalist, even more than the rest of us, is a social creation. The capitalists' sense of entitlement is out of touch with reality because it denies the social foundation of their wealth. Poor people's claims to society's help with the provision of basic needs, or to common courtesy and respect, are more in tune with the realities of our mutual responsibilities. But typically the poor are not militantly insistent about these claims. Too often, they are meek. It is the capitalists who adamantly demand respect, power, deference, a right to their wealth untouched. Whatever excessive claims to entitlement some poor people may make, it is a weak echo of the hubristic demands of the wealthy.

THE RISE OF "FAMILY VALUES"

In the 1980s and 1990s, as the living standards of the working class steadily deteriorated, "values" came to increasing prominence as a political issue. But values were separated from economic questions. Instead of considering economic justice and social responsibility, values came to mean what some called "family values." As right-wing political forces came to prominence, they redirected the focus of moral debate by asserting conservative responses to such vital questions as abortion, the rights of women, and homosexuality. The energy of these assertions, backed by grassroots mobilizations through many right-wing Christian churches, created a climate in which the moral character of political candidates and party platforms seemed to rest on their stands on these "family values" issues—not on policies to deal with poverty, inequality, military budgets, or the rights of workers to organize unions.

Liberal and pro-labor politicians have answered these attacks in policy terms. But these leaders have too often been on the defensive in the moral debate. They have not expressed a coherent moral code of their own to answer the right's claims of moral leadership. They have not articulated an ethical system to justify their policies, integrate their views on family values with workers' needs, and motivate broad political participation by people who seek moral leadership as well as improvements in their everyday lives....

Individualism has a powerful appeal to the American psyche, open as Americans are to the mythic history of struggling immigrants and pioneers surviving by their own wits and growing rich through initiative, hard work, and true grit. The notion resonates with the early history of this country, a time of small farmers, merchants, and individual artisans, before capitalism and its vast, impersonal social networks and institutions came into existence. Appeals to individualism are especially attractive to modern workers, who so often feel fenced in, without power, independence, and apparent future prospects in their daily lives. No one wants to be told they can't do what they want, especially after a long day at work; no one wants to believe that a better future is closed off to them, especially those for whom it is most likely true....

ETHICAL LIMITS ON CAPITALISM

The moral challenge capitalism poses operates in practical ways at every level of society. It is most obvious when the rigors of capitalist life first come to a community, before people come to accept capitalist norms as "human nature." But even in an advanced capitalist country like the United States we can see the moral corrosion capitalism entails, and find it appalling.

We see it when a rural community finds itself assaulted by waves of development radiating out from nearby cities. Small merchants are driven out of business by national retail chains in new malls. Farm land and beautiful vistas are destroyed when building advances with no regard for community character or traditions, when property values dominate community values. The pace of life changes, becomes more intense. Everyone notices. It's a new way of life.

This is what happens when HMOs push doctors to sacrifice patient care to protect the bottom line. It's what happens when university professors must find corporate support for their scholarship

in the new, entrepreneurial university. In particular, it's what shocked photographers working for *National Geographic*, when the venerable nonprofit magazine opened for-profit outlets for their photographers' work and demanded to keep all the proceeds from use of the photos, after years of respectful working relations with this vital part of their workforce.[7]

In matters great and small, most people think of these developments as wrong, not just unfortunate. We tend to see the naked workings of capitalism as morally degrading. "Money is the root of all evil" isn't about money; it's about putting money at the forefront. It's about allowing the drive for money to be all-consuming, as it becomes when society puts no restrictions on the drive to maximize profit, and self-interest turns to greed.

Market activity needs institutions and rules to guide it. The social institutions that the Russians and the Chinese must now create to protect themselves from raw market power, we in the United States must also protect *and strengthen* in our own way. The institutions and policies we create to limit capitalist behavior must be based on some ethical values. These values cannot be rooted in individualism, since it is exactly the excesses of individualism that need to be curbed.

The moral authority to limit individualism comes from the reality that the individual is also social. The individual has obligations to the social network that helps create, shape, sustain, and also has the power to destroy, individuals. Society can make claims on individuals to be responsible to that social reality, while the individual has a claim to fair and respectful treatment in the social network.

We cannot outlaw greed, any more than we can outlaw any other feeling or attitude. But we can outlaw some of the practical effects of greed, by requiring that the effects of pursuing self-interest not undermine the rights of others. The debate about values needs to be refocused, to articulate values and morality that can help limit capitalist power. This means product standards, labor standards, environmental standards, standards that have bite, enforced with real consequences for those who violate them. It also means some form of social control on investment and other strategic business decisions. These are not easy things to do, technically or politically;

they require concentrated will and careful thought. Looking at the problems with class in mind will help develop the moral compass we need to get it right.

Being against greed is not being against business. Many small, family-run businesses operate in socially responsible ways. Their owners want to make a living, but they also take pride in workmanship, treat their employees well, and respect the community and natural environments in which they do business. The same is true for some big business as well. But, too often, individual good intentions are overwhelmed by market imperatives, driving owners to socially irresponsible action out of the needs of survival. Some of my friends who own small businesses talk about this pressure with the pain and resentment typical of middle class experience. When market imperatives drive business to antisocial action—eat or be eaten, kill or be killed, do what is necessary or go broke—we have a moral problem with far-reaching consequences.

The fact that the capitalists' wealth is social means that the claim working people make on that wealth is not a request for charity. It is a claim for what they themselves have already created. And, if it is true that it is better to teach a person how to fish than to give that person a bucket of fish, it is also true that workers' demand for wealth need not be put in terms of redistributing existing wealth. Rather, workers' need for wealth is better served by a claim for power over the process and machinery of wealth creation itself.

Because capitalists have a hard time accepting limits, they must be imposed by an opposing power. As the majority in society, the working class can have that power. Unlike capitalists, workers have an interest in understanding and acting upon values that challenge individualism. Working class politics can be bound up with these values. And a working class person, so much more attuned to direct mutual aid on the job and in daily survival than the capitalist, has a greater potential for understanding the interdependent nature of social reality.

Looking at "family values" from a class perspective shows us that the values needed to support families are the values of economic justice, values that give their due to mutual obligations, values that put limits on capitalism and create institutions that promote the material and spiritual well-being of working class families, and all people.

Twenty-first century politics, if they are to improve the lives of working class people, will need to challenge the rule of the marketplace. It will take the working class as an organized political force to assert the values of economic justice and muster the power needed to implement policies that flow from those values. From the point of view of working people, the task now is to make class issues the wedge issues of the new century. Economic justice must become the new moral litmus test, the basic ethical standard against which we measure candidates, public officials, and our social institutions. In the concluding chapters of this book, I turn to the prospects for such a working class politics, already beginning to bubble up in the United States at the start of the twenty-first century.

NOTES

1. Adam Smith, *The Wealth of Nations* [1776] (New York: Modern Library, 1937), 14.
2. Ibid.
3. Leon Levy, interviewed by Jeff Madrick, in "Wall Street Blues," *New York Review of Books*, Vol. XLV, No. 15, October 8, 1998, 10. Levy was partner and is now chairman of the board of trustees of the Oppenheimer Funds.
4. This basic idea has been elaborated by John Rawls, *A Theory of Social Justice* (Cambridge, Mass.: Harvard University Press, 1971). Rawls, however, constructs his ethical principles outside of any particular society, before anyone knows his or her position in what will come. In reality, ethics are forged in the conflicts of interests among classes and other groups in actual societies. What is thought to be "right" and what "wrong" is complicated by the relative power of those who stand to win or lose according to the answer. This is why the debate over values and social ethics is not just a question of logic or the better argument. The debate over values is a contest of power.
5. Smith, *Wealth of Nations*, 48.
6. See, for example, T. Alterman, et al., "Decision Latitude, Psychological Demand, Job Strain, and Coronary Heart Disease in the Western Electric Study," *American Journal of Epidemiology*, No. 139 (1994), 620–627; R.L. Repetti, "The Effects of Workload and the Social Environment at Work on Health," in L. Goldberger and S. Breznitz (eds.), *Handbook of Stress: Theoretical and Clinical Aspects*, 2nd ed. (New York: Free Press, 1993), 368–385; P.L. Schnall, et al., "The Relationship

Between Job Strain, Workplace, Diastolic Blood Pressure, and Left Ventricular Mass Index," *Journal of the American Medical Association*, No. 263 (1990), 1929–1935; Cary L. Cooper and Michael J. Smith, *Job Stress and Blue Collar Work* (New York: John Wiley & Sons, 1985); Robert D. Caplan, et al., *Job Demands and Worker Health* (Washington, D.C.: U.S. Department of Health, Education, and Welfare, April 1975). Similar findings were reported in a nontechnical way in Erica Goode, "For Good Health, It Helps To Be Rich and Important," *New York Times*, June 1, 1999, F1.

7. Alex Kuczynski, "National Geographic Angers Its Photographers," *New York Times*, February 1, 1999, C1.

51. THE DOMINANCE OF THE CORPORATION

CARL BOGGS

The immense growth of corporate power is probably the most fundamental development of the past 20 or 30 years.

This selection comes from a book entitled *The End of Politics: Corporate Power and the Decline of the Public Sphere*. This title represents well the point of this selection. What Boggs is describing is the issue of power in society. For most people the word *power* is associated with government. To Boggs, and to most sociologists, power is much more than government. Boggs's point is that government has been overshadowed by the power of the modern corporation. He describes the "corporate colonization of the public sphere," a "depoliticized society," "corporate hegemony," "economic globalization," and "the twilight of the nation state" as the reality we exist in today.

Despite significant governmental changes, policy shifts, and evolving social patterns over several decades, one element of continuity in American life remains, namely, the persistent expansion of corporate power. Far from being a simple economic fact of life, this process takes on political, social, and cultural meanings that penetrate into the deepest regions of everyday life. In political terms growing corporate power has worked most of all to hollow out the public sphere, as huge industrial, technical, and financial institutions have won more freedom to mobilize enormous resources for the purpose of shaping public dialogue and social existence. Corporations foster a mood of antipolitics by means of their power to commodify virtually every human activity as well as through their ownership and control of the mass media, their capacity to manipulate electoral and legislative politics toward sought goals, and their key role in globalizing the economy.

Since the 1970s big business in the United States has developed well beyond its traditionally hegemonic status, filling large parts of the void left by weakened labor unions, deradicalized social movements, the waning of broad progressive coalitions, and the growing ennui of the Democratic Party. Today's corporate behemoths (IBM, General Motors, AT&T, Microsoft,

From Carl Boggs, *The End of Politics: Corporate Power and the Decline of the Public Sphere*. The Guilford Press, 2000. By permission.

General Electric, Disney) depart from their predecessors in that they are generally much larger, more far-flung and diversified, more organizationally streamlined, and far more technologically developed, even as they retain the same profit-driven agendas. At the same time, such giant entities actually begin to constitute a new public sphere of their own by virtue of having taken over many functions of political decision making, including investment and allocation of resources—but in a setting that allows for no internal democratic governance or popular accountability. Corporate networks dominate the state apparatus, own and control the mass media, profoundly shape education and medicine, and penetrate into even the most intimate realms of social life (e.g., the family, sexuality). Societal priorities relating to both domestic and foreign investment, foreign policy, technology, work, and culture are set or overwhelmingly influenced by a narrow stratum of industrial, financial, and technical elites.[1] For the most part, these elites now exercise far more control over the state than the state over the elites. And multinational corporations are relatively unconstrained by the strictures of democratic participation and the open exchange of ideas, being run as disciplined, centralized, and routinized hierarchies in the service of highly instrumental goals such as technical efficiency, material growth, and enhanced market shares. Viewed in this way, corporations function by their very raison d'etre to restrict development of an open, dynamic public sphere in which major issues of the day can be confronted. Much like quasi-feudal institutions, they are set up to guarantee elite domination, rank-and-file obedience, and minimal accountability to outside agencies and constituencies. The post-Fordist corporate system (like the capitalist legacy as a whole) is consciously designed in myriad ways to undercut citizenship, devalue politics, and resist the pull of democratic legitimating principles.[2]

The all-consuming "industrial civility" fostered by multinational corporations and Wall Street financial institutions has manifestly depoliticizing effects: not only are these structures themselves rigidly enclosed, but they exercise enough power to limit political debates and policy choices and also possess enough wealth to influence the entire field of candidates in electoral campaigns. Market principles, shaped and redefined by the modern technocratic apparatus, commodify and instrumentalize virtually all public discourses, practically everything that takes place in the political system. The "public good," insofar as it lives on in liberal discourse as a viable construct, does not exist outside of what elites may regard as contributing to efficient, pragmatic, and marketable outcomes; inevitably, economic discourse winds up conquering the public sphere, crowding out general societal concerns such as collective consumption, social planning, and ecological sustainability.

The immense growth of corporate power is probably the most fundamental development of the past 20 or 30 years. As economic globalization proceeds, more than 40,000 multinational companies have moved into a position to dominate the international and domestic landscape, controlling vast wealth, resources, and institutional power—and with it a greater capacity than ever to reshape the public sphere. The leading corporations build power plants, mine and distribute natural resources, control the flow of the world's oil, gas, and electricity, manage the circulation of money, manufacture and sell the world's automobiles, electronic goods, ships, planes, weapons, computers, chemicals, and satellite technology, and grow most of the world's agricultural goods. They supply the world's military and police forces with equipment, arms, and munitions. In the process of doing all this they have maintained control over about 90 percent of all technology, including what goes into the mass media, information systems, and popular culture. From this vantage point the largest corporations are able to dominate virtually every phase of economic, political, and cultural life; they set the agenda for nearly every dimension of public policy.

In the United States, huge corporations like Microsoft, AT&T, Time Warner, Disney/ABC, IBM, and General Electric have assumed unprecedented power to delimit, directly and indirectly, what takes place in the realm of public discourse. They can shape the images and exchanges that effectively engage mass audiences, in part by employing sophisticated opinion-polling, telemarketing, and public relations in order to manipulate discourse toward specific (private) ends, resulting in a subversion of the public interest (defined in even the loosest sense). The corporations use a wide array of media influences, lobbies, PAC campaigns, experts, and lawyers to undercut the threat from consumer groups, labor, social movements, and community interests.

Intensified corporate colonization of the public sphere took a dramatic turn with passage in February 1996 of the Telecommunications Act. This legislation was ostensibly designed to enhance market competition among rival communications firms, thus stimulating improved services, greater popular access, and technological innovation. It would unleash a new era of heightened deregulation in keeping with the Reaganesque "free market" ethos of the times; indeed, this epochal rewriting of the 1934 Communications Act occurred at the very crest of the deregulatory ideological tide, as Patricia Aufderheide makes clear in her book on this legislation.[3] The result, of course, was precisely the opposite of what the legislation's partisans had claimed: it served mainly to pave the way toward more complete economic control over communications networks by a relatively small number of corporate giants. With the regulatory power of government now minimized, the private interests could more easily take control and set agendas in the entire information realm, including the Internet. Thus, while the Telecommunications Act promised a more interactive, open, even democratic setting, in practice anything resembling the public interest wound up as mere whispering amidst the established players' loud clamor for increased market share and profits. As Aufderheide writes: "It makes the American public, and public life itself, a derivative of the vigor and appetites of large business."[4] In this case the public domain was even further eviscerated by a decision-making process that unfolded largely outside of the public's purview, in a narrow process that received little media attention and involved no input from community groups, labor, consumers, and others left outside the corporate orbit. In Robert W. McChesney's words, "The analysis of the commercialization of the Internet is predicated on the thorough absence of any political debate concerning how best to employ cyberspace."[5] The all-important Telecommunications Act was the product of a closed system in which political "differences"—for example, those between Newt Gingrich and Al Gore—more or less vanished in the powerful field of privileged interests.

One of the hallmarks of a depoliticized society is the largely taken-for-granted character of deeply entrenched forms of domination. Nowadays, the Washington establishment makes certain that oppositional currents are confined to the most limited corridors of debate and participation, where political choices are ultimately instrumentalized, reduced to matters of technique and efficiency. Critical issues that revolve around the undeniably *public* character of corporations—such matters as the structure of authority, what is produced, the rights of labor, trade policies, and so forth—are rarely posed in the political arena. Tobacco production, sales, and advertising are viewed as the prerogative of "private" companies functioning in a "free" market, answerable only to their "stockholders." Similarly, the U.S. military interventions in Iraq during 1991 and later, costing tens of thousands of lives, were undertaken to defend U.S. "security" interests and protect American markets' easy access to oil, to ensure "the American way of life" (in President George H. Bush's language). And continued large-scale worker layoffs and dislocations resulting from corporate downsizing are justified as necessary to keep capitalist firms internationally competitive—examples of that are legion.

Corporate power is reproduced and reinforced in two ways: through the perpetual rationalization of economic structures and through increased atomization of social life outside the confines of the corporation. The rather extreme individualism that has always infused America's liberal tradition, in effect, helps to reproduce corporate power. What needs to be emphasized here is that the celebrated "unity," cohesion, and purposive development of large corporations feeds on a high degree of mass inertia, much of it derived from popular belief in the fiction (again, rooted in liberalism) of a "private" ownership that confers nearly absolute "rights" and "freedoms" on the owners of capital. In this scheme of things "politics" represents an unwelcome challenge to managerial autonomy and flexibility at a time when intensified global competition seems to demand greater adaptation and fluidity. Elites want maximum "freedom" from state intervention that taxes, regulates, influences markets, and otherwise impedes the open flow of resources, goods, and profits. While corporations do not always succeed in fighting off government supervision in certain areas, the legitimating ethos of private firms maximizing their interests in a presumably self-regulating market economy still holds sway and has even enjoyed a resurgence in the 1990s. To the extent that politics is devalued in favor of such presumed economic rationality, the main possible counterweight to corporate power—a strong, dynamic public sector—is eviscerated, undermined by an appeal to laissez-faire ideology. By the end of the twentieth century the balance between governmental and corporate power had tipped strongly in favor of the latter, despite continued (and generally unconvincing) protests against the tyranny of "big government" by conservatives and neoliberals.

Modern corporations, stronger, more rationalized, more ideologically self-conscious, and increasingly global in scope, have stepped into the political breach, indeed, many nominally "private" firms have for some time performed governing functions normally the purview of the state. Greider describes General Electric as such a company, which not only manufactures light bulbs, jet engines, and nuclear power equipment but also plays a significant role in the mass media (it owns NBC and CNBC), the military, the environment, foreign trade, and of course the larger expanse of the international economy. It devotes huge resources to advertising, controls important segments of media programming, and influences election campaigns along with legislation, not only through its enormous power and wealth but through its ubiquitous institutional presence. Few other entities came close to duplicating such far-reaching activities or exercising such influence in the media. As Greider writes, "Given the failure of the other institutions to adapt and revitalize themselves, corporate politics has become the organizational core of the political process—the main connective tissue linking people to their government."[6] The great impact of corporations like GE, of course, is weighted overwhelmingly on the side of conservatism—in economics if not in social and cultural values. Such quasi-governing institutions hire large teams of lawyers,

lobbyists, public relations agents, and advertisers to protect their interests and propagate their values, all the while manufacturing the image of a "responsible corporate citizen" dedicated to human rights, democracy, environmental protection, Mom, and apple pie. The economic health of GE is naturally equated with and might pass for the common good: sustained growth and profits are presented as a necessary link to greater material affluence, proliferation of jobs, a better environment, a more powerful country. In this schema GE does maintain an extensive work force, much of it well-paid, with nearly 250,000 employees at 280 plants in the United States and overseas.

The political reality is that General Electric has worked aggressively, often ruthlessly, for a strong military, a fiercely nationalistic foreign policy, free trade, reductions in taxes and social programs, and loosened environmental regulations. As a major producer of nuclear power equipment it has, not surprisingly, been in the forefront of a pronuclear agenda. Further, with its multiple internal and external constituencies, GE has taken on the character of an expanded and updated urban political machine—though with far less accountability. GE executives and managers have been found guilty of corruption and criminal fraud, but penalties have rarely been harsh enough to deter repeated violations. Thus, in 1990 GE was convicted of criminal fraud for cheating the Army on a $254 million contract for battlefield computers, for which the corporation paid $16.1 million in criminal and civil fines—including $11.7 million to settle roughly 200 other government charges. At GE, as in the rest of the corporate economy, ethics have all too often been bypassed in favor of more instrumental pursuits; while fervently upheld in theory, in practice ethics have been quietly subordinated to the operational criteria of control, efficiency, and profits. And the influence of workers and consumers on vital areas of decision making at GE has been minimal, especially at a time when downsizing and layoffs further erode popular leverage. Managerial elites want to escape governmental regulations of *any* sort, and—at least since the later 1970s—there has been a major impetus toward the resurgence of laissez-faire ideology in the United States. By means of a sustained mobilization of professional expertise, moreover, these elites have been able to exercise pervasive influence over the flow of political and cultural information, seeking ever to suppress such tame liberal ideas as the free exchange of ideas, government involvement as needed, and active participation by all citizens in political decision making.

Corporate hegemony is further solidified by the workings of economic globalization, the information revolution, mass media, and the culture industry—all of which are interwoven in a matrix of commodified production. Multinational corporations exercise nearly total control over resource allocation, investment decisions, commerce, and world trade, severely reducing the role of specifically national actors (whether governments or firms).[7] "Global cities" like Tokyo, Mexico City, New York, Singapore, Los Angeles, and Sao Paolo, with no particular regional or national allegiances, become magnetic centers of capital and technology flows that resist the force of territorial boundaries. Working through the World Bank, World Trade Organization (WTO), and the International Monetary Fund (IMF), and aided by such trade arrangements as GATT and NAFTA, multinationals use their financial leverage to push for a market-centered capitalism featuring minimal governmental controls, fiscal austerity, and privatization wherever feasible. Any genuine form of political regulation is regarded as a threat to the "free market," which is glibly passed off as representative of a form of economic "democracy." The deep structural impacts of a highly globalized and interconnected market system have yet to be fully comprehended. On the downside, though, economic upheavals emanating from Asia from late 1997 through most of 1998 (the "Asian contagion" scare) may well offer some clues to the future. The first ripples of economic crisis already reveal momentous forces that are exacerbating class (and possibly racial) divisions in many countries. Meanwhile, globalization has led to a decline of national governmental power and local autonomy to such a degree that many basic economic decisions are being usurped by multinational corporations and allied international organizations. In the absence of effective multinational planning or regulation mechanisms, development

will surely have little in common with the utopian vision of elites who see—not chaos and polarization—but only unfettered economic growth, a worldwide strengthening of human freedoms and rights, and the increased technological capacity to solve the world's major problems.

We know that corporate power does in fact translate into dynamic economic development, but the penetration of capital into every region of the world brings with it highly uneven forms of growth, sharpened class divisions, social dislocations, and mounting ecological crises. The process reproduces the same emphasis on privatized modes of production and consumption, market priorities over social goods, technological manipulation of resources and information, and material growth for its own (and profits') sake—leading to the same extreme maldistribution of wealth, authoritarian governance, and familiar coupling of urban decay and violence. With global political instrumentalities lacking sufficient leverage, the public sphere—such as it is—inevitably succumbs to the ceaseless pressures of the economic powers that be, leaving no ethical or governing framework for solving urgent problems. (The failure of the U.N.-sponsored Earth Summit to deal decisively with the global ecological crisis at its meeting in Rio de Janeiro in 1992, among many other such failures, reflects this predicament.) The subordination of politics to the all-powerful commodity underpins the strong corporate drive toward a unified world economy where diversity means little more than capitalist rivalries, where genuine cultural and ideological pluralism are submerged by the homogenizing ethic of market relations.

Economic globalization creates a shrinking world even as markets expand, the flow of capital, technology, material resources, transportation, and telecommunications having generally increased at an accelerating pace since the 1970s. Further, goods and services are no longer produced in only one location but rather enter the market through what Robert Reich dubs the "global web" of producers, computers, and satellites that link designers, engineers, contractors, and distributors worldwide. Resources, knowledge, and customized services are more easily than ever exchanged instantaneously across manufacturing and distribution sectors, across national boundaries. Thus, in an evolving complex global and high-value economy, "fewer products have distinct nationalities. Quantities can be produced efficiently in many different locations, to be combined in all sorts of ways to serve customer needs in many places. Intellectual and financial capital can come from anywhere, and be added instantly."[8] This is just as true for cultural products like film and music as it is for such durable goods as autos, electronic goods, and computers. To be sure, there are still remnants of national economic identity in the multinational system—Japan versus the United States, competition among developing Asian powers for markets, conflict among Latin American countries, and so on—but the entire corporate system, while still tied to specific governments, is becoming more and more disconnected from the nation-state. In Reich's words, "The emerging American company knows no national boundaries, feels no geographic constraint."[9] Moreover, as interdependence weakens nationalism, it also renders national and local politics weaker and more vulnerable to the inexorable pressures of the cosmopolitan market.

We have thus reached what Jean-Marie Guehenno describes as "the twilight of the nation-state," a political construct that has ultimately adapted poorly to the web of economic interdependence and the vast power of global corporations. It follows that a politics organized historically around viable nation-states will be far less today a locus of a mass mobilization, legitimacy, and decision making than it has been for the past 200 years. The result is what Guehenno terms a "crisis of the spatial perception of power," in which the connection between the exercise of power (both economic and political) and territoriality is severely weakened.[10] As politics becomes increasingly subordinated to a mosaic of private interests, governing structures tend to simply follow a variety of short-term, instrumental agendas of the moment, bereft of any larger vision or public sense of purpose that might transcend the pull of corporate power. Globalization undermines the strong historical connection between capitalism and nationalism. As Greider argues: "The obsession with nations in competition misses the point of what is happening: The global economy divides every society into new camps of conflict-

ing economic interests. It undermines every nation's ability to maintain social cohesion. It mocks the assumption of shared political values that supposedly unite people in the nation-state."[11] Here globalism extends and deepens the domestic logic of corporate colonization, making a charade of democracy as it transforms the entire landscape....

What the analysis presented in these pages suggests, however, is that even in the event of the corporate hegemony becoming fragile—that is, even once its contradictions begin to explode—any future revival of politics at the level of mass publics will face tremendous obstacles. The deep, collective sense of empowerment that must catalyze such a political revival runs up against not only the awesome might of global capital but, closer to home, the devastating effects of a hollowed-out public sphere and civic culture. The problem is further complicated once we take into account the disabling limits of those formal liberal-democratic structures that remain from an earlier period; clearly any political rebirth will be forced to reappropriate and transcend that harshly compromised tradition, one that has lately run counter to the creative, empowering psychological energies needed to produce an engaged citizenry.[12] Lacking these energies, even the most ambitious radical-democratic ideals and arrangements, even the most celebrated participatory schemes, will ultimately lose their popular appeal. In an age of corporate colonization, unfortunately, the historical processes at work seem relentless in subverting what is needed for a revival of true participatory politics.

At the end of the twentieth century the corporate order appears more stable and in control than at any other time in the recent past, despite a series of mounting contradictions that might have been expected to undermine the whole edifice. This is so largely because the system, in its globalized incarnation, has been able to maintain an unprecedented degree of ideological and cultural hegemony over both state and civil society; opposition is subverted before it can fully confront the multiple contradictions of the system. Elites can more easily solidify their position since their claim to rule is rarely questioned enough to place their interests and priorities fundamentally into question. Unlike the popular strata involved with daily struggles and grassroots movements, elites typically do not suffer the well-known "postmodern" malaise of sharply fragmented identities and purposes; despite internal divisions, their overall class orientation is far more unified. As capital becomes more fluid, mobile, and global, as material and technological resources become more concentrated, the multinational corporations begin to enjoy new leverage, qualitatively, vis-à-vis virtually everything that stands before them (including even the most powerful nation-states). And where citizen participation and local sovereignty are already devalued in the domestic society, as in the case of the United States, such leverage expands even further. In the absence of strong global or national counterweights, the worldwide market is much freer to pursue its deadly course of expansionism (and ultimately destruction of the planet). A "new world order" built along these lines—that is, featuring the massive concentration of economic and political power—inevitably conflicts with even the most rudimentary requirements of democratic politics, namely, an open public sphere, a thriving civic culture, broad allocation of material resources, and minimal differences between rich and poor. After all, sustained citizen involvement in community life and political decision making hardly fits the corporate demands for hierarchy, profit maximization, cost cutting, and "market flexibility" in a period of heightened global competition. Whether corporate hegemony can be maintained in a world riven with economic crisis, social polarization, and civil strife—a world ultimately faced with ecological catastrophe—is yet another matter.

NOTES

1. Stanley A. Deetz, *Corporate Colonization* (Albany, NY: SUNY Press, 1992).
2. See Bowles and Gintis, *Capitalism and Democracy*, ch. 2, on this historic conflict between two competing forces.
3. Patricia Aufderheide, *Communications Policy and the Public Interest* (New York: Guilford Press, 1999), 22–23.
4. Ibid., 62.
5. Robert W. McChesney, *Corporate Media and the Threat to Democracy* (New York: Seven Stories Press, 1997), 34.
6. William Greider, *Who Will Tell the People?* (New York: Simon & Schuster, 1992), 336.
7. See Robert Reich, *The Work of Nations* (New York: Vintage, 1992), chs. 10, 11.
8. Ibid., 112.
9. Ibid., 124.
10. Jean-Marie Guehenno, *End of the Nation State* (Minneapolis: University of Minnesota Press, 1995), 20.
11. Greider, *One World, Ready or Not* (New York: Simon and Schuster, 1997), 18.
12. For an extended discussion of the requirements for a participatory citizenship, see Paul Barry Clarke, *Deep Citizenship* (London: Pluto, 1996), chs. 4,7.

52. JOBS—AND JOBLESSNESS—IN A TECHNOLOGICAL AMERICA

S. ARONOWITZ and W. DI FAZIO

...The shape of things to come—as well as those already in existence—signals the emerging proletarianization of work at every level below top management and a relatively few scientific and technical occupations.

There is a revolution going on in society concerning our economic institutions. Specifically, it has to do with work. This selection examines that revolution and ties it to a scientific-technological revolution. Aronowitz and Di Fazio show us what is happening and why. Jobs will never be the same as they were; incomes and standard of living for most people will be considerably lower than they are now; mobility will become more difficult, and a greater gap will be created between those at the top of the economic order and everyone else. This selection deserves careful examination and debate. It will probably happen in the classroom more than it will in the political order.

OVERVIEW

In 1992, the long-term shifts in the nature of paid work became painfully visible not only to industrial workers and those with technical, professional, and managerial credentials and job experience but also to the public. During that year, "corporate giants like General Motors and IBM announced plans to shed tens of thousands of workers." General Motors, which at first said it would close twenty-one U.S. plants by 1995, soon disclaimed any definite limit to the number of either plant closings or firings and admitted that the numbers of jobs lost might climb above the predicted 70,000, even if the recession led to increased car sales. IBM, which initially shaved about 25,000 blue- and white-collar employees, soon increased its estimates to possibly 60,000, in effect reversing the company's historic policy of no layoffs. Citing economic conditions, Boeing,

From *The Jobless Future: Sci-Tech and the Dogma of Work*, by S. Aronowitz and W. DiFazio. Copyright © 1994 by the Regents of the University of Minnesota. Reprinted by permission of the University of Minnesota Press.

the world's largest airplane producer, and Hughes Aircraft, a major parts manufacturer, were poised for substantial cuts in their well-paid workforces. In 1991 and 1992, major retailers, including Sears, either shut down stores or drastically cut the number of employees; in late January 1993, Sears announced that it was letting about 50,000 employees go. The examples could be multiplied. Millions, worldwide, were losing their jobs in the industrialized West and Asia. Homelessness was and is growing....

...The scientific-technological revolution of our time, which is not confined to new electronic processes but also affects organizational changes in the structure of corporations, has fundamentally altered the forms of work, skill, and occupation. The whole notion of tradition and identity of persons with their work has been radically changed.

Scientific and technological innovation is, for the most part, no longer episodic. Technological change has been routinized. Not only has abstract knowledge come to the center of the world's political economy, but there is also a tendency to produce and trade in symbolic significations rather than concrete products. Today, knowledge rather than traditional skill is the main productive force. The revolution has widened the gap between intellectual, technical, and manual labor, between a relatively small number of jobs that, owing to technological complexity, require more knowledge and a much larger number that require less; because the mass of jobs are "de-skilled," there is a resultant redefinition of occupational categories that reflects the changes in the nature of jobs. As these transformations sweep the world, older conceptions of class, gender, and ethnicity are called into question. For example, on the New York waterfront (until 1970, the nation's largest), Italians and blacks dominated the Brooklyn docks and the Irish and Eastern Europeans worked the Manhattan piers. Today, not only are the docks vanishing as sites of shipping, the workers are gone as well. For those who remain, the traditional occupation of longshoreman—dangerous, but highly skilled—has given way, as a result of containerization of the entire process, to a shrunken workforce that possesses knowledge but not the old skills[1] ...This is just an example of a generalized shift in the nature and significance of work.

As jobs have changed, so have the significance and duration of joblessness. Partial and permanent unemployment, except during the two great world depressions (1893–1898 and 1929–1939) largely episodic and subject to short-term economic contingencies, has increasingly become a mode of life for larger segments of the populations not only of less industrially developed countries, but for those in "advanced" industrial societies as well. Many who are classified in official statistics as "employed" actually work at casual and part-time jobs, the number of which has grown dramatically over the past fifteen years. This phenomenon, once confined to freelance writers and artists, laborers and clerical workers, today cuts across all occupations, including the professions. Even the once buoyant "new" profession of computer programmer is already showing signs of age after barely a quarter of a century. We argue that the shape of things to come—as well as those already in existence—signals the emerging proletarianization of work at every level below top management and a relatively few scientific and technical occupations.

At the same time, because of the permanent character of job cuts starting in the 1970s and glaringly visible after 1989, the latest recession has finally and irrevocably vitiated the traditional idea that the unemployed are an "industrial reserve army" awaiting the next phase of economic expansion. Of course, some laid-off workers, especially in union workplaces, will be recalled when the expansion, however sluggish, resumes. Even if one stubbornly clings to the notion of a reserve army, one cannot help but note that its soldiers in the main now occupy the part-time and temporary positions that appear to have replaced the well-paid full-time jobs.

Because of these changes, the "meaning" (in the survival, psychological, and cultural senses) of work—occupations and professions—as forms of life is in crisis. If the tendencies of the economy and the culture point to the conclusion that work is no longer significant in the formation of the self, one of the crucial questions of our time is what, if anything, can replace it. When layers of qualified—to say nothing of mass—labor are made redundant, obsolete, *irrelevant*, what, after five centuries during which work remained a, perhaps *the*, Western cultural ideal, can we mean by the "self"? Have we reached a large historical watershed, a climacteric that will be as devastating as natural climacterics of the past that destroyed whole species?

...Science and technology (of which organization is an instance) alter the nature of the labor process, not only the rationalized manual labor but also intellectual labor, especially the professions. Knowledge becomes ineluctably intertwined with, even dependent on, technology. Even so-called labor-intensive work becomes increasingly mechanized and begins to be replaced by capital- and technology-intensive—*capitech-intensive*—work. Today, the regime of world economic life consists of scratching every itch of everyday life with sci-tech: eye glasses, underarm deodorant, preservatives in food, braces on pets. Technology has become the universal problem solver, the postmodern equivalent of *deus ex machina*, the ineluctable component of education and play as much as of work. No level of schooling is spared: Students interact with computers to learn reading, writing, social studies, math, and science in elementary school through graduate school. Play, once and still the corner of the social world least subject to regimentation, is increasingly incorporated into computer software, especially the products of the Apple corporation. More and more, we, the service and professional classes, are chained to our personal computers; with the help of the modem and the fax, we can communicate, in seconds, to the farthest reaches of the globe. We no longer need to press the flesh: By e-mail, we can attend conferences, gain access to library collections, and write electronic letters to perfect strangers. And, of course, with the assistance of virtual reality, we can engage in electronic sex. The only thing the computer cannot deliver is touch, but who needs it, anyway?[2]

…The new electronic communication technologies have become the stock-in-trade of a relatively few people because newspapers, magazines, and television have simply refused to acknowledge that we live in a complex world. Instead, they have tended to *simplify* news, even for the middle class. Thus, an "unintended" consequence of the dissemination of informatics to personal use is a growing information gap already implied by the personal computer. A relatively small number of people—no more than ten million in the United States—will, before the turn of the century, be fully wired to world sources of information and new knowledge: libraries, electronic newspapers and journals, conferences and forums on specialized topics, and colleagues, irrespective of country or region around the globe. Despite the much-heralded electronic highway, which will be largely devoted to entertainment products, the great mass of the world's population, already restricted in its knowledge and power by the hierarchical division of the print media into tabloids and newspapers of record, will henceforth be doubly disadvantaged.

Of course, the information gap makes a difference only if one considers the conditions for a democratic—that is, a participatory—society. If popular governance even in the most liberal-democratic societies has been reduced in the last several decades to *plebiscitary* participation, the potential effect of computer-mediated knowledge is to exacerbate exclusion of vast portions of the underlying populations of all countries….

New uses of knowledge widen the gap between the present and the future; new knowledge challenges not only our collectively held beliefs but also the common ethical ground of our "civilization." The tendency of science to dominate the labor process, which emerged in the last half of the nineteenth century but attained full flower only in the last two decades, now heralds an entirely new regime of work in which almost no production *skills* are required. Older forms of technical or professional knowledge are transformed, incorporated, superseded, or otherwise eliminated by computer-mediated technologies—by applications of physical sciences intertwined with the production of knowledge: expert systems—leaving new forms of knowledge that are *inherently* labor-saving. But, unlike the mechanizing era of pulleys and electrically powered machinery, which retained the "hands-on" character of labor, computers have transferred most knowledge associated with the crafts and manual labor and, increasingly, intellectual knowledge, to the machine. As a result, although each generation of technological change makes some work more complex and interesting and raises the level of training or qualification required by a (diminishing) fraction of intellectual and manual labor force, for the overwhelming majority of workers, this process simplifies tasks or eliminates them, and thus eliminates the worker….

THINGS FALL APART

…Of course, the introduction of computer-mediated technologies in administrative services—especially banks and insurance companies and retail and wholesale trades—preceded that in goods production. From the early days of office computers in the 1950s, there has been a sometimes acrimonious debate about their effects. Perhaps the Spencer Tracy—Katharine Hepburn comedy *Desk Set* best exemplifies the issues: When a mainframe computer is introduced into the library of a large corporation, its professional and technical staff is at first alarmed, precisely because of their fear of losing their jobs. The film reiterates the prevailing view of the period (and ours?) that, far from posing a threat, computers promise to increase work by expanding needs. Significantly, the film asserts that the nearly inexhaustible desire for information inherent in human affairs will provide a fail-safe against professional and clerical redundancy. In contradistinction to these optimistic prognostications, new information technologies have enabled corporations, large law firms, and local governments to reduce the library labor force, including professional librarians. In turn, several library science schools have closed, including the prestigious library school at Columbia University.

By the 1980s, many if not most large and small businesses used electronic telephone devices to replace the live receptionist. A concomitant of these changes has been the virtual extinction of the secretary as an occupational category for all except top executives and department heads, if by that term we mean the individual service provided by a clerical worker to a single manager or a small group of managers. Today, at the levels of line and middle management, the "secretary" is a word-processing clerk; many middle managers have their own answering machines or voice mail and do their own word processing. They may have access to a word-processing pool only for producing extensive reports. Needless to say, after a quarter of a century during which computers displaced nearly all major office machines—especially typewriters, adding machines, and mechanical calculators—and all but eliminated the job category of file clerk, by the 1980s, many major corporations took advantage of the information "revolution" to decentralize their facilities away from cities to suburbs and exurbs. Once concentrated in large urban areas, data processing now can be done not only in small rural communities but also in satellite- and wire-linked, underdeveloped offshore sites. This has revived the once-scorned practice of working at home. Taken together, new forms of corporate organization, aided by the computer, have successfully arrested and finally reversed the steady expansion of the clerical labor force and have transferred many of its functions from the office to the bedroom.

Visiting a retail food supermarket in 1992, President George H. Bush was surprised to learn that the inventory label on each item enabled the checkout clerk to record the price by passing it through an electronic device, a feature of retailing that has been in place for at least fifteen years. This innovation has speeded the checkout process but has also relieved the clerk of punching the price on the register, which, in turn, saves time by adding the total bill automatically. The clerk in retail food and department stores works at a checkout counter and has been reduced to handling the product and observing the process, but intervenes only when it fails to function properly. Supermarket employers require fewer employees and, perhaps equally important, fewer workers in warehouses: An operator sits at a computer and identifies the quantity and location of a particular item rather than having to search for its location and count the numbers visually. The goods are loaded onto a vehicle by remote control and a driver operating a forklift takes them to the trucking dock, where they are mechanically loaded again. Whereas once the warehouse worker required a strong back, most of these functions are now performed mechanically and electronically.

Some of the contraction of clerical and industrial employment is, of course, a result of the general economic decline since the late 1980s. But given the astounding improvements in productivity of the manual industrial and clerical work force attributable to computerization, as we argued earlier, there is no evidence that a general economic recovery would restore most of the lost jobs in office and production sites—which raises the crucial issue of the relationship between measures designed to promote economic growth and job creation in the era of computer-mediated work....

The American cultural ideal is tied not only to consumer society but also to the expectation that, given average abilities, with hard work and a little luck almost anyone can achieve occupational and even social mobility. Professional, technical, and managerial occupations perhaps even more than the older aspiration of entrepreneurial success are identified with faith in American success, and the credentials acquired through post-secondary education have become cultural capital, the necessary precondition of mobility. Put another way, if scientifically based technical knowledge has become the main productive force, schooling becomes the major route to mobility. No longer just places where traditional culture is disseminated to a relatively small elite, universities and colleges have become the key repositories of the cultural and intellectual capital from which professional, technical, and managerial labor is formed.

For the first quarter century after World War II, the expansion of these categories in the labor force was sufficient to absorb almost all of those trained in the professional and technical occupations. In some cases—notably education, the health professions, and engineering—there were chronic shortages of qualified professionals and managers. Now there is growing evidence of permanent redundancy within the new middle class....

In the two decades beginning in the mid-1960s, the United States experienced the largest-scale restructuring and reforming of its industrial base in more than a century. Capital flight, which extended beyond U.S. borders, was abetted by technological change in administration and in production. Millions of workers, clerical and industrial, lost their high-paying jobs and were able to find employment only at lower wages. Well-paid union jobs became more scarce, and many, especially women, could find only part-time employment. But the American cultural ideal, buttressed by ideological—indeed, sometimes mythic—journalism and social theory, was barely affected in the wake of the elimination of millions of blue- and white-collar jobs. As C. Wright Mills once remarked in another context, these public issues were experienced as private troubles.

The persistence, if not so much the real and exponential growth, of poverty amid plenty was publicly acknowledged, even by mainstream politicians, but, like alienated labor, it was bracketed as a discrete "racial problem" that left the mainstream white population unaffected. Job creation precluded serious consideration of the old Keynesian solutions; these had been massively defeated by the state-backed, yet ideologically antistatist, free-market ideologies. We were told that deregulation would free up the market and ensure economic growth that eventually would employ the jobless, provided they cleaned up their act. Even in the halcyon days of the Great Society programs of the war-inflated Johnson years, the antipoverty crusade offered the long-term unemployed only literacy and job training and, occasionally, the chance to finish high school and enter college or technical school. The Great Society created few permanent jobs and relied on the vitality of the private sector to employ those trained by its programs....

The question now is not only what the consequences of the closing of routes to mobility of a substantial fraction of sons and daughters of manual and clerical workers may be, but also whether the professional and technical middle class can expect to reproduce itself at the same economic and social level under the new, deregulated conditions. For...the older and most prestigious professions of medicine, university teaching, law, and engineering are in trouble: Doctors and lawyers and engineers are becoming like assembly-line clerks ... proletarians. Although thus far there are only scattered instances of long-term unemployment among them, the historical expectation, especially among doctors and lawyers, that they will own their own practices, has for most of them been permanently shattered. More than half of each profession (and a substantially larger proportion of recent graduates) have become salaried employees of larger firms, hospitals, or group practices; with the subsumption of science and technology under large corporations and the state engineers have not, typically, been self-employed for over a century.

Similarly, the attainment of a Ph.D. in the humanities or the social or natural sciences no longer ensures an entry-level academic position or a well-paid research or administrative job. Over the past fifteen years, a fairly substantial number of Ph.D.s have entered the academic proletariat of part-time and adjunct faculty. Most full-time teachers have little time and energy for the research they were trained to perform. Of course, the reversal of fortune for American colleges and universities is overdetermined by the stagnation and, in some sectors, decline of some professions; by the long-term recession; by organizational and technological changes; and by twenty years of conservative hegemony, which often takes the cultural form of anti-intellectualism. Since the 1960s, universities have been sites of intellectual as well as political dissent and even opposition. A powerful element in the long-term budget crises, that many private as well as public institutions have suffered is at least partially linked to the perception among executive authorities that good money should not be thrown after bad.

And, with the steep decline in subprofessional and technical jobs, universities and colleges, especially the two-year community colleges, are re-examining their "mission" to educate virtually all who seek postsecondary education. In the past five years, we have seen the reemergence of the discourse of faculty "productivity," the reimposition of academic "standards," and other indicators that powerful forces are arrayed to impose policies of contraction in public education....

In the subprofessions of elementary and secondary school teaching, social work, nursing, and medical technology, to name only the most numerically important, salaries and working conditions have deteriorated over the past decade so that the distinction, both economically and at the workplace, between the living standards of skilled manual workers and these professionals has sharply narrowed. Increasingly, many in these categories have changed their psychological as well as political relationship to the performance of the job. The work of a classroom teacher, line social worker, or nurse is, despite efforts by unions and professional organizations to shore up their professional status, no longer seen as a "vocation" in the older meaning of the term. Put succinctly, many in these occupations regard their work as does any manual worker: They take the money and run. More and more, practicing professionals look toward management positions to obtain work satisfaction as well as improvements in their living standard because staying "in the trenches" is socially unappreciated and financially appears to be a dead end. Consequently, in addition to a mad race to obtain more credentials in order to qualify for higher positions, we have seen a definite growth in union organization among these groups even as union membership in the private sector, especially as a proportion of the manual labor force, has sharply declined....

The economic and technological revolutions of our time notwithstanding, work is of course not disappearing. Nor should it. Rebuilding the cities, providing adequate education and child care, and saving the environment are all labor-intensive activities. The unpaid labor of housekeeping and child rearing remain among the major social scandals of our culture. The question is whether work as a cultural ideal has not already been displaced by its correlates: status and consumption. Except for a small proportion of those who are affected by technological innovation—those responsible for the innovations, those involved in developing their applications, and those who run the factories and offices—most workers, including professionals, are subjugated by labor-saving, work-simplification, and other rationalizing features of the context within which technology is introduced. For the subjugated, paid work has already lost its intrinsic meaning. It has become, at best, a means of making a living and a site of social conviviality.

NOTES

1. William DiFazio, *Longshoremen: Community and Resistance on the Brooklyn Waterfront* (South Hadley, MA: Bergin and Garvey, 1985).
2. Phillip K. Dick, *The Three Stigmata of Palmer Eldritch* (London: Jonathan Cape and Granada Books, 1978). First published in 1964, Dick's novel foreshadows the development of virtual reality technology, linking it to a future when most people can no longer live on Earth but are afforded the means to simulate a life on this planet from a position somewhere in the galaxy.

PART XI

Social Institutions: Kinship, Religious, Educational

Institutions are most easily understood by dividing them into the areas of life they regulate. Part X of this book examined political and economic institutions; Part XI briefly looks at three more institutional areas.

Two selections are studies of marriage and the family in the United States. Arlene and Jerome Skolnick give us an excellent overview of the changes that have taken place in the American family, asking us always to consider the complexity, causes, and consequences of these changes. Richard Gelles and Murray Straus examine violence in the family and give us some unusual, interesting, and important reasons for this. One selection ties families to social class and examines the role of the family in perpetuating class.

Two selections introduce religious institutions. The first by Emile Durkheim, gives us a definition of religion and its role in society, and the second John Freie looks at how religion in the United States today tries to market itself in relation to people's search for meaning in community.

The last two selections examine educational institutions. Harry Gracey takes one institution, kindegarten—and shows its importance to socializing children to become citizens in school and society at large. Jonathan Kozol reports on New York City public schools, educational institutions characterized by "savage inequalities."

53. FAMILY IN TRANSITION, 1997

ARLENE and JEROME SKOLNICK

A knowledge of family history reveals that the solution to contemporary problems will not be found in some lost golden age. Families have always struggled with outside circumstances and inner conflict. Our current troubles inside and outside the family are genuine, but we should never forget that many of the most vexing issues confronting us derive from benefits of modernization few of us would be willing to give up.

To understand the history of the family in society is to become aware of the many ways it has changed. It is the product of change, and it is responsible for change. It adjusts to modern society, and it contributes to what modern society becomes. It is, the Skolnicks warn us, not something that used to be wonderful and no longer is, but something that is no longer what it used to be. For good or bad—and it depends on one's perspective—we have witnessed a very basic transformation. There are many themes that the Skolnicks highlight in this selection that are worth paying attention to: the diversity of family structures, nostalgia for a past that never was, the Victorian model of the family that emerged during the industrial revolution, the companionate model that eventually replaced the Victorian model in the early twentieth century, and a triple revolution in the mid-twentieth century that brought significantly new patterns—including a lot more choices for young people, changing female roles, and more emphasis on the ideals of emotional satisfaction in the family and democratic structure. The family is alive and well as we enter the twenty-first century; it has, however, undergone very important changes we need to understand.

It was one of the oddest episodes in America's political history—a debate between the vice president of the United States and a fictional television character. During the 1992 election campaign, former Vice President Dan Quayle set off a firestorm of debate with a remark denouncing a fictional television character for choosing to give birth out of wedlock. The *Murphy Brown* show, according to Quayle, was "mocking the importance of fathers." It reflected the "poverty of values" that was responsible for the nation's ills. From the talk shows to the front pages of newspapers to dinner tables across the nation, arguments broke out about the meaning of the vice president's remarks.

Comedians found Quayle's battle with a TV character good for laughs. But others saw serious issues being raised. Many people saw Quayle's comments as a stab at single mothers and working women. Some saw them as an important statement about the decline of family values and the importance of the two-parent family. In the opening show of the fall season, *Murphy Brown* fought back by poking fun at Quayle and telling the audience that families come in many different shapes and sizes. After the election, the debate seemed to fade away. It flared up again in the spring of 1993, after the *Atlantic Monthly* featured a cover story entitled "Dan Quayle was Right."

Why did a brief remark in a political speech set off such a heated and long-lasting debate? The Dan Quayle-Murphy Brown affair struck a nerve because it touched a central predicament in American society: the gap between the everyday realities of family life and our cultural images of how families ought to be. Contrary to the widespread notion that some flaw in American character or culture is to blame for these trends, comparable shifts are found throughout the industrialized world. All advanced modern countries have experienced shifts in women's roles, rising divorce rates, lower marriage and birth rates, and an increase in single-parent families. In no other country, however, has family change been so traumatic and divisive as ours.

The transformation of family life has been so dramatic that, to many Americans, it has seemed as if "an earthquake had shuddered through the American family" (Preston 1984). Divorce rates first skyrocketed, then stabilized at historically high levels. Women have surged into the workplace. Birth rates have declined. The women's movement has changed the way men and women think and act toward one another, both inside the home and in the world at large. Furthermore, social and sexual rules that once seemed carved in stone have crumbled away: Unmarried couples can live together openly; unmarried mothers can keep their babies. Abortion has become legal. Remaining single and remaining childless, once thought to be highly deviant (although not illegal), have both become acceptable lifestyle options.

Today, most people live in ways that do not conform to the cultural ideal that prevailed in the 1950s. The traditional breadwinner/housewife family with minor children today represents only a small minority of families. The "typical" American family in the last two decades of the twentieth century is likely to be one of four other kinds: the two-wage-earner family, the single-parent family, the "blended" family of remarriage, or the "empty nest" couple whose children have grown up and moved out. Indeed, in 1984, fully half of American families had no children under age 18 (Norton and Glick 1986: 9). Apart from these variations, large numbers of people will spend part of their lives living apart from their families—as single young adults, as divorced singles, as older people who have lost a spouse.

The changes of recent decades have affected more than the forms of family life; they have been psychological changes as well. A major study of American attitudes over two decades revealed a profound shift in how people think about family life, work, and themselves (Veroff, Douvan, and Kulka 1981). In 1957, four-fifths of respondents thought that a man or woman who did not want to marry was sick, immoral, and selfish. By 1976, only one-fourth of respondents thought that choice was bad. Two-thirds were neutral, and one-seventh viewed the choice as good. Summing up many complex findings, the authors conclude that America underwent a "psychological revolution" in the two decades between surveys. Twenty years earlier, people defined their satisfaction and problems—and indeed themselves—in terms of how well they lived up to traditional work and family roles. More recently, people have become more introspective, more attentive to inner experience. Fulfillment has come to mean finding intimacy, meaning, and self-definition, rather than satisfactory performance of traditional roles.

A DYING INSTITUTION?

All these changes, occurring as they did in a relatively short period of time, gave rise to fears about the decline of the family. Since the early 1970s, anyone watching television or reading newspapers and magazines would hear again and again that the family is breaking down, falling apart, disintegrating, and even becoming "an endangered species." There also began a great nostalgia for the "good old days" when Mom was in the kitchen, families were strong and stable, and life was uncomplicated. This mood of nostalgia mixed with anxiety contributed to the rise of the conservative New Right and helped propel Ronald Reagan into the White House.

In the early 1980s, heady with victory, the conservative movement hoped that by dismantling the welfare state and overturning the Supreme Court's abortion decision, the clock could be turned back and the "traditional" family restored.

As the 1990s began, it became clear that such hopes had failed. Women had not returned to full-time homemaking; divorce rates had not returned to the levels of the 1950s. The "liberated" sexuality of the 1960s and 1970s had given way to greater restraint, largely because of fear of AIDS, although the norms of the 1950s did not return.

Despite all the changes, however, the family in America is "here to stay" (Bane 1976). The vast majority of Americans—at least 90 percent—marry and have children, and surveys repeatedly show that family is central to the lives of most Americans. They find family ties their deepest source of satisfaction and meaning, as well as the source of their greatest worries (Mellman, Lazarus, and Rivlin 1990). In sum, family life in America is a complex mixture of both continuity and change.

Although the transformations of the past three decades do not mean the end of family life, they have brought a number of new difficulties. For example, most families now depend on the earnings of wives and mothers, but the rest of society has not caught up to the new realities. There is still an earnings gap between men and women. Employed wives and mothers still bear most of workload in the home. For both men and women, the demands of the job are often at odds with family needs. Debates about whether or not the family is "in decline" do little to solve these dilemmas.

During the same years in which the family was becoming the object of public anxiety and political debate, a torrent of new research on the family was pouring forth. The study of the family had come to excite the interest of scholars in a range of disciplines—history, demography, economics, law, psychology. As a result of this research, we now have much more information available about the family than ever before. Ironically, much of the new scholarship is at odds with the widespread assumption that the family had a long, stable history until hit by the social "earthquake" of the 1960s and 1970s. We have learned from historians that the "lost" golden age of family happiness and stability we yearn for never actually existed....

THE STATE OF THE CONTEMPORARY FAMILY

Part of the confusion surrounding the current status of the family arises from the fact that the family is a surprisingly problematic area of study; there are few if any self-evident facts, even statistical ones. Researchers have found, for example, that when the statistics of family life are plotted for the entire twentieth century, or back into the nineteenth century, a surprising finding emerges: Today's young people—with their low marriage, high divorce, and low fertility rates—appear to be behaving in ways consistent with long-term historical trends (Cherlin 1981; Masnick and Bane 1980). The recent changes in family life appear deviant only when compared to what people were doing in the 1940s and 1950s. But it was the postwar generation that married young, moved to the suburbs, and had three, four, or more children that departed from twentieth-century trends. As one study put it, "Had the 1940s and 1950s not happened, today's young adults, would appear to be behaving normally" (Masnick and Bane 1980: 2).

Thus, the meaning of "change" in a particular indicator of family life depends on the time frame in which it is placed. If we look at trends over too short a period of time—say ten or twenty years—we may think we are seeing a marked change, when, in fact, an older pattern may be reemerging. For some issues, even discerning what the trends are can be a problem. Whether or not we conclude that there is an "epidemic" of teenage pregnancy depends on how we define adolescence and what measure of illegitimacy we use. Contrary to the popular notion of skyrocketing teenage pregnancy, teen-aged childbearing has actually been on the decline during the past two decades (Luker). It is possible for the *ratio* of illegitimate births to all births to go up at the same time as there are declines in the *absolute number* of births and in the likelihood that an individual will bear an illegitimate child. This is not to say that concern about teenage pregnancy is unwarranted; but the reality is much more complex than the simple and scary notion an "epidemic" implies.

Given the complexities of interpreting data on the family, it is little wonder that, as Joseph Featherstone observes (1979: 37), the family is a "great intellectual Rorschach blot." One's conclusions about the current state of the family often derive from deeper values and assumptions one holds in the first place about the definition and role of the family in society....

THE MYTH OF A STABLE, HARMONIOUS PAST

Laments about the current state of decay of the family imply some earlier era in which the family was more stable and harmonious. But unless we can agree what "earlier time" should be chosen as a baseline and what characteristics of the family should be specified, it makes little sense to speak of family decline. Historians have not, in fact, located a golden age of the family.

Recent historical studies of family life also cast doubt on the reality of family tranquillity. Historians have found that premarital sexuality, illegitimacy, generational conflict, and even infanticide can best be studied as a part of family life itself rather than as separate categories of deviation. For example, William Kessen (1965), in his history of the field of child study, observes:

> Perhaps the most persistent single note in the history of the child is the reluctance of mothers to suckle their babies. The running war between the mother who does not want to nurse and the philosopher-psychologists who insist she must stretches over two thousand years (pp. 1–2).

The most shocking finding of the recent wave of historical studies is the prevalence of infanticide throughout European history. Infanticide has long been attributed to primitive peoples or assumed to be the desperate act of an unwed mother. It now appears that infanticide provided a major means of population control in all societies lacking reliable contraception, Europe included, and that it was practiced by families on legitimate children. Historians now believe that increases and decreases in recorded birth rates may actually reflect variations in infanticide rates.

Rather than being an instinctive trait, having tender feelings toward infants—regarding a baby as a precious individual—seems to emerge only when infants have a decent chance of surviving and adults experience enough security to avoid feeling that children are competing with them in a struggle for survival. Throughout many centuries of European history, both of these conditions were lacking.

Another myth about the family is that of changelessness—the belief that the family has been essentially the same over the centuries, until recently, when it began to come apart. Family life has always been in flux; when the world around them changes, families change in response. At periods when a whole society undergoes some major transformation, family change may be especially rapid and dislocating.

In many ways, the era we are living through today resembles two earlier periods of family crisis and transformation in American history (Skolnick 1991). The first occurred the early nineteenth century, when the growth of industry and commerce moved work out of the home. Briefly, the separation of home and work disrupted existing patterns of daily family life, opening a gap between the way people actually lived and the cultural blueprints for proper gender and generational roles (Ryan 1981). In the older pattern, when most people worked on farms, a father was not just the head of the household, but also the boss of the family enterprise. Mother and children and hired hands worked under his supervision. But when work moved out, father—along with older sons and daughters—went with it, leaving behind mother and the younger children. These dislocations in the functions and meaning of family life unleashed an era of personal stress and cultural confusion.

Eventually, a new model of family emerged that not only reflected the new separation of work and family, but glorified it. No longer a workplace, the household now became idealized as "home sweet home," an emotional and spiritual shelter from the heartless world outside. Although father remained the head of the family, mother was now the central figure in the home. The new model celebrated the "true woman's" purity, virtue, and selflessness. Many of our culture's most basic ideas about the family in American culture, such as "women's place is in the home," were formed at this time. In short, the family pattern we now think of as traditional was in fact the first version of the modern family.

Historians label this model of the family "Victorian" because it became influential in England and Western Europe as well as in the United States during the reign of Queen Victoria. It reflected, in idealized form, the nineteenth-century middle-class family. However, the Victorian model became the prevailing cultural definition of family. Few families could live up to the ideal in all its particulars; working-class, black, and ethnic families, for example, could not get by without the economic contributions of wives, mothers, and daughters. And even for middle-class families, the Victorian idea prescribed a standard of perfection that was virtually impossible to fulfill (Demos 1986).

Eventually, however, social change overtook the Victorian model. Beginning around the 1880s, another period of rapid economic, social, and cultural change unsettled Victorian family patterns, especially their gender arrangements. Several generations of so-called "new women" challenged Victorian notions of femininity. They became educated, pursued careers, became involved in political causes—including their own—and created the first wave of feminism. This ferment culminated in the victory of the women's suffrage movement. It was followed by the 1920s' jazz age era of flappers and flaming youth—the first, and probably the major, sexual revolution of the twentieth century.

To many observers at the time, it appeared that the family and morality had broken down. Another cultural crisis ensued, until a new cultural blueprint emerged—the companionate model of marriage and the family. The new model was a revised, more relaxed version of the Victorian family; companionship and sexual intimacy were now defined as central to marriage.

This highly abbreviated history of family and cultural change forms the necessary backdrop for understanding the family upheavals of the late twentieth century. As in earlier times, major changes in the economy and society have destabilized an existing model of family life and the everyday patterns and practices that have sustained it. We have experienced a triple revolution: First, the move toward a postindustrial service and information economy; second, a life course revolution brought about the reductions in mortality and fertility; and third, a psychological transformation rooted mainly in rising educational levels.

Although these shifts have profound implications for everyone in contemporary society, women have been the pacesetters of change. Most women's lives and expectations over the past three decades, inside and outside the family, have departed drastically from those of their own mothers. Men's lives today also are different from their fathers' generation, but to a much lesser extent.

THE TRIPLE REVOLUTION

The Postindustrial Family

The most obvious way the new economy affects the family is in its drawing women, especially married women, into the workplace. A service and information economy produces large numbers of jobs that, unlike factory work, seem suitable for women. Yet as Jessie Bernard (1982) once observed, the transformation of a housewife into a paid worker outside the home sends tremors through every family relationship. It creates a more "symmetrical" family, undoing the sharp contrast between men's and women's roles that marks the breadwinner/housewife pattern. It also reduces women's economic dependence on men, thereby making it easier for women to leave unhappy marriages.

Beyond drawing women into the workplace, shifts in the nature of work and a rapidly changing globalized economy have unsettled the lives of individuals and families at all class levels. The well-paying industrial jobs that once enabled a blue-collar worker to own a home and support a family are no longer available. The once-secure jobs that sustained the "organization men" and their families in the 1950s and 1960s have been made shaky by downsizing, an unstable economy, corporate takeovers, and a rapid pace of technological change.

The new economic climate has also made the transition to adulthood increasingly problematic. The reduction in job opportunities is in part responsible for young adults' lower fertility rates and for women flooding into the workplace. Further, the family formation patterns of the 1950s are out of step with the increased educational demands of today's postindustrial society. In the post-war years, particularly in the United States, young people entered adulthood in one giant step—going to work, marrying young, moving to a separate household from their parents, and having children quickly. Today, few young adults can afford to marry and have children in their late teens or early twenties. In an economy where a college degree is necessary to earn a living wage, early marriage impedes education for both men and women.

Those who do not go on to college have little access to jobs that can sustain a family. Particularly in the inner cities of the United States, growing numbers of young people have come to see no future for themselves at all in the ordinary world of work. In middle-class families, a narrowing opportunity structure has increased anxieties about downward mobility for offspring and parents as well. The "Hamlet syndrome" or the "incompletely launched young adult syndrome" has become common: Young adults deviate from their parents' expectations by failing to launch careers and become successfully independent adults, and may even come home to crowd their parents' empty nest (Schnaiberg and Goldenberg 1989).

The Life Course Revolution

The demographic transformations of the twentieth century are no less significant than the economic ones. We cannot hope to understand current predicaments of family life without understanding how radically the demographic and social circumstances of twentieth-century Americans have changed. In earlier times, mortality rates were highest among infants, and the possibility of death from tuberculosis, pneumonia, or other infectious diseases was an ever-present threat to young and middle-aged adults. Before the turn of this century, only 40 percent of

women lived through all the stages of a normal life course—growing up, marrying, having children, and surviving with a spouse to the age of 50 (Uhlenberg 1980).

Demographic and economic change has had a profound effect on women's lives. Women today are living longer and having fewer children. When infant and child mortality rates fall, women no longer have to have five or seven or nine children to make sure that two or three will survive to adulthood. After rearing children, the average woman can look forward to three or four decades without maternal responsibilities. Because traditional assumptions about women are based on the notion that they are constantly involved with pregnancy, child rearing, and related domestic concerns, the current ferment about women's roles may be seen as a way of bringing cultural attitudes in line with existing social realities.

As people live longer, they can stay married longer. Actually, the biggest change in twentieth-century marriage is not the proportion of marriages disrupted through divorce, but the potential length of marriage and the number of years spent without children in the home. By the 1970s, the statistically average couple would spend only 18 percent of their married lives raising young children, compared with 54 percent a century ago (Bane 1976). As a result, marriage is becoming defined less as a union between parents raising a brood of children and more as a personal relationship between two individuals.

A Psychological Revolution

The third major transformation is a set of psycho-cultural changes that might be described as "psychological gentrification" (Skolnick 1991). That is, cultural advantages once enjoyed only by the upper classes—in particular, education—have been extended to those lower down on the socioeconomic scale. Psychological gentrification also involves greater leisure time, travel, and exposure to information, as well as a general rise in the standard of living. Despite the persistence of poverty, unemployment, and economic insecurity in the industrialized world, far less of the population than in the historical past is living at the level of sheer subsistence.

Throughout Western society, rising levels of education and related changes have been linked to a complex set of shifts in personal and political attitudes. One of these is a more psychological approach to life—greater introspectiveness and a yearning for warmth and intimacy in family and other relationships (Veroff, Douvan, and Kulka 1981). There is also evidence of an increasing preference on the part of both men and women for a more companionate ideal of marriage and a more democratic family. More broadly, these changes in attitude have been described as a shift to "postmaterialist values," emphasizing self-expression, tolerance, equality, and a concern for the quality of life (Inglehart 1990).

The multiple social transformations of our era have brought both costs and benefits: Family relations have become both more fragile and more emotionally rich; mass longevity has brought us a host of problems as well as the gift of extended life. Although change has brought greater opportunities for women, persisting gender inequality means women have borne a large share of the costs of these gains. But we cannot turn the clock back to the family models of the past.

Paradoxically, after all the upheavals of recent decades, the emotional and cultural significance of the family persists. Family remains the center of most people's lives and, as numerous surveys show, a cherished value. Although marriage has become more fragile, the parent-child relationship—especially the mother-child relationship—remains a core attachment across the life course (Rossi and Rossi 1990). The family, however, can be both "here to stay" and beset with difficulties. There is widespread recognition that the massive social and economic changes we have lived through call for public and private sector policies in support of families. Most European countries have recognized for some time that governments must play a role in supplying an array of supports to families—health care, children's allowances, housing subsidies, support for working parents and children (such as child care, parental leave, and shorter workdays for parents), as well as an array of services for the elderly.

Each country's response to these changes ... has been shaped by its own political and cultural traditions. The United States remains embroiled in a cultural war over the family; many social

commentators and political leaders have promised to reverse the recent trends and restore the "traditional" family. In contrast, other Western nations, including Canada and the other English-speaking countries, have responded to family change by establishing policies aimed at mitigating the problems brought about by economic and social changes. As a result of these policies, these countries have been spared much of the poverty and social disintegration that has plagued the United States in the last decade (Edgar 1993, Smeeding 1992).

LOOKING AHEAD

The world at the end of the twentieth century is vastly different from what it was at the beginning, or even in the middle. Families are struggling to adapt to new realities. The countries that have been at the leading edge of family change still find themselves struggling with yesterday's norms, today's new realities, and an uncertain future. As we have seen, changes in women's lives have been a pivotal factor in recent family trends. In many countries, there is a considerable difference between men's and women's attitudes and expectations of one another. Even where both partners accept a more equal division of labor in the home, there is often a gap between attitudes and behavior. In no country have employers, the government, or men fully caught up to the changes in women's lives.

But a knowledge of family history reveals that the solution to contemporary problems will not be found in some lost golden age. Families have always struggled with outside circumstances and inner conflict. Our current troubles inside and outside the family are genuine, but we should never forget that many of the most vexing issues confronting us derive from benefits of modernization few of us would be willing to give up—for example, longer, healthier lives, and the ability to choose how many children to have and when to have them. There was no problem of the aged in the past, because most people never aged—they died before they got old. Nor was adolescence a difficult stage of the life cycle when children worked, education was a privilege of the rich, and a person's place in society was determined by heredity rather than choice. And when most people were hungry illiterates, only aristocrats could worry about sexual satisfaction and self-fulfillment.

In short, there is no point in giving in to the lure of nostalgia. There is no golden age of the family to long for, nor even some past pattern of behavior and belief that would guarantee us harmony and stability if only we had the will to return to it. Family life is bound up with the social, economic, and ideological circumstances of particular times and places. We are no longer peasants, Puritans, pioneers, or even suburbanites circa 1955. We face conditions unknown to our ancestors, and we must find new ways to cope with them.

REFERENCES

Bane, M. J. 1976. *Here to Stay.* New York: Basic Books.

Bernard, J. 1982. *The Future of Marriage.* New York: Bantam.

Blake, J. 1978. "Structural Differentiation and the Family: A Quiet Revolution." Presented at American Sociology Association, San Francisco.

Cherlin, A. J. 1981. *Marriage, Divorce, Remarriage.* Cambridge, MA: Harvard University Press.

Demos, John. 1986. *Past, Present, and Personal.* New York: Oxford University Press.

Featherstone, J. 1979. "Family Matters." *Harvard Educational Review* 49, no. 1: 20—52.

Gagnon, J. H., and W. Simon. 1970. *The Sexual Scene.* Chicago: Aldine/Transaction.

Inglehart, Ronald. 1990. *Culture Shift.* New Jersey: Princeton University Press.

Keller, S. 1971. "Does the Family Have a Future?" *Journal of Comparative Studies* Spring.

Kessen, E. W. 1965. *The Child.* New York: John Wiley.

Masnick, G., and M. J. Bane. 1980. *The Nation's Families: 1960—1990.* Boston: Auburn House.

Mellman, A., E. Lazarus, and A. Rivlin. 1990. "Family Time, Family Values." In *Rebuilding the Nest*, edited by D. Blankenhorn, S. Bayme, and J. Elshtain. Milwaukee: Family Service America.

Norton, A. J. and P. C. Glick. 1986. "One-Parent Families: A Social and Economic Profile." *Family Relations* 35: 9—17.

Preston, S. H. 1984. "Presidential Address to the Population Association of America." Quoted in *Family and Nation* by D. P. Moynihan (1986). San Diego: Harcourt Brace Jovanovich.

Rossi, A. S. and P. H. Rossi. 1990. *Of Human Bonding: Parent-Child Relations Across the Life Course.* Hawthorne, New York: Aldine de Gruyter.

Ryan, M. 1981. *The Cradle of the Middle Class.* New York: Cambridge University Press.

Schnaiberg, A. and S. Goldenberg. 1989. "From Empty Nest to Crowded Nest: The Dynamics of Incompletely Launched Young Adults." *Social Problems* 36, no. 3 (June) 251—69.

Skolnick, A. 1991. *Embattled Paradise: The American Family in an Age of Uncertainty.* New York: Basic Books.

Uhlenberg, P. 1980. "Death and the Family." *Journal of Family History* 5, no. 3: 313—20.

Veroff, J., E. Douvan, and R. A. Kulka. 1981. *The Inner American: A Self-Portrait from 1957 to 1976.* New York: Basic Books.

54. PROFILING VIOLENT FAMILIES

RICHARD GELLES and MURRAY STRAUS

Sometimes, the very characteristics that make the family a warm, supportive, and intimate environment also lead to conflict and violence.

This is indeed a very interesting approach to understanding family violence. It focuses not on the personality traits of violent offenders, but on the structural factors that affect the likelihood of family violence. In a typical sociological fashion, the authors ask us to look closely at the way our structures and institutions work in order to become more aware of the complexities of this problem in society—and also to become more alert to characteristics of own relationships.

VIOLENCE AND THE SOCIAL ORGANIZATION OF THE FAMILY

The myth that violence and love do not coexist in families disguises a great irony about intimacy and violence. There are a number of distinct organizational characteristics of the family that promote intimacy, but at the very same time contribute to the escalation of conflict to violence and injury. Sometimes, the very characteristics that make the family a warm, supportive, and intimate environment also lead to conflict and violence.

The time we spend with our family almost always exceeds the time we spend at work or with nonfamily members. This is particularly true for young children, men and women who are not in the work force, and the very old. From a strictly quantitative point of view, we are at greater risk in the home simply because we spend so much time there. But, time together is not sufficient to lead to violence. What goes on during these times is much more important than simply the minutes, hours, days, weeks, or years spent together.

Not only are we with our parents, partners, and children, but we interact with them over a wide range of activities and interests. Unless you

live (and love) with someone, the total range of activities and interests you share are much narrower than intimate, family involvements. Although the range of intimate interactions is great, so is the intensity. When the nature of intimate involvement is deep, the stakes of the involvement rise. Failures are more important. Slights, insults, and affronts hurt more. The pain of injury runs deeper. A cutting remark by a family member is likely to hurt more than the same remark in another setting.

We know more about members of our family than we know about any other individuals we ever deal with. We know their fears, wants, desires, frailties. We know what makes them happy, mad, frustrated, content. Likewise, they know the same about us. The depth of knowledge that makes intimacy possible also reveals the vulnerabilities and frailties that make it possible to escalate conflict. If, for instance, our spouse insults us, we know in an instant what to say to get even. We know enough to quickly support a family member, or to damage him. In no other setting is there a greater potential to support and help, or hurt and harm, with a gesture, a phrase, or a cutting remark. Over and over again, the people we talk to point to an attack on their partner's vulnerabilities as precipitating violence:

> If I want to make her feel real bad, I tell her how stupid she is. She can't deal with this, and she hits me.

Excerpt from *Physical Violence in American Families: Risk Factors and Adaptations to Violence in 8,145 Families*, by Richard J. Gelles and Murray A. Straus. By permission of Transaction Publishers, © 1990.

We tear each other down all the time. He says things just to hurt me—like how I clean the house. I complain about his work—about how he doesn't make enough money to support us. He gets upset, I get upset, we hit each other.

If I really want to get her, I call her dirty names or call her trash.

We found, in many of our interviews with members of violent families, that squabbles, arguments, and confrontations escalate rapidly to violence when one partner focused on the other's vulnerabilities. Jane, a thirty-two-year-old mother, found that criticizing her husband's child-care skills often moved an argument to violence:

Well, we would argue about something, anything. If it was about our kids I would say, "But you shouldn't talk, because you don't even know how to take care of them. If I wanted to hurt him I would use that. We use the kids in our fights and it really gets bad. He [her husband] doesn't think the baby loves him. I guess I contribute to that a bit. When the baby start's fussin' my husband will say "Go to your mom." When I throw it up to him that the baby is afraid of him, that's when the fights really get goin'."

It is perhaps the greatest irony of family relations that the quality that allows intimacy—intimate knowledge of social biographies—is also a potential explosive, ready to be set off with the smallest fuse.

The range of family activities includes deciding what television program to watch, who uses the bathroom first, what house to buy, what job to take, how to raise and discipline the children, or what to have for dinner. Whether the activities are sublime or ridiculous, the outcome is often "zero-sum" for the participants. Decisions and decision making across the range of family activities often mean that one person (or group) will win, while another will lose. If a husband takes a new job in another city, his wife may have to give up her job, while the children may have to leave their friends. If her job and the children's friends are more important, then the husband will lose a chance for job advancement or a higher income. Although the stakes over which television station to watch or which movie to go to may be smaller, the notion of winning and losing is still there. In fact, some of the most intense family conflicts are

over what seem to be the most trivial choices. Joanne, a twenty-five-year-old mother of two toddlers, remembers violent fights over whether she and her husband would talk or watch television:

When I was pregnant the violence was pretty regular. John would come home from work. I would want to talk with him, 'cause I had been cooped up' in the house with the baby and being pregnant. He would just want to watch the TV. So he would have the TV on and he didn't want to listen to me. We'd have these big fights. He pushed me out of the way. I would get in front of the TV and he would just throw me on the floor.

We talked to one wife who, after a fight over the television, picked the TV up and threw it at her husband. For a short time at least, they did not have a television to fight over.

Zero-sum activities are not just those that require decisions or choices. Less obvious than choices or decisions, but equally or sometimes more important, are infringements of personal space or personal habits. The messy wife and the neat husband may engage in perpetual zero-sum conflict over the house, the bedroom, and even closet space. How should meals be served? When should the dishes be washed? Who left the hairbrush in the sink? How the toothpaste should be squeezed from the tube and a million other daily conflicts and confrontations end with a winner and a loser.

Imagine that you have a co-worker who wears checkered ties with striped shirts, who cannot spell, and whose personal hygiene leaves much to be desired. How likely are you to: (1) tell him that he should change his habits; (2) order him to change; (3) spank him, send him to his room, or cut off his paycheck until he does change? Probably never. Yet, were this person your partner, child, or even parent, you would think nothing of getting involved and trying to influence his behavior. Although the odd behavior of a friend or co-worker may be cause for some embarrassment, we typically would not think of trying to influence this person unless we had a close relationship with him. Yet, family membership carries with it not only the right, but sometimes the obligation, to influence other members of the family. Consequently, we almost always get involved in interactions in the home that we would certainly ignore or make light of in other settings.

Few people notice that the social structure of the family is unique. First, the family has a balance of both males and females. Other settings have this quality—coeducational schools, for instance. But many of the social institutions we are involved in have an imbalance of males and females. Some settings—automobile assembly lines, for instance—may be predominantly male, while other groups—a typing pool, for instance—may be almost exclusively female. In addition to the fact that intimate settings almost always include males and females, families also typically include a range of ages. Half of all households have children under eighteen years of age in them. Thus the family, more so than almost any other social group or social setting, has the potential for both generational and sex differences and conflicts. The battle between the sexes and the generation gap have long been the source of intimate conflict.

Not only is the family made up of males and females with ages ranging from newborn to elderly, but the family is unique in how it assigns tasks and responsibilities. No other social group expects its members to take on jobs simply on the basis of their age or their sex. In the workplace, at school, and in virtually every other social setting, roles and responsibilities are primarily based on interest, experience, and ability. In the home, duties and responsibilities are primarily tied to age and gender. There are those who argue that there is a biological link between gender and task—that women make better parents than men. Also, the developmental abilities of children certainly preclude their taking on tasks or responsibilities they are not ready for. But, by and large, the fact that roles and responsibilities are age and gender linked is a product of social organization and not biological determinism.

When someone is blocked from doing something he or she is both interested in and capable of doing, this can be intensely frustrating. When the inequality is socially structured and sanctioned within a society that at the same time espouses equal opportunity and egalitarianism, it can lead to intense conflict and confrontation. Thus, we find that the potential for conflict and violence is especially high in a democratic and egalitarian society that sanctions and supports a male-dominated family system. Even if we did not have values that supported democracy and egalitarianism, the linking of task to gender would produce considerable conflict because not every man is capable of taking on the socially prescribed leadership role in the home; and not every woman is interested in and capable of assuming the primary responsibility for child care.

The greater the inequality, the more one person makes all the decisions and has all the power, the greater the risk of violence. Power, power confrontations, and perceived threats to domination, in fact, are underlying issues in almost all acts of family violence. One incident of nearly deadly family violence captures the meaning of power and power confrontations:

> My husband wanted to think of himself as the head of the household. He thought that the man should wear the pants in the family. Trouble was, he couldn't seem to get his pants on. He had trouble getting a job and almost never could keep one. If I didn't have my job as a waitress, we would have starved. Even though he didn't make no money, he still wanted to control the house and the kids. But it was my money, and I wasn't about to let him spend it on booze or gambling. This really used to tee him off. But he would get the maddest when the kids showed him no respect. He and I argued a lot. One day we argued in the kitchen and my little girl came in. She wanted to watch TV. My husband told her to go to her room. She said, "No, I don't have listen to you!" Well, my husband was red. He picked up a knife and threw it at my little girl. He missed. Then he threw a fork at her and it caught her in the chin. She was bloody and crying, and he was still mad and ran after her. I had to hit him with a chair to get him to stop. He ran out of the house and didn't come back for a week. My little girl still has a scar on her cheek.

You can choose whom to marry, and to a certain extent you may chose to end the marital relationship. Ending a marital relationship, even in the age of no-fault divorce, is not neat and simple. There are social expectations that marriage is a long-term commitment—"until death do us part." There are social pressures that one should "work on a relationship" or "keep the family together for the sake of the children." There are also emotional and financial constraints that keep families together or entrap one partner who would like to leave.

You can be an ex-husband or an ex-wife, but not an ex-parent or an ex-child. Birth relationships are quite obviously involuntary. You cannot choose your parents or your children (with the exception of adoption, and here your choices are still limited).

Faced with conflict, one can fight or flee. Because of the nature of family relations, it is not easy to choose the flight option when conflict erupts. Fighting, then, becomes a main option for resolving intimate conflict.

The organization of the family makes for stress. Some stress is simply developmental—the birth of a child, the maturation of children, the increasing costs of raising children as they grow older, illness, old age, and death. There are also voluntary transitions—taking a new job, a promotion, or moving. Stress occurring outside of the home is often brought into the home—unemployment, trouble with the police, trouble with friends at school, trouble with people at work. We expect a great deal from our families: love, warmth, understanding, nurturing, intimacy, and financial support. These expectations, when they cannot be fulfilled, add to the already high level of stress with which families must cope.

Privacy is the final structural element of modern families that makes them vulnerable to conflict, which can escalate into violence.... The nuclear structure of the modern family, and the fact that it is the accepted norm that family relations are private relations, reduces the likelihood that someone will be available to prevent the escalation of family conflict to intimate violence.

We have identified the factors that contribute to the high level of conflict in families. These factors also allow conflicts to become violent and abusive interchanges. By phrasing the discussion differently, we could have presented these factors as also contributing to the closeness and intimacy that people seek in family relations. People who marry and have families seek to spend large amounts of time together, to have deep and longlasting emotional involvement, to have an intimate and detailed knowledge of another person,

and to be able to create some distance between their intimate private lives and the interventions of the outside world.

There are a number of conclusions one can draw from the analysis of the structural factors that raise the risk of conflict and violence in the family. First, there is a link between intimacy and violence. Second is the classic sociological truism—structures affect people. Implicit in the discussion of these factors is that one can explain part of the problem of violence in the home without focusing on the individual psychological status of the perpetrators of violence and abuse. Violence occurs, not just because it is committed by weird, bad, different, or alien people, but because the structure of the modern household is conducive to violent exchanges.

FAMILY CHARACTERISTICS RELATED TO INTIMATE VIOLENCE

The structural arrangement of the family makes it possible for violence to occur in all households. However, not all homes are violent....

Economic adversity and worries about money pervade the typical violent home. Alicia, the 34-year-old wife of an assembly-line worker, has beaten, kicked, and punched both her children. So has her husband, Fred. She spoke about the economic problems that hung over their heads:

> He worries about what kind of a job he's going to get, or if he's going to get a job at all. He always worries about supporting the family. I think I worry about it more than he does.... It gets him angry and frustrated. He gets angry a lot. I think he gets angry at himself for not providing what he feels we need. He has to take it out on someone, and the kids and me are the most available ones.

We witnessed a more graphic example of the impact of economic stress during one of our in-home interviews with a violent couple. When we entered the living room to begin the interview, we could not help but notice the holes in the living room walls. During the course of the interview, Jane, the 24-year-old mother of three children, told us that her husband had been laid off from his job at a local shipyard and had come home, taken out his shotgun, and shot up the living room. Violence had not yet been directed at the children, but as we left and considered the family, we could not help but worry about the future targets of violent outbursts.

Stressful life circumstances are the hallmark of the violent family. The greater the stress individuals are under, the more likely they are to be violent toward their children. Our 1976 survey of violence in the American family included a measure of life stress. Subjects were asked whether they had experienced any of a list of 18 stressful events in the last year, ranging from problems at work, to death of a family member, to problems with children. Experience with stress ranged from households that experienced no stressful event to homes that had experienced 13 of the 18 items we discussed. The average experience with stress, however, was modest—about two stressful life events each year. Not surprisingly, the greater the number of stressful events experienced, the greater the rate of abusive violence toward children in the home. More than one out of three families that were unfortunate enough to encounter ten or more stressful events reported using abusive violence toward a child in the previous year. This rate was 100 percent

greater than the rate for households experiencing only one stressful incident.

Violent parents are likely to have experienced or been exposed to violence as children. Although this does not predetermine that they will be violent (and likewise, some abusive parents grew up in nonviolent homes), there is the heightened risk that a violent past will lead to a violent future.

A final characteristic of violent parents is that they are almost always cut off from the community they live in. Our survey of family violence found that the most violent parents have lived in their community for less than two years. They tend to belong to few, if any, community organizations and have little contact with friends and relatives. This social isolation cuts them off from any possible source of help to deal with the stresses of intimate living or economic adversity. These parents are not only more vulnerable to stress, their lack of social involvement also means that they are less likely to abandon their violent behavior and conform to community values and standards. Not only are they particularly vulnerable to responding violently to stress, they tend not to see this behavior as inappropriate.

55. FAMILIES AND CLASS PLACEMENT

DANIEL P. McMURRER and ISABEL V. SAWHILL

"Of the many possible reasons for the importance of family background (in relation to future success), we focus on three: genetic inheritance, material resources, and a good home environment.... If genetics are all-important ... public policy can do little to affect the degree of inequality other than to redistribute income after the fact. If material resources are crucial, it will help to proide the less advantaged with more money. If home environment is critical, greater efforts to ensure responsible childbearing and good parenting are in order.

Here is a selection that tries to summarize why families are important to the class placement of children. It nicely summarizes the issues and the research in this area. It raises questions, takes stands, and acts as a good introduction to a difficult and important topic.

HOW IMPORTANT IS FAMILY BACKGROUND?

As stressed in chapter 6, family background or class is important. (The term "family background" can be defined in different ways. It is more commonly understood to mean the economic and social status of the family in which one grew up, as measured by the income, occupation and/or education of one or both parents. But the definition can be expanded to include parents' marital status, number of siblings, race, residential location, and other descriptors of early environment.)

Although most studies find that family background matters, its effect should not be exaggerated. It cannot explain more than 20 to 30 percent[1] of the variation in an individual's economic status as an adult. This should not be surprising. Children with very similar family backgrounds often have different abilities, receive different amounts of schooling, and make different choices or confront different opportunities as they mature and enter their adult years. Even siblings raised in the same families often turn out quite differently, a fact that has been used by a number of researchers to study the influence of family environment versus factors external to the family in determining who gets ahead.[2] Some of these other factors, such as education, can be measured and have enabled researchers to explain, at most, 40 to 50 percent of the variation in various measures of adult success.

But this still leaves the glass half empty. Much is not explained by either family background or anything else we can measure. So we are a long way from having a full understanding of why some people succeed and others don't. It could be hard-to-measure qualities such as persistence, social skills, good judgment, or appearance. It could be historical events, such as a war or a depression occurring at a critical juncture in one's life. It could reflect institutional or cultural evaluations that favor some attributes (e.g., having

white skin or being a good athlete) over others. Or it could be just plain luck.[3]

Still, family background is at least as important to later success as anything else that can be measured, with the possible exception of education (which is indirectly affected by background in any case).[4] What is it about family background that explains its importance for later success?

Why Is Family Background Important?

Of the many possible reasons for the importance of family background, we focus on three: genetic inheritance, material resources, and a good home environment. In other words, we suspect that higher-income parents may produce more-successful children because they are more able, because they invest more money in their children, and because they are better parents.

A full-scale review of any one of these three topics could fill an entire book. We report some suggestive findings here, as a guide to understanding these extremely important issues. In the absence of such understanding, public policies aimed at improving opportunities for less-advantaged children are likely to produce disappointing results. If genetics are all-important, for example, public policy can do little to affect the degree of inequality other than to redistribute income after the fact. If material resources are crucial, it will help to provide the less advantaged with more money. If home environment is critical, greater efforts to ensure responsible childbearing and good parenting are in order.

GENETIC INHERITANCE

One frequent explanation for the importance of family background is that successful parents pass on good genes to their children. We know that individuals who share the same or similar genes (because they are identical twins or biologically related in some other way) are more similar in terms of their intelligence, sociability, health, and other characteristics than individuals who

From "Why Families Matter," in *Getting Ahead: Economic and Social Mobility in America*, by Daniel P. McMurrer and Isabel V. Sawhill, The Urban Institute Press, 1998. By permission.

are not related to each other—even when these individuals have been separated since birth and have experienced quite different environments. For example, children who are adopted end up with educations far more similar to their biological parents' than to those of their adoptive parents. Similarly, identical twins who have been raised apart and may never have known each other share many of the same characteristics.[5]

Of all the characteristics that matter for success, the genetic transmission of cognitive ability—or "intelligence"—has received the most attention. In their controversial and much discussed book, *The Bell Curve*, Richard Herrnstein and Charles Murray suggest that as much as 40 to 80 percent of differences in IQ across individuals are genetically based.[6] Moreover, they suggest that cognitive ability is a critical determinant of economic success and that its importance has increased as society has become more complex and the economy more technologically advanced. They believe we are moving toward a society which is increasingly stratified by intellectual ability, one in which the cognitively elite will receive the greatest rewards and the cognitively disadvantaged the fewest.

Both the substance and the implications of the Herrnstein-Murray argument have been questioned by other researchers. Some researchers argue that they overstate the extent to which ability is inherited, and suggest that a more accurate reading of the evidence on this question may be that 35 to 45 percent of IQ differences across individuals are related in some way to genetic factors.[7] Others cite evidence to support a larger role for genetics.[8] In the end, the importance of genetics in determining individual IQ remains an unresolved and intensely debated topic.

Lower estimates of the genetic component reflect the important interaction between "nature" and "nurture" in determining intelligence. There is evidence that IQ is malleable, with one of the most striking illustrations of this being the so-called "Flynn effect." James R. Flynn found that average IQ scores have been increasing—often dramatically—in every industrialized country for which data are available.[9] Because the gene pool cannot change nearly as quickly as scores have

increased throughout this century, the Flynn effect suggests that some significant component of cognitive ability must be shaped by environmental factors.

Whatever the proportion of IQ differences that is in fact genetically based, most research agrees that differences in educational attainment and other environmental factors are more important than IQ or test score differences in determining individual economic outcomes.[10] Recent estimates suggest that no more than 10 to 15 percent of differences in earnings or income is associated with differences in cognitive ability.[11] Still, it seems clear that some significant component of IQ is inherited, that this inherited advantage (or disadvantage) is one of the attributes parents pass on to their children, and that it has some effect on future success. When Thomas Jefferson wrote that "all men are created equal," he was expressing a political statement, not a scientific fact.

MATERIAL RESOURCES

Another possible explanation for the relationship between family background and economic success is that children from low-income families fare poorly because their parents lack the income to provide them with what money can buy—food and clothing, good schools, adequate health care, and housing in a safe neighborhood. In addition, lack of resources may create a stressful environment for the parent, leading to inadequate parenting and poor outcomes for the child.

Many studies find a link between family income during childhood and later measures of success during adolescence or adult life. For example, children from poor families are twice as likely as those from nonpoor families to drop out of high school, to repeat a grade, to be expelled or suspended from school, and to be "economically inactive" in their early 20s (not employed, in school, or taking care of preschool children). As adolescents, they are more likely to bear a child out of wedlock, to commit a crime, and to engage in other risky behaviors.[12] These correlations are frequently used to conclude that low income causes undesirable outcomes among children from poor families. But these correlations do not prove that low income *causes* poor outcomes any more than the World Series occurring in the fall proves that baseball causes cold weather.

To get around the problem of causation, researchers often control for the influence of other factors that may affect adult success but may also be correlated with income. One recent and very ambitious effort of this sort, led by Greg Duncan and Jeanne Brooks-Gunn, involved 13 different research teams, using different data and focusing on different child and adult outcomes but within a consistent analytical framework. Each team looked at the question of how much difference income makes. Their answers varied in size of effect but were consistent in suggesting that—even after controlling for parental education, family structure, and various demographic characteristics—living in poverty, especially persistent poverty, has an effect on later outcomes, especially on children's intellectual achievements when they are young (ages two through eight).[13] Fewer effects were found for older children, for adults, or for behavioral or health outcomes. In a slightly earlier but extremely comprehensive review of the literature, Robert Haveman and Barbara Wolfe noted that a 10 percent increase in parental income typically increases a child's adult earnings by between 1 and 3 percent, even after controlling for other variables.[14]

Even these carefully controlled studies may exaggerate the true effect of material resources on child outcomes, since income often serves as a marker for something else within a family—something that cannot be measured, and thus controlled for, using existing data but which is equally or more important to the welfare of children. Some of the same characteristics that enable adults to achieve success in the labor market and earn more income may also contribute to their being good parents. These difficult-to-measure characteristics could include their own intelligence, attitudes and values, diligence, good health, sense of responsibility, emotional maturity, parenting methods, and so forth.[15]

The general point, that income may be a marker for something else, has been especially well made by Susan Mayer,[16] who has used a variety of creative analytic techniques to ferret out the extent to which income is associated with better outcomes for children, because it is telling us something about their parents' unobserved characteristics rather than because it is having a direct impact on the welfare of children. She concludes that money does matter somewhat in determining child outcomes, but not nearly as much as most researchers have assumed. It has a small effect on each of a wide range of outcomes, but even a significant increase in the incomes of poor families (like a *doubling* of income for those in the bottom 20 percent of the income distribution) would result in only slight improvements in such later outcomes as educational attainment, dropping out of high school, and becoming pregnant as a teen.

Does this mean the nation can safely eliminate welfare and other parts of the safety net with no consequences? The answer is almost certainly no. For one thing, the research is quite clear that increasing the incomes of children in families below the poverty line has a bigger impact than increasing it for those higher up the income scale.[17] In large part, this is probably because parents with very limited incomes lead extremely stressful lives, may be depressed, and may take out some of their frustrations on their children.[18] Further, current safety net programs effectively protect most families from the kind of serious material hardship that might otherwise interfere with healthy child development—most poor children do get the basic necessities most of the time. It is not clear how generous this safety net needs to be to prevent damage to the next generation. One could easily argue, for example, that until a guarantee of adequate health care exists, children from lower-income families will remain at risk of poor health with all its attendant consequences. Mayer does find, however, that despite already wide variation across states in the size of the safety net, there are no clearly detectable effects on the next generation.

In short, whatever its other merits, it is doubtful that any politically feasible increase in the material resources provided to parents would appreciably change the life trajectories of their children. Mayer's research is hardly the last word on this topic, of course, but it should caution us against assuming that the inheritance of social position in our society is primarily a story about what money can buy.

From a policy perspective, the important point here is that providing greater income transfers to poor families without changing their other characteristics will not necessarily break the link between poverty in one generation and poverty in the next. It may be the right thing to do—as a simple matter of fairness—but it is not likely to transform future lives.

PARENTING AND HOME ENVIRONMENT[19]

As a child grows up, parents do much more, of course, than simply provide material resources. Good parents provide an appropriate mix of warmth and discipline. This is often referred to in the literature as "authoritative" parenting and is usually contrasted to two other styles, overly "permissive" and overly strict or "authoritarian" parenting. Good parenting is not just an abstraction. It has been found to produce better-adjusted and more-successful children.[20] In addition to warmth and discipline, good parents also tend to provide their children with intellectual stimulation (such as reading materials in the home), strong values, and a growing network of connections outside the family—all of which may also contribute to their success.

None of this would matter if good parenting and a stimulating home environment were randomly distributed across the population. But they are not. Most studies have shown that good parenting and a positive home environment often go hand in hand with higher levels of parental income and education.[21]

Further, the structure of the family itself has a significant effect on children's outcomes. Children who grow up with only one biological parent are less successful, on average, than children who grow up living with both parents. This is true across a broad range of outcomes, including labor market success as an adult. And these effects can be found even in families with similar levels of income. In fact, the effects of family structure on various outcomes seem to be due partly to the typically lower incomes in such families and partly to the absence of the second parent, with the two effects being roughly comparable in size.[22] Because about 40 percent of all children now live apart from one parent, up from 12 percent in 1960, the effects of this factor have likely increased.

Thus, some significant component of the effect of family background on success can be explained by factors that take place within the home itself. Disadvantaged children are less likely to experience desirable forms of parenting, to have access to learning experiences that are vital to their early cognitive development, and to grow up in a two-parent family. Overall, differences in parenting practices, home learning environment, and family structure across different family income groups may account for something like one-third to one-half of the overall relationship between family income and children's development.[23] Given the difficulty of measuring such intangibles as "good parenting," these and other figures from the literature are probably lower-bound estimates of the importance of home environment.

CONCLUSION

Genetic inheritance, material resources, and home environment are all correlated with family background and help to explain why it is a strong predictor of later success. The existing literature has not adequately sorted out their relative importance and leaves much unexplained. However, the evidence at least suggests that genetic factors and material resources account for a small part of the association between family background and later success. Home environment (including parenting practices, access to learning experiences, and family structure) appears to play a larger role. However, the three cluster in ways that make distinguishing their separate effects difficult. A single parent who is a high school dropout with few resources—and who out of frustration, despair, or ignorance mistreats or neglects her children—is a case in point. Providing her with additional resources would make her job as a mother easier, but it cannot replace an absent father or guarantee that she will know what to do as a parent to ensure a better future for her children.

NOTES

1. See, e.g., Christopher Jencks et al., *Who Gets Ahead? The Determinants of Economic Success in America* (New York: Basic Books, 1979), 292; Robert Haveman, *Poverty Policy and Poverty Research: The Great Society and the Social Sciences* (Madison, WI.: University of Wisconsin Press, 1987), 114–116; Robert Haveman and Barbara Wolfe, "The Determinants of Children's Attainments: A Review of Methods and Findings," *Journal of Economic Literature* 33:1829–1878 (December 1995); Robert M. Hauser and Megan M. Sweeney, "Does Poverty in Adolescence Affect the Life Chances of High School Graduates," ed. Greg J. Duncan and Jeanne Brooks-Gunn, *Consequences of Growing Up Poor* (New York: Russell Sage Foundation, 1997), 585.

2. Jencks et al. (1979); Gary Solon et al., "A Longitudinal Analysis of Sibling Correlations in Economic Status," *Journal of Human Resources* 26:509–534 (Summer 1991).

3. See, e.g., Christopher Jencks et al., *Inequality: A Reassessment of the Effect of Family and Schooling in America* (New York: Basic Books, 1972).

4. The relative impact of family background versus education depends on how well family background is measured, but when one includes in family background hard-to-measure influences that affect siblings similarly, the role of background looms at least at large as that of education. For further discussion and some evidence, see Jencks et al. (1979), 10, 214. The best recent reviews of the literature can be found in Haveman and Wolfe (1995) and Duncan and Brooks-Gunn (1997).

5. Edward F. Zigler and Matia Finn Stevenson, *Children in a Changing World: Development and Social Issues*, second edition (Pacific Grove, CA: Brooks/Cole Publishing Company, 1993), 105–112.

6. Richard Herrnstein and Charles Murray, *The Bell Curve: Intelligence and Class Structure in American Life* (New York: Free Press, 1994).

7. Bernie Devlin et al., "Galton Redux: Eugenics, Intelligence, Race, and Society: A Review of *The Bell Curve: Intelligence and Class Structure in American Life*," *Journal of the American Statistical Association*, 1483–1488 (1995).

8. Zigler and Stevenson (1993), 105–106.

9. Data for 20 industrialized countries suggest that IQ scores have been rising at a rate of about 15 points (or one standard deviation) per generation. James R. Flynn, "IQ Trends over Time: Intelligence, Race, and Meritocracy," *Meritocracy and Equality*, ed. Steven Durlauf (Princeton, NJ: Princeton University Press, forthcoming).

10. Claude S. Fischer et al., *Inequality by Design: Cracking the Bell Curve Myth* (Princeton, NJ: Princeton University Press, 1996), 84–86.

11. William Dickens, Thomas J. Kane, and Charles Schultze, *Does the Bell Curve Ring True? A Reconsideration* (Washington, D.C.: Brookings Institution, forthcoming); and McKinley L. Blackburn and David Neumark, "Omitted-Ability Bias and the Increase in Return to Schooling," *Journal of Labor Economics* 11:521–544 (1993). Similar results are reported using 1962 data in Jencks et al. (1972).

12. Jeanne Brooks-Gunn and Greg J. Duncan, "The Effects of Poverty on Children," Center for the Future of Children, The David and Lucile Packard Foundation, *The Future of Children* 7:58–59 (summer/fall 1997).

13. Greg J. Duncan and Jeanne Brooks-Gunn, "Income Effects across the Life Span: Integration and Interpretation," *Consequences of Growing Up Poor*, ed. Greg J. Duncan and Jeanne Brooks-Gunn (New York: Russell Sage Foundation, 1997).

14. Haveman and Wolfe (1995), 1864.

15. Duncan and Brooks-Gunn (1997), 601. Duncan and Brooks-Gunn appear to believe that the quality of the home environment—including the quality of mother-child interactions, the physical condition of the home, and opportunities to learn—is responsible for a substantial portion of the effects of income on cognitive outcomes. And although providing such things as educational toys, reading materials, or a safe play area can cost money, they are not necessarily large items in most family budgets.

16. Susan E. Mayer, *What Money Can't Buy: Family Income and Children's Life Chances* (Cambridge, MA: Harvard University Press, 1997).

17. Duncan and Brooks-Gunn (1997), 597. John Shea, "Does Parents' Money Matter?" Working paper 6026 (Cambridge, MA: National Bureau of Economic Research, Inc., May 1997).

18. Rand Conger et al., "A Family Process Model of Economic Hardship and Adjustment of Early Adolescent Boys," *Child Development* 63:526–541 (1992).

19. We are indebted to Deborah Phillips (Board on Children, Youth, and Families; Institute of Medicine; National Research Council) and Edward Zigler (Yale University) for their assistance in guiding us through some of the relevant literature on this topic.

20. This typology was developed by Diana Baumrind, who showed, in a series of studies, that parenting practices are a major influence on child development (Zigler and Stevenson [1993], 373). Also see Eleanor Maccoby, "Socialization in the Context of the Family: Parent-Child Interaction," *Handbook of Child Psychology*, ed. Paul H. Mussen (New York: John Wiley and Son, 1983), 39–51.

21. For further discussion and cites to the literature, see Thomas L. Hanson, Sara McLanahan, and Elizabeth Thomson, "Economic Resources, Parental Practices, and Children's Well-Being," in Duncan and Brooks-Gunn (1997), 190–238. These authors find that household income and debt are only weakly related to effective parenting, but note that "our results differ from those of other studies," which find stronger effects. The differences may re-

late to the peculiarities of the data used for this one study. Also see endnote 23.

22. Sara McLanahan, "Parent Absence or Poverty: Which Matters More?" in Duncan and Brooks-Gunn (1997), 35–48.

23. Duncan and Brooks-Gunn (1997) find that the home learning environment alone can explain up to one-third of the overall relationship.

56. THE MEANING OF RELIGION

EMILE DURKHEIM

This division of the world into two domains, the one containing all that is sacred, the other all that is profane, is the distinctive trait of religious thought....

What is religion? Here is a classic statement by an exciting social thinker who focuses on a single theme that characterizes all religion to him: the creation of a world apart from the everyday or profane, a world we call a "sacred" world.

The study which we are undertaking is therefore a way of taking up again, *but under new conditions*, the old problem of the origin of religion. To be sure, if by origin we are to understand the very first beginning, the question has nothing scientific about it, and should be resolutely discarded. There was no given moment when religion began to exist, and there is consequently no need of finding a means of transporting ourselves thither in thought. Like every human institution, religion did not commence anywhere. Therefore, all speculations of this sort are justly discredited; they can only consist in subjective and arbitrary constructions which are subject to no sort of control. But the problem which we raise is quite another one. What we want to do is to find a means of discerning the ever-present causes upon which the most essential forms of religious thought and practice depend....

The general conclusion of the book which the reader has before him is that religion is something eminently social. Religious representations

Reprinted and abridged with the permission of The Free Press, a Division of Simon & Schuster, Inc. from *The Elementary Forms of Religious Life* by Emile Durkheim, translated by Joseph Ward Swain. Copyright © 1915 by George Allen & Unwin; Copyright 1965 by The Free Press.

are collective representations which express collective realities; the rites are a manner of acting which take rise in the midst of the assembled groups and which are destined to excite, maintain or recreate certain mental states in these groups. So if the categories [through which we understand] are of religious origin, they ought to participate in this nature common to all religious facts; they too should be social affairs and the product of collective thought....

All known religious beliefs, whether simple or complex, present one common characteristic: they presuppose a classification of all the things, real and ideal, of which men think, into two classes or opposed groups, generally designated by two distinct terms which are translated well enough by the words *profane* and *sacred* (*profane, sacré*). This division of the world into two domains, the one containing all that is sacred, the other all that is profane, is the distinctive trait of religious thought; the beliefs, myths, dogmas and legends are either representations or systems of representations which express the nature of sacred things, the virtues and powers which are attributed to them, or their relations with each other and with profane things....

In all the history of human thought there exists no other example of two categories of things so profoundly differentiated or so radically opposed to one another. The traditional opposition of good and bad is nothing beside this; for the good and the bad are only two opposed species of the same class, namely morals, just as sickness and health are two different aspects of the same order of facts, life, while the sacred and the profane have always and everywhere been conceived by the human mind as two distinct classes, as two worlds between which there is nothing in common. The forces which play in one are not simply those which are met with in the other, but a little stronger; they are of a different sort. In different religions, this opposition has been conceived in different ways. Here, to separate these two sorts of things, it has seemed sufficient to localize them in different parts of the physical universe; there, the first have been put into an ideal and transcendental world, while the material world is left in full possession of the others. But howsoever much the forms of the contrast may vary, the fact of the contrast is universal....

The opposition of these two classes manifests itself outwardly with a visible sign by which we can easily recognize this very special classification, wherever it exists. Since the idea of the sacred is always and everywhere separated from the idea of the profane in the thought of men, and since we picture a sort of logical chasm between the two, the mind irresistibly refuses to allow the two corresponding things to be confounded, or even to be merely put in contact with each other; for such a promiscuity, or even too direct a contiguity, would contradict too violently the dissociation of these ideas in the mind. The sacred thing is *par excellence* that which the profane should not touch, and cannot touch with impunity. To be sure, this interdiction cannot go so far as to make all communication between the two worlds impossible; for if the profane could in no way enter into relations with the sacred, this latter could be good for nothing. But, in addition to the fact that this establishment of relations is always a delicate operation in itself, demanding great precautions and a more or less complicated initiation, it is quite impossible, unless the profane is to lose its specific characteristics and become sacred after a fashion and to a certain degree itself. The two classes cannot even approach each other and keep their own nature at the same time.

Thus we arrive at the first criterium of religious beliefs. Undoubtedly there are secondary species within these two fundamental classes which, in their turn, are more or less incompatible with each other. But the real characteristic of religious phenomena is that they always suppose a bipartite division of the whole universe, known and knowable, into two classes which embrace all that exists, but which radically exclude each other. Sacred things are those which the interdictions protect and isolate; profane things, those to which these interdictions are applied and which must remain at a distance from the first. Religious beliefs are the representations which express the nature of sacred things and the relations which they sustain, either with each other or with profane things. Finally, rites are the rules of conduct which prescribe how a man should comport himself in the presence of these sacred objects....

The really religious beliefs are always common to a determined group, which makes profession of adhering to them and of practicing the rites connected with them. They are not merely received individually by all the members of this group; they are something belonging to the group, and they make its unity. The individuals which compose it feel themselves united to each other by the simple fact that they have a common faith. A society whose members are united by the fact that they think in the same way in regard to the sacred world and its relations with the profane world, and by the fact that they translate these common ideas into common practices, is what is called a Church. In all history, we do not find a single religion without a Church. Sometimes the Church is strictly national, sometimes it passes the frontiers; sometimes it embraces an entire people (Rome, Athens, the Hebrews), sometimes it embraces only a part of them (the Christian societies since the advent of Protestantism); sometimes it is directed by a corps of priests, sometimes it is almost completely devoid of any official directing body. But wherever we observe the religious life, we find that it has a definite group as its foundation. Even the so-called private cults, such as the domestic cult or the cult of a corporation, satisfy this condition; for they are always celebrated by a group, the family or the corporation. Moreover, even these particular religions are ordinarily only special forms of a more general religion which embraces all; these restricted

Churches are in reality only chapels of a vaster Church which, by reason of this very extent, merits this name still more....

Thus we arrive at the following definition: A *religion is a unified system of beliefs and practices relative to sacred things, that is to say, things set apart and forbidden—beliefs and practices, which* *unite into one single moral community called a Church, all those who adhere to them.* The second element which thus finds a place in our definition is no less essential than the first; for by showing that the idea of religion is inseparable from that of the Church, it makes it clear that religion should be an eminently collective thing.

57. RELIGION AND COMMUNITY

JOHN F. FREIE

But as populations have shifted and as communities have eroded, religion in America has also become transformed. Fearing membership declines, congregations have changed their structures, their message, and their approach. Instead of attempting to transcend narrow individualism and consumerism, they have adapted to it, developing therapeutic rather than religious messages; instead of trying to counteract the forces that have undermined genuine community, they have created their own counterfeit versions disconnected from their own neighborhoods; and instead of acting as organizations that enhance the richness of the local community, they have focused on building loyalty to the congregation.

Freie sees the popularity of many religious congregations today as arising from a marketing strategy that promises community but creates what he calls "counterfeit communities" isolated from the larger local community.

RELIGIOUS PALAVER: CHURCH MARKETING

Many mainstream churches in America are facing declining memberships as a growing proportion of the population has become unchurched. Since 1965, mainstream Protestant denominations have experienced more than a 50 percent decline in membership, and surveys indicate that only a minority of adults consider the church to be "relevant for today." Running counter to this trend is the Catholic Church,

From John F. Freie. *Counterfeit Community: The Exploitation of Our Longings for Connectedness,* Rowan & Littlefield Publishers, Inc., 1998. By permission.

which has experienced an increase of about one-sixth (primarily because of higher birthrates and immigration from Latin America). In addition, the more conservative evangelical, fundamentalist, and Pentecostal groups have experienced a similar increase. Still, a feeling of crisis pervades most churches in America today.

All churches, whether mainstream or not, have attempted to respond to this perceived crisis. After years of study by a host of special councils set up by almost all denominations, religion in America has turned to marketing techniques to address membership concerns. As one expert on church marketing says: "The successful marketing-oriented church, by identifying the key concerns of its desired publics, will design the types of programs, worships, preaching, counseling, and relationships that their constituents are seeking (product)" (Considine 1995, 22).

A clever marketing strategy to lure potential customers into the flock is to offer them what they yearn for, but lack in their everyday lives. One important dimension of this marketing strategy is to offer them a sense of connectedness, a feeling of community: "As one of the big aspects of the product of the church is the offering of relationships with others, it is logical that the best way to promote the church is through the development and growth of meaningful relationships with others" (Considine 1995, 21). Another religious marketing advisor assessed the current situation this way: "*Gemeinshaft* (community) is disappearing. As a result, persons are experiencing a growing need for meaningful association with others, for fellowship.... Congregations are in a most opportune position to meet the growing hunger for fellowship" (Shawchuck et al. 1992, 27).

Using this marketing approach, churches have promoted themselves as religious communities, moral communities, pilgrim communities, prayer communities, fellowships, communities of worship, spiritual communities, Christian communities, church communities, or communities of believers. In a world where community has eroded, churches have attempted to exploit our desire for community and connectedness rather than play a vital role in rebuilding community. Rather than attempting to counter the broader, more fundamental, social trends that have led to the erosion of community, churches have done what other social institutions have done: they have exploited our desire for community to achieve short-term gains, that is, they have resorted to palaver.

One of the most successful church marketing ventures is the Willow Creek Community megachurch in South Barrington, Illinois. Based upon a marketing survey conducted in 1975, Pastor Bill Hybels founded a highly successful evangelical operation. Applying sound principles of market segmentation, Willow Creek offers its clientele a wide range of programs for children, teenagers, singles, adults, and the elderly. Short courses covering topics such as parenting skills,

marriage, and divorce are among the more than ninety different programs offered. The idea is to link people with those similar to them and thereby make them feel connected both to other, similar people and to the church.

Adjusting their Sunday services to the results revealed in their marketing surveys, Hybels avoids pulpits and robes (he preaches instead from a lectern in a business suit) and uses rock, jazz, folk, and Dixieland music as well as a theatrical troupe and an occasional modest-sized orchestra to entertain. There are no hymnals (the words to songs appear on huge video screens), and the messages are primarily therapeutic with only occasional references to the Bible. Sin is never mentioned, but improving communication skills is a frequent theme. As sociologist Stephen Warner has said of Willow Creek: "Hybels is preaching a very upbeat message. It's a salvationist message, but the idea is not so much being saved from the fires of hell. Rather, it's being saved from the meaninglessness and aimlessness in this life. It's more of a soft-sell" (quoted in Sullivan 1991, 14). Judging from membership and attendance figures—more than 6,000 "true believers" who are encouraged to tithe and attendance of about 15,000 for four weekend services—the soft sell works.

The modern marketing approach of religion today is to sell the church through the use of direct appeals to being part of a spiritual community or in a more indirect, soft sell fashion by promoting the church as a place where the development and growth of meaningful relationships with others takes place. This is the palaver of religious community.

COUNTERFEIT RELIGIOUS COMMUNITY IN CONGREGATIONS

Where genuine community existed, the congregation played an important role. In such communities the congregation became a gathering of believers (no matter what the denomination) who represented the interests of the community. The social fabric of the congregation emerged not so much from the activities of the church as from the community. Religious activities functioned to enhance and enrich the community. In many instances it was difficult to determine if activities organized and endorsed by the church were more activities of the surrounding community or church activities. There was, in those situations, no need to fabricate a community since the congregation existed because there already was a community.

In addition to the important representation function that congregations have played for community, they have also been instrumental in helping to transform the consciousness of its members so that they may overcome narrow conceptions of self-interest. Churches operating within genuine communal contexts help produce moral leadership that encourages mutuality, civility, and cooperation, which, in turn, helps to build communal bonds. In effect, religion is able to counter the natural narrowing effects of localism by encouraging action based upon ethical standards far nobler than self-interest and individualism.

But as populations have shifted and as communities have eroded, religion in America has also become transformed. Fearing membership declines, congregations have changed their structures, their message, and their approach. Instead of attempting to transcend narrow individualism and consumerism, they have adapted to it, developing therapeutic rather than religious messages; instead of trying to counteract the forces that have undermined genuine community, they have created their own counterfeit versions disconnected from their own neighborhoods; and instead of acting as organizations that enhance the richness of the local community, they have focused on building loyalty to the congregation.

CULTS AS COUNTERFEIT COMMUNITIES

While most congregations struggle with building membership by attempting to market themselves effectively, other religious organizations, namely cults, have gone even further. Most mainstream church marketing attempts would be classified as "soft sell," but cult approaches are at the very least "hard sell," and most could more accurately be described as brainwashing.

At the core of the cult experience, and initially one of its most attractive features for potential converts, is the feeling of community they get from recruiters. Although the cult belief system is a strong reinforcing mechanism once a person is a member, one of the important early attractions the cult has for new recruits is the feeling of community that they experience (Balch 1980). "People end up joining cults when events lead them to search for a deeper sense of belonging and for something more meaningful in their lives," says Harrary (1994, 20). While there are a host of psychological characteristics associated with cult members that are often used to explain their involvement, many of their concerns are addressed through the sense of belonging and the feeling of love and acceptance they receive as a result of the communal experience.

Recruiters for cults are well trained to exploit the longing for connectedness that exists among potential members. Once the prospect is lured to the initial meeting with other members, a process known as "love-bombing" begins. The prospect is greeted warmly, complimented on some aspect of his or her appearance, and repeatedly told in a variety of ways how wonderful they are. In that meeting, positive experiences are shared by all. At the conclusion of the meeting, the prospect is invited to a free weekend at a retreat or camp. It is at this intensive weekend retreat where the longings for connectedness that the recruit feels are more fully exploited.

In the fully controlled environment of the retreat, the recruit is brainwashed into believing that meaning in life may only be obtained by becoming a member of the cult. Recruits are food- and sleep-deprived, allowed to talk only with members of the group, made to listen to repetitive lectures, and impressed with the loving and caring nature of the group. Cults attempt to separate the recruits from all outside relationships (especially family) and link them emotionally to the cult.

Once the recruit has joined, the entire dimension of the counterfeit community becomes visible. Cults are run in an authoritarian manner with the leader or leaders usually claiming some sort of divinity. Those who violate any particular rule are often dealt with harshly (public beatings and public humiliation are common), and the ideological/spiritual beliefs are further imposed. The cult leaders are said to possess the only truths, and all who are not members of the cult are purveyors of lies. The roles that members play in the community are sketched out, and everything the member does is choreographed by the leader.

Certainly cults represent the minority of approaches to religion in America today. Because of their secretive nature, no one knows exactly how many there are or how many people are actually members. Estimates range from 600 to over 3,000 cults in operation today. However, more relevant for our purposes is the initial appeal that cults use to entice prospective members: the exploitation of longings for community. Once the recruit demonstrates an interest in becoming a member, the religious beliefs are introduced more completely to further solidify their attachment to the group, but the initial attraction is the feeling of community. The universalistic values and symbols that characterize the religious beliefs add legitimacy to the new patterns of communal interaction: "Gratifying interpersonal relationships among devotees in a cult crystallize a legitimating 'plausibility structure' for the symbol system of the movement, which in turn provides a symbolic mystique which enhances the perceived 'loving' quality of the spiritual fellowship" (Robbins and Anthony 1982, 66). In genuine community, religion encourages and complicates interactions among the members of the community, and usually there are many members of the community who may not be members of that particular religion. But in cults the religion structures and defines the entire communal experience—community and religion become inseparable.

CONCLUSION

Religion in America has not only failed to stem the tide that has led to a deterioration of commu-

nity, but it has adapted to it by accepting community's demise and attempting to survive by developing its own version of community, inherently counterfeit in nature. Instead of using the congregation as a building block for the maintenance of community, religion has accepted individualism as the dominant driving force in America and adapted by delivering therapeutic messages to its members in order to facilitate their ability to get along with each other as individuals. Instead of maintaining a presence in local neighborhoods and attempting to work with neighborhood organizations, congregations have turned toward the creation of the organizational church and attempted to provide a feeling of community by involving followers in "church work" to connect them to the church itself, rather than the local community. The result of these activities has been, at best, the expression of feelings of community among the members of the congregations while the congregations themselves remain disconnected from the neighborhoods of which they should be an organic part.

REFERENCES

Balch, Robert. 1980. "Looking Behind the Scenes in a Religious Cult: Implications for the Study of Conversion." *Sociological Analysis* 41: 137–43.

Considine, John J. 1995. *Marketing Your Church: Concepts and Strategies*. Kansas City MO: Sheed and Ward.

Harrary, Keith. 1994. "The Truth About Jonestown," in *Religious Cults in America*, ed. Robert Emmet Long. New York: The H. W. Wilson Company, pp. 10–20.

Robbins, Thomas, and Dick Anthony. 1982. "Cults, Culture, and Community," in *Cults and the Family*, ed. Florence Kaslow and Marvin B. Sussman. New York: The Haworth Press.

Shawchuck, Norman, Philip Kotler, Bruce Wrenn, and Gustave Rath. 1992. *Marketing for Congregations: Choosing to Serve People More Effectively*. Nashville: Abingdon Press.

Sullivan, Deidre. 1991. "Targeting Souls." *American Demographics* 13: 42–46; 56–59.

58. KINDERGARTEN AS ACADEMIC BOOT CAMP

HARRY L. GRACEY

By the end of the school year, the successful kindergarten teacher has a well-organized group of children. They follow classroom routines automatically, having learned all the command signals and the expected responses to them. They have, in our terms, learned the student role.

Kindergarten is preparation for school, and school is preparation for living in society. Gracey links citizenship in the bureaucratic school to taking on positions in a highly bureaucratic society—both expect obedience to rules. To make his point, Gracey describes one afternoon in a kindergarten class. The student learns routine, submission, and discipline. It is, according to Gracey, a preparation for life.

It is interesting to note that in this kindergarten class there is an attempt to weave some religious instruction into the secular. Gracey's article was written over twenty years ago. The separation of church and state, a very important U.S. institution was not always important in some classrooms at that time. It is not clear if Gracey is observing a private religious school or a public school. If it is indeed a public school, then it is important to recognize that the religious aspects of this classroom are no longer constitutional. My assumption has always been that it was indeed a public school, and the use of religious objects and prayers are indeed an issue that you should consider. In any case, it is fascinating how the religious and the political are intertwined here, highlighting the Durkheim idea that both areas of life are taught to children as the "sacred."

Education must be considered one of the major institutions of social life today. Along with the family and organized religion, however, it is a "secondary institution," one in which people are prepared for life in society as it is presently organized. The main dimensions of modern life, that is, the nature of society as a whole, is determined principally by the "primary institutions," which today are the economy, the political system, and the military establishment. Education has been defined by sociologists, classical and contemporary, as an institution that serves society by socializing people into it through a formalized, standardized procedure. At the beginning of this century Emile Durkheim told student teachers at the University of Paris that education "consists of a methodical socialization of the younger generation." He went on to add:

> It is the influence exercised by adult generations on those that are not ready for social life. Its object is to arouse and to develop in the child a certain number of physical, intellectual, and moral states that are demanded of him by the political society as a whole and by the special milieu for which he is specifically destined.... To the egotistic and asocial being that has just been born, [society] must, as rapidly as possible, add another, capable of leading a moral and social life. Such is the work of education.[1]

The education process, Durkheim said, "is, above all, the means by which society perpetually

Reprinted by permission of Harry L. Gracey, Cambridge, MA.

re-creates the conditions of its very existence."[2] The contemporary educational sociologist, Wilbur Brookover, offers a similar formulation in his recent textbook definition of education:

> Actually, therefore, in the broadest sense, education is synonymous with socialization. It includes any social behavior that assists in the induction of the child into membership in the society or any behavior by which the society perpetuates itself through the next generation.[3]

The educational institution is, then, one of the ways in which society is perpetuated through the systematic socialization of the young, while the nature of the society being perpetuated—its organization and operation, its values, beliefs, and ways of living—are determined by the primary institutions. The educational system, like other secondary institutions, *serves* the society that is *created* by the operation of the economy, the political system, and the military establishment.

Schools, the social organizations of the educational institution, are today for the most part large bureaucracies run by specially trained and certified people. There are few places left in modern societies in which formal teaching and learning is carried on in small, isolated groups, like the rural, one-room schoolhouses of the last century. Schools are large, formal organizations that tend to be parts of larger organizations, local community School Districts. These School Districts are bureaucratically organized, and their operations are supervised by state and local governments. In this context, as Brookover says:

> The term *education* is used ... to refer to a system of schools, in which specifically designated persons are expected to teach children and youth certain types of acceptable behavior. The school system becomes a...unit in the total social structure and is recognized by the members of the society as a separate social institution. Within this structure, a portion of the total socialization process occurs.[4]

Education is the part of the socialization process that takes place in the schools; and these are, more and more today, bureaucracies within bureaucracies.

Kindergarten is generally conceived by educators as a year of preparation for school. It is thought of as a year in which small children, five or six years old, are prepared socially and emotionally for the academic learning that will take place over the next twelve years. It is expected that a foundation of behavior and attitudes will be laid in kindergarten on which the children can acquire the skills and knowledge they will be taught in the grades. A booklet prepared for parents by the staff of a suburban New York school system says that the kindergarten experience will stimulate the child's desire to learn and cultivate the skills he will need for learning in the rest of his school career. It claims that the child will find opportunities for physical growth, for satisfying his "need for self-expression," acquire some knowledge, and provide opportunities for creative activity. It concludes, "The most important benefit that your five-year-old will receive from kindergarten is the opportunity to live and grow happily and purposefully with others in a small society." The kindergarten teachers in one of the elementary schools in this community, one we shall call the Wilbur Wright School, said their goals were to see that the children "grew" in all ways: physically, of course, emotionally, socially, and academically. They said they wanted children to like school as a result of their kindergarten experiences and that they wanted them to learn to get along with others.

None of these goals, however, is unique to kindergarten; each of them is held to some extent by teachers in the other six grades at Wright School. And growth would occur, but differently, even if the child did not attend school. The children already know how to get along with others, in their families and their play groups. The unique job of the kindergarten in the educational division of labor seems rather to be teaching children the *student role*. The student role is the repertoire of behavior and attitudes regarded by educators as appropriate to children in school. Observation in the kindergartens of the Wilbur Wright School revealed a great variety of activities through which children are shown and then drilled in the behavior and attitudes defined as appropriate for school and thereby induced to learn the role of student. Observations of the kindergartens and interviews with the teachers both pointed to the teaching and learning of classroom routines as the main element of the student role. The teachers expended most of their efforts, for the first half of the year at least, in training the children to follow the routines the teachers created. The children were, in a very real sense, *drilled* in tasks and activities created by the teachers for their own purposes and beginning and ending quite arbitrarily (from the child's point of view) at the command of the teacher. One teacher remarked that she hated September because during the first month "everything has to be done rigidly, and repeatedly, until they know exactly what they're supposed to do." However, "by January," she said, "they know exactly what to do [during the day] and I don't have to be after them all the time." Classroom routines were introduced gradually from the beginning of the year in all the kindergartens, and the children were drilled in them as long as was necessary to achieve regular compliance. By the end of the school year, the successful kindergarten teacher has a well-organized group of children. They follow classroom routines automatically, having learned all the command signals and the expected responses to them. They have, in our terms, learned the student role. The following observation shows one such classroom operating at optimum organization on an afternoon late in May. It is the class of an experienced and respected kindergarten teacher.

AN AFTERNOON IN KINDERGARTEN

At about 12:20 in the afternoon on a day in the last week of May, Edith Kerr leaves the teachers' room where she has been having lunch and walks to her classroom at the far end of the primary wing of Wright School. A group of five- and six-year-olds peers at her through the glass doors leading from the hall cloakroom to the play area outside. Entering her room, she straightens some material in the "book corner" of the room, arranges music on the piano, takes colored paper from her closet and places it on one of the shelves under the window. Her room is divided into a number of activity areas through the arrangement of furniture and play equipment. Two easels and a paint table near the door create a kind of passageway inside the room. A

wedge-shaped area just inside the front door is made into a teacher's area by the placing of "her" things there: her desk, file, and piano. To the left is the book corner, marked off from the rest of the room by a puppet stage and a movable chalkboard. In it are a display rack of picture books, a record player, and a stack of children's records. To the right of the entrance are the sink and clean-up area. Four large round tables with six chairs at each for the children are placed near the walls about halfway down the length of the room, two on each side, leaving a large open area in the center for group games, block building, and toy truck driving. Windows stretch down the length of both walls, starting about three feet from the floor and extending almost to the high ceilings. Under the windows are long shelves on which are kept all the toys, games, blocks, paper, paints, and other equipment of the kindergarten. The left rear corner of the room is a play store with shelves, merchandise, and cash register; the right rear corner is a play kitchen with stove, sink, ironing board, and bassinette with baby dolls in it. This area is partly shielded from the rest of the room by a large standing display rack for posters and children's art work. A sandbox is found against the back wall between these two areas. The room is light, brightly colored, and filled with things that adults feel five- and six-year-olds will find interesting and pleasing.

At 12:25, Edith opens the outside door and admits the waiting children. They hang their sweaters on hooks outside the door and then go to the center of the room and arrange themselves in a semi-circle on the floor, facing the teacher's chair, which she has placed in the center of the floor. Edith follows them in and sits in her chair checking attendance while waiting for the bell to ring. When she has finished attendance, which she takes by sight, she asks the children what the date is, what day and month it is, how many children are enrolled in the class, how many are present, and how many are absent.

The bell rings at 12:30 and the teacher puts away her attendance book. She introduces a visitor, who is sitting against the wall taking notes, as someone who wants to learn about schools and children. She then goes to the back of the room and takes down a large chart labeled "Helping

Hands." Bringing it to the center of the room, she tells the children it is time to change jobs. Each child is assigned some task on the chart by placing his name, lettered on a paper "hand," next to a picture signifying the task—for example, a broom, a blackboard, a milk bottle, a flag, and a Bible. She asks the children who wants each of the jobs and rearranges their "hands" accordingly. Returning to her chair, Edith announces, "One person should tell us what happened to Mark." A girl raises her hand, and when called on says, "Mark fell and hit his head and had to go to the hospital." The teacher adds that Mark's mother had written saying that he was in the hospital.

During this time, the children have been interacting among themselves in their semi-circle. Children have whispered to their neighbors, poked one another, made general comments to the group, waved to friends on the other side of the circle. None of this has been disruptive, and the teacher has ignored it for the most part. The children seem to know just how much of each kind of interaction is permitted—they may greet in a soft voice someone who sits next to them, for example, but may not shout greetings to a friend who sits across the circle, so they confine themselves to waving and remain well within understood limits.

At 12:35, two children arrive. Edith asks them why they are late and then sends them to join the circle on the floor. The other children vie with each other to tell the newcomers what happened to Mark. When this leads to a general disorder, Edith asks, "Who has serious time?" The children become quiet and a girl raises her hand. Edith nods and the child gets a Bible and hands it to Edith. She reads the Twenty-third Psalm while the children sit quietly. Edith helps the child in charge begin reciting the Lord's Prayer; the other children follow along for the first unit of sounds, and then trail off as Edith finishes for them. Everyone stands and faces the American flag hung to the right of the door. Edith leads the pledge to the flag, with the children again following the familiar sounds as far as they remember them. Edith then asks the girl in charge what song she wants and the child replies, "My Country." Edith goes to the piano and plays "America," singing as the children follow her words.

Edith returns to her chair in the center of the room and the children sit again in the semi-circle on the floor. It is 12:40 when she tells the children, "Let's have boys' sharing time first." She calls the name of the first boy sitting on the end of the circle, and he comes up to her with a toy helicopter. He turns and holds it up for the other children to see. He says, "It's a helicopter." Edith asks, "What is it used for?" and he replies, "For the army. Carry men. For the war." Other children join in, "For shooting submarines." "To bring back men from space when they are in the ocean." Edith sends the boy back to the circle and asks the next boy if he has something. He replies "No" and she passes on to the next. He says "Yes" and brings a bird's nest to her. He holds it for the class to see, and the teacher asks, "What kind of bird made the nest?" The boy replies, "My friend says a rain bird made it." Edith asks what the nest is made of and different children reply, "mud," "leaves" and "sticks." There is also a bit of moss woven into the nest and Edith tries to describe it to the children. They, however, are more interested in seeing if anything is inside it, and Edith lets the boy carry it around the semi-circle showing the children its insides. Edith tells the children of some baby robins in a nest in her yard, and some of the children tell about baby birds they have seen. Some children are asking about a small object in the nest which they say looks like an egg, but all have seen the nest now and Edith calls on the next boy. A number of children say, "I know what Michael has, but I'm not telling." Michael brings a book to the teacher and then goes back to his place in the circle of children. Edith reads the last page of the book to the class. Some children tell of books they have at home. Edith calls the next boy, and three children call out, "I know what David has." "He always has the same thing." "It's a bang-bang." David goes to his table and gets a box which he brings to Edith. He opens it and shows the teacher a scale-model of an old-fashioned dueling pistol. When David does not turn around to the class, Edith tells him, "Show it to the children" and he does. One child says, "Mr. Johnson [the principal] said no guns." Edith replies, "Yes, how many of you know that?" Most of the children in the circle raise their hands. She continues, "That you aren't supposed to bring guns to school?" She calls the next boy on the circle and he brings two large toy soldiers to her which the children enthusiastically identify as being from "Babes in Toyland." The next boy brings an American flag to Edith and shows it to the class. She asks him what the stars and stripes stand for and admonishes him to treat it carefully. "Why should you treat it carefully?" she asks the boy. "Because it's our flag," he replies. She congratulates him, saying, "That's right."

"Show and Tell" lasted twenty minutes and during the last ten, one girl in particular announced that she knew what each child called on had to show. Edith asked her to be quiet each time she spoke out, but she was not content, continuing to offer her comment at each "show." Four children from other classes had come into the room to bring something from another teacher or to ask for something from Edith. Those with requests were asked to return later if the item wasn't readily available.

Edith now asks if any of the children told their mothers about their trip to the local zoo the previous day. Many children raise their hands. As Edith calls on them, they tell what they liked in the zoo. Some children cannot wait to be called on, and they call out things to the teacher, who asks them to be quiet. After a few of the animals are mentioned, one child says, "I liked the spooky house," and the others chime in to agree with him, some pantomiming fear and horror. Edith is puzzled, and asks what this was. When half the children try to tell her at once, she raises her hand for quiet, then calls on individual children. One says, "The house with nobody in it"; another, "The dark little house." Edith asks where it was in the zoo, but the children cannot describe its location in any way she can understand. Edith makes some jokes, but they involve adult abstractions the children cannot grasp. The children have become quite noisy now, speaking out to make both relevant and irrelevant comments, and three little girls have become particularly assertive.

Edith gets up from her seat at 1:10 and goes to the book corner, where she puts a record on the player. As it begins a story about the trip to the zoo, she returns to the circle and asks the children to go sit at the tables. She divides them among the tables in such a way as to indicate that they don't have regular seats. When the children are all seated at the four tables, five or six to a table, the teacher asks, "Who wants to be the first one?" One of the noisy girls comes to the center of the room. The voice on the record is giving directions for imitating an ostrich and the girl follows them, walking around the center of the room holding her ankles with her hands. Edith replays the record, and all the children, table by table, imitate ostriches down the center of the room and back. Edith removes her shoes and shows that she can be an ostrich too. This is apparently a familiar game, for a number of children are calling out, "Can we have the crab?" Edith asks one of the children to do a crab "so we can all remember how," and then plays the part of the record with music for imitating crabs by. The children from the first table line up across the room, hands and feet on the floor and faces pointing toward the ceiling. After they have "walked" down the room and back in this posture, they sit at their table and the children of the next table play "crab." The children love this; they run from their tables, dance about on the floor waiting for their turns and are generally exuberant. Children ask for the "inch worm" and the game is played again with the children squirming down the floor. As a conclusion, Edith shows them a new animal imitation, the "lame dog." The children all hobble down the floor on three "legs," table by table, to the accompaniment of the record.

At 1:30, Edith has the children line up in the center of the room; she says, "Table one, line up in front of me," and children ask, "What are we going to do?" Then she moves a few steps to the side and says, "Table two over here, line up next to table one," and more children ask, "What for?" She does this for table three and table four and each time the children ask, "Why, what are we going to do?" When the children are lined up in four lines of five each, spaced so that they are not touching one another, Edith puts on a new record and leads the class in calisthenics, to the accompaniment of the record. The children just jump around every which way in their places instead of doing the exercises, and by the time the record is finished, Edith, the only one following it, seems exhausted. She is apparently adopting the President's new "Physical Fitness" program in her classroom.

At 1:35, Edith pulls her chair to the easels and calls the children to sit on the floor in front of her, table by table. When they are all seated she asks, "What are you going to do for work time today?" Different children raise their hands and tell Edith what they are going to draw. Most are going to make pictures of animals they saw in the zoo. Edith asks if they want to make pictures to send to Mark in the hospital, and the children agree to this. Edith gives drawing paper to the children, calling them to her one by one. After getting a piece of paper, the children go to the crayon box on the right-hand shelves, select a number of colors, and go to the tables, where they begin drawing. Edith is again trying to quiet the perpetually talking girls. She keeps two of them standing by her so they won't disrupt the others. She asks them, "Why do you feel you have to talk all the time," and then scolds them for not listening to her. Then she sends them to their tables to draw.

Most of the children are drawing at their tables, sitting or kneeling in their chairs. They are all working very industriously and, engrossed in their work, very quietly. Three girls have chosen to paint at the easels, and having donned their smocks, they are busily mixing colors and intently applying them to their pictures. If the children at the tables are primitives and neo-realists in their animal depictions, these girls at the easels are the class abstract-expressionists, with their broad-stroked, colorful paintings.

Edith asks of the children generally, "What color should I make the cover of Mark's book?" Brown and green are suggested by some children "because Mark likes them." The other children are puzzled as to just what is going on and ask, "What book?" or "What does she mean?" Edith explains what she thought was clear to them already, that they are all going to put their pictures together in a "book" to be sent to Mark. She goes to a small table in the play-kitchen corner and tells the children to bring her their pictures when they are finished and she will write their message for Mark on them.

By 1:50, most children have finished their pictures and given them to Edith. She talks with some of them as she ties the bundle of pictures together—answering questions, listening, carrying on conversations. The children are playing in various parts of the room with toys, games, and blocks they have taken off the shelves. They also move from table to table, examining each other's pictures, offering compliments and suggestions. Three girls at a table are cutting up colored paper for a collage. Another girl is walking about the room in a pair of high heels with a woman's purse over her arm. Three boys are playing in the center of the room with the large block set, with which they are building walk-ways and walking on them. Edith is very much concerned about their safety and comes over a number of times to fuss over them. Two or three other boys are pushing trucks around the center of the room, and mild altercations occur when they drive through the block constructions. Some boys and girls are playing at the toy store, two girls are serving "tea" in the play kitchen, and one is washing a doll baby. Two boys have elected to clean the room, and with large sponges they wash the movable blackboard, the puppet stage, and then begin on the tables. They run into resistance from the children who are working with construction toys on the tables and do not want to dismantle their structures. The class is like a room full of bees, each intent on pursuing some activity, occasionally bumping into one another, but just veering off in another direction without serious altercation. At 2:05, the custodian arrives pushing a cart loaded with half-pint milk containers. He places a tray of cartons on the counter next to the sink, then leaves. His coming and going is unnoticed in the room (as, incidentally, is the presence of the observer, who is completely ignored by the children for the entire afternoon).

At 2:15, Edith walks to the entrance of the room, switches off the lights, and sits at the piano and plays. The children begin spontaneously singing the song, which is "Clean up, clean up. Everybody clean up." Edith walks around the room supervising the clean-up. Some children put their toys, the blocks, puzzles, games, and so on back on their shelves under the windows. The children making a collage keep right on working. A child from another class comes in to borrow the 45—rpm adaptor for the record player. At more urging from Edith, the rest of the children shelve their toys and work. The children are sitting around their tables now and Edith asks, "What record would you like to hear while you have your milk?" There is some confusion and no general consensus, so Edith drops the subject and begins to call the children, table by table, to come get their milk. "Table one," she says, and the five children come to the sink, wash their hands and dry them, pick up a carton of milk and a straw, and take it back to their table. Two talking girls wander about the room interfering with the children getting their milk and Edith calls out to them to "settle down." As the children sit, many of them call out to Edith the name of the record they want to hear. When all the children are seated at tables with milk, Edith plays one of these records called "Bozo and the Birds" and shows the children pictures in a book that goes with the record. The record recites, and the book shows the adventures of a clown, Bozo, as he walks through a woods meeting many different kinds of birds who, of course, display the characteristics of many kinds of people or, more accurately, different stereotypes. As children finish their milk, they take blankets or pads from the shelves under the windows and lie on them in the center of the room, where Edith sits on her chair showing the pictures. By 2:30, half the class is lying on the floor on their blankets, the record is still playing and the teacher is turning the pages of the book. The child who came in previously returns the 45—rpm adaptor, and one of the kindergartners tells Edith what the boy's name is and where he lives.

The record ends at 2:40. Edith says, "Children, down on your blankets." All the class is lying on blankets now, Edith refuses to answer the various questions individual children put to her because, she tells them, "it's rest time now." Instead, she talks very softly about what they will do tomorrow. They are going to work with clay, she says. The children lie quietly and listen. One of the boys raises his hand and when called on tells Edith, "The animals in the zoo looked so hungry yesterday." Edith asks the children what they think about this and a number try to volunteer opinions, but Edith accepts only those offered in a "rest-time tone," that is, softly and quietly. After a brief discussion of animal feeding, Edith calls the names of the two children on milk detail and has them collect empty milk cartons from the tables and return them to the tray. She asks the two children on clean-up detail to clean up the room. Then she gets up from her chair

and goes to the door to turn on the lights. At this signal, the children all get up from the floor and return their blankets and pads to the shelf. It is raining (the reason for no outside play this afternoon), and cars driven by mothers clog the school drive and line up along the street. One of the talkative little girls comes over to Edith and pointing out the window says, "Mrs. Kerr, see my mother in the new Cadillac?"

At 2:50, Edith sits at the piano and plays. The children sit on the floor in the center of the room and sing. They have a repertoire of songs about animals, including one in which each child sings a refrain alone. They know these by heart and sing along through the ringing of the 2:55 bell. When the song is finished, Edith gets up and coming to the group says, "Okay, rhyming words to get your coats today." The children raise their hands and as Edith calls on them, they tell her two rhyming words, after which they are allowed to go into the hall to get their coats and sweaters. They return to the room with these and sit at their tables. At 2:59 Edith says. "When you have your coats on, you may line up at the door." Half of the children go to the door and stand in a long line. When the three o'clock bell rings, Edith returns to the piano and plays. The children sing a song called "Goodbye," after which Edith sends them out.

TRAINING FOR LEARNING AND FOR LIFE

The day in kindergarten at Wright School illustrates both the content of the student role as it has been learned by these children and the processes by which the teacher has brought about this learning, or, "taught" them the student role. The children have learned to go through routines and to follow orders with unquestioning obedience, even when these make no sense to them. They have been disciplined to do as they are told by an authoritative person without significant protest. Edith has developed this discipline in the children by creating and enforcing a rigid social structure in the classroom through which she effectively controls the behavior of most of the children for most of the school day. The "living with others in a small society" which the school pamphlet tells parents is the most important thing the children will learn in kindergarten can be seen now in its operational meaning, which is learning to live by the routines imposed by the school. This learning appears to be the principal content of the student role.

Children who submit to school-imposed discipline and come to identify with it, so that being a "good student" comes to be an important part of their developing identities, *become* the good students by the school's definitions. Those who submit to the routines of the school but do not come to identify with them will be adequate students who find the more important part of their identities elsewhere, such as in the play group outside school. Children who refuse to submit to the school routines are rebels who become known as "bad students" and often "problem children" in the school, for they do not learn the academic curriculum and their behavior is often disruptive in the classroom. Today, schools engage clinical psychologists in part to help teachers deal with such children.

In looking at Edith's kindergarten at Wright School, it is interesting to ask how the children learn this role of student—come to accept school-imposed routines—and what, exactly, it involves in terms of behavior and attitudes. The most prominent features of the classroom are its physical and social structures. The room is carefully furnished and arranged in ways adults feel will interest children. The play store and play kitchen in the back of the room, for example, imply that children are interested in mimicking these activities of the adult world. The only space left for the children to create something of their own is the empty center of the room, and the materials at their disposal are the blocks, whose use causes anxiety on the part of the teacher. The room, being carefully organized physically by the adults, leaves little room for the creation of physical organization on the part of the children.

The social structure created by Edith is a far more powerful and subtle force for fitting the children to the student role. This structure is established by the very rigid and tightly controlled set of rituals and routines through which the children are put during the day. There is first the rigid "locating procedure" in which the children are asked to find themselves in terms of the month, date, day of the week, and the number of the class who are present and absent. This puts

them solidly in the real world as defined by adults. The day is then divided into six periods whose activities are for the most part determined by the teacher. In Edith's kindergarten, the children went through Serious Time, which opens the school day, Sharing Time, Play Time (which, in clear weather, would be spent outside), Work Time, Clean-Up Time, after which they have their milk, and Rest Time, after which they go home. The teacher has programmed activities for each of these Times.

Occasionally, the class is allowed limited discretion to choose between proffered activities, such as stories or records, but original ideas for activities are never solicited from them. Opportunity for free individual action is open only once in the day, during the part of Work Time left after the general class assignment has been completed (on the day reported, the class assignment was drawing animal pictures for the absent Mark). Spontaneous interests or observations from the children are never developed by the teacher. It seems that her schedule just does not allow room for developing such unplanned events. During Sharing Time, for example, the child who brought a bird's nest told Edith, in reply to her question of what kind of bird made it, "My friend says it's a rain bird." Edith does not think to ask about this bird, probably because the answer is "childish," that is, not given in accepted adult categories of birds. The children then express great interest in an object in the nest, but the teacher ignores this interest, probably because the object is uninteresting to her. The soldiers from "Babes in Toyland" strike a responsive note in the children, but this is not used for a discussion of any kind. The soldiers are treated in the same way as objects that bring little interest from the children. Finally, at the end of Sharing Time, the child-world of perception literally erupts in the class with the recollection of "the spooky house" at the zoo. Apparently, this made more of an impression on the children than did any of the animals, but Edith is unable to make any sense of it for herself. The tightly imposed order of the class begins to break down as the children discover a universe of discourse of their own and begin talking excitedly with one another. The teacher is effectively excluded from this child's world of perception and for a moment she fails to dominate the classroom situation. She re-asserts control, however, by taking the children to the next activity she has planned for the day. It seems never to have occurred to Edith that there might be a meaningful learning experience for the children in re-creating the "spooky house" in the classroom. It seems fair to say that this would have offered an exercise in spontaneous self-expression and an opportunity for real creativity on the part of the children. Instead, they are taken through a canned animal imitation procedure, an activity that they apparently enjoy, but that is also imposed on them rather than created by them.

Although children's perceptions of the world and opportunities for genuine spontaneity and creativity are being systematically eliminated from the kindergarten, unquestioned obedience to authority and rote learning of meaningless material are being encouraged. When the children are called to line up in the center of the room they ask "Why?" and "What for?" as they are in the very process of complying. They have learned to go smoothly through a programmed day, regardless of whether parts of the program make any sense to them or not. Here the student role involves what might be called "doing what you're told and never mind why." Activities that might "make sense" to the children are effectively ruled out and they are forced or induced to participate in activities that may be "senseless," such as the calisthenics.

At the same time, the children are being taught by rote meaningless sounds in the ritual oaths and songs, such as the Lord's Prayer, the Pledge to the Flag, and "America." As they go through the grades, children learn more and more of the sounds of these ritual oaths, but the fact that they have often learned meaningless sounds rather than meaningful statements is shown when they are asked to write these out in the sixth grade; they write them as groups of sounds rather than as a series of words, according to the sixth grade teachers at Wright School. Probably much learning in the elementary grades is of this character, that is, having no intrinsic meaning to the children, but rather being tasks inexplicably required of them by authoritative adults. Listening to sixth grade children read social studies reports, for example, in which they

have copied material from encyclopedias about a particular country, an observer often gets the feeling that he is watching an activity that has no intrinsic meaning for the child. The child who reads, "Switzerland grows wheat and cows and grass and makes a lot of cheese" knows the dictionary meaning of each of these words but may very well have no conception at all of this "thing" called Switzerland. He is simply carrying out a task assigned by the teacher *because* it is assigned, and this may be its only "meaning" for him.

Another type of learning that takes place in kindergarten is seen in children who take advantage of the "holes" in the adult social structure to create activities of their own, during Work Time or out-of-doors during Play Time. Here the children are learning to carve out a small world of their own within the world created by adults. They very quickly learn that if they keep within permissible limits of noise and action, they can play as much as they please. Small groups of children formed during the year in Edith's kindergarten who played together at these times, developing semi-independent little groups in which they created their own worlds in the interstices of the adult-imposed physical and social world. These groups remind the sociological observer very much of the so-called "informal groups" adults develop in factories and offices of large bureaucracies.[5] Here too, within authoritatively imposed social organizations, people find "holes" to create little subworlds that support informal, friendly, unofficial behavior. Forming and participating in such groups seems to be as much part of the student role as it is of the role of bureaucrat.

The kindergarten has been conceived of here as the year in which children are prepared for their schooling by learning the role of student. In the classrooms of the rest of the school grades, the children will be asked to submit to systems and routines imposed by the teachers and the curriculum. The days will be much like those of kindergarten, except that academic subjects will be substituted for the activities of the kindergarten. Once out of the school system, young adults will more than likely find themselves working in large-scale bureaucratic organizations, perhaps on the assembly line in the factory, perhaps in the paper routines of the white-collar occupations, where they will be required to submit to rigid routines imposed by "the company" that may make little sense to them. Those who can operate well in this situation will be successful bureaucratic functionaries. Kindergarten, therefore, can be seen as preparing children not only for participation in the bureaucratic organization of large modern school systems, but also for the large-scale occupational bureaucracies of modern society.

NOTES

1. Emile Durkheim, *Sociology and Education* (New York: The Free Press, 1956), pp. 71—72.
2. Ibid., p. 123.
3. Wilbur Brookover, *The Sociology of Education* (New York: American Book Company, 1957), p. 4.
4. Ibid., p. 6.
5. See, for example, Peter M. Blau, *Bureaucracy in Modern Society* (New York: Random House, 1956), Chapter 3.

59. AMERICAN EDUCATION: SAVAGE INEQUALITIES

JONATHAN KOZOL

In effect, a circular phenomenon evolves: The richer districts…have more revenue, derived from taxing land and homes, to fund their public schools. The reputation of the schools, in turn, adds to the value of their homes, and this, in turn, expands the tax base for their public schools…. Few of the children [in the poorer districts will] be likely to compete effectively with kids [in the wealthier districts] for admissions to the better local colleges and universities of New York state. Even fewer will compete for more exclusive Ivy League admissions. And few of the graduates or dropouts of those poorer systems, as a consequence, are likely ever to earn enough to buy a home in [the wealthier districts]….

Jonathan Kozol's work, *Savage Inequalities*, is a detailed examination of the public schools in several American cities. The theme was the same wherever he looked: Some districts provide the best opportunities; others barely get by. This selection is an excerpt from his description of schools in New York City. Most of us probably have a hunch that public education is characterized by great inequalities; Kozol's description confirms these suspicions.

"In a country where there is no distinction of class," Lord Acton wrote of the United States 130 years ago, "a child is not born to the station of its parents, but with an indefinite claim to all the prizes that can be won by thought and labor. It is in conformity with the theory of equality … to give as near as possible to every youth an equal state in life." Americans, he said, "are unwilling that any should be deprived in childhood of the means of competition."[1]

It is hard to read these words today without a sense of irony and sadness. Denial of "the means of competition" is perhaps the single most consistent outcome of the education offered to poor children in the schools of our large cities; and nowhere is this pattern of denial more explicit or more absolute than in the public schools of New York City.

Average expenditures per pupil in the city of New York in 1987 were some $5,500. In the highest spending suburbs of New York (Great Neck or Manhasset, for example, on Long Island) funding levels rose above $11,000, with the highest districts in the state at $15,000. "Why," asks the city's Board of Education, "should our students receive less" than do "similar students" who live elsewhere? "The inequity is clear...."[2, 3]

New York City's public schools are subdivided into 32 school districts. District 10 encompasses a large part of the Bronx but is, effectively, two separate districts. One of these districts, Riverdale, is in the northwest section of the Bronx. Home to many of the city's most sophisticated and well-educated families, its elementary schools have relatively few low-income students. The other section, to the south and east, is poor and heavily nonwhite.

The contrast between public schools in each of these two neighborhoods is obvious to any visitor. At Public School 24 in Riverdale, the principal speaks enthusiastically of his teaching staff. At Public School 79, serving poorer children to the south, the principal says that he is forced to take the "tenth-best" teachers. "I thank God they're still breathing," he remarks of those from whom he must select his teachers....

Sometimes a school principal, whatever his background or his politics, looks into the faces of the children in his school and offers a disarming statement that cuts through official ambiguity. "These are the kids most in need," says Edward Flanery, the principal of one of the low-income schools, "and they get the worst teachers." For children of diverse needs in his overcrowded rooms, he says, "you need an outstanding teacher. And what do you get? You get the worst."

In order to find Public School 261 in District 10, a visitor is told to look for a mortician's office. The funeral home, which faces Jerome Avenue

in the North Bronx, is easy to identify by its green awning. The school is next door, in a former roller-skating rink. No sign identifies the building as a school. A metal awning frame without an awning supports a flagpole, but there is no flag.

In the street in front of the school is an elevated public transit line. Heavy traffic fills the street. The existence of the school is virtually concealed within this crowded city block.

In a vestibule between the outer and inner glass doors of the school is a sign with these words: "All children are capable of learning."

Beyond the inner doors, a guard is seated. The lobby is long and narrow. The ceiling is low. There are no windows. All the teachers I see at first are middle-aged white women. The principal, who is also a white woman, tells me that the school's "capacity" is 900, but that there are 1,300 children here. The size of classes for fifth and sixth grade children in New York, she says, is "capped" at 32, but she says that class size in the school goes "up to 34." (I later see classes, however, as large as 37.) Classes for younger children, she goes on, are "capped at 25," but a school can go above this limit if it puts an extra adult in the room. Lack of space, she says, prevents the school from operating a pre-kindergarten program.

I ask the principal where her children go to school. They are enrolled in private school, she says.

"Lunch time is a challenge for us," she explains. "Limited space obliges us to do it in three shifts, 450 children at a time."

Textbooks are scarce and children have to share their social studies books. The principal says there is one full-time pupil counselor and another who is here two days a week: A ratio of 930 children to one counselor. The carpets are patched and sometimes taped together to conceal an open space. "I could use some new rugs," she observes.

To make up for the building's lack of windows and the crowded feeling that results, the staff puts plants and fish tanks in the corridors. Some of the plants are flourishing. Two boys, released from class, are in a corridor beside a tank, their noses pressed against the glass. A school of pinkish fish inside the tank are darting back and forth.

Farther down the corridor a small Hispanic girl is watering the plants.

Two first-grade classes share a single room without a window, divided only by a blackboard. Four kindergartens and a sixth-grade class of Spanish-speaking children have been packed into a single room in which, again, there is no window. A second-grade bilingual class of 37 children has its own room, but again there is no window.

By eleven o'clock, the lunchroom is already packed with appetite and life. The kids line up to get their meals, then eat them in ten minutes. After that, with no place they can go to play, they sit and wait until it's time to line up and go back to class.

On the second floor, I visit four classes taking place within another undivided space. The room has a low ceiling. File cabinets and movable blackboards give a small degree of isolation to each class. Again, there are no windows.

The library is a tiny, windowless, and claustrophobic room. I count approximately 700 books. Seeing no reference books, I ask a teacher if encyclopedias and other reference books are kept in classrooms.

"We don't have encyclopedias in classrooms," she replies. "That is for the suburbs."

The school, I am told, has 26 computers for its 1,300 children. There is one small gym, and children get one period, and sometimes two, each week. Recess, however, is not possible because there is no playground. "Head Start," the principal says, "scarcely exists in District 10. We have no space."

The school, I am told, is 90 percent black and Hispanic; the other 10 percent are Asian, white, or Middle Eastern.

In a sixth-grade social studies class, the walls are bare of words or decorations. There seems to be no ventilation system, or, if one exists, it isn't working.

The class discusses the Nile River and the Fertile Crescent.

The teacher, in a droning voice: "How is it useful that these civilizations developed close to rivers?"

A child, in a good loud voice: "What kind of question is that?"

In my notes, I find these words: "An uncomfortable feeling—being in a building with no windows. There are metal ducts across the room. Do they give air? I feel asphyxiated...."

On the top floor of the school, a sixth grade of 30 children shares a room with 29 bilingual second graders. Because of the high class size, there is an assistant with each teacher. This means that 59 children and four grown-ups—63 in all—must share a room that, in a suburban school, would hold no more than 20 children and one teacher. There are, at least, some outside windows in this room—it is the only room with windows in the school—and the room has a high ceiling. It is a relief to see some daylight.

I return to see the kindergarten classes on the ground floor and feel stifled once again by lack of air and the low ceiling. Nearly 120 children and adults are doing what they can to make the best of things: 80 children in four kindergarten classes, 30 children in the sixth-grade class, and about eight grown-ups who are aides and teachers. The kindergarten children, sitting on the worn rug, which is patched with tape, look up at me and turn their heads to follow me as I walk past them.

As I leave the school, a sixth-grade teacher stops to talk. I ask her, "Is there air conditioning in warmer weather?"

Teachers, while inside the building, are reluctant to give answers to this kind of question. Outside, on the sidewalk, she is less constrained: "I had an awful room last year. In the winter, it was 56 degrees. In the summer, it was up to 90. It was sweltering."

I ask her, "Do the children ever comment on the building?"

"They don't say," she answers, "but they know."

I ask her if they see it as a racial message.

"All these children see TV," she says. "They know what suburban schools are like. Then they look around them at their school. This was a roller-rink, you know.... They don't comment on it, but you see it in their eyes. They understand."

On the following morning, I visit P.S. 79, another elementary school in the same district. "We work under difficult circumstances," says the principal, James Carter, who is black. "The school was built to hold one thousand students.

We have 1,550. We are badly overcrowded. We need smaller classes but, to do this, we would need more space. I can't add five teachers. I would have no place to put them."

Some experts, I observe, believe that class size isn't a real issue. He dismisses this abruptly. "It doesn't take a genius to discover that you learn more in a smaller class. I have to bus some 60 kindergarten children elsewhere, since I have no space for them. When they return next year, where do I put them?"

"I can't set up a computer lab. I have no room. I had to put a class into the library. I have no librarian. There are two gymnasiums upstairs, but they cannot be used for sports. We hold more classes there. It's unfair to measure us against the suburbs. They have 17 to 20 children in a class. Average class size in this school is 30."

"The school is 29 percent black, 70 percent Hispanic. Few of these kids get Head Start. There is no space in the district. Of 200 kindergarten children, 50 maybe get some kind of preschool."

I ask him how much difference preschool makes.

"Those who get it do appreciably better. I can't overestimate its impact but, as I have said, we have no space."

The school tracks children by ability, he says. "There are five to seven levels in each grade. The highest level is equivalent to 'gifted,' but it's not a full-scale gifted program. We don't have the funds. We have no science room. The science teachers carry their equipment with them."

We sit and talk in the nurse's room. The window is broken. There are two holes in the ceiling. About a quarter of the ceiling has been patched and covered with a plastic garbage bag.

"Ideal class size for these kids would be 15 to 20. Will these children ever get what white kids in the suburbs take for granted? I don't think so. If you ask me why, I'd have to speak of race and social class. I don't think the powers that be in New York City understand, or want to understand, that if they do not give these children a sufficient education to lead healthy and productive lives, we will be their victims later on. We'll pay the price someday—in violence, in economic costs. I despair of making this appeal in any terms but these. You cannot issue an appeal to conscience in New York today. The fair-play argu-

ment won't be accepted. So you speak of violence and hope that it will scare the city into action."

While we talk, three children who look six or seven years old come to the door and ask to see the nurse, who isn't in the school today. One of the children, a Puerto Rican girl, looks haggard. "I have a pain in my tooth," she says. The principal says, "The nurse is out. Why don't you call your mother?" The child says, "My mother doesn't have a phone." The principal sighs. "Then go back to your class." When she leaves, the principal is angry. "It's amazing to me that these children ever make it with the obstacles they face. Many *do* care and *they do* try, but there's a feeling of despair. The parents of these children want the same things for their children that the parents in the suburbs want. Drugs are not the cause of this. They are the symptom. Nonetheless, they're used by people in the suburbs and rich people in Manhattan as another reason to keep children of poor people at a distance."

I ask him, "Will white children and black children ever go to school together in New York?"

"I don't see it," he replies. "I just don't think it's going to happen. It's a dream. I simply do not see white folks in Riverdale agreeing to cross-bus with kids like these. A few, maybe. Very few. I don't think I'll live to see it happen."

I ask him whether race is the decisive factor. Many experts, I observe, believe that wealth is more important in determining these inequalities.

"This," he says—and sweeps his hand around him at the room, the garbage bag, the ceiling—"would not happen to white children...."

Two months later, on a day in May, I visit an elementary school in Riverdale. The dogwoods and magnolias on the lawn in front of P.S. 24 are in full blossom on the day I visit. There is a well-tended park across the street, another larger park three blocks away. To the left of the school is a playground for small children, with an innovative jungle gym, a slide, and several climbing toys. Behind the school are two playing fields for older kids. The grass around the school is neatly trimmed.

The neighborhood around the school, by no means the richest part of Riverdale, is nonetheless expensive and quite beautiful. Residences in the area—some of which are large, free-standing houses, others condominiums in solid red-brick buildings—sell for prices in the region of $400,000, but some of the larger Tudor houses on the winding and tree-shaded streets close to the school can cost up to $1 million. The excellence of P.S. 24, according to the principal, adds to the value of these homes. Advertisements in the *New York Times* will frequently inform prospective buyers that a house is "in the neighborhood of P.S. 24."

The school serves 825 children in the kindergarten through sixth grade. This is approximately half the student population crowded into P.S. 79, where 1,550 children fill a space intended for 1,000, and a great deal smaller than the 1,300 children packed into the former skating rink; but the principal of P.S. 24, a capable and energetic man named David Rothstein, still regards it as excessive for an elementary school.

The school is integrated in the strict sense that the middle- and upper-middle-class white children here occupy a building that contains some Asian and Hispanic and black children; but there is little integration in the classrooms because the vast majority of the Hispanic and black children are assigned to "special" classes on the basis of evaluations that have classified them EMR—"educable mentally retarded"—or else, in the worst of cases, TMR—"trainable mentally retarded."

I ask the principal if any of his students qualify for free-lunch programs. "About 130 do," he says. "Perhaps another 35 receive their lunches at reduced price. Most of these kids are in the special classes. They do not come from this neighborhood."

The very few nonwhite children that one sees in mainstream classes tend to be Japanese or of other Asian origins. Riverdale, I learn, has been the residence of choice for many years to members of the diplomatic corps.

The school therefore contains effectively two separate schools: one of about 130 children, most of whom are poor, Hispanic, black, assigned to one of the 12 special classes; the other of some 700 mainstream students, almost all of whom are white or Asian.

There is a third track also—this one for the students who are labeled "talented" or "gifted."

This is termed a "pull-out" program because the children who are so identified remain in mainstream classrooms but are taken out for certain periods each week to be provided with intensive and, in my opinion, excellent instruction in some areas of reasoning and logic often known as "higher-order skills" in the contemporary jargon of the public schools. Children identified as "gifted" are admitted to this program in first grade and, in most cases, will remain there for six years. Even here, however, there are two tracks of the gifted. The regular gifted classes are provided with only one semester of this specialized instruction yearly. Those very few children, on the other hand, who are identified as showing the most promise are assigned, beginning in the third grade, to a program that receives a full-year regimen.

In one such class, containing ten intensely verbal and impressive fourth-grade children, nine are white and one is Asian. The "special" class I enter first, by way of contrast, has twelve children of whom only one is white and none is Asian. These racial breakdowns prove to be predictive of the schoolwide pattern.

In a classroom for the gifted on the first floor of the school, I ask a child what the class is doing. "Logic and syllogisms," she replies. The room is fitted with a planetarium. The principal says that all the elementary schools in District 10 were given the same planetariums ten years ago, but that certain schools, because of overcrowding, have been forced to give them up. At P.S. 261, according to my notes, there was a domelike space that had been built to hold a planetarium, but the planetarium had been removed to free up space for the small library collection. P.S. 24, in contrast, has a spacious library that holds almost 8,000 books. The windows are decorated with attractive, brightly colored curtains and look out on flowering trees. The principal says that it's inadequate, but it appears spectacular to me after the cubicle that holds a meager 700 books within the former skating rink.

The district can't afford librarians, the principal says, but P.S. 24, unlike the poorer schools of District 10, can draw on educated parent volunteers who staff the room in shifts three days a week. A parent organization also raises independent funds to buy materials, including books, and will soon be running a fund-raiser to enhance the library's collection.

In a large and sunny first-grade classroom that I enter next, I see 23 children, all of whom are white or Asian. In another first grade, there are 22 white children and two others who are Japanese. There is a computer in each class. Every classroom also has a modern fitted sink.

In a second-grade class of 22 children, there are two black children and three Asian children. Again, there is a sink and a computer. A sixth-grade social studies class has only one black child. The children have an in-class research area that holds some up-to-date resources. A set of encyclopedias (World Book, 1985) is in a rack beside a window. The children are doing a Spanish language lesson when I enter. Foreign languages begin in sixth grade at the school, but Spanish is offered also to the kindergarten children. As in every room at P.S. 24, the window shades are clean and new, the floor is neatly tiled in gray and green, and there is not a single light bulb missing.

Walking next into a special class, I see twelve children. One is white. Eleven are black. There are no Asian children. The room is half the size of mainstream classrooms. "Because of overcrowding," says the principal, "we have had to split these rooms in half." There is no computer and no sink.

I enter another special class. Of seven children, five are black, one is Hispanic, one is white. A little black boy with a large head sits in the far corner and is gazing at the ceiling.

"Placement of these kids," the principal explains, "can usually be traced to neurological damage."

In my notes: "How could so many of these children be brain damaged?"

Next door to the special class is a woodworking shop. "This shop is only for the special classes," says the principal. The children learn to punch in time cards at the door, he says, in order to prepare them for employment.

The fourth-grade gifted class, in which I spend the last part of the day, is humming with excitement. "I start with these children in the first grade," says the teacher. "We pull them out of mainstream classes on the basis of their test re-sults and other factors such as the opinion of their teachers. Out of this group, beginning in third grade, I pull out the ones who show the most potential, and they enter classes such as this one."

The curriculum they follow, she explains, "emphasizes critical thinking, reasoning, and logic." The planetarium, for instance, is employed not simply for the study of the universe as it exists. "Children also are designing their own galaxies," the teacher says.

A little girl sitting around a table with her classmates speaks with perfect poise: "My name is Susan. We are in the fourth-grade gifted program."

I ask them what they're doing, and a child says, "My name is Laurie, and we're doing problem-solving."

A rather tall, good-natured boy who is half-standing at the table tells me that his name is David. "One thing that we do," he says, "is logical thinking. Some problems, we find, have more than one good answer. We need to learn not simply to be logical in our own thinking but to show respect for someone else's logic even when an answer may be technically incorrect."

When I ask him to explain this, he goes on, "A person who gives an answer that is not 'correct' may nonetheless have done some interesting thinking that we should examine. 'Wrong' answers may be more useful to examine than correct ones."

I ask the children if reasoning and logic are innate or if they're things that you can learn.

"You know some things to start with when you enter school," Susan says. "But we also learn some things that other children don't."

I ask her to explain this.

"We know certain things that other kids don't know because we're *taught* them."

She has braces on her teeth. Her long brown hair falls almost to her waist. Her loose white T-shirt has the word *TRI-LOGIC* on the front. She tells me that Tri-Logic is her father's firm.

Laurie elaborates on the same point: "Some things, you know. Some kinds of logic are inside of you to start with. There are other things that someone needs to teach you."

David expands on what the other two have said: "Everyone can think and speak in logical ways unless they have a mental problem. What this program does is bring us to a higher form of logic."

The class is writing a new "Bill of Rights." The children already know the U.S. Bill of Rights and they explain its first four items to me with precision. What they are examining today, they tell me, is the very *concept* of a "right." Then they will create their own compendium of rights according to their own analysis and definition. Along one wall of the classroom, opposite the planetarium, are seven Apple II computers on which children have developed rather subtle color animations that express the themes—of greed and domination, for example—that they also have described in writing.

"This is an upwardly mobile group," the teacher later says. "They have exposure to whatever New York City has available. Their parents may take them to the theater, to museums...."

In my notes: "Six girls, four boys. Nine white, one Chinese. I am glad they have this class. But what about the others? Aren't there ten black children in the school who could enjoy this also?"

The teacher gives me a newspaper written, edited, and computer-printed by her sixth-grade gifted class. The children, she tells me, are provided with a link to kids in Europe for transmission of news stories.

A science story by one student asks whether scientists have ever falsified their research. "Gregor Mendel," the sixth grader writes, "the Austrian monk who founded the science of genetics, published papers on his work with peas that some experts say were statistically too good to be true. Isaac Newton, who formulated the law of gravitation, relied on unseemly mathematical sleight of hand in his calculations.... Galileo Galilei, founder of modern scientific method, wrote about experiments that were so difficult to duplicate that colleagues doubted he had done them."

Another item in the paper, also by a sixth-grade student, is less esoteric: "The Don Cossacks dance company, from Russia, is visiting the United States. The last time it toured America was 1976.... The Don Cossacks will be in New York City for two weeks at the Neil Simon Theater. Don't miss it!"

The tone is breezy—and so confident! That phrase—"Don't miss it!"—speaks a volume about life in Riverdale.

"What makes a good school?" asks the principal when we are talking later on. "The building and teachers are part of it, of course. But it isn't just the building and the teachers. Our kids come from good families and the neighborhood is good. In a three-block area, we have a public library, a park, a junior high.... Our typical sixth grader reads at eighth-grade level." In a quieter voice he says, "I see how hard my colleagues work in schools like P.S. 79. You have children in those neighborhoods who live in virtual hell. They enter school five years behind. What do they get?" Then, as he spreads his hands out on his desk, he says: "I have to ask myself why there should be an elementary school in District 10 with fifteen hundred children. Why should there be an elementary school within a skating rink? Why should the Board of Ed allow this? This is not the way that things should be...."

The differences *between* school districts and *within* school districts in the city are, however, almost insignificant compared to those between the city and the world of affluence around it—in Westchester County, for example, and in largely prosperous Long Island.

Even in the suburbs, nonetheless, it has been noted that a differential system still exists, and it may not be surprising to discover that the differences are once again determined by the social class, parental wealth, and sometimes race, of the schoolchildren. A study, a few years ago, of 20 of the wealthiest and poorest districts of Long Island, for example, matched by location and size of enrollment, found that the differences in per-pupil spending were not only large but had approximately doubled in a five-year period. Schools, in Great Neck, in 1987, spent $11,265 for each pupil. In affluent Jericho and Manhasset, the figures were, respectively, $11,325 and $11,370. In Oyster Bay, the figure was $9,980. Compare this to Levittown, also on Long Island but a town of mostly working-class white families, where per-pupil spending dropped to $6,900. Then compare these numbers to the spending level in the town of Roosevelt, the poorest district in the county, where the schools are 99 percent nonwhite and where the figure dropped to $6,340. Finally, consider New York City, where, in the same year, $5,590 was invested in each pupil—less than half of what was spent in Great Neck. The pattern is almost identical to that which we have seen outside Chicago.

Again, look at Westchester County, where, in the same year, the same range of discrepancies was found. Affluent Bronxville, an attractive suburb just north of the Bronx, spent $10,000 for each pupil. Chappaqua's yearly spending figure rose above $9,000. Studying the chart again, we locate Yonkers—a blue-collar town that is predominantly white but where over half the student population is nonwhite—and we find the figure drops to $7,400. This is not the lowest figure, though. The lowest-spending schools within Westchester, spending a full thousand dollars less than Yonkers, serve the suburb of Mount Vernon, where three quarters of the children in the public schools are black.[4]

"If you're looking for a home," a realtor notes, "you can look at the charts for school expenditures and use them to determine if your neighbors will be white and wealthy or, conversely, black or white but poor...."

In effect, a circular phenomenon evolves: The richer districts—those in which the property lots and houses are more highly valued—have more revenue, derived from taxing land and homes, to fund their public schools. The reputation of the schools, in turn, adds to the value of their homes, and this, in turn, expands the tax base for their public schools. The fact that they can levy lower taxes than the poorer districts but exact more money, raises values even more; and this, again, means further funds for smaller classes and for higher teacher salaries within their public schools. Few of the children in the schools of Roosevelt or Mount Vernon will, as a result, be likely to compete effectively with kids in Great Neck and Manhasset for admissions to the better local colleges and universities of New York state. Even fewer will compete for more exclusive Ivy League admissions. And few of the graduates or dropouts of those poorer systems, as a consequence, are likely ever to earn enough to buy a home in Great Neck or Manhasset....

The point is often made that, even with a genuine equality of schooling for poor children, other forces still would militate against their school performance. Cultural and economic factors and the flight of middle-income blacks from inner cities still would have their consequences in the heightened concentration of the poorest children in the poorest neighborhoods. Teen-age pregnancy, drug use, and other problems still would render many families in these neighborhoods all but dysfunctional. Nothing I have said...should leave the misimpression that I do not think these factors are enormously important. A polarization of this issue, whereby some insist on the primacy of school, others on the primacy of family and neighborhood, obscures the fact that both are elemental forces in the lives of children.

The family, however, differs from the school in the significant respect that government is not responsible, or at least not directly, for the inequalities of family background. It *is* responsible for inequalities in public education. The school is the creature of the state; the family is not. To the degree, moreover, that destructive family situations may be bettered by the future acts of government, no one expects that this could happen in the years immediately ahead. Schools, on the other hand, could make dramatic changes almost overnight if fiscal equity were a reality.

If the New York City schools were funded, for example, at the level of the highest-spending suburbs of Long Island, a fourth-grade class of 36 children such as those I visited in District 10 would have had $200,000 *more* invested in their education during 1987.[5] Although a portion of this extra money would have gone into administrative costs, the remainder would have been enough to hire two extraordinary teachers at enticing salaries of $50,000 each, divide the class into *two classes* of some 18 children each, provide them with computers, carpets, air conditioning, new texts and reference books, and learning games—indeed, with everything available today in the most affluent school districts—and also pay the costs of extra counseling to help those children cope with the dilemmas that they face at home. Even the most skeptical detractor of "the worth of spending further money in the public schools" would hesitate, I think, to face a grade-school principal in the South Bronx and try to tell her that this "wouldn't make much difference."

It is obvious that urban schools have other problems in addition to their insufficient funding. Administrative chaos is endemic in some urban systems. (The fact that this in itself is a reflection of our low regard for children who depend on these systems is a separate matter.) Greater funding, if it were intelligently applied, could partially correct these problems—by making possible, for instance, the employment of some very gifted, high-paid fiscal managers who could ensure that money is well used—but it probably is also true that major structural reforms would still be needed. To polarize these points, however, and to argue, as the White House has been claiming for a decade, that administrative changes are a "better" answer to the problem than equality of funding and real efforts at desegregation is dishonest and simplistic. The suburbs have better administrations (sometimes, but not always), and they also have a lot more money in proportion to their children's needs. To speak of the former and evade the latter is a formula that guarantees that nothing will be done *today* for children who have no responsibility for either problem.

To be in favor of "good families" or of "good administration" does not take much courage or originality. It is hard to think of anyone who is opposed to either. To be in favor of redistribution of resources and of racial integration would require a great deal of courage—and a soaring sense of vision—in a president or any other politician. Whether such courage or such vision will someday become transcendent forces in our nation is by no means clear....

Until 1983, Mississippi was one of the few states with no kindergarten program and without compulsory attendance laws. Governor William Winter tried that year to get the legislature to approve a $60—million plan to upgrade public education. The plan included early childhood education, higher teacher salaries, a better math and science program for the high schools, and compulsory attendance with provisions for enforce-ment. The state's powerful oil corporations, facing a modest increase in their taxes to support the plan, lobbied vigorously against it. The Mid-Continent Oil and Gas Association began a television advertising campaign to defeat the bill, according to a *Newsweek* story.[6]

"The vested interests are just too powerful," a state legislator said. Those interests, according to *Newsweek,* are "unlikely" to rush to the aid of public schools that serve poor children.

It is unlikely that the parents or the kids in Rye or Riverdale know much about realities like these; and, if they do, they may well tell themselves that Mississippi is a distant place and that they have work enough to do to face inequities in New York City. But, in reality, the plight of children in the South Bronx of New York is almost as far from them as that of children in the farthest reaches of the South.

All of these children say the Pledge of Allegiance every morning. Whether in the New York suburbs, Mississippi, or the South Bronx, they salute the same flag. They place their hands across their hearts and join their voices in a tribute to "one nation indivisible" which promises liberty and justice to all people. What is the danger that the people in a town like Rye would face if they resolved to make this statement true? How much would it really harm their children to compete in a fair race?

NOTES

1. Lord Acton cited: George Alan Hickrod, "Reply to the 'Forbs' Article," *Journal of School Finance,* vol. 12 (1987).

2. Per-pupil Spending, New York City and Suburbs: Office for Policy Analysis and Program Accountability, New York State Board of Education, "Statistical Profiles of School Districts," (Albany: 1987).

3. Question Asked by New York City Board of Education and Response of Community Service Society: Community Service Society of New York, "Promoting Poverty: The Shift of Resources Away from Low-Income New York City School Districts," (New York: 1987).

4. Per-pupil Spending in Long Island and Westchester County: New York State Department of Education, "Statistical Profiles of School Districts," cited above.

Also see *Newsday*, May 18, 1986. According to Sandra Feldman, President of the United Federation of Teachers in New York City, "the average per-pupil expenditure is nearly $2,500 higher" in the suburbs "right outside the city." (*The School Administrator*, March 1991.) According to the *New York Times* (May 4, 1991), New York City now spends $7,000 for each pupil. The wealthiest suburbs spend approximately $15,000.

5. $200,000 More Each Year: In the school year ending in June 1987, per-pupil funding was $5,585 in New York City, about $11,300 in Jericho and Manhasset. For 36 children, the difference was over $200,000.

6. Mississippi Data: *Time*, November 14, 1988; *Newsweek*, December 13, 1982; *Governing Magazine*, January 1990.

PART XII

Social Change

Individuals must be understood within the context of social organization. We are located in structure, learn culture, are socialized, and are subject to institutions and social controls.

However, human beings also act back on society, and in those actions, they sometimes change society. Society is not simply a static entity; it is ever changing.

What causes society to change? Does violence produce change? According to William Gamson in the first selection, sometimes it does.

Lewis Killian shows us how difficult it is to assess change, giving the example of race relations in the United States. This selection is part of the final chapter in his autobiography as a sociologist.

Anthony Giddens describes a major source of change in all societies, called globalization. Karl Marx's classic statement describes the role of inequality and conflict in social change, and the selection by Michel Crozier reminds us how complex and interrelated all social change is.

60. VIOLENCE AND POLITICAL POWER: THE MEEK DON'T MAKE IT

WILLIAM A. GAMSON

The successful group is one that is ready and willing to fight like hell for goals that can be met without overturning the system.

There are always some in society who refuse to accept the way things are. Sometimes, such people perform individual acts of protest (such as refusing to pay that part of their income tax earmarked for war), and sometimes they join together with others to work for change. Americans have had a long tradition of protest movements, and it seems that in the 1960s, such movements were very influential in effecting change. Sometimes, social movements are diffuse and only slightly structured (such as the anti-Vietnam War movement) but are able to influence change through marches, demonstrations, boycotts, or acts of violence by individual protesters or authorities.

William A. Gamson's article discusses organized protest groups and their attempts to alter society. It asks a simple question: Do groups that end up using violence to achieve their ends succeed or are they doomed to fail? The answer is not a simple one, and it may be surprising.

Besides being a good introduction to social change, the article is also an example of how a sociologist might scientifically study this complex topic. One does not have to just *think* that violence works or that it does not. Here is a beginning to that long and difficult process of gathering evidence carefully and without serious bias. As in all good scientific reporting, the technique used by the researcher is carefully laid out for the reader, so that the reader has the necessary information to criticize the study or to do one of his or her own to show that the researcher is wrong.

Most political scientists view the American system as a pluralist democracy. The image is of a contest carried out under orderly rules. "You scratch my back and I'll scratch yours"; "If you want to get along, go along"; "Don't make permanent enemies because today's adversary may be your ally next time around."

It's a contest for power and recognition that any number can play. If you've got a problem, get organized, play the game, and work for change. Don't expect to win every time or to win the whole pot; compromise is the lifeblood of pluralist politics. More likely than not, you'll find some allies who are willing to help you because they think you can help them, now or in the future.

Of course, some people won't play by the rules. Instead of bargaining for advantages, forming coalitions with the powerful, writing peaceful propaganda, and petitioning, some groups get nasty. Contestants who misbehave, who resort to violence and, perish the thought, try to eliminate other contestants, must be excluded from the game.

In such a calculus, the Tobacco Night Riders should have failed. They began as a secret fraternal order, officially called the "Silent Brigade," whose purpose was to force tobacco growers to

From "Violence and Political Power: The Meek Don't Make It" by William Gamson, *Psychology Today*, July 1974. Reprinted with permission from *Psychology Today Magazine*. Copyright © 1974 (Sussex Publishers, Inc.)

join the Planters Protective Association, hold tobacco off the market, and bargain collectively
with the huge tobacco companies.

WHEN VIOLENCE PAID

The Night Riders didn't play by the rules of pluralist politics. On December 1, 1906, 250
masked and armed men swarmed into Princeton,
Kentucky, and took control. They disarmed the
police, shut off the water supply, and captured
the courthouse and telephone offices. They pa-
trolled the streets, ordered citizens to keep out of
sight, and shot at those who disobeyed. Then
they dynamited and burned two large tobacco
factories and rode off singing "the fire shines
bright in my old Kentucky home."

A year later, they struck again, at Hopkinsville,
Kentucky. They occupied strategic posts and
dragged a buyer from the Imperial Tobacco
Company from his home to pistol-whip him. As
usual, they marched out singing, but this time
the sheriff organized a posse to pursue the raiders
and attacked their rear. The pursuers killed one
man and wounded another before the raiders
drove the posse back into Hopkinsville.

Violence, we are told, doesn't pay, but the
Night Riders enjoyed a considerable measure of
success. By 1908, the Planters Protective
Association was handling nine-tenths of the crop
produced in its area. The power of the big tobacco companies was broken, and they were buying
their tobacco through the association at substantially increased prices. From the depressed conditions of a few years earlier, the black patch area of
Kentucky and Tennessee prospered. Mortgages
were paid off and new homes, new buggies, and
new barns appeared everywhere. The state of
Kentucky even passed a law providing a penalty
of "triple damages" for any association member
who sold his tobacco "outside."

FLAWS IN THE PLURALIST HEAVEN

In recent years, the body of criticism about the assumptions of pluralist theory has grown. Critics
such as C. Wright Mills, whose *The Power Elite*
was one of the earliest and most vocal attacks on

the theory, deny the pluralist premise that
America has no single center of power. "The flaw
in the pluralist heaven," writes political scientist
E. E. Schattschneider, "is that the heavenly chorus sings with a strong upper-class accent.
Probably about 90 percent of the people cannot
get into the pressure system."

To know who gets into the system, and how, is
to understand the central issue of American politics. In the last 200 years, hundreds of previously
unorganized groups here challenged the existing
powers. Many of them collapsed quickly and left
no trace; some died and rose again from the
ashes. Some were pre-empted by competitors,
some won the trappings of influence without its
substance. Some shoved their way into the political arena yelling and screaming, some walked in
on the arms of powerful sponsors, some wandered in unnoticed. The fate of these challenging groups reveals just how permeable the
American system is.

To see which groups make it, and what factors
contribute to their success, I picked a random
sample from the hundreds of challenging groups
that surfaced in America between 1800 and
1945. I drew the line after World War II because
the outcomes for current protest groups are still
unclear. I defined a *challenging group* by its relationship to two targets: its *antagonist* (the object
of actual or planned attempts at influence) and
its *constituency* (the individuals or organizations
whose resources and energy the group seeks to
organize and mobilize).

A challenging group must meet two problems
at the same time. Unlike an established interest
group such as the American Medical Association,
its membership is not already organized. A challenging group cannot send out a call to action
and expect that most of its loyal members will follow it into battle; it must create this loyalty from
scratch. Of course, many of today's established
groups went through a period of challenge and
we studied some of them during their early years.

Second, a challenging group must demand
some change that its own membership cannot provide. A messianic group that offered salvation to
members would not qualify unless the group wanted changes in laws or social institutions as well.

A challenge ends when one of three events occurs: The group disbands; the group stops trying

to win friends and influence people, even though it continues to exist; or the group's major antagonists accept it as a legitimate spokesman for its constituency.

I drew my sample from an exhaustive list of social movements and formal organizations. After eliminating those that did not fit the definition of a challenging group, we were left with 64 valid groups, and of these we were able to get sufficient information on 53.

CHALLENGES FROM BICYCLES TO BIRTH CONTROL

The 53 groups are a representative sample of challenging groups in American history…. Some failed, some won. Some had quite humble goals: The League of American Wheelmen formed in 1880 to get the right to bicycle on public highways. Others sought nothing less than revolution. Some groups, such as the American Birth Control League, started radical and became establishment. Others, like the Night Riders, appear more disreputable today than they probably seemed then.

Twenty of the groups were occupationally based, such as the American Federation of Teachers; 17 were reform oriented, such as the Federal Suffrage Association; 10 were socialist, such as the International Workingmen's Association (the First International); and 6 were some brand of right-wing or nativist group, such as the Christian Front Against Communism or the German-American Bund.

Definitions of success are complicated. We tried many and settled on two summary measures. The first focuses on whether other power holders came to accept the group as a valid representative of legitimate interests. The second measure focuses on whether the group gained new advantages for its constituents and beneficiaries and accomplished its goals.

The combination of these two definitions of success means that a group's efforts may have four possible outcomes. It may win many new advantages and full acceptance from its antagonists (complete success); no advantages but acceptance (co-optation); many advantages but no acceptance (preemption); or neither advantages

nor acceptance (failure). More than half of the groups, 58 percent, were successful on one measure or the other; only 38 percent were successful in both meanings.

Next, I explored the strategies and characteristics of the groups to see why some succeeded and others failed. I began with the touchiest issue of all, violence.

Most of the groups had no violence at all in their history, but 15 of them participated in some kind of violent exchange. It is misleading, however, to assume that these groups used violence as a tactic. In some cases, they were attacked by the police or by mobs with little or no provocation; in other cases, pitched battles took place but it is no easy matter to know who started in. Rather than trying to make that judgment, we divided the groups into two types—eight activist groups that, whether or not they initiated a fight, were willing to give and take if one started. The other seven were passive recipients; they were attacked and could not, or simply did not, fight back.

THE SUCCESS OF THE UNRULY

In the case of violence, it appears better to give than to receive if you want to succeed in American politics. The activist groups that fought back or, in some cases, initiated violence had a higher-than-average success rate; six of the eight won new advantages and five of the six were eventually accepted as well. The nonviolent recipients of attack, however, lost out completely. None of them met their goals, although one, the Dairymen's League, was co-opted.

Violence is even more certain to reap benefits when the group's goals are limited and when the group does not aim to displace its antagonists but rather to coexist with them. When I eliminated revolutionary groups that aimed to displace the opposition, I found that *every* violence user was successful in winning new advantages and *every* violence recipient was unsuccessful.

Several groups tried a strategy that we might call speaking loudly and carrying a small stick. They advocated violence but never actually used it. The Communist Labor Party, the Revolutionary Workers League, and the German-American Bund roared a good deal, but they never bit. This is the least effective strategy of all, for such groups pay the cost of violence without gaining its benefits. They are threatening but they are weak, which makes them an easy target for repression.

Violence is not the only kind of high-pressure tactic that brings success. Ten groups used other unruly strategies on their opposition; such as strikes, boycotts, and efforts to humiliate or embarrass their antagonists. For example, A. Philip Randolph's March on Washington Committee threatened a mass march on the Capitol in the spring of 1941 to push President Franklin D. Roosevelt into a more active role in ending racial discrimination in employment. The government was then arousing the country for war with appeals that contrasted U.S. democracy with Nazi racism, so such a march would have been a considerable embarrassment to the administration. A week before the march was scheduled to happen, President Roosevelt promised a policy of nondiscrimination in all federal hiring and, by executive order, created a Fair Employment Practices Committee to carry out this policy.

The League of Deliverance used the boycott against businesses that hired Chinese workers. They threatened worse. They notified "offenders" that after six days of non-compliance, their district would be declared "dangerous.... Should the Chinese remain within the proclaimed district after the expiration of...30 days, the General Executive Committee will be required to abate the danger in whatever manner seems best to them." The league, however, never had call to go beyond the boycott tactic. By firing its Chinese employees, a business could buy peace with the league; many did just that.

Forceful tactics are associated with success, as violence is. Eight out of the ten groups that applied such pressures were accepted and won new advantages, a percentage that is twice as great as the percentage for groups that avoided such tactics.

VIOLENCE COMES FROM CONFIDENCE

These data undermine the pluralist argument that violence is the product of frustration, desper-

ation, and weakness, that it is an act of last resort by those who are unable to attract a following and achieve their goals. Violence, pluralists assume, is unsuccessful as a tactic because it simply increases the hostility around it and invites the legitimate action of authorities against it.

My interpretation is nearly the opposite. Violence grows from an impatience born of confidence and a sense of rising power. It occurs when the challenging group senses that the surrounding community will condone it, when hostility toward the *victim* renders it a relatively safe strategy. In this sense, violence is as much a symptom of success as a cause.

Groups use violence to prevent being destroyed and to deter authorities from attack; less often, they use violence to gain a specific objective. Successful groups almost never used it as a primary tactic. Typically, the primary means of influence were strikes, bargaining, and propaganda. Violence, in short, is the spice of protest, not the meat and potatoes.

The size of the violent groups supports this interpretation. The active groups tend to be large; only one of the eight, the Night Riders, had fewer than 10,000 members, while five of the seven recipients of violence were this small. Such numbers seem more likely to breed confidence and impatience than desperation.

The successful group in American politics is not the polite petitioner who carefully observes all the rules. It is the rambunctious fighter, one with limited goals, that can elbow its way into the arena. But the willingness to fight is not enough. A group must be *able* to fight; it needs organization and discipline to focus its energies.

A challenging group faces antagonists that have control over their members, as established bureaucracies do. Challenging groups can overcome this disadvantage by adopting the structure of established organizations. They can deal on more equal terms if they are able to create their own apparatus of internal control—if they can turn *members* into *agents*.

Even when challenging groups have a committed membership, however, they may still lack unity of command. It is not enough to have agents if they have no direction, if some factions shout, "March!" and others cry, "Wait!"

THE READINESS IS ALL

One may convert members into soldiers, but soldiers fight civil wars as well as foreign ones. Thus a group needs a bureaucratic structure to help become ready for action, and centralized power to help it reach unified decisions.

I considered a group *bureaucratic* if it had three characteristics. It must have a constitution or charter that states the purposes of the group and rules for its operation; an ideological manifesto is not enough. It must keep a formal list of its members, which it distinguishes from mere sympathizers. And it must have at least three internal divisions; for example, executives, chapter heads, and the rank and file.

Twenty-four of the groups met all three criteria, and these were more likely than nonbureaucratic groups to win acceptance (71 percent to 28 percent) and new advantages (62 percent to 38 percent).

I defined a group as *centralized* if power resided in a single leader or central committee and local chapters had little autonomy. Slightly more than half of the groups, 28, had such a centralized structure; 19 of these had a single, dominant leader, and 9 had some form of collective leadership such as a national board or an executive committee. The rest of the groups had no one center of power.

Centralization is unrelated to bureaucracy as defined above; half of the bureaucratic groups and half of the nonbureaucratic groups had centralized power structures. Bureaucracy and centralization each contribute something to success, but it is the combination that really does the trick. Groups that were both bureaucratic *and* centralized had the best chance of achieving their goals; 75 percent of them were successful. Groups that were neither bureaucratic nor centralized had very little chance of winning anything. Only one, the Federal Suffrage Association, defied the odds and won both acceptance and advantages. The FSA was only one, and hardly the most important, of the groups that fought for women's suffrage. It achieved its objective, but it was neither alone nor always in the center of the struggle.

Thus modern protest groups that attempt to distribute authority among all their members and avoid hierarchy should take heed. If they are going to be involved with struggles with the authorities, they will have a difficult time avoiding factions in their ranks and reaching their goals.

JUNGLE LAWS VERSUS POLITE POLITICS

The pluralist image of orderly contest is a half-truth. It fits well enough into the bargaining and give-and-take that goes on inside the political arena. But there is another kind of contest going on at the same time between those outside the arena and those already inside. This conflict is a great deal less orderly than what happens in the lobbies, the board rooms, and the other corridors of established power.

This second locus of conflict has its own rules too, but they are more like the laws of the jungle. Whatever differences the powerful may have among themselves, they are on the same team in the struggle between insiders and outsiders. Challengers who try to play by the rules that members observe among themselves should realize two things. Insiders won't apply their rules to outsiders; and outsiders, being poor in resources, have little to offer the powerful in an alliance.

Challengers do better when they realize that they are in a political combat situation. They don't need to look for a fight, but they had better be ready to participate in one if the occasion arises. They must therefore be organized like a combat group—with willing, committed people who know what to do, and a command structure that can keep its people out of the wrong fight at the wrong time.

But this advice really only applies to groups with limited goals. I included revolutionary groups in my sample, but it should come as no surprise that none of them were successful. I can't say what makes for success among such groups because I had no successes to compare with the failures. A more complete picture of the successful group is one that is ready and willing to fight like hell for goals that can be met without overturning the system.

Perhaps it is disconcerting to discover that the meek do not inherit the earth—or at least that part of it presided over by the American political system. But those rambunctious groups that fight their way into the political arena escape misfor-

tune because they are prepared to withstand counterattack, and to make it costly to those who would keep them out.

61. SOCIAL CHANGE AND RACE RELATIONS

LEWIS M. KILLIAN

I rejoice that black citizens are so much freer than they were in my childhood and that I have been released from the bonds of a Jim Crow society. But my joy turns to despair when I must confront the fact that behind the facade of freedom in public places exists a structure of inequality that is in some aspects more hideous than that of the past, offering less hope of salvation to the victims.

Lewis Killian, a sociologist who has spent much of his professional career studying race relations in the United States, describes what he sees as he looks back at the mixed record of change as it relates to inequality between African Americans and whites.

The South I came home to was very different from the one I had left in 1968. The changes since my childhood introduction to race relations in Georgia were even vaster. It is an urban South, swept out of its rural past by the same winds that have changed the rest of the nation. The rural charm disappeared along with the rural problems that, during the Great Depression, seemed to epitomize the South—according to FDR, "the nation's economic problem number one." The people are far more heterogeneous than was the two-toned population in which I grew to manhood; Latinos of various sorts, Southeast Asians, Koreans, and Asian Indians are familiar compatriots, particularly in a navy community such as Pensacola. So are transplanted Yankees, born anywhere from Boston to California but long since retired to the Sunbelt. It is dismaying to me, a born-and-bred southern Democrat who rejoiced in Jimmy Carter's elec-

tion and am still angry over his subsequent defeat, that now so many southerners are Republicans. Even by the time I published the first edition of my book, *White Southerners*, in 1970, white voters living in the South had become one of the bulwarks of Republican strength in presidential contests.

Sociologists and historians who have devoted much study to the South as a region now debate whether there remains a distinctive southern culture. I stay out of the discussion but feel personally that there is still enough different about the South and many of its people to make me feel that I have indeed come home. There is always a "new South," but enough of the old persists to remind me of the one I once knew and have always loved in spite of its faults.

Along with the growth of the crowded cities, the most visible evidence of change in the region is in race relations. As a Cracker who knew and accepted segregation when it was at its cruelest and most extensive, I now suffer from culture shock when I see the changes that were so violently resisted during the civil rights movement.

From *Black and White: Reflections of a White Southern Sociologist*, by Lewis M. Killian. Dix Hills, NY: General Hall, 1994.

The "Colored" restrooms and drinking fountains are gone. A few, very few, black families worship regularly in my parish church; there is still a black Episcopal parish in Pensacola. Blacks appear to shop freely with whites, and both are often served by stylishly dressed black salespeople and cashiers. In the past two years, I have formed a close friendship with a black man of about my age. Henry Burrell, who grew up in the slums of Detroit, is a veteran of the U.S. Air Force and now is a permanent deacon in the Roman Catholic church. We work together as members of the Human Rights Advocacy Committee in northwest Florida. When, after a meeting, Henry and I want to have lunch together, we don't have to wonder where it will be safe for us to go. All we have to decide is what kind of food we want.

As an adjunct professor at the University of West Florida, I have occasionally taught classes in minority relations. Rarely have I encountered a student, even one raised in the South, who retains even the dimmest memory of segregation. These students, white and black, are as intrigued and shocked by my lecture describing "the way it was" as were the audiences to whom I gave the same lecture in Massachusetts. I, in turn, experienced a bit of shock one day when a beautiful young white woman casually informed the class that her husband was a black air force pilot on duty in Korea. I still am subject to a twinge of anxiety when I see an interracial couple on Pensacola Beach, remembering how blacks were beaten when they tried to desegregate the beaches near St. Augustine, Florida, in the early 1960s.

I rejoice that black citizens are so much freer than they were in my childhood and that I have been released from the bonds of a Jim Crow society. But my joy turns to despair when I must confront the fact that behind the facade of freedom in public places exists a structure of inequality that is in some aspects more hideous than that of the past, offering less hope of salvation to the victims.

The statistics sociologists and economists present in their endless outpouring of books and articles tell a story of persistent residential segregation, the resegregation of public schools, and an almost invariant gap between the incomes of white and black families. They confirm the reality of disproportionate rates of delinquency, ille-

gitimacy, and welfare dependence among minority ethnic groups, even though the rates are also increasing in the white population and the white poor still outnumber the black.

But I do not have to study the tables and graphs to find evidence of the enduring consequences of slavery, segregation, and exploitation. As I drive along the freeway that bisects Pensacola from south to north, there are places where I can see black slum dwellings on either side. Only a few blocks away I can find the all-black public housing projects where the poor but decent residents live in fear of the drug dealers who prey on their children. With Henry Burrell, I visit the juvenile detention center and see children as young as twelve years old awaiting trial for armed robbery, car theft, or worse felonies. There are young white felons there, too, but I know that society still offers more opportunities for whites if they are reformed than for the blacks. I see machines, from mechanical cottonpickers and ditchdiggers to my wife's washing machine, doing the work that once provided employment for many blacks who, though underpaid, enjoyed the dignity of a job. At the same time, I know that despite nearly a quarter of a century of affirmative action, only a well-qualified minority of black workers have been able to move into the professional and high-tech jobs that each year become more important in our economy. Although the small city of Pensacola is far removed in space and population from Chicago, I can see in my new home in the South the same trends toward greater segregation and inequality that Bill Wilson and his students are discovering in the northern industrial metropolis.

Worse yet, I am condemned by the fact that in spite of the dismantling of *de jure* segregation, I still live in a white world that is, in a way, more segregated than was my environment in Macon. With the disappearance of domestic servants and black yardmen such as "Black Lewis," I do not have the daily close contact with blacks that I once knew. The domestics have not been replaced by black neighbors, although the law says that they could be. Only once in our lives have we enjoyed the fellowship of a black family in an American neighborhood. That was in Amherst, where an army officer whom I knew at the University of Massachusetts, James Faison, bought a house on our little cul-de-sac. He and his wife, Martha, lived there for a few years before building a grander house in another part of the town. Kay and I would welcome neighbors such as the Faisons again and would go to great lengths to defend their exercise of their rights. But we are not about to embark on a quixotic crusade that would entail inviting a black friend, or a stranger, to endure the tribulations of being a test case.

In the early days of my professional study of race relations, my theoretical views were quite clear to me, and my faith in progress was firm. Once awakened to the dangers of the myth of race and the evils of segregation, I cherished the naive belief that the tide of history was flowing slowly but inexorably toward erasing them. The very concept of race and the divisions rationalized by it were, I had learned, relatively recent developments in the long history of human culture. Although I did not anticipate their immediate demise, I was confident that every move, scientific, theological, or legal, to destroy them would be a sure step in the direction of racial democracy, to be realized perhaps even in my lifetime. In my teaching at the University of Oklahoma and at Florida State University, I preached a simple but powerful gospel of assimilation.

Then the mixed and inadequate accomplishments of the civil rights movement and the unmasking of the deep economic problems that remain little affected by civil rights laws all thrust a haze of doubt into my theoretical view and cast a pall of gloom over my hopes for progress. I still preferred an assimilationist outcome, but I no longer had faith that it would come in my lifetime, if ever. The ethnic divisions and the hostilities that were revived and magnified in the 1960s, not only in the United States but throughout the world, suggested that the tide flowed toward unending conflict, not assimilation or even peaceful, harmonious pluralism.

My record of theoretical and personal devotion to assimilation suggests that I should be an enthusiastic advocate of affirmative action in the form of compensatory discrimination. I cannot, however, join the ranks of my friends who believe that it will lead eventually to the disappearance of color consciousness. The evidence I have assiduously examined leads me to conclude that such a program leads only to a form of "supertokenism" benefiting a fortunate few but changing neither the distribution of power nor the concentration of wealth that together keep poor blacks outside the mainstream and even increase their numbers. At the same time, the issue, wielded as a political weapon, perpetuates and deepens the rift between white and black Americans. I see no inclination on the part of white voters and their elected representatives to support or even propose the radical economic reforms that would be necessary to reverse the decades-long trend for the rich to get richer and the poor, poorer. It is easier for politicians to unite white voters in opposition to new taxes, to welfare programs, and to "quotas" than to inspire them with a vision of a society in which the vast wealth of the nation is distributed more equally.

Equally confusing and discouraging is the disarray among black Americans. There are no contemporary counterparts of Washington and Du Bois or of Martin Luther King, Jr., and Malcolm X, with opposing but inspiring philosophies and calls to action. The current "black establishment," the NAACP, the Urban League, and the greatly shrunken Southern Christian Leadership Conference, year after year advocate measures that have proven inadequate and that depend on the goodwill of whites, a goodwill that is diminishing. A small but growing number of black intellectuals—hardly "leaders"—criticize the shopworn solutions proposed by the established "leaders" and advocate self-help programs reminiscent of the Black Power era. No contemporary social movement has emerged, however. Although there are frequent cries of anguish from black Americans, the black protest movement that stretches back to the slave revolts and the Underground Railroad appears to be moribund or, at the least, quiescent....

62. GLOBALIZATION

ANTHONY GIDDENS

We are the first generation to live in this [global cosmopolitan] society, whose contours we can as yet only dimly see. It is shaking up our existing ways of life, no matter where we happen to be. This is not—at least at the moment—a global order driven by collective human will. Instead, it is emerging in an anarchic, haphazard, fashion, carried along by a mixture of influences.

Globalization is more than an economic revolution. It changes every aspect of people's lives. This is the central point of Gidden's selection.

A friend of mine studies village life in central Africa. A few years ago, she paid her first visit to a remote area where she was to carry out her fieldwork. The day she arrived, she was invited to a local home for an evening's entertainment. She expected to find out about the traditional pastimes of this isolated community. Instead, the occasion turned out to be a viewing of *Basic Instinct* on video. The film at that point hadn't even reached the cinemas in London.

Such vignettes reveal something about our world. And what they reveal isn't trivial. It isn't just a matter of people adding modern paraphernalia—videos, television sets, personal computers and so forth—to their existing ways of life. We live in a world of transformations, affecting almost every aspect of what we do. For better or worse, we are being propelled into a global order that no one fully understands, but which is making its effects felt upon all of us.

Globalisation may not be a particularly attractive or elegant word. But absolutely no one who wants to understand our prospects at century's end can ignore it. I travel a lot to speak abroad. I haven't been to a single country recently where globalisation isn't being intensively discussed. In France, the word is *mondialisation*. In Spain and Latin America, it is *globalización*. The Germans say *Globalisierung*.

The global spread of the term is evidence of the very developments to which it refers. Every business guru talks about it. No political speech is complete without reference to it. Yet even in the late 1980s the term was hardly used, either in academic literature or in everyday language. It has come from nowhere to be almost everywhere.

Given its sudden popularity, we shouldn't be surprised that the meaning of the notion isn't always clear, or that an intellectual reaction has set in against it. Globalisation has something to do with the thesis that we now all live in one world—but in what ways exactly, and is the idea really valid? Different thinkers have taken almost completely opposite views about globalisation in debates that have sprung up over the past few years. Some dispute the whole thing. I'll call them the sceptics.

According to the sceptics, all the talk about globalisation is only that—just talk. Whatever its benefits, its trials and tribulations, the global economy isn't especially different from that which existed at previous periods. The world carries on much the same as it has done for many years.

Most countries, the sceptics argue, gain only a small amount of their income from external trade. Moreover, a good deal of economic exchange is between regions, rather than being truly world-wide. The countries of the European

From Anthony Giddens. *Runaway World.* © 2000. Reproduced by permission of Routledge, Inc.

Union, for example, mostly trade among themselves. The same is true of the other main trading blocs, such as those of Asia-Pacific or North America.

Others take a very different position. I'll label them the radicals. The radicals argue that not only is globalisation very real, but that its consequences can be felt everywhere. The global market-place, they say, is much more developed than even in the 1960s and 1970s and is indifferent to national borders. Nations have lost most of the sovereignty they once had, and politicians have lost most of their capability to influence events. It isn't surprising that no one respects political leaders any more, or has much interest in what they have to say. The era of the nation-state is over. Nations, as the Japanese business writer Kenichi Ohmae puts it, have become mere "fictions". Authors such as Ohmae see the economic difficulties of the 1998 Asian crisis as demonstrating the reality of globalisation, albeit seen from its disruptive side.

The sceptics tend to be on the political left, especially the old left. For if all of this is essentially a myth, governments can still control economic life and the welfare state remain intact. The notion of globalisation, according to the sceptics, is an ideology put about by free-marketeers who wish to dismantle welfare systems and cut back on state expenditures. What has happened is at most a reversion to how the world was a century ago. In the late nineteenth century there was already an open global economy, with a great deal of trade, including trade in currencies.

Well, who is right in this debate? I think it is the radicals. The level of world trade today is much higher than it ever was before, and involves a much wider range of goods and services. But the biggest difference is in the level of finance and capital flows. Geared as it is to electronic money—money that exists only as digits in computers—the current world economy has no parallels in earlier times.

In the new global electronic economy, fund managers, banks, corporations, as well as millions of individual investors, can transfer vast amounts of capital from one side of the world to another at the click of a mouse. As they do so, they can destabilise what might have seemed rock-solid economies—as happened in the events in Asia.

The volume of world financial transactions is usually measured in US dollars. A million dollars is a lot of money for most people. Measured as a stack of hundred-dollar notes, it would be eight inches high. A billion dollars—in other words, a thousand million—would stand higher than St Paul's Cathedral. A trillion dollars—a million million—would be over 120 miles high, 20 times higher than Mount Everest.

Yet far more than a trillion dollars is now turned over *each day* on global currency markets. This is a massive increase from only the late 1980s, let alone the more distant past. The value of whatever money we may have in our pockets, or our bank accounts, shifts from moment to moment according to fluctuations in such markets.

I would have no hesitation, therefore, in saying that globalisation, as we are experiencing it, is in many respects not only new, but also revolutionary. Yet I don't believe that either the sceptics or the radicals have properly understood either what it is or its implications for us. Both groups see the phenomenon almost solely in economic terms. This is a mistake. Globalisation is political, technological and cultural, as well as economic. It has been influenced above all by developments in systems of communication, dating back only to the late 1960s.

In the mid-nineteenth century, a Massachusetts portrait painter, Samuel Morse, transmitted the first message, 'What hath God wrought?', by electric telegraph. In so doing, he initiated a new phase in world history. Never before could a message be sent without someone going somewhere to carry it. Yet the advent of satellite communications marks every bit as dramatic a break with the past. The first commercial satellite was launched only in 1969. Now there are more than 200 such satellites above the earth, each carrying a vast range of information. For the first time ever, instantaneous communication is possible from one side of the world to the other. Other types of electronic communication, more and more integrated with satellite transmission, have also accelerated over the past few years. No dedicated transatlantic or transpacific cables existed at all until the late 1950s. The first held fewer than 100 voice paths. Those of today carry more than a million.

On 1 February 1999, about 150 years after Morse invented his system of dots and dashes, Morse Code finally disappeared from the world stage. It was discontinued as a means of communication for the sea. In its place has come a system using satellite technology, whereby any ship in distress can be pinpointed immediately. Most countries prepared for the transition some while before. The French, for example, stopped using Morse Code in their local waters in 1997, signing off with a Gallic flourish: "Calling all. This is our last cry before our eternal silence."

Instantaneous electronic communication isn't just a way in which news or information is conveyed more quickly. Its existence alters the very texture of our lives, rich and poor alike. When the image of Nelson Mandela may be more familiar to us than the face of our next-door neighbour, something has changed in the nature of our everyday experience.

Nelson Mandela is a global celebrity, and celebrity itself is largely a product of new communications technology. The reach of media technologies is growing with each wave of innovation. It took 40 years for radio in the United States to gain an audience of 50 million. The same number was using personal computers only 15 years after the personal computer was introduced. It needed a mere 4 years, after it was made available, for 50 million Americans to be regularly using the Internet.

It is wrong to think of globalisation as just concerning the big systems, like the world financial order. Globalisation isn't only about what is "out there", remote and far away from the individual. It is an "in here" phenomenon too, influencing intimate and personal aspects of our lives. The debate about family values, for example, that is going on in many countries might seem far removed from globalising influences. It isn't. Traditional family systems are becoming transformed, or are under strain, in many parts of the world, particularly as women stake claim to greater equality. There has never before been a society, so far as we know from the historical record, in which women have been even approximately equal to men. This is a truly global revolution in everyday life, whose consequences are being felt around the world in spheres from work to politics.

Globalisation thus is a complex set of processes, not a single one. And these operate in a contradictory or oppositional fashion. Most people think of globalisation as simply "pulling away" power or influence from local communities and nations into the global arena. And indeed this is one of its consequences. Nations do lose some of the economic power they once had. Yet it also has an opposite effect. Globalisation not only pulls upwards, but also pushes downwards, creating new pressures for local autonomy. The American sociologist Daniel Bell describes this very well when he says that the nation becomes not only too small to solve the big problems, but also too large to solve the small ones.

Globalisation is the reason for the revival of local cultural identities in different parts of the world. If one asks, for example, why the Scots want more independence in the UK, or why there is a strong separatist movement in Quebec, the answer is not to be found only in their cultural history. Local nationalisms spring up as a response to globalising tendencies, as the hold of older nation-states weakens.

Globalisation also squeezes sideways. It creates new economic and cultural zones within and across nations. Examples are the Hong Kong region, northern Italy, and Silicon Valley in California. Or consider the Barcelona region. The area around Barcelona in northern Spain extends into France. Catalonia, where Barcelona is located, is closely integrated into the European Union. It is part of Spain, yet also looks outwards.

These changes are being propelled by a range of factors, some structural, others more specific and historical. Economic influences are certainly among the driving forces—especially the global financial system. Yet they aren't like forces of nature. They have been shaped by technology, and cultural diffusion, as well as by the decisions of governments to liberalise and deregulate their national economies.

The collapse of Soviet communism has added further weight to such developments, since no significant group of countries any longer stands outside. That collapse wasn't just something that just happened to occur. Globalisation explains both why and how Soviet communism met its end. The former Soviet Union and the East European countries were comparable to the

West in terms of growth rates until somewhere around the early 1970s. After that point, they fell rapidly behind. Soviet communism, with its emphasis upon state-run enterprise and heavy industry, could not compete in the global electronic economy. The ideological and cultural control upon which communist political authority was based similarly could not survive in an era of global media.

The Soviet and the East European regimes were unable to prevent the reception of Western radio and television broadcasts. Television played a direct role in the 1989 revolutions, which have rightly been called the first "television revolutions." Street protests taking place in one country were watched by television audiences in others, large numbers of whom then took to the streets themselves.

Globalisation, of course, isn't developing in an even-handed way, and is by no means wholly benign in its consequences. To many living outside Europe and North America, it looks uncomfortably like Westernisation—or, perhaps, Americanisation, since the US is now the sole superpower, with a dominant economic, cultural and military position in the global order. Many of the most visible cultural expressions of globalisation are American—Coca-Cola, McDonald's, CNN.

Most of the giant multinational companies are based in the US too. Those that aren't all come from the rich countries, not the poorer areas of the world. A pessimistic view of globalisation would consider it largely an affair of the industrial North, in which the developing societies of the South play little or no active part. It would see it as destroying local cultures, widening world inequalities and worsening the lot of the impoverished. Globalisation, some argue, creates a world of winners and losers, a few on the fast track to prosperity, the majority condemned to a life of misery and despair.

Indeed, the statistics are daunting. The share of the poorest fifth of the world's population in global income has dropped, from 2.3 per cent to 1.4 per cent between 1989 and 1998. The proportion taken by the richest fifth, on the other hand, has risen. In sub-Saharan Africa, 20 countries have lower incomes per head in real terms than they had in the late 1970s. In many less developed countries, safety and environmental regulations are low or virtually non-existent. Some transnational companies sell goods there that are controlled or banned in the industrial countries—poor-quality medical drugs, destructive pesticides or high tar and nicotine content cigarettes. Rather than a global village, one might say, this is more like global pillage.

Along with ecological risk, to which it is related, expanding inequality is the most serious problem facing world society. It will not do, however, merely to blame it on the wealthy. It is fundamental to my argument that globalisation today is only partly Westernisation. Of course the Western nations, and more generally the industrial countries, still have far more influence over world affairs than do the poorer states. But globalisation is becoming increasingly decentred—not under the control of any group of nations, and still less of the large corporations. Its effects are felt as much in Western countries as elsewhere.

This is true of the global financial system, and of changes affecting the nature of government itself. What one could call "reverse colonisation" is becoming more and more common. Reverse colonisation means that non-Western countries influence developments in the West. Examples abound—such as the latinising of Los Angeles, the emergence of a globally oriented high-tech sector in India, or the selling of Brazilian television programmes to Portugal.

Is globalisation a force promoting the general good? The question can't be answered in a simple way, given the complexity of the phenomenon. People who ask it, and who blame globalisation for deepening world inequalities, usually have in mind economic globalisation and, within that, free trade. Now, it is surely obvious that free trade is not an unalloyed benefit. This is especially so as concerns the less developed countries. Opening up a country, or regions within it, to free trade can undermine a local subsistence economy. An area that becomes dependent upon a few products sold on world markets is very vulnerable to shifts in prices as well as to technological change.

Trade always needs a framework of institutions, as do other forms of economic development. Markets cannot be created by purely economic means, and how far a given economy should be exposed to the world market-place must depend upon a range of criteria. Yet to oppose economic globalisation, and to opt for economic protectionism, would be a misplaced tactic for rich and poor nations alike. Protectionism may be a necessary strategy at some times and in some countries. In my view, for example, Malaysia was correct to introduce controls in 1998, to stem the flood of capital from the country. But more permanent forms of protectionism will not help the development of the poor countries, and among the rich would lead to warring trade blocs.

The debates about globalisation I mentioned at the beginning have concentrated mainly upon its implications for the nation-state. Are nation-states, and hence national political leaders, still powerful, or are they becoming largely irrelevant to the forces shaping the world? Nation-states are indeed still powerful and political leaders have a large role to play in the world. Yet at the same time the nation-state is being reshaped before our eyes. National economic policy can't be as effective as it once was. More importantly, nations have to rethink their identities now the older forms of geopolitics are becoming obsolete. Although this is a contentious point, I would say that, following the dissolving of the Cold War, most nations no longer have enemies. Who are the enemies of Britain, or France, or Brazil? The war in Kosovo didn't pit nation against nation. It was a conflict between old-style territorial nationalism and a new, ethically driven interventionalism.

Nations today face risks and dangers rather than enemies, a massive shift in their very nature.

It isn't only of the nation that such comments could be made. Everywhere we look, we see institutions that appear the same as they used to be from the outside, and carry the same names, but inside have become quite different. We continue to talk of the nation, the family, work, tradition, nature, as if they were all the same as in the past. They are not. The outer shell remains, but inside they have changed—and this is happening not only in the US, Britain, or France, but almost everywhere. They are what I call "shell institutions". They are institutions that have become inadequate to the tasks they are called upon to perform.

As the changes I have described in this chapter gather weight, they are creating something that has never existed before, a global cosmopolitan society. We are the first generation to live in this society, whose contours we can as yet only dimly see. It is shaking up our existing ways of life, no matter where we happen to be. This is not—at least at the moment—a global order driven by collective human will. Instead, it is emerging in an anarchic, haphazard, fashion, carried along by a mixture of influences.

It is not settled or secure, but fraught with anxieties, as well as scarred by deep divisions. Many of us feel in the grip of forces over which we have no power. Can we reimpose our will upon them? I believe we can. The powerlessness we experience is not a sign of personal failings, but reflects the incapacities of our institutions. We need to reconstruct those we have, or create new ones. For globalisation is not incidental to our lives today. It is a shift in our very life circumstances. It is the way we now live.

63. CLASS, SOCIAL CONFLICT, AND SOCIAL CHANGE

KARL MARX

The history of all hitherto existing society is the history of class struggles....

The bourgoisie, historically, has played a most revolutionary part....[Eventually] it creates a world after its own image ... and more massive and more colossal productive forces than have all preceding generations together....

What the bourgeoisie ... produces above all, is its own grave-diggers. Its fall and the victory of the proletariat are equally inevitable.

The *Communist Manifesto*, published in 1848, was meant to be a propoganda tract rather than a scholarly essay. It simplifies Marx's view of social change, but, at the same time, makes his argument clear. Real social change arises because of class conflict. In his world he identified two dominant classes: the bourgeoisie and the proletariat (the capitalists and the workers). Here is a description of the rise of both classes and the inevitable conflict that he foresees.

The history of all hitherto existing society is the history of class struggles.

Freeman and slave, patrician and plebeian, lord and serf, guild-master and journeyman—in a word, oppressor and oppressed, stood in constant opposition to one another, carried on an uninterrupted, now hidden, now open fight, a fight that each time ended either in a revolutionary re-constitution of society at large or in the common ruin of the contending classes.

In the earlier epochs of history, we find almost everywhere a complicated arrangement of society into various orders, a manifold gradation of social rank. In ancient Rome we have patricians, knights, plebeians, slaves; in the Middle Ages, feudal lords, vassals, guild-masters, journeymen, apprentices, serfs; in almost all of these classes, again, subordinate gradations.

The modern bourgeois society that has sprouted from the ruins of feudal society has not done

From *The Communist Manifesto*, from *Karl Marx: Selected Writings*, ed. D. McLellan, Oxford University Press, 1977. © David McLellan 1977. Reprinted with the permission of Oxford University Press.

away with class antagonisms. It has but established new classes, new conditions of oppression, new forms of struggle in place of the old ones.

Our epoch, the epoch of the bourgeoisie, possesses, however, this distinctive feature: it has simplified the class antagonisms. Society as a whole is more and more splitting up into two great hostile camps, into two great classes directly facing each other: Bourgeoisie and Proletariat.

From the serfs of the Middle Ages sprang the chartered burghers of the earliest towns. From these burgesses the first elements of the bourgeoisie were developed.

The discovery of America, the rounding of the Cape, opened up fresh ground for the rising bourgeoisie. The East Indian and Chinese markets, the colonization of America, trade with the colonies, the increase in the means of exchange and in commodities generally, gave to commerce, to navigation, to industry, an impulse never before known, and thereby, to the revolutionary element in the tottering feudal society, a rapid development.

The feudal system of industry, under which industrial production was monopolized by closed guilds, now no longer sufficed for the growing wants of the new markets. The manufacturing system took its place. The guild-masters were pushed on one side by the manufacturing middle class; division of labour between the different corporate guilds vanished in the face of division of labour in each single workshop.

Meantime the markets kept ever growing, the demand ever rising. Even manufacture no longer sufficed. Thereupon, steam and machinery revolutionized industrial production. The place of manufacture was taken by the giant, Modern Industry, the place of the industrial middle class, by industrial millionaires, the leaders of whole industrial armies, the modern bourgeois.

Modern industry has established the world-market, for which the discovery of America paved the way. This market has given an immense development to commerce, to navigation, to communication by land. This development has, in its turn, reacted on the extension of industry; and in proportion as industry, commerce, navigation, railways extended, in the same proportion the bourgeoisie developed, increased its capital, and pushed into the background every class handed down from the Middle Ages.

We see, therefore, how the modern bourgeoisie is itself the product of a long course of development, of a series of revolutions in the modes of production and of exchange.

Each step in the development of the bourgeoisie was accompanied by a corresponding political advance of that class. An oppressed class under the sway of the feudal nobility, an armed and self-governing association in the medieval commune; here independent urban republic (as in Italy and Germany), there taxable 'third estate' of the monarchy (as in France), afterwards, in the period of manufacture proper, serving either the semi-feudal or the absolute monarchy as a counterpoise against the nobility, and, in fact, cornerstone of the great monarchies in general, the bourgeoisie has at last, since the establishment of Modern Industry and of the world-market, conquered for itself, in the modern representative State, exclusive political sway. The executive of the modern State is but a committee for managing the common affairs of the whole bourgeoisie.

The bourgeoisie, historically, has played a most revolutionary part.

The bourgeoisie, wherever it has got the upper hand, has put an end to all feudal, patriarchal, idyllic relations. It has pitilessly torn asunder the motley feudal ties that bound man to his 'natural superiors', and has left remaining no other nexus between man and man than naked self-interest, than callous 'cash payment'. It has drowned the most heavenly ecstasies of religious fervour, of chivalrous enthusiasm, of philistine sentimentalism, in the icy water of egotistical calculation. It has resolved personal worth into exchange value, and in place of the numberless indefeasible chartered freedoms, has set up that single, unconscionable freedom - Free Trade. In one word, for exploitation, veiled by religious and political illusions, it has substituted naked, shameless, direct, brutal exploitation.

The bourgeoisie has stripped of its halo every occupation hitherto honoured and looked up to with reverent awe. It has converted the physician, the lawyer, the priest, the poet, the man of science into its paid wage-labourers.

The bourgeoisie has torn away from the family its sentimental veil, and has reduced the family relation to a mere money relation....

The need of a constantly expanding market for its products chases the bourgeoisie over the whole surface of the globe. It must nestle everywhere, settle everywhere, establish connections everywhere....

The bourgeoisie, by the rapid improvement of all instruments of production, by the immensely facilitated means of communication, draws all, even the most barbarian, nations into civilization. The cheap prices of its commodities are the heavy artillery with which it batters down all Chinese walls, with which it forces the barbarians' intensely obstinate hatred of foreigners to capitulate. It compels all nations, on pain of extinction, to adopt the bourgeois mode of production; it compels them to introduce what it calls civilization into their midst, i.e., to become bourgeois themselves. In one word, it creates a world after its own image.

The bourgeoisie has subjected the country to the rule of the towns. It has created enormous cities, has greatly increased the urban population as compared with the rural, and has thus rescued a considerable part of the population from the idiocy of rural life. Just as it has made the country dependent on the towns, so it has made barbarian and semi-barbarian countries dependent on the civilized ones, nations of peasants on nations of bourgeois, the East on the West.

The bourgeoisie keeps more and more doing away with the scattered state of the population, of the means of production, and of property. It has agglomerated population, centralized means of production, and has concentrated property in a few hands. The necessary consequence of this was political centralization. Independent or but loosely connected provinces, with separate interests, laws, governments, and systems of taxation, became lumped together into one nation, with one government, one code of laws, one national class-interest, one frontier, and one customs-tariff.

The bourgeoisie, during its rule of scarcely one hundred years, has created more massive and more colossal productive forces than have all preceding generations together. Subjection of Nature's forces to man, machinery, application of chemistry to industry and agriculture, steam-navigation, railways, electric telegraphs, clearing of whole continents for cultivation, canalization of rivers, whole populations conjured out of the ground—what earlier century had even a presentiment that such productive forces slumbered in the lap of social labour?…

We see then that the means of production and of exchange, on whose foundation the bourgeoisie built itself up, were generated in feudal society. At a certain stage in the development of these means of production and of exchange, the conditions under which feudal society produced and exchanged, the feudal organization of agriculture and manufacturing industry, in one word, the feudal relations of property become no longer compatible with the already developed productive forces; they became so many fetters. They had to be burst asunder; they were burst asunder.

Into their place stepped free competition, accompanied by a social and political constitution adapted to it, and by the economical and political sway of the bourgeois class.…

In proportion as the bourgeoisie, i.e., capital, is developed, in the same proportion is the proletariat, the modern working class, developed—a class of labourers, who live only so long as they find work, and who find work only so long as their labour increases capital. These labourers, who must sell themselves piecemeal, are a commodity, like every other article of commerce, and are consequently exposed to all the vicissitudes of competition, to all the fluctuations of the market.

Owing to the extensive use of machinery and to division of labour, the work of the proletarians has lost all individual character, and, consequently, all charm for the workman. He becomes an appendage of the machine, and it is only the most simple, most monotonous, and most easily acquired knack, that is required of him. Hence, the cost of production of a workman is restricted, almost entirely, to the means of subsistence that he requires for his maintenance, and for the propagation of his race. But the price of a commodity, and therefore also of labour, is equal to its cost of production. In proportion, therefore, as the repulsiveness of the work increases, the wage decreases. Nay more, in proportion as the use of machinery and division of labour increases, in the same proportion the burden of toil also increases, whether by prolongation of the working hours, by increase of the work exacted in a given time or by increased speed of the machinery, etc.

Modern industry has converted the little workshop of the patriarchal master into the great factory of the industrial capitalist. Masses of labourers, crowded into the factory, are organized like soldiers. As privates of the industrial army they are placed under the command of a perfect hierarchy of officers and sergeants. Not only are they slaves of the bourgeois class, and of the bourgeois State; they are daily and hourly enslaved by the machine, by the overlooker, and, above all, by the individual bourgeois manufacturer himself. The more openly this despotism proclaims gain to be its end and aim, the more petty, the more hateful, and the more embittering it is.…

The lower strata of the middle class—the small tradespeople, shopkeepers, and retired tradesmen generally, the handicraftsmen and peasants—all these sink gradually into the proletariat, partly because their diminutive capital does not suffice for the scale on which Modern Industry is carried on, and is swamped in the competition with the large capitalists, partly because their specialized skill is rendered worthless by new methods of production. Thus the proletariat is recruited from all classes of the population.

The proletariat goes through various stages of development. With its birth begins its struggle with the bourgeoisie. At first the contest is carried on by individual labourers, then by the workpeople of a factory, then by the operatives of one trade, in one locality, against the individual bourgeois who directly exploits them. They direct their attacks not against the bourgeois conditions of production, but against the instruments of production themselves; they destroy imported wares that compete with their labour, they smash to pieces machinery, they set factories ablaze, they seek to restore by force the vanished status of the workman of the Middle Ages.

At this stage the labourers still form an incoherent mass scattered over the whole country, and broken up by their mutual competition. If anywhere they unite to form more compact bodies, this is not yet the consequence of their own active union, but of the union of the bourgeoisie, which class, in order to attain its own political ends, is compelled to set the whole proletariat in motion, and is moreover yet, for a time, able to do so. At this stage, therefore, the proletarians do not fight their enemies, but the enemies of their enemies, the remnants of absolute monarchy, the landowners, the non-industrial bourgeois, the petty bourgeoisie. Thus the whole historical movement is concentrated in the hands of the bourgeoisie; every victory so obtained is a victory for the bourgeoisie.

But with the development of industry the proletariat not only increases in number; it becomes concentrated in greater masses, its strength grows, and it feels that strength more. The various interests and conditions of life within the ranks of the proletariat are more and more equalized, in proportion as machinery obliterates all distinctions of labour, and nearly everywhere reduces wages to the same low level. The growing competition among the bourgeois, and the resulting commercial crises, make the wages of the workers ever more fluctuating. The unceasing improvement of machinery, ever more rapidly developing, makes their livelihood more and more precarious; the collisions between individual workmen and individual bourgeois take more and more the character of collisions between two classes. Thereupon the workers begin to form combinations (Trades' Unions) against the bourgeois; they club together in order to keep up the rate of wages; they found permanent associations in order to make provision beforehand for these occasional revolts. Here and there the contest breaks out into riots.

Now and then the workers are victorious, but only for a time. The real fruit of their battles lies, not in the immediate result, but in the ever-expanding union of the workers. This union is helped on by the improved means of communication that are created by modern industry and that place the workers of different localities in contact with one another. It was just this contact that was needed to centralize the numerous local struggles, all of the same character, into one national struggle between classes.

Of all the classes that stand face to face with the bourgeoisie today, the proletariat alone is a really revolutionary class. The other classes decay and finally disappear in the face of Modern Industry; the proletariat is its special and essential product.

The lower middle class, the small manufacturer, the shopkeeper, the artisan, the peasant, all these fight against the bourgeoisie, to save from extinction their existence as fractions of the middle class. They are therefore not revolutionary, but conservative. Nay more, they are reactionary, for they try to roll back the wheel of history. If by chance they are revolutionary, they are so only in view of their impending transfer into the proletariat; they thus defend not their present, but their future interests, they desert their own standpoint to place themselves at that of the proletariat.

The 'dangerous class', the social scum, that passively rotting mass thrown off by the lowest layers of old society, may, here and there, be swept into the movement by a proletarian revolution; its conditions of life, however, prepare it far more for the part of a bribed tool of reactionary intrigue....

All previous historical movements were movements of minorities, or in the interests of minorities. The proletarian movement is the self-conscious, independent movement of the immense majority, in the interests of the immense majority. The proletariat, the lowest stratum of our present society, cannot stir, cannot raise itself up, without the whole superincumbent strata of official society being sprung into the air.

Though not in substance, yet in form, the struggle of the proletariat with the bourgeoisie is at first a national struggle. The proletariat of each country must, of course, first of all settle matters with its own bourgeoisie.

In depicting the most general phases of the development of the proletariat, we traced the more or less veiled civil war, raging within existing society, up to the point where that war breaks out into open revolution, and where the violent overthrow of the bourgeoisie lays the foundation for the sway of the proletariat....

The essential condition for the existence, and for the sway of the bourgeois class, is the formation and augmentation of capital; the condition for capital is wage-labour. Wage-labour rests exclusively on competition between the labourers. The advance of industry, whose involuntary promoter is the bourgeoisie, replaces the isolation of the labourers, due to competition, by their revolutionary combination, due to association. The development of Modern Industry, therefore, cuts from under its feet the very foundation on which the bourgeoisie produces and appropriates products. What the bourgeoisie, therefore, produces, above all, is its own grave-diggers. Its fall and the victory of the proletariat are equally inevitable.

64. SOCIETY AND CHANGE

MICHEL CROZIER

We will never succeed in changing society the way we want.... Every society is a complex system, and this is why it cannot be changed or renewed simply by a decision, even one arrived at democratically by majority rule.

Michel Crozier, a French sociologist, regards social change as very complex. Although we may think that society changes because someone is successful in doing so, it rarely changes because of the will of the individual. Our efforts may bring unintended consequences and even have the opposite effect of what we intended. Yet it is still important to try to make change because retreat from attempting change will bring even worse problems.

We will never succeed in changing society the way we want. Even if we were to persuade the majority of our fellow citizens to follow our lead, we would not succeed in enacting a plan for society because society, human relations, and social systems are too complex. We would

From "The Future of French Society," by Michel Crozier, in *Strategies for Change*, MIT Press, Trans. William R. Beer, 1982. English translation copyrighted © 1982 by the Massachusetts Institute of Technology.

have succeeded in mobilizing nothing but an abstract and unsubstantial agreement, the awakened dreams of our fellow men. This desire, this fantasy, never determines how people really act.

It is possible to work within a system only by understanding its characteristics. This assertion is not as self-evident as it may appear because all too often we are not willing to understand society as it is. Instead, we spend our time making social blueprints that do not have the slightest chance of success because they do not take into account the complex working of human relationships and everyday social interaction.

Every society is a complex system, and this is why it cannot be changed or renewed simply by a decision, even one arrived at democratically by majority rule. This is not to say that there are fixed laws of society, imposed on humanity like a sort of divine will. This all-too-human construction is the product of human history, and so it can be shaped, reworked, and changed. But at the same time, it is a system, an interdependent framework of relations that is beyond the conscious will of individual people.

Of course, neither these relations nor the whole system are unalterable. They do change as a result of human action, but the overall result of this action is different from the wishes of individual people. It is possible to bring about change more consciously and effectively, but it is not possible to impose a specific program simply through the agreement of individual people. This may seem contradictory, particularly if the profound difference that exists between people's individual preferences and their real behavior toward others is not appreciated.

Behavior in social relationships is like a game in which each person depends on the other. To win, or simply not to lose, you have to take the possible reactions of others into account. The games of social life make us obey rules that are independent of us. These games are regulated, commanded, corrected, and maintained by mechanisms to which we do not have direct access. These games are the building blocks of systems that organize every one of our activities, including the biggest and most complex, society itself.

When a warehouse worker sets aside a special supply of goods to meet unexpected requests of production workers, while at the same time politely refusing to provide for the maintenance workers, he is neither obeying his boss nor hoping for the final victory of the working class. It is not because of some personal character trait that he is easy-going with his old assistant and strict with his new one. This is the only way he can succeed in keeping the wheels turning in the department that is his world of work, while at the same time keeping the respect of his peers and influencing

events that affect him. This is as true at the level of society as it is at the level of a business.

Games, systems, and society are the necessary mediators of all human action, but they are structured in such a way that this mediation can have an effect opposite to what most participants want or think they want. The road to hell, as everyone knows, is paved with good intentions. To set up the rule of virtue, hypocrisy and eavesdropping are brought in, and have been from the time of Savonarola to Mao; the control of excess profits strengthens the black market. And very often in the attempt to free people, new chains are forged for them. Every organized human action, every collective effort, and even ideological movements lead to what can be called the *perverse effect*, effects that are the opposite of what the participants wanted. These perverse effects cannot be blamed on some force of evil—neither on the powerful at the top of the social scale nor on agitators at the bottom. They are the necessary consequence of interdependent relationships among people.

This will come as a surprise to those who still believe in the myth of the social contract, who believe that the collective will of people, the sum of their individual wishes, naturally produces rational decisions. The use of opinion polls has given new respectability and weight to this idealistic view of democracy. In fact, we are prisoners of our social situation, of our relationships, of our need to exist for, with, and against other people. Outside of this situation and these interactions, we cannot decide what we want because we literally do not know. This is why abstract opinion, cut off from the real context of social relations, only partially indicates what our real behavior is. In the spring of 1968, opinion polls registered satisfaction in France, and the pollsters said that the students had never been so happy.

It would be tempting to conclude that it is better not to try to intervene at all because every social action leads to a series of effects that can be the exact opposite of what was intended. This is the temptation of pessimism that has recently reappeared among the "new philosophers." It must be resisted, not simply because it leads people to give up but also because it leads to an even worse state of affairs. Every situation in which we do not intervene tends to deteriorate. Every analysis of businesses or institutions that are not working reveals that the same rules and principles that were successful twenty or thirty years ago are the cause of disorder and failure today.

So it is not a question of choosing between action and retreat but of finding the means and direction of the action that cannot be avoided. In everyday life, we continually make choices on the basis of tested rules based on our experience. Unfortunately, we cannot transpose this principle to a broader area because individually we are helpless against large-scale organizations, nationwide societies, and the world order. The inescapable recognition of our limitations leads us to examine two principles of action.

The first principle is that of giving priority to the understanding of real systems, not to the discussion of aims and ideals. We can find out what we want only if we know what we are doing. As long as we are not aware of what is really going on, our ideals and goals are nothing but projections of our inadequacies and inabilities. We can progress only by bringing the ideal back to earth, by putting the system of relations on its feet: reality first, ideals later.

The second principle, a consequence of understanding the perverse effect, is that we have to get away from the guesswork of everyday activity. We have to spend as much energy on the ongoing operation of the system as we do on utopian projects for changing the whole system radically and idealistically. We cannot do our job as responsible people and citizens unless we go beyond the sort of blind empiricism that led an English minister of foreign affairs to declare shortly before the war in 1914, "You know, nothing really ever happens."

PART XIII

The Importance of Sociology

In this final part we turn our attention to why sociology is important. Of what use is it? Why bother with it? It is hoped that after reading many of the selections in this reader, the student will recognize that sociology is both a scientific and a humanistic perspective, useful for understanding ourselves and our society. Although I debated leaving Part XIII out entirely, I decided to express a personal and explicit statement about what sociology means to me. Throughout this reader, however, there should be many examples of how important it is for all people to examine their lives and their society within a sociological perspective.

65. SOCIOLOGY AND DEMOCRACY

JOEL M. CHARON

…The theme of democracy stands out. One might, in truth, argue that the study of sociology is the study of issues relevant to understanding democratic society.

The study of sociology is important if democratic society is going to thrive. The issues that matter in a democratic society are studied in sociology. This is the point of view of this selection.

In the final analysis, it may be true that ignorance is bliss. It may be true that people should be left alone with the myths they happen to pick up in interaction with one another. It may be true that a liberal arts education that does not have immediate practical value is worthless.

SOCIOLOGY AND A LIBERAL ARTS EDUCATION

I do not believe any of these ideas, but I wonder about them a lot. One can more easily make a case for mathematics, foreign languages, writing, speech, psychology, and economics on the level of practical use. "The student needs to know these if he or she is to get along in life," the argument goes. It is far more difficult to make a case for sociology on the basis of practical use—unless, of course, by *practical use* one means *thinking about and understanding the world*. If a college education is ultimately an attempt to encourage people to wonder, investigate, and carefully examine their lives, then sociology is one of the most important disciplines.

Note its purpose: To get students to examine an aspect of life carefully and systematically that most people only casually and occasionally think about. It is to get people to understand what culture is and to recognize that what they believe is largely a result of their culture. It is to get them to see that they are born into a society that has a long history, that they are ranked and given roles in that society, and that ultimately they are told who they are, what to think, and how to act. It is to get them to see that the institutions they follow and normally accept are not the only ways in which society can function—that there are always alternatives. It is to get them to realize that those whom they regard as sick, evil, or criminal are often simply different. It is to get them to see that those they hate are often a product of social circumstances that should be understood more carefully and objectively.

In short, the purpose of sociology is to get people to examine objectively their lives and their society. This process is uncomfortable and sometimes unpleasant. I keep asking myself, as I teach the insights of sociology, "Why not just leave those students alone?" And, quite frankly, I do not usually know how to answer this question. We are socialized into society. Shouldn't we simply accept that which we are socialized to believe? Isn't it better for society if people believe myth? Isn't it better for people's happiness to let them be?

I usually come back to what many people profess to be one primary purpose of a university education: "liberal arts." To me, the liberal arts should be "liberating." A university education should be liberating: It should help the individual escape the bonds of his or her imprisonment by bringing an understanding of that prison. We

From *Ten Questions: A Sociological Perspective*, 3rd Edition, by Joel M. Charon. © 1998. Reprinted with permission of Brooks/Cole an imprint of the Wadsworth Group, a division of Thomson Learning. Fax 800-730-2215.

should read literature, understand art, and study biology and sociology in order to break through what those who defend society want us to know to reach a plane from which we can see reality in a more careful and unbiased way. In the end, sociology probably has the greatest potential for liberation in the academic world: At its best, it causes individuals to confront their ideas, actions, and being. We are never the same once we bring sociology into our lives. Life is scrutinized. Truth becomes far more tentative.

SOCIOLOGY AND DEMOCRACY

The Meaning of Democracy

Liberation, as you probably realize, has something to do with democracy. Although democracy is clearly an ideal that Americans claim for themselves, it is not usually clearly defined or deeply explored.

Sociology, however, explores democracy, and it asks rarely examined questions about the possibility for democracy in this—or any—society. To many people, democracy simply means "majority rule," and we too often superficially claim that if people go to a voting booth, then democracy has been established and the majority does, in fact, rule. Democracy, however, is far more than majority rule, and majority rule is far more than the existence of voting booths.

Democracy is very difficult to achieve. No society can become perfectly democratic; few societies really make much progress in that direction. Alexis de Tocqueville, a great French social scientist who wrote *Democracy in America* (1840) after traveling throughout much of the United States in 1831, believed that here was a thriving democracy, one with great future potential. Tocqueville pointed out many of our shortcomings—most important, the existence of slavery—but he believed that we probably had a more democratic future than any other society in the world. What Tocqueville did was examine the nature of our society—our structure, culture, and institutions—and then show what qualities of our society encouraged the development of democracy. For example, he identified our willingness to join voluntary associations that would impact

government, strong local ties, and the little need we had for a central government. Although much has changed since Tocqueville wrote, his lasting importance was to remind us that democracy is a very difficult social state to achieve, that certain social conditions make it possible and certain patterns support its continued existence. It is also, he wrote, very easy to lose.

Democracy is difficult to define. When I try, I usually end up listing four qualities. These describe a whole society, not just the government in that society. Although everyone will not agree that these are the basic qualities of a democracy, I think they offer a good place to begin:

1. *A democratic society is one in which the individual is free in both thinking and action.* People are in control of their own lives. To the extent that a society encourages freedom, we can call it a democratic society.
2. *A democratic society is one in which the government is effectively limited.* Those who control government do not do what they choose to do. Voting, law, organizations of people, and constitutions effectively limit their power. To the extent that government is effectively limited, we call it a democratic society.
3. *A democratic society is one in which human differences are respected and protected.* There is a general agreement that no matter what the majority favors, certain rights are reserved for the individual and for minorities who are different from the majority. Diversity is respected and even encouraged. To the extent that diversity and individuality is respected and protected, we call it a democratic society.
4. *A democratic society is one in which all people have an equal opportunity to live a decent life.* That is, privilege is not inherited, people have equality before the law, in educational opportunity, in opportunity for material success, and in whatever is deemed to be important in society. To the extent that real equality of opportunity exists, we call it a democratic society.

These four qualities that make up the definition of democracy described here must be tentative descriptions, and people should debate their relative significance. Some will regard other qualities to be more important, and some will regard only one or two of these qualities as necessary. I am only trying here to list four qualities that make sense to me and that guide my own estimate of whether the United States and other societies are democratic.

If these qualities do capture what democracy means, however, it should be obvious by now that the questions and thinking [that sociologists investigate]…are relevant to both the understanding of and the working toward a democratic society. Because sociology focuses on social organization, structure, culture, institutions, social order, social class, social power, social conflict, socialization, and social change, *sociology must continually examine issues that are relevant to understanding a democratic society.* And, on top of this, because *sociology critically examines people and their society, it encourages the kind of thinking that is necessary for people living in and working for a democratic society.…* One might, in truth, argue that the study of sociology is the study of issues relevant to understanding democratic society.

Sociology: An Approach to Understanding Democratic Society

[Sociology deals] with the nature of the human being and the role of socialization and culture in what we all become. To ask questions about human nature is to ask simultaneous questions about the possibility for democratic society, a society built on qualities that are not often widespread in society: respect for individual differences, compromise, and concern over inequality and lack of freedom. The sociological approach to the human being makes no assumption of fixed qualities, but it has a strong tendency to see human beings as living within social conditions that are responsible for forming many of their most important qualities. A society tends to produce certain types of people and certain social conditions, encouraging one value or another, one set of morals or another, one way of doing things or another. Conformity, control of the human being, tyranny, and pursuit of purely selfish interests can be encouraged; but so, too, can freedom, respect for people's rights, limited government, and equality. *The possibilities for and the limits to a human being who can live democratically are part of what sociology investigates through its questions concerning culture, socialization, and human nature.*

Those who think about society must inevitably consider the central problem of social order: How much freedom and how much individuality can we allow and still maintain society…? Those who favor greater freedom will occasionally wonder: How can there really be meaningful freedom in any society? As long as society exists, how much freedom can we encourage without destroying the underlying order? Are there limits? If so, how can we discover them? What are the costs, if any, of having a democratic society? Those who fear disorder and the collapse of society might ask: How much does the individual owe to society? Such questions are extremely difficult to answer, but they are investigated with the discipline of sociology, and they push the serious student to search for a delicate balance between order and freedom. Too often, people are willing to sell out freedom in the name of order; too often, people claim so much freedom that they do not seem to care about the continuation of society. The sociologist studies these problems and causes the student to reflect again and again on this dilemma inherent in all societies, especially those that claim to be part of the democratic tradition. There can be no freedom without society, Emile Durkheim reminds us, because a basic agreement over rules must precede the exercise of freedom. *But the problem is, How many rules? How much freedom? There is no more basic question for those who favor democracy, and there is no question more central to the discipline of sociology.*

The question of social order also leads us to the questions of what constitutes a nation and what constitutes a society…. These issues may not seem at first to have much relevance to democracy, but they surely do. It is easy for those who profess democracy to favor majority rule. It is much more difficult for any nation to develop institutions that respect the rights of all societies within its borders. A nation is a political state that rules over one—or more—societies. If it is democratic, the nation does not simply rule these societies but responds to their needs and rights, from true political representation to a decent standard of living. If it is democratic, the question the nation faces is *not* "How can we mold that society to be like the dominant society?" but "How can we create an order in which many societies can exist?" If it is democratic, the nation must balance the needs of each society's push for independence with the need for maintaining social order. *The whole meaning of what it is to be a society, as well as the associated problems of order and independence, are central sociological—and democratic—concerns.*

It is the question of control by social forces over the human being that places sociology squarely within the concerns of democracy. Much of sociology questions the possibility for substantial freedom. Democracy teaches that human beings should and can think for themselves. Much of the purpose of sociology, however, is to show us that our thinking is created by our social life; that, although we may claim that our ideas are our own, they really result from our cultures, from our positions in social structure, and from powerful and wealthy people.... Even to claim that "we are a democracy" can simply be part of an ideology, an exaggeration we accept because we are victims of various social forces. Our actions, too, result from a host of social forces that few of us understand or appreciate: institutions, opportunities, class, roles, social controls—to name only some—that quietly work on the individual, pushing him or her in directions not freely chosen.... Sociology seems to make democracy an almost impossible dream, and to some extent, the more sociology one knows, the more difficult democracy seems. *Indeed, sociology tends to simply uncover more and more ways in which human beings are shaped and controlled. This, in itself, makes sociology very relevant for understanding the limits of democracy. It causes one to seriously wonder whether human beings can be free in any sense.*

As I said earlier in this chapter, however, *sociology as a part of a liberal education is an attempt to liberate the individual from many of these controls.* The first step in liberation is understanding: It is really impossible to think for oneself or to act according to free choice unless one understands the various ways in which we are controlled. For example, it is only when I begin to see that my ideas of what it means to be a "man" have been formed through a careful and calculated process throughout society that I can begin to act in the way I choose. Only when I begin to understand how powerful advertising has become in develop-

ing my personal tastes as well as my personal values can I begin to step back and direct my own life. And even then, an important sociological question continuously teases the thoughtful person: Can society exist if people are truly liberated? If people question everything, can there still be the unity necessary for order?

The study of social inequality—probably the central concern within all sociology—is, of course, an issue of primary importance to understanding the possibility for a democratic society.... It seems that it is the nature of society to be unequal. Many forces create and perpetuate inequality. Indeed, even in our groups and our formal organizations, great inequalities are the rule. Why? Why does it happen? And what are its implications for democracy? If society is characterized by great inequalities of wealth and power, then how can free thought and free action prevail among the population? If a society—in name, a democracy—has a small elite that dominates the decision making, what difference does going to the polls make? If large numbers of people must expend all their energy to barely survive because of their poverty, where is their freedom, their opportunity to influence the direction of society, their right to improve their lives? If society is characterized by racist and sexist institutions, how is democracy possible for those who are victims? *More than any other perspective, sociology makes us aware of many problems standing in the way of a democratic society, not the least of which are social, economic, and political inequality.*

This focus on social inequality will cause many individuals to look beyond the political arena to understand democracy. A democratic society requires not only limited government but also a limited military, a limited upper class, limited corporations, and limited interest groups. Limited government may bring freedom to the individual, but it also may simply create more unlimited power for economic elites in society, which is often an even more ruthless tyranny over individual freedom. *Sociology, because its subject is society, broadens our concerns, investigates the individual not only in relation to political institutions but also in relation to many other sources of power that can and do limit real democracy and control much of what we think and do.*

The democratic spirit cares about the welfare of all people. It respects life, values individual rights, encourages quality of life, and seeks justice for all. Sociology studies social problems.... Many people live lives of misery, characterized by poverty, crime, bad jobs, exploitation, lack of self-worth, stress, repressive institutions, violent conflict, inadequate socialization, and alienation of various kinds. These are more than problems caused by human biology or human genes; these are more than problems caused by the free choices of individual actors. Something social has generally caused misery to occur. *Although it is impossible for sociology — or a democratic society — to rid the world of such problems, it is part of the spirit of both to understand them, to suggest and to carry out ways to deal with them.* Democracy is shallow and cold if large numbers of people continue to live lives of misery.

...Ethnocentrism, although perhaps inevitable and even necessary to some extent, is a way of looking at one's own culture and others in a manner antagonistic to a basic principle of democracy: respect for human diversity and individuality. To claim that our culture is superior to others is to treat other cultures without respect, to reject them for what they are, to believe that everyone must be like us. Such ideas encourage violent conflict and war and justify discrimination, segregation, and exploitation. Sociology challenges us to be careful with ethnocentrism. We must understand what it is, what its causes are, and how it functions. An understanding of ethnocentrism will challenge us to ask: "When are my judgments of others simply cultural and when are they based on some more defensible standards (such as democratic standards)?" "When are my judgments narrow and intolerant; when are they more careful and thought out?" Even then, an understanding of ethnocentrism will not allow us to judge people who are different without seriously questioning our judgments. *Sociology and democracy are perspectives that push us to understand human differences and to be careful in condemning those differences.*

[Sociology also examines] social change and the power of the individual. This discussion, too, challenges many of our taken-for-granted "truths" concerning democracy. The sociologist's faith in the individual as an agent of change is not great. Democracy is truly an illusion if it means that the individual has an important say in the direction of society. But if sociology teaches us anything about change that has relevance for democracy, it is that intentionally created change is possible only through a power base. If a democracy is going to be more than a description in a book, people who desire change in society — ideally, toward more freedom, limited government, equality of opportunity, and respect for individual rights — must work together and act from a power base, recognizing that the existing political institutions are usually fixed against them. And before we go off armed with certainty, we should remember that our certainty was probably also socially produced and that, through our efforts, we may bring change we never intended and may even lose whatever democracy we now have. Social change is complex, depends on social power, and is difficult to bring about in a way we would like. *The sociologist will examine the possibility for intentional social change in a democratic society and will be motivated to isolate the many barriers each society establishes to real social change.*

SUMMARY AND CONCLUSION

Democracy exists at different levels. For some, it is a simplistic, shallow idea. For others, however, it is a complex and challenging idea to investigate and a reality worthwhile to create. If it is going to be more than a shallow idea, however, people should understand the nature of all society, the nature of power, ethnocentrism, inequality, change, and all the other concepts discussed and investigated in sociology. Whereas other disciplines may study issues relevant to understanding democracy and encourage people to think democratically, in a very basic sense, this study is the heart of sociology.

...Democracy means that one must understand reality not by accepting authority but by careful, thoughtful investigation. It is through evidence, not bias, that one should understand. It is through open debate, not a closed belief system, that one should try to understand. *The principles of science and democracy are similar. There is no greater test of those principles than the discipline of sociology: an attempt to apply scientific principles to that for which we are all taught to feel a special reverence.*

Because it is a critical perspective that attempts to question what people have internalized from their cultures, sociology is a threat to those people who claim to know the truth. It punctures myth and asks questions that many of us would rather not hear. To see the world sociologically is to wonder about all things human. To see the world sociologically is to see events in a much larger context than the immediate situation, to think of individual events in relation to the larger present, to the past, and to the future. To see the world sociologically is to be suspicious of what those in power do (in our society and in our groups), and it is constantly to ask questions about what is and what can be.

The sociologist wonders about society and asks questions that get at the heart of many of our most sacred ideas. Perhaps this is why it seems so threatening to "those who know"; and perhaps this is why it is so exciting to those who take it seriously.